BD Chaurasia's

Human Anatomy

Regional and Applied Dissection and Clinical

Fifth Edition

Volume **2**

LOWER LIMB
ABDOMEN and PELVIS

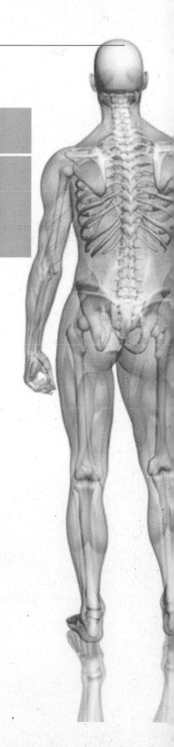

Dr. B.D. Chaurasia
1937–1985

BD Chaurasia's
Human Anatomy

Regional and Applied   Dissection and Clinical

Fifth Edition

Volume 2

LOWER LIMB
ABDOMEN and PELVIS

Edited by

Krishna Garg

MBBS, MS, PhD, FIMSA, FIAMS, FAMS

Ex-Professor and Head
Department of Anatomy
Lady Hardinge Medical College, New Delhi

CBS

CBS Publishers & Distributors Pvt Ltd

New Delhi • Bangalore • Pune • Cochin • Chennai

BD Chaurasia's

Human Anatomy Volume **2**

Regional and Applied
Dissection and Clinical

Copyright © Publisher and author

Fifth Edition: 2010

ISBN: 978-81-239-1864-8

First Edition: 1979
Reprinted: 1980, 1981, 1982, 1983, 1984, 1985, 1986, 1987, 1988
Second Edition: 1989
Reprinted: 1990, 1991, 1992, 1993, 1994
Third Edition: 1995
Reprinted: 1996, 1997, 1998, 1999, 2000, 2001, 2002, 2003, 2004
Fourth Edition: 2004
Reprinted: 2005, 2006, 2007, 2008, 2009

Published by Satish Kumar Jain and produced by Vinod K. Jain for
CBS Publishers & Distributors Pvt Ltd
Head off: CBS Plaza 4819/XI Prahlad Street, 24 Ansari Road, Daryaganj,
New Delhi 110 002, India.
Ph: 23289259, 23266861/67

www.cbspd.com
Fax: +91-11-23243014
e-mail: delhi@cbspd.com; cbspubs@vsnl.com;
cbspubs@airtelmail.in.

Branches

• **Bangalore:** Seema House 2975, 17th Cross, K.R. Road,
  Banasankari 2nd Stage, Bangalore 560 070, Karnataka
  Ph: +91-80-26771678/79   Fax: +91-80-26771680   e-mail: bangalore@cbspd.com

• **Pune:** Shaan Brahmha Complex, 631/632 Basement,
  Appa Balwant Chowk, Budhwar Peth, Next To Ratan Talkies,
  Pune 411 002, Maharashtra
  Ph: +91-20-24464057/58   Fax: +91-20-24464059   e-mail: pune@cbspd.com

• **Cochin:** 36/14 Kalluvilakam, Lissie Hospital Road,
  Cochin 682 018, Kerala
  Ph: +91-484-4059061-65   Fax: +91-484-4059065   e-mail: cochin@cbspd.com

• **Chennai:** 20, West Park Road, Shenoy Nagar, Chennai 600 030, TN
  Ph: +91-44-26260666, 26208620   Fax: +91-44-45530020   email: chennai@cbspd.com

Printed at: Thomson Press (India) Ltd.

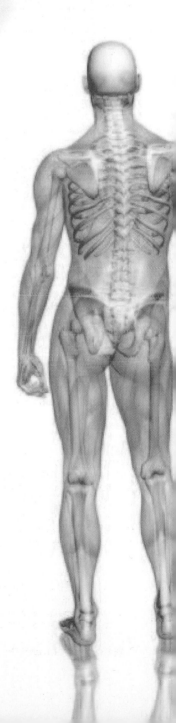

Dedicated to

my teacher

Shri Uma Shankar Nagayach

BD Chaurasia's

Human Anatomy

Regional and Applied   Dissection and Clinical

Fifth Edition

Volume **1**

UPPER LIMB and THORAX

Volume **2**

LOWER LIMB, ABDOMEN and PELVIS

Volume **3**

HEAD, NECK and BRAIN

This human anatomy is not systemic but regional
Oh yes, it is theoretical as well as practical
Besides the gross features, it is chiefly clinical
Clinical too is very much diagrammatical.

Lots of tables for the muscles are provided
Even methods for testing are incorporated
Improved colour illustrations are added
So that right half of brain gets stimulated

Tables for muscles acting on joints are given
Tables for branches of nerves & arteries are given
Hope these volumes turn highly useful
Editor's hardwork under Almighty's guidance prove fruitful

Preface to the Fifth Edition

The fourth edition of *BD Chaurasia's Human Anatomy* was completed and got published in 2004 with the guidance of Mr YN Arjuna of CBS Publishers & Distributors. His constructive suggestions have been incorporated in this edition as well.

The volumes of fourth edition have been doing well. One expected them to last for about 5 to 7 years. It was a pleasant surprise when Mr SK Jain, Chairman, possessing a broad vision, requested me in 2007 to bring out the fifth edition soon. A new challenge awaited me.

My foremost thoughts had been to make these volumes still more student-friendly even during their clinical tenure. So hallmark of this edition has been to put colour illustrations of clinical anatomy at the end of each chapter. These figures would help the students during their clinical years before they revise the subject for their postgraduate entrance examinations.

As a pilot project, videos of bones of the whole body and thoracic organs have been prepared at Kathmandu University School of Medical Sciences and Dhulikhel Hospital, Near Kathmandu, Nepal. Liberty provided by Dr Rajendra Koju, Chief Executive Officer, has been monumental. The video is added to the existing CD of questions and answers and is given with each volume.

A number of multiple choice questions have been increased for wider testing of the subject. Important clinical terms, mnemonics and references have been added to make volumes holistic. All these additions have added pages, dedicated to figures for visual treat.

The diagrams of the volumes have been critically evaluated by respected Dr Mohini Kaul, Ex-Professor and Head, Department of Anatomy, Maulana Azad Medical College. She had monumental patience to go through these books and provided lots of suggestions. It seems as if she came from USA to do this job for me and CBS. Accordingly diagrams have been improved, freshly coloured by dedicated and aggressive Mr Chand S Naagar of Limited Colors. Page layout of the book has been diligently done by Ms Nishi Verma of Limited Colors. She has tried to be economical on paper without compromising on quality.

My heartfelt thanks are for Mr SK Jain, Chairman, who has always taken personal interest in these books. He has ever been immensely helpful. I am obliged to Mr Vinod K Jain, Director, CBS for his guidance.

Suggestions for rectification and improvement are welcome.

Krishna Garg
dr.krishnagarg@gmail.com

Preface to the Fifth Edition

Preface to the First Edition
(Excerpts)

The necessity of having a simple, systematized and complete book on anatomy has long been felt. The urgency for such a book has become all the more acute due to the shorter time now available for teaching anatomy, and also to the falling standards of English language in the majority of our students in India. The national symposium on "Anatomy in Medical Education" held at Delhi in 1978 was a call to change the existing system of teaching the unnecessary minute details to the undergraduate students.

This attempt has been made with an object to meet the requirements of a common medical student. The text has been arranged in small classified parts to make it easier for the students to remember and recall it at will. It is adequately illustrated with simple line diagrams which can be reproduced without any difficulty, and which also help in understanding and memorizing the anatomical facts that appear to defy memory of a common student. The monotony of describing the individual muscles separately, one after the other, has been minimised by writing them out in tabular form, which makes the subject interesting for a lasting memory. The relevant radiological and surface anatomy have been treated in separate chapters. A sincere attempt has been made to deal, wherever required, the clinical applications of the subject. The entire approach is such as to attract and inspire the students for a deeper dive in the subject of anatomy.

The book has been intentionally split in three parts for convenience of handling. This also makes a provision for those who cannot afford to have the whole book at a time.

It is quite possible that there are errors of omission and commission in this mostly single-handed attempt. I would be grateful to the readers for their suggestions to improve the book from all angles.

I am very grateful to my teachers and the authors of numerous publications, whose knowledge has been freely utilised in the preparation of this book. I am equally grateful to my professor and colleagues for their encouragement and valuable help. My special thanks are due to my students who made me feel their difficulties, which was a great incentive for writing this book. I have derived maximum inspiration from Prof. Inderbir Singh (Rohtak), and learned the decency of work from Shri SC Gupta (Jiwaji University, Gwalior).

I am deeply indebted to Shri KM Singhal (National Book House, Gwalior) and Mr SK Jain (CBS Publishers and Distributors, Delhi), who have taken unusual pains to get the book printed in its present form. For giving it the desired get-up, Mr VK Jain and Raj Kamal Electric Press are gratefully acknowledged. The cover page was designed by Mr Vasant Paranjpe, the artist and photographer of our college; my sincere thanks are due to him. I acknowledge with affection the domestic assistance of Munne Miyan and the untiring company of my Rani, particularly during the odd hours of this work.

BD CHAURASIA

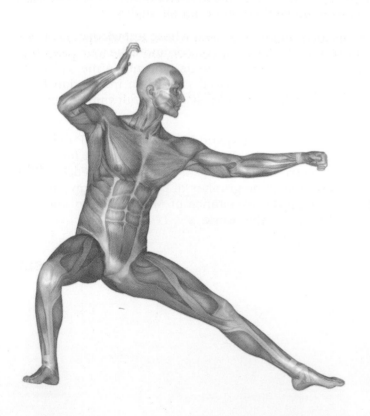

Acknowledgements

First acknowledgement is to Almighty for guiding the intellect along the correct path. Hope it is a continuous process.

Prof. Nafis Ahmad Faruqi, Chairman, Department of Anatomy, JLN Medical College, AMU, Aligarh and Prof. Shoukat N Kazi, Ex-Professer of Anatomy, DY Patil Medical College, Pune, have been generous to let me take material from their popular books. Their generosity is gratefully acknowledged.

Prof. Ved Prakash, Prof. Indira Bahl, Prof. Surinder Himmat Singh, Prof. DP Garg, Prof. Shashi L Malik, Director Prof. Suvira Gupta, Prof. Gayatri Rath, Prof. Shashi Raheja and Dr Anjali Dhamangaonkar of Mumbai have been guiding me whenever required.

Thanks are due to Prof. Mangala Kohli, Asstt. Director General, Medical Education, DGHS, Dr Shah Alam Khan, AIIMS, Dr Naresh Chand, Dr Preeti Srivastava, Dr Neeta Rani Garg, Dr Veena Aggarwal, Dr Kiran Vasudeva, all friends and our children for encouraging me. Rekha's contribution really needs much appreciation. Meenakshi Saran has been providing moral support and Dr Shilpa Garg has been appreciating my efforts.

The following students of various institutions have been kind enough to provide me feedback for the improvement of the volumes. They are Mr Saurabh Kumar, Amit Kumar Singh (2007–2008 batch) of Banarasi Das Chandiwala Institute of Physiotherapy; Sakshi, Shubham, Anant, Amrik of Ist year BDS of Shri Bankey Bihari Dental College; Rachit Chawla 2nd year student of Manipal College of Medical Sciences, Pokhran, Nepal; Mahesh Nepal of KUSMS, Nepal. I am indebted to them for their suggestions.

Heartfelt thanks to orchestra of "Limited Colors" for repeated textual corrections and artfully colouring the diagrams. I am obliged to Dr Medha Joshi of Krishna Dental College for reading the text and providing necessary suggestions.

Remembrances are due to Late Mr BR Sharma of CBS for encouraging me in all the endeavours.

Last, thanks are also due to Almighty.

Krishna Garg

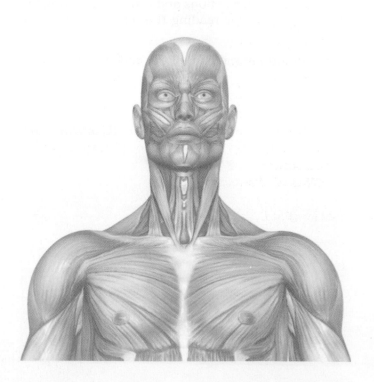

Contents

Section 2: ABDOMEN AND PELVIS

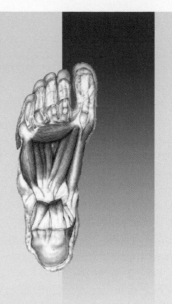

SECTION 1

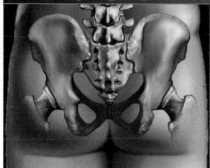

LOWER LIMB

CHAPTER 1

Introduction

The lower limb in its basic structure is similar to the upper limb because both of them formerly (as in animals) were used for locomotion. Each limb has a girdle, hip girdle or shoulder girdle, by which it is attached to the axial skeleton. The girdle supports three main segments of the limb, a proximal thigh or arm, a middle leg or forearm and a distal foot or hand. The similarity between the two limbs is not only outward, but to a great extent it is also found in the bones, joints, muscles, vessels, nerves and lymphatics.

However, with the evolution of erect or plantigrade posture in man, the two limbs despite their basic similarities have become specialized in different directions to meet the new functional needs. The emancipated upper limb is specialized for prehension and free mobility whereas the lower limb is specialized for support and locomotion. In general, the lower limbs attain stability at the cost of some mobility, and the upper limbs attain freedom of mobility at the cost of some stability. Thus the lower limbs are bulkier and stronger than the upper limbs (Fig. 1.1). A few of the distinguishing features of the lower limbs are listed below.

1. During early stages of development, the lower limb buds rotate medially through 90 degrees, so that their preaxial or tibial border faces medially and the extensor surface forwards (Fig. 1.2). The upper limb buds, on the other hand, rotate laterally through 90 degrees, so that their preaxial or radial border faces laterally and the extensor surface backwards (Fig. 1.3).

2. The antigravity muscles in the lower limb are much better developed than in the upper limb because they have to lift the whole body up during attaining the erect posture and also in walking up the staircase. These muscles are the gluteus maximus, extensor of hip (Fig. 1.4); the quadriceps femoris, extensor of knee (Fig. 1.5);

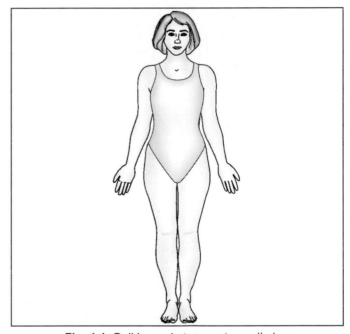

Fig. 1.1: Bulkier and stronger lower limbs.

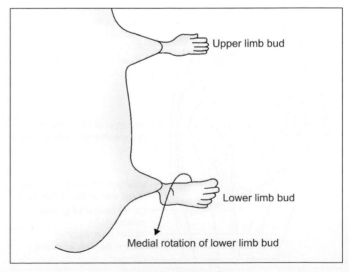

Upper limb bud

Lower limb bud

Medial rotation of lower limb bud

Fig. 1.2: Limb buds.

and the gastrocnemius and soleus, plantar flexors of ankle (Fig. 1.6). They have an extensive origin and a large, bulky fleshy belly.

3. The distal end or insertion of the muscles of lower limb moves only when feet are off the ground; this is known as the action from above. But when feet are supporting the body weight, the muscles act in reverse from below, i.e. the proximal end or origin moves towards the distal end or insertion. This is typically seen while rising up from a sitting posture, and in going

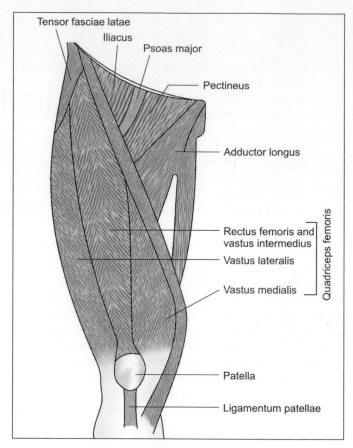

Fig. 1.5: The quadriceps femoris.

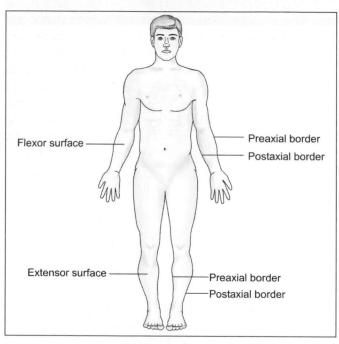

Fig. 1.3: Change in position of the preaxial and postaxial borders and surfaces.

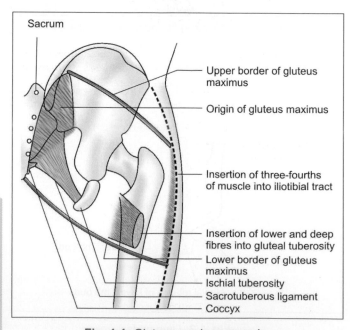

Fig. 1.4: Gluteus maximus muscle.

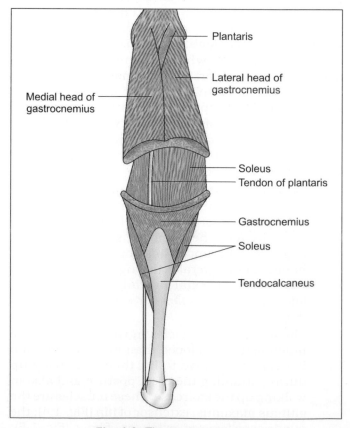

Fig. 1.6: The tendocalcaneus.

upstairs. Maintenance of posture in erect attitude, both at rest and in walking, running, etc., also involves the reverse action when the antagonist muscles must balance against each other. Reverse muscular actions are far less common in the upper limb.

4. The postaxial bone or fibula of the leg does not take part in the formation of knee joint (Fig. 1.7). Patella or knee cap is a large sesamoid bone developed in the tendon of quadriceps femoris. It articulates with the lower end of femur anteriorly, and takes part in the formation of knee joint (Fig. 1.8).

5. The foot in lower primates is a prehensile organ. The apes and monkeys can very well grasp the boughs with their feet. Their great toe can be opposed over the lesser toes. In man, however, the foot has changed from a grasping to a supporting organ. In fact, foot has undergone maximum change during evolution. The great toe comes in line with the other toes, loses its power of opposition, and is greatly enlarged to become the principal support of the body (Fig. 1.9). The four lesser toes, with the loss of prehensile function, have become vestigial and reduced in size. The tarsal bones become large, strong and wedge-shaped, which contribute to the stable support on one hand, and form the elastic arches of the foot on the other hand. The small and insignificant heel of the grasping primate foot becomes greatly enlarged and elongated to which is attached the tendocalcaneus that can lift the heel in walking. The bony alterations are associated with numerous ligamentous and muscular modifications which aim at the maintenance of the arches of foot.

6. Certain diseases, like varicose veins and Buerger's disease, occur specifically in the lower limb (Fig. 1.10). The developmental deformities of the foot like talipes equinovarus are more common than those of the hand.

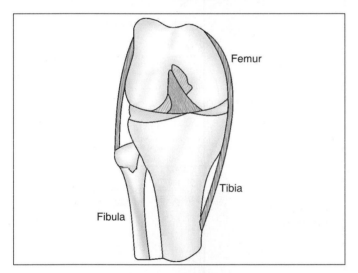

Fig. 1.7: Fibula not forming part of the knee joint.

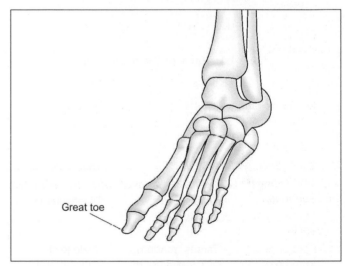

Fig. 1.9: The great toe of foot has lost the power of opposition.

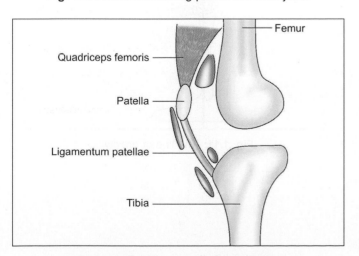

Fig. 1.8: Patella with its attachments.

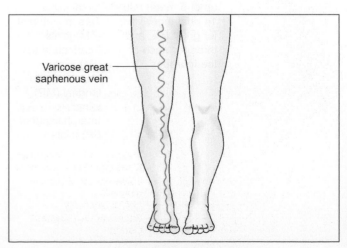

Fig. 1.10: Varicose veins.

PARTS OF THE LOWER LIMB

The parts of the lower limb are shown in Table 1.1.

Related Terms

1. The *hip bone* is made up of three elements, ilium, pubis and ischium, which are fused at the acetabulum. Two hip bones form the *hip girdle* which articulates posteriorly with the sacrum at the sacroiliac joints. The bony *pelvis* includes the two hip bones, a sacrum and a coccyx. *Hip joint* is an articulation between the hip bone and femur.

2. The *gluteal region,* overlying the side and back of the pelvis, includes the hip and the buttock which are not sharply distinguished from each other. *Hip* or *coxa* is the superolateral part of the gluteal region presented in a side view, while the *buttock* or *natis* is the inferomedial rounded bulge of the region presented in a back view.

3. The junction of thigh and anterior abdominal wall is indicated by the groove of groin or inguinal region. The *gluteal fold* is the upper limit of the thigh posteriorly.

4. *Ham* or *poples* is the lower part of the back of thigh and the back of the knee.

5. *Calf* or *sura* is the soft, bulky posterior part of the leg. The bony prominences, one on each side of the ankle, are called the *malleoli.* These are formed by the lower ends of tibia and fibula.

6. The foot or *pes* has an upper surface, called the *dorsal surface,* and a lower surface, called the *sole* or *plantar surface.* Sole is homologous with the palm of the hand.

The line of gravity passes through cervical and lumbar vertebrae. In the lower limbs, it passes behind the hip joint and in front of knee and ankle joints (Fig. 1.11).

Table 1.1: Parts of the lower limb		
Parts	**Bones**	**Joints**
1. Gluteal region, covers the side and back of the pelvis	• Hip bone	• Hip joint
2. Thigh, from hip to knee	• Femur • Patella	• Knee joint
3. Leg or crus, from knee to ankle	• Tibia • Fibula	• Tibiofibular joints
4. Foot or pes, from heel to toes	• Tarsus, made up of 7 tarsal bones • Metatarsus, made up of 5 metatarsals • 14 phalanges, two for great toe, and three for each of the four toes	• Ankle joint • Subtalar and transverse tarsal joints • Tarsometatarsal (TM) joints • Intermetatarsal (IM) joints • Metatarsophalangeal (MP) joints • Interphalangeal (IP) joints

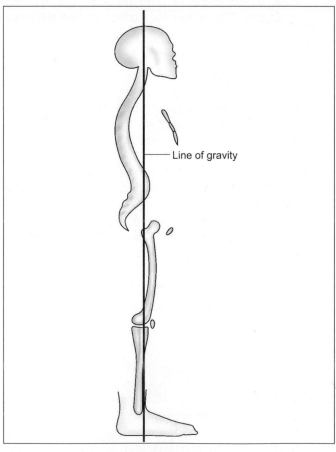

Fig. 1.11: The line of gravity.

CHAPTER 2

Bones of Lower Limb

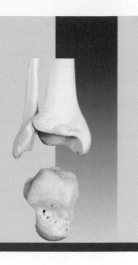

The various bones of the lower limb have been enumerated in the previous chapter. The bones are described one by one below. The description of each bone is given in two parts. The first part introduces the main features and the second part describes the attachments.

HIP BONE

Hip bone is a large irregular bone. It is made up of three parts. These are the *ilium* superiorly, the *pubis* anteroinferiorly, and the *ischium* posteroinferiorly. The three parts are joined to each other at a cup-shaped hollow, called the *acetabulum*. The pubis and ischium are separated by a large oval opening called the *obturator foramen*.

The acetabulum articulates with the head of the femur to form the *hip joint*. The pubic parts of the two hip bones meet anteriorly to form the *pubic symphysis*. The two hip bones form the *pelvic* or hip girdle. The bony pelvis is formed by the two hip bones along with the sacrum and coccyx.

Side Determination

1. The acetabulum is directed laterally.
2. The flat, expanded ilium forms the upper part of the bone, that lies above the acetabulum.
3. The obturator foramen lies below the acetabulum. It is bounded anteriorly by the thin pubis, and posteriorly by the thick and strong ischium.

Anatomical Position

1. The pubic symphysis and anterior superior iliac spine lie in the same coronal plane.
2. The pelvic surface of the body of the pubis is directed backwards and upwards.

3. The symphyseal surface of the body of the pubis lies in the median plane.

ILIUM

The ilium or *flank* forms the upper expanded plate like part of the hip bone. Its lower part forms the upper two-fifths of the acetabulum. The ilium has the following:

1. An upper end which is called the iliac crest.
2. A lower end which is smaller, and is fused with the pubis and the ischium at the acetabulum. The ilium forms the upper two-fifths of the acetabulum.
3. Three borders—anterior, posterior and medial.
4. Three surfaces—gluteal surface, iliac surface or iliac fossa, and a sacropelvic surface.

Iliac Crest

The iliac crest (Figs 2.1 to 2.3) is a broad convex ridge forming the upper end of the ilium. It can be felt in the living at the lower limit of the flank.

Curvatures: Vertically it is convex upwards, anteroposteriorly, it is concave inwards in front and concave outwards behind (Fig. 2.1).

The highest point of the iliac crest is situated a little behind the midpoint of the crest. It lies at the level of the interval between the spines of vertebrae L3 and L4.

Ends: The anterior end of the iliac crest is called the *anterior superior iliac spine* (ASIS). This is a prominent landmark that is easily felt in the living. The posterior end of the crest is called the *posterior superior iliac spine*. Its position on the surface of the body is marked by a dimple 4 cm lateral of the second sacral spine (Fig. 5.1).

Morphological divisions: Morphologically, the iliac crest is divided into a long *ventral segment* and a short *dorsal segment*.

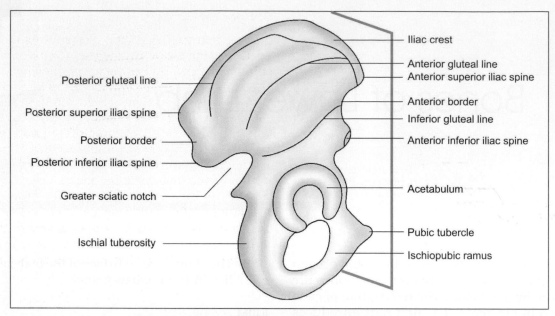

Fig. 2.1: General features of outer surface of hip bone.

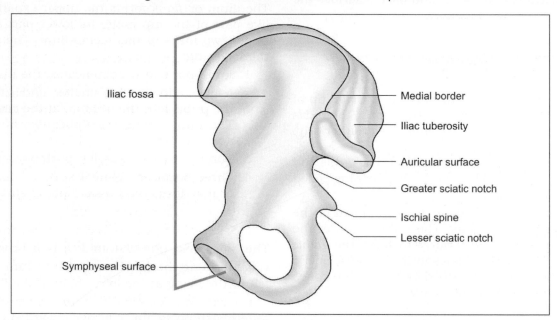

Fig. 2.2: General features of inner surface of hip bone.

The ventral segment forms more than the anterior two-thirds of the crest. It has an outer lip, an inner lip, and an intermediate area. The tubercle of the iliac crest is an elevation that lies on the outer lip about 5 cm behind the anterior superior iliac spine (Fig. 2.3).

The dorsal segment forms less than the posterior one-third of the crest. It has a lateral and a medial slope separated by a ridge.

Anterior Border of Ilium

Anterior border starts at the anterior superior iliac spine and runs downwards to the acetabulum. The upper part of the border presents a notch, while its lower part shows an elevated area called the *anterior inferior iliac spine*. The lower half of this spine is large, triangular and rough.

Posterior Border of Ilium

Posterior border extends from the posterior superior iliac spine to the upper end of the posterior border of the ischium. A few centimeters below the posterior superior iliac spine it presents another prominence called the *posterior inferior iliac spine*. Still lower down the posterior border is marked by a large deep notch called the *greater sciatic notch*.

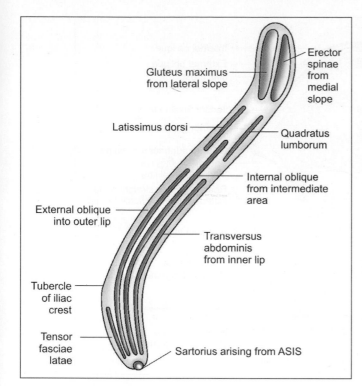

Fig. 2.3: Scheme to show the attachments on the right iliac crest (as seen from above).

Medial Border

Medial border extends on the inner or pelvic surface of the ilium from the iliac crest to the iliopubic eminence. It separates the iliac fossa from the sacropelvic surface. Its lower rounded part forms the iliac parts of the arcuate line or inlet of pelvis.

Gluteal Surface

Gluteal surface is the outer surface of the ilium, which is convex in front and concave behind, like the iliac crest. It is divided into four areas by three gluteal lines (Fig. 2.1). The *posterior gluteal line,* the shortest, begins 5 cm in front of the posterior superior spine, and ends just in front of the posterior inferior spine. The *anterior gluteal line,* the longest, begins about 2.5 cm behind the anterior superior iliac spine, runs backwards and then downwards to end at the middle of the upper border of the greater sciatic notch. The *inferior gluteal line,* the most ill-defined, begins a little above and behind the anterior inferior spine, runs backwards and downwards to end near the apex of the greater sciatic notch.

Iliac Fossa

Iliac fossa is the large concave area on the inner surface of the ilium, situated in front of its medial border. It forms the lateral wall of the false pelvis (Fig. 2.2).

Sacropelvic Surface

Sacropelvic surface is the uneven area on the inner surface of the ilium, situated behind its medial border. It is subdivided into three parts; the iliac tuberosity, the auricular surface and the pelvic surface. The *iliac tuberosity* is the upper, large, roughened area, lying just below the dorsal segment of the iliac crest. It is raised in the middle and depressed both above and below. The *auricular surface* is articular but pitted. It lies anteroinferior to the iliac tuberosity. It articulates with the sacrum to form the sacroiliac joint. The *pelvic surface* is smooth and lies anteroinferior to the auricular surface. It forms a part of the lateral wall of the true pelvis. Along the upper border of the greater sciatic notch, this surface is marked by the *preauricular sulcus.* This sulcus is deeper in females than in males.

Particular Features

Attachments on the Ilium

1. The *anterior superior iliac spine* gives attachment to the lateral end of the inguinal ligament. It also gives origin to the sartorius muscle; the origin extends onto the upper half of the notch below the spine (Figs 2.3 to 2.5).

2. The *outer lip of the iliac crest* provides:
   (a) Attachment to the fascia lata in its whole extent.
   (b) Origin to the tensor fasciae latae in front of the tubercle.
   (c) Insertion to the external oblique muscle in its anterior two-thirds.
   (d) Origin to the latissimus dorsi just behind the highest point of the crest. The tubercle of the crest gives attachment to the iliotibial tract (Figs 2.3 and 3.9).

3. The *inner lip of the iliac crest* provides:
   (a) Origin to the transversus abdominis in its anterior two-thirds (Fig. 16.11).
   (b) Attachment to the fascia transversalis and to the fascia iliaca in its anterior two-thirds, deep to the attachment of the transversus abdominis.
   (c) Origin to the quadratus lumborum in its posterior one-third (Fig. 2.9).
   (d) Attachment to the thoracolumbar fascia around the attachment of the quadratus lumborum.

4. The *intermediate area of the iliac crest* gives origin to the internal oblique muscle in its anterior two-thirds (Figs 2.3 and 2.4).

5. The attachments on the *dorsal segment of the iliac crest* are as follows.

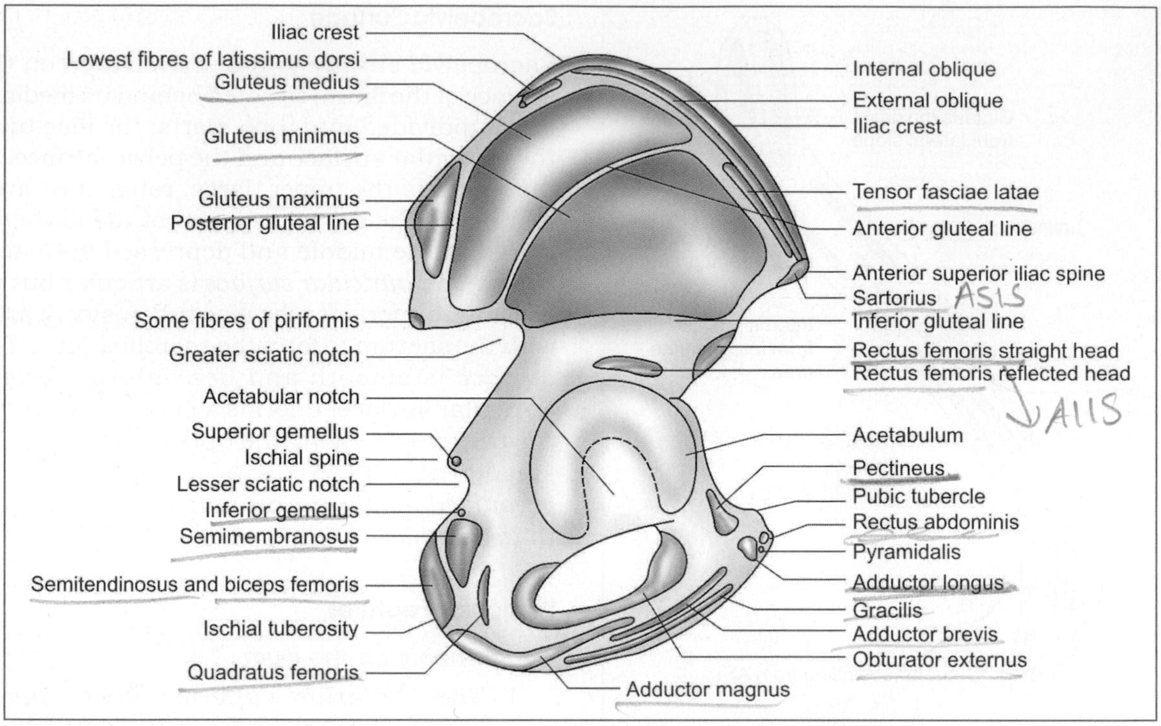

Iliac crest
Lowest fibres of latissimus dorsi
Gluteus medius
Gluteus minimus
Gluteus maximus
Posterior gluteal line
Some fibres of piriformis
Greater sciatic notch
Acetabular notch
Superior gemellus
Ischial spine
Lesser sciatic notch
Inferior gemellus
Semimembranosus
Semitendinosus and biceps femoris
Ischial tuberosity
Quadratus femoris

Internal oblique
External oblique
Iliac crest
Tensor fasciae latae
Anterior gluteal line
Anterior superior iliac spine
Sartorius *ASLS*
Inferior gluteal line
Rectus femoris straight head
Rectus femoris reflected head
↓AIIS
Acetabulum
Pectineus
Pubic tubercle
Rectus abdominis
Pyramidalis
Adductor longus
Gracilis
Adductor brevis
Obturator externus
Adductor magnus

Fig. 2.4: Attachments on the outer surface of the right hip bone.

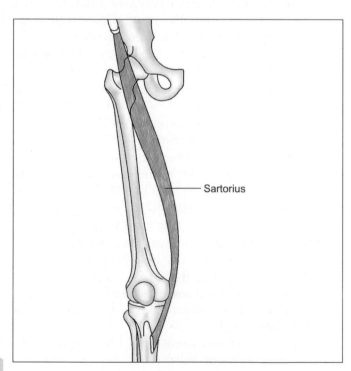

Sartorius

Fig. 2.5: Sartorius muscle.

(a) The lateral slope gives origin to the gluteus maximus (Fig. 2.3).

(b) The medial slope gives origin to the erector spinae.

(c) The interosseous and dorsal sacroiliac ligaments are attached to the medial margin

deep to the attachment of the erector spinae (Fig. 2.9).

6. The upper half of the *anterior inferior iliac spine* gives origin to the straight head of the rectus femoris. The rough lower part of this spine gives attachment to the iliofemoral ligament (Figs 2.4 and 2.22).

7. The *posterior border of the ilium* provides:

   (a) Attachment to upper fibres of the sacro-tuberous ligament above the greater sciatic notch (Fig. 2.6).

   (b) Origin to few fibres of the piriformis from upper margin of the greater sciatic notch.

8. The attachments on the *gluteal surface* are as follows.

   (a) The area behind the posterior gluteal line gives origin to upper fibres of the gluteus maximus (Fig. 2.7).

   (b) The gluteus medius arises from the area between the anterior and posterior gluteal lines.

   (c) The gluteus minimus arises from the area between the anterior and inferior gluteal lines.

   (d) Below the inferior gluteal line, the reflected head of the rectus femoris arises from the groove above the acetabulum (Fig. 2.4).

   (e) The capsular ligament of the hip joint is attached along the margin of acetabulum.

9. The iliac fossa gives origin to the iliacus from its upper two-thirds (Fig. 2.8). The lower grooved part of the fossa is covered by the iliac bursa.

10. The *iliac tuberosity* provides attachment to:

   (a) The interosseous sacroiliac ligament in its greater part (Fig. 2.9).

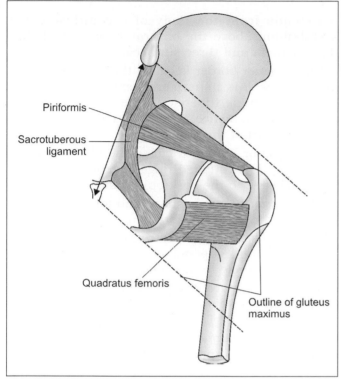

Fig. 2.6: Dotted lines outline gluteus maximus.

Piriformis

Sacrotuberous ligament

Quadratus femoris

Outline of gluteus maximus

   (b) The dorsal sacroiliac ligament posteriorly.

   (c) The iliolumbar ligament superiorly.

11. The convex margin of the *auricular surface* gives attachment to ventral sacroiliac ligament.

12. The attachments on the pelvic surface are as follows.

   (a) The preauricular sulcus provides attachment to the lower fibres of the ventral sacroiliac ligament.

   (b) The part of the pelvic surface lateral to the preauricular sulcus gives origin to a few fibres of the piriformis.

   (c) The rest of the pelvic surface gives origin to the upper half of the obturator internus (Fig. 2.9).

PUBIS

It forms the anteroinferior part of the hip bone and the anterior one-fifth of the acetabulum, forms the anterior boundary of the obturator foramen. It has:

   (a) A *body* anteriorly.

   (b) A *superior ramus* superolaterally.

   (c) An *inferior ramus* inferolaterally (Figs 2.1 and 2.2).

Body of Pubis

This is flattened from before backwards, and has:

   1. A superior border called the pubic crest.

   2. A pubic tubercle at the lateral end of the pubic crest.

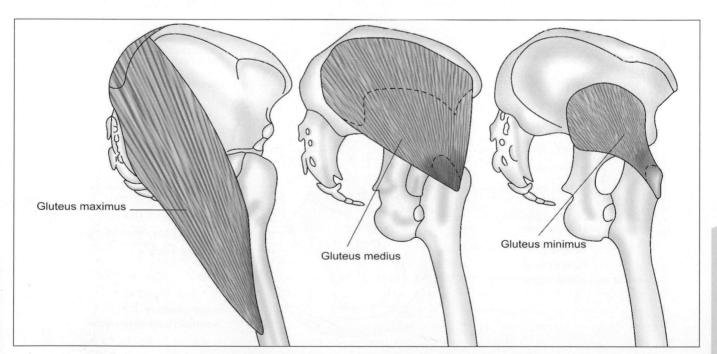

Gluteus maximus

Gluteus medius

Gluteus minimus

Fig. 2.7: The gluteus maximus, gluteus medius and gluteus minimus.

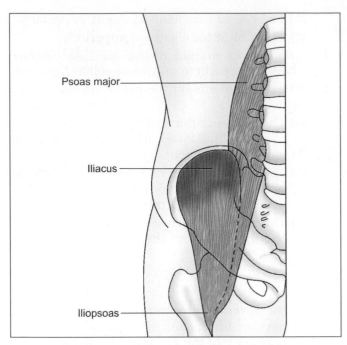

Fig. 2.8: Psoas major and iliacus muscles.

3. Three surfaces, viz. anterior, posterior and medial.

The *pubic tubercle* is the lateral end of the pubic crest, forming an important landmark (Fig. 2.9).

The *anterior surface* is directed downwards, forwards and slightly laterally. It is rough supero-medially and smooth elsewhere.

The *posterior* or *pelvic surface* is smooth. It is directed upwards and backwards. It forms the anterior wall of the true pelvis, and is related to the urinary bladder.

The *medial* or *symphyseal surface* articulates with the opposite pubis to form the pubic symphysis.

Superior Ramus

It extends from the body of the pubis to the acetabulum, above the obturator foramen. It has three borders and three surfaces.

The superior border is called the *pectineal line* or *pecten pubis.* It is a sharp crest extending from just behind the pubic tubercle to the posterior part of the iliopubic eminence. With the pubic crest it forms the pubic part of the arcuate line.

The anterior border is called the *obturator crest.* The border is a rounded ridge, extending from the pubic tubercle to the acetabular notch.

The *inferior border* is sharp and forms the upper margin of the obturator foramen.

The *pectineal surface* is a triangular area between the anterior and superior borders, extending from the pubic tubercle to the iliopubic eminence.

The *pelvic surface* lies between the superior and inferior borders. It is smooth and is continuous with the pelvic surface of the body of the pubis.

The *obturator surface* lies between the anterior and inferior borders. It presents the obturator groove.

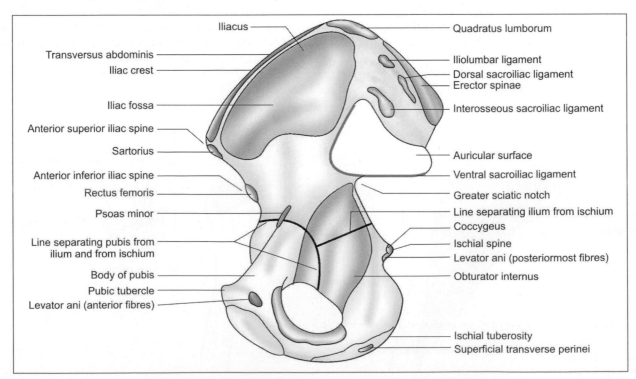

Fig. 2.9: Attachments of the inner surface of the right hip bone.

Inferior Ramus

It extends from the body of the pubis to the ramus of the ischium, medial to the obturator foramen. It unites with the ramus of the ischium to form the conjoined ischiopubic rami. For convenience of description, the conjoined rami will be considered together at the end.

Particular Features

Attachments and Relations of the Pubis

1. The *pubic tubercle* provides attachment to the medial end of the inguinal ligament and to ascending loops of the cremaster muscle. In males, the tubercle is crossed by the spermatic cord (Figs 3.2 and 4.3).
2. The medial part of the *pubic crest* is crossed by the medial head of the rectus abdominis. The lateral part of the crest gives origin to the lateral head of the rectus abdominis, and to the pyramidalis (Fig. 2.4).
3. The anterior surface of the body of the pubis provides:
   (a) Attachment to the anterior pubic ligament medially.
   (b) Origin to the adductor longus in the angle between the crest and the symphysis.
   (c) Origin to the gracilis, from the margin of symphysis, and from the inferior ramus.
   (d) Origin to the adductor brevis lateral to the origin of the gracilis (Fig. 2.4).
   (e) Origin to the obturator externus near the margin of the obturator foramen (Figs 2.10 and 2.11).

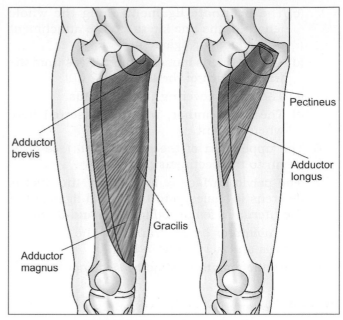

Fig. 2.10: The adductor muscles.

4. The *posterior surface* of the body of the pubis provides:
   (a) Origin to the levator ani from its middle part.
   (b) Origin to the obturator internus laterally (Fig. 2.9).
   (c) Attachment to the puboprostatic ligaments medial to the attachment of the levator ani.
5. The *pectineal line* provides attachment to:
   (a) The conjoint tendon at the medial end.
   (b) The lacunar ligament at the medial end, in front of the attachment of the conjoint tendon (Fig. 16.13).

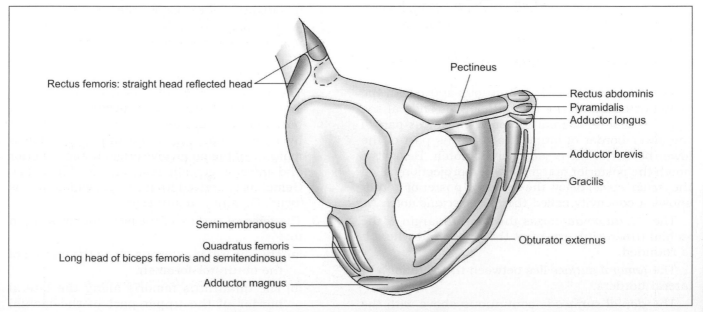

Fig. 2.11: Attachments of pubis and ischium.

(c) The pectinate ligament along the whole length of the line lateral to the attachment of the lacunar ligament

(d) The pectineus muscle which arises from the whole length of the line (Fig. 2.10).

(e) The fascia covering the pectineus.

(f) The psoas minor, which is inserted here when present.

6. The upper part of the *pectineal surface* gives origin to the pectineus (Fig. 2.11).

7. The pelvic surface is crossed by the ductus deferens in males, and the round ligament of the uterus in females (Figs 32.2 and 31.8).

8. The *obturator groove* transmits the obturator vessels and nerve (Fig. 4.6).

9. See attachments on conjoined ischiopubic rami.

ISCHIUM

The ischium forms the posteroinferior part of the hip bone, and the adjoining two-fifths of the acetabulum. It forms the posterior boundary of the obturator foramen. The ischium has a body and a ramus (Figs 2.1, 2.2 and 2.4).

Body of the Ischium

This is a thick and massive mass of bone that lies below and behind the acetabulum. It has two ends, upper and lower; three borders, anterior, posterior and lateral; and three surfaces, femoral, dorsal and pelvic.

The *upper end* forms the posteroinferior two-fifths of the acetabulum. The ischium, ilium and pubis fuse with each other in the acetabulum.

The *lower end* forms the *ischial tuberosity*. It gives off the ramus of the ischium which forms an acute angle with the body.

The *anterior border* forms the posterior margin of the obturator foramen.

The *posterior border* is continuous above with the posterior border of the ilium. Below, it ends at the upper end of the ischial tuberosity. It forms part of the lower border of ilium. It also forms part of the lower border of the greater sciatic notch. Below the notch the posterior margin shows a projection called the *ischial spine*. Below the spine the posterior border shows a concavity called the *lesser sciatic notch*.

The *lateral border* forms the lateral margin of the ischial tuberosity, except at the upper end where it is rounded.

The *femoral surface* lies between the anterior and lateral borders.

The *dorsal surface* is continuous above with the gluteal surface of the ilium. From above downwards

it presents a convex surface adjoining the acetabulum, a wide shallow groove, and the upper part of the ischial tuberosity.

The *ischial tuberosity* is divided by a transverse ridge into an upper and a lower area. The upper area is subdivided by an oblique ridge into a superolateral area and an inferomedial area. The lower area is subdivided by a longitudinal ridge into outer and inner area (Fig. 2.14).

The *pelvic surface* is smooth and forms part of the lateral wall of the true pelvis.

Conjoined Ischiopubic Rami

The inferior ramus of the pubis unites with the ramus of the ischium on the medial side of the obturator foramen. The site of union may be marked by a localized thickening. The conjoined rami have:

1. Two borders, upper and lower

2. Two surfaces, outer and inner.

The *upper border* forms part of the margin of the obturator foramen.

The *lower border* forms the pubic arch along with the corresponding border of the bone of the opposite side.

The *inner surface* is convex and smooth. It is divided into three areas, upper, middle and lower, by two ridges.

Particular Features

Attachments and Relations of the Ischium

1. The *ischial spine* provides:

    (a) Attachment to the sacrospinous ligament along its margins.

    (b) Origin for the posterior fibres of the levator ani from its pelvic surface. Its dorsal surface is crossed by the internal pudendal vessels and by the nerve to the obturator internus (Figs 2.9 and 5.12).

2. The *lesser sciatic notch* is occupied by the tendon of the obturator internus. There is a bursa deep to the tendon. The notch is lined by hyaline cartilage. The upper and lower margins of the notch give origin to the superior and inferior gemelli respectively (Fig. 2.12). Gemellus is derived from gemini, which means 'twin'. Gemini is a sun sign.

3. The *femoral surface* of the ischium gives origin to:

    (a) The obturator externus along the margin of the obturator foramen.

    (b) The quadratus femoris along the lateral border of the upper part of the ischial tuberosity (Fig. 2.11).

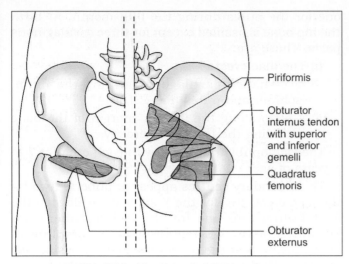

Fig. 2.12: Muscles of gluteal region.

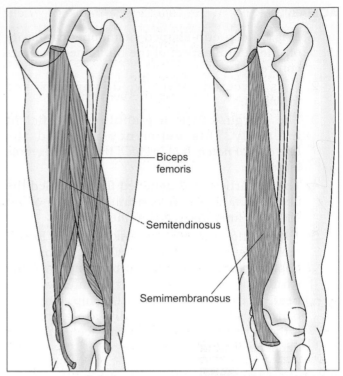

Fig. 2.13: Hamstring muscles.

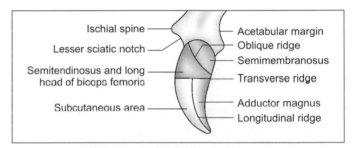

Fig. 2.14: Posterior view of the right ischial tuberosity and its attachments.

4. The *dorsal surface* of the ischium has the following relationships. The upper convex area is related to the piriformis, the sciatic nerve, and the nerve to the quadratus femoris. The groove transmits the tendon of the obturator internus (Fig. 2.12).
5. The attachments on the *ischial tuberosity* are as follows.

   The superolateral area gives origin to the semimembranosus, the inferomedial area to the semitendinosus and the long head of the biceps femoris, and the outer lower area to the adductor magnus (Figs 2.13 and 2.14). The inner lower area is covered with fibrofatty tissue which supports body weight in the sitting position. The sharp medial margin of the tuberosity gives attachment to the sacrotuberous ligament. The lateral border of the ischial tuberosity provides attachment to the ischiofemoral ligament, just below the acetabulum.
6. The greater part of the pelvic surface of the ischium gives origin to the obturator internus. The lower end of this surface forms part of the lateral wall of the ischioanal fossa (Fig. 2.9).
7. The attachments on the *conjoined ischiopubic rami* are as follows.
   (a) The upper border gives attachment to the obturator membrane.
   (b) The lower border provides attachment to the fascia lata, and to the membranous layer of superficial fascia or Colles' fascia of the perineum.
   (c) The muscles taking origin from the outer surface are:
      (i) The obturator externus, near the obturator margin of both rami.
      (ii) The adductor brevis, chiefly from the pubic ramus.
      (iii) The gracilis, chiefly from the pubic ramus.
      (iv) The adductor magnus, chiefly from the ischial ramus (Fig. 2.4).
   (d) The attachments on the inner surface are as follows. The perineal membrane is attached to the lower ridge. The upper area gives origin to the obturator internus. The middle area gives origin to the deep transverse perinei, and is related to the dorsal nerve of the penis, and to the internal pudendal vessels. The lower area provides attachment to crus penis, and gives origin to the ischiocavernosus and to superficial transverse perinei (Fig. 2.15).

ACETABULUM

1. It is a deep cup-shaped hemispherical cavity on the lateral aspect of the hip bone, about its centre.
2. It is directed laterally, downwards and forwards.
3. The margin of the acetabulum is deficient inferiorly, this deficiency is called the *acetabular notch.* It is bridged by the transverse ligament.
4. The nonarticular roughened floor is called the acetabular fossa. It contains a mass of fat which is lined by synovial membrane.
5. A horseshoe-shaped articular surface or lunate surface is seen on the anterior, superior, and posterior parts of the acetabulum. It is lined with hyaline cartilage, and articulates with the head of the femur to form the hip joint. The fibrocartilaginous acetabular labrum is attached to the margins of the acetabulum; it deepens the acetabular cavity.

OBTURATOR FORAMEN

1. This is a large gap in the hip bone, situated anteroinferior to acetabulum, between the pubis and the ischium.
2. It is large and oval in males, and small and triangular in females.
3. It is closed by the obturator membrane which is attached to its margins, except at the obturator groove where the obturator vessels and nerve pass out of the pelvis.

Ossification: The hip bone ossifies in cartilage from three primary centres and five secondary centres. The primary centres appear, one for the ilium during the second month of intrauterine life; one for the ischium during the fourth month; and

one for the pubis during the fifth month. At birth the hip bone is ossified except for three cartilaginous parts. These are:

(i) The iliac crest.
(ii) A Y-shaped cartilage separating the ilium, ischium and pubis (Fig. 2.16).
(iii) A strip along the inferior margin of the bone including the ischial tuberosity.

The ischiopubic rami fuse with each other at 7 to 8 years of age.

The secondary centres appear at puberty, two for the iliac crest, two for the Y-shaped cartilage of the acetabulum and one for the ischial tuberosity. Ossification in the acetabulum is complete at 16–17 years, and the rest of the bone is ossified by 20–25 years. The anterior superior iliac spine, pubic tubercle and crest and the symphyseal surface may have separate secondary centres of ossification.

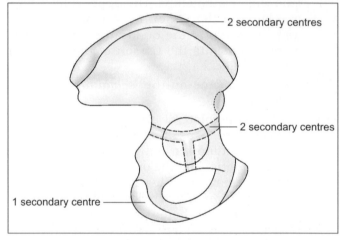

Fig. 2.16: Ossification of the hip bone.

FEMUR

The femur or thigh bone is the longest and the strongest bone of the body. Like any other long bone it has two ends upper and lower, and a shaft (Figs 2.17 and 2.18).

Side Determination

1. The upper end bears a rounded head whereas the lower end is widely expanded to form two large condyles.
2. The head is directed medially.
3. The cylindrical shaft is convex forwards.

Anatomical Position

1. The head is directed medially upwards and slightly forwards.

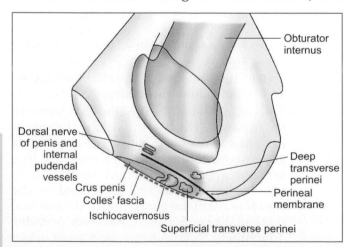

Fig. 2.15: Attachments on the inner surfaces of the right ischiopubic rami.

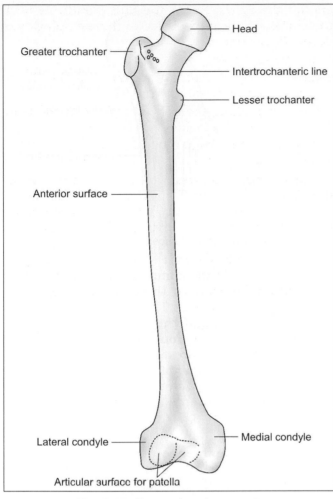

Fig. 2.17: Femur: Anterior aspect.

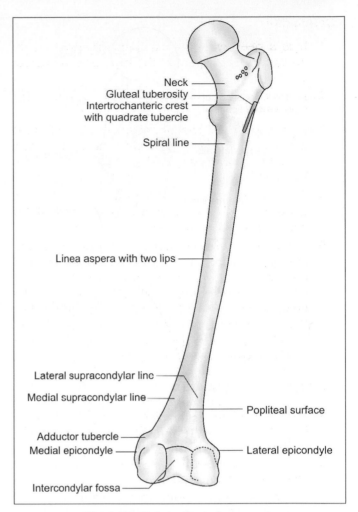

Fig. 2.18: Femur: Posterior aspect.

2. The shaft is directed obliquely downwards and medially so that the lower surfaces of two condyles of femur lie in the same horizontal plane.

Upper End

The upper end of the femur includes the head, the neck, the greater trochanter, the lesser trochanter, the intertrochanteric line, and the intertrochanteric crest. These are described as follows.

Head

1. The head forms more than half a sphere, and is directed medially, upwards and slightly forwards (Fig. 2.19).
2. It articulates with the acetabulum to form the hip joint.
3. A roughened pit is situated just below and behind the centre of the head. This pit is called the fovea.
4. *Blood supply*
   (a) The smaller, medial part of the head, near the fovea, is supplied by medial *epiphyseal*

arteries derived from the posterior division of the obturator artery and from the ascending branch of the *medial circumflex femoral artery*. These arterial twigs enter the acetabular notch and then pass along the round ligament to reach the head (Fig. 4.8).

(b) The larger, lateral part of the head is supplied by *lateral epiphyseal arteries* which are derived from the retinacular branches of the medial circumflex femoral artery. This set constitutes the main supply and damage to it results in necrosis of the head following intracapsular fractures of the neck of the femur. After epiphyseal fusion, the lateral epiphyseal arteries anastomose freely with the metaphyseal arteries.

Neck

1. It connects the head with the shaft and is about 3.7 cm long.
2. The neck makes an angle with the shaft. The *neck-shaft angle* is about 125° in adults. It is

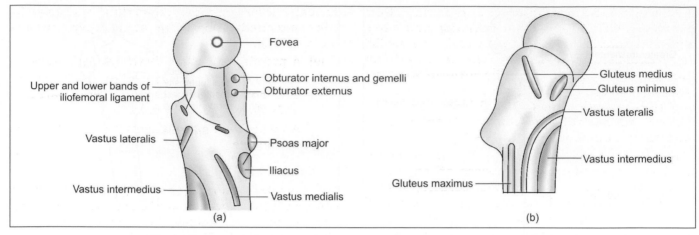

Fig. 2.19: Upper end of the right femur: (a) Medial aspect, (b) Lateral aspect.

less in females due to their wider pelvis. The angle facilitates movements of the hip joint. It is strengthened by a thickening of bone called the *calcar femorale* present along its concavity.

3. The neck has two borders and two surfaces. The *upper border,* concave and horizontal, meets the shaft at the greater trochanter. The *lower border,* straight and oblique, meets the shaft near the lesser trochanter. The *anterior surface* is flat. It meets the shaft at the intertrochanteric line. It is entirely intracapsular. The articular cartilage of the head may extend to this surface. The *posterior surface* is convex from above downwards and concave from side to side. It meets the shaft at the intertrochanteric crest. Only a little more than its medial half is intracapsular. The posterior surface is crossed by a horizontal groove for the tendon of the obturator externus to be inserted into the trochanteric fossa.

4. The *angle of femoral torsion* or angle of anteversion is formed between the transverse axes of the upper and lower ends of the femur. It is about 15 degrees.

5. *Blood supply:* The intracapsular part of the neck is supplied by the retinacular arteries derived chiefly from the trochanteric anastomosis. The vessels produce longitudinal grooves and foramina directed towards the head, mainly on the anterior and posterosuperior surfaces. The extracapsular part of the neck is supplied by the ascending branch of the medial circumflex femoral artery.

Greater Trochanter

1. This is large quadrangular prominence located at the upper part of the junction of neck with the shaft. The upper border of the trochanter lies at the level of the centre of the head.

2. The greater trochanter has an upper border with an apex, and three surfaces, anterior, medial and lateral. The *apex* is the inturned posterior part of the posterior border. The *anterior surface* is rough in its lateral part. The *medial surface* presents a rough impression above, and a deep *trochanteric fossa* below. The *lateral surface* is crossed by an oblique ridge directed downwards and forwards.

Lesser Trochanter

It is a conical eminence directed medially and backwards from the junction of the posteroinferior part of the neck with the shaft.

Intertrochanteric line

It marks the junction of the anterior surface of the neck with the shaft of the femur. It is a prominent roughened ridge which begins above, at the anterosuperior angle of the greater trochanter as a tubercle, and is continuous below with the spiral line in front of the lesser trochanter. The spiral line winds round the shaft below the lesser trochanter to reach the posterior surface of the shaft (Fig. 2.18).

Intertrochanteric crest

It marks the junction of the posterior surface of the neck with the shaft of the femur. It is a smoothrounded ridge, which begins above at the posterosuperior angle of the greater trochanter and ends at the lesser trochanter. The rounded elevation, a little above its middle, is called the *quadrate tubercle.*

Shaft

The shaft is more or less cylindrical. It is narrowest in the middle, and is more expanded inferiorly than superiorly. It is convex forwards and is directed obliquely downwards and medially, because the upper ends of two femora are separated by the width of the pelvis, and their lower ends are close together.

In the *middle one-third,* the shaft has three borders, medial, lateral and posterior and three surfaces, anterior, medial and lateral. The medial and lateral borders are rounded and ill-defined, but the posterior border is in the form of a broad roughened ridge, called the *linea aspera.* The linea aspera has distinct medial and lateral lips. The medial and lateral surfaces are directed more backwards than towards the sides.

In the *upper one-third of the shaft,* the two lips of the linea aspera diverge to enclose an additional posterior surface. Thus it has four borders, medial, lateral, spiral line and the lateral lip of the gluteal tuberosity and four surfaces anterior, medial, lateral and posterior. The gluteal tuberosity is a broad roughened ridge on the lateral part of the posterior surface.

In the *lower one-third of the shaft* also, the two lips of the linea aspera diverge as supracondylar lines to enclose an additional, popliteal surface. Thus, this part of the shaft has four borders, medial, lateral, medial supracondylar line and lateral supracondylar line and four surfaces, anterior, medial, lateral and popliteal. The medial border and medial supracondylar line meet inferiorly to obliterate the medial surface.

Lower End

The lower end of the femur is widely expanded to form two large condyles, one medial and one lateral. Anteriorly, the two condyles are united and are in line with the front of the shaft. Posteriorly, they are separated by a deep gap, termed the intercondylar fossa or intercondylar notch, and project backwards much beyond the plane of the popliteal surface.

Articular Surface

The two condyles are partially covered by a large articular surface which is divisible into patellar and tibial parts. The *patellar surface* covers the anterior surfaces of both condyles, and extends more on the lateral condyle than on the medial (Fig. 2.17). Between the two condyles, the surface is grooved vertically. It is separated from the tibial surfaces by two faint grooves. The *tibial surfaces* cover the inferior and posterior surfaces of the two condyles, and merge anteriorly with the patellar surface. The part of the surface over the lateral condyle is short and straight anteroposteriorly. The part over the medial condyle is longer and is curved with its convexity directed medially.

Lateral Condyle

The lateral condyle is flat laterally, and is more in line with the shaft. It, therefore, takes greater part in the transmission of body weight to the tibia.

Though it is less prominent than the medial condyle, it is stouter and stronger. The lateral aspect presents the following.

(a) A prominence called the *lateral epicondyle.*
(b) The *popliteal groove* which lies just below the epicondyle. It has a deeper anterior part and a shallower posterior part.
(c) A *muscular impression* posterosuperior to the epicondyle.

Medial Condyle

This condyle is convex medially. The most prominent point on it is called the *medial epicondyle.* Postero-superior to the epicondyle there is a projection, the *adductor tubercle.* This tubercle is an important landmark. The epiphyseal line for the lower end of the femur passes through it.

Intercondylar Fossa or Intercondylar Notch

This notch separates the lower and posterior parts of the two condyles. It is limited anteriorly by the patellar articular surface, and posteriorly by the intercondylar line which separates the notch from the popliteal surface.

Particular Features

Attachments on the Femur

1. The fovea on the head of the femur provides attachment to the ligament of the head of femur or round ligament, or ligamentum teres (Figs 4.8 and 12.2).
2. The following are attached to the *greater trochanter.*
   (a) The *piriformis* is inserted into the apex.
   (b) The *gluteus minimus* is inserted into the rough lateral part of the anterior surface (Fig. 2.19a).
   (c) The *obturator internus* and the *two gemelli* are inserted into the upper rough impression on medial surface.
   (d) The obturator externus is inserted into the trochanteric fossa.
   (e) The gluteus medius is inserted into the ridge on the lateral surface (Fig. 2.19b). The trochanteric bursa of the gluteus maximus lies behind the ridge.
3. The attachments on the *lesser trochanter* are as follows.
   (a) The psoas major is inserted on the apex and medial part of the rough anterior surface (Figs 2.8, 2.20 and 2.21).
   (b) The iliacus is inserted on the anterior surface of the base of the trochanter and on the area below it.

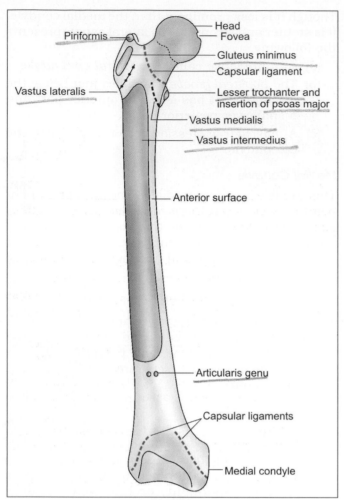

Fig. 2.20: Attachments on the anterior aspect of the right femur.

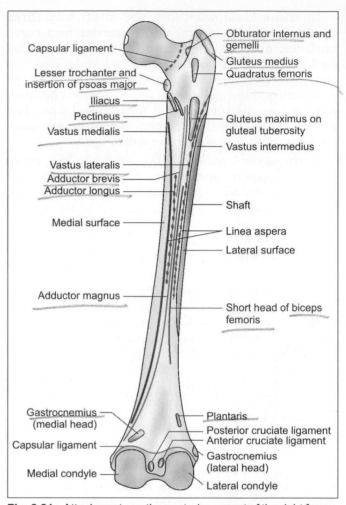

Fig. 2.21: Attachments on the posterior aspect of the right femur.

(c) The smooth posterior surface of the lesser trochanter is covered by a bursa that lies deep to the upper horizontal fibres of the adductor magnus.

4. The *intertrochanteric line* provides:
   (a) Attachment to the capsular ligament of the hip joint.
   (b) Attachment to the upper band of the iliofemoral ligament in its upper part.
   (c) Attachment to the lower band of iliofemoral ligament in its lower part (Fig. 2.22).
   (d) Origin to the highest fibres of the vastus lateralis from the upper end.
   (e) Origin to the highest fibres of the vastus medialis from the lower end of the line.
5. The *quadrate tubercle* receives the insertion of the quadratus femoris (Fig. 2.21).
6. The attachments on the *shaft* are as follows.
   (a) The medial and popliteal surfaces are bare, except for a little extension of the origin of the medial head of the gastrocnemius to the popliteal surface.

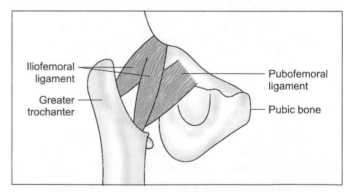

Fig. 2.22: Attachment of iliofemoral ligament.

(b) The *vastus intermedius* arises from the upper three-fourths of the anterior and lateral surfaces (Fig. 2.20).
(c) The *articularis genu* arises just below the vastus intermedius.
(d) The lower 5 cm of the anterior surface are related to *suprapatellar bursa* (Fig. 3.7).
(e) The *vastus lateralis* arises from the upper part of the intertrochanteric line, anterior

and inferior borders of the greater trochanter, the lateral lip of the gluteal tuberosity, and the upper half of the lateral lip of the linea aspera.

(f) The *vastus medialis* arises from the lower part of intertrochanteric line, the spiral line, medial lip of the linea aspera, and the upper one-fourth of medial supracondylar line.

(g) The deeper fibres of the lower half of the *gluteus maximus* are inserted into the gluteal tuberosity.

(h) The *adductor longus* is inserted along the medial lip of the linea aspera between the vastus medialis and the adductors brevis and magnus.

(i) The *adductor brevis* is inserted into a line extending from the lesser trochanter to the upper part of the linea aspera, behind the pectineus and the upper part of the adductor longus.

(j) The *adductor magnus* is inserted into the medial margin of the gluteal tuberosity, the linea aspera, the medial supracondylar line, and the adductor tubercle, leaving a gap for the popliteal vessels (Fig. 4.2a).

(k) The *pectineus* is inserted on a line extending from the lesser trochanter to the linea aspera.

(l) The *short head of the biceps femoris* arises from the lateral lip of the linea aspera between the vastus lateralis and the adductor magnus, and from the upper two-thirds of the lateral supracondylar line.

(m) The medial and lateral *intermuscular septa* are attached to the lips of the linea aspera and to the supracondylar lines. They separate the extensor muscles from the adductors medially, and from the flexors laterally (Fig. 3.10).

(n) The lower end of the lateral supracondylar line gives origin to the *plantaris* above and the upper part of the *lateral head of the gastrocnemius* below.

(o) The popliteal surface is covered with fat and forms the floor of the popliteal fossa (Fig. 6.3b). The origin of the *medial head of the gastrocnemius* extends to the popliteal surface just above the medial condyle.

7. The attachments on the *lateral condyle* are:
   (a) The fibular collateral ligament of the knee joint is attached to the lateral epicondyle (Figs 2.23 and 12.10).
   (b) The popliteus arises from the deep anterior part of the popliteal groove. When the knee

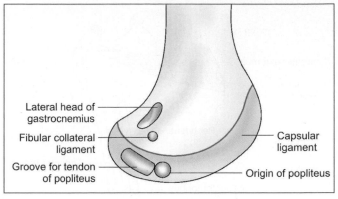

Fig. 2.23: Attachments on the lateral surface of the lateral condyle of the femur.

is flexed the tendon of this muscle lies in the shallow posterior part of the groove.

(c) The muscular impression near the lateral epicondyle gives origin to the lateral head of the gastrocnemius.

8. The attachments on the *medial condyle* are as follows.
   (a) The tibial collateral ligament of the knee joint is attached to the medial epicondyle (Fig. 12.9).
   (b) The adductor tubercle receives the insertion of the hamstring part or the ischial head of the adductor magnus (Fig. 2.24).

9. The attachments on the *intercondylar notch* are as follows.
   (a) The *anterior cruciate ligament* is attached to the posterior part of the medial surface of the lateral condyle, on a smooth impression.
   (b) The *posterior cruciate ligament* is attached to the anterior part of the lateral surface of medial condyle, on a smooth impression (Fig. 2.21).
   (c) The *intercondylar line* provides attachment to the capsular ligament and laterally to the oblique popliteal ligament. The *infra-patellar synovial fold* is attached to the anterior border of the intercondylar fossa.

Nutrient Artery to the Femur

This is derived from the *second perforating artery*. The nutrient foramen is located on the medial side of the linea aspera, and is directed upwards.

Ossification: The femur ossifies from one primary and four secondary centres. The primary centre for the shaft appears in the seventh week of intrauterine life. The secondary centres appear, one for the lower end at the end of the ninth month of intrauterine life, one for the head during the first six months of

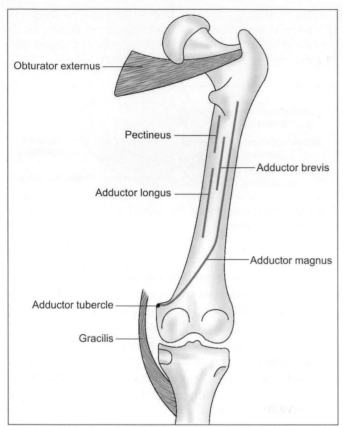

Fig. 2.24: The linear insertion of the adductors extends from the trochanteric fossa above to the medial surface of the tibia below.

life, one for the greater trochanter during the fourth year, and one for the lesser trochanter during the twelfth year (Fig. 2.25).

There are three epiphyses at the upper end and one epiphysis at the lower end. The upper epiphyses; lesser trochanter, greater trochanter and head, in that order, fuse with the shaft at about eighteen years. The lower epiphysis fuses by the twentieth year.

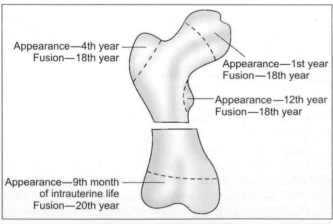

Fig. 2.25: Ossification of femur.

The following points are noteworthy.

1. The neck represents the upper end of the shaft because it ossifies from the primary centre.
2. Ossification of the lower end of the femur is of medicolegal importance. Presence of its centre in a newly born child found dead indicates that the child was viable, i.e. it was capable of independent existence.
3. The lower end of the femur is the growing end.
4. The lower epiphyseal line passes through the adductor tubercle.
5. The epiphyseal line of the head coincides with the articular margins, except superiorly where a part of the non-articular area is included in the epiphysis for passage of blood vessels to the head. In addition, the plane of this epiphysis changes with age from an oblique to a more vertical one.

Structure

The angles and curvatures of the femur are strengthened on their concave sides by bony buttresses. The concavity of the neck-shaft angle is strengthened by a thickened buttress of compact bone, known as the *calcar femorale*. Similarly, the linea aspera is also supported by another buttress. This mechanism helps in resisting stresses including that of body weight.

PATELLA

The patella is the largest sesamoid bone in the body, developed in the tendon of the quadriceps femoris. It is situated in front of the lower end of the femur about 1 cm above the knee joint (Fig. 2.26).

Side Determination

1. The patella is triangular in shape with its apex directed downwards. The apex is non-articular posteriorly.
2. The anterior surface is rough and non-articular. The upper three-fourths of the posterior surface are smooth and articular.
3. The posterior articular surface is divided by a vertical ridge into a larger lateral area and a smaller medial area. The bone laid on a table rests on the broad lateral area and determines the side of the bone.

Features

The patella has an apex, three borders, superior, lateral and medial, and two surfaces, anterior and posterior.

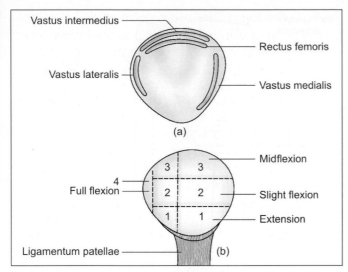

Fig. 2.26: Features of the right patella, (a) Anterior view, and (b) Posterior view. Areas of patella in contact with patellar surface of femur during movement.

The *apex* directed downwards, is rough and vertically ridged. It is covered by an expansion from the tendon of the rectus femoris, and is separated from the skin by the prepatellar bursa. The *posterior surface* is articular in its upper three-fourths and non-articular in its lower one-fourth.

The articular area is divided by a vertical ridge into a larger lateral and smaller medial portion. Another vertical ridge separates a medial strip from the medial portion. This strip articulates with a reciprocal strip on the medial side of the inter-condylar notch of the femur during full flexion. The rest of the medial portion and the lateral portion of the articular surface are divided by two transverse lines into three pairs of facets.

During different phases of movements of the knee, different portions of the patella articulate with the femur. The lower pair of articular facets articulates during extension; middle pair during beginning of flexion; upper pair during midflexion; and the medial strip during full flexion of the knee (Fig. 12.6).

Attachments on the Patella

The *superior border* or base provides insertion to the rectus femoris in front and to the vastus intermedius behind. The *lateral border* provides insertion to vastus lateralis in its upper one-third or half. The *medial border* provides insertion to the vastus medialis in its upper two-thirds.

The non-articular area on the posterior surface provides attachment to the ligamentum patellae below, and is related to infrapatellar pad of fat above.

Ossification: The patella ossifies from several centres which appear during 3 to 6 years of age. Fusion is complete at puberty.

One or two centres at the superolateral angle of the patella may form separate pieces of bone. Such a patella is known as bipartite or tripartite patella. The condition is bilateral and symmetrical (Fig. 2.27).

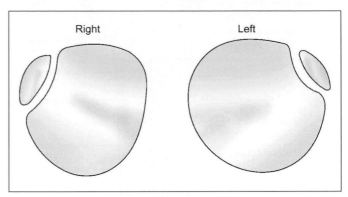

Fig. 2.27: Bipartite patella.

TIBIA

The tibia is the medial and larger bone of the leg. It is homologous with the radius of the upper limb.

Side Determination

1. The upper end is much larger than the lower end.
2. The medial side of the lower end projects downwards beyond the rest of the bone. The projection is called the medial malleolus.
3. The anterior border of the shaft is most prominent and crest-like. It is sinuously curved and terminates below at the anterior border of the medial malleolus.

Features

The tibia has an upper end, a shaft and a lower end (Figs 2.28 and 2.29).

Upper End

The upper end of the tibia is markedly expanded from side to side, to form two large condyles which overhang the posterior surface of the shaft. The upper end includes:

(a) A medial condyle,
(b) A lateral condyle,
(c) An intercondylar area,
(d) A tuberosity (Fig. 2.30).

Medial condyle

Medial condyle is larger than the lateral condyle. Its superior surface articulates with the medial condyle of the femur. The articular surface is oval and its long axis is anteroposterior. The central part of the

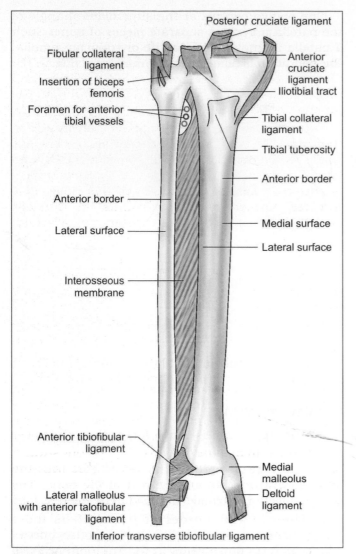

Fig. 2.28: Anterior view of right tibia and fibula including the ligaments.

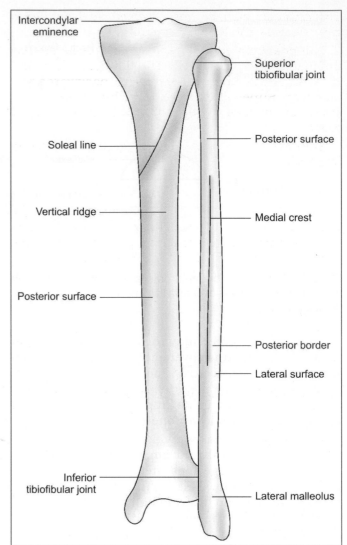

Fig. 2.29: Posterior view of tibia and fibula.

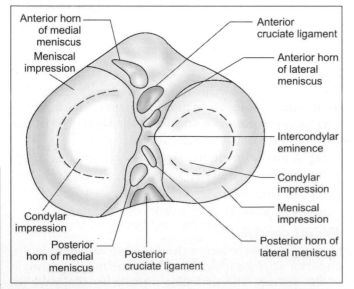

Fig. 2.30: Superior view of the upper end of the right tibia.

surface is slightly concave and comes into direct contact with the femoral condyle. The peripheral part is flat and is separated from the femoral condyle by the medial meniscus. The lateral margin of the articular surface is raised to cover the medial intercondylar tubercle.

The posterior surface of the medial condyle has a groove. The anterior and medial surfaces are marked by numerous vascular foramina.

Lateral condyle

The lateral condyle overhangs the shaft more than the medial condyle. The superior surface of the condyle articulates with the lateral condyle of the femur. The articular surface is nearly circular. As in the case of the medial condyle, the central part is slightly concave and comes in direct contact with the femur, but the peripheral part is flat and is separated from the femur by the lateral meniscus.

The articular surface has a raised medial margin which covers the lateral intercondylar tubercle.

The posteroinferior aspect of the lateral condyle articulates with the fibula. The fibular facet is flat, circular, and is directed downwards, backwards and laterally. Superomedial to the fibular facet, the posterior surface of the condyle is marked by a groove.

The anterior aspect of the condyle bears a flattened impression.

Intercondylar Area

Intercondylar area is the roughened area on the superior surface, between the articular surfaces of the two condyles. The area is narrowest in its middle part. This part is elevated to form the intercondylar eminence which is flanked by the medial and lateral intercondylar tubercles.

Tuberosity of the tibia

Tuberosity of the tibia is a prominence located on the anterior aspect of the upper end of the tibia. It forms the anterior limits of the intercondylar area. Inferiorly it is continuous with the anterior border of the shaft. The tuberosity is divided into an upper smooth area and a lower rough area. The epiphyseal line for the upper end of the tibia passes through the junction of these two parts.

Shaft

The shaft of the tibia is prismoid in shape. It has three borders, anterior, medial and interosseous; and three surfaces, lateral, medial and posterior.

Borders

The *anterior border* is sharp and S-shaped being convex medially in the upper part and convex laterally in the lower part. It extends from the tibial tuberosity above to the anterior border of the medial malleolus below. It is subcutaneous and forms the *shin.*

The *medial border* is rounded. It extends from the medial condyle, above, to the posterior border of the medial malleolus, below.

The *interosseous* or *lateral border* extends from the lateral condyle a little below and in front of the fibular facet, to the anterior border of the fibular notch.

Surfaces

The *lateral surface* lies between the anterior and interosseous borders. In its upper three-fourths, it is concave and is directed laterally, and in its lower one-fourth it is directed forwards.

The *medial surface* lies between the anterior and medial borders. It is broad, and most of it is subcutaneous.

The *posterior surface* lies between the medial and interosseous borders. It is widest in its upper part. This part is crossed obliquely by a rough ridge called the *soleal line.* The soleal line begins just behind the fibular facet, runs downwards and medially, and terminates by joining the medial border at the junction of its upper and middle thirds (Fig. 2.29).

Above the soleal line, the posterior surface is in the form of a triangular area. The area below the soleal line is elongated. It is divided into medial and lateral parts by a vertical ridge. A *nutrient foramen* is situated near the upper end of this ridge. It is directed downwards and transmits the nutrient artery which is a branch of the posterior tibial artery.

Lower End

The lower end of the tibia is slightly expanded. It has five surfaces. Medially, it is prolonged downwards as the medial malleolus.

The anterior surface of the lower end has an upper smooth part, and a lower rough and grooved part. The medial surface is subcutaneous and is continuous with the medial surface of the medial malleolus. The lateral aspect of the lower end presents a triangular fibular notch to which the lower end of the fibula is attached. The upper part of the notch is rough. The lower part is smooth and may be covered with hyaline cartilage. The inferior surface of the lower end is articular. It articulates with the superior trochlear surface of the talus and thus takes part in forming the ankle joint. Medially the articular surface extends on to the medial malleolus.

The *medial malleolus* is a short but strong process which projects downwards from the medial surface of the lower end of the tibia. It forms a subcutaneous prominence on the medial side of the ankle.

Particular Features

Attachments on the Tibia

Figures 2.31 and 2.32 show the attachments on the tibia.

1. Attachments on the medial condyle
   (a) The *semimembranosus* is inserted into the groove on the posterior surface.
   (b) The capsular ligament of the knee joint is attached to the upper border, which also gives attachment to the deeper fibres of the tibial collateral ligament (Fig. 12.9).
   (c) The medial patellar retinaculum is attached to the anterior surface.

2. Attachments on lateral condyle
   (a) The *iliotibial tract* is attached to the flattened impression on the anterior surface (Fig. 2.28).

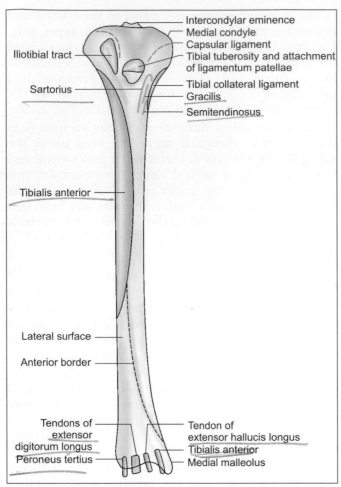

Fig. 2.31: Attachments on the anterior aspect of the right tibia.

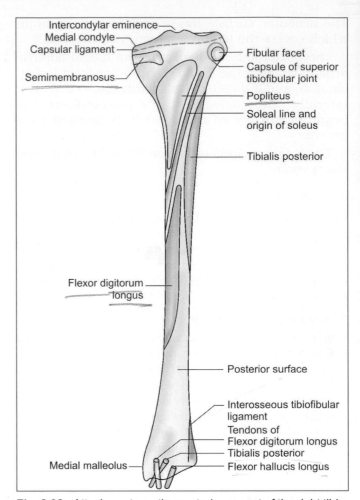

Fig. 2.32: Attachments on the posterior aspect of the right tibia.

(b) The capsular ligament of the superior tibiofibular joint is attached around the margins of the fibular facet.

(c) The groove on the posterior surface of the lateral condyle is occupied by the tendon of the popliteus with a bursa intervening.

3. Attachments on the intercondylar area

The following are attached from before backwards.

(a) The *anterior horn of the medial meniscus*, just in front of the medial articular surface (Fig. 2.30).

(b) The anterior cruciate ligament on a smooth area just behind the previous attachment.

(c) The *anterior horn of the lateral meniscus*, to the front of the intercondylar eminence, and lateral to the anterior cruciate ligament.

(d) The *posterior horn of the lateral meniscus*, to the posterior slope of the intercondylar eminence.

(e) The *posterior horn of the medial meniscus*, to the depression behind the base of the medial intercondylar tubercle.

(f) The *posterior cruciate ligament*, to the posterior-most smooth area.

4. Attachment on tibial tuberosity

The *ligamentum patellae* is attached to the upper smooth part of the *tibial tuberosity*. The lower rough area of the tuberosity is subcutaneous, but is separated from the skin by the subcutaneous infrapatellar bursa (Fig. 3.7).

5. Attachment on the shaft

(a) The *tibialis anterior* arises from the upper two-thirds of the lateral surface (Fig. 2.33).

(b) The upper part of the medial surface receives the insertions of the *sartorius*, the *gracilis* and the *semitendinosus*, from before backwards (Fig. 2.34). Still further posteriorly this surface gives attachment to the *tibial collateral ligament* along the medial border (Fig. 2.31).

(c) The *soleus* arises from the soleal line (Fig. 2.32). The soleal line also gives attachment to the fascia covering the soleus, the fascia covering the popliteus, and the transverse fascial septum. The tendinous

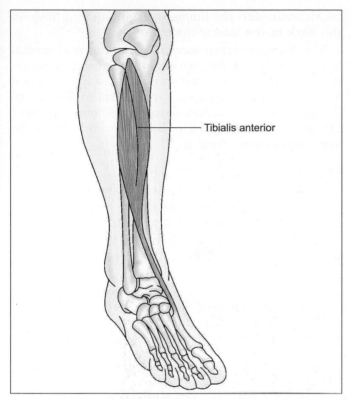

Fig. 2.33: Tibialis anterior.

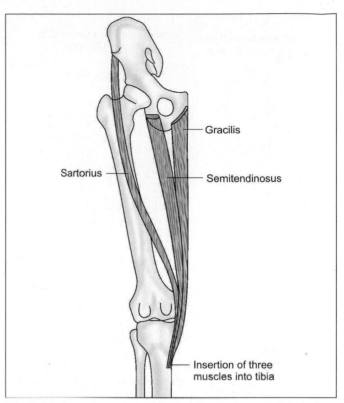

Fig. 2.34: Insertion of muscles on the upper medial surface of tibia.

arch for origin of the soleus is attached to a tubercle at the upper end of the soleal line.

(d) The *popliteus* is inserted on the posterior surface, into the triangular area above the soleal line.

(e) The medial area of the posterior surface below the soleal line gives origin to the flexor digitorum longus while the lateral area gives origin to the tibialis posterior.

(f) The anterior border of the tibia gives attachment to the deep fascia of the leg and, in its lower part, to the superior extensor retinaculum.

(g) The rough upper part of the fibular notch gives attachment to the interosseous tibiofibular ligament.

(h) The capsular ligament of the ankle joint is attached to the lower end along the margins of articular surface. The deltoid ligament of the ankle joint is attached to the lower border of the medial malleolus (Figs 12.16 and 2.28).

Blood Supply

The nutrient artery to the tibia is the largest nutrient artery in the body. It is a branch of the posterior tibial artery which enters the bone on its posterior surface.

Ossification: The tibia ossifies from one primary and two secondary centres. The primary centre appears in the shaft during the seventh week of intrauterine life. A secondary centre for the upper end appears just *before birth,* and fuses with the shaft at 16–18 years. The upper epiphysis is prolonged downwards to form the tibial tuberosity. A secondary centre for the lower end appears during the first year, forms the medial malleolus by the seventh year, and fuses with the shaft by 15–17 years (Fig. 2.35).

FIBULA

The fibula is the lateral and smaller bone of the leg. It is very thin as compared to the tibia. It is homologous with the ulna of the upper limb.

Side Determination

1. The upper end, or head, is slightly expanded in all directions. The lower end or lateral malleolus is expanded anteroposteriorly and is flattened from side to side.

2. The medial side of the lower end bears a triangular articular facet anteriorly, and a deep or malleolar fossa posteriorly.

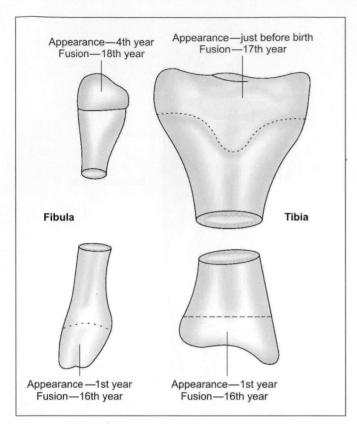

Appearance—4th year
Fusion—18th year

Appearance—just before birth
Fusion—17th year

Fibula

Tibia

Appearance—1st year
Fusion—16th year

Appearance—1st year
Fusion—16th year

Fig. 2.35: Ossification of tibia and fibula.

Features

The fibula has an upper end, a shaft and a lower end.

Upper End or Head

It is slightly expanded in all directions. The superior surface bears a circular articular facet which articulates with the lateral condyle of the tibia. The *apex* of the head or the styloid process projects upwards from its posterolateral aspect.

The constriction immediately below the head is known as the *neck* of the fibula (Figs 2.36 and 2.37).

Shaft

The shaft shows considerable variation in its form because it is moulded by the muscles attached to it. It has three borders—anterior, posterior and interosseous; and three surfaces—medial, lateral and posterior.

Borders

The *anterior border* begins just below the anterior aspect of the head. At its lower end it divides to enclose an elongated triangular area which is continuous with the lateral surface of the lateral malleolus.

The *posterior border* is rounded. Its upper end lies in line with the styloid process. Below, the border is

continuous with the medial margin of the groove on the back of the lateral malleolus.

The *interosseous* or *medial border* lies just medial to the anterior border, but on a more posterior plane. It terminates below at the upper end of a roughened area above the talar facet of the lateral malleolus. In its upper two-thirds, the interosseous border lies very close to the anterior border and may be indistinguishable from it.

Surfaces

The *medial surface* lies between the anterior and interosseous borders. In its upper two-thirds, it is very narrow, measuring 1 mm or less.

The *lateral surface* lies between the anterior and posterior borders. It is twisted backwards in its lower part.

The *posterior surface* is the largest of the three surfaces. It lies between the interosseous and posterior borders. In its upper two-thirds, it is divided into two parts by a vertical ridge called the *medial crest* (Fig. 2.37a).

Lower End or Lateral Malleolus

The tip of the lateral malleolus is 0.5 cm lower than that of the medial malleolus, and its anterior surface is 1.5 cm posterior to that of the medial malleolus. It has the following four surfaces.

The anterior surface is rough and rounded. The posterior surface is marked by a groove. The lateral surface is subcutaneous. The medial surface bears a triangular articular facet for the talus anteriorly and the malleolar fossa posteriorly.

Particular Features

Attachments and Relations of the Fibula

1. The medial surface of the shaft gives origin to:
   (a) The extensor digitorum longus, from the whole of the upper one-fourth, and from the anterior half of the middle two-fourths.
   (b) The extensor hallucis longus, from the posterior half of its middle two-fourths.
   (c) The peroneus tertius, from its lower one-fourth (Figs 2.36 and 2.38).
2. The part of the posterior surface between the medial crest and the interosseous border, the grooved part, gives origin to the tibialis posterior.
3. The part of the posterior surface between the medial crest and the posterior border gives origin to:
   (a) Soleus from the upper one-fourth.
   (b) Flexor hallucis longus from its lower three-fourths (Figs 2.39 and 2.40).

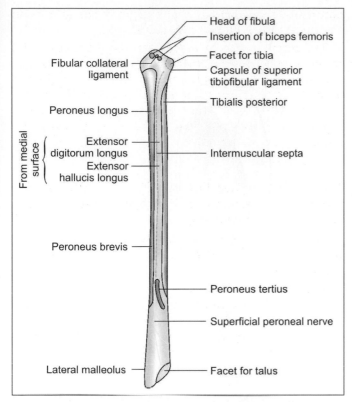

Fig. 2.36: Right fibula: Anterior aspect.

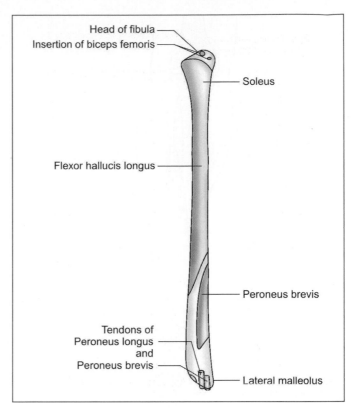

Fig. 2.37: Right fibula: Posterior aspect.

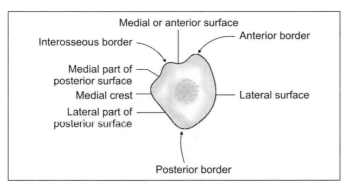

Fig. 2.37a: T.S. through shaft of fibula to show its borders and surfaces.

4. The lateral surface of the shaft gives origin to:
   (a) Peroneus longus, from its upper one-third, and posterior half of the middle one-third.
   (b) The peroneus brevis from the anterior half of its middle one-third, and the whole of lower one-third. The common peroneal nerve terminates in relation to the neck of fibula (Fig. 2.42).

5. The head of the fibula receives the insertion of the biceps femoris on the anterolateral slope of the apex. This insertion is C-shaped. The fibular collateral ligament of the knee joint is attached within the C-shaped area (Fig. 2.42). The origins of the extensor digitorum, the peroneus longus, and the soleus, described

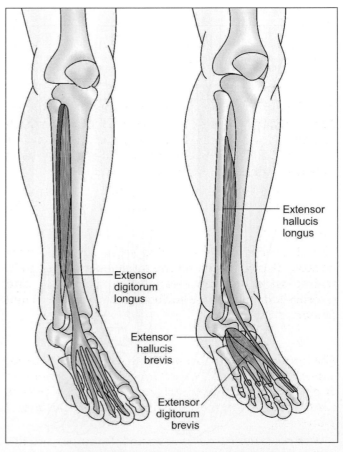

Fig. 2.38: Anterolateral view of leg.

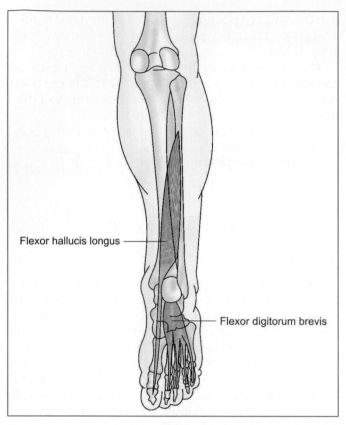

Fig. 2.39: Flexor hallucis longus in the calf and flexor digitorum brevis in the sole.

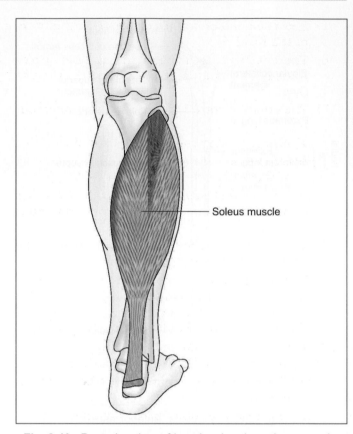

Fig. 2.40: Posterior view of leg showing the soleus muscle.

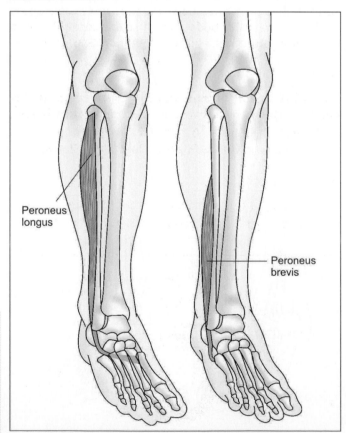

Fig. 2.41: Anterolateral view of leg.

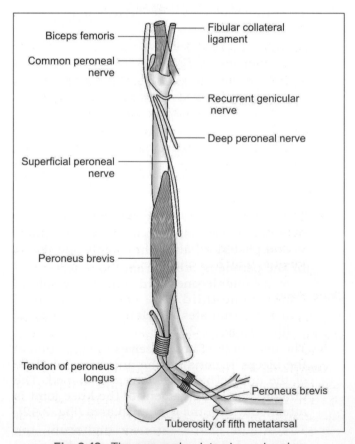

Fig. 2.42: The peroneal or lateral crural region.

above, extend on to the corresponding aspects of the head.

6. The capsular ligament of the superior tibio-fibular joint is attached around the articular facet.

7. The anterior border of fibula gives attachment to:
   (a) Anterior intermuscular septum of the leg.
   (b) Superior extensor retinaculum, to lower part of the anterior margin of triangular area.
   (c) Superior peroneal retinaculum, to the lower part of the posterior margin of triangular area.

8. The posterior border gives attachment to the posterior intermuscular septum.

9. The interosseous border gives attachment to the interosseous membrane. The attachment leaves a gap at the upper end for passage of the anterior tibial vessels (Fig. 2.28).

10. The triangular area above the medial surface of the lateral malleolus gives attachment to:
    (a) The interosseous tibiofibular ligament, in the middle.
    (b) The anterior tibiofibular ligament, ante-riorly (Fig. 2.28).
    (c) The posterior tibiofibular, posteriorly.

11. The attachments on the lateral malleolus are as follows.
    (a) Anterior talofibular ligament to the anterior surface (Fig. 2.28).
    (b) Inferior transverse tibiofibular ligament above and posterior talofibular ligament below to the malleolar fossa (Fig. 12.21).
    (c) The capsule of the ankle joint along the edges of the malleolar articular surface.
    (d) Slight notch on the lower border gives attachment to calcaneofibular ligament (Fig. 12.20).

12. The groove on the posterior surface of the malleolus lodges the tendon of the peroneus brevis, which is deep, and of the peroneus longus, which is superficial (Fig. 2.37).

Blood Supply

The peroneal artery gives off the nutrient artery for the fibula, which enters the bone on its posterior surface.

Ossification: The fibula ossifies from one primary and two secondary centres. The primary centre for the shaft appears during the eighth week of intrauterine life. A secondary centre for the lower end appears during the first year, and fuses with the shaft by about sixteen years. A secondary centre for the upper end appears during the fourth year, and fuses with the shaft by about eighteen years (Fig. 2.35).

The fibula *violates* the law of ossification because the secondary centre which appears first in the lower end does not fuse last. The reasons for this violation are:

1. The secondary centre appears first in the lower end because it is a pressure epiphysis.
2. The upper epiphysis fuses last because this is the growing end of the bone.

BONES OF THE FOOT

TARSUS

The tarsus is made up of seven tarsal bones, arranged in two rows. In the proximal row, there is the talus above, and the calcaneus below. In the distal row, there are four tarsal bones lying side by side. From medial to lateral side these are the medial cuneiform, the intermediate cuneiform, the lateral cuneiform and the cuboid. Another bone, the navicular, is interposed between the talus and the three cuneiform bones. In other words, it is interposed between the proximal and distal rows (Figs 2.43 and 2.44).

The tarsal bones are much larger and stronger than the carpal bones because they have to support and distribute the body weight. Each tarsal bone is roughly cuboidal in shape, having six surfaces.

TALUS

The talus is the second largest tarsal bone. It lies between the tibia above and the calcaneum below, gripped on the sides by the two malleoli.

It has a head, a neck and a body (Fig. 2.45).

Side Determination

1. The rounded head is directed forwards.
2. The trochlear articular surface of the body is

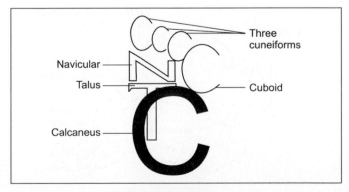

Fig. 2.43: Tarsus.

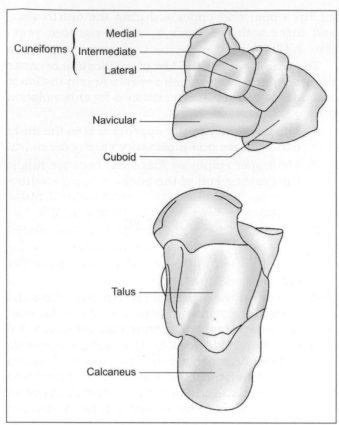

Fig. 2.44: Bones of the foot: Dorsal aspect.

directed upwards, and the concave articular surface downwards.

3. The body bears a large triangular, facet laterally, and a comma-shaped facet medially.

Features

Head

1. It is directed forwards and slightly downwards and medially.
2. Its anterior surface is oval and convex. The long axis of this surface is directed downwards and medially. It articulates with the posterior surface of the navicular bone.
3. The inferior surface is marked by three articular areas separated by indistinct ridges. The posterior facet is largest, oval and gently convex; it articulates with the middle facet on sustentaculum tali of the calcaneum. The anterolateral facet articulates with the anterior facet of the calcaneum, and the medial facet with the spring ligament (Fig. 12.19).

Neck

1. This is the constricted part of the bone between the head and the body.
2. It is set obliquely on the body, so that inferiorly it extends further backwards on the medial side than on the lateral side. However, when viewed

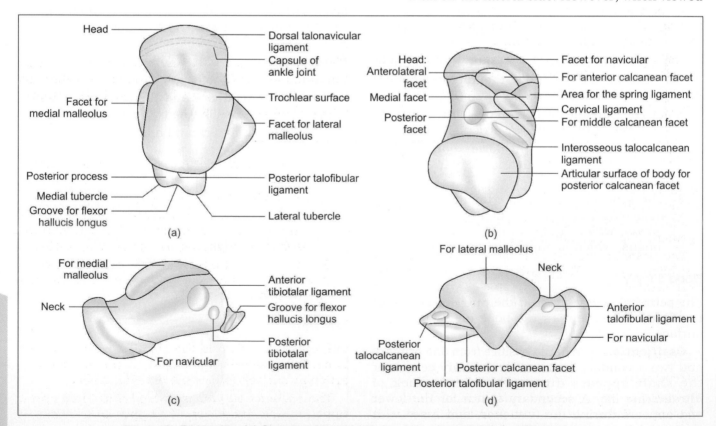

Fig. 2.45: Right talus: (a) Superior view, (b) inferior view, (c) medial view, (d) lateral view.

from dorsal side, the long axis of the neck is directed downwards, forwards and medially. The *neck–body angle* is 130 to 140 degrees in infants and 150 degrees in adults. The smaller angle in young children accounts for the inverted position of their feet.

3. The medial part of its plantar surface is marked by a deep groove termed the *sulcus tali*. The sulcus tali lies opposite the sulcus calcanei on the calcaneum, the two together enclosing a space called the *sinus tarsi*.

4. In habitual squatters, a squatting facet is commonly found on the upper and lateral part of the neck. The facet articulates with the anterior margin of the lower end of the tibia during extreme dorsiflexion of the ankle.

Body

The body is cuboidal in shape and has five surfaces.

The *superior surface* bears an articular surface, which articulates with the lower end of the tibia to form the ankle joint. This surface is also called the *trochlear surface*. It is convex from before backwards and concave from side to side. It is wider anteriorly than posteriorly. The medial border of the surface is straight, but the lateral border is directed forwards and laterally. The trochlear surface articulates with the inferior surface of lower end of tibia.

The *inferior surface* bears an oval, concave articular surface which articulates with the posterior facet of the calcaneum to form the subtalar joint (Fig. 12.22a).

The *medial surface* is articular above and non-articular below. The articular surface is comma-shaped and articulates with the medial malleolus of tibia.

The *lateral surface* bears a triangular articular surface for the lateral malleolus. The surface is concave from above downwards, and its apex forms the lateral tubercle of the talus. The posterior part of the lateral surface is separated from the trochlea by an ill-defined, small triangular area which articulates with the inferior transverse tibiofibular ligament (Figs 2.28 and 12.21).

The *posterior process* is small and is marked by an oblique groove. The groove is bounded by medial and lateral tubercles. The lateral tubercle is occasionally separate (5%) and is then called the *os trigonum*.

Particular Features

Attachments on the Talus

The talus is devoid of muscular attachments, but numerous ligaments are attached to it because it takes part in three joints (Fig. 2.45).

1. The following ligaments are attached to the neck:
   (a) The distal part of the dorsal surface provides attachment to the capsular ligament of the ankle joint and to the dorsal talonavicular ligament. The proximal part of the dorsal surface lies within the ankle joint.
   (b) The inferior surface provides attachment to the interosseous talocalcanean and cervical ligaments.
   (c) The lateral part of the neck provides attachment to the anterior talofibular ligament (Figs 2.45, 12.16 and 12.20).

2. The lower, non-articular part of the medial surface of the body gives attachment to the deep fibres of the deltoid or anterior tibiotalar ligament (Fig. 2.45c).

3. The groove on the posterior surface lodges the tendon of the flexor hallucis longus. The medial tubercle provides attachment to the superficial fibres of the deltoid ligament, (posterior tibiotalar) above and the medial talocalcanean ligament below (Fig. 2.45c). Posterior talofibular ligament is attached to upper part of posterior process while posterior talocalcanean ligament is attached to its plantar border.

Ossification: The talus ossifies from one centre which appears during the 6th month of intrauterine life.

CALCANEUS OR CALCANEUM

The calcaneus is the largest tarsal bone. It forms the prominence of the heel. Its long axis is directed forwards, upwards and laterally. It is roughly cuboidal and has six surfaces.

Side Determination

1. The anterior surface is small and bears a concavoconvex articular facet for the cuboid. The posterior surface is large and rough.

2. The dorsal or upper surface bears a large convex articular surface in the middle. The plantar surface is rough and triangular (Fig. 2.46a).

3. The lateral surface is flat, and the medial surface concave from above downwards (Fig. 2.46d).

Features

The *anterior surface* is the smallest surface of the bone. It is covered by a concavoconvex, sloping articular surface for the cuboid (Fig. 2.46c).

The *posterior surface* is divided into three areas, upper, middle and lower. The upper area is smooth while the others are rough.

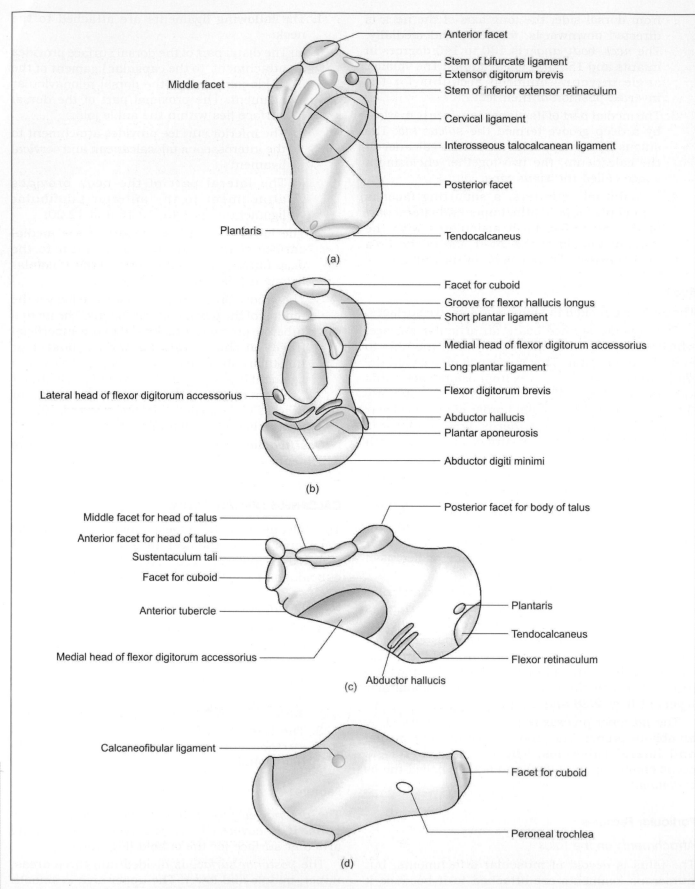

Fig. 2.46: Right calcaneous: (a) Superior view, (b) inferior view, (c) medial view, (d) lateral view.

The *dorsal* or *superior surface* can be divided into three areas. The posterior one-third is rough. The middle one-third is covered by the posterior facet for articulation which facet on inferior surface of body of talus. This facet is oval, convex and oblique. The anterior one-third is articular in the anteromedial part, and non-articular in its posterolateral part. The articular part is in the form of an elongated middle facet present on the sustentaculum tali and anterior facet. These two facets articulate respectively with posterior facet and anteromedial facets on inferior aspect of head of talus.

The *plantar surface* is rough and marked by three tubercles. The medial and lateral tubercles are situated posteriorly, whereas the anterior tubercle lies in the anterior part. The *lateral surface* is rough and almost flat. It presents in its anterior part, a small elevation termed the *peroneal trochlea* or *tubercle*.

The *medial surface* is concave from above downwards. The concavity is accentuated by the presence of a shelf-like projection of bone, called the *sustentaculum tali,* which projects medially from its anterosuperior border. The upper surface of this process assists in the formation of the talocalcaneonavicular joint. Its lower surface is grooved; and the medial margin is in the form of a rough strip convex from before backwards.

Particular Features

Attachments and Relations of the Calcaneus

1. The middle rough area on the posterior surface receives the insertion of the tendocalcaneus and of the plantaris. The upper area is covered by a bursa. The lower area is covered by dense fibrofatty tissue and supports the body weight while standing. It can be compared to the attachment of ligamentum patellae (Fig. 2.47).

2. The lateral part of the non-articular area on the anterior part of the dorsal surface provides:

(a) Origin to the extensor digitorum brevis (Fig. 2.48).

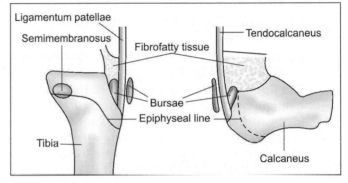

Fig. 2.47: Comparison of the tendocalcaneous and the ligamentum patellae.

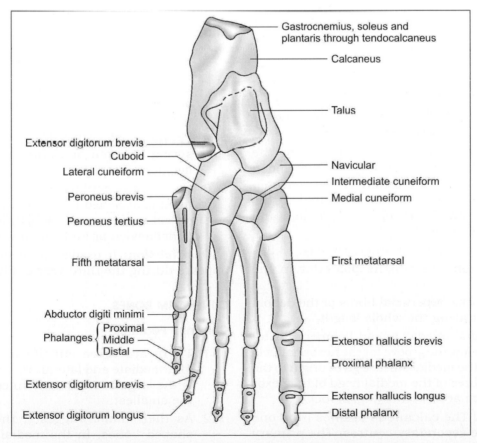

Fig. 2.48: Skeleton of the foot as seen from the dorsal aspect.

(b) Attachment to the stem of the inferior extensor retinaculum.

(c) Attachment to the stem of the bifurcate ligament. The medial, narrow part of the non-articular area forms the sulcus calcanei, and provides attachment to the interosseous talocalcanean ligament medially and the cervical ligament laterally (Fig. 12.16).

3. The attachments on the plantar surface are: The *medial tubercle* provides:

(a) Origin for the abductor hallucis medially.

(b) Attachment to the flexor retinaculum medially.

(c) Origin to the flexor digitorum brevis anteriorly.

(d) Attachment to the plantar aponeurosis anteriorly (Fig. 10.3).

The *lateral tubercle* gives origin to the *abductor digiti minimi*, the origin extending to the front of the tubercle. The *anterior tubercle* and the rough area in front of it provide attachment to the *short plantar ligament*. The rough strip between the three tubercles affords attachment to the *long plantar ligament* (Fig. 2.49).

4. The attachments and relations of the lateral surface are as follows. The peroneal tubercle lies between the tendons of the peroneus brevis above and the peroneus longus below (Fig. 8.19). The trochlea itself gives attachment to a slip from the inferior peroneal retinaculum. The calcaneofibular ligament is attached about 1 cm behind the peroneal trochlea.

5. The attachments and relations of the medial surface are as follows.

The groove on the lower surface of the sustentaculum tali is occupied by the tendon of the flexor hallucis longus. The medial margin of the sustentaculum tali is related to the tendon of the *flexor digitorum longus* and provides attachment to:

(a) The spring ligament anteriorly (Fig. 13.5).

(b) A slip from the tibialis posterior in the middle.

(c) Some of the superficial fibres of the deltoid ligament along the whole length.

(d) The medial talocalcanean ligament posteriorly. Below the groove for the flexor hallucis longus, the medial surface gives origin to the fleshy fibres of the medial head of the flexor digitorum accessorius (Fig. 2.46c).

Ossification: The calcaneus ossifies from one primary and one secondary centres. The primary centre appears during the 3rd month of intrauterine life. The secondary centre appears between 6–8 years to form a scale-like epiphysis on the posterior surface, which fuses with the rest of the bone by 14–16 years.

NAVICULAR BONE

The navicular bone is boat-shaped. It is situated on the medial side of the foot, in front of the head of the talus, and behind the three cuneiform bones.

Features

1. The anterior surface is convex, is divided into three facets for the three cuneiform bones.

2. The posterior surface is concave and oval for articulation with the head of the talus.

3. The dorsal surface is broad and convex from side to side. It is rough for the attachment of ligaments.

4. The plantar surface is small and slightly concave from side to side. It is rough and non-articular.

5. The medial surface has a blunt and prominent tuberosity, directed downwards, the tuberosity is separated from the plantar surface by a groove.

6. The lateral surface is rough and irregular, but frequently has a facet for the cuboid.

Attachments

1. Tuberosity of the navicular bone receives the principal insertion of the tibialis posterior. The groove below the tuberosity transmits a part of the tendon of this muscle to other bones (Fig. 13.9).

2. Plantar surface provides attachment to the spring ligament or plantar calcaneonavicular ligament (Fig. 13.5).

3. Calcaneonavicular part of the bifurcate ligament is attached to the lateral surface. To the dorsal surface are attached the talonavicular, cuneonavicular and cubonavicular ligaments.

Ossification: It ossifies from one centre which appears during the third year of life.

CUNEIFORM BONES

Common Features

1. There are three cuneiform bones, medial, intermediate and lateral. The medial cuneiform is the largest and the intermediate cuneiform, the smallest.

2. As their name suggests, these are wedge-shaped bones. In the medial cuneiform, the edge of the wedge forms the dorsal surface.

In the intermediate and lateral cuneiforms, the thin edge of wedge forms the plantar surface.

3. The anterior parts of the medial and lateral cuneiforms projects further forwards than the intermediate cuneiform. This forms a deep recess for the base of second metatarsal bone.

MEDIAL CUNEIFORM

Features

1. Dorsal surface is formed by the rough edge of the wedge.
2. Plantar surface is formed by the base of the wedge.
3. Distal surface has a large kidney-shaped facet for the base of the first metatarsal bone, with its hilum directed laterally.
4. Proximal surface is a pyriform facet for the navicular.
5. Medial surface is rough and subcutaneous.
6. Lateral surface is marked by an inverted L-shaped facet along the posterior and superior margins for the intermediate cuneiform bone. The anterosuperior part of the facet is separated by a vertical ridge. This part is for the base of second metatarsal bone. The anteroinferior part of the lateral surface is roughened.

Attachments

1. The greater part of the tibialis anterior is inserted into an impression on the antero-inferior angle of the medial surface (Figs 2.49 and 8.7).
2. The plantar surface receives a slip from the tibialis posterior.
3. A part of the peroneus longus is inserted into the rough anteroinferior part of the lateral surface (Fig. 2.49).

INTERMEDIATE CUNEIFORM

Features

1. The proximal and distal surfaces bear triangular articular facets.
2. The lateral surface is marked by a vertical facet along its posterior margin. This facet is for the lateral cuneiform bone. It is indented in the middle.
3. The plantar surface is formed by the edge of the wedge.

Attachments

The plantar surface receives a slip from the tibialis posterior.

LATERAL CUNEIFORM

Additional Features

1. The proximal surface is rough in its lower one-third, and has a triangular facet in its upper two-thirds for the navicular bone.
2. The lateral surface is marked in its post-erosuperior part by a triangular or oval facet for the cuboid. At the anteroinferior angle, a small facet may be present for the fourth metatarsal bone.
3. The plantar surface is formed by the edge of the wedge.

Attachments

The plantar surface receives a slip from the tibialis posterior.

Ossification: Each cuneiform bone ossifies from one centre, which appears during the first year in the lateral cuneiform, during the second year in the medial cuneiform, and during the third year in the intermediate cuneiform bone.

CUBOID

The cuboid is the lateral bone of the distal row of the tarsus, situated in front of the calcaneum and behind the fourth and fifth metatarsal bones. It has six surfaces.

Features

1. The proximal surface is concavoconvex for articulation with the calcaneum.
2. The distal surface is also articular. It is divided by a vertical ridge into two areas for the fourth and fifth metatarsal bones.
3. The dorsal surface is rough for the attachment of ligaments. It is directed upwards and laterally.
4. The plantar surface is crossed anteriorly by an oblique groove. The groove is bounded posteriorly by a prominent ridge.
5. The lateral surface is short and notched.
6. The medial surface is extensive, being partly articular and partly non-articular. An oval facet in the middle articulates with the lateral cuneiform bone. Proximal to this a small facet may present for the navicular bone.

Attachments

1. The notch on the lateral surface, and the groove on the plantar surface, are occupied by the tendon of the peroneus longus (Fig. 2.41).
2. The ridge posterior to the groove gives

attachment to the deep fibres of the long plantar ligament (Fig. 2.49).

3. The short plantar ligament is attached to the posterior border of the plantar surface.

4. The posteromedial part of the plantar surface provides:
   (a) Insertion to a slip from the tibialis pos-terior.
   (b) Origin to the flexor hallucis brevis.

5. The non-articular part of the medial surface provides attachment to ligaments, including the lateral limb of the bifurcate ligament.

Ossification: The cuboid bone ossifies from one centre which appears just before birth.

METATARSUS

1. The metatarsus is made up of 5 metatarsal bones, which are numbered from medial to lateral side.

2. Each metatarsal is a miniature long bone and has the following parts.

(a) The *shaft* which is slightly convex dorsally and concave ventrally in its longitudinal axis. It is prismoid in form, and tapers from base to the head.

(b) The *base* or proximal end is set obliquely in such a way that it projects backwards and laterally.

(c) The *head* or distal end is flattened from side to side.

Metacarpals versus Metatarsals

The metatarsals are quite similar to metacarpals. For the differences between the metacarpals and metatarsals refer Table 2.1.

Identification

First Metatarsal

1. This is the shortest, thickest and stoutest of all metatarsal bones and is adapted for transmission of the body weight (Fig. 2.48).

2. The proximal surface of the base has a kidney-shaped facet, which is concave outwards.

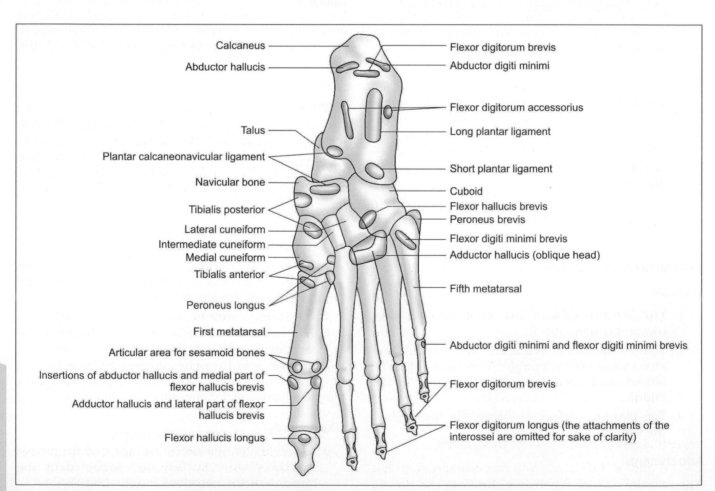

Fig. 2.49: Skeleton of the foot as seen from the plantar aspect.

Table 2.1: Differences between metacarpals and metatarsals	
Metacarpal	**Metatarsal**
1. The head and shaft are prismoid	1. The head and shaft are flattened from side to side
2. The shaft is of uniform thickness	2. The shaft tapers distally
3. The dorsal surface of the shaft has an elongated, flat triangular area	3. The dorsal surface of the shaft is uniformly convex
4. The base is irregular	4. The base appears to be cut sharply and obliquely

Second Metatarsal

1. This is the longest metatarsal. It has a wedge-shaped base (Fig. 2.49).
2. The lateral side of the base has two articular facets, a larger dorsal, and a smaller plantar each of which is subdivided into a proximal part for the lateral cuneiform bone and a distal part for the third metatarsal.
3. The medial side of the base bears one facet, placed dorsally, for the medial cuneiform.

Third Metatarsal

1. The lateral side of the base has one facet, placed dorsally, for the fourth metatarsal bone.
2. The medial side of the base has two facets, dorsal and plantar for second metatarsal bone.

Fourth Metatarsal

1. The proximal surface of the base is quadrangular. It articulates with the cuboid bone.
2. The lateral side of the base has one facet, placed dorsally, for the fifth metatarsal bone.
3. The medial side of the base has one facet placed dorsally, which is subdivided into a proximal part for the lateral cuneiform and a distal part, for third metatarsal bone.

Fifth Metatarsal

1. The lateral side of the base has a large tuberosity or styloid process projecting backwards and laterally.
2. The medial side of the base has one facet for the fourth metatarsal bone.
3. The plantar surface of the base is grooved by the tendon of the abductor digiti minimi.

Important Attachments to Metatarsal Bones

1. A part of the tibialis anterior is inserted on the medial side of the base of the first metatarsal bone (Fig. 8.7).
2. The greater part of the peroneus longus is inserted on a large impression at the inferior angle of the lateral surface of the base of the first metatarsal bone (Fig. 2.49).
3. The peroneus brevis is inserted on the dorsal surface of the tuberosity of the fifth metatarsal bone (Fig. 2.48).
4. The peroneus tertius is inserted on the medial part of the dorsal surface of the base and the medial border of the shaft of the fifth metatarsal bone (Fig. 2.48).
5. The flexor digiti minimi brevis arises from the plantar surface of the base of the fifth metatarsal bone (Fig. 2.49).
6. The shaft of metatarsal bones gives origin to interossei (Figs 10.9 and 10.10).

Ossification: Each metatarsal bone ossifies from one primary and one secondary centre. The primary centre appears in the shaft during the tenth week of foetal life in the first metatarsal, and during the ninth week of foetal life in the rest of the metatarsals.

A secondary centre appears for the base of the first metatarsal during the third year, and for the heads of the other metatarsals between three and four years. All secondary centres unite with the shaft by 18th year. A separate centre for the tuberosity of the fifth metatarsal bone may be present (Fig. 2.50).

PHALANGES

There are 14 phalanges in each foot; 2 for the great toe and 3 for each of the other toes. As compared to the phalanges of the hand, these are much smaller in size, and the shafts particularly of first row are compressed from side to side. Otherwise their arrangement and features are similar in two limbs.

Attachments

A. On bases of distal phalanges

(a) Lateral four toes, flexor digitorum longus on the plantar surface, and the extensor expansion on the dorsal surface (Fig. 10.6).
(b) Great toe, flexor hallucis longus on the plantar surface, and the extensor hallucis longus on the dorsal surface (Figs 2.48 and 2.49).

B. On shaft and bases of middle phalanges

Flexor digitorum brevis on each side of the shaft on plantar surface (Fig. 10.5); and extensor expansion on the dorsal surface.

C. On bases of proximal phalanges

(a) Second, third and fourth toes, a lumbrical muscle on the medial side, and an interosseous muscle on each side (Figs 10.6, 10.9 and 10.10).

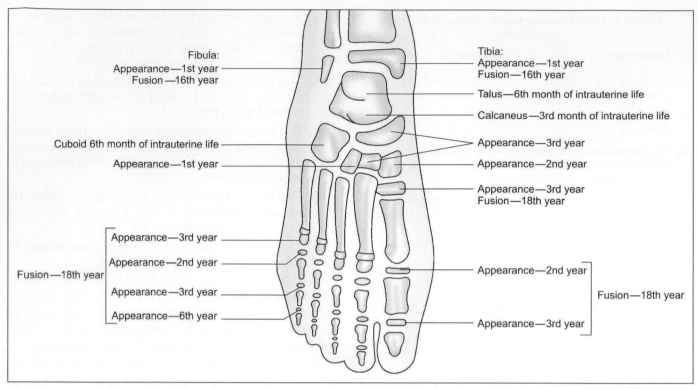

Fig. 2.50: Ossification of foot bones.

(b) Fifth toe, a plantar interosseous muscle on the medial side, and the abductor digiti minimi and the flexor digiti minimi brevis on the lateral side (Fig. 2.49).

(c) Great toe, abductor hallucis and part of the flexor hallucis medially, adductor hallucis and the remaining part of the flexor hallucis brevis laterally.

D. The *fibrous flexor sheath* is attached to the margins of the proximal and middle phalanges of the lateral four toes.

Ossification: Phalanx ossifies by one primary centre for the shaft which appears in tenth week of foetal life. The single secondary centre appears in the base. It appears in the proximal phalanx in second year, middle phalanx in third year and in distal phalanx in the sixth year. These fuse with the respective shafts by eighteenth year. The big toe has two phalanges and their secondary centres appear in second and third years to fuse with shaft in 18th year (Fig. 2.50).

SESAMOID BONES

These are located at the following sites.

1. The patella is, by far, the largest sesamoid bone.
2. There is one sesamoid bone in the tendon of peroneus longus. It articulates with the cuboid.
3. Sesamoid bones may be present in the tendons of the tibialis anterior, the tibialis posterior, the lateral head of the gastrocnemius, the psoas major, and the gluteus maximus.
4. There are two small sesamoids in the tendon of the flexor hallucis brevis. They articulate with the head of the first metatarsal bone.
5. Other tendons crossing the metatarsal, phalangeal and interphalangeal joints may have sesamoids.

CLINICAL ANATOMY

• Iliac crest is used for taking bone marrow biopsy in cases of anaemia or leukaemia.

• Weaver's bottom—persons sitting for a long period of time may get inflammation of their ischial tuberosity bursa.

• Tripping over minor obstructions or other accidents causing forced medial rotation of the thigh and leg during the fall results in:

(a) The fracture of the shaft of femur in persons below the age of 16 years (Fig. 2.51).

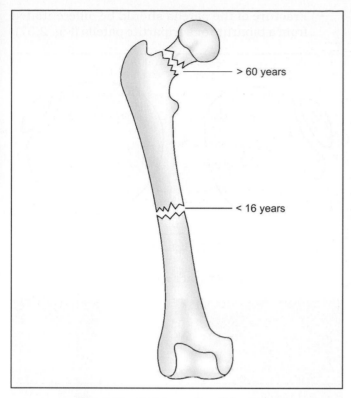

Fig. 2.51: Common sites of fracture.

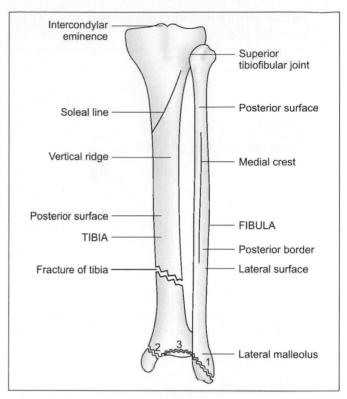

Fig. 2.53: 3 stages of Pott's fracture and fracture of tibia.

(b) Bucket-handle tear of the medial meniscus between the ages of 14 and 40 years (Fig. 2.52).

(c) Pott's fracture of the leg between the ages of 40 and 60 years (Fig. 2.53).

(d) Fracture of neck of the femur over the age of 60 years (Fig. 2.54). This is common in females due to osteoporosis and degeneration of calcar femorale.

- The head of femur is supplied by an artery along the ligamentum teres. Main arterial supply is from retinacular arteries, branches of medial femoral circumflex artery. These arteries get

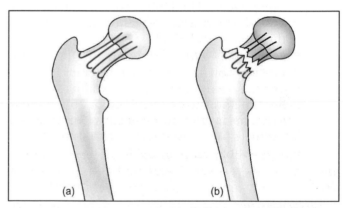

Fig. 2.54: (a) Normal arterial supply of the head of femur, (b) avascular necrosis of head in fracture neck femur.

injured in intracapsular fracture of neck of femur, leading to avascular necrosis of the head (Fig. 2.54). In such cases hip joint need to be replaced.

- The centre of ossification in lower end of femur and even in upper end of tibia seen by X-ray is used as a medicolegal evidence to prove that the newborn (found dead) was nearly full term and was viable.

- In fracture of upper third of shaft of femur, proximal segment is flexed by iliopsoas, laterally rotated by muscles attached to greater trochanter. Distal segment is pulled upwards

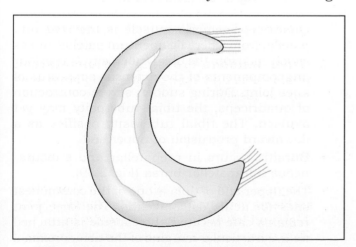

Fig. 2.52: Bucket handle tear of medial meniscus.

by hamstrings and laterally rotated by adductor muscles (Fig. 2.55).

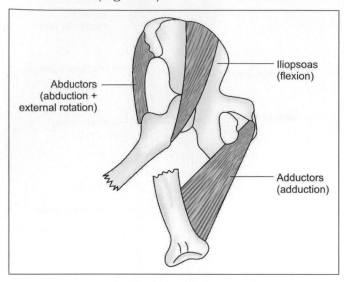

Fig. 2.55: Fracture of upper 3rd of shaft of femur.

- The patella has a natural tendency to dislocate outwards because of the outward angulation between the long axes of the thigh and leg. This is prevented by:
  (a) *Bony factor:* The lateral edge of the patellar articular surface of the femur is deeper than the medial edge and
  (b) *Muscular factor:* Insertion of the vastus medialis on the medial border of patella extends lower than that of vastus lateralis on the lateral border (Fig. 2.26). Vastus medialis is first to degenerate and last to recover in diseases of the knee joint (Fig. 2.56).

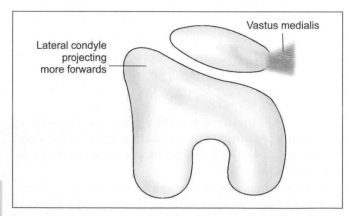

Fig. 2.56: Projecting lateral edge of patellar articular surface.

- Patella probably improves leverage of the quadriceps femoris by increasing the angulation of the line of pull on the leg. However, removal of the patella does not interfere with the function of the patella.

- Fracture of the patella should be differentiated from a bipartite or a tripartite patella (Fig. 2.57).

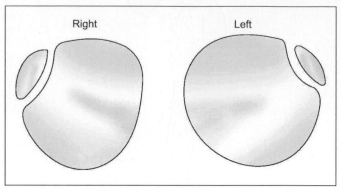

Fig. 2.57: Bipartite patella.

- Patella may get fractured (Fig. 2.58).

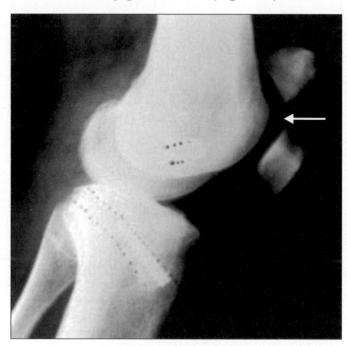

Fig. 2.58: Fracture of patella.

- Quadriceps femoris muscle is inserted into patella, from where ligamentum patellae arises which ends into the tibial tuberosity. These four are components of the extensor apparatus of knee joint. During sudden severe contraction of quadriceps, the tibial tuberosity may get avulsed. The tibial tuberosity ossifies as a downward protrusion of upper end.
- Bursitis occurs in prepatellar and subcutaneous infrapatellar bursa (Fig. 2.59).
- The upper end of tibia is one of the commonest sites for acute osteomyelitis. The knee joint remains safe because the capsule is attached near the articular margins of the tibia, proximal to the epiphyseal line (Fig. 2.60).

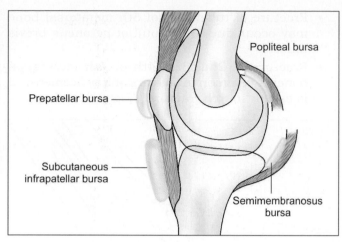

Fig. 2.59: Bursitis in prepatellar and subcutaneous infrapatellar bursa.

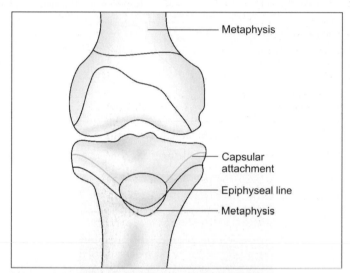

Fig. 2.60: The epiphyseal line is distal to the capsular attachment.

- The tibia is commonly fractured at the junction of upper two-thirds and lower one-third of the shaft as the shaft is most slender here. Such fractures may unite slowly, or may not unite at all as the blood supply to this part of the bone is poor. This may also be caused by tearing of the nutrient artery (Fig. 2.53).

- Sometimes a surgeon takes a piece of bone from the part of the body and uses it to repair a defect in some other. This procedure is called a *bone graft*. For this purpose pieces of bone are easily obtained from the subcutaneous medial aspect of tibia.

- If the foot gets caught in a hole in the ground, there is forcible abduction and external rotation. In such an injury, first there occurs a spiral fracture of lateral malleolus, then fracture of the medial malleolus. Finally the posterior margin of the lower end of tibia shears off. These

stages are termed 1st, 2nd and 3rd degrees of Pott's fracture (Fig. 2.53).

- Forward dislocation of the tibia on the talus produces a characteristic prominence of the heel. This is the commonest type of injury of the ankle.

- The upper and lower ends of the fibula are subcutaneous and palpable (Fig. 2.61).

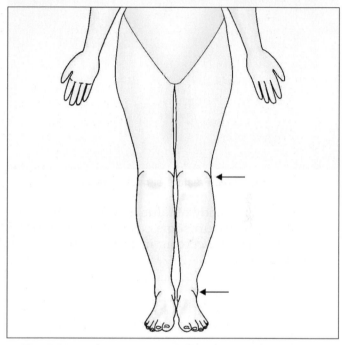

Fig. 2.61: Subcutaneous upper and lower ends of fibula.

- The common peroneal nerve can be rolled against the neck of fibula. This nerve is commonly injured here (Fig. 2.42).

- Fibula is an ideal spare bone for a bone graft.

- Though fibula does not bear any weight, the lateral malleolus and the ligaments attached to it are very important in maintaining stability at the ankle joint (Fig. 2.62).

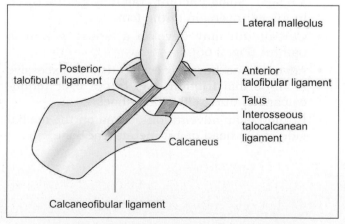

Fig. 2.62: Ligament attached to lateral malleolus.

- Forced dorsiflexion may cause fracture of the neck of the talus (Fig. 2.63).

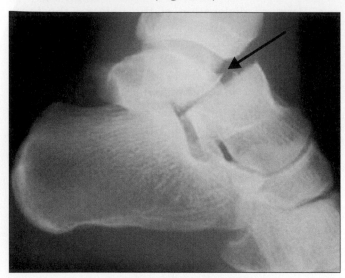

Fig. 2.63: Fracture of neck of talus.

- If arteries to body of talus go through the neck only as occurs in some cases, the body would get avascular necrosis in fracture of its neck (Fig. 2.64).

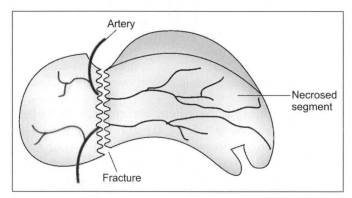

Fig. 2.64: Avascular necrosis of body of talus in some cases.

- Fracture of the calcaneum results by a fall from a height. Sustentaculum tali may get fractured in forced inversion of the foot.
- Calcaneum may develop a 'spur', which is painful (Fig. 2.65).
- Adventitious bursae develop due to excessive or abnormal friction, e.g. bursa over tendo-calcaneus due to ill fitting shoes.
- Bunion is an adventitious bursa on the medial side of the head of 1st metatarsal bone.

- Fracture of tuberosity of 5th metatarsal bone may occur due to the pull of peroneus brevis muscle.
- Fracture of 2nd, 3rd, 4th or 5th metatarsal bones is common in soldiers and policemen and is called "march fracture" (Fig. 2.66).

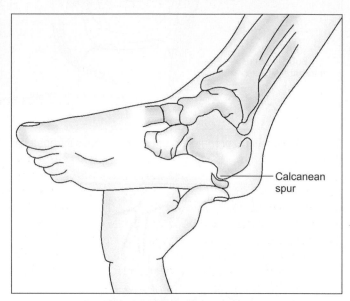

Fig. 2.65: Calcaneum spur.

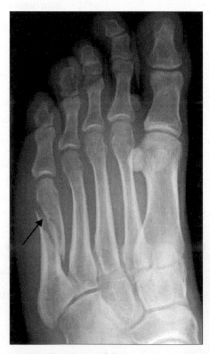

Fig. 2.66: Fracture of 5th metatarsal bone.

CHAPTER 3

Front of Thigh

Front of thigh extends between the hip and knee joints. The superficial fascia contains one big vein, the great saphenous vein, besides the cutaneous nerves, vessels, lymphatics and lymph nodes. The upper third of thigh medially contains the femoral triangle, middle third carries the femoral vessels through the adductor canal. Front of thigh also contains a vast four-headed muscle, the quadriceps femoris, besides the iliopsoas in the uppermost region and adductor muscles on its medial side. Femoral hernia if occurs is seen in the upper medial region of front of thigh.

SURFACE LANDMARKS

Iliac crest is a thick, curved bony margin, forming laterally the lower margin of the waist. The hands are often supported on the iliac crests in a relaxed standing posture. *Anterior superior iliac spine* is the anterior end of the iliac crest. *Tubercle* of the iliac crest is a low bony prominence situated on the outer lip of the iliac crest about 2.5 cm behind the anterior superior iliac spine.

Fold of groin is a shallow curved groove which separates the front of the thigh from the anterior abdominal wall. It represents the flexion crease of the thigh and overlies the inguinal ligament which extends from the anterior superior iliac spine to the pubic tubercle. The downward convexity of the ligament is due to the pull exerted by the fascia lata of the thigh.

Pubic tubercle is a small bony projection felt at the medial end of the fold of groin. Pubic symphysis is formed in the median plane between the right and left pubic bones. Pubic crest is a short bony ridge between the pubic tubercle and pubic symphysis (Fig. 3.1).

The *greater trochanter* of femur lies a hand's-breadth (about 12.5 cm) below the tubercle of *iliac*

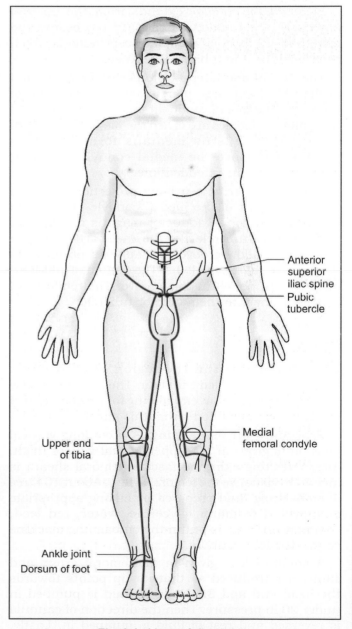

Fig. 3.1: Lines of dissection.

crest, forming a wide (4.5 cm) prominence just in front of the hollow on the side of the hip. The upper margin of the trochanter lies about the same level as the pubic crest.

Midinguinal point lies midway between the anterior superior iliac spine and the pubic symphysis. The femoral artery and the head of the femur lie beneath the midinguinal point.

Patella (knee cap) is the largest sesamoid bone of the body, developed in the tendon of quadriceps femoris. It is easily seen and felt in front of the knee. It can be moved freely in a fully extended knee.

Tibial tuberosity is a blunt prominence in front of the upper end of tibia, marking the upper end of the shin.

Ligamentum patellae extends from the apex of patella to the tibial tuberosity. It represents the tendon (5 × 2.5 cm) of the quadriceps femoris which can be felt best in a half flexed knee.

The medial and lateral *condyles of the femur* and of the tibia form large bony masses at the sides of the knee. The most prominent points on the sides of the femoral condyles are called the medial and lateral epicondyles. Vastus medialis forms a fleshy prominence above the medial condyle of femur, particularly in an extended knee.

Adductor tubercle is a bony projection from the uppermost part of the medial condyle of femur to which the tendon of adductor magnus is attached. To palpate the tubercle, flex the knee partly and note the wide, shallow groove that appears posterior to the mass of vastus medialis. The tendon of adductor magnus can be felt in this groove. The tendon can be traced down to the adductor tubercle.

SKIN OF THIGH

The skin of thigh in the region around pubic symphysis, is studded with hair. The presence of few stitches indicates that embalming for preservation of the body has been done from this site.

Procedure for embalming: A 6 cm long vertical incision is given in the upper medial side of thigh. After reflecting skin and fasciae, femoral sheath is incised to visualise the femoral artery. About 10 litres of embalming fluid prepared by mixing appropriate amounts of formalin, glycerine, water, red lead, common salt, etc. is put in the embalming machine connected to a cannula.

A small nick is given in the femoral artery and cannula introduced so that its tip points towards the head end and 8.5 litres of fluid is pumped in under 20 lb pressure. Then the direction of cannula is reversed and rest of fluid is pumped in. Lastly, the skin is stitched.

DISSECTION

Make a curved incision from anterior superior iliac spine to the pubic tubercle. Give a curved incision around the scrotum/pudendal cleft towards upper medial side of thigh. Extend it vertically down below the medial condyle of tibia till the level of tibial tuberosity. Now make a horizontal incision below the tibial tuberosity till the lateral side of leg (Fig. 3.1). Reflect the skin laterally, exposing the superficial fatty and deeper membranous layers of superficial fascia. Remove the fatty layer.

Identify the great saphenous vein in the medial part of anterior surface of thigh. Draining into its upper part are its three superficial tributaries, namely superficial circumflex iliac, superficial epigastric and superficial external pudendal. The vertical group of superficial inguinal lymph nodes lie along the upper part of great saphenous vein.

Dissect the superficial inguinal ring 1 cm above and lateral to the pubic tubercle. The spermatic cord and ilioinguinal nerve leave the abdomen through this ring.

Trace the great saphenous vein backwards till it pierces the specialised deep fascia known as cribriform fascia to drain into the femoral vein enclosed in the femoral sheath.

SUPERFICIAL FASCIA

The superficial fascia has *two layers*, a superficial fatty layer and a deep membranous layer, which are continuous with the corresponding layers of the anterior abdominal wall. The two layers are most distinct in the uppermost part of the thigh, near the groin, where the cutaneous nerves, vessels and lymph nodes lie between the two layers.

The membranous layer is loosely attached to the deep fascia of the thigh except near the inguinal ligament, where it is firmly attached along a horizontal line. The line of firm attachment is called *Holden's line*. It begins a little lateral to the pubic tubercle and extends laterally for about 8 cm (Fig. 3.2).

The importance of this line is as follows.

When the urethra is injured in the perineum, urine may flow out or extravasate into the interval deep to the membranous layer of superficial fascia. This urine can pass up into the anterior abdominal wall from where it can enter the upper part of the thigh. However, the firm attachment of the membranous layer of superficial fascia to the deep fascia along Holden's line prevents urine from descending into the thigh beyond the line (Fig. 28.26).

The superficial fascia contains cutaneous nerves, cutaneous arteries, the great saphenous vein and its tributaries, and the superficial inguinal lymph nodes. The nerves and vessels are described below. The inguinal lymph nodes are described later.

CUTANEOUS NERVES

The skin of the front of the thigh is supplied by seven cutaneous nerves derived directly, or indirectly, from the lumbar plexus (Fig. 3.3). In addition, the skin over the upper lateral part of the thigh is supplied by the lateral cutaneous branch of the subcostal nerve (Fig. 5.3).

The *ilioinguinal nerve* (L1) emerges at the superficial inguinal ring, and supplies the skin at the root of the penis or over the mons pubis in the female, the anterior one-third of the scrotum or labium majus, and the supromedial part of the thigh (Fig. 3.4).

The *femoral branch of genitofemoral nerve* (L1, L2) pierces the femoral sheath and the overlying deep fascia 2 cm below the midinguinal point, and supplies most of the skin over the femoral triangle (Fig. 3.5).

The *lateral cutaneous nerve of thigh* (L2, L3) is a branch of the lumbar plexus. It emerges behind the lateral end of the inguinal ligament, divides into anterior and posterior branches, and supplies the skin on the anterolateral side of the thigh and on the anterior part of the gluteal region.

The *intermediate cutaneous nerve of thigh* (L2, L3) is a branch of the anterior division of the femoral nerve. It pierces the deep fascia at the junction of the upper one-third and middle one-third of the thigh. It divides into two or more branches and supplies a strip of skin on the front of the thigh extending from the sartorius to the knee.

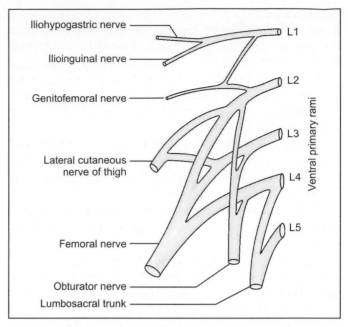

Fig. 3.3: The lumbar plexus and its branches.

The *medial cutaneous nerve of the thigh* (L2, L3) is a branch of the anterior division of the femoral nerve. It divides into anterior and posterior divisions. The nerve supplies the skin on the medial side of the lower two-thirds of the thigh.

The *saphenous nerve* (L3, L4) is a branch of the posterior division of the femoral nerve. It pierces the deep fascia on the medial side of the knee, runs down in front of the great saphenous vein, and supplies the skin on the medial side of the leg and foot up to the ball of the big toe (Fig. 8.3).

Before piercing the deep fascia the saphenous nerve gives off the *infrapatellar branch* which runs downwards and laterally, and supplies the skin over the ligamentum patellae.

Patellar Plexus

It is a plexus of fine nerves situated in front of the patella, the ligamentum patellae and the upper end of the tibia. It is formed by contributions from:

(a) The anterior division of the lateral cutaneous nerve
(b) The intermediate cutaneous nerve
(c) The anterior division of the medial cutaneous nerve
(d) The infrapatellar branch of the saphenous nerve.

CUTANEOUS ARTERIES

Three small arteries arising from the femoral artery can be seen a little below the inguinal ligament (Fig. 3.12).

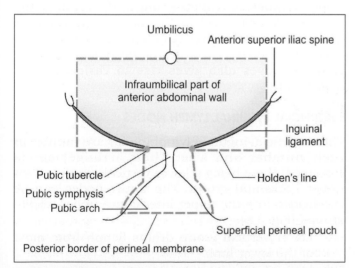

Fig. 3.2: The superficial area into which urine may pass when urethra is injured. The areas within the interrupted lines have a well-defined membranous layer of superficial fascia.

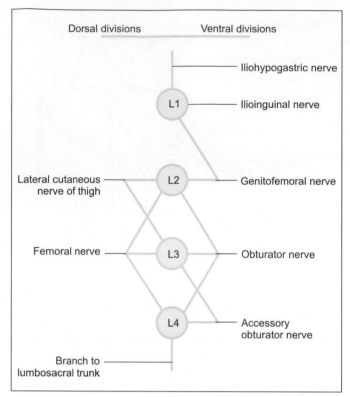

Fig. 3.4: Diagrammatic scheme of lumbar plexus.

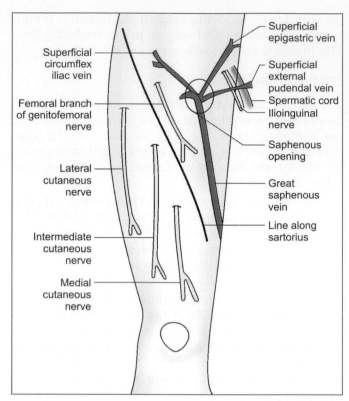

Fig. 3.5: Superficial vessels and nerves seen on the front of the thigh.

1. *Superficial external pudendal artery* pierces the cribriform fascia, runs medially in front of the spermatic cord, and supplies the external genitalia.
2. *Superficial epigastric artery* pierces the cribriform fascia, runs towards the umbilicus, and supplies the lower part of anterior abdominal wall.
3. *Superficial circumflex iliac artery* pierces the fascia lata lateral to saphenous opening, runs upwards below the inguinal ligament, and anastomoses at the anterior superior iliac spine with deep circumflex iliac, superior gluteal and lateral circumflex femoral arteries.

Great or Long Saphenous Vein

This is the largest and longest superficial vein of the lower limb (*Saphes* = easily seen).

It begins on the dorsum of the foot from the medial end of the dorsal venous arch, and runs upwards in front of the medial malleolus, along the medial side of the leg, and behind the knee. In the thigh, it inclines forwards to reach the saphenous opening where it pierces the cribriform fascia and opens into the femoral vein. Before piercing the cribriform fascia, it receives three named tributaries corres-ponding to the three cutaneous arteries, and also many unnamed tributaries (Figs 3.5, 8.2 and 9.1).

It contains about 10 to 15 valves which prevent back flow of the venous blood, which tends to occur because of gravity. One valve is always present at the saphenofemoral junction. Incompetence of these valves makes the vein dilated and tortuous leading to varicose veins.

The vein is also connected to the deep veins of the limb by perforating veins. There are three medial perforators just above the ankle, one perforator just below the knee, and another one in the region of the adductor canal (Fig. 11.5). The perforating veins are also provided with valves which permit flow of blood only from the superficial to the deep veins. Failure of these valves also gives rise to varicose veins (Fig. 11.11).

SUPERFICIAL INGUINAL LYMPH NODES

The superficial inguinal lymph nodes are variable in their number and size. Their arrangement is T-shaped, there being a lower vertical group and an upper horizontal group. The upper nodes can be subdivided into the upper lateral and upper medial groups (Fig. 3.6).

- Lower vertical group drains lymph from most of the lower limb.
- Upper lateral group drains lymph from infra-umbilical part of anterior abdominal wall and gluteal region.

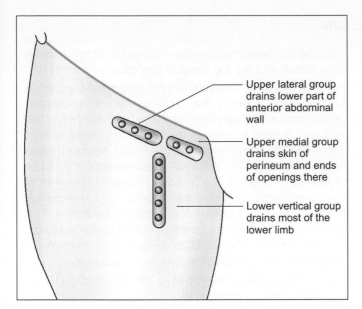

Fig. 3.6: Superficial inguinal lymph nodes.

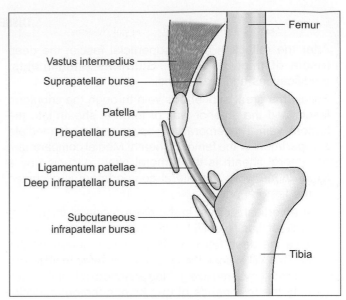

Fig. 3.7: The patellar bursae.

- Upper medial group drains lymph from external genital organs including the terminal ends of the urethra, anal canal and vagina.

SUBCUTANEOUS BURSAE

Bursae are lubricating mechanisms which are provided at sites of friction to smoothen movement. Undue pressure on them may cause their pathological enlargement. Bursae present in relation to the patella are described here (Fig. 3.7).

Prepatellar Bursa

It lies in front of the lower part of the patella and of the upper part of the ligamentum patellae.

Subcutaneous Infrapatellar Bursa

It lies in front of lower part of the tibial tuberosity and of the lower part of the ligamentum patellae.

Two deep bursae are also present. These are suprapatellar bursa and deep infrapatellar bursa.

DEEP FASCIA OF THIGH/FASCIA LATA

The fascia lata is a tough fibrous sheath that envelops the whole of the thigh like a sleeve. Its attachments, shown in Fig. 3.8, are as follows.

Superiorly it is attached to the boundary line between the lower limb and the pelvis. Thus anteriorly it is attached to the inguinal ligament; laterally to the iliac crest; posteriorly, through the gluteal fascia to the sacrum, coccyx and sacro-tuberous ligament; and medially to the pubis, the pubic arch and the ischial tuberosity.

Inferiorly, on the front and sides of the knee, the fascia lata is attached to subcutaneous bony

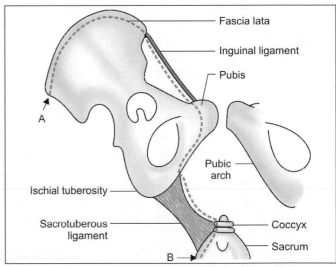

Fig. 3.8: The upper attachments of the fascia lata. Points A and B are continuous with each other.

prominences and the capsule of the knee joint. Posteriorly, it forms the strong popliteal fascia which is continuous below with the fascia of the back of the leg.

Modifications of Fascia Lata

Iliotibial Tract

The fascia lata is thickened laterally where it forms a 5 cm wide band called the iliotibial tract (Fig. 3.9). Superiorly the tract splits into two layers. The superficial lamina is attached to tubercle of iliac crest, and deep lamina to the capsule of hip joint. Inferiorly, the tract is attached to a smooth area on anterior surface of the lateral condyle of tibia. The importance of the iliotibial tract is as follows.

DISSECTION

After the reflection of the superficial fascia, the deep fascia of thigh is visible. Study its attachments, modifications and extensions.

Follow the great saphenous vein through the cribriform fascia and the anterior wall of femoral sheath into the femoral vein. The femoral vein occupies the intermediate compartment of the femoral sheath. Medial compartment of femoral sheath is the femoral canal occupied by a lymph node while the lateral compartment is occupied by the femoral artery.

Give a vertical incision in the deep fascia of thigh from tubercle of iliac crest till the lateral condyle of femur and remove the deep fascia or fascia lata in lateral part of thigh. This will expose the tensor fascia latae muscle and gluteus maximus muscle getting attached to iliotibial tract. Identify the four heads of quadriceps femoris muscle.

Learn about these muscles from Table 3.1. Do the actions on yourself and try the patellar jerk on your friends.

Remove the entire deep fascia from upper one-third of the front of thigh. Identify the sartorius muscle stretching gently across the thigh from lateral to medial side and the adductor longus muscle extending from medial side of thigh towards lateral side into the femur, being crossed by the sartorius. This triangular depression in the upper one-third of thigh is the femoral triangle. The medial border of sartorius forms lateral boundary and medial border of adductor longus forms medial boundary. The base of this triangle is formed by the inguinal ligament. Dissect its boundaries, and contents, e.g. femoral nerve, artery and vein, and accompanying structures.

Expose the sartorius muscle till its insertion into the upper medial surface of shaft of tibia.

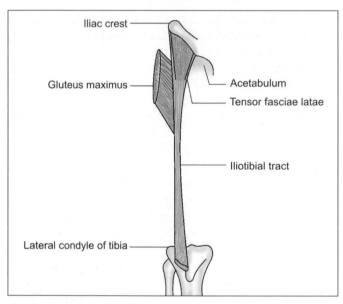

Fig. 3.9: The iliotibial tract with insertion of two muscles.

(a) Two important muscles are inserted into its upper part, between the superficial and deep laminae. These are the three-fourths part of the gluteus maximus; and the tensor fasciae latae.

(b) The iliotibial tract stabilizes the knee both in extension and in partial flexion; and is, therefore, used constantly during walking and running. In leaning forwards with slightly flexed knees, the tract is the main support of the knee against gravity.

Saphenous Opening

This is an oval opening in the fascia lata. The centre of the opening is 4 cm below and 4 cm lateral to the pubic tubercle. It is about 2.5 cm long and 2 cm broad with its long axis directed downwards and laterally. The opening has a sharp crescentic lateral margin or falciform margin which lies in front of the femoral sheath. The medial margin of the opening lies at a deeper level. It is formed by the fascia overlying the pectineus. The fascia passes behind the femoral sheath (Fig. 3.5).

The saphenous opening is closed by the *cribriform fascia* which covers the opening.

Intermuscular Septa

Three intermuscular septa divide the thigh into three compartments (Fig. 3.10).

The *lateral intermuscular septum* is the thickest of these septa. It extends from the iliotibial tract to the lateral lip of the linea aspera. It separates the anterior compartment of the thigh from the posterior compartment.

The *medial intermuscular septum* is attached to the medial lip of the linea aspera, and separates the anterior compartment of the thigh from the medial compartment.

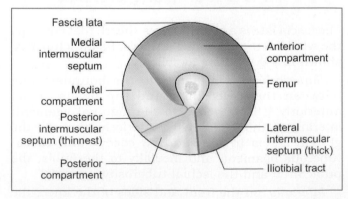

Fig. 3.10: Intermuscular septa and compartments of thigh.

The *posterior intermuscular septum* is poorly defined. It separates the medial compartment of the thigh from the posterior compartment.

FEMORAL TRIANGLE

It is a triangular depression on the front of the upper one-third of the thigh immediately below the inguinal ligament.

Boundaries

The femoral triangle is bounded *laterally* by the medial border of sartorius; and *medially* by the medial border of the adductor longus (Fig. 3.11). Its *base* is formed by the inguinal ligament. The *apex,* which is directed downwards, is formed by the point where the medial and lateral boundaries meet.

The apex is continuous, below, with the adductor canal.

The *roof* of the femoral triangle is formed by:

(i) Skin.

(ii) Superficial fascia containing the superficial inguinal lymph nodes, the femoral branch of the genitofemoral nerve, branches of the ilioinguinal nerve, superficial branches of the femoral artery with accompanying veins, and the upper part of the great saphenous vein.

(iii) *Deep fascia*, with the saphenous opening and the cribriform fascia (Fig. 3.12).

The *floor* of the triangle is formed medially by the adductor longus and pectineus, and laterally by the psoas major and iliacus (Fig. 3.13a and b).

Contents

The contents of the femoral triangle (Fig. 3.14) are as follows.

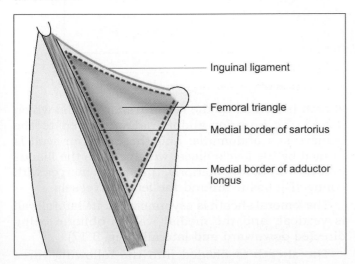

Fig. 3.11: Boundaries of the femoral triangle.

Inguinal ligament

Femoral triangle

Medial border of sartorius

Medial border of adductor longus

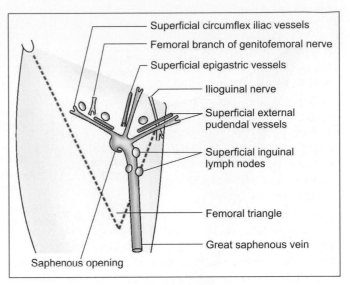

Superficial circumflex iliac vessels

Femoral branch of genitofemoral nerve

Superficial epigastric vessels

Ilioinguinal nerve

Superficial external pudendal vessels

Superficial inguinal lymph nodes

Femoral triangle

Great saphenous vein

Saphenous opening

Fig. 3.12: Structures in the roof of femoral triangle.

1. *Femoral artery and its branches:* The femoral artery traverses the triangle from its base at the midinguinal point to the apex. In the triangle, it gives off six branches, three superficial and three deep.

2. *Femoral vein and its tributaries:* The femoral vein accompanies the femoral artery. The vein is medial to the artery at base of triangle, but posteromedial to artery at the apex.

   The femoral vein receives the great saphenous vein, circumflex veins and veins corresponding to the branches of femoral artery.

3. The *femoral sheath* encloses the upper 4 cm of the femoral vessels (Fig. 3.15).

4. *Nerves:*

   (a) The *femoral nerve* lies lateral to the femoral artery, *outside the femoral sheath*, in the groove between the iliacus and the psoas major muscles. It is described later.

   (b) The *nerve to the pectineus* arises from the femoral nerve just above the inguinal ligament. It passes behind femoral sheath to reach the anterior surface of pectineus.

   (c) The *femoral branch of the genitofemoral nerve* occupies the lateral compartment of the femoral sheath along with the femoral artery. It supplies most of the skin over the femoral triangle.

   (d) The *lateral cutaneous nerve of the thigh* crosses the lateral angle of the triangle. Runs on the lateral side of thigh and ends by dividing into anterior and posterior branches. These supply anterolateral aspect of front of thigh and lateral aspect of gluteal region respectively.

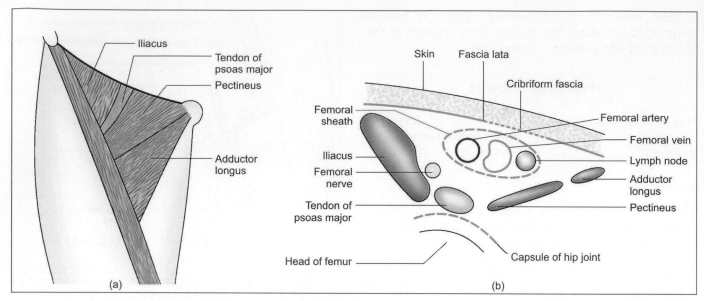

Fig. 3.13: Floor of the femoral triangle: (a) Surface view, (b) sectional view.

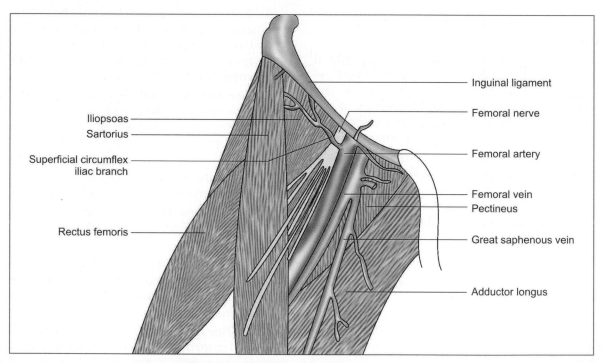

Fig. 3.14: Contents of the femoral triangle.

5. The *deep inguinal lymph nodes* lie deep to the deep fascia. These lie medial to upper part of femoral vein and receive lymph from superficial inguinal lymph nodes, from glans penis or clitoris and deep lymphatics of lower limb.

Femoral Sheath

This is a funnel-shaped sleeve of fascia enclosing the upper 3 to 4 cm of the femoral vessels. The sheath is formed by downward extension of two layers of the fascia of the abdomen. The anterior wall of the sheath is formed by the fascia transver-salis which lies in the anterior abdominal wall deep to the transversus abdominis; and the posterior wall is formed by the fascia iliaca, which covers the iliacus muscle (Fig. 3.16). Inferiorly, the sheath merges with connective tissue around the femoral vessels.

The femoral sheath is asymmetrical. Its lateral wall is vertical, and the medial wall is oblique being directed downward and laterally (Fig. 3.17).

The sheath is divided into the following three compartments by septa (Fig. 3.18).

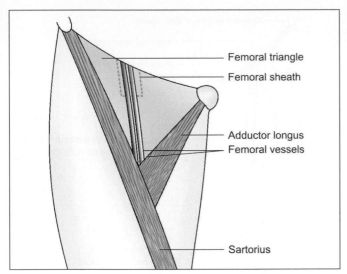

Fig. 3.15: Femoral sheath enclosing the upper parts of the femoral vessels.

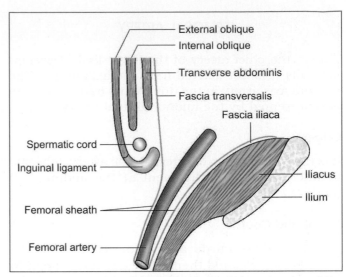

Fig. 3.16: Formation of the femoral sheath by extension of the fascia transversalis and the fascia iliaca into the thigh.

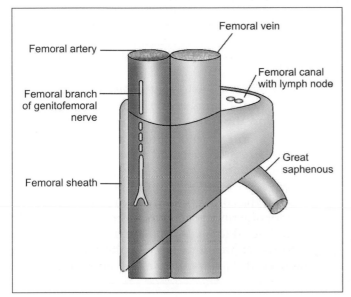

Fig. 3.17: Asymmetry of the femoral sheath.

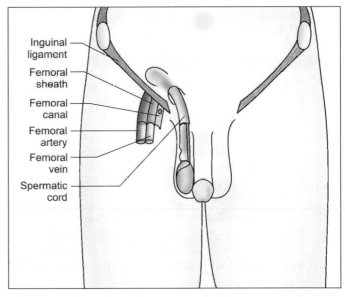

Fig. 3.18: Three compartments of femoral sheath.

1. The *lateral* or *arterial compartment* contains the femoral artery and the femoral branch of the genitofemoral nerve.
2. The *intermediate* or *venous compartment* contains the femoral vein.
3. The *medial* or *lymphatic compartment* is the smallest of all, and is known as the *femoral canal* which is described below.

Femoral Canal

This is the medial compartment of the femoral sheath. It is conical in shape, being wide above or at base and narrow below. It is about 1.5 cm long, and about 1.5 cm wide at the base (Figs 3.13, 3.17 and 3.18).

The base or upper end of femoral canal is called *femoral ring*. The boundaries of ring are important.

It is *bounded* anteriorly by the inguinal ligament, posteriorly by pectineus and its covering fascia, medially by the concave margin of lacunar ligament, and laterally by the septum separating it from femoral vein.

The inferior epigastric vessels are closely related to junction of the anterior and lateral walls of ring. The femoral ring is closed by a condensation of extraperitoneal connective tissue called the *femoral septum*.

The parietal peritoneum covering septum from above shows a depression called *femoral fossa*.

The femoral canal contains a lymph node of Cloquet or of Rosenmüller, lymphatics, and a small amount of areolar tissue. The lymph node drains the glans penis in males and the clitoris in females.

FEMORAL ARTERY

This is the chief artery of the lower limb. Developmentally it is not derived from the axis artery. The original axis artery in the uppermost part of the limb is represented by the inferior gluteal artery.

Origin

It is the continuation of external iliac artery. It begins behind the inguinal ligament at the midinguinal point.

Extent and Course

It passes downwards and medially, first in the femoral triangle, and then in the adductor canal. At the lower end of the adductor canal, i.e. at the junction of the middle and lower thirds of the thigh it passes through an opening in the adductor magnus to become continuous with the popliteal artery (Fig. 3.19).

Relations of Femoral Artery in Femoral Triangle

1. The main anterior relations are the skin, superficial fascia, deep fascia and the anterior wall of the femoral sheath.
2. Posteriorly, the artery rests, from above downwards on the psoas major, the pectineus, and the adductor longus. The posterior wall of the femoral sheath intervenes between these structures and the artery (Fig. 3.20).
3. The femoral artery is accompanied by the femoral vein. Just below the inguinal ligament the vein is medial to the artery. However, the vein gradually crosses to the lateral side

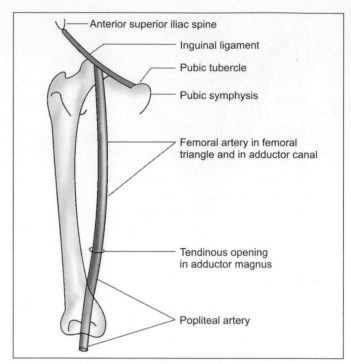

Fig. 3.19: Course and extent of the femoral artery.

posterior to the artery. It is directly behind the artery at the apex of the femoral triangle, and lateral to the lower end of the artery.

4. The femoral nerve is lateral to the upper part of the artery. Lower down the artery is related to the branches of the nerve, some of which cross it. The branch to the pectineus crosses behind the upper part of the artery. The medial cutaneous nerve of the thigh crosses the artery from lateral to medial side near the apex of the femoral triangle. The saphenous branch crosses the artery within the adductor canal.

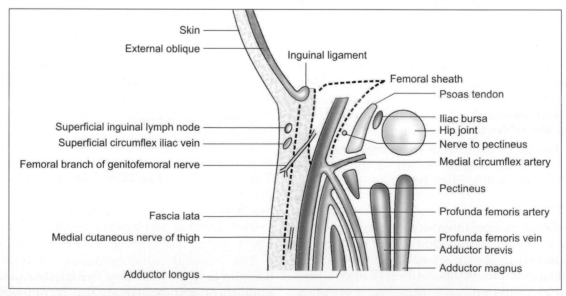

Fig. 3.20: Anterior and posterior relations of the femoral artery in the femoral triangle.

The nerve to the vastus medialis is lateral to the artery in the adductor canal.

5. The femoral branch of the genitofemoral nerve is also lateral to the upper part of the femoral artery, within the femoral sheath, but lower down it passes to the front of the artery (Fig. 3.17).

6. The profunda femoris artery a branch of the femoral artery itself, and its companion vein, lie behind the upper part of the femoral artery, where it lies on the pectineus. Lower down, however, the femoral and profunda arteries are separated by the adductor longus.

The relations of the femoral artery in the adductor canal are given later.

Branches in the Femoral Triangle

The femoral artery gives off three superficial and three deep branches in the femoral triangle.

The superficial branches are:

(i) Superficial external pudendal supplies the skin of external genital organs (Fig. 3.12).

(ii) Superficial epigastric for skin and fasciae of lower part of anterior abdominal wall.

(iii) Superficial circumflex iliac for skin along the iliac crest.

The deep branches are:

(i) Profunda femoris.

(ii) Deep external pudendal.

(iii) Muscular branches.

Profunda Femoris Artery

This is the largest branch of the femoral artery (Fig. 3.20). It is the chief artery of supply to all the three compartments of the thigh. It arises from the lateral side of the femoral artery about 4 cm below the inguinal ligament. The origin lies in front of the iliacus. As the artery descends, it passes posterior to the femoral vessels. It leaves the femoral triangle by passing deep to the adductor longus. Continuing downwards, it passes first between the adductor longus and the adductor brevis, and then between the adductor longus and the adductor magnus. Its terminal part pierces the adductor magnus to anastomose with upper muscular branches of the popliteal artery.

The profunda femoris artery gives off the medial and lateral circumflex femoral arteries, and four perforating arteries (Figs 7.7 and 7.8).

The *medial circumflex femoral artery* leaves the femoral triangle by passing posteriorly, between the pectineus and the psoas major muscles. It supplies adductor muscles and head of femur.

The *lateral circumflex femoral artery* runs laterally between the anterior and posterior divisions of the femoral nerve, passes behind the sartorius and the rectus femoris, and divides into ascending, transverse and descending branches.

The ascending branch runs deep to the tensor fasciae latae, gives branches to the hip joint and the greater trochanter, and anastomoses with the superior gluteal artery.

The transverse branch pierces the vastus lateralis and takes part in the cruciate anastomosis on the back of the thigh just below the greater trochanter.

The descending branch runs down along the anterior border of the vastus lateralis, accompanied by the nerve to that muscle.

Four *perforating arteries* are described in Chapter 7. These supply muscles attached to linea aspera.

Deep External Pudendal Artery

This branch of the femoral artery passes deep to the spermatic cord, or the round ligament of the uterus, and supplies the scrotum or the labium majus.

Muscular Branches

Numerous *muscular branches* arise from the femoral and profunda femoris artery, or its branches, to supply the muscles of the thigh.

FEMORAL VEIN

It begins as an upward continuation of the popliteal vein at the lower end of the adductor canal, and ends by becoming continuous with the external iliac vein behind the inguinal ligament, medial to the femoral artery (Fig. 3.14).

Tributaries: It receives:

1. The great saphenous vein.

2. Veins accompanying three deep branches of femoral artery in femoral triangle, i.e. profunda, deep external pudendal, and muscular.

3. Lateral and medial circumflex femoral veins.

4. The descending genicular and muscular veins in the adductor canal.

FEMORAL NERVE

The femoral nerve is the chief nerve of the anterior compartment of the thigh.

Origin and Root Value

It is the largest branch of the lumbar plexus. It is formed by the dorsal divisions of the anterior primary rami of spinal nerves L2, L3 and L4 (Figs 3.3 and 3.4).

Course

It enters the femoral triangle by passing behind the inguinal ligament just lateral to the femoral artery. In the thigh, it lies in the groove between the iliacus and the psoas major, outside the femoral sheath, and lateral to the femoral artery. After a short course of about 4 cm below the inguinal ligament, the nerve divides into anterior and posterior divisions which are separated by the lateral circumflex femoral artery (Figs 3.14 and 3.21).

Branches and Distribution

Muscular

1. The anterior division supplies the sartorius.
2. The posterior division supplies the rectus femoris, the three vasti and the articularis genu. The articularis genu is supplied by a branch from the nerve to vastus intermedius.

Cutaneous

1. The anterior division gives two cutaneous branches, the intermediate and the medial cutaneous nerves of the thigh.

2. The posterior division gives only one cutaneous branch, the saphenous nerve. Their areas of distribution are shown in Fig. 3.5.

Articular

1. The hip joint is supplied by the nerve to the rectus femoris.
2. The knee joint is supplied by the nerves to the three vasti. The nerve to the vastus medialis contains numerous proprioceptive fibres from the knee joint, accounting for the thickness of the nerve. This is in accordance with *Hilton's law*: Nerve supply to a muscle which lies across a joint, not only supplies the muscle, but also supplies the joint beneath and the skin overlying the muscle.

Vascular

To the femoral artery and its branches.

Note: The nerve to the pectineus arises from the medial side of the femoral nerve just above the inguinal ligament. It passes obliquely downwards and medially, behind the femoral sheath, to reach the anterior surface of the muscle.

MUSCLES OF FRONT OF THE THIGH

The muscles of the anterior compartment of the thigh are the sartorius, the quadriceps femoris, and the articularis genu (Figs 3.22 to 3.24). In addition to these, some muscles belonging to other regions are also encountered on the front of the thigh. The iliacus and psoas major muscles, which form part of the floor of the femoral triangle, have their origin within the abdomen. The pectineus and adductor longus, also seen in relation to the femoral triangle, are muscles of the medial compartment of the thigh. They are described in Chapter 4. In the upper lateral corner of the front of the thigh, we see the tensor fasciae latae. This is a muscle of the gluteal region and is described in Chapter 5.

The *sartorius* is long, narrow and ribbon-like. It runs downwards and medially across the front of the thigh. It is the longest muscle in the body. Its attachments are given in Table 3.1. Its nerve supply and actions are given in Table 3.2.

The *quadriceps femoris* is so called because it consists of four parts. These are the rectus femoris, the vastus lateralis, the vastus medialis, and the vastus intermedius. The rectus femoris is fusiform. It runs more or less vertically on the front of the thigh superficial to the vasti. The three vasti are wrapped around the shaft of the femur in the positions indicated by their names. The attachments of the components of the quadriceps femoris are

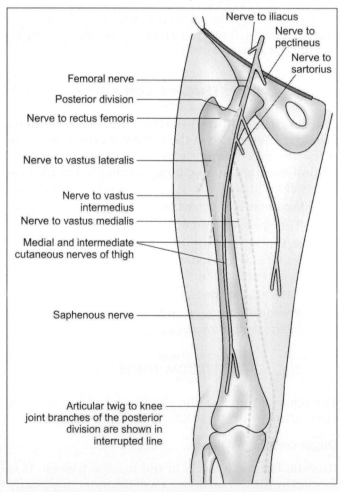

Fig. 3.21: The branches and distribution of femoral nerve.

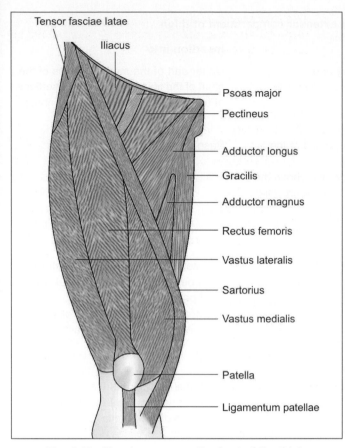

Fig. 3.22: Muscles seen on the front of the thigh.

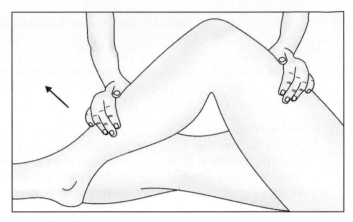

Fig. 3.23: Shows how to test the quadriceps femoris muscle.

given in Table 3.1. Their nerve supply and actions are given below.

The *articularis genu* consists of a few muscular slips that arise from the anterior surface of the shaft of the femur, a few centimeters above the patellar articular margin. They are inserted into the upper part of the synovial membrane of the knee joint. They pull the synovial membrane upwards during extension of the knee, thus preventing damage to it.

Iliacus and Psoas Major

These muscles form the lateral part of the floor of the femoral triangle. They are classified as muscles of the iliac region, and also among the muscles of the posterior abdominal wall. Since the greater parts of their fleshy bellies lie in the posterior abdominal wall, they will be described in detail in the section on the abdomen. However on account of their principal action on the hip joint, the following points may be noted.

1. Both have a common insertion on the lesser trochanter of the femur and are the chief and powerful flexors of the hip joint.

2. Because of their common insertion and action, the two muscles are often referred to by a common name, the iliopsoas.

3. Both are supplied by spinal segments L2 and L3. The psoas is supplied by the branches from the nerve roots, whereas the iliacus is supplied by the femoral nerve.

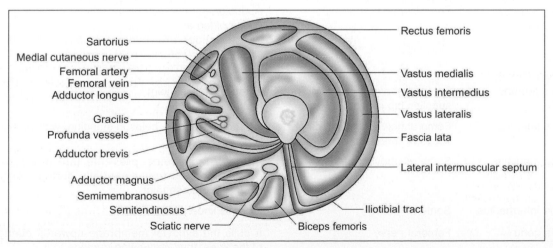

Fig. 3.24: Transverse section through the upper third of the thigh.

Table 3.1: Muscles of the anterior or extensor compartment of thigh

Muscle	Origin from	Insertion into
1. **Sartorius** (Fig. 3.22)	• Anterior superior iliac spine and • Upper half of the notch below the spine	Upper part of the medial surface of the shaft of the tibia in front of the insertions of the gracilis and the semitendinosus
2. **Quadriceps femoris**		
A. Rectus femoris (Fig. 3.22) fusiform, superficial fibres bipennate, deep fibres straight	• Straight head: from the upper half of the anterior inferior iliac spine • Reflected head: from the groove above the margin of the acetabulum and the capsule of the hip joint	Base of patella
B. Vastus lateralis (Fig. 3.22) forms large part of quadriceps femoris	The origin is linear The line runs along: • Upper part of intertrochanteric line • Anterior and inferior borders of greater trochanter • Lateral lip of gluteal tuberosity • Upper half of lateral lip of linea aspera	• Lateral part of the base of patella • Upper one-third of the lateral border of patella • Expansion to the capsule of knee joint, tibia and iliotibial tract
C. Vastus medialis (Fig. 3.22)	The origin is linear The line runs along: • Lower part of intertrochanteric line • Spiral line • Medial lip of linea aspera • Upper one-fourth of medial supracondylar line	Medial one-third of the base and upper two-thirds of the medial border of the patella
D. Vastus intermedius (Fig. 3.24)	• Upper three-fourths of the anterior and lateral surfaces of the shaft of femur	Base of patella *Note.* The patella is a sesamoid bone in the tendon of the quadriceps femoris. The ligamentum patellae is the actual tendon of the quadriceps femoris, which is inserted into the upper part of tibial tuberosity

Table 3.2: Muscles of the anterior or extensor compartment of thigh

Muscle	Nerve supply	Actions
1. Sartorius (Sartor = tailor)	Femoral nerve	Abductor and lateral rotator of thigh Flexor of leg at knee joint These actions are involved in assuming the position in which a tailor work, i.e. palthi posture
2. Quadriceps femoris		
A. Rectus femoris	Femoral nerve, this branch also supplies hip joint	Extensor of knee joint Flexor of hip joint
B. Vastus lateralis	Femoral nerve, this branch also supplies knee joint	Extends knee joint, helps in standing, walking and running
C. Vastus medialis	Same as above	Extends knee joint, prevents lateral displacement of patella. Rotates femur medially during locking stage of extension of knee joint
D. Vastus intermedius	Same as above	Extends knee joint
3. Articularis genu	Femoral nerve	It pulls the synovial membrane upwards during extension of the knee, thus preventing damage to it

ADDUCTOR/ HUNTER'S/ SUBSARTORIAL CANAL

This is also called the subsartorial canal or Hunter's canal. John Hunter (1729–1793) was an anatomist and surgeon at London. Hunter's operation for the treatment of popliteal aneurysm by ligating the femoral artery in the adductor canal is a landmark in the history of vascular surgery. The adductor canal is an intermuscular space situated on the medial side of the middle one-third of the thigh (Figs 3.25 and 3.26).

Extent

The canal extends from the apex of the femoral triangle, above, to the tendinous opening in the adductor magnus, below.

Shape

The canal is triangular on cross-section.

Boundaries

It has anterior, posterior and medial walls. The anterior wall is formed by the vastus medialis. The posterior wall or floor is formed by the adductor longus, above, and the adductor magnus, below. The medial wall or roof is formed by a strong fibrous membrane joining the anterior and posterior walls. The roof is overlapped by the sartorius.

The *subsartorial plexus* of nerves lies on the fibrous roof of the canal under cover of the sartorius. The plexus is formed by branches from the medial cutaneous nerve of the thigh, the saphenous nerve, and the anterior division of the obturator nerve. It supplies the overlying fascia lata and the neighbouring skin.

Contents

These are as follows (Fig. 3.27).

1. The *femoral artery* enters the canal at the apex of the femoral triangle. Within the canal it gives off muscular branches and a descending

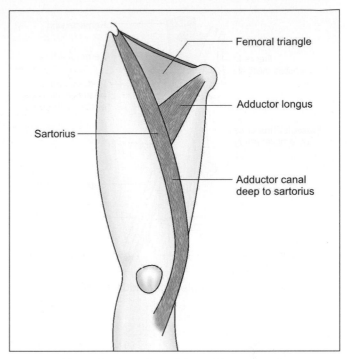

Fig. 3.25: Location of the adductor canal.

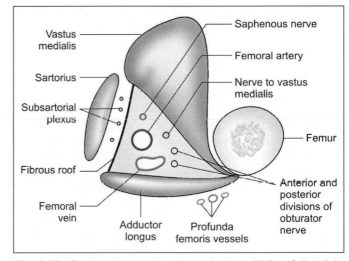

Fig. 3.26: Transverse section through the middle of the right adductor canal, seen from above. Note the boundaries and contents of the canal.

DISSECTION

Upper one-third of sartorius forms the lateral boundary of the femoral triangle. On lifting the middle one-third of sartorius, a part of deep fascia stretching between vastus medialis and adductor muscles is exposed. On longitudinal division of this strong fascia, the adductor canal/subsartorial canal/Hunter's canal is visualised. Dissect its contents, e.g. femoral vessels, saphenous nerve and nerve to vastus medialis, and distal parts of both divisions of obturator nerve.

---

genicular branch. The *descending genicular artery* is the last branch of the femoral artery arising just above the hiatus magnus. It divides into a superficial saphenous branch that accompanies the saphenous nerve, and a deep muscular branch that enters the vastus medialis and reaches the knee.

2. The *femoral vein* lies posterior to the femoral artery in the upper part, and lateral to the artery in the lower part of the canal.

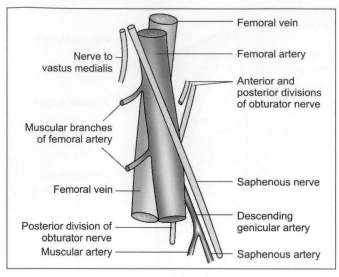

Fig. 3.27: Contents of the adductor canal.

3. The *saphenous nerve* crosses the femoral artery anteriorly from lateral to medial side. It leaves the canal with the saphenous artery by piercing the fibrous roof.

4. The *nerve* to the *vastus medialis* lies lateral to the femoral artery, and enters the vastus medialis in the upper part of the canal.

5. *Two divisions of obturator nerve:* The anterior division emerges at the lower border of the adductor longus, gives branches to the subsartorial plexus, and ends by supplying the femoral artery. The posterior division of the obturator nerve runs on the anterior surface of the adductor magnus, accompanies the femoral and popliteal arteries, and ends by supplying the knee joint (Fig. 4.5).

CLINICAL ANATOMY

- The fascia lata is attached to the inguinal ligament. Extension of the thighs pulls the abdominal wall downwards and makes it tense. To relax the abdomen fully for palpation by an examining physician, the patient is asked to draw the legs up. This overcomes the pull of the fascia lata on the abdominal wall.

- *Femoral hernia:* The femoral canal is an area of potential weakness in the abdominal wall through which abdominal contents may bulge out forming a femoral hernia. A femoral hernia is more common in females because the femoral canal is wider in them than in males. This is associated with the wider pelvis, and the smaller size of the femoral vessels, in the female (Fig. 3.28).

Hernia comprises a neck and a sac. Coverings are the layers on the sac. Mostly the content of hernial sac is a loop of bowel (Fig. 3.29).

- The course of an enlarging hernial sac is typical. First it passes downwards through the femoral canal, then forwards through the saphenous opening, and finally upwards along the superficial epigastric and superficial circumflex iliac vessels. For reduction of such a hernia the reverse course has to be followed (Fig. 3.30).

- In cases of strangulation of a femoral hernia, the surgeon has to enlarge the femoral ring. This is possible only by cutting the lacunar ligament; which forms the medial boundary of the ring. Normally this can be done without danger. Occasionally, however, an abnormal obturator

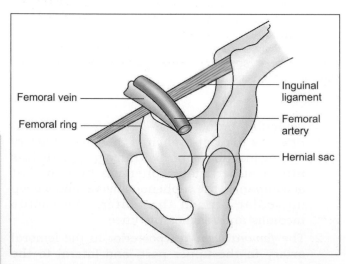

Fig. 3.28: Femoral hernia.

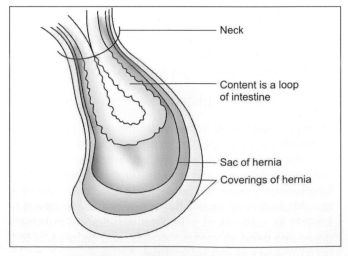

Fig. 3.29: Hernial sac with loop of bowel.

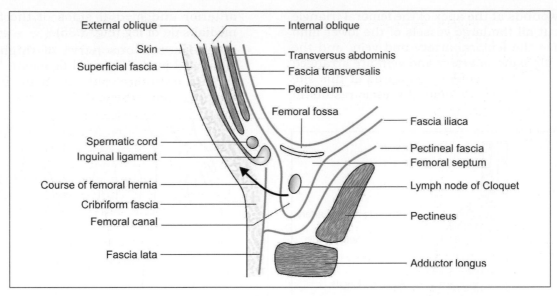

Fig. 3.30: Femoral canal and the course of a femoral hernia.

artery may lie along the edge of the lacunar ligament; and cutting it may cause alarming haemorrhage (Fig. 3.31).

- *Abnormal obturator artery:* The normal obturator artery is a branch of the internal iliac. It gives a pubic branch which anastomoses with the pubic branch of the inferior epigastric artery. Occasionally, this anastomosis is large and the obturator artery then appears to be a branch of the inferior epigastric. Usually, the abnormal artery passes lateral to the femoral canal in contact with the femoral vein and is safe in an operation to enlarge the femoral ring. Sometimes, however, the abnormal obturator artery may lie along the medial margin of the femoral ring, i.e. along the free margin of the lacunar ligament. Such an artery is likely to be cut if an attempt is made to enlarge the femoral ring cutting lacunar ligament (Fig. 3.31).

- The femoral artery can be compressed at the midinguinal point against the head of the femur or against the superior ramus of the pubis to control bleeding from the distal part of the limb in the thigh or leg.

- Pulsations of the femoral artery can be felt at the midinguinal point, against the head of the femur and the tendon of the psoas major. A bilateral absence or feebleness of the femoral pulse may result from coarctation or narrowing of the aorta, or thrombosis, i.e. clotting of blood within the aorta (Fig. 3.32).

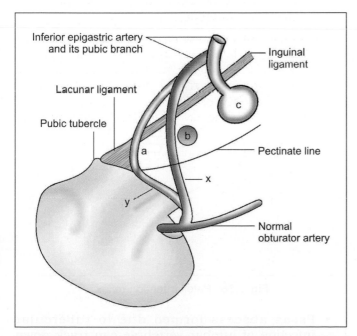

Fig. 3.31: Pubic region seen from behind to show the course of an abnormal obturator artery: a = femoral canal; b = femoral vein; c = junction of external iliac and femoral arteries; x = usual safe course of abnormal obturator artery; y = occasional dangerous position of artery.

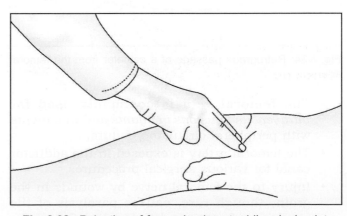

Fig. 3.32: Palpation of femoral pulse at midinguinal point.

- Stab wounds at the apex of the femoral triangle may cut all the large vessels of the lower limb because the femoral artery and vein, and the profunda femoris artery and vein are arranged in one line from before backwards at this site (Fig. 3.33). Injury to femoral vessels results in fatal haemorrhage.

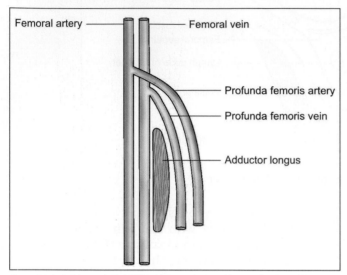

Fig. 3.33: Sagittal sectional view of four vessels.

- Since the femoral artery is quite superficial in the femoral triangle, it can be easily exposed for ligation, i.e. tying, or for passing a cannula or a thick needle. Catheters are passed upwards till the heart for certain minor operation (Fig. 3.34).

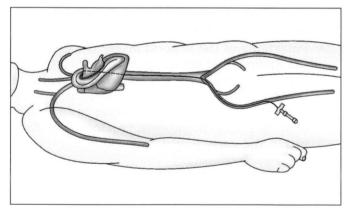

Fig. 3.34: Retrograde passage of a catheter from the femoral artery.

- The femoral vein is commonly used for *intravenous infusions in infants* and in patients with peripheral circulatory failure.
- The femoral artery is exposed in the adductor canal for various surgical procedures.
- Injury to the femoral nerve by wounds in the groin, though rare, causes paralysis of the quadriceps femoris and a sensory deficit on the anterior and medial sides of the thigh and medial side of leg (Fig. 3.35).
- Lateral cutaneous nerve of thigh may get entangled in the inguinal ligament. This leads to pain on lateral side of thigh. It is called "meralgia parasthetica" (Fig. 3.35).

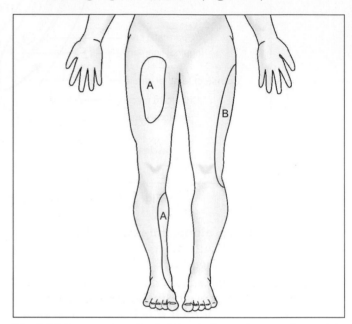

Fig. 3.35: Sensory loss due to injury to femoral nerve–A,meralgia parasthetica–B.

- Patellar tendon reflex or knee jerk (L3, L4). The knee joint gets extended on tapping the ligamentum patellae (Fig. 3.36).

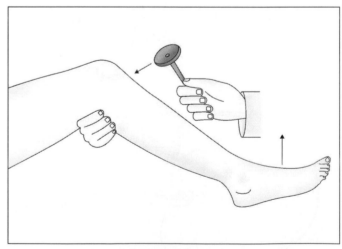

Fig. 3.36: Patellar tendon reflex.

- Psoas abscess formed due to tubercular infection of lumbar vertebrae can track down between psoas major muscles and its fascia to reach behind the inguinal ligament into the femoral triangle. It may be mistaken for enlarged lymph nodes (Fig. 3.37).

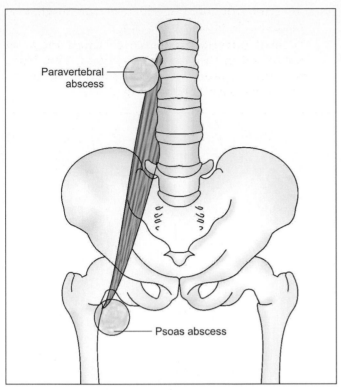

Fig. 3.37: Course of psoas abscess.

- Anterolateral region of thigh is used for giving intramuscular injections in children and infants. It is given below and lateral to anterior superior iliac spine in vastus lateralis muscle. This is a safe area. This site is also a preferred

site in adults, especially in case of "self injection" (Fig. 3.38).

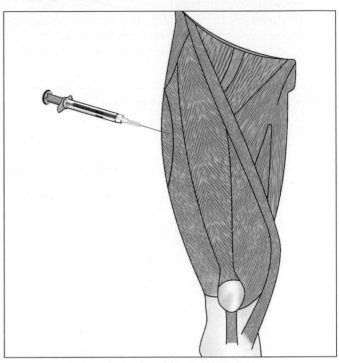

Fig. 3.38: Anterolateral region of thigh.

- Prepatellar bursitis is called "housemaids knee" or miner's knee (Fig. 2.59).
- Subcutaneous infrapatellar bursitis is called "clergyman's knee."

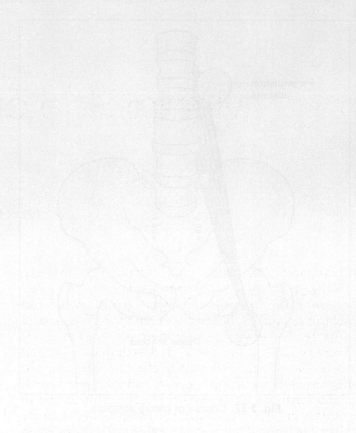

CHAPTER 4

Medial Side of Thigh

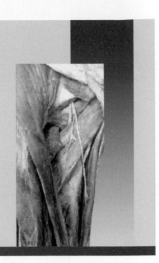

This chapter deals with the adductor muscles of thigh. The biggest of these is the adductor magnus, supplied by two different motor nerves, i.e. obturator and sciatic nerves and hence is a composite or hybrid muscle. The obturator nerve arises from anterior primary rami of lumbar 2, 3, 4 segments of spinal cord. The ventral divisions of the above mentioned segments form obturator nerve, and their dorsal divisions form the larger femoral nerve. This is due to rotation of this limb, so that the extensors of knee are placed in front of thigh while flexors are positioned on back of thigh and adductors on medial side.

INTRODUCTION

The adductor or medial compartment of thigh is very well developed and is derived, as indicated by its nerve supply from both the flexors and extensors between which it lies. Its counterpart in the arm is represented only by coracobrachialis muscle, as the arm can be adducted by pectoralis major and latissimus dorsi muscles.

BOUNDARIES

The adductor or medial compartment of the thigh is bounded anteriorly by the medial intermuscular septum which separates it from the extensor (anterior) compartment; and posteriorly by an ill-defined posterior intermuscular septum which separates it from the flexor (posterior) compartment (Fig. 3.10).

The structures to be studied in this region are muscles, nerves and arteries. These are as follows.

Muscles

Intrinsic

   (i) Adductor longus
   (ii) Adductor brevis
   (iii) Adductor magnus
   (iv) Gracilis
   (v) Pectineus.

Extrinsic

The obturator externus lies deep in this region. It is functionally related to the gluteal region.

Nerves

   1. Obturator nerve.
   2. Accessory obturator nerve.

DISSECTION

The triangular adductor longus was seen to form the medial boundary of femoral triangle (Fig. 4.1). Cut this muscle 3 cm below its origin and reflect the distal part laterally. On its deep surface, identify the anterior division of obturator nerve which supplies both adductor longus and gracilis muscles. Lateral to adductor longus on the same plane is the pectineus muscle. Cut it close to its origin and reflect laterally, tracing the occasional branch of anterior division of obturator nerve to this muscle. Obturator nerve is accompanied by the branches of obturator artery and medial femoral circumflex arteries.

Deeper to adductor longus and pectineus is the adductor brevis. Look for its nerve supply either from anterior/posterior division. Divide adductor brevis close to its origin. Deepest plane of muscles comprises adductor magnus (Fig. 4.2) and obturator externus, both supplied by posterior division of obturator nerve. Lying vertically along the medial side of thigh is the *graceful* gracilis. Study these muscles and the course of obturator nerve. Look for accessory obturator nerve. If present, it supplies pectineus.

Lastly, remove the obturator externus from its origin to expose the obturator artery and its branches.

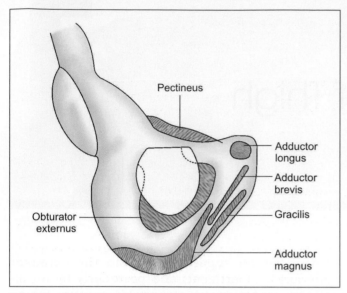

Fig. 4.1: Origin of muscles of medial compartment of the thigh.

Arteries

1. Obturator artery.
2. Medial circumflex femoral artery.

MUSCLES OF ADDUCTOR COMPARTMENT OF THIGH

The attachments of the muscles are given in Table 4.1. Their nerve supply and actions are given in Table 4.2. The obturator externus is described in Chapter 5.

Relations of Adductor Longus

The relations of the adductor longus are important. They are as follows.

Anterior Surface

1. Spermatic cord
2. Great saphenous vein with fascia lata
3. Femoral vessels
4. Sartorius (Fig. 4.3).

Posterior Surface

1. Adductor brevis
2. Adductor magnus
3. Anterior division of obturator nerve
4. Profunda femoris vessels (Fig. 4.4).

Lateral Border: Pectineus.

Medial Border: Gracilis.

Figure 4.5 shows the procedure of testing the adductors against resistance.

OBTURATOR NERVE

The obturator nerve is the chief nerve of the medial compartment of the thigh.

Origin and Root Value

It is a branch of the lumbar plexus. It is formed by the ventral divisions of the anterior primary rami of spinal nerves L2, L3, L4. The upper part of the nerve lies in the pelvis. It enters the thigh by passing through the obturator canal (Fig. 4.6).

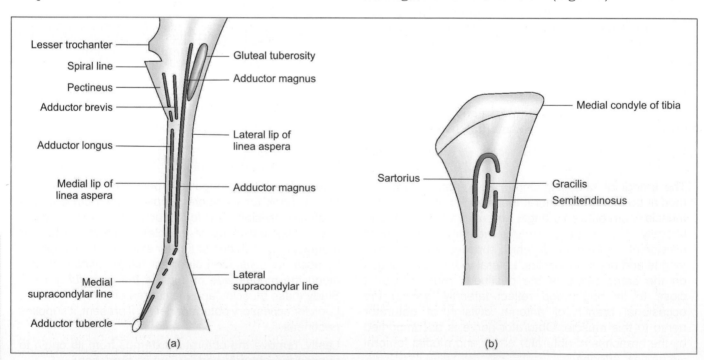

Fig. 4.2: Insertion of muscles: (a) Posterior aspect of femur, (b) upper part of medial surface of tibia.

Table 4.1: Muscles of the medial compartment of thigh

Muscles	Origin from	Insertion into
Adductor longus (Fig. 4.1) This is a triangular muscle, forming the medial part of the floor of the femoral triangle. It lies in the plane of the pectineus	It arises by a narrow, flat tendon from the front of the body of the pubis in the angle between the pubic crest and the pubic symphysis	The linea aspera in middle one-third of the shaft of the femur between the vastus medialis and the adductor brevis and magnus (Fig. 4.2)
Adductor brevis (Fig. 4.1) The muscle lies behind the pectineus and adductor longus	(a) Anterior surface of body of the pubis (b) Outer surface of inferior ramus of the pubis between the gracilis and obturator externus (c) Outer surface of ramus of the ischium between gracilis and the adductor magnus	Line extending from the lesser trochanter to upper part of linea aspera, behind the upper part of adductor longus
Adductor magnus (Fig. 4.1) This is the largest muscle of this compartment. Because of its double nerve supply, it is called a hybrid muscle	(a) Inferolateral part of the ischial tuberosity (b) Ramus of the ischium (c) Lower part of inferior ramus of the pubis	(a) Medial margin of gluteal tuberosity (b) Linea aspera (c) Medial supracondylar line (d) Adductor tubercle
Gracilis (Fig. 4.1)	(a) Medial margin of the lower half of the body of the pubis (b) Inferior ramus of the pubis (c) Adjoining part of the ramus of the ischium	Upper part of the medial surface of tibia behind the sartorius and in front of the semitendinosus
Pectineus (Figs 3.22 and 4.1) This is flat, quadrilateral muscle It forms a part of the floor of the femoral triangle	(a) Pecten pubis (b) Upper half of the pectineal surface of superior ramus of the pubis (c) Fascia covering the pectineus	Line extending from lesser trochanter to the linea aspera

Table 4.2: Muscles of the medial compartment of thigh

Muscles	Nerve supply	Actions
Adductor longus	Anterior division of obturator nerve	Powerful adductor of thigh of hip joint These act as posture controllers
Adductor brevis	Anterior or posterior division of obturator nerve	Adductor longus, adductor brevis and upper part of adductor magnus help in flexion of thigh
Adductor magnus (hybrid muscle) (Fig. 4.5)	Double nerve supply: Adductor part by posterior division of obturator nerve Hamstring part by tibial part of sciatic nerve	Lower part of adductor magnus helps in extension of hip and flexion of knee
Gracilis	Anterior division of obturator nerve	Flexor and medial rotator of thigh. It is a weak adductor of thigh
Pectineus (hybrid or composite muscle)	Double nerve supply: Anterior fibres by femoral nerve Posterior fibres by anterior division of obturator nerve	Flexor of thigh Adductor of thigh

Course and Relations in Thigh

1. Within the obturator canal the nerve divides into anterior and posterior divisions.
2. The *anterior division* passes downwards in front of the obturator externus being separated from the posterior division by a few fibres of this muscle. It then descends behind the pectineus and the adductor longus, and in front of the adductor brevis. The anterior division supplies the following muscles.

(a) Pectineus
(b) Adductor longus
(c) Gracilis
(d) Adductor brevis if it is not supplied by the posterior division.

The anterior division also gives a branch to the hip joint. Below the lower border of the adductor longus, it supplies a twig to the subsartorial plexus, and ends by supplying the femoral artery in the adductor canal.

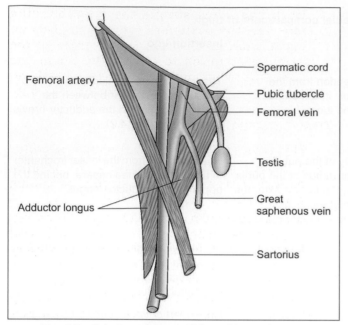

Fig. 4.3: Anterior relations of the adductor longus.

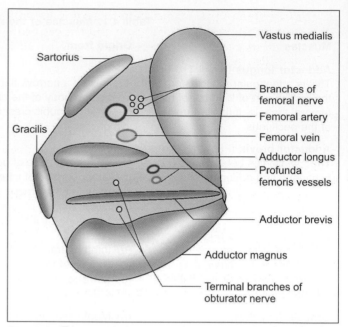

Fig. 4.4: Transverse section through the femoral triangle showing the relations of the adductor longus.

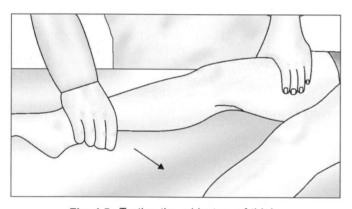

Fig. 4.5: Testing the adductors of thigh.

3. The *posterior division* enters the thigh by piercing the upper border of the obturator externus muscle. It descends behind the adductor brevis and in front of the adductor magnus. It gives branches to the following muscles.

   (a) Obturator externus

   (b) Adductor magnus

   (c) Adductor brevis if not supplied by the anterior division.

   In the adductor canal, it is reduced to a thin genicular branch which enters the popliteal

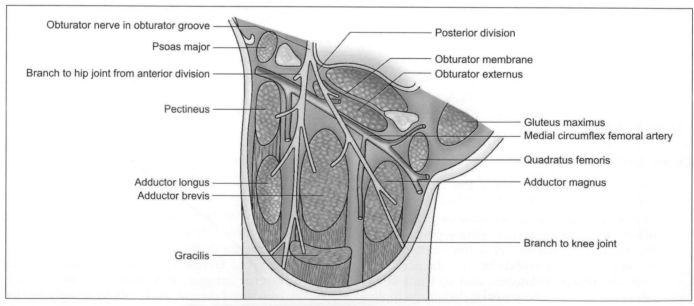

Fig. 4.6: The course and distribution of the obturator nerve.

fossa, pierces the oblique popliteal ligament and ends by supplying the capsule and the cruciate ligaments of the knee joint. Some of its fibres end by innervating the popliteal artery.

ACCESSORY OBTURATOR NERVE

This nerve is present in about 30% of subjects. It is a branch of the lumbar plexus, and is formed by the ventral divisions of the anterior primary rami of spinal nerves L3 and L4. It descends along the medial border of the psoas major, crosses the superior ramus of the pubis behind the pectineus, and terminates by dividing into three branches. One branch supplies the deep surface of the pectineus, another supplies the hip joint, and the third communicates with the anterior division of the obturator nerve. Sometimes the nerve is very small, and ends by supplying the pectineus only (Fig. 4.7).

OBTURATOR ARTERY

1. The obturator artery is a branch of the internal iliac, and accompanies (lies below) the obturator nerve in the pelvis.
2. At the upper margin of the obturator foramen, the obturator artery divides into anterior or medial and posterior or lateral branches which form a circle over the obturator membrane and anastomoses with the medial circumflex femoral artery.
3. Both branches supply the neighbouring muscles, the posterior branch also gives an *acetabular branch* which passes through the acetabular notch to supply the fat in the acetabular fossa and sends a twig to the head of the femur along the round ligament (Fig. 4.8).

MEDIAL CIRCUMFLEX FEMORAL ARTERY

1. This artery arises from the profunda femoris.
2. It leaves the femoral triangle by passing backwards and ends by dividing into ascending and transverse branches.
3. Ascending branch of medial femoral circumflex anastomoses with ascending branch of lateral femoral circumflex and superior gluteal artery to form "trochanteric anastomoses". This gives retinacular branches which lie along the retinacula of capsular of hip joint to supply head of femur. Transverse branch anastomoses with transverse branch of lateral femoral circumflex, inferior gluteal and first perforating branch of profunda femoris to form "cruciate anastomoses" (Fig. 4.8).
4. Before giving off the terminal branches, the artery gives off many muscular branches, and an *acetabular branch* which passes through the acetabular notch to supply fat in the acetabular fossa. It also sends a twig to the head of the femur along the round ligament (Fig. 4.8).

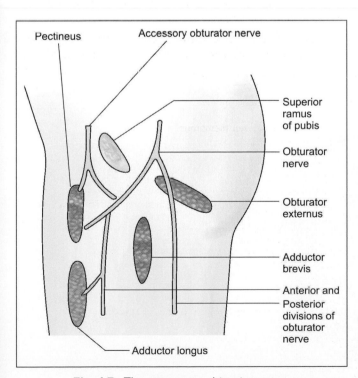

Fig. 4.7: The accessory obturator nerve.

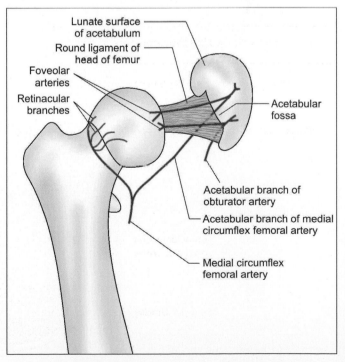

Fig. 4.8: Acetabular arteries and their foveolar branches.

CLINICAL ANATOMY

- Spasm of the adductors of thigh in certain intractable cases of spastic paraplegia may be relieved by surgical division of the obturator nerve.

- A disease of the hip joint may cause referred pain in the knee and on the medial side of the thigh because of their common nerve supply by the obturator nerve.

- Obturator nerve may be involved with femoral nerve in retroperitoneal tumours. A nerve entrapment syndrome leading to chronic pain on the medial side of thigh may occur in athletes with big adductor muscles.

- The gracilis muscles is most superficial muscle of the adductor compartment. This muscle is often used for transplantation of any damaged muscle.

- Intracapsular fracture of neck of femur causes damage to the retinacular branches (which supply head of femur), leading to avascular necrosis of head of femur (Fig. 2.54).

CHAPTER 5

Gluteal Region

The gluteal region forms the prominence at the upper posterior parts of lower limb. Gluteus maximus is the largest muscle of the region which indirectly extends till the tibia bone, so that it can act simultaneously on both the hip and knee joints.

The ischial tuberosity on which one sits underlies this muscle. The gateway to the gluteal region, the greater sciatic notch; the thickest nerve of the body, the sciatic nerve also lie beneath this huge antigravity postural muscle. One neurovascular bundle formed by pudendal nerve and vessels just appear into the gluteal region from the greater sciatic notch to disappear fast through the lesser sciatic notch to supply anything and everything in the region of the perineum.

INTRODUCTION

The gluteal region overlies the side and back of the pelvis, extending from the iliac crest above to the gluteal fold below. The lower part of the gluteal region which presents a rounded bulge due to excessive amount of subcutaneous fat is known as the buttock or natis. The anterosuperior part of the region seen in a side view is called the hip. The muscles, nerves and vessels emerging from pelvis are covered by gluteus maximus and buttock.

Morphologically, the erect posture of man has led to extension at the hip and appearance of gluteal fold, which is a transverse skin crease of the hip joint. This puts greater responsibility on gluteus maximus which makes the body erect and maintains it in erect posture at the hip; this involves raising and supporting the trunk against gravity. The gluteus maximus, covering the hip joint is, therefore, one of the most powerful and bulkiest muscles in man.

SURFACE LANDMARKS

1. *Buttock* is the rounded bulge in the lower part of the gluteal region. The two buttocks are separated from each other in the posterior median line by the *natal cleft* which begins at the third sacral spine and deepens inferiorly. The gluteal fold marks the lower limit of the buttock. Note that the *gluteal fold* is the transverse skin crease of the hip joint and that it does not correspond to the lower border of gluteus maximus which crosses the fold obliquely downwards and laterally (Fig. 5.1).

2. *Ischial tuberosity* is a large bony prominence which lies deep to the lower border of gluteus maximus about 5 cm from the median plane and about the same distance above the gluteal fold. It can be felt by placing the fingers in the medial part of the gluteal fold and pressing them upwards.

3. *Greater trochanter* of femur is a large bony prominence situated immediately in front of the hollow on the side of the hip and about a hands breadth below the tubercle of iliac crest.

4. *Iliac crest* is a thick curved bony ridge felt in a groove in the lower margin of the waist. The hands spanning the waist are often supported by the iliac crest. The *highest point* of iliac crest corresponds to the interval between the spines of the third and fourth lumbar vertebrae; site of lumbar puncture.

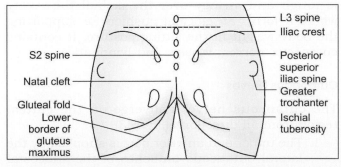

Fig. 5.1: Landmarks of the gluteal region.

71

DISSECTION

Make a curved incision from spine of second sacral spine: (i) along the iliac crest till its tubercle (ii); make a vertical incision from the second sacral spine downwards till the natal cleft (iii); taking it further laterally with downward convexity till the middle of the back of thigh (iv) (Fig. 5.2).

Reflect the thick skin and fascia towards the lateral aspect. The cutaneous nerves and vessels are difficult to find. Study them from the text. After removing the deep fascia from gluteus maximus muscle, define the attachments of this muscle. Perform the actions on yourself.

The anterior end of iliac crest is known as the *anterior superior iliac spine.* A line drawn from here to the front of the greater trochanter marks the junction between gluteal region and the front of thigh.

The posterior end of iliac crest is known as the *posterior superior iliac spine.* It lies in the floor of a dimple about 5 cm from the median plane and at the level of second sacral spine opposite the middle of sacroiliac joint.

5. *Sacrum* lies posteriorly between the two hip bones. The upper three sacral spines are usually palpable in the median plane. The *second spine,* lying between the *two posterior superior iliac spines*, is the guide to the other two spines. The lower part of sacrum and the coccyx lie in the floor of the natal cleft.

6. *Coccyx* lies just behind the anus. It is slightly mobile under pressure.

7. The *sacrotuberous ligament* lying deep to the lower border of gluteus maximus can be felt by a firm pressure between the lower part of sacrum and ischial tuberosity (Fig. 2.6).

SUPERFICIAL FASCIA

It is heavily laden with fat, more so in females, and is tough and stringy over the ischial tuberosity where it forms an efficient cushion for supporting the body weight in the sitting posture. It contains cutaneous nerves, vessels and lymphatics.

Cutaneous Nerves

The cutaneous nerves converge on the gluteal region from all directions (Fig. 5.3).

1. The upper and anterior part is supplied by the lateral cutaneous branches of the subcostal T12 and iliohypogastric L1 nerves.

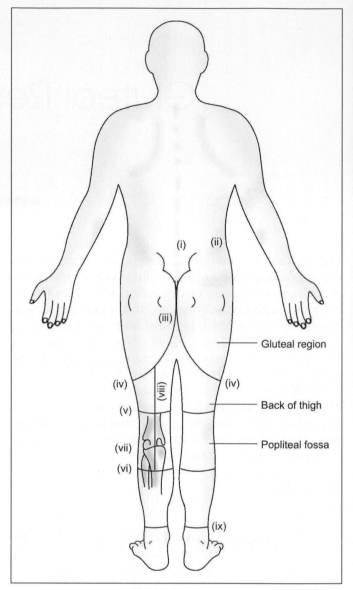

Fig. 5.2: Lines for dissection.

2. The upper and posterior part is supplied by the posterior primary rami of spinal nerves L1, L2, L3 and S1, S2, S3.

3. The lower and anterior part is supplied by branches from the posterior division of the lateral cutaneous nerve of the thigh (L2, L3).

4. The lower and posterior part is supplied by branches from the posterior cutaneous nerve of the thigh (S1, S2, S3) and the perforating cutaneous nerve (S2, S3).

Cutaneous Vessels and Lymphatics

The *blood supply* of the skin and subcutaneous tissue is derived from perforating branches of the superior and inferior gluteal arteries.

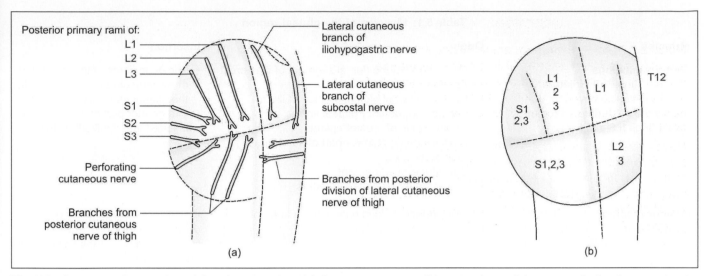

Fig. 5.3: Cutaneous innervation of the gluteal region: (a) Cutaneous nerves, (b) root values of the nerves in the four quadrants.

The *lymphatics* from the gluteal region drain into the lateral group of the superficial inguinal lymph nodes.

DEEP FASCIA

The deep fascia above and in front of the gluteus maximus, i.e. over the gluteus medius, is thick, dense, opaque and pearly white. Over the gluteus maximus, however, it is thin and transparent. The deep fascia splits and encloses the gluteus maximus musclc (Fig. 5.4).

MUSCLES OF GLUTEAL REGION

These muscles are the gluteus maximus, the gluteus medius, the gluteus minimus, the piriformis, the superior and inferior gemelli, the obturator internus obturator externus, and quadratus femoris. The tensor fasciae latae which lies on the lateral side of thigh, just in front of gluteal region, is also considered here. The attachments and nerve supply of these muscles are given in Tables 5.1 and 5.2. Their actions and some other features are considered below.

STRUCTURES UNDER COVER OF GLUTEUS MAXIMUS

These are numerous as follows.

Muscles

1. Gluteus medius.
2. Gluteus minimus.
3. Reflected head of the rectus femoris.
4. Piriformis.
5. Obturator internus with two gemelli.
6. Quadratus femoris.
7. Obturator externus.

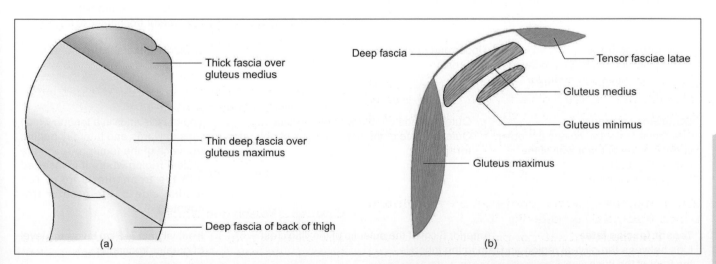

Fig. 5.4: Deep fascia of the gluteal region. (a) Surface view, (b) in vertical section.

Table 5.1: Muscles of the gluteal region

Muscles	Origin	Insertion
Gluteus maximus This is a large, quadrilateral powerful muscle covering mainly the posterior surface of pelvis (Figs 5.6 and 2.7)	• Outer slope of the dorsal segment of iliac crest • Posterior gluteal line • Posterior part of gluteal surface of ilium behind the posterior gluteal line • Aponeurosis of erector spinae • Dorsal surface of lower part of sacrum • Side of coccyx • Sacrotuberous ligament • Fascia covering gluteus medius	• The deep fibres of the lower part of the muscle are inserted into the gluteal tuberosity • The greater part of the muscle is inserted into the iliotibial tract
Gluteus medius It is fan-shaped, and covers the lateral surface of the pelvis and hip (Fig. 2.7)	Gluteal surface of ilium between the anterior and posterior gluteal lines	Into the greater trochanter of femur, on oblique ridge on the lateral surface. The ridge runs downwards and forwards
Gluteus minimus It is fan-shaped, and is covered by the gluteus medius (Fig. 2.7)	Gluteal surface of ilium between the anterior and inferior gluteal lines	Into greater trochanter of femur, on a ridge on the lateral part of the anterior surface
Piriformis Lies below and parallel to the posterior border of the gluteus medius (Fig. 2.12)	It arises within the pelvis from: • Pelvic surface of the middle three pieces of the sacrum, by three digitations • Upper margin of the greater sciatic notch	The rounded tendon is inserted into the apex of the greater trochanter of the femur
Gemellus superior Small muscle lying along the upper border of the tendon of the obturator internus (Fig. 2.12)	Upper part of lesser sciatic notch	Blends with tendon of obturator internus, and gets inserted into medial surface of greater trochanter of femur
Gemellus inferior Small muscle lying along the lower border of the tendon of the obturator internus (Fig. 5.7)	Lower part of lesser sciatic notch	Same as above
Obturator internus Fan-shaped, flattened belly lies in pelvis and the tendon in the gluteal region	• Pelvic surface of obturator membrane • Pelvic surface of the body of the ischium, ischial tuberosity, ischiopubic rami, and ilium below the pelvic brim • Obturator fascia	The tendon of the obturator internus leaves the pelvis through the lesser sciatic foramen. Here it bends at a right angle around the lesser sciatic notch and runs laterally to be inserted into the medial surface of the greater trochanter of the femur
Quadratus femoris Quadrilateral muscle lying between inferior gemellus and adductor magnus (Fig. 5.8)	Upper part of the outer border of ischial tuberosity	Quadrate tubercle and the area below it
Obturator externus Triangular in shape, covers the outer surface of the anterior wall of the pelvis (Fig. 5.9)	• Outer surface of obturator membrane • Outer surface of the bony margins of obturator foramen	The muscle ends in a tendon which runs upwards and laterally behind the neck of the femur to reach the gluteal region where it is inserted into the trochanteric fossa (on medial side of the greater trochanter)
Tensor fasciae latae Lies between the gluteal region and the front of the thigh	Anterior 5 cm of the outer lip of the iliac crest up to the tubercle	Iliotibial tract 3–5 cm below the level of greater trochanter

Table 5.2: Muscles of the gluteal region

Muscles	Nerve supply	Actions
Gluteus maximus	Inferior gluteal nerve (L5, S1, S2)	Chief extensor of the thigh at the hip joint. This action is very important in rising from a sitting position. It is essential for maintaining the erect posture. Other actions are: (a) Lateral rotation of the thigh (b) Abduction of the thigh (by upper fibres) (c) Along with the tensor fasciae latae the muscle stabilises the knee through the iliotibial tract It supports both the hip and the knee when these joints are slightly flexed. It is an antigravity muscle as well. Figure 5.5 (a) shows how to test the muscle. It is done by extending the thigh and palpating the muscle
Gluteus medius **Gluteus minimus**	Superior gluteal nerve (L4, L5, S1) Superior gluteal nerve (L4, L5, S1)	The *gluteus medius* and *gluteus minimus* are powerful abductors of the thigh. Their anterior fibres are also medial rotators. However, their most important action is to maintain the balance of the body when the opposite foot is off the ground, as in walking and running. They do this by preventing the opposite side of the pelvis from tilting downwards under the influence of gravity. Figure 5.5 (b) shows how to test the gluteus medius muscle. It is done by abducting thigh against resistance and palpating for the contracting muscle
Piriformis	Ventral rami of S1, S2	
Gemellus superior	Nerve to obturator internus (L5, S1, S2)	
Gemellus inferior	Nerve to quadratus femoris (L4, L5, S1)	
Obturator internus	Nerve to obturator internus (L5, S1, S2)	Lateral rotators of thigh at the hip joint
Quadratus femoris	Nerve to quadratus femoris (L4, L5, S1)	
Obturator externus	Posterior division of obturator nerve (L2, L3, L4)	
Tensor fasciae latae	Superior gluteal nerve (L4, L5, S1)	Abductor and medial rotator of thigh and an extensor of knee joint

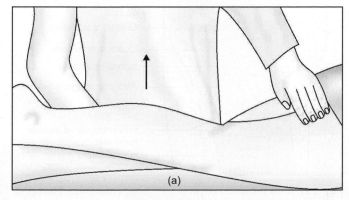 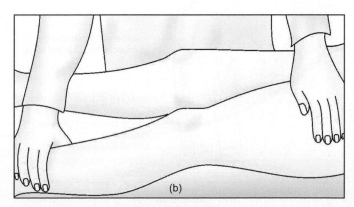

Fig. 5.5: (a) and (b) show how the gluteus maximus and gluteus medius are tested.

DISSECTION

Reflect the gluteus maximus to examine the underlying structures. For this, identify the lower border of muscle. Insert a forceps on the deep surface of muscle which is to be cut from below upwards midway between its origin and insertion. Reflect two parts on either side. Piriformis is *key muscle* of the region, define its margins. Identify the structures above and below this muscle, most important being the sciatic nerve. Above piriformis are superior gluteal vessels and nerve. Below piriformis are inferior gluteal vessels and nerve. The thickest nerve of the body, sciatic nerve also enters the gluteal region through the greater sciatic notch. Pudendal nerve and vessels appear here through greater sciatic notch and disappear through the lesser sciatic notch (Fig. 5.10).

Under the lower and medial part of the gluteus maximus muscle, ischial tuberosity is easily palpable. Separate the hamstring muscles from the ischial tuberosity. Identify long vertical sacrotuberous ligament and smaller horizontal sacrospinous ligament to demarcate the greater and lesser sciatic foramina and structures entering and leaving them. Greater sciatic notch is the 'door' of the gluteal region.

Define the borders of the gluteus medius muscle. Cut through the muscle 5 cm above its insertion into the greater trochanter of femur. The superior gluteal vessels and nerve are now exposed which are to be traced into gluteus minimus and tensor fascia latae. Reflect gluteus minimus from its origin towards the insertion to expose the straight and reflected heads of rectus femoris muscle and the capsule of the hip joint.

8. Origin of the four hamstrings from the ischial tuberosity.
9. Insertion of the upper or pubic fibres of the adductor magnus (Figs 5.6 to 5.8).

Vessels

1. Superior gluteal vessels (Fig. 5.9).
2. Inferior gluteal vessels.
3. Internal pudendal vessels.
4. Ascending branch of the medial circumflex femoral artery.
5. Trochanteric anastomoses, formed by the descending branch of the superior gluteal artery, the ascending branches of the medial and lateral circumflex femoral arteries, and often the inferior gluteal artery.
6. Cruciate anastomoses, formed by the transverse branches of the medial and lateral circumflex femoral arteries, the descending branch of the inferior gluteal artery, and the ascending branch of the first perforating artery.
7. The first perforating artery itself.

Nerves

1. Superior gluteal (L4, L5, S1) as in Fig. 5.9.
2. Inferior gluteal (L5, S1, S2).
3. Sciatic (L4, S5, S1, S2, S3).
4. Posterior cutaneous nerve of thigh (S1, S2, S3).

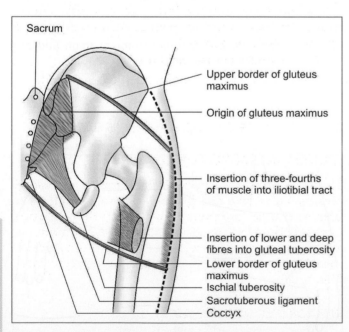

Fig. 5.6: Origin and insertion of gluteus maximus muscle.

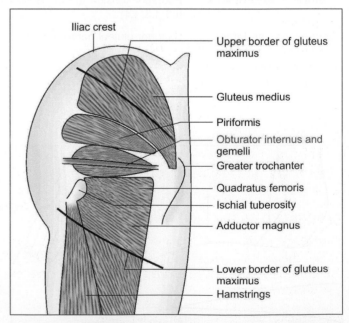

Fig. 5.7: Muscles under cover of the gluteus maximus. The upper and lower borders of this muscle are indicated in thick lines.

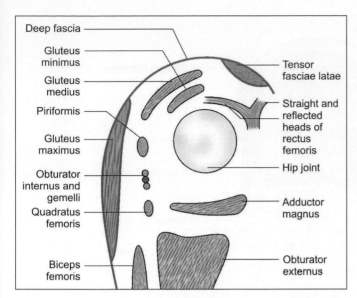

Fig. 5.8: Scheme of an oblique vertical section showing muscles of the gluteal region.

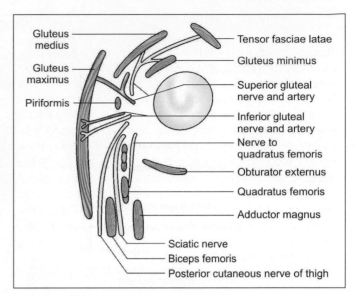

Fig. 5.9: Structures under cover of the gluteus maximus.

5. Nerve to the quadratus femoris (L4, L5, S1).
6. Pudendal nerve (S2, S3, S4).
7. Nerve to the obturator internus (L5, S1, S2).
8. Perforating cutaneous nerves (S2, S3).

Bones and Joints

1. Ilium.
2. Ischium with ischial tuberosity.
3. Upper end of femur with the greater trochanter.
4. Sacrum and coccyx.
5. Hip joint.
6. Sacroiliac joint.

Ligaments

1. Sacrotuberous (Fig. 5.10).
2. Sacrospinous.
3. Ischiofemoral (Fig. 12.4).

Bursae

1. Trochanteric bursa of gluteus maximus.
2. Bursa over the ischial tuberosity.
3. Bursa between the gluteus maximus and vastus lateralis.

STRUCTURES DEEP TO THE GLUTEUS MEDIUS

The gluteus medius covers the superior gluteal nerve, the deep branch of the superior gluteal artery, the gluteus minimus, and the trochanteric bursa of the gluteus medius.

STRUCTURES DEEP TO THE GLUTEUS MINIMUS

Structures lying deep to the gluteus minimus

include the reflected head of the rectus femoris, and the capsule of the hip joint.

SACROTUBEROUS AND SACROSPINOUS LIGAMENTS

These two ligaments convert the greater and lesser sciatic notches of the hip bone into foramina of the same name.

The *sacrotuberous ligament* is a long and strong ligament extending between the medial margin of ischial tuberosity and the posterior iliac spines. It forms the posterolateral boundary of the outlet of the pelvis (Fig. 5.10).

The *sacrospinous ligament* is a short, thick, triangular band situated deep to the sacrotuberous ligament. It is attached:

(a) Laterally to the ischial spine
(b) Medially to the sacrococcygeal junction.

NERVES OF THE GLUTEAL REGION

SUPERIOR GLUTEAL NERVE (L4, L5, S1)

The superior gluteal nerve is a branch of the sacral plexus. It enters the gluteal region through the greater sciatic foramen, above the piriformis, runs forwards between the gluteus medius and minimus, and supplies three muscles, viz., the gluteus medius, the gluteus minimus and the tensor fasciae latae (Fig. 5.10).

INFERIOR GLUTEAL NERVE (L5, S1, S2)

This is also a branch of the sacral plexus given off in the pelvis. It enters the gluteal region through

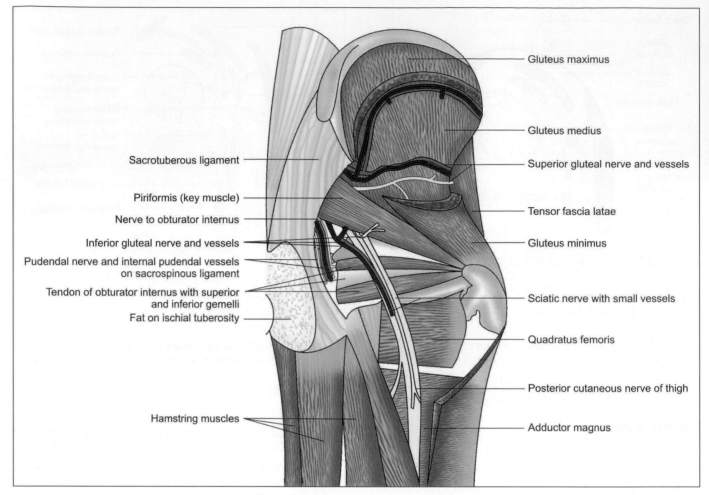

Labels (clockwise from top right):
- Gluteus maximus
- Gluteus medius
- Superior gluteal nerve and vessels
- Tensor fascia latae
- Gluteus minimus
- Sciatic nerve with small vessels
- Quadratus femoris
- Posterior cutaneous nerve of thigh
- Adductor magnus
- Hamstring muscles
- Fat on ischial tuberosity
- Tendon of obturator internus with superior and inferior gemelli
- Pudendal nerve and internal pudendal vessels on sacrospinous ligament
- Inferior gluteal nerve and vessels
- Nerve to obturator internus
- Piriformis (key muscle)
- Sacrotuberous ligament

Fig. 5.10: Structures in gluteal region.

the greater sciatic foramen below the piriformis, and ends by supplying the gluteus maximus only, to which it is fully committed (Fig. 5.10).

SCIATIC NERVE (L4, L5; S1 S2 S3)

Course

This is the thickest nerve in the body. It is the main continuation of the sacral plexus. It enters the gluteal region through the greater sciatic foramen below the piriformis, runs downwards between the greater trochanter and the ischial tuberosity, and enters the back of the thigh at the lower border of the gluteus maximus. It does not give any branches in the gluteal region (Fig. 5.10).

POSTERIOR CUTANEOUS NERVE OF THE THIGH (S1, S2, S3)

It is a branch of the sacral plexus. It enters the gluteal region through the greater sciatic foramen, below the piriformis, and runs downwards medial or posterior to the sciatic nerve. It continues in the back of the thigh immediately deep to the deep fascia.

The nerve gives:
1. A perineal branch which crosses the ischial tuberosity, enters the urogenital triangle of the perineum, and supplies the skin of the posterior two-thirds of the scrotum, or labium majus.
2. Gluteal branches which wind upwards round the lower border of the gluteus maximus, and supply the skin of the posteroinferior quadrant of the gluteal region.

NERVE TO QUADRATUS FEMORIS (L4, L5, S1)

This nerve arises from the sacral plexus, enters the gluteal region through the greater sciatic foramen below the piriformis, and runs downwards deep to the sciatic nerve, the obturator internus and the gemelli. It supplies the quadratus femoris, the gemellus inferior and the hip joint (Fig. 5.9).

PUDENDAL NERVE (S2, S3, S4)

This is a branch of the sacral plexus. Only a small part of this nerve is seen in the gluteal region. It enters this region through the greater sciatic foramen. It then crosses the apex or lateral end of the sacrospinous ligament, medial to the internal pudendal vessels. It leaves the gluteal region by passing into the lesser sciatic foramen through which it enters the ischioanal fossa.

NERVE TO THE OBTURATOR INTERNUS (L5, S1, S2)

This is a branch of the sacral plexus. It enters the gluteal region through the greater sciatic foramen and crosses the ischial spine, lateral to the internal pudendal vessels, to re-enter the pelvis. It supplies both the obturator internus and the gemellus superior muscles.

PERFORATING CUTANEOUS NERVE (S2, S3)

This is a branch of the sacral plexus. It pierces the lower part of the sacrotuberous ligament, winds round the lower border of the gluteus maximus, and supplies the skin of the posteroinferior quadrant of the gluteal region.

ARTERIES OF GLUTEAL REGION

SUPERIOR GLUTEAL ARTERY

It is a branch of the posterior division of the internal iliac artery.

Course and Distribution

It enters the gluteal region through the greater sciatic foramen passing above the piriformis along with the superior gluteal nerve. In the foramen, it divides into superficial and deep branches. The *superficial branch* supplies the gluteus maximus (Fig. 5.11).

The *deep branch* subdivides into superior and inferior branches, which run along the anterior and inferior gluteal lines respectively, between the gluteus medius and the gluteus minimus. The superior branch ends at the anterior superior iliac spine by anastomosing with the ascending branch of the lateral circumflex femoral artery and with branches from the deep circumflex iliac artery. The inferior branch takes part in formation of the trochanteric anastomoses.

INFERIOR GLUTEAL ARTERY

It is a branch of the anterior division of the internal iliac artery.

Course and Distribution

It enters the gluteal region by passing through the greater sciatic foramen, below the piriformis, along with the inferior gluteal nerve. It supplies:

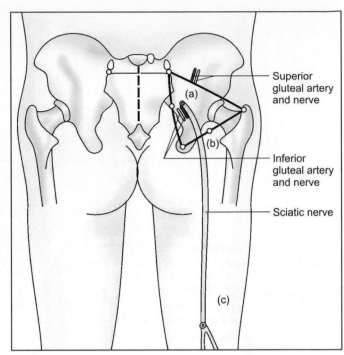

Fig. 5.11: Position of sciatic nerve and gluteal arteries.

1. *Muscular branches* to gluteus maximus and to all the muscles deep to it below the piriformis.
2. *Cutaneous branches* to the buttock and the back of the thigh.
3. An *articular branch* to the hip joint.
4. A *cruciate anastomotic branch.*
5. An *artery to the sciatic nerve,* which represents the axis artery in this region, and may at times be quite large.
6. A *coccygeal branch* which supplies the area over the coccyx.

INTERNAL PUDENDAL ARTERY

This is a branch of the anterior division of the internal iliac artery.

It enters the gluteal region through the greater sciatic foramen (Fig. 5.12). It has a very short course in the gluteal region.

It crosses the ischial spine and leaves the gluteal region by passing into the lesser sciatic foramen through which it reaches the ischioanal fossa.

TROCHANTERIC ANASTOMOSES

This is situated near the trochanteric fossa, and supplies branches to the head of the femur. It is formed by:

(a) The inferior division of the deep branch of the superior gluteal artery.

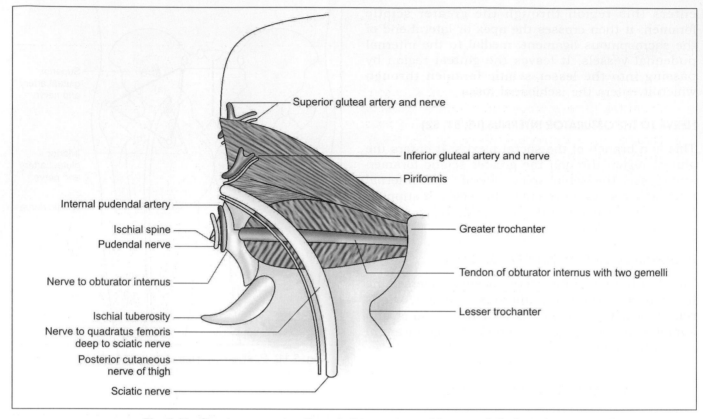

Superior gluteal artery and nerve

Inferior gluteal artery and nerve

Piriformis

Internal pudendal artery

Ischial spine

Pudendal nerve

Greater trochanter

Nerve to obturator internus

Tendon of obturator internus with two gemelli

Ischial tuberosity

Lesser trochanter

Nerve to quadratus femoris deep to sciatic nerve

Posterior cutaneous nerve of thigh

Sciatic nerve

Fig. 5.12: Structures passing through the greater and lesser sciatic foramina.

(b) The ascending branch of the medial circumflex artery.

(c) The ascending branch of the lateral circumflex artery.

CRUCIATE ANASTOMOSES

This anastomosis is situated over the upper part of the back of the femur at the level of the middle of the lesser trochanter. It is formed:

(a) From above by the anastomotic branch of the inferior gluteal artery.

(b) From below by the ascending branch of the first perforating artery.

(c) Medially by the transverse branch of the medial circumflex femoral artery.

(d) Laterally by the transverse branch of the lateral circumflex femoral artery. This anastomosis is a connection between the internal iliac and femoral arteries.

Structures Passing through the Greater Sciatic Foramen (Gateway of Gluteal Region)

A. The piriformis, emerging from the pelvis fills the foramen almost completely. It is the key muscle of the region.

B. Structures passing above the piriformis are:
   1. Superior gluteal nerve.
   2. Superior gluteal vessels (Fig. 5.10).
C. Structures passing below the piriformis are:
   1. Inferior gluteal nerve.
   2. Inferior gluteal vessels.
   3. Sciatic nerve.
   4. Posterior cutaneous nerve of thigh.
   5. Nerve to quadratus femoris.
   6. Pudendal nerve.
   7. Internal pudendal vessels.
   8. Nerve to obturator internus.

The last three structures, after a short course in the gluteal region, enter the lesser sciatic foramen, where the pudendal nerve and internal pudendal vessels run in the pudendal canal.

Structures Passing through the Lesser Sciatic Foramen

   1. Tendon of obturator internus.
   2. Pudendal nerve.
   3. Internal pudendal vessels.
   4. Nerve to obturator internus.

The upper and lower parts of the foramen are filled up by the origins of the two gemelli muscles.

CLINICAL ANATOMY

Gluteal Muscles

- *Intramuscular injections* are given in the anterosuperior quadrant of the gluteal region, i.e. in the glutei medius and minimus, to avoid injury to large vessels and nerves which pass through the lower part of this region (Fig. 5.13). Gluteal region is not the prominence of the buttock only. It is a very big area over the iliac bone.

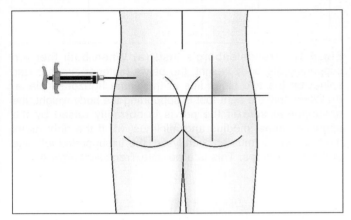

Fig. 5.13: Site of intramuscular injection.

- *When the gluteus maximus is paralysed* as in muscular dystrophy, the patient cannot stand up from a sitting posture without support. Such patients, while trying to stand up, rise gradually, supporting their hands first on legs and then on the thighs; they climb on themselves (Fig. 5.14).

Fig. 5.14: Trying to stand up in paralysis of gluteus maximus muscle.

- *When the glutei medius and minimus (of right side) are paralysed,* the patient cannot walk normally. He bends or waddles on the right side or paralysed side to clear the opposite foot, i.e. left, off the ground. This is known as *lurching gait;* when bilateral, it is called *waddling gait* (Fig. 5.15).

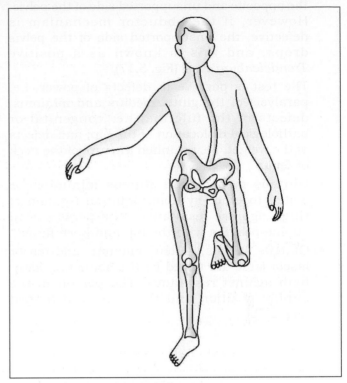

Fig. 5.15: Lurching gait.

- The normal gait depends on the proper abductor mechanism at both hips (Fig. 5.16). This mechanism comprises:
  - (a) The adequate power, provided by the glutei medius and minimus.
  - (b) The fulcrum, formed by a normal relationship of the head of the femur with the acetabulum.
  - (c) The weight transmitted by the head and neck of the femur.

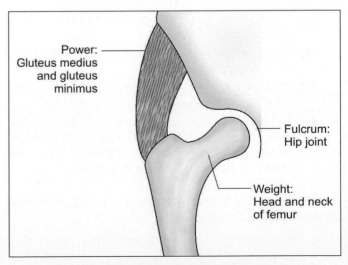

Power:
Gluteus medius and gluteus minimus

Fulcrum: Hip joint

Weight: Head and neck of femur

Fig. 5.16: Abductor mechanism at the hip joint.

- Normally when the body weight is supported on one limb, the glutei of the supported side raise the opposite and unsupported side of the pelvis. However, if the abductor mechanism is defective, the unsupported side of the pelvis drops, and this is known as a positive *Trendelenburg's test* (Fig. 5.17).

  The test is positive in defects of power, i.e. paralysis of the glutei medius and minimus; defects of the fulcrum, i.e. congenital or pathological dislocation of the hip; and defects of the weight, i.e. ununited fracture of the neck of femur.

- Gluteus medius and gluteus minimus are tested together by doing internal rotation of thigh against resistance. The person is in supine position with the hip and knee flexed.

- Gluteus medius, gluteus minimus and tensor fascia latae are tested by the abducting lower limb against resistance. The person in the supine position and the knee is extended (Fig. 5.5b).

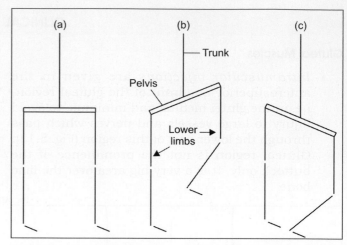

Fig. 5.17: Trendelenburg's test. (a) When both feet are supporting the body weight, the pelvis (anterior superior iliac spine) on the two sides lies in the same horizontal plane. (b) When only the right foot is supporting the body weight, the unsupported side of the pelvis is normally raised by the opposite gluteal medius and minimus. (c) If the right glutei medius and minimus are paralysed, the unsupported left side of the pelvis drops. This is a positive Trendelenburg's test.

Popliteal Fossa

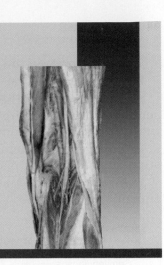

INTRODUCTION

The popliteal fossa, a diamond-shaped depression felt at the back of semi-flexed knee joint, contains the popliteal vessels and the two terminal branches of the sciatic nerve. Popliteal artery is used for auscultating while taking blood pressure in the lower limb. Common peroneal nerve lies on the neck of fibula and is the most frequently injured nerve in the lower limb. Its paralysis leads to "foot drop" position with inability to dorsiflex and evert the foot.

Popliteal fossa is a shallow depression felt best at the back of knee joint, when the joint is semi-flexed. It corresponds to the cubital fossa of the forearm.

SURFACE LANDMARKS

1. *Lateral* and *medial condyles* of femur and tibia can be identified easily on the sides and front of the knee.
2. *Head of the fibula* is a bony prominence situated just below the posterolateral aspect of the lateral condyle of tibia.
3. *Common peroneal nerve* can be palpated against the posterolateral aspect of the neck of fibula, medial to the tendon of biceps femoris, by moving the finger from below upwards.
4. *Fibular collateral ligament* of the knee joint is felt like a rounded cord just above the head of the fibula in a flexed knee.
5. When the knee is flexed against resistance, the *hamstrings* can be seen and palpated easily right up to their insertion. Medially, the rounded tendon of the *semitendinosus* lies superficial to the flat tendon of *semimembranosus.* In front of these tendons there is a groove bounded anteriorly by the tendon of *adductor magnus.* Laterally, there is the tendon of *biceps femoris.*

In front of this tendon there is a shallow groove bounded anteriorly by the *iliotibial tract.*
6. Pulsations of the *popliteal artery* can be felt in the middle of the popliteal fossa by applying deep pressure.
7. In the lower part of popliteal fossa, two heads of the *gastrocnemius* form rounded cushions that merge inferiorly into the calf.

DISSECTION

Make a horizontal incision across the back of thigh at its junction of upper two-thirds with lower one-third and another horizontal incision at the back of leg at its junction of upper one-third and lower two-thirds (v), (vi).

Draw a vertical incision joining the midpoints of the two horizontal incisions made (vii) (Fig. 5.2). Reflect the skin and fascia on either side. Find the cutaneous nerves, e.g. posterior cutaneous nerve of thigh, posterior division of medial cutaneous nerve, sural communi-cating nerve and short saphenous vein. Cut and clean the deep fascia. Identify the boundaries and contents of the fossa.

Trace the tibial nerve as it courses through the centre of the popliteal fossa. Its three delicate articular branches are given off in the upper part of the fossa, cutaneous branch in the middle part and muscular branches in lower part of the fossa. Common peroneal nerve is lying just medial to the tendon of biceps femoris muscle. Trace its branches. Popliteal vein is deep to the tibial nerve and popliteal artery is the deepest as seen from the back. Trace all the muscular, cutaneous, genicular and terminal branches of the popliteal artery.

POPLITEAL FOSSA

The popliteal fossa is a diamond-shaped depression lying behind the knee joint, the lower part of the femur, and the upper part of the tibia.

The *boundaries* of the fossa are as follows.

Superolaterally: The biceps femoris (Fig. 6.1).

Superomedially: The semitendinosus and the semimembranosus, supplemented by the gracilis, the sartorius and the adductor magnus.

Inferolaterally: Lateral head of the gastrocnemius supplemented by the plantaris.

Inferomedially: Medial head of the gastrocnemius.

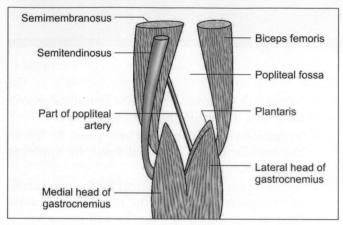

Semimembranosus — Biceps femoris

Semitendinosus — Popliteal fossa

Part of popliteal artery — Plantaris

Lateral head of gastrocnemius

Medial head of gastrocnemius

Fig. 6.1: Boundaries of the right popliteal fossa. Part of popliteal artery shown.

The **roof** of the fossa is formed by deep fascia or popliteal fascia (Fig. 6.2). The superficial fascia over the roof contains:

1. The small saphenous vein.
2. Three cutaneous nerves, namely, the branches and terminal part of the posterior cutaneous nerve of the thigh, the posterior division of the medial cutaneous nerve of the thigh, and the peroneal or sural communicating nerve.

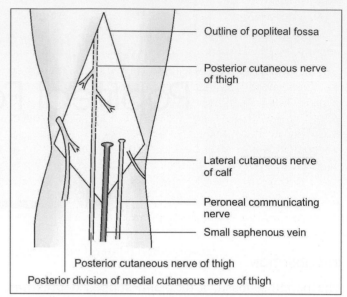

Outline of popliteal fossa

Posterior cutaneous nerve of thigh

Lateral cutaneous nerve of calf

Peroneal communicating nerve

Small saphenous vein

Posterior cutaneous nerve of thigh

Posterior division of medial cutaneous nerve of thigh

Fig. 6.2: Structures on the roof of the popliteal fossa.

The **floor** of the popliteal fossa is formed from above downwards by:

1. The popliteal surface of the femur.
2. The capsule of the knee joint and the oblique popliteal ligament.
3. The strong popliteal fascia covering the popliteus muscle (Fig. 6.3).

The main **contents** of the fossa are:

1. The popliteal artery and its branches.
2. The popliteal vein and its tributaries.
3. The tibial nerve and its branches.
4. The common peroneal nerve and its branches.

The fossa also contains the following.

5. The posterior cutaneous nerve of the thigh.

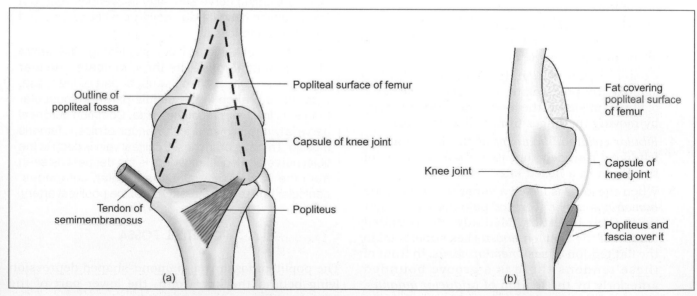

Outline of popliteal fossa

Popliteal surface of femur

Capsule of knee joint

Tendon of semimembranosus

Popliteus

Fat covering popliteal surface of femur

Knee joint

Capsule of knee joint

Popliteus and fascia over it

(a)

(b)

Fig. 6.3: Floor of the popliteal fossa: (a) Surface view, (b) vertical sectional view.

6. The genicular branch of the obturator nerve.

7. The popliteal lymph nodes.

8. Fat.

The popliteal vessels and the tibial nerve cross the fossa vertically, and are arranged one over the other. The tibial nerve is most superficial; the popliteal vein lies deep or anterior to tibial nerve; and the popliteal artery is deepest of all. The artery is crossed posteriorly by the vein and by the nerve. The relative position of these structures is as follows.

In the upper part of the fossa, from medial to lateral side: artery, vein and nerve.

In the middle part, from behind forwards: nerve, vein and artery.

In the lower part, from medial to lateral side: nerve, vein and artery (Fig. 6.4).

The common peroneal nerve crosses the fossa obliquely from the superior angle to the lateral angle, along the medial border of the biceps femoris, lying in the same superficial plane as the tibial nerve.

POPLITEAL ARTERY

Beginning, Course and Termination

Popliteal artery is the continuation of the femoral artery. It begins at the opening in the adductor magnus or hiatus magnus, i.e. at the junction of middle one-third with the lower one-third of thigh.

It runs downwards and slightly laterally, to reach the lower border of the popliteus.

It terminates at the lower border of popliteus by dividing into the anterior and posterior tibial arteries (Fig. 6.5).

Relations

The popliteal artery is the deepest structure in the popliteal fossa. It has the following relations.

Anterior or *deep* to the artery, from above downwards, there are:

(i) The popliteal surface of the femur.

(ii) the back of the knee joint.

(iii) the fascia covering the popliteus muscle (Fig. 6.3).

Posteriorly or *superficially*, the artery is related to the popliteal vein, and further posteriorly, to the tibial nerve (Fig. 6.4).

Laterally, the upper part of the artery is related to the biceps femoris and the lateral condyle of the femur. The lower part of the artery is related to the plantaris and the lateral head of the gastrocnemius.

Medially, the upper part of the artery is related to the semimembranosus and the medial condyle of the femur. The lower part of the artery is related to the tibial nerve, the popliteal vein, and the medial head of the gastrocnemius (Fig. 6.1).

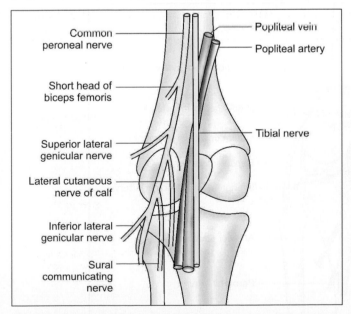

Fig. 6.4: The arrangement of the main nerves and vessels in the popliteal fossa.

Labels: Common peroneal nerve; Short head of biceps femoris; Superior lateral genicular nerve; Lateral cutaneous nerve of calf; Inferior lateral genicular nerve; Sural communicating nerve; Popliteal vein; Popliteal artery; Tibial nerve

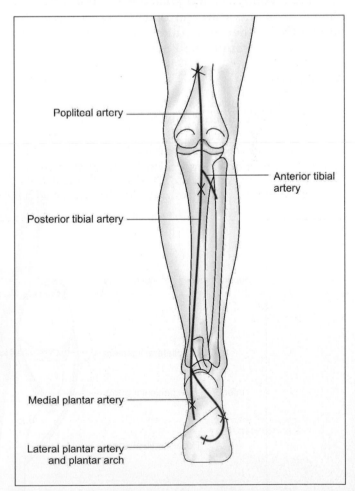

Fig. 6.5: Position of popliteal, posterior and anterior tibial, medial and lateral plantar arteries.

Labels: Popliteal artery; Posterior tibial artery; Anterior tibial artery; Medial plantar artery; Lateral plantar artery and plantar arch

Branches

Several large *muscular* branches are given off. The upper (two or three) muscular branches supply the adductor magnus and the hamstrings, and terminate by anastomosing with the fourth perforating artery. The lower muscular or sural branches supply the gastrocnemius, the soleus and the plantaris.

Cutaneous branches arise either directly from the popliteal artery, or indirectly from its muscular branches. One cutaneous branch usually accompanies the small saphenous vein.

Genicular branches are five in number, two superior, two inferior and one middle. The *middle genicular artery* pierces the oblique popliteal ligament of the knee, and supplies the cruciate ligaments and the synovial membrane of the knee joint (Fig. 6.6).

The medial and lateral *superior genicular arteries* wind round the corresponding sides of the femur immediately above the corresponding condyle, and pass deep to the hamstrings. The medial and lateral *inferior genicular arteries* wind round the corresponding tibial condyles, and pass deep to the collateral ligaments of the knee. All these arteries reach the front of the knee and take part in forming the anastomoses around the knee.

POPLITEAL VEIN

It begins at the lower border of the popliteus by the union of veins accompanying the anterior and posterior tibial arteries. It is medial to the popliteal artery in the lower part of the fossa; posterior to the artery in the middle; and posterolateral to it in the upper part of the fossa. The vein continues as the femoral vein at the opening in the adductor magnus. The popliteal vein receives:

1. The small saphenous vein.
2. The veins corresponding to the branches of the popliteal artery (Fig. 6.4).

TIBIAL NERVE

Root Value: (L4, L5, S1, S2, S3).

Course

This is the larger terminal branch of the sciatic nerve. It lies superficial or posterior to the popliteal vessels (Fig. 6.7). It extends from the superior angle to the inferior angle of the popliteal fossa, crossing the popliteal vessels from lateral to medial side.

Branches

1. Three genicular or articular branches arise in the upper part of the fossa;
   (i) Superior medial genicular nerve lies above the medial condyle of femur, deep to the muscles.
   (ii) Middle genicular nerve pierces the posterior part of the capsule of the knee joint to supply structures in the intercondylar notch of femur (Fig. 6.8).
   (iii) Inferior medial genicular nerve lies along the upper border of popliteus and reaches inferior to the medial condyle of tibia.
2. Cutaneous nerve is called sural which originates in the middle of the fossa and leaves

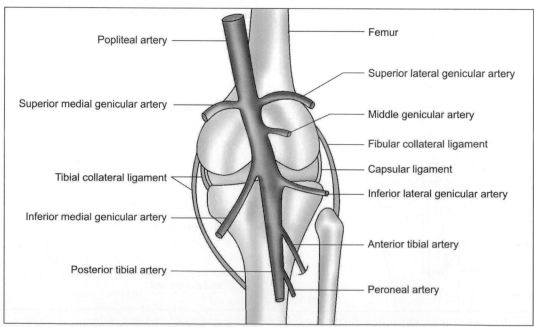

Fig. 6.6: Course of the genicular branches of the popliteal artery.

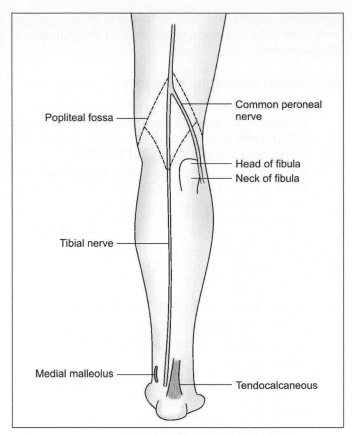

Fig. 6.7: Tibial and common peroneal nerves.

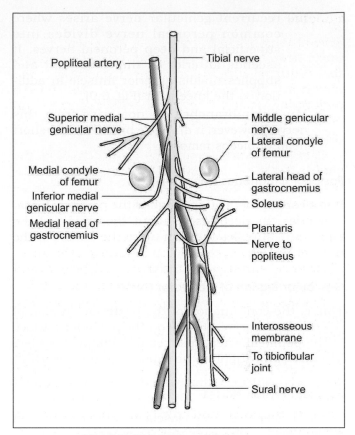

Fig. 6.8: Distribution of tibial nerve.

it at the inferior angle. It supplies the skin of lower half of back of leg and whole of lateral border of the foot till the tip of little toe.

3. Muscular branches arise in the distal part of the fossa for the lateral and medial heads of gastrocnemius, soleus, plantaris and popliteus.

The nerve to the popliteus crosses the popliteal artery, runs downwards and laterally, winds round the lower border of the popliteus, and supplies it from its deep (anterior) surface. In addition to the popliteus, the nerve also supplies the tibialis posterior, the superior tibiofibular joint, the tibia, the interosseous membrane, and the inferior tibiofibular joint.

Since the muscular branches except to the medial head of gastrocnemius arise from the lateral side, the medial side of the nerve is "safe side", while operating. This nerve usually does not get injured.

COMMON PERONEAL NERVE

Root Value: (L4, L5, S1, S2)

Course

This is the smaller terminal branch of the sciatic nerve. It lies in the same superficial plane as the tibial nerve (Fig. 6.7). It extends from the superior angle of the fossa to the lateral angle, along the medial border of the biceps femoris. Continuing downwards and forwards, it winds round the posterolateral aspect of the neck of the fibula, pierces the peroneus longus, and divides into the superficial and deep peroneal nerves.

Branches

1. Cutaneous branches are two:
   (i) Lateral cutaneous nerve of the calf descends to supply the skin of the upper two-thirds of the lateral side of the leg (Fig. 9.2).
   (ii) peroneal communicating nerve arises in the upper part of the fossa. It runs on the posterolateral aspect of calf and joins the sural nerve (Fig. 6.4).

2. Articular branches:
   (i) Superior lateral genicular nerve accompanies the artery of the same name and lies above the lateral femoral condyle.
   (ii) inferior lateral genicular nerve also runs with the artery of the same name to the lateral aspect of knee joint above the head of fibula (Fig. 6.4).

(iii) recurrent genicular nerve arises where common peroneal nerve divides into superficial and deep peroneal nerves. It ascends anterior to the knee joint and supplies tibialis anterior muscle in addition to the knee joint (Fig. 6.9).

3. Muscular branches do not arise from this nerve. However, it may give branch to the short head of biceps femoris.

Posterior Cutaneous Nerve of Thigh

It is a content of the upper half of the popliteal fossa. It pierces the deep fascia about the middle of the fossa, and supplies the skin up to the middle of the back of the leg.

Genicular Branch of Obturator Nerve

This is the continuation of the posterior division of the obturator nerve. It runs on the posterior surface of the popliteal artery, pierces the oblique popliteal ligament, and supplies the capsule of the knee joint.

Popliteal Lymph Nodes

These lie deep to the deep fascia near the termination of the small saphenous vein. They receive afferents from both superficial and deep parts of back of leg and knee joint. The efferents end in deep inguinal lymph nodes.

Anastomoses around the Knee Joint

1. Anastomoses around the knee joint is a complicated, arterial network situated around the patella and around the lower end of the femur and the upper end of the tibia.

2. The network is divisible into a superficial and a deep part. The *superficial part* lies partly in the superficial fascia around the patella and partly in fat behind the ligamentum patellae. The *deep part* lies on the femur and the tibia all around their adjoining articular surfaces.

3. It is formed:
   Medially, by
   (a) the descending genicular (Fig. 6.10).
   (b) the superior medial genicular.
   (c) the inferior medial genicular arteries.
   Laterally, by
   (a) the descending branch of the lateral circumflex femoral artery.
   (b) the superior lateral genicular.
   (c) inferior lateral genicular.

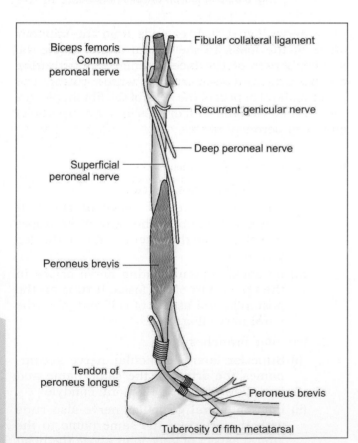

Fig. 6.9: The peroneal or lateral crural region.

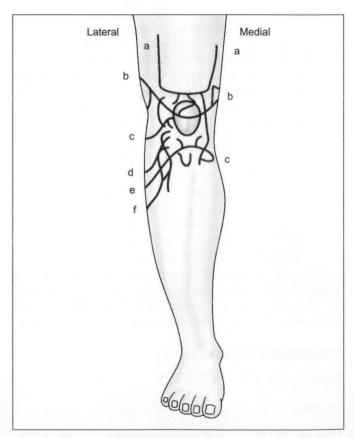

Fig. 6.10: Anastomoses around the knee joint.

(d) Anterior tibial recurrent.

(e) Posterior tibial recurrent.

(f) Circumflex fibular arteries.

The medial and lateral arteries form longitudinal anastomoses on each side of the patella. The longitudinal anastomoses are inter-connected to form transverse anastomoses just above and below the patella and above the tibial tuberosity.

4. The anastomoses supplies bones taking part in forming the knee joint, and the capsule and synovial membrane of the knee joint.

CLINICAL ANATOMY

- Blood pressure in the lower limb is recorded from the popliteal artery. In coarctation of the aorta, the popliteal pressure is lower than the brachial pressure (Fig. 6.11).

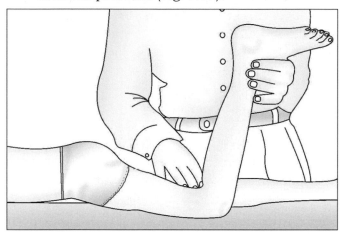

Fig. 6.11: Palpating the left popliteal artery.

- Constant pulsations of the popliteal artery against the unyielding tendon of the adductor magnus may cause changes in the vessel wall, leading to narrowing and occlusion of the artery. Sudden occlusion of the artery may cause gangrene up to the knee, but this is usually prevented by the collateral circulation through the profunda femoris artery.

- Common peroneal nerve can get injured easily by a stick blow on posterolateral aspect of neck of the fibula. Since its two terminal branches, e.g. superficial peroneal supplies evertors of the foot and deep peroneal supplies dorsiflexors, these actions are lost. This condition is called "Foot drop" (Figs 6.9 and 6.12).

- The popliteal artery is fixed to the capsule of the knee joint by a fibrous band present just above the femoral condyles. This may be a source of continuous traction or stretching on the artery, causing primary thrombosis of the artery in young subjects.

- Popliteal lymph nodes get enlarged in infection on lateral side of sole/foot. These are lying along the short saphenous vein. Short saphenous vein pierces deep fascia to drain into popliteal vein (Fig. 6.13).

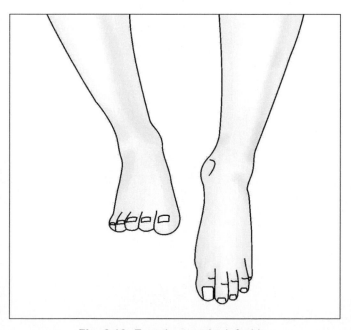

Fig. 6.12: Foot drop on the left side.

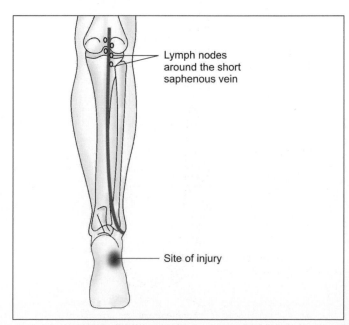

Lymph nodes around the short saphenous vein

Site of injury

Fig. 6.13: Enlarged popliteal lymph nodes.

- When the popliteal artery is affected by atherosclerosis, the lower part of artery usually remains patent where grafts can be tried.
- The popliteal artery is more prone to aneurysm than many other arteries of the body.
- The common peroneal nerve can be palpated against the posterolateral side of the neck of the fibula. It may be injured in this area. It is the most frequently injured nerve in the lower limb (Fig. 2.42). This nerve is relatively unprotected. It may get entrapped between the attachments of peroneus longus to the head and shaft of fibula. Patients present foot drop which is usually painless. There is weakness of dorsiflexion of ankle and of eversion of the foot. Inversion and plantar flexion are normal and ankle jerk is intact.
- Damage to tibial nerve causes motor and sensory loss.
  (a) **Motor loss:** Superficial and deep muscles of calf and intrinsic muscles of sole.
  (b) **Sensory loss:** Loss of sensation on whole of sole of foot, plantar aspect of digits and nail beds on dorsum of foot.

Back of Thigh

The back of thigh contains the hamstring muscles. These muscles arise in the gluteal region and course through the back of thigh to be inserted into the region of the popliteal fossa. Sciatic nerve supplies all these muscles including part of the composite or hybrid muscle, the adductor magnus.

The artery accompanying or running in the sciatic nerve represents part of the axial artery of the lower limb.

INTRODUCTION

The posterior compartment of the thigh is also called the flexor compartment. It is incompletely separated from the medial compartment by the poorly defined posterior intermuscular septum. The adductor magnus is a component of both these compartments.

CUTANEOUS INNERVATION

The skin over the back of the thigh is supplied by branches from the posterior cutaneous nerve of the thigh (Fig. 6.2).

MUSCLES OF BACK OF THE THIGH

The muscles of the back of the thigh are called the *hamstring muscles*. They are the semitendinosus, the semimembranosus, the long head of the biceps femoris, and the ischial head of the adductor magnus.

The hamstrings share the following characters.

(i) Origin from the ischial tuberosity (Fig. 7.1).
(ii) Insertion into one of the bones of the leg.

The adductor magnus reaches only up to the adductor tubercle of the femur, but is included amongst the hamstrings because the tibial collateral ligament of the knee joint is, morphologically, the degenerated tendon of this muscle.

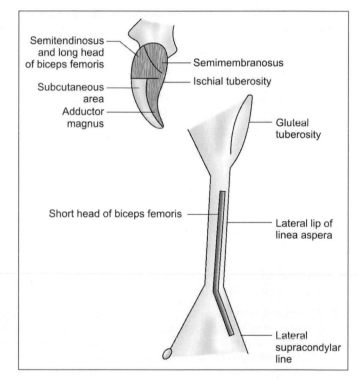

Fig. 7.1: Origin of the hamstring muscles.

(iii) Nerve supply from the tibial part of the sciatic nerve.
(iv) The muscles act as flexors of the knee and extensors of the hip.

The attachments hamstrings are given in Tables 7.1 and 7.2.

SCIATIC NERVE

The sciatic nerve is the thickest nerve in the body. In its upper part, it forms a band about 2 cm wide. It begins in the pelvis and terminates at the superior angle of the popliteal fossa by dividing into the tibial and common peroneal nerves.

Give a vertical incision on the back of intact skin left after the dissections of gluteal region and the popliteal fossa (viii) (Fig. 5.2). Reflect the skin and fasciae on either side. Clean the hamstring muscles and study their features from the Tables 7.1 and 7.2.

Sciatic nerve was seen in the gluteal region. Identify its branches in back of thigh to each of the hamstring muscles including the short head of biceps femoris muscle. Trace the two terminal divisions of this nerve.

Separate the hamstring muscles to expose the ischial part of the composite or hybrid adductor magnus muscle. Look for insertion of adductor longus, into the linea aspera of femur. Trace the profunda femoris vessels behind adductor longus including its perforating branches.

Origin and Root Value

This is the largest branch of the sacral plexus. Its root value is L4, L5, S1, S2, S3. It is made up of two parts, the tibial part and the common peroneal part. The tibial part is formed by the ventral divisions of the anterior primary rami of L4, L5, S1, S2, S3. The common peroneal part is formed by the dorsal divisions of the anterior primary rami of L4, L5, S1, S2 (Figs 7.4 and 7.5).

Course and Relations

1. **In the pelvis:** The nerve lies in front of the piriformis, under cover of its fascia.
2. **In the gluteal region:** The sciatic nerve enters the gluteal region through the greater sciatic foramen below the piriformis. It runs downwards with a slight lateral convexity, passing between the ischial tuberosity and the greater trochanter. It has the following relations in the gluteal region.

Superficial or posterior: Gluteus maximus. (Figs 5.9 and 7.6).

Deep or anterior:

(a) Body of the ischium.

(b) Tendon of the obturator internus with the gemelli.

(c) Quadratus femoris, obturator externus.

(d) The capsule of the hip joint.

Table 7.1: Muscles of the back of thigh		
Muscle	**Origin from**	**Insertion into**
1. Semitendinosus It is so named because it has a long tendon of insertion. It lies postero-medially in the thigh, superficial to the semimembranosus (Fig. 7.3)	From the inferomedial impression on the upper part of the ischial tuberosity, in common with the long head of the biceps femoris (Fig. 7.1)	Into the upper part of the medial surface of the tibia behind the sartorius and the gracilis (Fig. 4.2b)
2. Semimembranosus It is so named because it has a flat tendon of origin. It lies posteromedially in the thigh, deep to the semitendinosus	From the superolateral impression on the upper part of the ischial tuberosity. Expansions from the tendon form the oblique popliteal ligament, and the fascia covering the popliteus (Fig. 6.3)	Into the groove on the posterior surface of the medial condyle of the tibia (Fig. 2.32)
3. Biceps femoris It has two heads of origin long and short. It lies posterolaterally in the thigh (Fig. 7.6)	(a) *Long head:* From the inferomedial impression on the upper part of the ischial tuberosity; in common with the semitendinosus, and also from the lower part of the sacrotuberous ligament (b) *Short head:* From the lateral lip of the linea aspera between the adductor magnus and the vastus lateralis, from the upper two-thirds of the lateral supracondylar line, and from the lateral intermuscular septum	The tendon is either folded around, by the fibular collateral ligament. It is inserted into the head of the fibula in front of its apex or styloid process (Figs 2.42 and 6.9)
4. Adductor magnus (Fig. 4.1) This is the largest muscle of this compartment. Because of its double nerve supply, it is called a hybrid muscle	(a) Inferolateral part of the ischial tuberosity (b) Ramus of the ischium (c) Lower part of the inferior ramus of the pubis	(a) Medial margin of gluteal tuberosity (b) Linea aspera (c) Medial supracondylar line (d) Adductor tubercle

Table 7.2: Muscles of the back of thigh

Muscles	Nerve supply	Action
1. Semitendinosus	Tibial part of sciatic nerve (L5, S1, S2)	Chief flexor of the knee and medial rotator of the leg in semiflexed knee. Weak extensor of the hip
2. Semimembranosus	Tibial part of sciatic nerve (L5, S1, S2)	Chief flexor of the knee and medial rotator of the leg in semiflexed knee. Weak extensor of the hip
3. Biceps femoris	(a) Long head, by tibial part of sciatic nerve (b) Short head, by common peroneal part of sciatic nerve (L5, S1, S2)	Chief flexor of the knee and lateral rotator of leg in semiflexed knee. Weak extensor of the hip
4. Adductor magnus (hybrid muscle) (Fig. 4.5)	Double nerve supply: Adductor part by posterior division of obturator nerve Hamstring part by tibial part of sciatic nerve	Lower part of adductor magnus helps in extension of hip and flexion of knee Figure 7.2 shows the testing of the hamstring muscles, by flexing the knee against resistance and palpating the contracting muscles

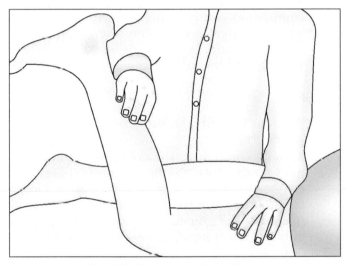

Fig. 7.2: Testing the hamstrings.

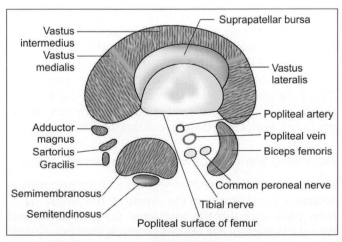

Fig. 7.3: Muscles of back of the thigh. Cross-section above the adductor tubercle.

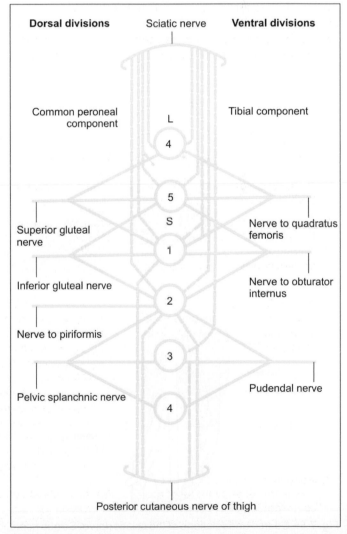

Fig. 7.4: Diagrammatic scheme of the lumbosacral plexus.

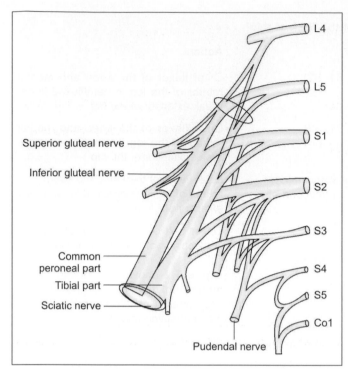

Superior gluteal nerve

Inferior gluteal nerve

Common peroneal part

Tibial part

Sciatic nerve

Pudendal nerve

L4

L5

S1

S2

S3

S4

S5

Co1

Fig. 7.5: Scheme to show the sacral plexus and its branches.

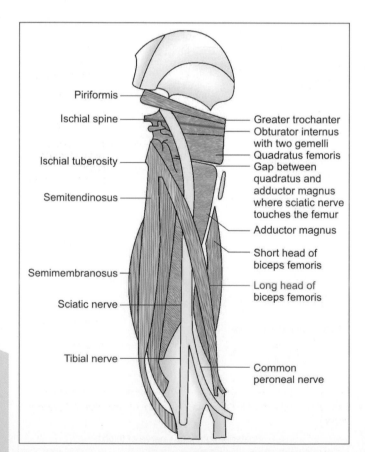

Piriformis

Ischial spine

Ischial tuberosity

Semitendinosus

Semimembranosus

Sciatic nerve

Tibial nerve

Greater trochanter

Obturator internus with two gemelli

Quadratus femoris

Gap between quadratus and adductor magnus where sciatic nerve touches the femur

Adductor magnus

Short head of biceps femoris

Long head of biceps femoris

Common peroneal nerve

Fig. 7.6: Course and relations of the sciatic nerve. Sciatic nerve in contact with femur between lower border of quadratus femoris and upper border of adductor magnus.

(e) The upper, transverse fibres of the adductor magnus.

Medial: Inferior gluteal nerve and vessels.

3. **In the thigh:** The sciatic nerve enters the back of the thigh at the lower border of the gluteus maximus. It runs vertically downwards up to the superior angle of the popliteal fossa, at the junction of the upper two-thirds and lower one-third of the thigh, where it terminates by dividing into the tibial and the common peroneal nerves. It has the following relations in the thigh:

Superficial or posterior: The sciatic nerve is crossed by the long head of the biceps femoris.

Deep or anterior: The nerve lies on the adductor magnus (Fig. 7.6).

Medial: The semimembranosus, and the semitendinosus.

Lateral: Biceps femoris.

The sciatic nerve is accompanied by a small companion artery which is a branch of the inferior gluteal artery. The artery runs along the sciatic nerve for some distance before sinking into its substance.

Branches

1. *Articular* branches to the hip joint arise in the gluteal region.

2. *Muscular* branches: The *tibial part* of the sciatic nerve supplies the semitendinosus, the semimembranosus, the long head of the biceps femoris, and the ischial head of the adductor magnus. The *common peroneal part* supplies only the short head of the biceps femoris.

ARTERIES OF THE BACK OF THIGH

The arteries on the back of the thigh are terminal parts of the branches of the profunda femoris. The lateral circumflex femoral branch of the profunda femoris divides into ascending, transverse and descending branches. The medial circumflex femoral artery divides into ascending and transverse branches (Fig. 7.7a and b). The main supply to the back of the thigh is through the perforating branches of the profunda femoris. These are described below.

Perforating Branches of the Profunda Femoris Artery

The profunda femoris artery gives off four perforating arteries. They arise on the front of the thigh. They then pass through the adductor magnus and wind round the back of the femur, piercing the aponeurotic origins of other muscles attached to the linea aspera. They ultimately end in the vastus lateralis.

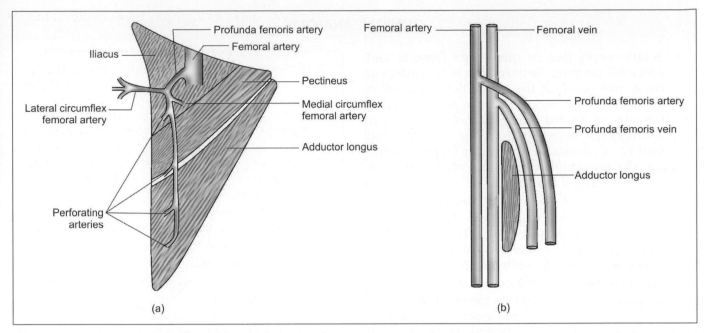

Fig. 7.7: Origin and course of the profunda femoris artery. (a) Surface view, (b) sagittal sectional view. Note that the femoral and profunda vessels straddle the adductor longus.

The *first* perforating artery arises just above, or on the upper border of the adductor brevis, the second in front of the adductor brevis, the third immediately below the adductor brevis, and the fourth is the termination of the profunda femoris artery. The muscles perforated by each artery are shown in Fig. 7.8. The perforating arteries give off muscular branches. They also give off cutaneous and anastomotic branches. The second perforating artery, gives off the nutrient artery to the femur.

ANASTOMOSES ON THE BACK OF THIGH

At least two distinct chains of anastomoses can be made out in the back of the thigh. One lies partly on the surface of the adductor magnus and partly in its substance. The other lies close to the linea aspera of femur. These longitudinal anastomotic chains are formed by the branches of internal iliac, the femoral and popliteal arteries. Thus from above downwards:

(a) The gluteal arteries anastomose with each other and with the circumflex femoral arteries.

(b) The circumflex femorals anastomose with the first perforating artery (cruciate anastomoses).

(c) The perforating arteries anastomose with one another.

(d) The fourth perforating artery anastomoses with the upper muscular branches of the popliteal artery (Fig. 7.8).

Another anastomosis is found on the sciatic nerve. This is formed by the companion artery of the sciatic nerve and the perforating arteries.

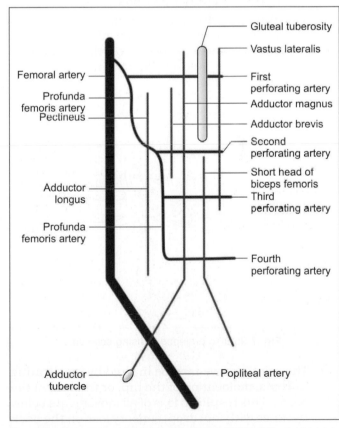

Fig. 7.8: Scheme to show the relations of the profunda femoris artery.

These longitudinal anastomoses provide an alternative route of blood supply to the lower limb, bypassing the external iliac and femoral arteries.

CLINICAL ANATOMY

- Sciatic nerve lies on quadratus femoris and adductor magnus. Between the thin borders of these two muscles the nerve lies for a short distance on the femur. When a person sits on the edge of a hard table/chair, the nerve gets compressed between the edge of table and femur. It results in numbness of lower limb. But the sensations come back when foot is hit on the ground a few times.

- Compression of the sciatic nerve against the femur, between quadratus femoris and adductor magnus (Fig. 7.6), after sitting for a long time, may give rise to a *sleeping foot*. Foot wakes up when it is patted or pinched.

- Shooting pain along the cutaneous distribution of the sciatic nerve and its terminal branches, chiefly the common peroneal, is known as sciatica. Pain usually begins in the gluteal region or even higher, and radiates along the back of the thigh, and the lateral side of the leg, to the dorsum of the foot.

  This is usually due to compression and irritation of one or more nerve roots forming the sciatic nerve. The cause may be osteoarthritis, lumbar disc prolapse, spondylolisthesis, fibrositis, neuritis, etc. (Fig. 7.9).

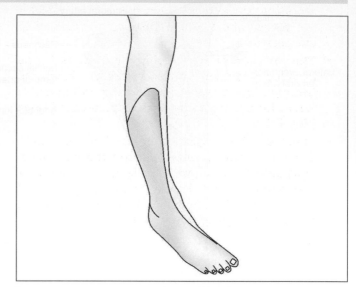

Fig. 7.10: Sensory loss on most of the leg due to injury to sciatic nerve.

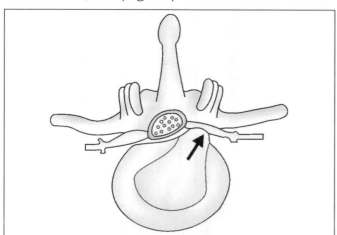

Fig. 7.9: Disc prolapse causing sciatica.

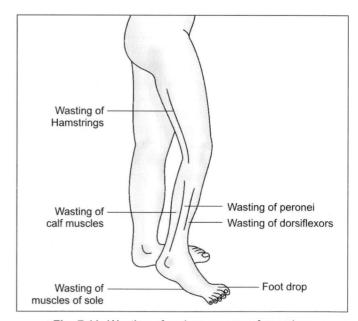

Wasting of Hamstrings

Wasting of calf muscles

Wasting of peronei

Wasting of dorsiflexors

Wasting of muscles of sole

Foot drop

Fig. 7.11: Wasting of various groups of muscles.

- The sciatic nerve may be injured by penetrating wounds, dislocation of the hip, or fracture of the pelvis. This results in loss of all movements below the knee with foot drop; sensory loss on the back of the thigh, the whole of the leg, and the foot except the area innervated by the saphenous nerve (Figs 7.10 and 7.11).

- Motor loss includes loss of hamstring muscles, loss of dorsiflexors, plantarflexors, evertors and muscles of sole.

- Hamstring muscles lying at the back of the knee can be accidently or deliberately slashed or cut. If cut, the person cannot run, as these muscles are required for extension of the hip and flexion of the knee, movements essential in walking/running.

- Paralysis of gluteus medius and minimus by poliomylitis affects proper locomotion. It leads to lurching gait (Fig. 5.15).

- Bursae associated with gluteus maximus are prone to bursitis. Bursitis over ischial tuberosity is called "weaver's bottom".

- Hamstrings have variable length. Some persons cannot touch their toes with fingers while standing straight as their hamstring muscles are rather short. They cannot do very well in gymnastics.
- The inflammation of semimembranous bursa is called semimembranosus bursitis. The bursa becomes more prominent during extension of knee, and disappears during flexion of knee (Fig. 7.12).
- There are four muscles in the back of thigh. Three of them are inserted into the leg bones. Only adductor magnus ends in the adductor tubercle of femur. Tibial collateral ligament of knee joint is the morphological continuation of the adductor magnus muscle.

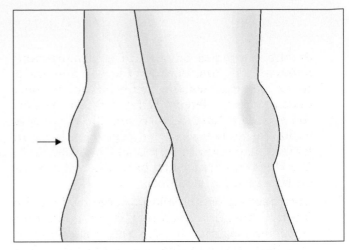

Fig. 7.12: Semimembranosus bursitis.

CHAPTER 8

Front, Lateral and Medial Sides of Leg and Dorsum of Foot

The great saphenous vein starts on the medial side of the dorsum of the foot and runs up just anterior to the medial malleolus, where it can be "slit open" for transfusion purposes. Dorsalis pedis artery, the distal continuation of the anterior tibial artery, is used for palpation in some clinical conditions. The dorsiflexors of foot supplied by deep peroneal nerve lie in the anterior compartment of leg. Tibialis anterior is an invertor of the foot as well. The two big evertors of the foot with superficial peroneal nerve are placed in the lateral compartment of the leg. The tendons of all these muscles are retained in position by two extensor and two peroneal retinacula. The three muscles inserted on the upper medial surface of tibia stabilise the pelvis on the thigh and leg (Fig. 4.2b).

SURFACE LANDMARKS

1. *Medial and lateral condyles of tibia* are felt better in a flexed knee with the thigh flexed and laterally rotated (Fig. 8.1).
2. *Tibial tuberosity* is a bony prominence on the front of the upper part of tibia, 2.5 cm distal to the knee joint line passing through the upper margins of the tibial condyles. The tuberosity provides attachment to ligamentum patellae above, and is continuous with the shin below.
3. *Head of the fibula* lies posterolaterally at the level of tibial tuberosity. It serves as a guide to common peroneal nerve which winds around the posterolateral aspect of the neck of fibula.
4. *Shin* is the subcutaneous anterior border of tibia. It is sinuously curved and extends from the tibial tuberosity to the anterior margin of the medial malleolus. It is better defined in the upper part than in the lower part.
5. *Medial surface of tibia* is subcutaneous, except in the uppermost part where it is crossed by

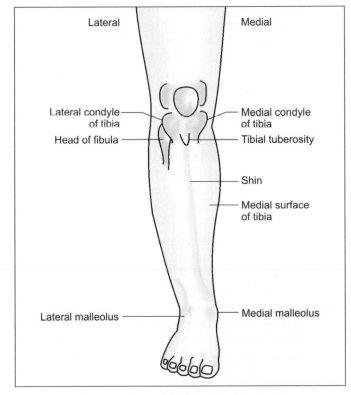

Fig. 8.1: Landmarks on leg and foot.

the tendons of sartorius, gracilis and semi-tendinosus. Great saphenous vein crosses lower one-third of the surface, running obliquely upwards and backwards from the anterior border of medial malleolus.

6. *Medial border of tibia* is palpable throughout its whole extent. The saphenous nerve and great saphenous vein run partly along it.
7. *Gastrocnemius* and the underlying *soleus* form the fleshy prominence of the *calf*. These muscles become prominent when heel is raised as standing on toes. *Tendocalcaneus* is the strong, thick tendon of these muscles; it is

attached below to the posterior surface of calcaneum.

8. *Medial malleolus* is the bony prominence on the medial side of ankle. It is formed by a downwards projection from the medial surface of the lower end of tibia.

9. *Lateral malleolus* is the bony prominence on the lateral side of ankle. It is formed by the lower end of fibula. It is larger but narrower than the medial malleolus, and its tip is 0.5 cm below that of the medial malleolus. The posterior borders of two malleoli are in the same coronal plane, but the anterior border of lateral malleolus is about 1.5 cm behind that of the medial malleolus.

10. *Peroneal trochlea,* when present, is felt as a little prominence about a finger-breadth below the lateral malleolus. Peroneus brevis passes above and the peroneus longus below the trochlea.

11. *Sustentaculum tali* can be felt about a thumb-breadth below the medial malleolus.

12. *Tuberosity of navicular bone* is a low bony prominence felt 2.5 to 3.75 cm anteroinferior to the medial malleolus, about midway between the back of the heel and root of the big toe, at the level of the lip of the shoe.

13. *Head of the talus* lies above the line joining the sustentaculum tali and tuberosity of navicular bone.

14. *Tuberosity of the base of fifth metatarsal bone* is the most prominent landmark on the lateral border of the foot. It lies midway between the point of the heel and the root of the little toe.

15. *Posterior tibial artery* pulsations can be felt against calcaneum about 2 cm below and behind the medial malleolus (Fig. 9.12).

16. *Dorsalis pedis artery* pulsations can be felt best on the dorsum of foot about 5 cm distal to the malleoli, lateral to the tendon of extensor hallucis longus, over the intermediate cunei-form bone (Fig. 8.14).

17. *Tendon of tibialis anterior* becomes prominent on active inversion of the foot, passing downwards and medially across the medial part of the anterior surface of ankle.

18. *Tendon of extensor hallucis longus* becomes prominent when the foot is dorsiflexed.

19. *Extensor digitorum brevis* produces an elevation on the lateral part of the dorsum of foot when the toes are dorsiflexed or extended (Fig. 8.13).

20. *First metatarsophalangeal joint* lies a little in front of the centre of the ball of big toe. The *other metatarsophalangeal joints* are placed about 2.5 cm behind the webs of the toes.

SUPERFICIAL FASCIA

The superficial fascia of the front of the leg and the dorsum of the foot contains: The superficial veins; cutaneous nerves; lymphatics, and small unnamed arteries.

DISSECTION

1. Make a horizontal incision across the leg at its junction with foot (Fig. 3.1).
2. Provide a vertical incision from the centre of incision (1) to the middle of incision drawn just below the level of tibial tuberosity.
3. Carry this vertical incision on to the dorsum of foot till the middle of the second toe.

   Reflect the skin on both the sides. Look for various veins and cutaneous nerves in the leg and foot according to the description given in the text.

Superficial Veins

1. The *dorsal venous arch* lies on the dorsum of the foot over the proximal parts of the metatarsal bones. It receives four dorsal metatarsal veins each of which is formed by the union of two dorsal digital veins (Fig. 8.2).

2. The *great* or *long saphenous vein* is formed by the union of the medial end of the dorsal venous

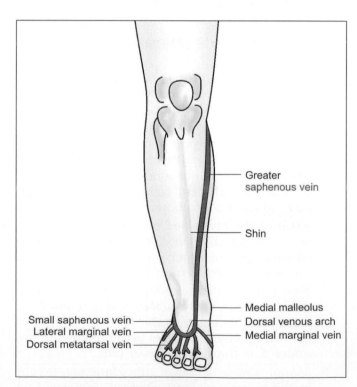

Greater saphenous vein

Shin

Medial malleolus
Dorsal venous arch
Medial marginal vein

Small saphenous vein
Lateral marginal vein
Dorsal metatarsal vein

Fig. 8.2: Superficial veins on the front of the leg.

arch with the medial marginal vein which drains the medial side of the great toe. It passes upwards in front of the medial malleolus, crosses the lower one-third of the medial surface of tibia obliquely, and runs along its medial border to reach the back of the knee. The saphenous nerve runs in front of the great saphenous vein.

3. The *small* or *short saphenous vein* is formed by the union of the lateral end of the dorsal venous arch with the lateral marginal vein, draining the lateral side of the little toe. It passes upwards behind the lateral malleolus to reach the back of the leg. The sural nerve accompanies the small saphenous vein.

Both saphenous veins are connected to the deep veins through the perforating veins.

Cutaneous Nerves

1. The *infrapatellar branch of the saphenous nerve* pierces the sartorius and the deep fascia on the medial side of the knee, curves downwards and forwards, and supplies the skin over the ligamentum patellae (Fig. 8.3).

2. The *saphenous nerve* is a branch of the posterior division of the femoral nerve. It pierces

the deep fascia on the medial side of the knee between the sartorius and the gracilis, and runs downwards in front of the great saphenous vein. It supplies the skin of the medial side of the leg and the medial border of the foot up to the ball of the great toe.

3. The *lateral cutaneous nerve of the calf* is a branch of the common peroneal nerve. It pierces the deep fascia over the lateral head of the gastrocnemius, and descends to supply the skin of the upper two-thirds of the lateral side of the leg.

4. The *superficial peroneal nerve* is a branch of the common peroneal nerve. It arises on the lateral side of the neck of the fibula deep to the fibres of the peroneus longus. It descends between the peroneal muscles, pierces the deep fascia at the junction of the upper two-thirds and lower one-third of the lateral side of the leg, and divides into medial and lateral branches. These branches supply the following.

(a) The skin over the lower one-third of the lateral side of the leg.

(b) The skin over the entire dorsum of the foot with the exception of the following areas.
   – Lateral border, supplied by sural nerve.
   – Medial border up to the base of the great toe, supplied by the saphenous nerve.
   – Cleft between the first and second toes, supplied by the deep peroneal nerve.

5. The *sural nerve* is a branch of the tibial nerve. It arises in the middle of the popliteal fossa. It runs vertically downwards, pierces the deep fascia in the middle of the back of leg, accompanies the small saphenous vein, and supplies the skin of the lower half of the back of leg and of the whole of the lateral border of the foot up to the tip of the little toe (Fig. 9.1).

6. The *deep peroneal nerve* terminates by supplying the skin adjoining the cleft between the first and second toes.

7. The *digital branches of the medial and lateral plantar nerves* curve upwards and supply the distal parts of the dorsum of the toes. Medial plantar nerve supplies medial 3½ toes; lateral plantar nerve supplies lateral 1½ toes.

DEEP FASCIA OF THE LEG

The following points about the fascia are noteworthy.

1. In the leg, tibia and fibula are subcutaneous at places, the most notable being the medial surface of the tibia, and the malleoli. Over these subcutaneous areas, the deep fascia is replaced by periosteum.

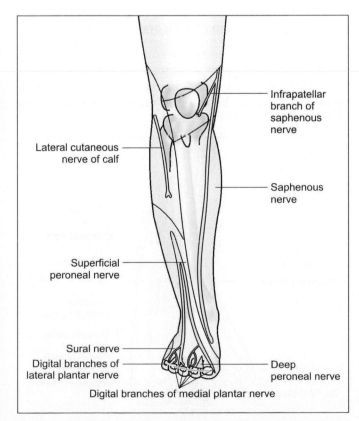

Fig. 8.3: Cutaneous nerves on the front of the leg and dorsum of foot.

2. Extensions of deep fascia form intermuscular septa that divide the leg into compartments (Fig. 8.4).

The *anterior* and *posterior* intermuscular septa are attached to the anterior and posterior borders of the fibula. They divide the leg into three compartments, *anterior, lateral,* and *posterior.* The posterior compartment is subdivided into superficial, intermediate and deep parts by *superficial* and *deep transverse fascial septa.*

3. Around the ankle, the deep fascia is thickened to form bands called *retinacula.* These are so called because they retain tendons in place. On the front of the ankle there are the *superior and inferior extensor retinacula.* Laterally, there are the *superior and inferior peroneal retinacula.* Posteromedially, there is the *flexor retinaculum.* The extensor retinacula are described below. The peroneal retinacula are considered with the lateral compartment of the leg and the flexor retinaculum with the posterior compartment.

DISSECTION

Underlying the superficial fascia is the dense deep fascia of leg. Divide this fascia longitudinally as it stretches between tibia and fibula. Expose the superior extensor retinaculum 5 cm above the ankle joint and the inferior extensor retinaculum in front of the ankle joint.

Superior Extensor Retinaculum

Attachments

Medially, it is attached to the lower part of the anterior border of the tibia, and *laterally* to the lower part of the anterior border of the fibula forming the anterior boundary of the elongated triangular area just above the lateral malleolus (Fig. 8.5).

Inferior Extensor Retinaculum

This is a Y-shaped band of deep fascia, situated in front of the ankle joint and over the posterior part of the dorsum of the foot. The stem of the Y lies laterally, and the upper and lower bands, medially (Fig. 8.6).

Attachments

1. The *stem* is attached to the anterior non-articular part of the superior surface of the calcaneum, in front of the sulcus calcanei.
2. The *upper band* passes upwards and medially, and is attached to the anterior border of the medial malleolus.
3. The *lower band* passes downwards and medially and is attached to the plantar aponeurosis.

The structures passing under cover of the extensor retinacula are as follows (Fig. 8.6).

1. Tibialis anterior.
2. Extensor hallucis longus.
3. Anterior tibial vessels.
4. Deep peroneal nerve
5. Extensor digitorum longus.
6. The peroneus tertius.

MUSCLES OF ANTERIOR COMPARTMENT OF THE LEG

The muscles of the anterior compartment of the leg are the tibialis anterior, the extensor hallucis longus, the extensor digitorum longus and the peroneus tertius (Fig. 8.7). The attachments of these muscles are given in Tables 8.1 and 8.2.

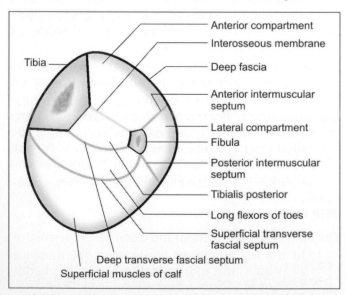

Fig. 8.4: Transverse section through the middle of the leg showing the intermuscular septa and the compartments.

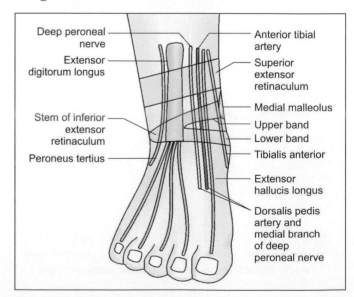

Fig. 8.5: Superior and inferior extensor retinacula of the ankle: Surface view.

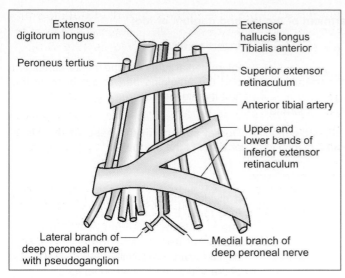

Fig. 8.6: Tendons, vessels and nerves related to the extensor retinacula.

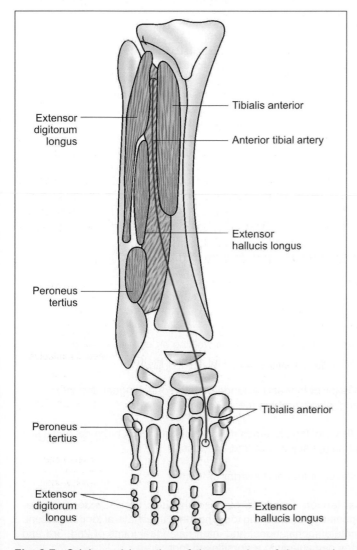

Fig. 8.7: Origin and insertion of the muscles of the anterior compartment of the leg.

ANTERIOR TIBIAL ARTERY

Introduction

This is the main artery of the anterior compartment of the leg (Figs 8.9 and 8.10). The blood supply to the anterior compartment of the leg is reinforced by the perforating branch of the peroneal artery, the size of which is inversely proportional to that of the anterior tibial artery.

Beginning, Course and Termination

The anterior tibial artery is the smaller terminal branch of the popliteal artery.

It begins on the back of the leg at the lower border of the popliteus, opposite the tibial tuberosity.

It enters the anterior compartment of the leg by passing forwards close to the fibula, through an opening in the upper part of the interosseous membrane.

In the anterior compartment, it runs vertically downwards to a point midway between the two malleoli where it changes its name to become the dorsalis pedis artery (Figs 8.11 and 8.12).

Relations

In the upper one-third of the leg, the artery lies between the tibialis anterior and the extensor digitorum longus (Fig. 8.7).

In the middle one-third it lies between the tibialis anterior and the extensor hallucis longus.

In the lower one-third it lies between the extensor hallucis longus and the extensor digitorum longus. In understanding these relations note that the artery is crossed from lateral to medial side by the tendon of the extensor hallucis longus (Fig. 8.5).

The artery is accompanied by the two venae comitantes.

Table 8.1: Muscles of the anterior compartment of the leg and dorsum of foot

Muscles	Origin from	Insertion into
1. **Tibialis anterior** It has a spindle-shaped belly with multipennate fibres (Fig. 8.7)	(a) Lateral condyle of tibia (b) Upper two-thirds or less of the lateral surface of the shaft of the tibia (c) Adjoining part of interosseous membrane	Inferomedial surface of the medial cuneiform and the adjoining part of the base of the first metatarsal bone
2. **Extensor hallucis longus**	(a) Posterior half of the middle 2/4 of the medial surface of the shaft of the fibula, medial to the extensor digitorum longus (b) Adjoining part of the interosseous membrane	Dorsal surface of the base of the distal phalanx of the big toe
3. **Extensor digitorum longus**	(a) Lateral condyle of tibia (b) Whole of upper one-fourth and anterior half of middle 2/4 of the medial surface of the shaft of the fibula (c) Upper part of interosseous membrane	It divides into four tendons for the lateral four toes. Each tendon is joined on the lateral side by a tendon of the extensor digitorum brevis, and forms the dorsal digital expansion. It is inserted on the bases of the middle and distal phalanges
4. **Peroneus tertius** It is a separated part of the extensor digitorum longus, and may be regarded as its fifth tendon. It may be absent	(a) Lower one-fourth of the medial surface of the shaft of the fibula (b) Adjoining part of the interosseous membrane	Medial part of the dorsal surface of the base of the fifth metatarsal bone
5. **Extensor digitorum brevis** This is a small muscle situated on the lateral part of the dorsum of foot, deep to the tendons of the extensor digitorum longus (Fig. 8.13)	The muscle arises from anterior part of the superior surface of the calcaneum	The muscle divides into four tendons for the medial four toes. The medial most part of the muscle, which is distinct, is known as the extensor hallucis brevis. The extensor hallucis brevis is inserted into the dorsal surface of the base of the proximal phalanx of the great toe. The lateral three tendons join the lateral sides of the tendons of the extensor digitorum longus to form the dorsal digital expansion for the second, third and fourth toes

Note: The above muscles also take origin from the deep surface of the deep fascia, and from adjoining intermuscular septa.

Table 8.2: Muscles of the anterior compartment of the leg and dorsum of foot (Fig. 8.8)

Muscles	Nerve supply	Action
1. **Tibialis anterior**	Deep peroneal nerve	(a) Dorsiflexor of foot (b) Invertor of the foot (c) Keeps the leg vertical while walking on uneven ground (d) Maintains medial longitudinal arch of the foot
2. **Extensor hallucis longus**	Deep peroneal nerve	Dorsiflexor of foot and extends metatarsophalangeal and interphalangeal joints of big toe
3. **Extensor digitorum longus**	Deep peroneal nerve	Dorsiflexor of foot. Extends metatarsophalangeal, proximal and distal interphalangeal joints of 2nd–5th toes
4. **Peroneus tertius**	Deep peroneal nerve	Dorsiflexor of foot and evertor of foot
5. **Extensor digitorum brevis**	Lateral terminal branch of the deep peroneal nerve	Medial tendon known as extensor hallucis brevis, extends metatarsophalangeal joint of big toe. The other three lateral tendons extend the metatarsophalangeal and interphalangeal joints of 2nd, 3rd and 4th toes particularly in a dorsiflexed foot

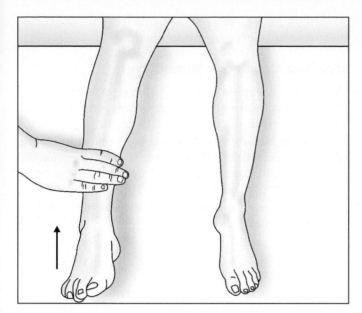

Fig. 8.8: How to test the dorsiflexors of the ankle joint.

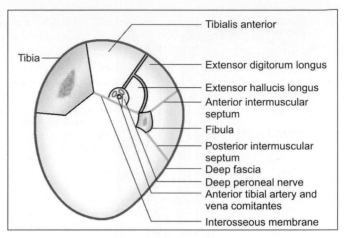

Fig. 8.10: Transverse section through the middle of leg showing the arrangement of structures in the anterior compartment.

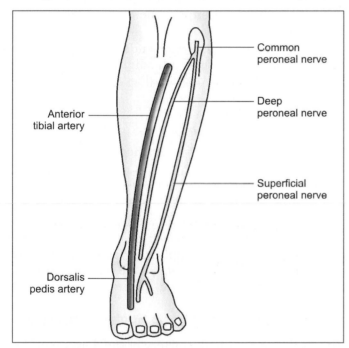

Fig. 8.9: Course of anterior tibial, dorsalis pedis arteries, deep and superficial peroneal nerves.

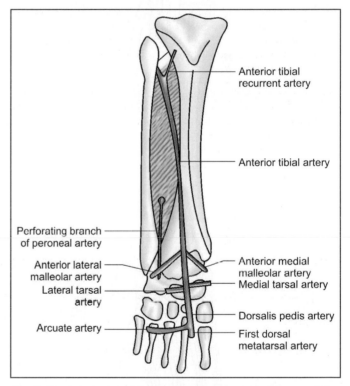

Fig. 8.11: Arteries on the front of the leg and dorsum of the foot.

The deep peroneal nerve is lateral to it in its upper and lower thirds, and anterior to it in its middle one-third.

Branches

1. *Muscular* branches supply adjacent muscles.
2. *Anastomotic* branches are given to the knee and ankle. The *anterior* and *posterior tibial recurrent branches* take part in the anastomoses round the knee joint. The *anterior medial malleolar* and *anterior lateral malleolar branches* take part in the anastomoses round the ankle joint or malleolar networks.

The *lateral malleolar network* lies just below the lateral malleolus.

The *medial malleolar network* lies just below the medial malleolus.

DEEP PERONEAL NERVE

Deep peroneal nerve is the nerve of the anterior compartment of the leg and the dorsum of the foot. This is one of the two terminal branches of common

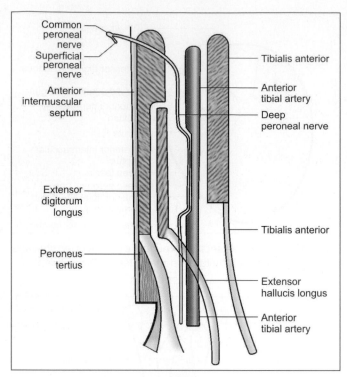

Fig. 8.12: Relations of the anterior tibial artery (schematic).

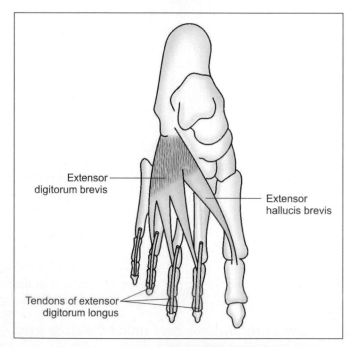

Fig. 8.13: The extensor digitorum brevis.

DISSECTION

Identify the small muscle extensor digitorum brevis situated on the lateral side of dorsum of foot. Its tendons are deep to the tendons of extensor digitorum longus. Its most medial tendon in called extensor hallucis brevis. Dissect the dorsalis pedis artery and its branches on the dorsum of the foot.

---

peroneal nerve. It corresponds to the posterior interosseous nerve of the forearm.

Beginning, Course and Termination

Deep peroneal nerve is one of the terminal branches of common peroneal nerve. It *begins* on the lateral side of the neck of the fibula.

It *enters the anterior compartment* by piercing the anterior intermuscular septum. It then pierces the extensor digitorum longus and comes to lie next to the anterior tibial artery (Fig. 8.12).

In the leg, it accompanies the anterior tibial artery and has similar relations.

The nerve ends on the dorsum of the foot, close to the ankle joint, by dividing into the lateral and medial terminal branches (Fig. 8.6).

The *lateral terminal branch* turns laterally and ends in a *pseudoganglion* deep to the extensor digitorum brevis. Branches proceed from the pseudoganglion and supply the extensor digitorum brevis and the tarsal joints.

The *medial terminal branch* ends by supplying the skin adjoining the first interdigital cleft and the proximal joints of the big toe (Fig. 8.3).

Branches

Muscular branches supply:
  (i) Four muscles of the anterior compartment of the leg (Fig. 8.10).
  (ii) The extensor digitorum brevis on the dorsum of the foot (Fig. 8.13).

A *cutaneous branch* supplies adjacent sides of the first and second toes (Fig. 8.3).

Articular branches supply the ankle joint, the tarsal joints, the tarsometatarsal and metatarsophalangeal joints of the big toe.

DORSALIS PEDIS ARTERY (DORSAL ARTERY OF THE FOOT)

This is the chief palpable artery of the dorsum of the foot (Fig. 8.14). It is commonly palpated in patients with vasoocclusive diseases of the lower limb. It is a continuation of the anterior tibial artery on to the dorsum of the foot.

Beginning, Course and Termination

The artery begins in front of the ankle between the two malleoli. It passes forwards along the medial side of the dorsum of the foot to reach the proximal end of the first intermetatarsal space. Here it dips downwards between the two heads of the first dorsal interosseous muscle, and ends in the sole by completing the plantar arterial arch (Figs 8.15 and 8.16).

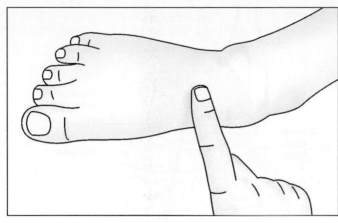

Fig. 8.14: The dorsalis pedis artery being palpated.

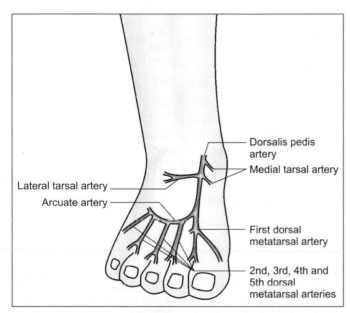

Fig. 8.15: Course of the dorsalis pedis artery on the dorsum of the foot.

Relations

Superficial

1. Skin, fasciae, and inferior extensor retinaculum.
2. Extensor hallucis brevis, which crosses the artery from the lateral to medial side (Fig. 8.17).

Deep

1. Capsular ligament of the ankle joint.
2. The talus, navicular and intermediate cuneiform bones and the ligaments connecting them (Fig. 8.18).

Medial

Extensor hallucis longus.

Lateral

1. First tendon of the extensor digitorum longus.
2. The medial terminal branch of the deep peroneal nerve.

Branches

1. The *lateral tarsal artery* is larger than the medial and arises over the navicular bone. It passes deep to the extensor digitorum brevis, supplies this muscle and neighbouring tarsal joints, and ends in the lateral malleolar network (Fig. 8.15).
2. The *medial tarsal branches* are two to three small twigs which join the medial malleolar network.
3. The *arcuate artery* is a large branch that arises opposite the medial cuneiform bone. It runs laterally over the bases of the metatarsal bones, deep to the tendons of the extensor digitorum longus and the extensor digitorum brevis, and

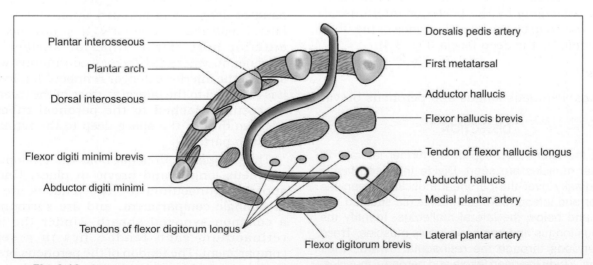

Fig. 8.16: Scheme to show how the dorsalis pedis artery becomes continuous with the plantar arch.

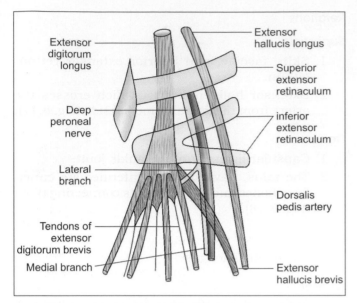

Fig. 8.17: Superficial, medial and lateral relations of the dorsalis pedis artery.

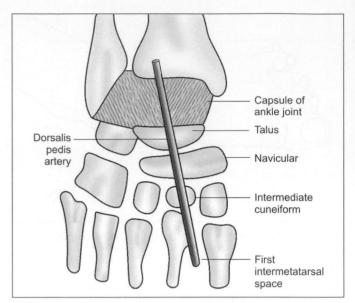

Fig. 8.18: Deep relations of the dorsalis pedis artery.

ends by anastomosing with the lateral tarsal and lateral plantar arteries. It gives off the *second, third* and *fourth dorsal metatarsal arteries,* each of which divides into dorsal digital branches for adjoining toes. The dorsal meta-tarsal arteries are joined by proximal and distal perforating arteries from the sole (Fig. 8.15).

4. The *first dorsal metatarsal artery* arises just before the dorsalis pedis artery dips into the sole. It gives a branch to the medial side of the big toe, and divides into dorsal digital branches for adjacent sides of the first and second toes.

LATERAL SIDE OF THE LEG

The lateral or peroneal compartment of the leg is bounded *anteriorly* by the anterior intermuscular septum, *posteriorly* by the posterior intermuscular septum, *medially* by the lateral surface of the fibula, and *laterally* by the deep fascia (Fig. 8.4).

Contents

Muscles: Peroneus longus and peroneus brevis.

DISSECTION

Reflect the lateral skin flap of leg further laterally till peroneal muscles are seen. Divide the deep fascia longitudinally over the peroneal muscles. Clean the superior and inferior peroneal retinacula situated just above and below the lateral malleolus. Identify the peroneus longus and peroneus brevis muscles. Trace their tendons through the retinacula towards their insertion. Study the deep fascia and peroneal muscles.

Nerve: Superficial peroneal nerve.

Vessels: The arterial supply is derived from the branches of the peroneal artery which reach the lateral compartment by piercing the flexor hallucis longus and the posterior intermuscular septum. The veins drain into the small saphenous vein.

PERONEAL RETINACULA

The *superior peroneal retinaculum* is a thickened band of deep fascia situated just behind the lateral malleolus. It holds the peroneal tendons in place against the back of the lateral malleolus. It is attached anteriorly to the posterior margin of the lateral malleolus, and posteriorly to the lateral surface of the calcaneum and to the superficial transverse fascial septum of the leg (Figs 8.4 and 8.19).

The *inferior peroneal retinaculum* is a thickened band of deep fascia situated anteroinferior to the lateral malleolus. Superiorly, it is attached to the anterior part of the superior surface of the calcaneum, where it becomes continuous with the stem of the inferior extensor retinaculum. Inferiorly, it is attached to the lateral surface of the calcaneum. A septum attached to the peroneal tubercle or trochlea divides the space deep to the retinaculum into two parts.

The peroneal retinacula hold the tendons of the peroneus longus and brevis in place. Under the superior retinaculum the two tendons are lodged in a single compartment, and are surrounded by a common synovial sheath. Under the inferior retinaculum each tendon lies in a separate compartment. The tendon of the peroneus brevis lies in the superior compartment and that of the peroneus longus in the inferior compartment. Here each tendon is enclosed in a separate extension of the synovial sheath (Fig. 8.19).

PERONEAL MUSCLES

These are the peroneus longus and the peroneus brevis. Their attachments are given in Tables 8.3 and 8.4.

SUPERFICIAL PERONEAL NERVE

Superficial peroneal nerve (Fig. 8.23) is the main nerve of the lateral compartment of the leg.

Origin

It is a smaller terminal branch of the common peroneal nerve.

Course

The nerve begins on the lateral side of neck of fibula, runs through the peroneal muscles and becomes superficial at the junction of upper two-thirds and lower one-third of leg.

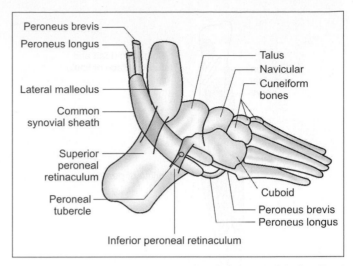

Fig. 8.19: The peroneal retinacula and the synovial sheath of the peroneal tendons.

Relations

It begins on the lateral side of the neck of the fibula, under cover of the upper fibres of the peroneus longus.

Table 8.3: The peroneal muscles		
Muscle	**Origin from**	**Insertion**
1. Peroneus longus It lies superficial to the peroneus brevis (Fig. 8.20)	(a) Head of the fibula, and sometimes the adjoining part of the lateral condyle of the tibia (b) Upper one-third, and posterior half of the middle one-third of the lateral surface of the shaft of the fibula	The tendon passes deep to the peroneal retinacula, runs through a tunnel in the cuboid, and is inserted into (a) the lateral side of the base of the first metatarsal bone and (b) the adjoining part of the medial cuneiform bone. The tendon changes its direction below the lateral malleolus and again on the cuboid bone. A sesamoid is present in the tendon in the latter situation
2. Peroneus brevis Lies deep to the peroneus longus (Figs 8.21 and 8.22)	(a) Anterior half of the middle one-third and the lower one-third of the lateral surface of the shaft of fibula (b) Anterior and posterior intermuscular septa of the leg	The tendon passes deep to the peroneal retinacula, and is inserted into the lateral side of the base of the fifth metatarsal bone

Table 8.4: The peroneal muscles		
Muscles	**Nerve supply**	**Action**
1. Peroneus longus	Superficial peroneal nerve	(a) Evertor of foot especially when foot is off the ground (b) Maintain lateral longitudinal arch and transverse arch of the foot Peroneus longus and tibialis anterior are inserted into the same two bones, the two together form a 'stirrup' beneath the middle of the sole. The presence of the sling keeps the middle of foot pulled up and prevents flattening of its arches.
2. Peroneus brevis	Superficial peroneal nerve	Evertor of foot

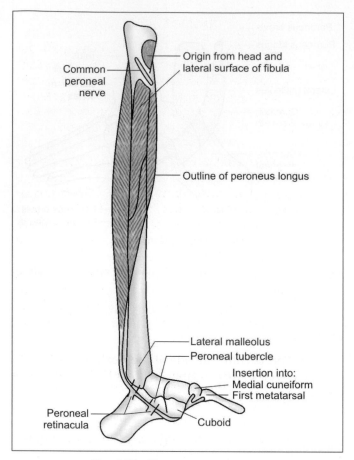

Fig. 8.20: The peroneus longus.

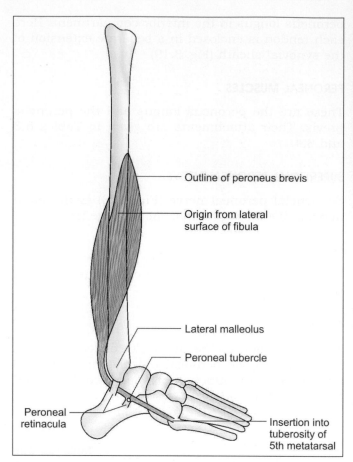

Fig. 8.21: The peroneus brevis.

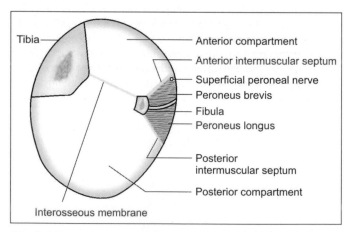

Fig. 8.22: Transverse section through the middle of the leg, showing the contents of the lateral compartment.

DISSECTION

Carefully look for common peroneal nerve in relation to the neck of fibula. Superficial peroneal nerve one of the terminal branches of common peroneal nerve supplies both the peroneus longus and brevis muscles and in lower one-third of leg it becomes cutaneous to supply most of the dorsum of foot.

In the upper one-third of the leg, it descends through the substance of the peroneus longus. In the middle one-third, it first descends for a short distance between the peroneus longus and brevis muscles, reaches the anterior border of the peroneus brevis, and the descends in a groove between the peroneus brevis and the extensor digitorum longus under cover of deep fascia.

At the junction of the upper two-thirds and lower one-third of the leg, it pierces the deep fascia to become superficial. It divides into a medial and a lateral branch which descend into the foot.

Branches and Distribution

Muscular branches are given off to the peroneus longus and the peroneus brevis.

Cutaneous branches: Through its terminal branches, the superficial peroneal nerve supplies the lower one-third of the lateral side of the leg and the greater part of the dorsum of the foot, except for the territories supplied by the saphenous, sural, deep peroneal nerves and plantar nerves (Fig. 8.3).

The *medial branch* crosses the ankle and divides into two dorsal digital nerves—one for the medial

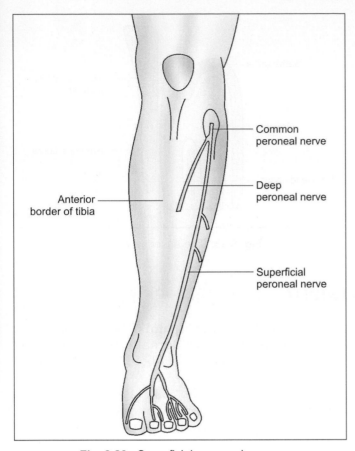

Fig. 8.23: Superficial peroneal nerve.

side of the big toe, and the other for the adjoining sides of the second and third toes.

The *lateral branch* also divides into two dorsal digital nerves for the adjoining sides of the third and fourth, and fourth and fifth toes.

Communicating branches. The medial branch communicates with the saphenous and deep peroneal nerves and the lateral branch with the sural nerve.

MEDIAL SIDE OF THE LEG

Medial side of the leg is formed by the medial surface of the shaft of tibia. The greater part of this surface is subcutaneous and is covered only by the skin and superficial fascia. In the upper part, however, the surface provides attachment to tibial collateral ligament near the medial border, and provides insertion to sartorius, gracilis and semitendinosus in front of the ligament, all of which are covered by a thin layer of deep fascia. The great saphenous vein and the saphenous nerve lie in the superficial fascia as they cross the lower one-third of this surface.

1. The skin, fasciae and periosteum on this surface are supplied by saphenous nerve.

2. The *tibial collateral ligament,* morphologically, represents degenerated part of the tendon of adductor magnus. Partly it covers the insertion of semimembranosus, and is itself crossed superficially by the tendons of sartorius, gracilis and semitendinosus, with anserine bursa around them.

3. *Guy ropes:* The three muscles inserted into the upper part of the medial surface of tibia represent one muscle from each of the three compartments of thigh, corresponding to the three elements of the hip bone.

   Sartorius belongs to anterior compartment of thigh, and is supplied by the nerve of ilium or femoral nerve; *gracilis* belongs to medial compartment of thigh, and is supplied by the nerve of pubis or obturator nerve.

   Semitendinosus belongs to posterior compartment of thigh, and is supplied by the nerve of ischium or sciatic nerve.

   These three muscles are anchored below at one point, and spread out above to span the pelvis, like three strings of a tent. From this arrangement it appears that they act as "guy ropes", to stabilize the bony pelvis on the femur (Fig. 8.24).

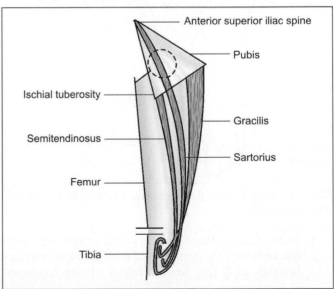

Fig. 8.24: Sartorius, gracilis and semitendinosus form the guy ropes, for the tent of pelvis.

4. *Anserine bursa:* This is a large, complicated bursa, with several diverticula. It separates the tendons of sartorius, gracilis and semitendinosus at their insertion from one another, from the bony surface of tibia, and from the tibial collateral ligament (Fig. 8.25).

5. The *great saphenous vein* ascends in front of the medial malleolus, and crosses lower one-third of the medial surface of tibia obliquely, with a backward inclination. The saphenous nerve runs downwards just in front of the great saphenous vein. The vein is accompanied by lymphatics from the foot, which drain into the vertical group of superficial inguinal lymph nodes.

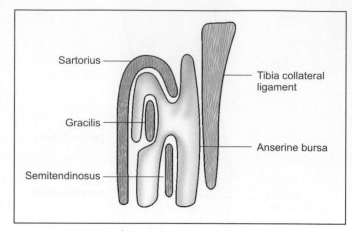

Fig. 8.25: The anserine bursa.

CLINICAL ANATOMY

- Paralysis of the muscles of the anterior compartment of the leg due to injury to deep peroneal nerve results in loss of the power of dorsiflexion of the foot. As a result the foot is plantar flexed. The condition is called *foot drop*. This is usually caused by injury or disease of the common peroneal nerve due to trauma, leprosy or peripheral neuritis (Fig. 8.26). Sensory loss is confined to first interdigital cleft.

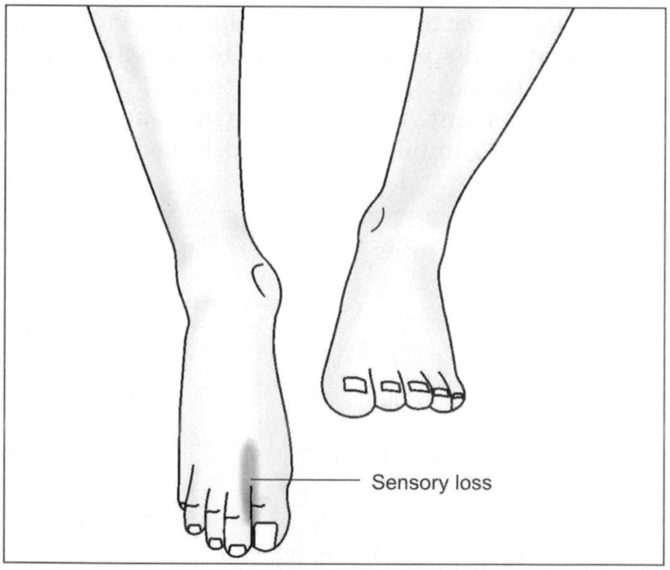

Fig. 8.26: Foot drop on the right side. Sensory loss in the first interdigital cleft.

- Pulsations of the dorsalis pedis artery are easily felt between the tendons of the extensor hallucis longus and the first tendon of the extensor digitorum longus. It must be remembered, however, that the dorsalis pedis artery is congenitally absent in about 14% of subjects (Fig. 8.14).

- Saphenous nerve may be subjected to entrapment neuropathy as it leaves the adductor canal, leading to pain in the area of its supply (Fig. 3.27).

- Superficial peroneal nerve supplies both peronei and then divides into medial and lateral cutaneous branches for supplying dorsum of foot. Superficial peroneal nerve can get entrapped as it penetrates the deep fascia of leg. It may also be involved in lateral compartment syndrome. Its paralysis causes loss of eversion of foot at subtalar joint (Fig. 8.23).

- Anterior tibial compartment syndrome/freshers's syndrome: The muscles of anterior compartment of leg get painful because of too much sudden exercise. The muscles are tender to touch (Fig. 8.10).

- Tenosynovitis of peronei tendon is the inflammation of the tendon sheaths of the peroneal muscles (Fig. 8.19). If superior peroneal retinaculum is torn, the tendons can get dislocated to front of lateral malleolus.

- Bursa anserina between insertion of sartorius, gracilis, semitendinosus and tibial collateral ligament may get inflamed.

- Paralysis of peroneus brevis and peroneus longus occurs due to injury to superficial peroneal nerve. The foot cannot be everted at subtalar joint.

CHAPTER 9

Back of Leg

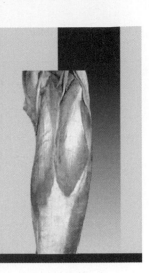

The short saphenous vein starts on the lateral side of the foot and ascends up on the back of leg to end in the popliteal vein. The back of leg contains superficial and deep muscles with tibial nerve and posterior tibial vessels. The superficial muscles get inserted into the strongest tendon of the body—the tendocalcaneus. Out of these the soleus is called the "peripheral heart". So there are two peripheral hearts and one central heart in the human body. The "peripheral heart" from each calf pumps only venous blood towards the heart, while the "central heart" receives venous blood, gets it oxygenated and pumps it to the whole body. Thus the peripheral heart is a "half hearted heart". Out of the four deep muscles, the popliteus acts as the key of the locked knee joint. The three pass down between the medial malleolus and calcaneum where these are retained in position by the single flexor retinaculum to reach the sole of the foot. These three muscles cause plantar flexion at the ankle joint. Tibialis posterior like tibialis anterior in addition causes inversion as well.

INTRODUCTION

The back or posterior compartment of the leg is also called the calf, corresponds to the front of forearm. This is the bulkiest of the three compartments of leg, because of the powerful antigravity superficial muscles, e.g. gastrocnemius, and soleus, and are quite large in size. They raise the heel during walking. These muscles are inserted into the heel. The deeper muscles cross the ankle medially to enter the sole.

Corresponding to the two bones of the leg, there are two arteries, the posterior tibial and peroneal, but there is only one nerve, the tibial, which represents both the median and ulnar nerves of the forearm.

SUPERFICIAL FASCIA

The superficial fascia of the back of the leg contains: The small and great saphenous veins and their

DISSECTION

Give a horizontal incision (ix) in the skin about 6 cm above the heel (Fig. 5.2). Carry this incision along the lateral and medial borders of the leg. Reflect whole skin of the back of leg distally. Identify the structures, e.g. great and small saphenous veins, medial and lateral calcanean arteries, and nerves in the superficial fascia.

tributaries, several cutaneous nerves, and the medial and lateral calcanean arteries.

Small or Short Saphenous Vein

The vein is formed on the dorsum of the foot by the union of the lateral end of the dorsal venous arch with the lateral marginal vein (Fig. 8.2). It enters the back of the leg by passing behind the lateral malleolus. In the leg, it ascends lateral to the tendocalcaneus, and then along the middle line of the calf, to the lower part of the popliteal fossa. Here it pierces the deep fascia and opens into the popliteal vein (Fig. 9.1). It drains the lateral border of the foot, the heel, and the back of the leg. It is connected with the great saphenous and with the deep veins, and is accompanied by the sural nerve.

Great or Long Saphenous Vein

This vein begins on the dorsum of the foot by union of the medial end of the dorsal venous arch with the medial marginal vein (Figs 8.2 and 3.5). It ascends in front of the medial malleolus. In the lower one-third of the leg, it passes obliquely across the medial surface of the tibia. In the upper two-thirds of the leg, the vein ascends along the medial border of the tibia, to the posteromedial side of the knee. It is accompanied by the saphenous nerve.

Cutaneous Nerves

The skin of the calf can be divided into three vertical areas, medial, central and lateral (Fig. 9.2). Roughly

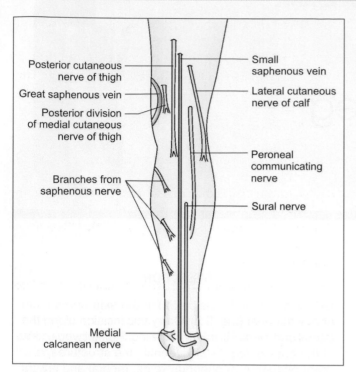

Fig. 9.1: Superficial veins and cutaneous nerves of the back of the leg and the heel.

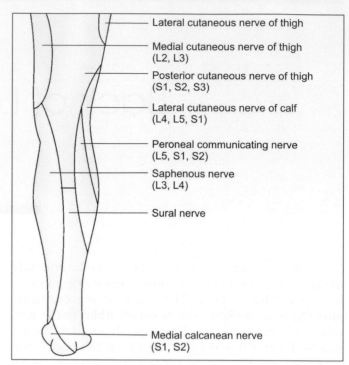

Fig. 9.2: Areas of cutaneous innervation of the back of the leg and the heel.

there are two nerves for each area, with an additional nerve for the heel. The medial area is supplied by the saphenous nerve and by the posterior branch of the medial cutaneous nerve of the thigh; the central area by the posterior cutaneous nerve of the thigh and by the sural nerve; the lateral area by the lateral cutaneous nerve of the calf and the peroneal communicating nerve. The lower part of the lateral area is supplied by the sural nerve. The heel is supplied by the medial calcanean branches of the tibial nerve.

1. The *saphenous nerve* (L3, L4) is a branch of the posterior division of the femoral nerve (Fig. 9.2). It arises in the femoral triangle. It pierces the deep fascia on the medial side of the knee between the sartorius and the gracilis, and descends close to the great saphenous vein. It supplies the skin of most of the medial area of the leg, and the medial border of the foot up to the ball of the big toe. During venesection this nerve should not be injured.

2. The *posterior division of the medial cutaneous nerve of the thigh* (L2, L3) supplies the skin of the upper most part of the medial area of the calf.

3. The *posterior cutaneous nerve of the thigh* (S1, S2, S3) is a branch of the sacral plexus and descends along with the small saphenous vein, to supply the skin of the upper half of the central area of the calf.

4. The *sural nerve* (L5, S1, S2) is a branch of the tibial nerve in the popliteal fossa. It descends between the two heads of the gastrocnemius. It accompanies the small saphenous vein. It is joined by the peroneal communicating nerve about 5 cm above the heel. After passing behind the lateral malleolus, the nerve runs forwards along the lateral border of the foot, and ends at the lateral side of the little toe. It supplies the skin shown in Fig. 9.2.

5. The *lateral cutaneous nerve of the calf* (L4, L5, S1) is a branch of the common peroneal nerve in the popliteal fossa. It supplies the skin of the upper two-thirds of the lateral area of the leg (both in front and behind).

6. The *peroneal* or *sural communicating nerve* (L5, S1, S2) is a branch of the common peroneal nerve. It descends to join the sural nerve about 5 cm above the heel. Before joining the latter it supplies the skin of the lateral area of calf.

7. The *medial calcanean branches* (S1, S2) of the tibial nerve perforate the flexor retinaculum and supply the skin of the heel and the medial side of the sole of the foot.

DEEP FASCIA

The posterior compartment of leg is bounded and subdivided by the deep fascia. It is thin above but thick near the ankle, where it forms the flexor and superior peroneal retinacula.

DISSECTION

Incise the deep fascia vertically and reflect it. Define the flexor retinaculum posteroinferior to the medial malleolus and identify the tendons enclosed in synovial sheaths passing deep to it. Identify the medial and lateral bellies of gastrocnemius muscle. Cut the medial belly 5 cm distal to the origin. Reflect it laterally to locate the popliteal vessels and tibial nerve. Identify plantaris muscle with its longest tendon situated posteromedial to lateral head to gastrocnemius. Reflect the lateral head of gastrocnemius 5 cm distal to its origin. Both the bellies now can be turned distally. Deep to gastrocnemius, expose the strong soleus muscle. The popliteal vessels and tibial nerve pass deep or anterior to the fibrous arch between the upper parts of the two leg bones.

Boundaries and Subdivisions of Posterior Compartment

The boundaries of the posterior compartment of the leg are as follows.

Anteriorly: Posterior surfaces of

1. Tibia,
2. The interosseous membrane,
3. The fibula, and
4. The posterior intermuscular septum.

Posteriorly: Deep fascia of the leg.

The posterior compartment is subdivided into three parts—superficial, middle and deep, by two strong fascial septa.

The *superficial transverse fascial septum* (Fig. 8.4) separates the superficial and deep muscles of the back of the leg, and encloses the posterior tibial vessels and tibial nerve. It is attached:

(a) *Above,* to the soleal line of the tibia and the back of the fibula, below the origin of the soleus.

(b) *Below,* it becomes continuous with the flexor and superior peroneal retinacula.

(c) *Medially,* it is attached to the medial border of the tibia.

(d) *Laterally,* to the posterior border of the fibula.

The *deep transverse fascial septum* separates the tibialis posterior from the long flexors of the toes. Attachments:

(a) *Above,* it blends with the interosseous membrane.

(b) *Below,* it blends with the superficial fascial septum.

(c) *Medially,* it is attached to the vertical ridge on the posterior surface of the tibia.

(d) *Laterally,* to the medial crest of the fibula.

Flexor Retinaculum

Some important facts about the retinaculum are as follows.

1. **Attachments:** The flexor retinaculum is attached *anteriorly* to the posterior border and tip of the medial malleolus and *posteriorly* and *laterally* to the medial tubercle of the calcaneum (Figs 9.3 and 9.4).

   Septa pass from the retinaculum to the underlying bone and divide the space deep to the retinaculum into four compartments.

2. **Structures passing deep to the retina-culum:** These are from medial to lateral side.

   (a) The tendon of the tibialis posterior.

   (b) The tendon of the flexor digitorum longus.

   (c) The posterior tibial artery and its terminal branches, along with the accompanying veins.

   (d) The tibial nerve and its terminal branches.

   (e) The tendon of the flexor hallucis longus. Each tendon occupies a separate compartment which is lined by a synovial sheath.

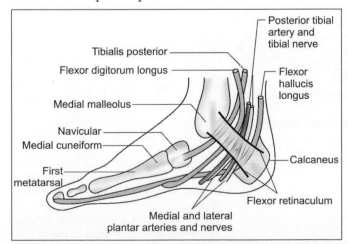

Fig. 9.3: Flexor retinaculum of the ankle, and the structures passing deep to it.

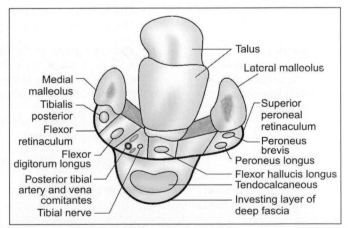

Fig. 9.4: Transverse section through the ankle showing the flexor retinaculum, the superior peroneal retinaculum, and related structures.

The nerve and artery share a common compartment.

These structures (a) to (e) lie in a *tarsal tunnel*. If the nerve gets pressed, it leads to *tarsal tunnel syndrome*.

3. The lower part of the deep surface of the flexor retinaculum gives origin to the greater part of the abductor hallucis muscle.

4. Near the calcaneum, the retinaculum is pierced by the medial calcanean vessels and nerves.

SUPERFICIAL MUSCLES

The muscles of the back of leg are classified into two groups—superficial and deep. The superficial muscles are the gastrocnemius, the soleus, and the plantaris. The attachments of these muscles are described in Tables 9.1 and 9.2.

Additional Points of Interest

1. The large size of the gastrosoleus is a human character, and is directly related to the adoption of an erect posture, and to the bipedal gait of man. Soleus is homologous with flexor digitorum superficialis of the front of forearm.

2. From an evolutionary point of view the long plantar ligament is the divorced tendon of the gastrocnemius; and the flexor digitorum brevis is the divorced distal part of the soleus.

3. A small sesamoid called the fabella is present in the tendon of origin of the lateral head of the gastrocnemius.

4. A bursa Brodie's bursa lies deep to the medial head of the gastrocnemius. The bursa is also deep to the semimembranosus and may communicate with the cavity of the knee joint.

5. The muscles of the calf play an important role in circulation. Contractions of these muscles help in the venous return from the lower limb. The soleus is particularly important in this respect.

There are large, valveless, venous sinuses in its substance. When the muscle contracts the blood in these sinuses is pumped out. When it relaxes, it sucks the blood from the superficial veins through the perforates. The soleus is, therefore, called the *peripheral heart*.

Table 9.1: Superficial muscles of the back of the leg		
Muscles	**Origin**	**Insertion**
1. **Gastrocnemius** This is a large powerful muscle. It has two heads, medial and lateral. It lies superficial to the soleus. The two heads of the gastrocnemius, and the soleus, are together referred to as the gastrosoleus or the triceps surae (Figs 9.5 and 9.6)	(a) The *medial head* is larger than the lateral It arises by a broad flat tendon from: • The posterosuperior depression on the medial condyle of the femur, behind the adductor tubercle • The adjoining raised area on the popliteal surface of the femur • The capsule of the knee joint (b) The *lateral head* arises by a broad flat tendon from: • The lateral surface of the lateral condyle of the femur; • The lateral supracondylar line; and • The capsule of the knee joint	The tendon of this muscle fuses with the tendon of the soleus to form the tendocalcaneus or tendoachilles, which is inserted into the middle one-third of the posterior surface of the calcaneum
2. **Soleus** It is a sole-shaped multipennate muscle, which lies deep to the gastrocnemius (Fig. 9.5)	It has a dome-shaped origin from: (a) The fibula: back of head, and upper one-fourth of the posterior surface of the shaft (b) Tibia: soleal line and middle one-third of the medial border of the shaft (c) The tendinous soleal arch that stretches between the tibia and the fibula	See gastrocnemius
3. **Plantaris** It is vestigeal in human beings. It has a short belly and a long tendon	(a) Lower part of the lateral supracondylar line of the femur (b) Oblique popliteal ligament	The tendon is thin and long. It lies between the gastrocnemius and the soleus, crossing from lateral to medial side It is inserted on the posterior surface of the calcaneum, medial to the tendo-calcaneus. Plantar aponeurosis is the estranged part of the plantaris

Table 9.2: Superficial muscles of the back of the leg

	Muscles	Nerve supply	Action
1.	Gastrocnemius	All the superficial muscles of the back of the leg are supplied by the tibial nerve (S1, S2)	The gastrocnemius and soleus are strong plantar flexors of the foot, at the ankle joint. The gastrocnemius is also a flexor of the knee. Plantar flexion, produced by the gastrocnemius and the soleus, is very important in walking and running
2.	Soleus	All the superficial muscles of the back of the leg are supplied by the tibial nerve (S1, S2)	The soleus is more powerful than the gastrocnemius, but the latter is faster acting. In walking, the soleus overcomes the inertia of the body weight, like the bottom gear of a car. When movement is under way, the quicker acting gastrocnemius increases the speed like the top gear of a car. Soleus is chiefly a postural muscle, to steady the leg on the foot
3.	Plantaris	All the superficial muscles of the back of the leg are supplied by the tibial nerve (S1, S2)	The plantaris is a rudimentary muscle, and is accessory to the gastrocnemius. Its functional importance is of transplantation

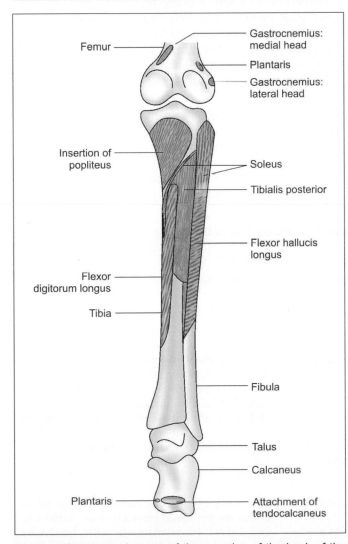

Fig. 9.5: Some attachments of the muscles of the back of the leg. The tibialis posterior also arises from the fibula, but this area cannot be seen in this view.

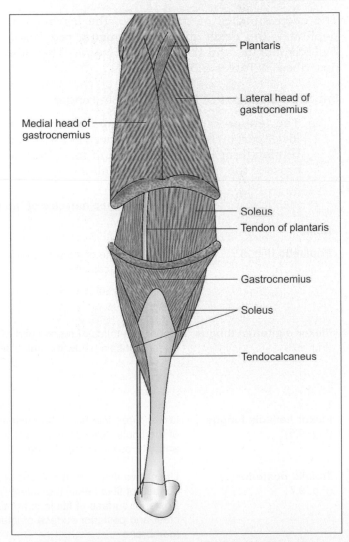

Fig. 9.6: Superficial muscles of the back of the leg.

6. The *tendocalcaneus* is the thickest and strongest tendon of the body. It is about 15 cm long. It begins near the middle of the leg, but its anterior surface receives fleshy fibres of the soleus almost up to its lower end. It is narrow and thick in the middle, and expanded at both ends.

7. Tendocalcaneus is also known as tendo-Achilles. According to a Greek legend, Achilles was an irresistible and invincible warrior. His mother, the sea Goddess, had dipped him in the underground river, Styx. No weapon could harm the body which had been covered by the waters of Styx. But the warrior was ultimately killed in the war of Trojans, by the arrows hitting his vulnerable heel which was the only unprotected part of his body. His mother had held him by one heel, and the water over this heel had not flowed.

DEEP MUSCLES

The deep muscles of the back of the leg are the popliteus, the flexor digitorum longus, the flexor hallucis longus, and the tibialis posterior. They are described in Tables 9.3 and 9.4.

Important Relations of Flexor Digitorum Longus

(a) The tendon crosses the tibialis posterior in lower part of the leg. It passes deep to the flexor retinaculum to enter the sole of foot. Here it crosses the tendon of flexor hallucis longus.

DISSECTION

Once the soleus has been studied, separate it from its attachment on tibia and reflect it laterally. Look for a number of deep veins which emerge from this muscle. Identify popliteus, situated above the soleus muscle. Deep to soleus is the first intermuscular septum. Incise this septum vertically to reach the long flexors of the toes, e.g. flexor hallucis longus laterally and flexor digitorum longus medially. Trace these tendons till the flexor retinaculum. Turn the flexor hallucis longus laterally and expose the second intermuscular septum. Divide this septum to reveal the deepest muscle of the posterior compartment of leg, e.g. tibialis posterior. Trace its tendon also till flexor retinaculum. Study these deep muscles. Clean the lowest part of popliteal vessels and trace its two terminal branches, anterior tibial into anterior compartment and posterior tibial into the posterior compartment of leg. Identify posterior tibial vessels and tibial nerve in fibrofatty tissue between the two long flexors of the leg deep to the first intermuscular septum. Peroneal vessels are identified in the connective tissue of the second intermuscular septum. Study their origin, course and branches from the following text.

The nerve to popliteus deserves special mention. Being a branch of tibial nerve it descends over the popliteus to reach its distal border. There it supplies the muscle after winding around its distal border. It also supplies a branch to tibialis posterior muscle, both tibiofibular joints and interosseous membrane.

Table 9.3: Deep muscles of the posterior compartment of the leg

Name	Origin	Insertion
Popliteus (Fig. 9.7)	Lateral surface of lateral condyle of femur; origin is intracapsular Outer margin of lateral meniscus of the knee joint	Posterior surface of shaft of tibia above soleal line
Flexor digitorum longus (Fig. 9.8)	Upper two-thirds of medial part of posterior surface of tibia below the soleal line	Bases of distal phalanges of shaft of lateral four toes. Muscle ends in a tendon which divides into four slips, one for each of the lateral four toes. Each slip is attached to the plantar surface of the distal phalanx of the digit concerned
Flexor hallucis longus (Fig. 9.5)	Lower three-fourths of the posterior surface of the fibula, (except the lowest 2.5 cm) and interosseous membrane	Plantar surface of base of distal phalanx of big toe
Tibialis posterior (Fig. 9.7)	Upper two-thirds of lateral part of posterior surface of tibia below the soleal line Posterior surface of fibula in front of the medial crest and posterior surface of interosseous membrane	Tuberosity of navicular bone and other tarsal bones except talus. Insertion is extended into 2nd, 3rd and 4th metatarsal bones at their bases

Table 9.4: Deep muscles of the posterior compartment of the leg

Name	Nerve supply	Action
Popliteus	Tibial nerve	Unlocks knee joint by lateral rotation of femur on tibia prior to flexion
Flexor digitorum longus	Tibial nerve	Flexes distal phalanges, plantar flexor of ankle joint; supports medial and lateral longitudinal arches of foot
Flexor hallucis longus	Tibial nerve	Flexes distal phalanx of big toe; plantar flexor of ankle joint; supports medial longitudinal arch of foot
Tibialis posterior	Tibial nerve	Plantar flexor of ankle joint; inverts foot at subtalar joint, supports medial longitudinal arch of foot (Fig. 9.9)

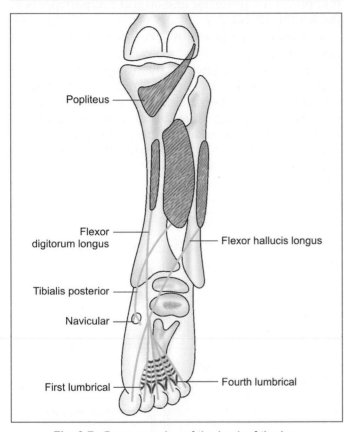

Fig. 9.7: Deep muscles of the back of the leg.

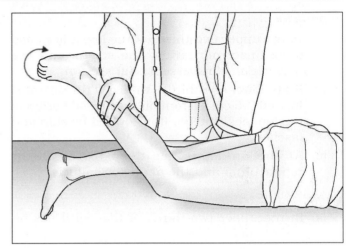

Fig. 9.9: Testing the deep muscles of the calf by plantar flexing the foot.

(b) The tendon receives the insertion of the flexor digitorum accessorius.

(c) The slips for the digits give origin to the four lumbrical muscles.

Important Relations of Flexor Hallucis Longus

The tendon runs across the lower part of the posterior surface of the tibia. Reaching the calcaneus it turns forwards below the sustentaculum tali which serves as a pulley for it. As the tendon lies on the medial side of calcaneum, it runs deep to the flexor retinaculum and is surrounded by a synovial sheath. The tendon then runs forwards in the sole when it is crossed by the tendon of flexor digitorum longus.

Important Relations of Tibialis Posterior

The tendon passes behind the medial malleolus, grooving it. The tendon then passes deep to the flexor retinaculum. The terminal part of the tendon supports the spring ligament.

POSTERIOR TIBIAL ARTERY

Beginning, Course and Termination

It begins at the lower border of the popliteus, between the tibia and the fibula, deep to the gastrocnemius.

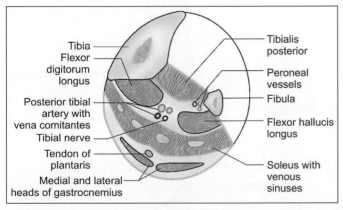

Fig. 9.8: Transverse section through the middle of the leg showing the arrangement of structures in the posterior compartment.

It enters the back of leg by passing deep to the tendinous arch of the soleus.

In the leg, it runs downwards and slightly medially, to reach the posteromedial side of the ankle, midway between the medial malleolus and the medial tubercle of the calcaneum.

It terminates deep to flexor retinaculum (and the origin of the abductor hallucis) by dividing, into the lateral and medial plantar arteries.

Relations

Superficial

(a) In the upper two-thirds of the leg, it lies deep to the gastrocnemius, the soleus and the superficial transverse fascial septum.

(b) In the lower one-third of the leg, it runs parallel to, and 2.5 cm in front of, the medial border of the tendocalcaneus. It is covered by skin and fasciae.

(c) At the ankle, it lies deep to the flexor retinaculum and the abductor hallucis.

Deep

(a) In the upper two-thirds of the leg, it lies on the tibialis posterior.

(b) In the lower one-third of the leg, it lies on the flexor digitorum longus and on the tibia.

(c) At the ankle, it lies directly on the capsule of the ankle joint between the flexor digitorum longus and the flexor hallucis longus (Figs 9.4 and 9.8).

The artery is *accompanied* by two venae comitantes and by the tibial nerve.

Branches

1. The *peroneal artery* (Fig. 9.10) is the largest branch of the posterior tibial artery. It is described later.
2. Several *muscular branches* are given off to muscles of the back of the leg.
3. A *nutrient artery* is given off to the tibia.
4. The *anastomotic branches* of the posterior tibial artery are as follows.
   (a) The circumflex fibular branch winds round the lateral side of the neck of the fibula to reach the front of the knee where it takes part in the anastomoses around the knee joint.
   (b) A communicating branch forms an arch with a similar branch from the peroneal artery about 5 cm above the ankle.
   (c) A malleolar branch anastomoses with other arteries over the medial malleolus.

(d) Calcaneal branches anastomose with other arteries in the region.

5. *Terminal branches:* These are the medial and lateral plantar arteries. They will be studied in the sole (Fig. 6.5).

PERONEAL ARTERY

Beginning, Course and Termination

This is the largest branch of the posterior tibial artery. It supplies the posterior and lateral compartments of the leg (Fig. 9.10).

It begins 2.5 cm below the lower border of the popliteus.

It runs obliquely towards the fibula, and descends along the medial crest of the fibula, accompanied by the nerve to the flexor hallucis longus. It passes behind the inferior tibiofibular and ankle joints, medial to peroneal tendons. It terminates by dividing into a number of lateral calcanean branches (Fig. 9.10).

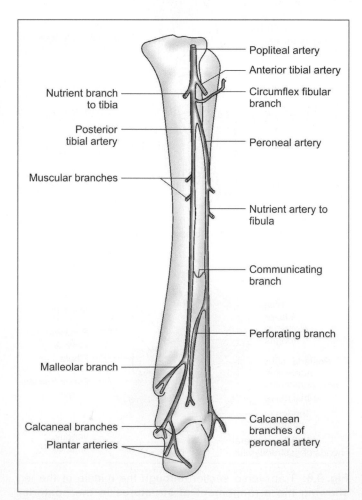

Fig. 9.10: Course of the posterior tibial and peroneal arteries.

Branches

1. *Muscular branches,* to the posterior and lateral compartments.
2. *Nutrient artery,* to the fibula.
3. *Anastomotic branches:*
   (a) The large perforating branch pierces the interosseous membrane 5 cm above the ankle, and joins the lateral malleolar network.
   (b) The communicating branch anastomoses with a similar branch from the posterior tibial artery, about 5 cm above the lower end of the tibia.
   (c) The calcanean branches join the lateral malleolar network.

The perforating branch of the peroneal artery may reinforce, or even replace the dorsalis pedis artery.

TIBIAL NERVE

Course

The course and relations of the tibial nerve in the leg are similar to those of the posterior tibial artery (Pages 119 and 120). Like the artery, the tibial nerve also terminates by dividing into the medial plantar and lateral plantar nerves (Fig. 9.3).

The tibial nerve crosses the posterior tibial artery and accompanying vena comitantes from medial to lateral side (Fig. 6.9).

Branches

Muscular

To the tibialis posterior, the flexor digitorum longus; the flexor hallucis longus, and the deep part of the soleus.

Cutaneous

Medial calcanean branches pierce the flexor retinaculum, and supply the skin on the back and lower surface of the heel.

Articular

To the ankle joint.

Terminal

Medial plantar and lateral plantar nerves (Fig. 10.13).

CLINICAL ANATOMY

- Tibial nerve can be injured at:
  (a) In upper part of calf from fracture of tibia.
  (b) In middle of calf from tight plasters.
  (c) Under flexor retinaculum. This is called *tarsal tunnel syndrome* (Fig. 9.11).

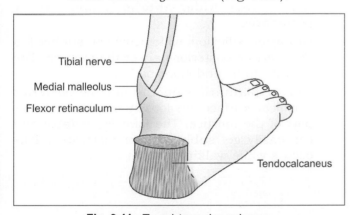

Fig. 9.11: Tarsal tunnel syndrome.

Sensory loss: Distal and middle phalanges including nail beds of all toes (Fig. 8.3). The sensory loss is in the skin over sole of foot.

Motor loss if injured at upper part of calf:
(a) superficial muscles of calf
(b) deep muscles of calf
(c) intrinsic muscles of sole

- Sural nerve has a tendency to form painful neuroma.

  Sural nerve can be grafted, as it is only sensory, is superficial and is easily identified lying between tendon of tendocalcaneus and lateral malleolus.

- The posterior tibial pulse can be felt against the calcaneum about 2 cm below and behind the medial malleolus (Fig. 9.12).

- Tendoachilles reflex or ankle jerk (S1, S2): The foot gets plantar flexed on tapping the tendocalcaneus (Fig. 9.13).

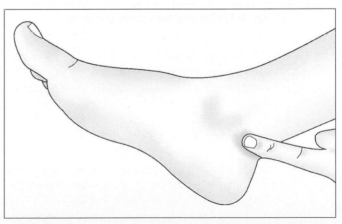

Fig. 9.12: Shows where to palpate the posterior tibial artery.

- The posterior tibial pulse is palpated in doubtful cases of intermittent claudication where a person gets cramps and severe pain in calf muscles due to lack of blood supply.
- For thrombangitis obliterans or occlusive disease of lower limb arteries, sympathetic fibres to the arteries are removed, so as to denervate the arteries. Lumbar 2 and 3 ganglia with intervening sympathetic trunk is removed, as these supply the arteries of lower limb.
- In long distance air travel, sitting immobile can lead to thrombosis of soleal venous sinuses. The thrombus may get dislodged to block any other artery. One must stretch the legs frequently.
- Tendon of plantaris is used for transplantation in the body. The tendon is long and can be used comfortably.
- Tendocalcaneus can rupture in tennis players 5 cm above its insertion. Plantar flexion is not possible. The two ends must be stitched.
- Tendocalcaneus can be tested by tendocalcaneus reflex (Fig. 9.13).

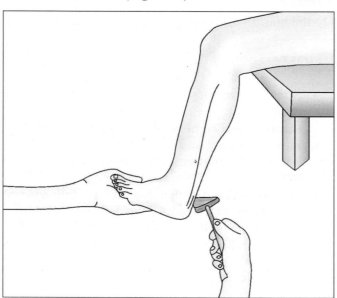

Fig. 9.13: Testing the tendocalcaneus.

- High heels for long periods causes change in posture. Knees are excessively bent, with lumbar vertebrae pushed forwards. There is a lot of stress on the muscles of back and those of the calf. So many fashionable ladies wear high heels for short time and change to flat ones soon (Fig. 9.14).

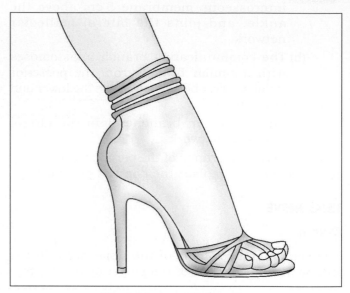

Fig. 9.14: Smart high heels.

- Dislocation or subluxation of ankle is common during plantarflexion. Lower end of the leg bones, i.e. medial malleolus, tibia, thin fibula and lateral malleous form tibiofibular mortice. This is wider anteriorly and narrow posteriorly.

The trochlear surface of talus forming ankle joint is also wider anteriorly and narrow posteriorly.

During dorsiflexion, wider trochlear surface fits into narrow posterior part of the mortice. The joint is stable and close packed.

During plantarflexion the narrow posterior trochlear surface lies loosely in wider anterior part of the mortice. The joint is unstable and can easily get subluxated or dislocated. This occurs while walking in high heels.

Sole of Foot

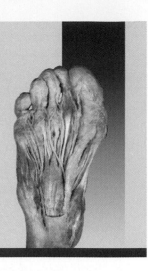

The sole of the foot is the counterpart of the hand. Muscles are arranged in four layers with the neurovascular bundles between first and second layers and then between third and fourth layers. There are no opponens muscles as opposition is not required in foot. But to straighten the action of flexor digitorum longus, there is flexor digitorum accessorius. There is only one plantar arch in the sole. Big toe with its two sesamoid bones in the tendon of flexor hallucis brevis bears double the weight than any of the other four toes. All the intrinsic muscles, i.e. muscles confined to the sole only are supplied by either of the two plantar nerves. The extrinsic muscles of the sole are supplied by the nerve of the respective compartment. The tendons and muscles of the sole maintain the arches of the foot.

INTRODUCTION

The structure of the sole is similar to that of the palm. The skin, superficial fascia, deep fascia, muscles, vessels and nerves, are all comparable in these two homologous parts. However, unlike the hand, the foot is an organ of support and locomotion. Accordingly, the structures of the foot get modified. The great toe has lost its mobility and its power of prehension; the lesser four toes are markedly reduced in size; and the tarsal bones and the first metatarsal are enlarged to form a broad base for better support. The arches of the foot serve as elastic springs for efficient walking, running, jumping and supporting of body weight.

DISSECTION

Skin of the sole usually becomes very hard. To remove it, the incision is given from heel through the root to the tip of the middle toe. Reflect the skin and fatty superficial fascia to each side of the sole. Look for cutaneous nerves and vessels.

SKIN

The skin of the sole, like that of the palm, is:
   (i) Thick for protection;
  (ii) Firmly adherent to the underlying plantar aponeurosis; and
 (iii) Creased. These features increase the efficiency of the grip of the sole on the ground.

The skin is supplied by three cutaneous nerves (Fig. 10.1). The nerves are:
  (a) Medial calcanean branches of the tibial nerve, to the posterior and medial portions;
  (b) Branches from the medial plantar nerve to the larger, anteromedial portion including the medial three and a half digits; and
  (c) Branches from the lateral plantar nerve to the smaller anterolateral portion including the lateral one and a half digits.

These nerves are derived from spinal nerves L4, L5 and S1. The segmental distribution is shown in Fig. 10.2. In eliciting the plantar reflex, the area supplied by segment S1 is stimulated.

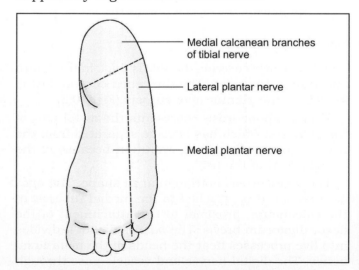

Fig. 10.1: Cutaneous nerves supplying the sole.

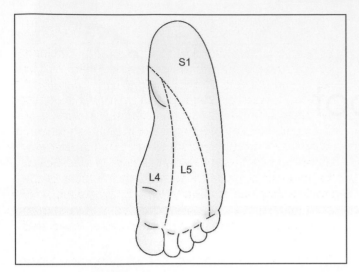

Fig. 10.2: Dermatomes on the sole.

SUPERFICIAL FASCIA

The superficial fascia of the sole is fibrous and dense. Fibrous bands bind the skin to the deep fascia or plantar aponeurosis, and divide the subcutaneous fat into small tight compartments which serve as water-cushions and reinforce the spring-effect of the arches of the foot during walking, running and jumping. The fascia is very thick and dense over the weight-bearing points. It contains cutaneous nerves and vessels. Thickened bands of superficial fascia stretch across the roots of the toes forming the superficial transverse metatarsal ligaments.

DEEP FASCIA

The deep fascia of the sole is specialized to form:
 (i) the plantar aponeurosis in the sole.
 (ii) the deep transverse metatarsal ligaments between the metatarsophalangeal joints.
 (iii) the fibrous flexor sheaths in the toes.

Plantar Aponeurosis

The deep fascia covering the sole is thick in the centre and thin at the sides. The thickened central part is known as the plantar aponeurosis (Fig. 10.3).

Plantar aponeurosis represents the distal part of the plantaris which has become separated from the rest of the muscle during evolution because of the enlargement of the heel.

The aponeurosis is triangular in shape. The *apex* is proximal. It is attached to the medial tubercle of the calcaneum, proximal to the attachment of the flexor digitorum brevis. The *base* is distal. It divides into five processes near the heads of the metatarsal bones. The digital nerves and vessels pass through the intervals between the processes.

DISSECTION

The deep fascia on the plantar aspect of toes is thickened to form fibrous flexor sheaths; proximally it is continuous with the plantar aponeurosis. Identify the cutaneous branches from medial and lateral plantar arteries and nerves on the respective sides of plantar aponeurosis. Between the five distal slips of the aponeurosis trace the digital nerves and vessels from medial plantar nerve and vessels for three and a half medial toes and from lateral plantar nerve and vessels for lateral one and a half toes.

Divide the plantar aponeurosis 4 cm distal to the heel. Reflect the cut ends both proximally and distally. This exposes the three muscles of the first layer of sole. Medial plantar nerve and vessels are easily visualised close to the medial border of sole. Stems of lateral plantar nerve and vessels including its superficial division are also seen.

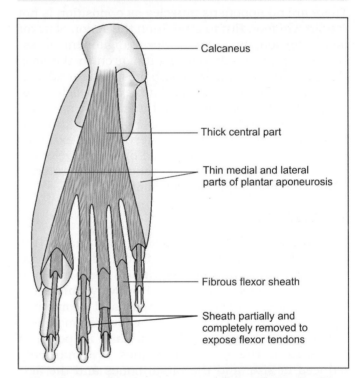

Fig. 10.3: Plantar aponeurosis and fibrous flexor sheaths.

Each process splits, opposite the metatarsophalangeal joints, into a *superficial and a deep slip.* The superficial slip is attached to skin. The deep slip divides into two parts which embrace the flexor tendons, and blend with the fibrous flexor sheaths and with the deep transverse metatarsal ligaments.

From the margins of the aponeurosis, lateral and medial *vertical intermuscular septa* pass deeply, and divide the sole into three compartments. Thinner *transverse septa* arise from the vertical septa and divide the muscles of the sole into four layers.

Functions

1. It fixes the skin of the sole.
2. It protects deeper structures.
3. It helps in maintaining the longitudinal arches of the foot.
4. It gives origin to muscles of the first layer of the sole.

The plantar aponeurosis differs from the palmar aponeurosis in giving off an additional process to the great toe, which restricts the movements of the latter.

Deep Transverse Metatarsal Ligaments

These are four short, flat bands which connect the plantar ligaments of the adjoining metatarsophalangeal joints. They are related dorsally to the interossei, and ventrally to the lumbricals and the digital vessels and nerves.

Fibrous Flexor Sheaths

These are made up of the deep fascia of the toes. Their structure is similar to that of the fibrous flexor sheaths of the fingers. They retain the flexor tendons in position during flexion of the toes (Figs 10.3 and 10.4).

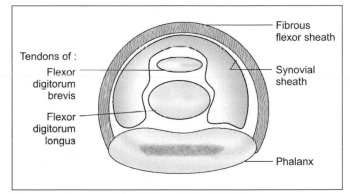

Tendons of :
Flexor digitorum brevis

Flexor digitorum longus

Fibrous flexor sheath

Synovial sheath

Phalanx

Fig. 10.4: Transverse section across a digit to show the fibrous flexor sheath.

MUSCLES OF THE FIRST LAYER OF THE SOLE

The muscles of the sole are arranged in four layers, which will be considered one by one.

The muscles of the first layer are the flexor digitorum brevis, the abductor hallucis, and the abductor digiti minimi. These muscles are described in Tables 10.1 and 10.2 (Fig. 10.5).

MUSCLES AND TENDONS OF THE SECOND LAYER OF THE SOLE

The contents of this layer are the tendons of the flexor digitorum longus, and of the flexor hallucis longus;

DISSECTION

Cut through the flexor digitorum brevis near its middle taking care to preserve the underlying lateral plantar nerve and vessels. Reflect the distal part distally till the toes. Detach the abductor digiti minimi and identify the lateral head of the flexor digitorum accessorius till its insertion into the tendon of flexor digitorum longus. Trace the long flexor tendons through the fibrous flexor sheath into the base of distal phalanges of toes. Follow the lumbricals to their insertion into the base of the proximal phalanx and into the extensor expansion of the dorsum of toes. Study the muscles of second layer comprising the long flexor tendons and associated muscles.

Cut through both the long flexor tendon and flexor digitorum accessorius where all the three are united to each other. Reflect the ends proximally and distally to reveal the muscles of third layer of sole.

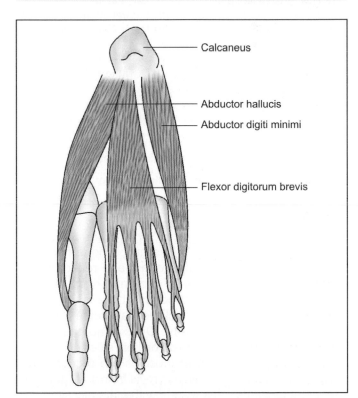

Calcaneus

Abductor hallucis
Abductor digiti minimi

Flexor digitorum brevis

Fig. 10.5: Muscles of the first layer of the sole.

and the flexor digitorum accessorius and lumbrical muscles. The muscles are described in Tables 10.3 and 10.4.

MUSCLES OF THE THIRD LAYER OF THE SOLE

The third layer of the sole contains three muscles. These are the flexor hallucis brevis, the flexor digiti minimi brevis, and the adductor hallucis. They are described in Tables 10.5 and 10.6.

Table 10.1: Muscles of the first layer of the sole

Muscles	Origin from	Insertion
1. **Flexor digitorum brevis** This muscle lies deep to the plantar aponeurosis (Fig. 10.5)	(a) Medial tubercle of calcaneum (b) Plantar aponeurosis (c) Medial and lateral intermuscular septa	The muscle ends in four tendons for the lateral four toes. Opposite the base of the proximal phalanx each tendon divides into two slips. The tendon of the flexor digitorum longus (for that digit) passes through the gap between the two slips. The two slips unite and partially decussate to form a grooved surface for the long flexor tendon. Finally the tendon again divides into two parts that are inserted into the margins of the middle phalanx. Note that the insertion is similar to that of the flexor digitorum superficialis of the hand
2. **Abductor hallucis** This muscle lies along the medial border of foot, and covers the origin of the plantar vessels and nerves	(a) Medial tubercle of calcaneum (b) Flexor retinaculum (c) Deep fascia covering it (d) Medial intermuscular septum	The tendon fuses with the medial portion of the tendon of the flexor hallucis brevis. It is inserted into the medial side of the base of the proximal phalanx of the great toe
3. **Abductor digiti minimi** This muscle lies along the lateral border of foot	(a) Medial and lateral tubercles of calcaneum (b) Lateral intermuscular septum (c) Deep fascia covering it	The tendon fuses with the tendon of the flexor digiti minimi brevis. It is inserted into the lateral side of the base of the proximal phalanx of the little toe

Table 10.2: Muscles of the first layer of the sole

Muscles	Nerve supply	Actions
1. **Flexor digitorum brevis**	Medial plantar nerve	Flexion of the toes at the proximal interphalangeal joints and metatarsophalangeal joints
2. **Abductor hallucis**	Medial plantar nerve	Abduction of the great toe away from the second toe
3. **Abductor digiti minimi**	Main trunk of lateral plantar nerve	Abduction of the little toe

DISSECTION

Separate flexor hallucis brevis and oblique head of adductor hallucis from their origin and reflect them distally. Preserve the plantar arch and deep plantar nerve. Look for sesamoid bones at the insertion of flexor hallucis brevis. Reflect the transverse head of adductor hallucis medially. On cutting the deep transverse metatarsal ligament on both sides of second toe, tendons of interossei muscles are recognised. Detach the flexor digiti minimi brevis from its origin and reflect it forwards. This will show the laterally situated interossei muscles. Identify and examine the attachment of tendon of tibialis posterior on the medial side of foot. Trace the course of tendon of peroneus longus through the groove in the cuboid bone.

MUSCLES OF THE FOURTH LAYER OF THE SOLE

The structures present in the fourth layer of the sole are the interosseous muscles, and the tendons of the tibialis posterior (Fig. 9.7) and of the peroneus longus (Fig. 8.20).

Interosseous Muscles of the Foot

These are small muscles placed between the metatarsal bones. There are three plantar and four dorsal interossei (Figs 10.8 to 10.10). Each plantar interosseous muscle arises from the plantar surface of the shaft of one metatarsal bone. It is inserted into the base of the proximal phalanx, and into the dorsal digital expansion of the corresponding digit. Each dorsal interosseous muscle arises from the shafts of two adjoining metatarsal bones. They are inserted into the bases of the proximal phalanges, and into the dorsal digital expansions. Details of the attachments of individual interosseous muscles are easily remembered if their actions are understood (Tables 10.7 and 10.8).

The interossei adduct or abduct the toes with reference to an axis passing through the *second digit*. The plantar interossei are *adductors* of the third, fourth and fifth toes. The dorsal interossei are *abductors*. The first dorsal interosseous muscle is inserted into the medial side of the proximal phalanx of the second digit; and the second muscle into the lateral side of the proximal phalanx of the second digit.

Table 10.3: Muscles and tendons of the second layer of the sole

Muscles	Origin from	Insertion
1. **Flexor digitorum longus** (Fig. 10.6)	From upper two-thirds of the medial part of the posterior surface of tibia below the soleal line	The muscle divides into four tendons. Each is inserted to the plantar surface of distal phalanx of second to fifth digit
2. **Flexor digitorum accessorius** It is so called because it is accessory to the flexor digitorum longus	It arises by two heads (a) *Medial head* is large and fleshy; it arises from the medial concave surface of the calcaneum and from its medial tubercle (b) Lateral head is smaller and tendinous; it arises from the calcaneum in front of the lateral tubercle, and from the long plantar ligament The two heads unite at an acute angle	The muscle fibres are inserted into the lateral side of the tendon of the flexor digitorum longus
3. **Lumbricals** There are four of them, numbered from medial to lateral side	They arise from the tendons of the flexor digitorum longus. The first lumbrical is unipennate, and the others are bipennate First lumbrical arises from medial side of 1st tendon of flexor digitorum longus Second lumbrical arises from adjacent sides of 1st and 2nd tendons of flexor digitorum longus Third lumbrical arises from adjacent sides of 2nd and 3rd tendons of flexor digitorum longus Fourth lumbrical arises from adjacent sides of 3rd and 4th tendons of flexor digitorum longus	Their tendons pass forwards on the medial sides of the metatarsophalangeal joints of the lateral four toes, and then dorsally for insertion into the extensor expansion
4. **Flexor hallucis longus**	Lower three-fourths of the posterior surface of fibula except lowest 2.5 cm and adjoining interosseous membrane	Plantar surface of the base of the distal phalanx of the great toe

Table 10.4: Muscles and tendons of the second layer of the sole

Muscles	Nerve supply	Actions
1. **Flexor digitorum longus** (Fig. 10.6)	Tibial nerve	Plantar flexion of lateral four toes Plantar flexion of ankle Maintains medial longitudinal arch
2. **Flexor digitorum accessorius**	Main trunk of lateral plantar nerve	1. Straightens the pull of the long flexor tendons 2. Flexes the toes through the long tendons
3. **Lumbricals**	The first muscle by the medial plantar nerve; and the other three by the deep branch of lateral plantar nerve	They maintain extension of the digits at the interphalangeal joints so that in walking and running the toes do not buckle under
4. **Flexor hallucis longus**	Tibial nerve	Plantar flexor of the big toe, plantar flexor of ankle joint, maintains medial longitudinal arch

Table 10.5: Muscles of the third layer of the sole

Muscles	Origin from	Insertion
1. **Flexor hallucis brevis** It covers the plantar surface of the first metatarsal bone (Fig. 10.7)	It arises by a Y-shaped tendon: (a) The *lateral limb,* from the medial part of the plantar surface of the cuboid bone, behind the groove for the peroneus longus and from the adjacent side of the lateral cuneiform bone (b) The *medial limb* is a direct continuation of the tendon of tibialis posterior into the foot	The muscle splits into medial and lateral parts, each of which ends in a tendon. Each tendon is inserted into the corresponding side of the base of the proximal phalanx of the great toe
2. **Adductor hallucis**	It arises by two heads: (a) The *oblique head* is large, and arises from the bases of the second, third, and fourth metatarsals, from the sheath of the tendon of the peroneus longus (b) The *transverse head* is small, and arises from the deep metatarsal ligament, and the plantar ligaments of the metatarsophalangeal joints of the third, fourth and fifth toes (transverse head has no bony origin)	On the lateral side of the base of the proximal phalanx of the big toe, in common with the lateral tendon of the flexor hallucis brevis
3. **Flexor digiti minimi brevis:** It lies along the fifth metatarsal bone	(a) Base of the fifth metatarsal bone (b) Sheath of the tendon of the peroneus longus	Into the lateral side of the base of the proximal phalanx of the little toe

Table 10.6: Muscles of the third layer of the sole

Muscles	Nerve supply	Actions
1. **Flexor hallucis brevis**	Medial plantar nerve	Flexes the proximal phalanx at the metatarsophalangeal joint of the great toe
2. **Adductor hallucis**	Deep branch of lateral plantar nerve, which terminates in this muscle	1. Adductor of great toe towards the second toe 2. Maintains transverse arches of the foot
3. **Flexor digiti minimi brevis**	Superficial branch of lateral plantar nerve	Flexes the proximal phalanx at the metatarsophalangeal joint of the little toe

PLANTAR VESSELS AND NERVES

1. The chief arteries of the sole are the medial and lateral plantar arteries. They are terminal branches of the posterior tibial artery (Fig. 6.5).

2. The chief nerves of the sole are the medial and lateral plantar nerves. They are terminal branches of the tibial nerve.

3. These arteries and nerves begin deep to the flexor retinaculum. The posterior tibial artery divides into the medial and lateral plantar arteries a little higher than the division of tibial nerve. As a result the arteries are closer to the margins of the sole than the corresponding nerves.

4. The medial plantar vessels and nerve lie between the abductor hallucis and the flexor digitorum brevis (Fig. 10.11).

5. The lateral plantar vessels and nerve run obliquely towards the base of the 5th metatarsal bone, between the first and second layers of the sole. Here the artery turns medially

DISSECTION

Dissect the medial plantar nerve and vessels on the medial side of sole. Lateral plantar nerve and vessels also enter the sole from the medial side. These cross the sole to reach the lateral side. Here lateral plantar artery forms a plantar arch across the sole which gives numerous branches. The lateral plantar nerve divides into a superficial and deep branch. The latter runs in the concavity of the plantar arch. The course branches of nerves and vessels are given in the text.

Table 10.7: Muscles of the fourth layer of the sole

Muscles	Origin from	Insertion
1. **Dorsal interossei** (Fig. 10.8) (four bellies), bipennate, muscle bellies, fills up gaps between metatarsals	Adjacent sides of metatarsal bones	Bases of proximal phalanges and dorsal digital expansion of toes; first on medial side of 2nd toe; second on lateral side of 2nd toe; third on lateral side of 3rd toe and fourth on lateral side of 4th toe
2. **Plantar interossei** (three bellies), unipennate, slender muscle bellies. Tendons pass on medial sides of third, fourth and fifth toes (Fig. 10.9)	Bases and medial sides of third, fourth and fifth metatarsals	Medial sides of bases of proximal phalanges and dorsal digital expansions of 3rd, 4th and 5th toes
3. **Tibialis posterior**	Posterior surfaces of leg bones	Tuberosity of navicular (Table 9.3)
4. **Peroneus longus**	Upper part of lateral surface of fibula	Base of 1st metatarsal (Table 8.3)

Table 10.8: Muscles of the fourth layer of the sole

Muscles	Nerve supply	Actions
1. **Dorsal interossei** (Fig. 10.8)	First, second, third by lateral plantar (deep branch), fourth dorsal interosseous by superficial branch of lateral plantar	Abductors of toes from axis of second toe. First and second cause medial and lateral abduction of second toe. Third and fourth for abduction of 3rd and 4th toes
2. **Plantar interossei** (Fig. 10.9)	First and second by lateral plantar (deep branch). Third by lateral plantar (superficial branch)	Adductors of third, fourth and fifth toes toward the axis. Flexor of metatarsophalangeal and extensor of interphalangeal joints of third, fourth and fifth toes
3. **Tibialis posterior**	Tibial nerve	Plantar flexor of ankle (Table 9.4)
4. **Peroneus longus**	Superficial peroneal nerve	Evertor of foot (Table 9.4)

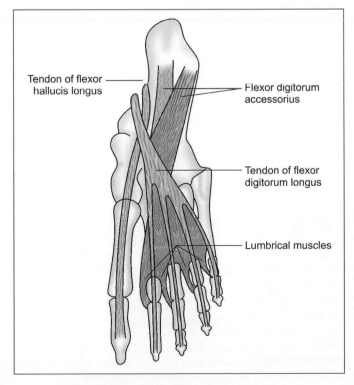

Fig. 10.6: The second layer of the sole.

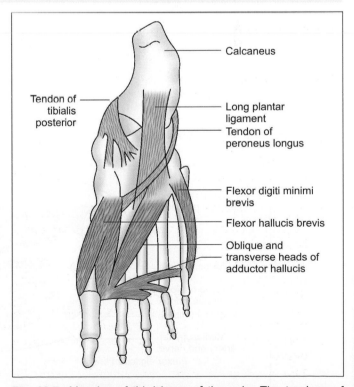

Fig. 10.7: Muscles of third layer of the sole. The tendons of tibialis posterior and peroneus longus belong to the fourth layer.

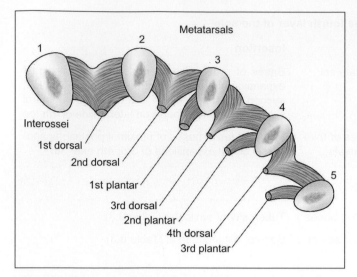

Fig. 10.8: Schematic transverse section through the metatarsal bones to show the origins of the interossei.

and becomes continuous with the plantar arch. This arch lies between the third and fourth layers of the sole (Fig. 10.11). The plantar arch is accompanied by the deep branch of the lateral plantar nerve.

Medial Plantar Nerve

Origin and Course

Medial plantar nerve is the larger terminal branch of the tibial nerve. It passes forwards between abductor hallucis and flexer digitorum brevis and divides into its branches. In its distribution, it resembles the median nerve of the hand (Fig. 10.12).

Branches

Its *muscular branches* supply four muscles as follows.

1. The abductor hallucis.

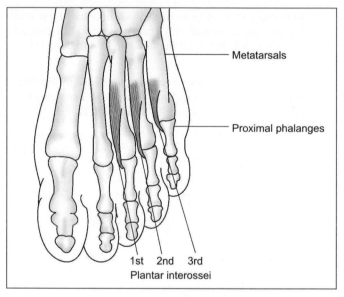

Fig. 10.9: The plantar interossei.

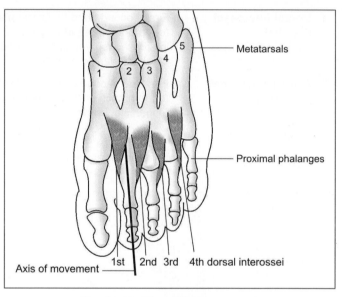

Fig. 10.10: The dorsal interossei.

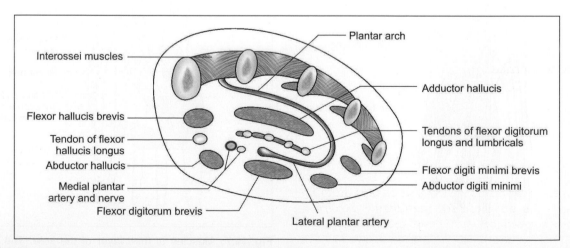

Fig. 10.11: Transverse section of the foot through the metatarsals showing the arrangement of structures in the sole.

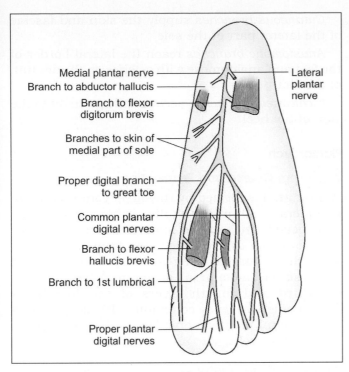

Fig. 10.12: Scheme to show the distribution of the medial plantar nerve.

2. The flexor digitorum brevis receive branches from the main trunk of the nerve, near its origin.
3. The flexor hallucis brevis receives a branch from the first digital nerve.
4. The first lumbrical muscle receives a branch from the second digital nerve.

Cutaneous branches supply the skin of the medial part of the sole, and of the medial three and a half toes through four digital branches. The first digital nerve supplies the medial side of the great toe; the second nerve supplies the adjacent sides of the first and second toes; the third nerve supplies the adjacent sides of the second and third toes; and the fourth nerve supplies the adjacent sides of the third and fourth toes. Each digital nerve gives off a dorsal branch which supplies structures around the nail of the digit concerned.

Articular branches supply joints of the tarsus and metatarsus.

Lateral Plantar Nerve

Origin

Lateral plantar nerve (Fig. 10.13) is the smaller terminal branch of the tibial nerve. It passes laterally and forwards till base of fifth metatarsal, where it divides into superficial and deep branches. In its distribution, it resembles the ulnar nerve in the hand.

Branches

The *main trunk* supplies two muscles, the flexor digitorum accessorius and the abductor digiti minimi, and the skin of the sole. The main trunk ends by dividing into superficial and deep branches (Fig. 10.14).

The *superficial branch* divides into two branches, lateral and medial. The *lateral* branch supplies three muscles—flexor digiti minimi brevis, the third plantar and fourth dorsal interossei, and the skin on the lateral side of the little toe. The *medial* branch

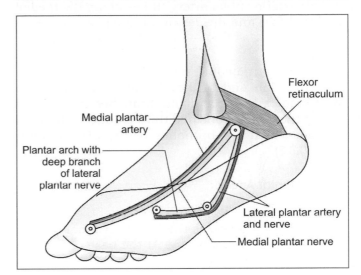

Fig. 10.13: Position of medial and lateral plantar nerves and vessels, including the plantar arch.

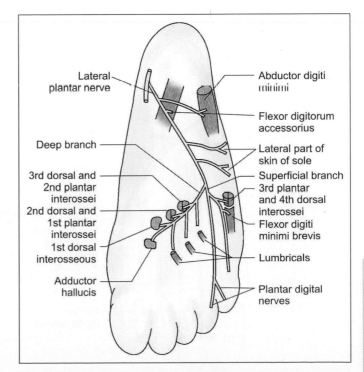

Fig. 10.14: Scheme to show the distribution of the lateral plantar nerve.

communicates with the medial plantar nerve, and supplies the skin lining the fourth interdigital cleft.

The *deep branch* supplies nine muscles, including the second, third and fourth lumbricals; first, second and third dorsal interossei; first and second plantar interossei and adductor hallucis.

Medial Plantar Artery

Beginning, Course and Termination

Medial plantar artery is a smaller terminal branch of the posterior tibial artery. It lies along the medial border of foot and divides into branches.

Branches

It gives off cutaneous, muscular branches to the overlying skin and to the adjoining muscles, and three small superficial digital branches that end by joining the first, second and third plantar metatarsal arteries which are branches of the plantar arch (Fig. 10.15).

Lateral Plantar Artery

Beginning, Course and Termination

Lateral plantar artery is the larger terminal branch of the posterior tibial artery. At the base of the fifth metatarsal bone it gives a superficial branch and then continues as the plantar arch (Fig. 10.13).

Branches

Muscular branches supply the adjoining muscles.

Cutaneous branches supply the skin and fasciae of the lateral part of the sole.

Anastomotic branches reach the lateral border of the foot and anastomose with arteries on the dorsum of the foot.

A *calcanean branch* is occasionally given off to the skin of the heel.

Plantar Arch

Beginning, Course and Termination

Plantar arch is formed by the direct continuation of the lateral plantar artery after it has given off the superficial branch and is completed medially by the dorsalis pedis artery. It extends from the base of the fifth metatarsal bone to the proximal part of the first intermetatarsal space, and lies between the third and fourth layers of the sole. It is accompanied by venae comitantes. The deep branch of the lateral plantar nerve lies in the concavity of the plantar arch.

Branches of the Plantar Arch

(i) Four *plantar metatarsal* arteries run distally, one in each intermetatarsal space. Each artery ends by dividing into two *plantar digital* branches for adjacent sides of two digits. The first artery also gives off a branch to the medial side of the great toe. The lateral side of the little toe gets a direct branch from the lateral plantar artery.

(ii) The plantar arch gives off three *proximal perforating arteries* that pass through the second, third and fourth intermetatarsal spaces and communicate with the dorsal metatarsal arteries which are the branches of the arcuate artery.

The distal end of each plantar metatarsal artery gives off a *distal perforating artery* which joins the distal part of the corresponding dorsal metatarsal artery (Fig. 10.16).

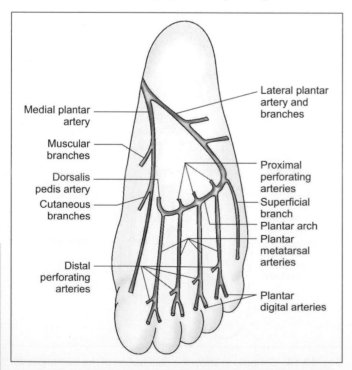

Fig. 10.15: Medial and lateral plantar arteries and their branches.

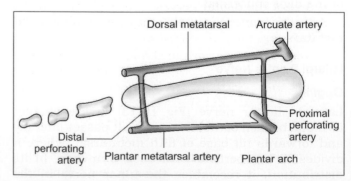

Fig. 10.16: The proximal and distal perforating arteries.

CLINICAL ANATOMY

- A neuroma may be formed on the branch of medial plantar nerve between 3rd and 4th metatarsal bones. It is called Morton's neuroma (Fig. 10.17). This causes pain between third and fourth metatarsals. It may be also due to pressure on digital nerve between 3rd and 4th metatarsals.

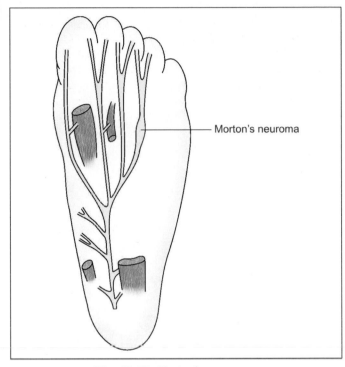

Fig. 10.17: Morton's neuroma.

- Fracture of shaft of 2nd/3rd/4th/metatarsal bones is called "march fracture". It is seen in army personnel, policemen as they have to march a lot.
- Plantar fasciaitis occurs in policemen due to stretching of the plantar aponeurosis. This results in pain in the heel region, especially during standing.
- Any of the digital nerves, especially the one in the third interdigital cleft may develop neuroma. This is a painful condition (Fig. 10.17).
- Normal architecture of the foot is subjected to insults due to "high heels". Females apparently look taller, smarter, but may suffer from sprains of the ankle joint (Fig. 9.14).
- Toes may be spread out or splayed.
- Longitudinal arches are exaggerated leading to pes cavus.
- If foot is dorsiflexed, person walks on the heel condition is called "pes calcaneus" (Fig. 10.18).

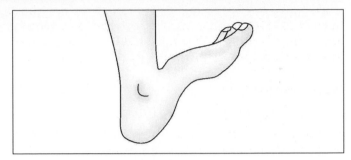

Fig. 10.18: Pes calcaneus.

- If foot is plantar flexed, person walks on toes. The condition is called "pes equinus" (Fig. 10.19).

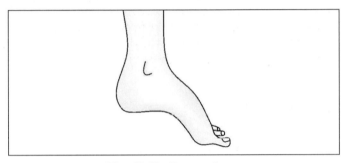

Fig. 10.19: Pes equinus.

- If medial border of foot is raised, person walks on lateral border of foot. The condition is "pes varus" (Fig. 10.20).

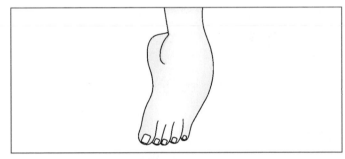

Fig. 10.20: Pes varus.

- If lateral border of foot is raised, person walks on medial border of foot. The condition is called "pes valgus" (Fig. 10.21).

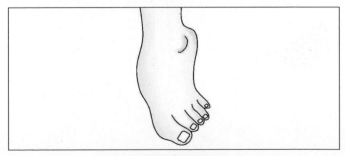

Fig. 10.21: Pes valgus.

Venous and Lymphatic Drainage; Comparison of Lower and Upper Limbs

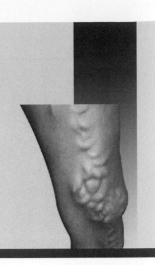

The saphenous veins can be "easily seen" in the leg. The varicose veins, if occur, look quite ugly under the skin. Effort should be made not to develop the varicose veins. Venous drainage acquires importance as blood has to flow up against the gravity. The lymph travels mostly to the inguinal group of lymph nodes. The sensory nerves are derived only from ventral rami of L1 to L5 and S1 to S3 segments of spinal cord.

Lower limb bud rotates medially, so that extensor compartment lies on front, while flexor compartment is present on the back of thigh. Tibia and big toe lie along the pre-axial border while fibula and little toe are along the post-axial border of the limb.

VENOUS DRAINAGE

Consideration of the venous drainage is of great importance because in the lower limb venous blood has to ascend against gravity. This is aided by a number of local factors, the failure of which gives rise to varicose veins.

Factors Helping Venous Return

General Factors

1. Negative intrathoracic pressure, which is made more negative during inspiration;
2. Arterial pressure and overflow from the capillary bed;
3. Compression of veins accompanying arteries by arterial pulsation; and
4. The presence of valves, which support the long column of blood, and maintain a unidirectional flow.

Local Factors

These are venous, muscular and fascial.
1. *Venous:* The veins of the lower limb are more muscular than the veins of any other part of the body. They have greater number of valves.

Superficial veins are connected to deep veins by perforators.
2. *Muscular:* When the limb is active, muscular contraction compresses the deep veins and drives the blood in them upwards.
3. *Fascial:* The tight sleeve of deep fascia makes muscular compression of the veins much more effective by limiting outward bulging of the muscles.

VEINS OF LOWER LIMB (Fig. 11.1)

The veins may be classified into three groups: superficial, deep and perforating.

Superficial Veins

They include the great and small saphenous veins, and their tributaries. They lie in the superficial fascia, on the surface of deep fascia (Figs 3.5 and 9.1). They are thick-walled because of the presence of smooth muscle and some fibrous and elastic tissues in their walls. Valves are more numerous in the distal parts of these veins than in their proximal parts. A large proportion of their blood is drained into the deep veins through the perforating veins.

Deep Veins

These are the medial plantar, lateral plantar, dorsalis pedis, anterior and posterior tibial, peroneal, popliteal, and femoral veins, and their tributaries. They accompany the arteries, and are supported by powerful surrounding muscles. The valves are more numerous in deep veins than in superficial veins. They are more efficient channels than the superficial veins because of the driving force of muscular contraction.

Perforating Veins

They connect the superficial with the deep veins. Their valves permit only one way flow of blood, from

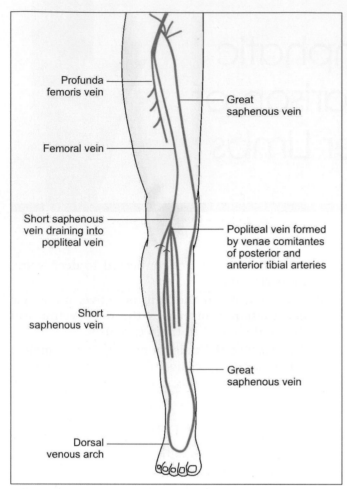

Profunda femoris vein

Great saphenous vein

Femoral vein

Short saphenous vein draining into popliteal vein

Popliteal vein formed by venae comitantes of posterior and anterior tibial arteries

Short saphenous vein

Great saphenous vein

Dorsal venous arch

Fig. 11.1: Scheme to show the arrangement of the veins of lower limb. Popliteal, short saphenous and venae comitantes of posterior tibial artery are on posterior aspect.

the superficial to the deep veins. There are about five perforators along the great saphenous vein, and one perforator along the small saphenous vein.

The relevant details of these veins are given below.

Long Saphenous Vein

It contains about 10–20 valves. There is one valve that lies just before the vein pierces the cribriform fascia and another at its termination into the femoral vein.

Tributaries

At the commencement: Medial marginal vein from the sole.

In the leg: It communicates freely with the small saphenous vein and with deep veins.

Just below the knee:

1. The anterior vein of the leg runs upwards, forwards and medially, from the lateral side of the ankle.
2. The posterior arch vein is large and constant. It begins from a series of small venous arches

which connect the medial ankle perforators, and runs upwards to join the great saphenous vein just below the knee.

3. A vein from the calf: This vein also communicates with the small saphenous vein.

In the thigh:

1. The accessory saphenous vein drains the posteromedial side of the thigh. It may communicate with the small saphenous vein.
2. The anterior cutaneous vein of the thigh drains the lower part of the front of the thigh.

Just before piercing the cribriform fascia:

1. Superficial epigastric,
2. Superficial circumflex iliac, and
3. Superficial external pudendal.

Just before termination: Deep external pudendal vein.

The *thoracoepigastric vein* runs along the anterolateral wall of the trunk. It connects the superficial epigastric vein with the lateral thoracic vein. Thus it is an important connection between the veins of the upper and lower limbs.

Small or Short Saphenous Vein

The vein is formed on the dorsum of the foot by the union of the lateral end of the dorsal venous arch with the lateral marginal vein (Fig. 9.1). It enters the back of the leg by passing behind the lateral malleolus. In the leg, it ascends lateral to the tendocalcaneus, and then along the middle line of the calf, to the lower part of the popliteal fossa. Here it pierces the deep fascia and opens into the popliteal vein. It drains the lateral border of the foot, the heel, and the back of the leg. It is connected with the great saphenous and with the deep veins, and is accompanied by the sural nerve.

Perforating Veins

As already mentioned, they connect the superficial with the deep veins (Fig. 11.2). These are classified as follows.

Indirect perforating veins

Indirect perforating veins connect the superficial veins with the deep veins through the muscular veins (Fig. 11.3).

Direct perforating veins

Direct perforating veins (Fig. 11.4) connect the superficial veins directly with the deep veins. The great and small saphenous veins are the large direct perforators. The small direct perforating veins (Fig. 11.5) are summarised below.

(a) *In the thigh:* The *adductor canal perforator* connects the great saphenous vein with the

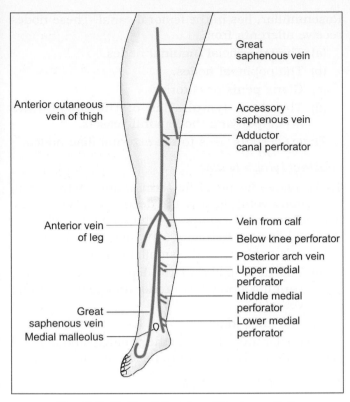

Fig. 11.2: Perforating veins of the lower limb.

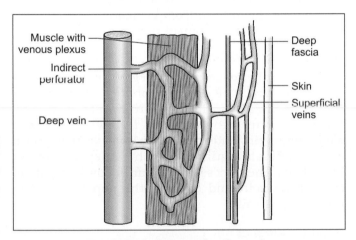

Fig. 11.3: Indirect perforating vein.

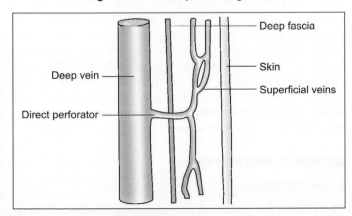

Fig. 11.4: Direct perforating vein.

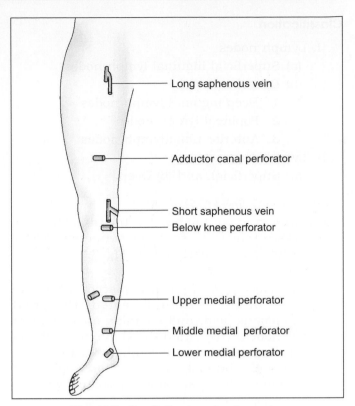

Fig. 11.5: Small direct perforating vein.

femoral vein in the lower part of the adductor canal.

(b) *Below the knee:*

One perforator connects the great saphenous vein or the posterior arch vein with the posterior tibial vein.

(c) *In the leg:*

A *lateral perforator* is present at the junction of the middle and lower thirds of the leg. It connects the small saphenous vein, or one of its tributaries with the peroneal vein.

Medially there are three perforators which connect the posterior arch vein with the posterior tibial vein.

1. The *upper medial perforator* lies at the junction of the middle and lower thirds of the leg.

2. The *middle medial perforator* lies above the medial malleolus.

3. The *lower medial perforator* lies posteroinferior to the medial malleolus.

LYMPHATIC DRAINAGE

Most of the lymph from the lower limb drains into the inguinal lymph nodes, either mostly directly or partly indirectly through the popliteal and anterior tibial nodes. The deep structures of the gluteal region and the upper part of the back of the thigh drain into the internal iliac nodes along the gluteal vessels.

Classification

I. Lymph nodes
   (a) Superficial inguinal lymph nodes.
   (b) Deep:
      1. Deep inguinal lymph nodes
      2. Popliteal lymph nodes
      3. Anterior tibial lymph nodes.
II. Lymphatics
   (a) Superficial, and (b) Deep.

Superficial Inguinal Lymph Nodes

These are very important because they drain the skin and fasciae of the lower limb; the perineum and the trunk below the umbilical plane (Fig. 3.6). They are divided into three sets.

1. The *lower vertical group* is placed along both sides of the terminal part of the great saphenous vein, and contains about four or five nodes. They drain the skin and fasciae of the lower limb (great saphenous territory), except the buttock and the short saphenous territory. A few lymphatics, accompanying the short saphenous vein, cross the leg, accompany the great saphenous vein, and drain into this group of nodes.

2. The *upper lateral group* is placed below the lateral part of the inguinal ligament, and contains about two or three nodes. They drain the skin and fasciae of the upper part of the lateral side of the thigh, the buttock, the flank and the back below the umbilical plane.

3. The *upper medial group* is placed below the medial end of the inguinal ligament. One or two nodes may lie above the inguinal ligament along the course of the superficial epigastric vessels. The group contains two to three nodes. They drain:
   (a) The anterior abdominal wall below the level of the umbilicus.
   (b) The perineum, including external genitalia, except the glans, the anal canal below the pectinate line, the vagina below hymen and the penile part of the male urethra.
   (c) The superolateral angle of the uterus, via the round ligament.

Efferents from all superficial inguinal nodes pierce the cribriform fascia, and terminate in the deep inguinal nodes. A few may pass directly to the external iliac nodes.

Deep Inguinal Lymph Nodes

These are about four to five in number, and lie medial to the upper part of the femoral vein. The most proximal node of this group; gland of Cloquet or of Rosenmüllar, lies in the femoral canal. These nodes receive afferents from:
   (a) The superficial inguinal nodes.
   (b) The popliteal nodes.
   (c) Glans penis or clitoris.
   (d) The deep lymphatics of the lower limb accompanying the femoral vessels.

Their efferents pass to the external iliac nodes.

Popliteal Lymph Nodes

These nodes lie near the termination of the small saphenous vein, deep to the deep fascia. One node lies between the popliteal artery and the oblique popliteal ligament. They receive afferents from:
   (a) The territory of the small saphenous vein.
   (b) The deep parts of the leg (through vessels running along the anterior and posterior tibial vessels).
   (c) The knee joint.

Their efferents run along the popliteal and femoral vessels, and terminate in the deep inguinal nodes.

Anterior Tibial Lymph Node

One inconstant node may lie along the upper part of the anterior tibial artery. When present, it collects lymph from the anterior compartment of the leg, and passes it on to the popliteal nodes.

Superficial Lymphatics

These lymph vessels are larger and are more numerous than the deep lymphatics. They run in the superficial fascia and ultimately form two streams. The main stream follows the great saphenous vein, and ends in the lower vertical group of superficial inguinal lymph nodes shown in Fig. 11.6a. The accessory stream follows the small saphenous vein and ends in the popliteal lymph nodes (Fig. 11.6b).

Deep Lymphatics

These are smaller and fewer than the superficial lymphatics, although they drain all structures lying deep to the deep fascia. They run along the principal blood vessels, and terminate mostly into the deep inguinal nodes, either directly or indirectly through the popliteal nodes. The deep lymphatics from the gluteal region and from the upper part of the back of the thigh accompany the gluteal vessels and end in the internal iliac nodes.

SEGMENTAL INNERVATION

1. Dermatomes

The principles involved are the same as described in the upper limb.

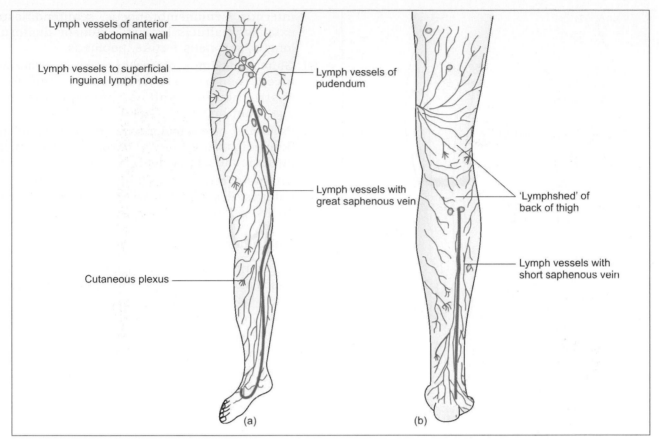

Fig. 11.6: Superficial lymphatics of the lower limb: (a) Anterior aspect, (b) posterior aspect.

The area of skin supplied by one spinal segment is called a dermatome.

Important Features

1. The cutaneous innervation of the lower limb is derived:
   (a) Mainly from segments L1 to L5 and S1 to S3 of the spinal cord; and
   (b) Partly from segments T12 and S4 (Fig. 11.7).

2. As a rule, the limb is supplied only by anterior primary rami. The exception to this rule is that the skin of the superomedial quadrant of the gluteal region is supplied by the posterior primary rami of nerves L1 to L3 and S1 to S3.

3. There is varying degree of overlap of adjoining dermatomes, so that the area of sensory loss following damage to the spinal cord or nerve roots is always less than the actual area of the dermatome.

4. Initially, each limb bud has a cephalic border, and a caudal border. These are known as the preaxial and the postaxial borders, respectively. In the embryo, the great toe and tibia lie along the preaxial border, and the little toe and fibula along the postaxial border. Later, the limb bud rotates medially through 90°, so that the great toe and tibia are carried medially, and the little toe and fibula laterally. Thus, the tibial border is the original preaxial border, and the fibular border, the postaxial border, of the lower limb.

5. The dermatomes of the lower limb are distributed in an orderly numerical sequence (Fig. 11.7).

   Along the preaxial border from above downwards, there are dermatomes T12, L1 to L4.

   The middle three toes, the adjoining area of the dorsum of the foot and the lateral side of the leg are supplied by segment L5.

   Along the postaxial border from below upwards, there are dermatomes S1, S2, S3.

6. As the limb elongates, the central dermatomes (L4, L5, S1) get pulled in such a way that these are represented only in the distal part of the limb, and are buried proximally. The line along which the central dermatomes are buried is known as the *axial line*. In fact, an axial line is defined as a line along which certain dermatomes are buried (missing) so that distant dermatomes adjoin each other. Overlapping of the dermatomes is minimal across the axial line. There are *two axial lines*, one ventral and one dorsal, both of which

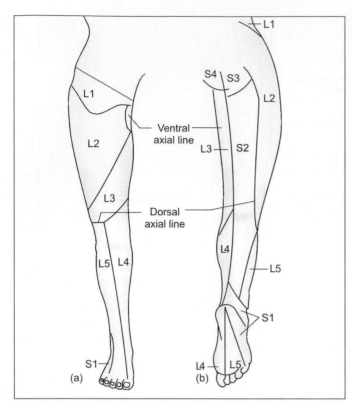

Fig. 11.7: Dermatomes of the lower limb: (a) Anterior view, (b) posterior view.

extend largely on the back of the limb. On the posterior surface of the limb, the *ventral axial line* extends up to the heel, whereas the *dorsal axial line* ends at a higher level, at the junction of the upper two-thirds and lower one-third of the leg. On the anterior surface of the limb, the ventral axial line crosses the scrotum, and the dorsal axial line encroaches on the lateral side of the knee. Some workers deny the existence of the dorsal axial line.

2. Myotomes

A spinal nerve supplies muscles that are derived from one myotome. Most of the muscles are supplied by more than one segment of the spinal cord, the supply by some segments being predominant. Damage of the predominant segments results in maximum paralysis of the muscle. The chart given below is accurate enough for use in clinical examination.

L1 Psoas major.

L2 Psoas major, iliacus, sartorius, gracilis, pectineus, adductor longus, adductor brevis.

L3 Quadriceps, adductors (longus, brevis, magnus).

L4 Quadriceps, tensor fasciae latae, adductor magnus, obturator externus, tibialis anterior, tibialis posterior.

L5 Gluteus medius, gluteus minimus, obturator

internus, semimembranosus, semitendinosus, extensor hallucis longus, extensor digitorum longus, peroneus tertius, popliteus.

S1 Gluteus maximus, obturator internus, piriformis, biceps femoris, semitendinosus, popliteus, gastrocnemius, soleus, peronei, extensor digitorum brevis.

S2 Piriformis, biceps femoris, gastrocnemius, soleus, flexor digitorum longus, flexor hallucis longus, intrinsic muscles of foot.

S3 Intrinsic muscles of foot (except abductor hallucis, flexor hallucis brevis, flexor digitorum brevis, extensor digitorum brevis).

Joint Movements

The segmental innervation of muscles can also be expressed in terms of movements of joints (Fig. 11.8).

Hip	Flexors, adductors and medial rotators	...L1, L2, L3
	Extensors, abductors and lateral rotators	...L5, S1
Knee	Extensors	...L3, L4
	Flexors	...L5, S1
Ankle	Dorsiflexors	...L4, L5
	Plantar flexors	...S1, S2
Foot	Invertors	...L4, L5
	Evertors	...L5, S1

SYMPATHETIC INNERVATION

1. Sympathetic innervation of the lower limb is derived from the lower three thoracic and upper two lumbar (T10 to L2) segments of the spinal cord. The fibres arise from the lateral horn cells, and pass out with the ventral roots as preganglionic (white rami) fibres. These pass down the sympathetic chain to relay in the lumbar and upper two or three sacral ganglia.

2. The postganglionic fibres emerge from the lumbar sympathetic ganglia and pass through grey rami to reach the lumbar nerves. From these nerves they pass into the femoral nerve. They supply the femoral artery and its branches in the thigh. Some postganglionic sympathetic fibres emerge from the upper two or three sacral ganglia. They travel through the tibial nerve to supply the popliteal artery and its branches in the leg and foot.

3. The blood vessels to skeletal muscles are dilated by sympathetic activity. These nerves are vasomotor, sudomotor and pilomotor to the skin.

4. Sympathetic denervation of the lower limb can be produced by removing the second, third and

fourth lumbar ganglia with the intermediate chain. This divides all preganglionic fibres to the lower limb. The first lumbar ganglion is preserved because it controls the proximal urethral sphincter mechanism. Its removal is followed by dry coitus. Bilateral lumbar sympathectomy is done in patients with Buerger's disease.

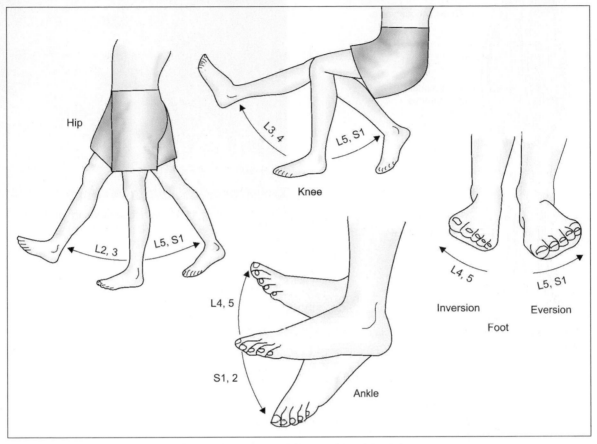

Fig. 11.8: Segmental innervation of the joints.

CLINICAL ANATOMY

- *Calf pump* and *peripheral heart*. In the upright position of the body, the venous return from the lower limb depends largely on the contraction of calf muscles. These muscles are, therefore, known as the "calf pump".

  For the same reason the soleus is called the *peripheral heart* (Fig. 9.8). When this muscle contracts, blood contained in large sinuses within it is pumped into the deep veins; and when the muscle relaxes, blood flows into the sinuses from the superficial veins. Unidirectional blood flow is maintained by the valves in the perforating veins (Fig. 11.9).

- "Cut open procedure" is done on the great saphenous vein as it lies in front of medial malleolus. This vein is used for transfusion of blood/fluids in case of non-availability or collapse of other veins. Saphenous nerve is identified and not injured as it lies anterior to the great saphenous vein (Fig. 11.10).

- Great saphenous vein is used for bypassing the blocked coronary arteries. The vein is reversed so that valves do not block the passage of blood.

- *Varicose veins and ulcers:* If the valves in perforating veins or at the termination of superficial veins become incompetent, the defective veins become "high pressure leaks" through which the high pressure of the deep veins produced by muscular contraction is transmitted to the superficial veins. This results in dilatation of the superficial veins and to gradual degeneration of their walls producing varicose veins and varicose ulcers (Figs 11.11 and 11.12).

- Varicose veins often occur during third trimester of pregnancy, as the iliac vein get pressed due to enlarged uterus. These mostly subside after delivery.

- *Trendelenburg's test:* This is done to find out the site of leak or defect in a patient with

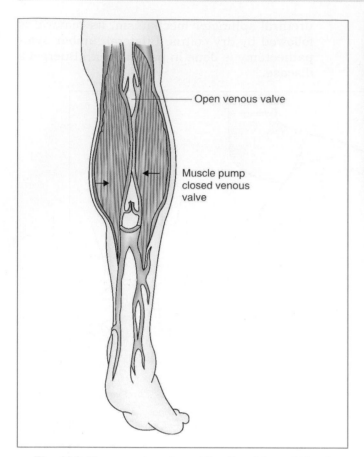

Fig. 11.9: Venous valves for unidirectional flow of blood.

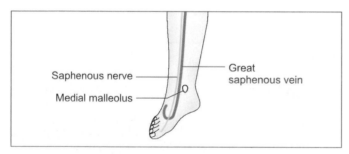

Fig. 11.10: Cut open procedure on great saphenous vein.

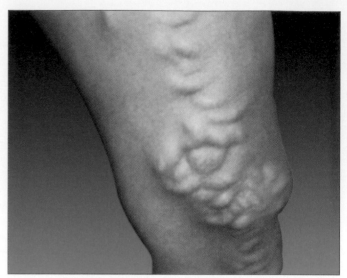

Fig. 11.11: Varicose veins in the thigh.

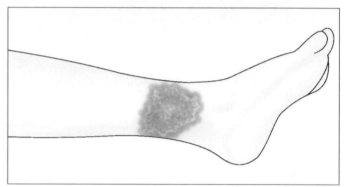

Fig. 11.12: Varicose ulcer.

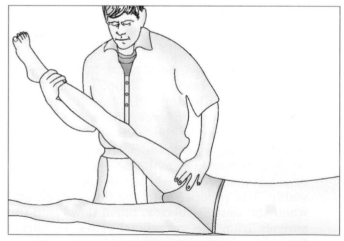

Fig. 11.13: Vein being emptied by raising the right leg.

varicose veins. Only the superficial veins and the perforating veins can be tested, not the deep veins.

The patient is made to lie down, and the veins are emptied by raising the limb and stroking the varicose veins in a proximal direction (Fig. 11.13). Now pressure is applied with the thumb at the saphenofemoral junction, and the patient is asked to stand up quickly. To test the superficial veins, the pressure is released. Quick filling of the varicose veins from above indicates incompetency of the superficial veins (Fig. 11.14).

To test the perforating veins, the pressure at the saphenofemoral junction is not released, but maintained for about a minute. Gradual filling of the varices indicates incompetency of the perforating veins, allowing the blood to pass from deep to superficial veins (Fig. 11.15).

- *Perthe's test:* This is employed to test the deep veins. A tourniquet is tied round the upper part

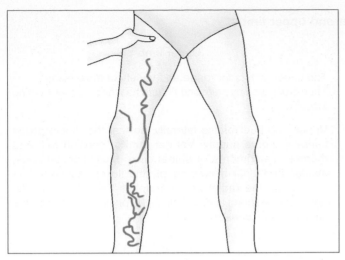

Fig. 11.14: Testing of the superficial veins.

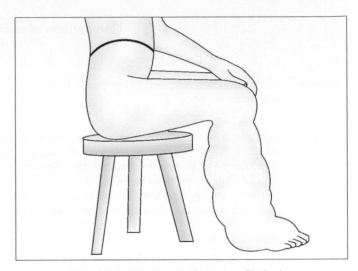

Fig. 11.16: Elephantiasis due to filariasis.

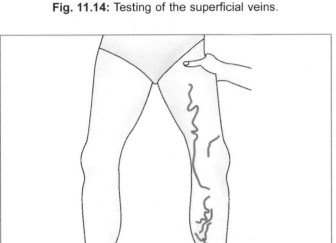

Fig. 11.15: Incompetency of the perforating veins.

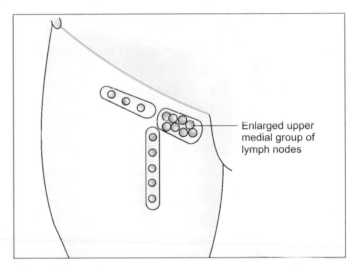

Enlarged upper medial group of lymph nodes

Fig. 11.17: Lymphadenitis due to infection in the perineum.

of thigh, tight enough to prevent any reflux down the vein. The patient is asked to walk quickly for a while, with the tourniquet in place. If the perforating and deep veins are normal, the varicose veins shrink, whereas if they are blocked, the varicose veins become more distended.

- *Elephantiasis:* Lymphatic obstruction caused by the parasite filaria is very common in the lower limb. This results in great hypertrophy of the skin and of subcutaneous tissue (elephantiasis) (Fig. 11.16).
- The commonest cause of a swelling in the inguinal area is enlargement of the inguinal lymph nodes. This can be caused by infection, or carcinoma, anywhere in the area drained by these nodes (Fig. 11.17).
- Like dermatomes, the myotomes are also helpful in determination of the level of a lesion in the spinal cord (Fig. 11.8).

- After a deep vein thrombosis affecting the perforators, they recanalise without valves. So the muscle pump will force blood from deep to superficial veins, causing varicosity of the veins.
- Varicose veins are treated with sclerosing injections or laser treatment.
- Comparison between long saphenous and short saphenous veins is as follows.

	Long saphenous vein	Short saphenous vein
Beginning	Medial end of dorsal venous plexus	Lateral end of dorsal venous plexus
Position	Anterior to medial malleolus	Posterior to lateral malleolus
Number of valves	15–20 valves	8–10 valves
Relation of a sensory nerve	Saphenous nerve	Sural nerve
Termination	Femoral vein	Popliteal vein

Comparison of lower and upper limbs	
Lower limb	**Upper limb**
General Lower limb with long and heavy bones supports and stabilises the body	The upper limb is for range and variety of movements. Thumb assisted by palm and fingers has the power of holding articles
Lower limb bud rotates medially, so that big toe points medially. Nerve supply: Ventral rami of lumbar 2–5 and sacral 1–3 segments of spinal cord. Sciatic and one of its terminal branch the tibial nerve supplies the flexor aspect of the limb. The other terminal branch of sciatic nerve, i.e. common peroneal, supplies the extensors of ankle joint (dorsiflexors) through its deep peroneal branch. Its superficial branch supplies the peroneal muscles of the leg. Femoral supplies the quadriceps femoris (extensor of knee) while obturator nerve supplies the adductors	Upper limb bud rotates laterally, so that the thumb points laterally. Nerve supply: Ventral rami of cervical 5–8 and thoracic 1 segments of spinal cord. Musculocutaneous, median and ulnar nerves supply the flexor aspects of the limb, while the radial nerve supplies the triceps brachii (extensor of elbow) and its branch the posterior interosseous supplies the extensors of wrist
Thigh	**Arm**
Bones Femur is the longest bone of lower limb and of the body	Humerus is the longest bone of upper limb
Joints Hip joint is a multiaxial joint	Shoulder joint is also multiaxial joint
Muscles Posteriorly: Hamstrings supplied by sciatic Anteriorly: Quadriceps by femoral Medially: Adductors by obturator nerve	Anteriorly: Biceps, brachialis and coracobrachialis supplied by musculocutaneous nerve Posteriorly: Triceps brachii supplied by radial nerve
Nerves Sciatic for posterior compartment of thigh, femoral for anterior compartment of thigh, obturator for adductor muscles of medial compartment of thigh	Musculocutaneous for anterior compartment of arm Radial for posterior compartment. Coracobrachialis equivalent to medial compartment of arm also supplied by musculocutaneous nerve
Branches Muscular, cutaneous, articular/genicular, vascular and terminal branches	Muscular, cutaneous, articular/genicular, vascular and terminal branches
Arteries Femoral, popliteal and profunda femoris (deep)	Axillary, brachial, profunda (deep) brachii
Leg	**Forearm**
Bones Tibia: Preaxial bone Fibula: Postaxial bone	Radius: Preaxial bone Ulna: Postaxial bone
Joints Knee joint formed by femur, tibia and patella. Fibula does not participate in knee joint. An additional bone (sesamoid) patella makes its appearance. This is an important weight-bearing joint	Elbow joint formed by humerus, radius and ulna, communicates with superior radioulnar joint. Forearm is characterised by superior and inferior radioulnar joints. These are both pivot variety of synovial joints permitting rotatory movements of pronation and supination, e.g. meant for picking up food and putting it in the mouth
Muscles Plantaris Flexor digitorum longus Flexor hallucis longus Soleus and flexor digitorum brevis Gastrocnemius (medial head) Gastrocnemius (lateral head) Tibialis anterior Extensor digitorum longus Extensor hallucis longus	Palmaris longus Flexor digitorum profundus Flexor pollicis longus Flexor digitorum superficialis Flexor carpi ulnaris Flexor carpi radialis Abductor pollicis longus Extensor digitorum Extensor pollicis longus

	Lower limb	Upper limb
General	Anterior aspect: Dorsiflexors of ankle joint Posterior aspect: Plantar flexors (flexors) of ankle joint Lateral aspect: Evertors of subtalar joint	Anterior aspect: Flexors of wrist and pronators of forearm Posterior aspect: Extensors of wrist, and supinator
Nerves	Tibial nerve for all the plantar flexors of the ankle joint. Common peroneal winds around neck of fibula (postaxial bone) and divides into superficial and deep branches. The deep peroneal supplies dorsiflexors (extensors) of the ankle joint. The superficial peroneal nerve supplies a separate lateral compartment of leg	Median nerve for 6½ muscles and ulnar nerve for 1½ muscles of anterior aspect of forearm. These are flexors of wrist and pronators of forearm. Posterior interosseous nerve or deep branch of radial supplies the extensors of the wrist and the supinator muscle of forearm. It winds around radius (preaxial bone) and corresponds to deep peroneal nerve. The superficial branch of radial nerve corresponds to the superficial peroneal nerve
Arteries	Popliteal divides into anterior tibial and posterior tibial in the popliteal fossa. Posterior tibial corresponds to ulnar artery	Brachial divides into radial and ulnar branches in the cubital fossa. Radial corresponds to anterior tibial artery

	Foot	Hand
Bones and joints	7 big tarsal bones occupying half of the foot. There are special joints between talus, calcaneus and navicular, i.e. subtalar and talocalcaneonavicular joints. They permit the movements of inversion and and eversion (raising the medial border/lateral border of the foot) for walking on the uneven surfaces. This movement of inversion is similar to supination and of eversion to pronation of forearm. Flexor digitorum accessorius is a distinct muscle to straighten the action of flexor digitorum longus tendons in line with the toes on which these act. Tibialis anterior and tibialis posterior and peroneus longus reach the foot and sole for the movements of inversion (first two) and eversion (last one) respectively	There are 8 small carpal bones occupying very small area of the hand. First carpometacarpal joint, i.e. joint between trapezium and base of 1st metacarpal is a unique joint. It is of saddle variety and permits a versatile movement of opposition in addition to other movements. This permits the hand to hold things, e.g. doll, pencil, food, bat, etc. Opponens pollicis is specially for opposition
Nerves	Medial plantar supplies four muscles of the sole including 1st lumbrical (abductor hallucis, flexor hallucis brevis, flexor digitorum brevis, 1st lumbrical) Lateral plantar corresponds to ulnar nerve and supplies 14 intrinsic muscles of the sole	Median nerve supplies 5 muscles of hand including 1st and 2nd lumbricals (abductor pollicis brevis, flexor pollicis brevis, opponens pollicis, 1st and 2nd lumbricals) Ulnar nerve corresponds to lateral plantar nerve and supplies 15 intrinsic muscles of the hand
Muscles	Muscles which enter the sole from the leg, e.g. flexor digitorum longus, flexor hallucis longus, tibialis posterior, peroneus longus are supplied by the nerves of the leg. 1st lumbrical is unipennate and is supplied by medial plantar, 2nd–4th are bipennate being supplied by deep branch of lateral plantar nerve Extensor digitorum brevis present on dorsum of foot	Muscles which enter the palm from forearm, e.g. flexor digitorum superficialis, flexor digitorum profundus, flexor pollicis longus are supplied by the nerves of the forearm. 1st and 2nd lumbricals are unipennate and are supplied by median nerve. 3rd and 4th are bipennate being supplied by deep branch of ulnar nerve No muscle on dorsum of hand
Blood vessels	Posterior tibial artery divides into medial plantar and lateral plantar branches. There is only one arch, the plantar arch formed by lateral plantar and dorsalis pedis (continuation of anterior tibial) arteries The great sphenous vein with perforators lies along the preaxial border. The short saphenous vein, lies along the postaxial border but it terminates in the popliteal fossa	Radial artery corresponds to anterior tibial while ulnar artery corresponds to posterior tibial artery. Ulnar artery divides into superficial and deep branches. There are two palmar arches, superficial and deep. The superficial arch mainly is formed by ulnar artery and deep arch is formed mainly by the radial artery. Cephalic vein is along the preaxial border. Basilic vein runs along the postaxial border of the limb and terminates in the middle of the arm
Axis	The axis of movement of adduction and abduction passes through the 2nd digit. So 2nd toe possesses two dorsal interossei muscles	The axis of movement of adduction and abduction is through the third digit or middle finger. So the middle finger has two dorsal interossei muscles

	Sole	Palm
I Layer	Abductor hallucis brevis Flexor digitorum brevis Abductor digiti minimi	Abductor pollicis brevis Flexor pollicis brevis Flexor digiti minimi Abductor digiti minimi
Between I & II layers	Superficial plantar arch is not present Branches of medial plantar nerve and artery Branches of superficial branch of lateral plantar nerve	Superficial palmar arch Branches of median nerve Branches of superficial branch of ulnar nerve
II Layer	— Tendon of flexor digitorum longus, lumbricals and flexor digitorum accessories Tendon of flexor hallucis longus	Tendons of flexor digitorum superficialis Tendons of flexor digitorum profundus and lumbricals Tendon of flexor pollicis longus
III Layer	Flexor hallucis brevis Adductor hallucis Flexor digiti minimi brevis	Opponens pollicis Adductor pollicis Opponens digiti minimi
Between III & IV layers	Plantar arch with deep branch of lateral plantar nerve	Deep palmar arch and deep branch of ulnar nerve
IV Layer	2–4 plantar interossei 1–4 dorsal interossei Tendons of tibialis posterior and peroneus longus	1–4 palmar interossei 1–4 dorsal interossei

CHAPTER 12

Joints of Lower Limb

The weight-bearing joints of the lower limb are more stable. Hip joint allows the same movement as the mobile shoulder joint, but the range of movement is restricted.

Knee joint allows similar movements as the elbow besides the very important locking of the joint for long time standing. The leg bones do not permit the movements of supination and pronation for reasons of stability.

The ankle joint also allows limited movements for the same reason. The additional movements of inversion and eversion provided at the subtalar joints are to adjust the foot to the uneven ground.

HIP JOINT

Type

Ball and socket variety of synovial joint.

Articular Surfaces

The head of the femur articulates with the acetabulum of the hip bone to form the hip joint. The *head of the femur* forms more than half a sphere, and is covered with hyaline cartilage except at the fovea capitis. The *acetabulum* presents a horseshoe-shaped, lunate articular surface, an acetabular notch and an acetabular fossa (Fig. 12.1). The lunate surface is covered with cartilage. Though the articular surfaces on the head of the femur and on the acetabulum are reciprocally curved, they are not co-extensive.

The hip joint is unique in having a high degree of stability as well as mobility. The *stability* or *strength* depends upon:

1. Depth of the acetabulum and the narrowing of its mouth by the acetabular labrum.
2. Tension and strength of ligaments.
3. Strength of the surrounding muscles.
4. Length and obliquity of the neck of the femur.

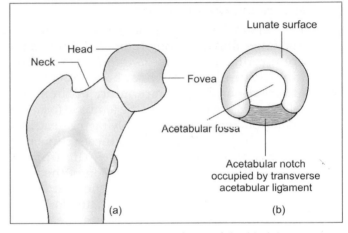

Fig. 12.1: Articular surfaces of the hip joint.

5. Atmospheric pressure: A fairly wide range of mobility is possible because of the fact that the femur has a long neck which is narrower than the equatorial diameter of the head.

Ligaments

The ligaments include:

1. The fibrous capsule,
2. The iliofemoral ligament,
3. The pubofemoral ligament,

4. The ischiofemoral ligament,
5. The ligament of the head of the femur,
6. The acetabular labrum, and
7. The transverse acetabular ligament.

1. The *fibrous capsule* is attached *on the hip bone* to the acetabular labrum including the transverse acetabular ligament, and to bone above and behind the acetabulum; and *on the femur* to the intertrochanteric line in front, and 1 cm medial to the intertrochanteric crest behind (Fig. 12.2).

Anterosuperiorly, the capsule is thick and firmly attached. This part is subjected to maximum tension in the standing posture. Posteroinferiorly, the capsule is thin and loosely attached to bone.

The capsule is made up of two types of fibres. The outer fibres are longitudinal and the inner are circular called as *zona orbicularis*. The longitudinal fibres are best developed anterosuperiorly, where many of them are reflected along the neck of the femur to form the *retinacula.* Blood vessels supplying the head and neck of the femur, travel along these retinacula. The synovial membrane lines the fibrous capsule, the intracapsular portion of the neck of the femur, both surfaces of the acetabular labrum, the transverse ligament, and fat in the acetabular fossa. It also invests the round ligament of the head of the femur (Fig. 12.2).

The joint cavity communicates with a bursa lying deep to the tendon of psoas major, through a circular opening in the capsule located between the pubofemoral ligament and vertical band of the iliofemoral ligament (Fig. 12.3).

2. The *iliofemoral ligament,* or inverted Y-shaped ligament of Bigelow, lies anteriorly. It is one of the strongest ligaments in the body. It prevents the trunk from falling backwards in the standing posture. The ligament is triangular in shape. Its apex is attached to the lower half of the anterior inferior iliac spine; and the base to the intertrochanteric line. The upper oblique and lower vertical fibres form thick and strong bands, while the middle fibres are thin and weak (Fig. 12.3).

3. The *pubofemoral ligament* supports the joint inferomedially. It is also triangular in shape. Superiorly, it is attached to the iliopubic eminence, the obturator crest and the obturator membrane. Inferiorly, it merges with the anteroinferior part of the capsule and with the lower band of the iliofemoral ligament.

4. The *ischiofemoral ligament* is comparatively weak. It covers the joint posteriorly. Its fibres are twisted and extend from the ischium to the acetabulum. The fibres of the ligament form the zona orbicularis. Some of them are attached to the greater trochanter (Fig. 12.4).

5. The *ligament of the head of the femur,* round ligament or ligamentum teres is a flat and triangular ligament. The apex is attached to the fovea capitis, and the base to the transverse ligament and the margins of the acetabular notch. It may be very thin, or even absent. It transmits arteries to the head of the femur, from the acetabular branches of the obturator and medial circumflex femoral arteries (Fig. 4.8).

6. The *acetabular labrum* is a fibrocartilaginous rim attached to the margins of the acetabulum.

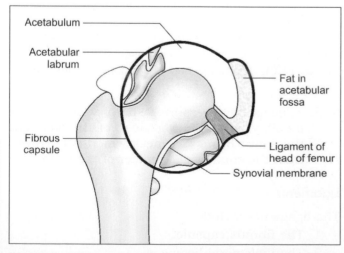

Fig. 12.2: Fibrous capsule of the hip joint and the synovial membrane.

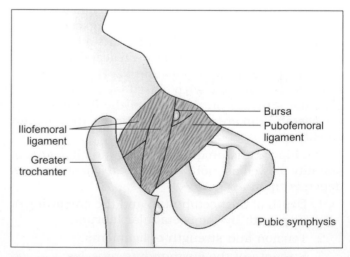

Fig. 12.3: The iliofemoral and pubofemoral ligaments.

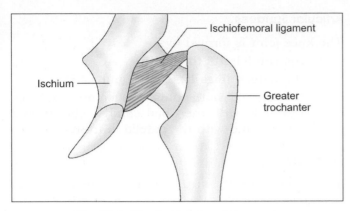

Fig. 12.4: The ischiofemoral ligament.

It narrows the mouth of the acetabulum. This helps in holding the head of the femur in position.

7. The *transverse ligament of the acetabulum* is a part of the acetabular labrum which bridges the acetabular notch. The notch is thus converted into a foramen which transmits acetabular vessels and nerves to the joint.

Relations of the Hip Joint

Anterior Relations (Fig. 12.5)

Tendon of the iliopsoas separated from the joint by a bursa and femoral vein, femoral artery and femoral nerve.

Posterior Relations

The joint, from below upwards, is related to the following muscles: Tendon of obturator externus covered by the quadratus femoris, obturator internus and gemelli, piriformis, sciatic nerve and the gluteus maximus muscle.

Superior Relations

Reflected head of the rectus femoris covered by the gluteus minimus, gluteus medius and partly by gluteus maximus.

Inferior Relations

Lateral fibres of the pectineus and the obturator externus. In addition there are gracilis, adductors longus, brevis, magnus and hamstring muscles.

Blood Supply

The hip joint is supplied by the obturator artery, two circumflex femoral and two gluteal arteries. The medial and lateral circumflex femoral arteries form an arterial circle around the capsular attachment on the neck of the femur. Retinacular arteries arise from this circle and supply the intracapsular part of the neck and the greater part of the head of the femur. A small part of the head, near the fovea capitis is supplied by the acetabular branches of the obturator and medial circumflex femoral arteries (Fig. 4.8).

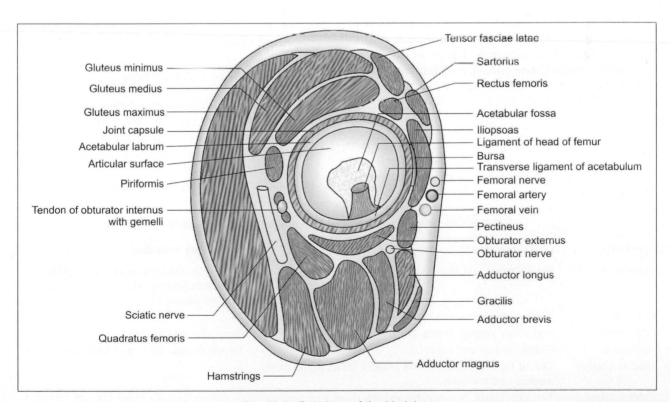

Fig. 12.5: Relations of the hip joint.

Nerve Supply

The hip joint is supplied by the femoral nerve, through the nerve to the rectus femoris; the anterior division of the obturator nerve; the nerve to the quadratus femoris; and the superior gluteal nerve.

Movements

1. Flexion and extension occur around a transverse axis.
2. Adduction and abduction occur around an anteroposterior axis.
3. Medial and lateral rotation occur around a vertical axis.
4. Circumduction is a combination of the foregoing movements.

In general, all axes pass through the centre of the head of the femur, but none of them is fixed because the head is not quite spherical.

Flexion is limited by contact of the thigh with the anterior abdominal wall. Similarly, adduction is limited by contact with the opposite limb. The range of the other movements is different from one another: Extension 15°, abduction 50°, medial rotation 25°, and lateral rotation 60°.

The muscles producing these movements are given in Table 12.1.

KNEE JOINT

The knee is the largest and most complex joint of the body. The complexity is the result of fusion of three joints in one. It is formed by fusion of the lateral femorotibial, medial femorotibial, and femoropatellar joints.

Type

It is compound synovial joint, incorporating two condylar joints between the condyles of the femur and tibia, and one saddle joint between the femur and the patella.

Articular Surfaces

The knee joint is formed by:

1. The condyles of the femur.
2. The patella (Figs 12.6, 12.7 and 12.8).
3. The condyles of the tibia. The femoral condyles articulate with the tibial condyles below and behind, and with the patella in front.

Ligaments

The knee joint is supported by the following ligaments.

1. Fibrous capsule.
2. Ligamentum patellae.
3. Tibial collateral or medial ligament.
4. Fibular collateral or lateral ligament.
5. Oblique popliteal ligament.
6. Arcuate popliteal ligament.
7. Anterior cruciate ligament.
8. Posterior cruciate ligament.
9. Medial meniscus.
10. Lateral meniscus.
11. Transverse ligament.

1. Fibrous (Articular) Capsule

The fibrous capsule is very thin, and is deficient anteriorly, where it is replaced by the quadriceps femoris, the patella and the ligamentum patellae.

Femoral attachment: It is attached about half to one centimeter beyond the articular margins. The attachment has three special features.

DISSECTION

Strip the extra structures around the knee joint, leaving behind the fibrous capsule, ligaments and parts of muscles/tendons attached to the bones/ligaments. Study the articular surfaces, articular capsule, medial and lateral collateral ligaments, oblique popliteal ligament and arcuate popliteal ligament.

Table 12.1: Muscles producing movements at the hip joint

Movement	Chief muscles	Accessory muscles
1. Flexion	Psoas major and iliacus	Pectineus, rectus femoris, and sartorius; adductors (mainly adductor longus) participate in early stages
2. Extension	Gluteus maximus and hamstrings	—
3. Adduction	Adductors longus, brevis and magnus	Pectineus and gracilis
4. Abduction	Glutei medius and minimus	Tensor fasciae latae and sartorius
5. Medial rotation	Tensor fasciae latae and the anterior fibres of the glutei medius and minimus	—
6. Lateral rotation	Two obturators, two gemelli and the quadratus femoris	Piriformis, gluteus maximus and sartorius

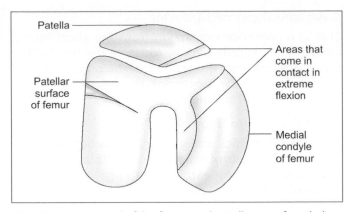

Fig. 12.6: Lower end of the femur and patella seen from below.

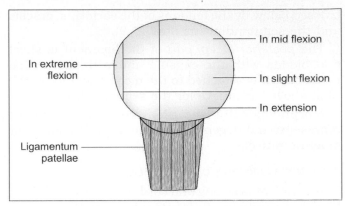

Fig. 12.7: Patella as seen from behind.

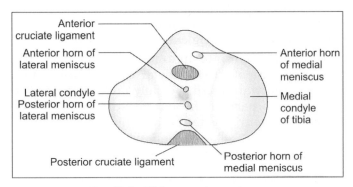

Fig. 12.8: Tibia seen from above.

(a) Anteriorly, it is deficient.

(b) Posteriorly, it is attached to the intercondylar line.

(c) Laterally, it encloses the origin of the popliteus.

Tibial attachment: It is attached about half to one centimeter beyond the articular margins. The attachment has three special features.

(a) Anteriorly, it descends along the margins of the condyles to the tibial tuberosity, where it is deficient.

(b) Posteriorly, it is attached to the intercondylar ridge which limits the attachment of the posterior cruciate ligament.

(c) Posterolaterally, there is a gap behind the lateral condyle for passage of the tendon of the popliteus.

Some terms applied to parts of the capsule are as follows.

Coronary ligament: The fibrous capsule is attached to the periphery of the menisci. The part of the capsule between the menisci and the tibia is sometimes called the coronary ligament.

Short lateral ligament: This is a cord-like thickening of the capsule deep to the fibular collateral ligament. It extends from the lateral epicondyle of femur, where it blends with the tendon of popliteus, to the medial border of the apex of the fibula.

The capsular ligament is weak. It is strengthened anteriorly by the medial and lateral patellar retinacula, which are extensions from the vastus medialis and lateralis; laterally by the iliotibial tract; medially by expansions from the tendons of the sartorius and semimembranosus; and posteriorly, by the oblique popliteal ligament.

Openings

The capsule has two constant gaps.

(a) One leading into the suprapatellar bursa.

(b) Another for the exit of the tendon of the popliteus.

Sometimes there are gaps that communicate with the bursae deep to the medial head of the gastrocnemius, and deep to the semimembranosus.

2. Ligamentum Patellae

This is the central portion of the common tendon of insertion of the quadriceps femoris; the remaining portions of the tendon form the medial and lateral patellar retinacula. The ligamentum patellae is about 7.5 cm long and 2.5 cm broad. It is attached above to the margins and rough posterior surface of the apex of the patella, and below to the *smooth, upper part* of the tibial tuberosity. The superficial fibres pass in front of the patella. The ligamentum patellae is related to the superficial and deep infrapatellar bursae, and to the infrapatellar pad of fat.

3. Tibial Collateral or Medial Ligament

This is a long band of great strength. Superiorly, it is attached to the medial epicondyle of the femur just below the adductor tubercle. Inferiorly, it divides into anterior and posterior parts.

The *anterior* or *superficial part* is about 10 cm long and 1.25 cm broad, and is separated from the capsule by one or two bursae. It is attached below to the medial border and posterior part of the medial surface of the shaft of the tibia. It covers the inferior medial genicular vessels and nerve, and the anterior part of the tendon of the semimembranosus, and is crossed below by the tendons of the sartorius, gracilis and the semitendinosus (Fig. 12.9).

The *posterior (deep) part* of the ligament is short and blends with the capsule and with the medial meniscus. It is attached to the medial condyle of the tibia above the groove for the semimembranosus.

Morphologically, the tibial collateral ligament represents the degenerated tendon of the adductor magnus muscle.

4. Fibular Collateral or Lateral Ligament

This ligament is strong and cord-like. It is about 5 cm long. Superiorly, it is attached to the lateral epicondyle of the femur just above the popliteal groove. Inferiorly, it is embraced by the tendon of the biceps femoris, and is attached to the head of the fibula in front of its apex. It is separated from the lateral meniscus by the tendon of the popliteus. It is free from the capsule. The inferior lateral genicular vessels and nerve separate it from the capsule (Fig. 12.10).

Morphologically, it represents the femoral attachment of the peroneus longus.

5. Oblique Popliteal Ligament

This is an expansion from the tendon of the semimembranosus. It runs upwards and laterally, blends with the posterior surface of the capsule, and is attached to the intercondylar line and lateral condyle of the femur. It is closely related to the popliteal artery, and is pierced by the middle genicular vessels and nerve, and the terminal part of the posterior division of the obturator nerve.

6. Arcuate Popliteal Ligament

This is a posterior expansion from the short lateral ligament. It extends backwards from the head of the fibula, arches over the tendon of the popliteus, and is attached to the posterior border of the intercondylar area of the tibia.

7 and 8. Cruciate Ligaments

These are very thick and strong fibrous bands, which act as direct bonds of union between tibia and femur, to maintain anteroposterior stability of knee joint. They are named according to the attachment on tibia.

Anterior cruciate ligament begins from anterior part of intercondylar area of tibia, runs upwards, backwards and laterally and is attached to the posterior part of medial surface of lateral condyle of femur. It is taut during extension of knee.

Posterior cruciate ligament begins from the posterior part of intercondylar area of tibia, runs upwards, forwards and medially and is attached to the anterior part of the lateral surface of medial condyle of femur. It is taut during flexion of the knee.

These are supplied by middle genicular vessels and nerves (Figs 12.8, 12.11 to 12.13).

9 and 10. Menisci or Semilunar Cartilages

The menisci are two fibrocartilaginous discs. They are shaped like crescents. They deepen the articular surfaces of the condyles of the tibia, and partially divide the joint cavity into upper and lower compartments. Flexion and extension of the knee take place in the *upper* compartment, whereas rotation takes place in the *lower* compartment.

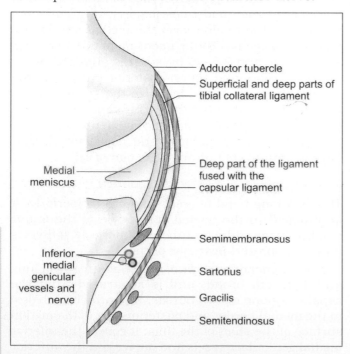

Fig. 12.9: Tibial collateral ligament.

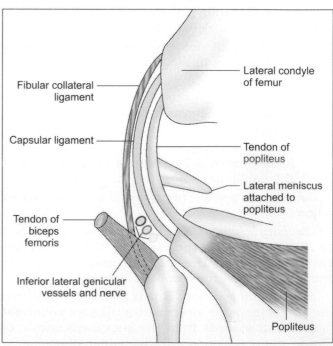

Fig. 12.10: Fibular collateral ligament.

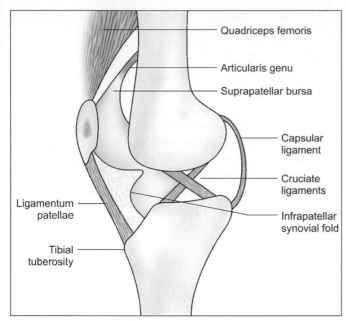

Fig. 12.11: Sagittal section through the knee joint to show the reflection of the synovial membrane (note the cruciate ligaments).

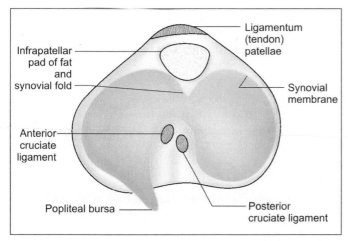

Fig. 12.12: Transverse section through the knee joint to show the arrangement of the synovial membrane.

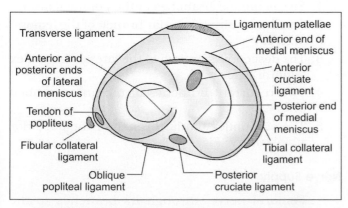

Fig. 12.13: The menisci and their important relations.

Each meniscus has the following.
1. *Two ends:* Both of which are attached to the tibia.
2. *Two borders:* The 'outer' border is thick, convex and fixed to the fibrous capsule; while the 'inner' border is thin, concave and free.
3. *Two surfaces:* The upper surface is concave for articulation with the femur. The lower surface is flat and rests on the peripheral two-thirds of the tibial condyle. The peripheral thick part is vascular. The inner part is avascular and is nourished by synovial fluid.

The *medial meniscus* is nearly semicircular, being wider behind than in front. The posterior fibres of the anterior end are continuous with the transverse ligament. Its peripheral margin is adherent to the deep part of the tibial collateral ligament.

The *lateral meniscus* is nearly circular. The posterior end of the meniscus is attached to the femur through two meniscofemoral ligaments. The tendon of the popliteus and the capsule separate this meniscus from the fibular collateral ligament. The more medial part of the tendon of the popliteus is attached to the lateral meniscus. The mobility of the posterior end of this meniscus is controlled by the popliteus and by the two meniscofemoral ligaments.

Functions of menisci
1. They help in making the articular surfaces more congruent. Because of their flexibility they can adapt their contour to the varying curvature of the different parts of the femoral condyles, as the latter glide over the tibia.
2. The menisci serve as shock absorbers.
3. They help in lubricating the joint cavity.
4. Because of their nerve supply, they also have a sensory function. They give rise to proprioceptive impulses.

11. Transverse Ligament

It connects the anterior ends of the medial and lateral menisci (Fig. 12.13).

DISSECTION

Cut through the tendon of quadriceps femoris muscle just above the knee joint. Extend this incision on either side of patella and ligamentum patellae anchored to the tibial tuberosity. Reflect patella downwards to peep into the cavity of knee joint.

Note the huge infrapatellar synovial fold and pad of fat in it. Remove the fat and posterior part of fibrous capsule so that the cruciate ligaments and menisci are visualised.

Synovial Membrane

The synovial membrane of the knee joint lines the capsule, except posteriorly where it is reflected forwards by the cruciate ligaments, forming a common covering for both the ligaments (Figs 12.11 and 12.12).

In front, it is absent from the patella. Above the patella, it is prolonged upwards for 5 cm or more as the suprapatellar bursa. Below the patella, it covers the deep surface of the infrapatellar pad of fat, which separates it from the ligamentum patellae. A median fold, the *infrapatellar synovial fold,* extends backwards from the pad of fat to the intercondylar fossa of the femur. An alar fold diverges on each side from the median fold to reach the lateral edges of the patella (Figs 12.12 and 12.14).

Bursae around the Knee

As many as 13 bursae have been described around the knee—four anterior, four lateral, and five medial. These bursae are as follows.

Anterior (Fig. 3.7)

1. Subcutaneous prepatellar bursa.
2. Subcutaneous infrapatellar bursa.
3. Deep infrapatellar bursa.
4. Suprapatellar bursa.

Lateral

1. A bursa deep to the lateral head of the gastrocnemius.
2. A bursa between the fibular collateral ligament and the biceps femoris.
3. A bursa between the fibular collateral ligament and the tendon of the popliteus.

4. A bursa between the tendon of the popliteus and the lateral condyle of the tibia.

Medial

1. A bursa deep to the medial head of the gastrocnemius.
2. The *anserine bursa* is a complicated bursa which separates the tendons of the sartorius, the gracilis and the semitendinosus from one another, from the tibia, and from the tibial collateral ligament (Fig. 8.26).
3. A bursa deep to the tibial collateral ligament.
4. A bursa deep to the semimembranosus.

Relations of Knee Joint

Anteriorly

Anterior bursae (Fig. 3.7), ligamentum patellae (Fig. 12.15), and patellar plexus of nerves.

Posteriorly

(a) *At the middle:* Popliteal vessels, tibial nerve.
(b) *Posterolaterally:* Lateral head of gastrocnemius, plantaris, and common peroneal nerve.
(c) *Posteromedially:* Medial head of gastrocnemius, semitendinosus, semimembranosus, gracilis, and popliteus at its insertion (Fig. 9.7).

Medially

Sartorius, gracilis and semitendinosus.
Great saphenous vein with saphenous nerve.
Semimembranosus (Fig. 12.15).

Laterally

Biceps femoris, and tendon of origin of popliteus.

Blood Supply

The knee joint is supplied by the anastomoses around it. The chief sources of blood supply are:

1. Five genicular branches of the popliteal artery.
2. The descending genicular branch of the femoral artery.
3. The descending branch of the lateral circumflex femoral artery.
4. Two recurrent branches of the anterior tibial artery.
5. The circumflex fibular branch of the posterior tibial artery (Fig. 6.10).

Nerve Supply

1. Femoral nerve, through its branches to the vasti, especially the vastus medialis.

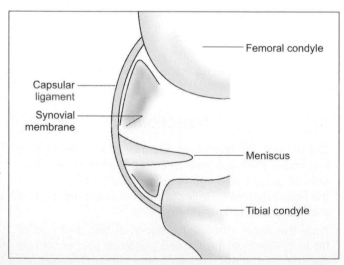

Fig. 12.14: Coronal section through part of the knee joint to show the synovial membrane.

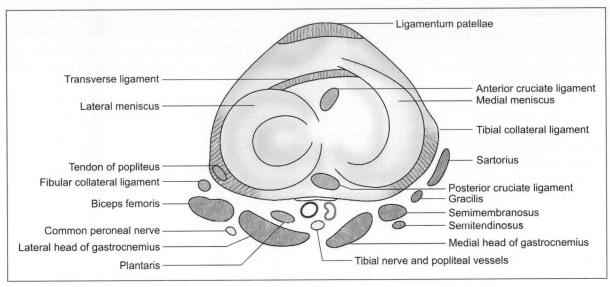

Fig. 12.15: Transverse section through the left knee joint showing its relations.

2. Sciatic nerve, through the genicular branches of the tibial and common peroneal nerves.
3. Obturator nerve, through its posterior division.

Movements at the Knee Joint

Active movements at the knee are flexion, extension, medial rotation and lateral rotation (Table 12.2).

Flexion and *extension* are the chief movements. These take place in the upper compartment of the joint, above the menisci. They differ from the ordinary hinge movements in two ways.

1. The transverse axis around which these movements take place is not fixed. During extension, the axis moves forwards and upwards, and in the reverse direction during flexion.
2. These movements are invariably accompanied by rotations or conjunct rotation. Medial rotation of the femur occurs during the last 30 degrees of extension, and lateral rotation of the femur occurs during the initial stages of flexion. When the foot is off the ground, the tibia rotates instead of the femur, in the opposite direction.

Rotatory movements at the knee are of a small range. Rotations take place around a vertical axis, and are permitted in the lower compartment of the joint, below the menisci. Rotatory movements may be combined with flexion and extension or conjunct rotations, or may occur independently in a partially flexed knee or adjunct rotations. The conjunct rotations are of value in locking and unlocking of the knee.

DISSECTION

Clean the articular surfaces of femur, tibia and patella on the soft specimen and on dried bones. Analyse the movements on them. Try all these movements on yourself and on your friends as well.

Table 12.2: Muscles producing movements at the knee joint

Movement	Principal muscles	Accessory muscles
A. Flexion	1. Biceps femoris 2. Semitendinosus 3. Semimembranosus	1. Gracilis 2. Sartorius 3. Popliteus
B. Extension	Quadriceps femoris	Tensor fasciae latae
C. Medial rotation of flexed leg	1. Popliteus 2. Semimembranosus 3. Semitendinosus	1. Sartorius 2. Gracilis
D. Lateral rotation of flexed leg	Biceps femoris	—

Locking and Unlocking of the Knee Joint

Locking is a mechanism that allows the knee to remain in the position of full extension as in standing without much muscular effort.

Locking occurs as a result of medial rotation of the femur during the last stage of extension. The anteroposterior diameter of the lateral femoral condyle is less than that of the medial condyle. As a result, when the lateral condylar articular surface is fully 'used up' by extension, part of the medial condylar surface remains unused. At this stage the lateral condyle serves as an axis around which the medial condyle rotates backwards, i.e. medial rotation of the femur occurs, so that the remaining part of the medial condylar surface is also 'taken up'. This movement locks the knee joint. Locking is aided by the oblique pull of ligaments during the last stages of extension. When the knee is locked, it is completely rigid and all ligaments of the joint are taut. Locking is produced by continued action of the same muscles that produce extension, i.e. the quadriceps femoris, especially the vastus medialis part.

The locked knee joint can be flexed only after it is unlocked by a reversal of the medial rotation, i.e. by lateral rotation of the femur. Unlocking is brought about by the action of the popliteus muscle.

Accessory or *passive movements* can be performed in a partially flexed knee. These movements include:

1. A wider range of rotation.
2. Anteroposterior gliding of the tibia on the femur.
3. Some adduction and abduction.
4. Some separation of the tibia from the femur.

Morphology of Knee Joint

1. The tibial collateral ligament is the degenerated tendon of the adductor magnus.

2. The fibular collateral ligament is the degenerated tendon of the peroneus longus.
3. Cruciate ligaments represent the collateral ligaments of the originally separate femorotibial joints.
4. Infrapatellar synovial fold indicates the lower limit of the femoropatellar joint.

ANKLE JOINT

This is a synovial joint of the hinge variety.

Articular Surfaces

The upper articular surface is formed by:

(i) The lower end of the tibia including the medial malleolus.
(ii) The lateral malleolus of the fibula, and
(iii) The inferior transverse tibiofibular ligament. These structures form a deep socket (Figs 12.16 and 12.21).

The inferior articular surface is formed by articular areas on the upper, medial and lateral aspects of the talus (Fig. 12.17).

Structurally, the joint is very strong. The stability of the joint is ensured by:

(i) Close interlocking of the articular surfaces.
(ii) Strong collateral ligaments on the sides.

DISSECTION

Define the margins of both extensor retinacula, one flexor retinaculum and both peroneal retinacula. Identify the tendons enclosed in synovial sheaths, nerves and blood vessels passing under them. Displace these structures without removing them. Clean and define the strong medial and lateral ligaments of ankle joint. Also demarcate the thin anterior and posterior parts of the capsule of the joint.

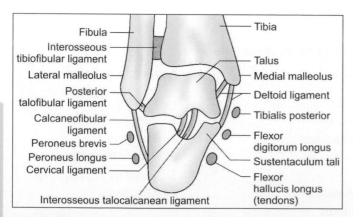

Fig. 12.16: Anterior view of a coronal section through the right ankle to show its articular surfaces.

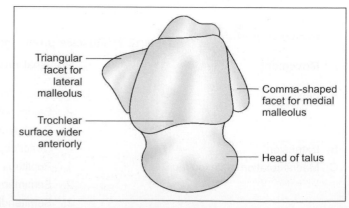

Fig. 12.17: Right talus seen from above showing the articular surface taking part in forming the ankle joint.

(iii) The tendons that cross the joint, four in front, and five behind (Fig. 12.18).

The depth of the superior articular socket is contributed by:

(i) The downward projection of medial and lateral malleoli, on the corresponding sides of talus.

(ii) By the inferior transverse tibiofibular ligament that bridges across the gap between the tibia and the fibula behind the talus. The socket is provided flexibility by strong tibiofibular ligaments and by slight movements of the fibula at the superior tibiofibular joint.

There are two factors, however, that tend to displace the tibia and fibula forwards over the talus. These factors are:

(a) The forward pull of tendons which pass from the leg to the foot.

(b) The pull of gravity when the heel is raised. Displacement is prevented by the following factors.

(i) The talus is wedge-shaped, being wider anteriorly. The malleoli are oriented to fit this wedge (Fig. 12.18).

(ii) The posterior border of the lower end of the tibia is prolonged downwards.

(iii) The presence of the inferior transverse tibiofibular ligament.

(iv) The tibiocalcanean, posterior tibiotalar, calcaneofibular and posterior talofibular ligaments pass backwards and resist forward movement of the tibia and fibula.

Ligaments

The joint is supported by:

(i) Fibrous capsule.

(ii) The deltoid or medial ligament.

(iii) A lateral ligament.

Fibrous Capsule

It surrounds the joint and is attached all around the articular margins with two exceptions.

(a) Posterosuperiorly, it is attached to the inferior transverse tibiofibular ligament.

(b) Anteroinferiorly, it is attached to the dorsum of the neck of the talus at some distance from the trochlear surface.

The anterior and posterior parts of the capsule are loose and thin to allow hinge movements. On each side, however, it is supported by strong collateral ligaments.

The synovial membrane lines the capsule. The joint cavity ascends for some distance between the tibia and the fibula.

Deltoid or Medial Ligament

This is a very strong triangular ligament present on the medial side of the ankle. The ligament is divided into a superficial and a deep part. Both parts have a common attachment above to the apex and margins of the medial malleolus. The lower attachment is indicated by the name of the fibres (Fig. 12.19).

Superficial part:

1. Anterior fibres or *tibionavicular* are attached to the tuberosity of the navicular bone and to the medial margin of the spring ligament.

2. The middle fibres or *tibiocalcanean* are attached to the whole length of the sustentaculum tali.

3. The posterior fibres or *posterior tibiotalar* are attached to the medial tubercle and to the adjoining part of the medial surface of the talus.

Deep part or *anterior tibiotalar* is attached to the anterior part of the medial surface of the talus.

The deltoid ligament is crossed by the tendons of the tibialis posterior and flexor digitorum longus.

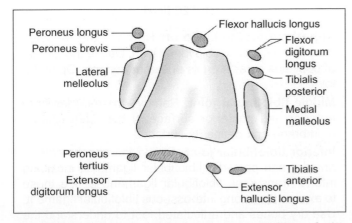

Fig. 12.18: Tendons maintaining the stability of the ankle joint.

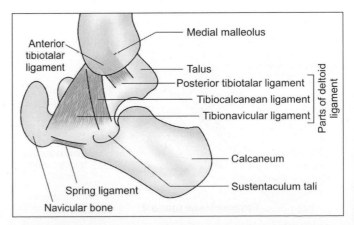

Fig. 12.19: Medial side of the ankle joint showing the parts of deltoid ligament.

Lateral Ligament

This ligament consists of three bands as follows.

1. The *anterior talofibular ligament* is a flat band which passes from the anterior margin of the lateral malleolus to the neck of the talus, just in front of the fibular facet (Fig. 12.20).
2. The *posterior talofibular ligament* passes from the lower part of the malleolar fossa of the fibula to the lateral tubercle of the talus.
3. The *calcaneofibular ligament* is a long rounded cord which passes from the notch on the lower border of the lateral malleolus to the tubercle on the lateral surface of the calcaneum. It is crossed by the tendons of the peroneus longus and brevis.

Relations of the Ankle Joint

Anteriorly, from medial to lateral side, there are the tibialis anterior, the extensor hallucis longus, the anterior tibial vessels, the deep peroneal nerve, the extensor digitorum longus, and the peroneus tertius (Fig. 12.18).

Posteriorly, from medial to lateral side, there are the tibialis posterior, the flexor digitorum longus, the posterior tibial vessels, the tibial nerve, the flexor hallucis longus, the peroneus brevis, and the peroneus longus.

Movements

1. *Active movements* are dorsiflexion and plantar flexion (Table 12.3).
   (a) In *dorsiflexion* the forefoot is raised, and the angle between the front of the leg and the dorsum of the foot is diminished. It is a close-pack position with maximum congruence of the joint surfaces. The wider anterior trochlear surface of the talus fits

Table 12.3: Muscles producing movements		
Movement	Principal muscles	Accessory muscles
A. Dorsiflexion	Tibialis anterior	1. Extensor digitorum longus 2. Extensor hallucis longus 3. Peroneus tertius
B. Plantar flexion	1. Gastrocnemius 2. Soleus	1. Plantaris 2. Tibialis posterior 3. Flexor hallucis longus 4. Flexor digitorum longus

into lower end of narrow posterior part of the lower end of tibia. There are no chances of dislocation in dorsiflexion.

(b) In *plantar flexion,* the forefoot is depressed, and the angle between the leg and the foot is increased. The narrow posterior part of trochlear surface of talus loosely fits into the wide anterior part of the lower end of tibia. High heels cause plantar flexion of ankle joint and its dislocations (Fig. 9.14).

Blood Supply

From anterior tibial, posterior tibial, and peroneal arteries.

Nerve Supply

From deep peroneal and tibial nerves.

TIBIOFIBULAR JOINTS

The tibia and fibula articulate at three joints, the superior, middle and inferior tibiofibular joints.

DISSECTION

Superior tibiofibular joint: Remove the muscles around the superior tibiofibular joint. Define the tendon of popliteus muscle on its posterior surface. Open the joint.

Middle tibiofibular joint: Remove the muscles from anterior and posterior surface of the interosseous membrane and define its surfaces.

Inferior tibiofibular joint: Define the attachments of anterior and posterior tibiofibular ligaments including inferior transverse tibiofibular ligament. Divide these to expose the strong interosseous tibiofibular ligament. Use dry bones and articulated foot to understand the attachments of the ligaments.

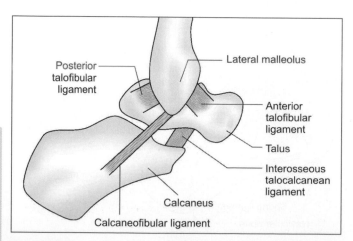

Fig. 12.20: Lateral side of the ankle joint showing the lateral ligament.

Superior Tibiofibular Joint

This is a small synovial joint of the plane variety. It is formed by articulation of small, rounded, flat facets present on the head of the fibula, and on the lateral condyle of the tibia. The joint permits slight gliding or rotatory movements that help in adjustment of the lateral malleolus during movements at the ankle joint.

The bones are united by a fibrous capsule which is strengthened by anterior and posterior ligaments. These ligaments are directed forwards and laterally. The cavity of the joint may communicate with the knee joint through the popliteal bursa. The joint is supplied by the nerve to the popliteus, and by the recurrent genicular nerve (Fig. 2.42).

Middle Tibiofibular Joint

This is a fibrous joint formed by the interosseous membrane connecting the shafts of the tibia and the fibula. The interosseous membrane is attached to the interosseous borders of the two bones. Its fibres are directed downwards and laterally. It is wide above and narrow below where it is continuous with the interosseous ligament of the inferior tibiofibular joint. It presents a large opening at the upper end for the passage of the anterior tibial vessels, and a much smaller opening near its lower end for the passage of the perforating branch of the peroneal artery (Fig. 2.28).

Relations

Anteriorly: Tibialis anterior, extensor digitorum longus, extensor hallucis longus, peroneus tertius, anterior tibial vessels and deep peroneal nerve.

Posteriorly: Tibialis posterior and flexor hallucis longus.

Nerve supply: Nerve to popliteus.

Functions:

1. The membrane provides additional surface for attachment of muscles.
2. Binds the tibia and the fibula.
3. Resists the downward pull exerted on the fibula by the powerful muscles attached to the bone. Note that the biceps femoris is the only muscle that pulls the fibula upwards.

Inferior Tibiofibular Joint

This is a syndesmosis uniting the lower ends of the tibia and the fibula (Figs 12.21, 2.28 and 2.29). The bony surfaces are connected by a very strong *interosseous ligament,* which forms the chief bond of union between the lower ends of these bones. The interosseous ligament is concealed both in front and behind by the *anterior* and *posterior tibiofibular ligaments,* whose fibres are directed downwards and laterally. The posterior tibiofibular ligament is stronger than the anterior. Its lower and deep portion forms the *inferior transverse tibiofibular ligament,* which is a strong thick band of yellowish fibres passing transversely from the upper part of the malleolar fossa of the fibula to the posterior border of the articular surface of the tibia, reaching up to the medial malleolus (Fig. 12.21).

Blood supply: Perforating branch of the peroneal artery; and the malleolar branches of the anterior and posterior tibial arteries (Fig. 9.10).

Nerve supply: Deep peroneal, tibial and saphenous nerves.

The joint permits slight movements, so that the lateral malleolus can rotate laterally during dorsi-flexion of the ankle.

JOINTS OF THE FOOT

The joints of the foot are numerous. They can be classified as:

(a) Intertarsal,

(b) Tarsometatarsal,

(c) Intermetatarsal,

(d) Metatarsophalangeal, and

(e) Interphalangeal.

The main intertarsal joints are the subtalar or talocalcanean joint, the talocalcaneonavicular joint and the calcaneocuboid joint. Smaller intertarsal joints include the cuneonavicular, cuboidonavicular, intercuneiform and cuneocuboid joints.

The movements permitted at these joints are as follows.

1. The intertarsal, tarsometatarsal and intermetatarsal joints permit gliding and rotatory movements, which jointly bring about inversion, eversion, supination and pronation of the foot.

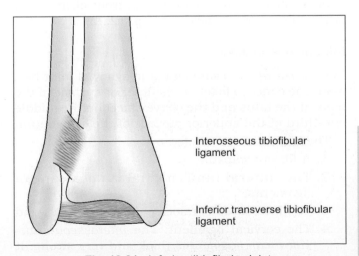

Fig. 12.21: Inferior tibiofibular joint.

Pronation is a component of eversion, while supination is a component of inversion.

2. The metatarsophalangeal joints are similar to the metacarpophalangeal joints of the hand. They permit flexion, extension, adduction and abduction of the toes.

3. The interphalangeal joints of hinge variety permit flexion and extension of the distal phalanges.

A brief description of the relevant joints is given below.

DISSECTION

Remove all the tendons, muscles from both dorsal and plantar aspects of the tarsal, metatarsal and phalanges. Define, identify the ligaments joining the various bones. Ligaments are stronger on the plantar aspect than the dorsal aspect.

Subtalar joint

Divide the ligaments which unite the talus and calcaneus together at the talocalcanean, talocalcaneonavicular joints. Study these joints carefully to understand the movements of inversion and eversion. On the lateral side of foot, define the attachments of long plantar ligament. Reflect this ligament from its proximal attachment to see the deeper plantar calcaneocuboid ligament.

SUBTALAR OR TALOCALCANEAN JOINT

There are two joints, posterior and anterior, between the talus and the calcaneum. The posterior joint is named the talocalcanean or subtalar joint. The anterior joint is a part of the talocalcaneonavicular joint. Since the two joints form a single functional unit, clinicians often include both joints under the term subtalar joint. However, the two joints are separated by the sinus tarsi. The greater part of the talocalcaneonavicular joint lies in front of the head of the talus and not below it (Fig. 12.22).

Talocalcanean Joint

The *talocalcanean joint* is a plane synovial joint between the concave facet on the inferior surface of the body of the talus and the convex facet on the middle one-third of the superior surface of the calcaneum.

The bones are connected by:

1. A fibrous capsule,
2. The lateral and medial talocalcanean ligaments,
3. The interosseous talocalcanean ligament, and
4. The cervical ligament: The *interosseous talocalcanean ligament* is thick and very strong. It is the chief bond of union between the talus

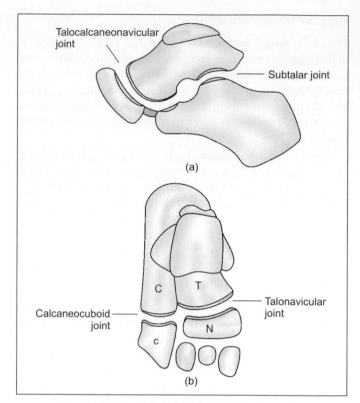

Fig. 12.22: The joint permitting movements of inversion and eversion: (a) Main joints, (b) accessory joints.

and the calcaneum. It occupies the sinus tarsi, and separates the talocalcanean joint from the talocalcaneonavicular joint. It becomes taut in eversion, and limits this movement. The *cervical ligament* is placed lateral to the sinus tarsi. It passes upwards and medially, and is attached above to a tubercle on the inferolateral aspect of the neck of the talus. It becomes taut in inversion, and limits this movement.

Movements

The joint participates in the movements of inversion and eversion of the foot described at the end of chapter.

Talocalcaneonavicular Joint

The joint has some of the features of a ball and socket joint. The head of the talus fits into a socket formed partly by the navicular bone, and partly by the calcaneum (Fig. 12.22). Two ligaments also take part in forming the socket: these are the spring ligament medially, and the medial limb of the bifurcate ligament laterally.

The bones taking part in forming the joint are connected by a fibrous capsule. The capsule is supported posteriorly by the interosseous talocalcanean ligament; dorsally by the dorsal talonavicular ligament; ventromedially by the spring ligament; and laterally by the medial limb of the bifurcate ligament. The spring ligament is described below. The bifurcate ligament is described with the calcaneocuboid joint.

Movements

The movements permitted at this joint are those of inversion and eversion. They are described below.

The *spring ligament* or *plantar calcaneonavicular ligament* is powerful. It is attached posteriorly to the anterior margin of the sustentaculum tali, and anteriorly to the plantar surface of the navicular bone between its tuberosity and articular margin. The head of the talus rests directly on the upper surface of the ligament, which is covered by fibrocartilage. The plantar surface of the ligament is supported by the tendon of tibialis posterior medially, and by the tendons of flexor hallucis longus and flexor digitorum longus, laterally.

The spring ligament is the most important ligament for maintaining the medial longitudinal arch of the foot.

CALCANEOCUBOID JOINT

This is a saddle joint. The opposed articular surfaces of the calcaneum and the cuboid are concavoconvex. On account of the shape of articular surfaces, medial movement of the forefoot is accompanied by its lateral rotation and adduction or inversion. Lateral movement of the forefoot is accompanied by medial rotation and abduction or eversion. The bones are connected by:

1. A fibrous capsule,
2. The lateral limb of the bifurcate ligament,
3. The long plantar ligament, and
4. The short plantar ligament.

The *bifurcate ligament* is Y-shaped. Its stem is attached to the anterolateral part of the sulcus calcanei; the medial limb or calcaneonavicular ligament, to the dorsolateral surface of the navicular bone; and the lateral limb or calcaneocuboid ligament, to the dorsomedial surface of the cuboid bone. Thus each limb of the ligament strengthens a separate joint.

The *long plantar ligament* (Fig. 12.23) is a long and strong ligament whose importance in maintaining the arches of foot is surpassed only by the spring ligament. It is attached posteriorly to the plantar surface of the calcaneum, and anteriorly to the lips of the groove on the cuboid bone, and to the bases of the middle three metatarsals. It converts the groove on the plantar surface of the cuboid into a tunnel for the tendon of the peroneus longus. Morphologically, it represents the divorced tendon of the gastrocnemius.

The *short plantar ligament* or *plantar calcaneocuboid ligament* lies deep to the long plantar ligament. It is broad and strong ligament extending from the anterior tubercle of the calcaneum to the plantar surface of the cuboid, behind its ridge.

Transverse Tarsal or Midtarsal Joint

This includes the calcaneocuboid and the talonavicular joints (Fig. 12.22). The talonavicular joint is a part of the talocalcaneonavicular joint, and hence the transverse tarsal joint may be said to be made

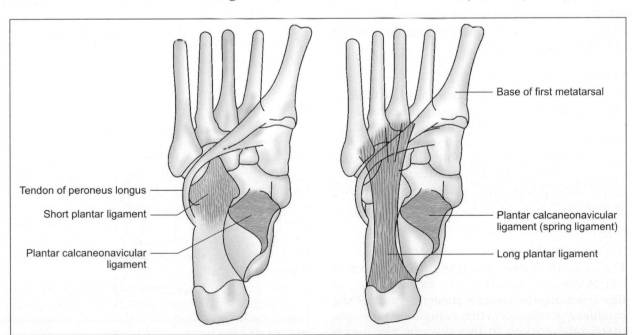

Base of first metatarsal

Tendon of peroneus longus

Short plantar ligament

Plantar calcaneonavicular ligament

Plantar calcaneonavicular ligament (spring ligament)

Long plantar ligament

Fig. 12.23: Some ligaments of the foot with the tendons of peroneus longus.

up of only one and a half joints. These joints are grouped together only by virtue of being placed in nearly the same transverse plane. In any case, the two joints do not form a functional unit. They have different axes of movements. It demarcates the forefoot from the hindfoot. Its movements help in inversion and eversion of the foot.

Inversion and Eversion of the Foot

Inversion is a movement in which the medial border of the foot is elevated, so that the sole faces medially.

Eversion is a movement in which the lateral border of the foot is elevated, so that the sole faces laterally. These movements can be performed voluntarily only when the foot is off the ground. When the foot is on the ground these movements help to adjust the foot to uneven ground.

In inversion and eversion, the entire part of the foot below the talus moves together. The movement takes place mainly at the subtalar and talocalcaneonavicular joints and partly at the transverse tarsal joint. The calcaneum and the navicular bone, move medially or laterally round the talus carrying the forefoot with them. Inversion is accompanied by plantar flexion of the foot and adduction of the forefoot. Eversion is accompanied by dorsiflexion of the foot and abduction of the forefoot.

Joints taking Part

Main

1. Subtalar (talocalcanean).
2. Talocalcaneonavicular.

Accessory

Transverse tarsal which includes calcaneocuboid and talonavicular joints.

Axis of Movements

Inversion and eversion take place around an oblique axis which runs forwards, upwards and medially, passing from the back of the calcaneum, through the sinus tarsi, to emerge at the superomedial aspect of the neck of the talus. The obliquity of the axis partly accounts for adduction, abduction, plantar flexion and dorsiflexion which are associated with these movements (Fig. 12.24).

Range of Movements

1. Inversion is much more free than eversion.
2. The range of movements is appreciably increased in plantar flexion of the foot because, in this position, the narrow posterior part of the trochlear surface of the talus occupies the tibiofibular socket. In this position slight side to side movements of the talus are permitted.

Muscles producing Movements

Inversion is produced by the actions of the tibialis anterior and the tibialis posterior, helped by the flexor hallucis longus and the flexor digitorum longus (Table 12.4).

Pronation and Supination of the Foot

These are really components of the movements of inversion and eversion. In pronation and supination, the forefoot (i.e. the distal part of the tarsus and metatarsus) moves on the calcaneum and talus. The medial border or the forefoot is elevated in supination (which is thus a part of inversion), while

Table 12.4: Muscles producing movements of inversion and eversion		
Movement	**Principal muscles**	**Accessory muscles**
A. Inversion	Tibialis anterior	Flexor hallucis longus
	Tibialis posterior	Flexor digitorum longus
B. Eversion	Peroneus longus	Peroneus tertius
	Peroneus brevis	

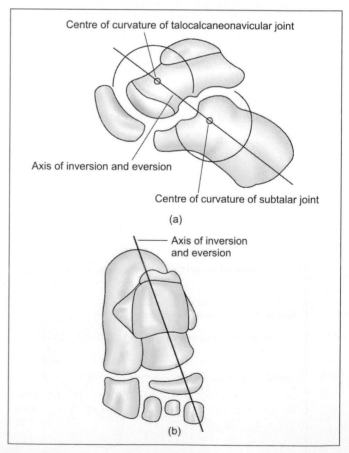

Fig. 12.24: Axis of movements of inversion and eversion: (a) Side view, (b) superior view.

the reverse occurs in pronation (and the eversion). These movements take place chiefly at the transverse tarsal joint and partly at smaller intertarsal, tarsometatarsal and intermetatarsal joints.

Limiting Factors

Inversion is limited by:
1. Tension of peronei
2. Tension of cervical ligament.

Eversion is limited by:
1. Tension of tibialis anterior
2. Tension of tibialis posterior
3. Tension of deltoid ligament.

Functional Significance

Inversion and eversion greatly help the foot in adjusting to uneven and slippery ground. When feet are supporting the body weight, these movements occur in a modified form called supination and pronation, which are forced on the foot by the body weight.

SMALLER JOINTS OF FOREFOOT

These are plane joints between the navicular, the cuneiform, the cuboid and the metatarsal bones. They permit small gliding movements, which allow elevation and depression of the heads of the metatarsals, as well as pronation and supination of the foot.

Joint Cavities of Foot

There are only six joint cavities in the intertarsal, tarsometatarsal and intermetatarsal joints. These are:
1. Talocalcanean
2. Talocalcaneonavicular
3. Calcaneocuboid
4. First cuneometatarsal
5. Cubometatarsal
6. Cuneonavicular with extensions (Fig. 12.25), i.e. navicular with three cuneiforms and second and third cuneometatarsal joints.

Metatarsophalangeal and Interphalangeal Joints

The structure of these joints is similar to the corresponding joints of the hand, with two exceptions.
1. The deep transverse ligaments of the foot connect all the five toes instead of only four fingers in the hand.
2. The toes are adducted and abducted with reference to the second toe and not the third finger as in the hand.

Morphologic Significance

In intrauterine life and early infancy, the soles of the feet are turned inwards, so that they face each others. As growth proceeds, the feet are gradually everted to allow a plantigrade posture. Such eversion does not occur in apes.

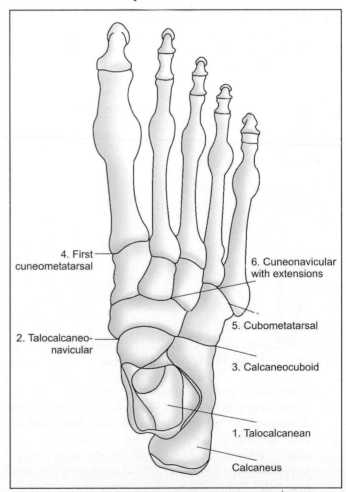

Fig. 12.25: Joint cavities of the foot.

CLINICAL ANATOMY

- *Congenital dislocation* is more common in the hip than in any other joint of the body. The head of the femur slips upwards on to the gluteal surface of the ilium because the upper margin of the acetabulum is developmentally deficient (Fig. 12.26). This causes lurching gait, and Trendelenburg's test is positive (Fig. 5.15).

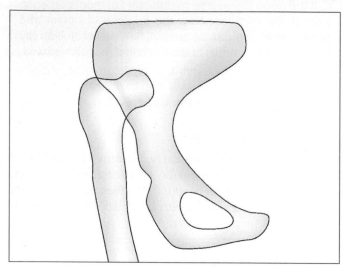

Fig. 12.26: Congenital dislocation of hip joint.

- *Perthes' disease* or pseudocoxalgia is characterized by destruction and flattening of the head of the femur, with an increased joint space in X-ray pictures (Fig. 12.27).

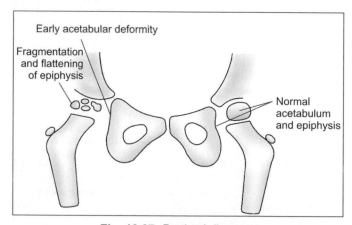

Fig. 12.27: Perthes' disease.

Coxa vera is a condition in which the neck-shaft angle is reduced from the normal angle of about 150° in a child, and 127° in an adult (Fig. 12.28).

- *Osteoarthritis* is a disease of old age, characterized by growth of osteophytes at the articular ends, which make movements limited and painful (Fig. 12.29).

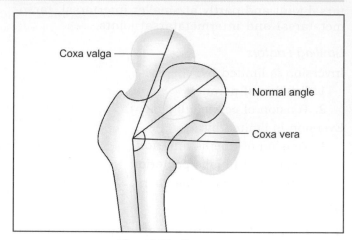

Fig. 12.28: Coxa vera.

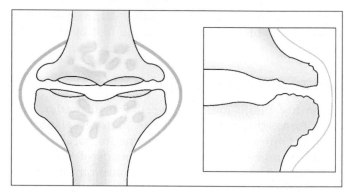

Fig. 12.29: Osteoarthritis.

- *Dislocation of the hip* may be posterior (more common), anterior (less common), or central (rare). The sciatic nerve may be injured in posterior dislocations (Fig. 12.5).
- Injuries in the region of hip joint may produce shortening of the lower limb. The length of lower limb is measured from the anterior superior iliac spine to the medial malleolus (Fig. 12.30).
- Disease of the hip like tuberculosis, may cause *referred pain* in the knee because of the common nerve supply of the two joints.
- *Aspiration of the hip joint* can be done by passing a needle from a point 5 cm below the anterior superior iliac spine, upwards, backwards and medially. It can also be done from the side by passing the needle from the posterior edge of the greater trochanter, upwards and medially, parallel with the neck of the femur.
- Hip diseases show an interesting age pattern:
  - (a) Below 5 years : Congenital dislocation and tuberculosis (Fig. 12.31)
  - (b) 5 to 10 years : Perthes' disease (Fig. 12.27)

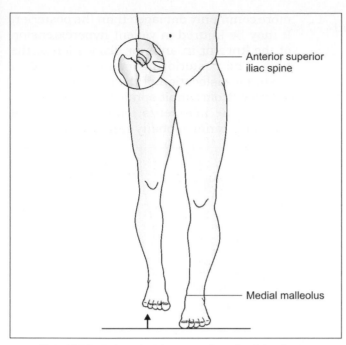

Fig. 12.30: Subcapital fracture of neck of the femur.

(c) 10 to 20 years : Coxa vera (Fig. 12.28)
(d) Above 40 years : Osteoarthritis (Fig. 12.29)

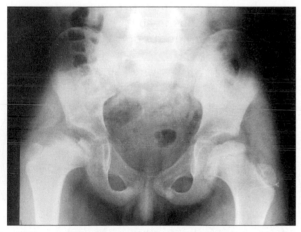

Fig. 12.31: TB of right hip joint.

- In arthritis of hip joint, the position of joint is partially flexed, abducted and laterally rotated.
- Fracture of the neck of the femur may be subcapital, near the head (Fig. 12.30), cervical in the middle, or basal near the trochanters. Damage to retinacular arteries causes avascular necrosis of the head. Such a damage is maximal in subcapital fractures and least in basal fractures. These fractures are common in old age, between the age of 40 and 60 years. Femur–neck–fracture is usually produced by trivial injuries (Figs 2.54 and 12.32).

Trochanteric fracture may be intertrochanteric, i.e. between the trochanters or subtrochanteric,

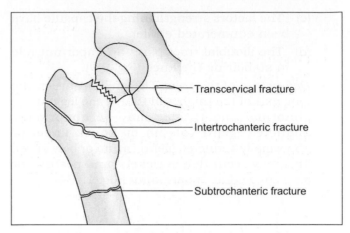

Fig. 12.32: Fracture of neck and trochanteric fracture.

i.e. below the trochanters. These fractures occur in strong, adult subjects, and are produced by severe, violent injuries (Fig. 12.32).

- Shenton's line, in an X-ray picture, is a continuous curve formed by the upper border of the obturator foramen and the lower border of the neck of the femur. In fracture neck femur, line becomes abnormal (Fig. 12.33).

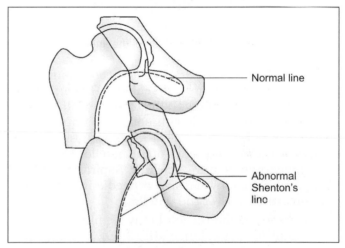

Fig. 12.33: Shenton's line.

- Structurally, the knee is a weak joint because the articular surfaces are not congruent. The tibial condyles are too small and shallow to hold the large, convex, femoral condyles in place. The femoropatellar articulation is also quite insecure because of the shallow articular surfaces, and because of the outward angulation between the long axis of the thigh and of the leg.

The stability of the joint is maintained by a number of factors.

(a) The cruciate ligaments maintain antero-posterior stability.

(b) The collateral ligaments maintain side to side stability.

(c) The factors strengthening the capsule have been enumerated earlier.

(d) The iliotibial tract plays an important role in stabilizing the knee (Fig. 3.9).

- *Deformities of the knee:* The angle between the long axis of the thigh and that of the leg may be abnormal and the leg may be abnormally abducted (genu valgum or knock knee) or abnormally adducted (genu varum or bow knee). This may occur due to rickets, and posture, or as a congenital abnormality (Fig. 12.34).

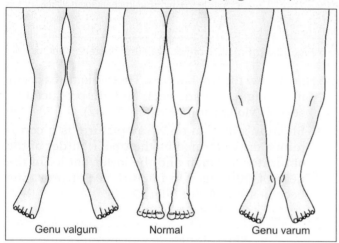

Genu valgum   Normal   Genu varum

Fig. 12.34: Deformities of the knee.

- *Diseases of the knee:* The knee joint may be affected by various diseases. These include osteoarthritis and various infections. Infections may be associated with collections of the fluid in the joint cavity. This gives rise to swelling above, and at the sides of the patella. The patella appears to float in the fluid. Aspiration of fluid can be done by passing a needle into the joint on either side of the patella.

Bursae around the joint may get filled with fluid resulting in swellings (Fig. 2.59).

- *Injuries to the knee:*
  (a) *Injuries to menisci* strains in a slightly flexed knee, as in kicking a football, the meniscus may get separated from the capsule, or may be torn longitudinally (bucket-handle tear) or transversely (Fig. 2.52).

  The medial meniscus is more vulnerable to injury than the lateral because of its fixity to the tibial collateral ligament, and because of greater excursion during rotatory movements. The lateral meniscus is protected by the popliteus which pulls it backwards so that it is not crushed between the articular surfaces.

  (b) *Injuries to cruciate ligaments* are also common. The anterior cruciate ligament is

more commonly damaged than the posterior. It may be injured in violent hyperextension of the knee or in anterior dislocation of the tibia. The posterior ligament is injured in posterior dislocation of the tibia. The injury may vary from simple sprain to complete tear. Tear of the ligaments leads to abnormal anteroposterior mobility (Fig. 12.35).

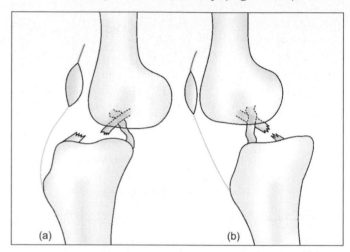

(a)   (b)

Fig. 12.35: (a) Anterior and (b) posterior cruciate ligaments.

(c) *Injuries to collateral ligaments* are less common, and may be produced by severe abduction and adduction strains (Fig. 12.36).

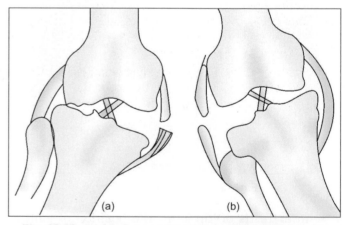

(a)   (b)

Fig. 12.36: (a) Medial and (b) lateral collateral ligaments.

- Semimembranosus bursitis is quite common. It causes a swelling in the popliteal fossa region on the posteromedial aspect (Fig. 7.12).
- Baker's cyst is a central swelling, occurs due to osteoarthritis of knee joint. The synovial membrane protrudes through a hole in the posterior part of capsule of knee joint.
- Hip joint and knee joint may need to be replaced if beyond repair (Fig. 12.37).
- In knee joint disease vastus medialis is first to atrophy and last to recover.

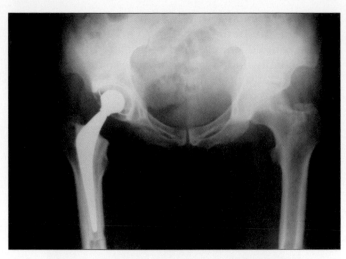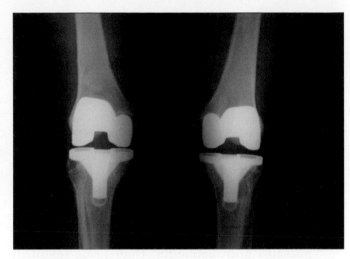

Fig. 12.37: Hip and knee joint replacement.

- The so-called *sprains of the ankle* are almost always abduction sprains of the subtalar joints, although a few fibres of the deltoid ligament are also torn. True sprains of the ankle joint are caused by forced plantar flexion, which leads to tearing of the anterior fibres of the capsule. The joint is unstable during plantar flexion.

- *Dislocations of the ankle* are rare because joint is very stable due to the presence of deep tibio-fibular socket. Whenever dislocation occurs, it is accompanied by fracture of one of the malleoli.

- Acute sprains of lateral ankle occur when the foot is plantar flexed and excessively inverted. The lateral ligaments of ankle joint are torn giving rise to pain and swelling.

- Acute sprains of medial ankle occur in excessive eversion, leading to tear of strong deltoid ligament. These cases are less common.

- The *optimal position* of the ankle to avoid ankylosis is one of slight plantar flexion.

- For injections into the ankle joint, the needle is introduced between tendons of extensor hallucis longus and tibialis anterior with the ankle partially plantar flexed.

- During walking, the plantar flexors raise the heel from the ground. When the limb is moved forwards the dorsiflexors help the foot in clearing the ground. The value of the ankle joint resides in this hinge action, in this to and fro movement of the joint during walking.

- The inferior tibiofibular joint is strong. The strength of the ligaments uniting the lower ends of the tibia and fibula is an important factor in maintaining the integrity of the ankle joint.

- The slight movements of the lateral malleolus taking place at this joint provide suppleness to the ankle joint.

- Gait is a motion which carries the body forwards. There are two phases: Swing and stance (Fig. 12.38).

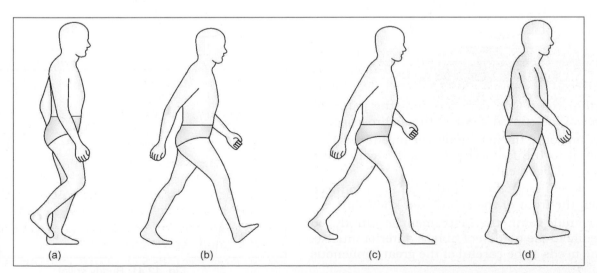

(a) (b) (c) (d)

Fig. 12.38: Phases of gait: (a) and (b) Swing phase; (c) and (d) Stance phase.

Swing phase:

(a) Flexion of hip, flexion of knee and plantar flexion of ankle.

(b) Flexion of hip, extension of knee and dorsi-flexion of ankle.

Stance phase:

(c) Flexion of hip, extension of knee and foot on the ground.

(d) Extension of hip, extension of knee and foot on the ground.

- Females wearing high heels (more than 5 cm), put stress on their back and lower limbs. The spine is pushed forwards, knees are excessively bent, resulting in too much pull on some muscles and ligaments. High heels result in shift in position of centre of gravity. The problems caused by high heels are "fashionable diseases". The sprains of the medial and lateral ligaments of ankle joint are almost always due to high heels.

- Joints of the foot lead to various deformities like mallet toe, hammer toe and claw toe (Fig. 12.39).

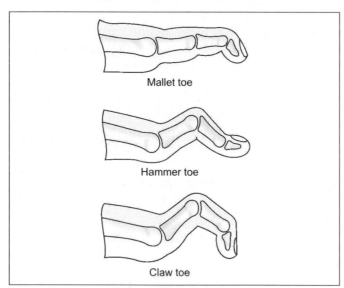

Fig. 12.39: Deformities of toes.

- *Arthroscopy:* One can look into the joints by special instruments called the arthroscopes.

  For hip joint, the instrument is introduced 4 cm lateral to the femoral pulse and 4 cm below inguinal ligament.

  For knee joint, the arthroscope is introduced from the front of the semiflexed knee joint.

  For ankle joint, the instrument is introduced medial to the tendon of tibialis anterior muscle. One needs to be careful of the great saphenous vein.

- *Hallux valgus:* Due to ill-fitting shoes great toe gets pushed laterally, even dislocating the sesamoid bone. Head of 1st metatarsal points medially and adventitious bursa develops there. Toes may be deformed at their joints resulting in claw toe (Fig. 12.40).

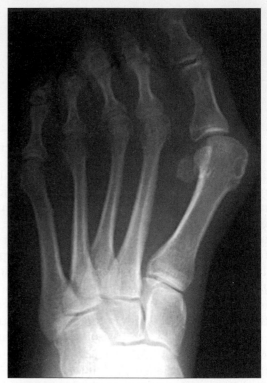

Fig. 12.40: X-ray showing hallux valgus.

- Fractured toe is taped with the adjacent toe, this is called buddy splint (Fig. 12.41).

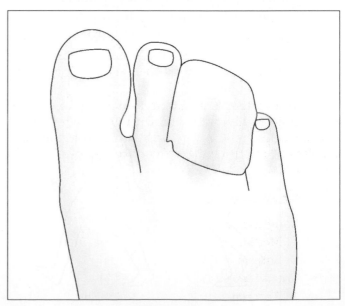

Fig. 12.41: Buddy splint.

CHAPTER 13

Arches of Foot

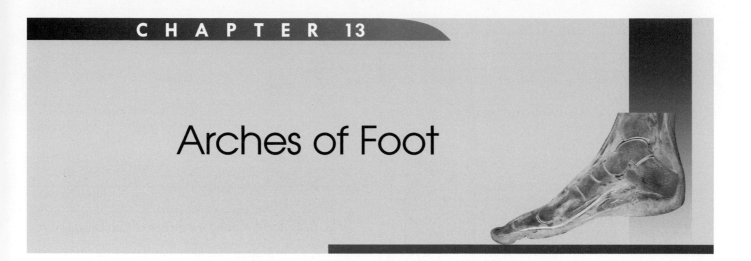

Arches of the foot help in fast walking, running and jumping. In addition, these help in weight-bearing and in providing upright posture. The foot is really unique to human being. Arches are supported by intrinsic and extrinsic muscles of the sole in addition to ligaments, aponeurosis and shape of the bones. Foot prints are not complete due to the arches. The foot has to suffer from many disorders because of tight shoes or high heels which one wears for various reasons.

INTRODUCTION

The foot has to act:

1. As a pliable platform to support the body weight in the upright posture, and
2. As a lever to propel the body forwards in walking, running or jumping. To meet these requirements, the human foot is designed in the form of elastic arches or springs. These arches are segmented, so that they can best sustain the stresses of weight and of thrusts. The presence of the arches makes the sole concave. This is best appreciated by examining foot prints which show the weight-bearing parts of the sole (Fig. 13.1).

An arched foot is a distinctive feature of man. It distinguishes him from other primates. The arches are present right from birth, although they are masked in infants by the excessive amount of fat in their soles.

CLASSIFICATION OF ARCHES

    A. Longitudinal
        1. Medial
        2. Lateral
    B. Transverse
        1. Anterior
        2. Posterior

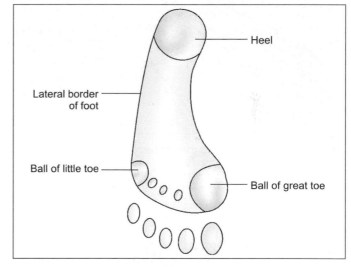

Fig. 13.1: Right foot print showing the weight-bearing points of the sole.

FORMATION OR STRUCTURE OF ARCHES

Medial Longitudinal Arch

This arch is considerably higher, more mobile and resilient than the lateral. Its constitution is as follows.

Ends: The *anterior end* is formed by the heads of the first, second and third metatarsals. The phalanges do not take part in forming the arches. The posterior end of this arch is formed by the medial tubercle of the calcaneum (Fig. 13.2).

Summit: The summit of the arch is formed by the superior articular surface of the body of the talus.

Pillars: The *anterior pillar* is long and weak. It is formed by the talus, the navicular, the three cuneiform bones, and the first three metatarsal bones. The *posterior pillar* is short and strong. It is formed by the medial part of the calcaneum (Fig. 13.3).

The *main joint* of the arch is the talocalcaneonavicular joint.

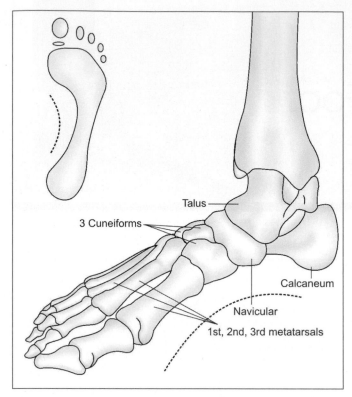

Fig. 13.2: Bones forming the arches of foot: Superior view.

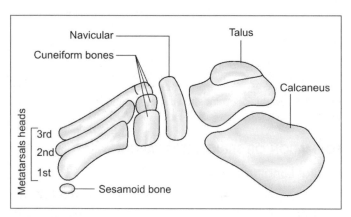

Fig. 13.3: Bones forming the arches of foot: Medial view.

Lateral Longitudinal Arch

This arch is characteristically low, has limited mobility, and is built to transmit weight and thrust to the ground. This is in contrast to the medial longitudinal arch which acts as a shock absorber. The constitution of the lateral longitudinal arch is as follows.

Ends

The *anterior end* of the arch is formed by the heads of the 4th and 5th metatarsal bones. The *posterior end* is formed by the lateral tubercle of the calcaneum (Fig. 13.4).

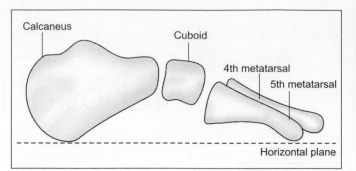

Fig. 13.4: Bones forming the arches of foot: Lateral view.

Summit

The *summit* lies at the level of the articular facets on the superior surface of the calcaneum at the level of the subtalar joint.

Pillars

The *anterior pillar* is long and weak. It is formed by the cuboid bone and by the 4th and 5th metatarsals. The *posterior pillar* is short and strong. It is formed by the lateral half of the calcaneum.

Main Joint

The *main joint* of the arch is the calcaneocuboid joint.

Anterior Transverse Arch

The *anterior transverse arch* is formed by the heads of the five metatarsal bones. It is complete because the heads of the first and fifth metatarsals both come in contact with the ground, and form the two ends of the arch.

Posterior Transverse Arch

The *posterior transverse arch* is formed by the greater parts of the tarsus and metatarsus. It is incomplete because only the lateral end comes in contact with the ground, the arch forming a 'half dome' which is completed by a similar half dome of the opposite foot.

FACTORS RESPONSIBLE FOR MAINTENANCE OF ARCHES

In general, the factors helping in maintaining the various arches are as follows.

1. Shape of the bones concerned.
2. *Intersegmental ties* or ligaments (and muscles) that hold the different segments of the arch together.
3. *Tie beams* or *bowstrings* that connect the two ends of the arch.
4. *Slings* that keep the summit of the arch pulled up. Each of these factors is considered below.

1. Bony Factor

The posterior transverse arch is formed, and maintained mainly because of the fact that many of the tarsal bones involved (e.g. the cuneiform bones), and the heads of the metatarsal bones, are wedge-shaped, the apex of the wedge pointing downwards.

The bony factor is not very important in the case of the other arches.

2. Intersegmental Ties

All arches are supported by the ligaments uniting the bones concerned. The most important of these are as follows.

(i) The spring ligament for the medial longitudinal arch (Figs 13.5 and 13.6).

(ii) The long and short plantar ligaments for the lateral longitudinal arch (Fig. 13.7).

(iii) In the case of the transverse arch, the metatarsal bones are held together by the interosseous muscles also.

3. Tie Beams

The longitudinal arches are prevented from flattening by the plantar aponeurosis, and by the muscles of the first layer of the sole. These structures keep the anterior and posterior ends of these arches pulled together. In the case of the transverse arch, the adductor hallucis acts as a tie beam (Figs 10.5 and 10.7).

4. Slings

(a) The summit of the medial longitudinal arch is pulled upwards by tendons passing from the posterior compartment of the leg into the sole, i.e. tibialis posterior, flexor hallucis longus, flexor digitorum longus (Fig. 13.6).

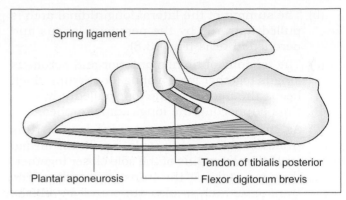

Fig. 13.5: Scheme showing some factors maintaining the medial longitudinal arch of the foot. There are the spring ligament and the tendon of the tibialis posterior which support the head of the talus; and the tie-beams formed by the plantar aponeurosis and the flexor digitorum brevis.

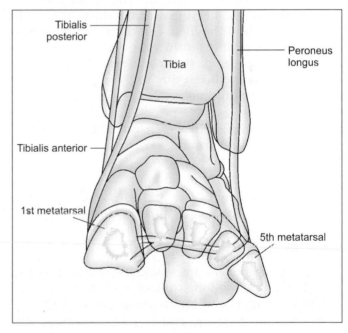

Fig. 13.6: Tendons supporting the medial longitudinal arch of the foot.

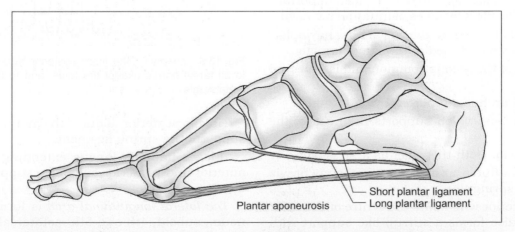

Fig. 13.7: Plantar ligaments that help to support the lateral longitudinal arch of the foot.

(b) The summit of the lateral longitudinal arch is pulled upwards by the peroneus longus and peroneus brevis (Fig. 13.8).

(c) The tendons of tibialis anterior and peroneus longus together form a sling (or stirrup) which keeps the middle of the foot pulled upwards, thus supporting the longitudinal arches.

(d) As the tendon of the peroneus longus runs transversely across the sole, it pulls the medial and lateral margins of the sole closer together, thus maintaining the transverse arches. The transverse arch is also supported by tibialis posterior which grips many of the bones of the sole through its slips (Figs 10.7 and 13.9).

FUNCTIONS

1. The arches of the foot distribute body weight to the weight-bearing areas of the sole, mainly the heel and the toes. Out of the latter, weight is borne mainly on the first and fifth toes. The lateral border of the foot bears some weight, but this is reduced due to the presence of the lateral longitudinal arch.
2. The arches act as springs (chiefly the medial longitudinal arch) which are of great help in walking and running.
3. They also act as shock absorbers in stepping and particularly in jumping.
4. The concavity of the arches protects the soft tissues of the sole against pressure.

SUMMARY

The arches of the foot are well known features of the foot. There are two longitudinal arches, i.e. medial longitudinal arch and lateral longitudinal arch.

In addition there are two transverse arches, i.e. posterior transverse arch and an anterior transverse arch.

The medial longitudinal arch is the most important and is primarily affected in pes planus and pes cavus.

This arch is formed by the calcaneus, navicular, three cuneiforms and medial three metatarsals.

Flattening of the arch is common and is assessed clinically.

The medial arch is supported by:

Spring ligament which supports the head of the talus.

Plantar fascia: Both these act as a tie beam.

Abductor hallucis and flexor digitorum brevis which act as spring ties.

Tibialis anterior which lifts the centre of the arch. This muscle also forms a stirrup like support with the help of peroneus longus muscle.

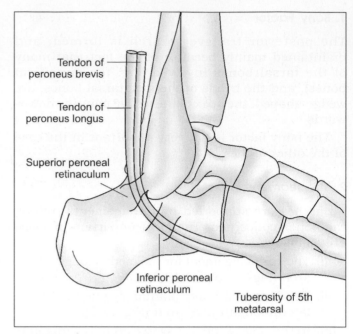

Fig. 13.8: Peroneal tendons helping to support the lateral longitudinal arch of the foot.

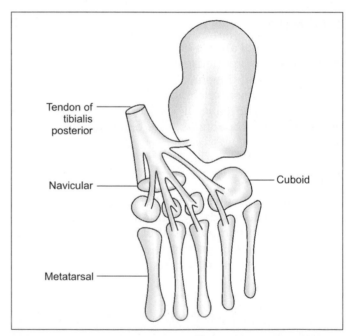

Fig. 13.9: Insertion of the tibialis posterior. Note the slips passing to all tarsal bones except the talus, and to the middle three metatarsals.

Tibialis posterior adducts the mid-tarsal joint and supports the spring ligament.

Flexor hallucis longus extending between the anterior and posterior ends also supports the head of talus.

The lateral longitudinal arch is formed by calcaneum, cuboid, 4th and 5th metatarsals. It is rather shallow and gets flattened on weight bearing.

This arch is supported by long plantar ligament, short plantar ligament. Plantar fascia acts as a tie beam.

Flexor digitorum brevis, flexor digiti minimi and abductor digiti minimi act as tie beams.

Peroneus longus, peroneus brevis and peroneus tertius support this arch.

Posterior transverse arch is formed by three cuneiforms and cuboid. This arch extends across the sole in a coronal plane. It is only a half arch, the other half gets completed by the other foot. This arch is supported by the ligaments binding the bones. It gets specific support from the tendon of peroneus longus as it extends from the lateral side to the medial side of the sole

Anterior transverse arch also lies in coronal plane. It is formed by the heads of five metatarsals. During weight bearing, the metatarsal heads flatten out.

This arch is supported by intermetatarsal ligaments and the intrinsic muscles of the sole. The transverse head of adductor hallucis holds the heads of metatarsals together (Fig. 10.7).

Table 13.1: Comparison of medial longitudinal arch and lateral longitudinal arch

	Medial longitudinal arch	Lateral longitudinal arch
Features	Higher, more mobile, resilient and shock absorber	Lower, limited mobility transmits weight
Anterior end	Heads of 1st, 2nd, 3rd metatarsal bones	Heads of 4th, 5th metatarsals
Posterior end	Medial tubercle of calcaneum	Lateral tubercle of calcaneum
Summit	Superior articular surface of talus	Articular facet on superior surface of calcaneum at level of subtalar joint
Anterior pillar	Talus, navicular, 3 cuneiforms and 1–3 metatarsal	Cuboid and 4th, 5th metatarsals
Posterior pillar	Medial half of calcaneum	Lateral half of calcaneum
Main joint	Talocalcaneonavicular joint	Calcaneocuboid joint
Bony factor	Wedge-shaped	Wedge-shaped
Intersegmental ties	Spring ligament	Long plantar ligament
		Short plantar ligament
Tie beams	Plantar aponeurosis (medial part)	Plantar aponeurosis (lateral part)
	Abductor hallucis	Abductor digiti minimi
	Medial part of flexor digitorum brevis	Lateral part of flexor digitorum brevis
Slings	Tibialis posterior	Peroneus longus
	Flexor hallucis longus	Peroneus brevis
	Flexor digitorum longus	
	Sling formed by tibialis anterior and peroneus longus	Sling formed by tibialis anterior and peroneus longus

Table 13.2: Comparison of anterior transverse arch and posterior transverse arch

	Anterior transverse arch	Posterior transverse arch
Formation	Heads of 1st to 5th metatarsals	Navicular, 3 cuneiforms, bases and shafts of metatarsals
Features	Complete arch	Incomplete. Arch is half dome raised medially
Bony factor	Round-shaped	Wedge-shaped
Intersegmental ties	Dorsal interosseous muscles	Dorsal interosseous muscles
Tie beams	Adductor hallucis	Flexor hallucis brevis
	Deep transverse metatarsal ligaments	Intertarsal and tarsometatarsal ligaments
Slings	Peroneus longus	Peroneus longus
	Tibialis posterior	Tibialis posterior

CLINICAL ANATOMY

- Absence or collapse of the arches leads to flat foot (pes planus), which may be congenital or acquired. The effects of a flat foot are as follows.
  - (a) Loss of spring in the foot leads to a clumsy, shuffling gait.
  - (b) Loss of shock absorbing function makes the foot more liable to trauma and osteoarthritis.
  - (c) Loss of the concavity of the sole leads to compression of the nerves and vessels of the sole. Compression of the communication between the lateral and medial plantar nerves causes neuralgic pain in the forefoot (metatarsalgia). Compression of blood vessels may cause vascular disturbances in the toes (Figs 13.10 and 13.11).
- Exaggeration of the longitudinal arches of the foot is known as *pes cavus*. This is usually a result of contracture (plantar flexion) at the transverse tarsal joint. When dorsiflexion of the metatarsophalangeal joints, and plantar flexion of the interphalangeal joints (due to atrophy of lumbricals and interossei) are superadded, the condition is known as *claw-foot*. The common causes of pes cavus and claw-foot are spina bifida and poliomyelitis (Fig. 13.12).

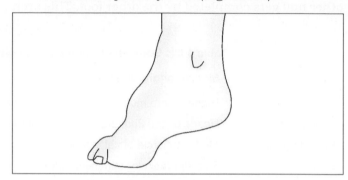

Fig. 13.12: Claw-foot or pes cavus.

- Other deformities of the foot are as follows.
  - (a) *Talipes equinus* in which the patient walks on toes, with the heel raised (Fig. 10.19).
  - (b) *Talipes calcaneus* in which the patient walks on heel, with the forefoot raised (Fig. 10.18).
  - (c) *Talipes varus* in which the patient walks on the outer border of foot (foot is inverted and adducted) (Fig. 10.20).
  - (d) *Talipes valgus* in which the patient walks on inner border of foot (foot is everted and abducted) (Fig. 10.21). Commonest deformity of the foot is *talipes equinovarus* (*club foot*). In this condition the foot is inverted, adducted and plantar flexed. The condition may be associated with spina bifida.
- Talipes (club foot) may be of two types: Talipes calcaneovalgus—foot is dorsiflexed at ankle joint, everted at midtarsal joints. Talipes equinovarus—foot is plantar flexed at ankle joint and inverted at midtarsal joints (Fig. 13.13).

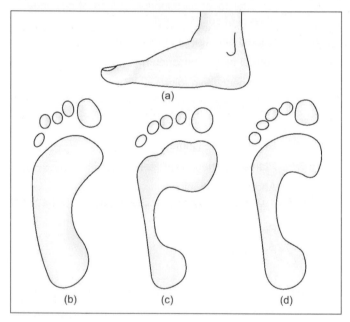

Fig. 13.10: (a), (b) Flat feet, (c) pes cavus and (d) normal.

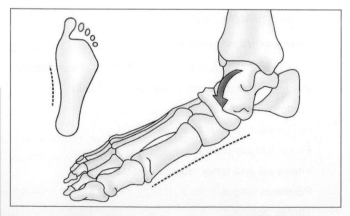

Fig. 13.11: Fallen arches of the foot.

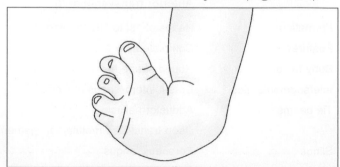

Fig. 13.13: Club foot—talipes equinovarus.

Surface and Radiological Anatomy

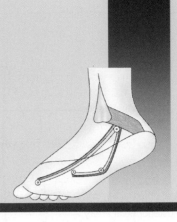

SURFACE MARKING OF ARTERIES

Femoral Artery

It corresponds to the upper two-thirds of a line joining the following two points.

(a) *Midinguinal point:* A point midway between the anterior superior iliac spine and the pubic symphysis (Fig. 14.1).

(b) *Adductor tubercle:* It lies at the lower end of the cord-like tendon of the adductor magnus. The tendon can be felt in a shallow groove just behind the prominence of the vastus medialis when the thigh is semiflexed, abducted and laterally rotated.

The upper one-third of the line represents the upper half of the artery lying in the femoral triangle. The middle one-third of the line represents the lower half of the artery lying in the adductor canal. The lower one-third of the line represents the descending genicular and saphenous branches of the artery.

Profunda Femoris Artery

First mark the femoral artery. The profunda artery is then marked by joining the following two points on the femoral artery.

(a) *First point:* 3.5 cm below the midinguinal point.

(b) *Second point:* 10 cm below the midinguinal point.

The artery is slightly convex laterally in its upper part.

Popliteal Artery

It is marked by joining the following points.

(a) *First point:* At the junction of the middle and lower thirds of the thigh, 2.5 cm medial to the midline on the back of the limb (Fig. 14.2).

(b) *Second point:* On the midline of the back of the knee.

(c) *Third point:* On the midline of the back of leg at the level of the tibial tuberosity.

Superior Gluteal Artery

Mark the following points.

(a) *First point:* At the posterior superior iliac spine.

(b) *Second point:* At the apex of the greater trochanter (Fig. 14.3).

The superior gluteal artery enters the gluteal region at the junction of the upper and middle thirds of the line joining points (a) and (b).

Anterior superior iliac spine
Midinguinal point
Femoral nerve
Femoral artery
Sartorius

Inguinal ligament
Femoral vein
Pubic tubercle
Pubic symphysis
Apex of femoral triangle
Adductor longus
Femoral vein
Descending genicular artery
Adductor tubercle

Fig. 14.1: Surface marking of femoral vessels, and femoral nerve.

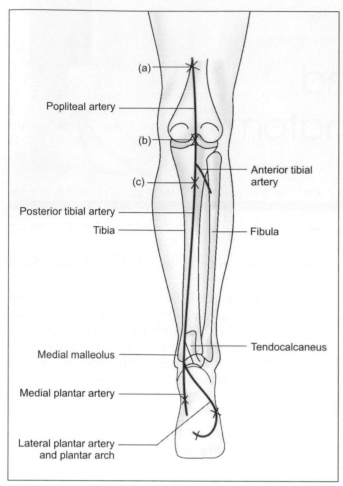

Fig. 14.2: Surface marking of popliteal, posterior tibial, medial and lateral plantar arteries.

Inferior Gluteal Artery

Mark the following points.

(a) *First point:* Posterior superior iliac spine.

(b) *Second point:* Ischial tuberosity.

Then mark a third point 2.5 cm lateral to the midpoint of the line joining (a) and (b). The sciatic nerve enters the gluteal region at this point. The inferior gluteal artery appears just medial to the entry of the sciatic nerve (Fig. 14.3).

Anterior Tibial Artery

It is marked by joining the following two points.

(a) *First point:* 2.5 cm below the medial side of the head of the fibula (Fig. 14.4).

(b) *Second point:* Midway between the two malleoli.

The artery passes downwards and slightly medially.

Posterior Tibial Artery

It is marked by joining the following two points.

(a) *First point:* On the midline of the back of the calf at the level of the tibial tuberosity.

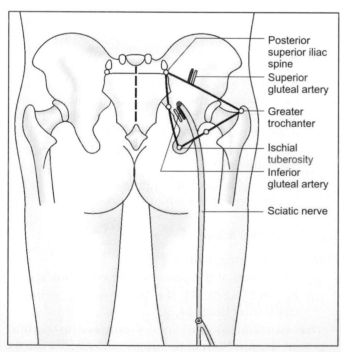

Fig. 14.3: Surface marking of sciatic nerve and gluteal arteries.

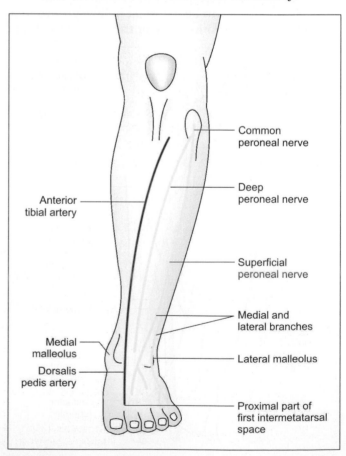

Fig. 14.4: Surface marking of anterior tibial, dorsalis pedis arteries; deep and superficial peroneal nerves.

(b) *Second point:* Midway between the medial malleolus and the tendocalcaneus (Fig. 14.2).

Dorsalis Pedis Artery

It is marked by joining the following two points.
(a) *First point:* Midway between the two malleoli.
(b) *Second point:* At the proximal end of the first intermetatarsal space (Fig. 14.4).

Medial Plantar Artery

It is marked by joining the following two points.
(a) *First point:* Midway between the medial malleolus and the prominence of the heel.
(b) *Second point:* On the navicular bone which lies midway between the back of the heel and the root of the big toe. The artery runs in the direction of the first interdigital cleft (Fig. 14.5).

Lateral Plantar Artery

It is marked by joining the following two points.
(a) *First point:* Midway between the medial malleolus and the prominence of the heel.
(b) *Second point:* 2.5 cm medial to the tuberosity of the fifth metatarsal bone (Fig. 14.5).

Plantar Arch

It is marked by joining the following two points.
(a) *First point:* 2.5 cm medial to the tuberosity of the fifth metatarsal bone.
(b) *Second point:* At the proximal end of the first intermetatarsal space, 2.5 cm distal to the tuberosity of the navicular bone (Fig. 14.5).

The arch is slightly curved with its convexity directed forwards.

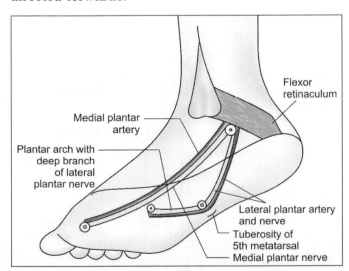

Fig. 14.5: Surface marking of medial and lateral plantar nerves and vessels, including the plantar arch.

VEINS

Femoral Vein

Its marking is same as that of the femoral artery, except that the upper point is taken 1 cm medial to the midinguinal point, and the lower point 1 cm lateral to the adductor tubercle. The vein is medial to the artery at the upper end, posterior to it in the middle, and lateral to it at the lower end (Fig. 14.1).

Great Saphenous Vein

It can be marked by joining the following points, although it is easily visible in living subjects.
(a) *First point:* On the dorsum of the foot at the medial end of the dorsal venous arch.
(b) *Second point:* On the anterior surface of the medial malleolus.
(c) *Third point:* On the medial border of the tibia at the junction of the upper two-thirds and lower one-third of the leg.
(d) *Fourth point:* At the adductor tubercle.
(e) *Fifth point:* Just below the centre of the saphenous opening (Fig. 14.6).

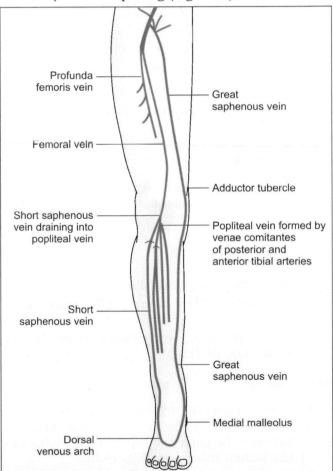

Fig. 14.6: Scheme to show the arrangement of the veins of the lower limb.

Small Saphenous Vein

It can be marked by joining the following points, although this vein is also easily visible in its lower part (Fig. 14.7).

(a) *First point:* On the dorsum of the foot at the lateral end of the dorsal venous arch.

(b) *Second point:* Behind the lateral malleolus.

(c) *Third point:* Just lateral to the tendocalcaneus above the lateral malleolus.

(d) *Fourth point:* At the centre of the popliteal fossa.

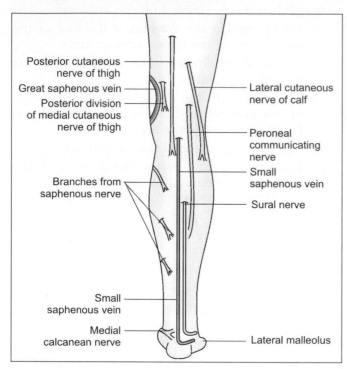

Fig. 14.7: Surface marking of small saphenous vein. The cutaneous nerves of the back of the leg and the heel also.

NERVES

Femoral Nerve

It is marked by joining the following two points.

(a) *First point:* 1.2 cm lateral to the midinguinal point.

(b) *Second point:* 2.5 cm vertically below the first point (Fig. 14.1).

Sciatic Nerve

It is marked by joining the following points.

(a) *First point:* 2.5 cm lateral to the midpoint between the posterior superior iliac spine and the ischial tuberosity (Fig. 14.3).

(b) *Second point:* Just medial to the midpoint between the ischial tuberosity and the greater trochanter.

(c) *The third point:* In the midline of the back of the thigh at the junction of its upper two-thirds and lower one-third, i.e. at the apex of the popliteal fossa.

Tibial Nerve

Mark the following points.

(a) *First point:* In the midline of back of the thigh at the junction of its upper two-thirds and lower one-third, i.e. at the apex of the popliteal fossa.

(b) *Second point:* In the midline of back of the leg at the level of tibial tuberosity (Fig. 14.8).

(c) *Third point:* Midway between the medial malleolus and tendocalcaneus.

The line joining (a) and (b) represents the tibial nerve in the popliteal fossa, and the line joining (b) and (c) represents it in the back of the leg.

Common Peroneal Nerve

It is marked by joining the following two points.

(a) *First point:* At the upper angle of the popliteal fossa (Fig. 6.7).

(b) *Second point:* On the back of the neck of the fibula (Fig. 2.42).

At the lower end the nerve turns forwards and ends deep to the upper fibres of the peroneus longus.

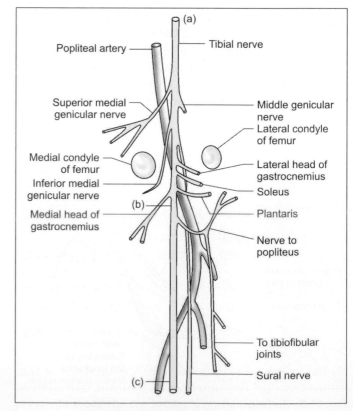

Fig. 14.8: Distribution of tibial nerve.

Deep Peroneal Nerve

It is marked by joining the following two points.

(a) *First point:* On the lateral aspect of the neck of the fibula (Fig. 14.4).

(b) *Second point:* In front of the ankle, midway between the two malleoli.

The nerve lies lateral to the anterior tibial artery in its upper and lower thirds, but anterior to the artery in its middle-third.

Superficial Peroneal Nerve

It is marked by joining the following two points.

(a) *First point:* On the lateral aspect of the neck of the fibula (Fig. 14.4).

(b) *Second point:* On the anterior border of the peroneus longus at the junction of the upper two-thirds and lower one-third of the leg.

At the lower point the nerve pierces the deep fascia and divides into medial and lateral branches.

Medial Plantar Nerve

It is marked in a manner similar to the medial plantar artery (Fig. 14.5). Lies lateral to the artery.

Lateral Plantar Nerve

It is marked in a manner similar to that for the lateral plantar artery (Fig. 14.5). Lies medial to the artery.

MISCELLANEOUS STRUCTURES

Saphenous Opening

Its centre lies 4 cm below and 4 cm lateral to the pubic tubercle. It is about 2.5 cm long and 2 cm broad, with its long axis directed downwards and laterally.

Femoral Ring

It is represented by a horizontal line 1.25 cm long over the inguinal ligament, 1.25 cm medial to the midinguinal point.

Superior Extensor Retinaculum

The retinaculum is about 3 cm broad vertically. It is drawn from the anterior border of the triangular subcutaneous area of the fibula to the lower part of the anterior border of the tibia, running medially and slightly upwards (Fig. 14.9).

Inferior Extensor Retinaculum

The *stem* is about 1.5 cm broad. It extends from the anterior part of the upper surface of the calcaneum to a point medial to the tendon of the extensor digitorum longus on the dorsum of the foot.

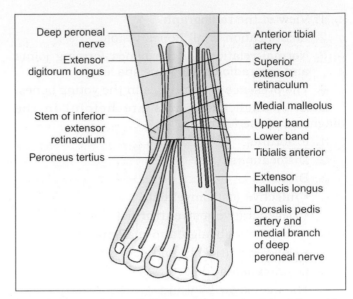

Fig. 14.9: Superior and inferior extensor retinacula of the ankle, surface view.

The *upper band* is about 1 cm wide, and extends from the medial end of the stem to the anterior border of the medial malleolus (Fig. 14.9).

The *lower band* is also about 1 cm wide. It extends from the medial end of the stem to the medial side of the foot, extending into the sole.

Flexor Retinaculum

It is about 2.5 cm broad, and extends from the medial malleolus to the medial side of the heel, running downwards and backwards (Fig. 14.10).

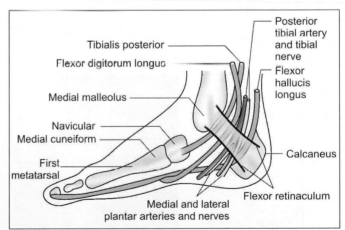

Fig. 14.10: Flexor retinaculum of the ankle, and the structures passing deep to it.

RADIOLOGICAL ANATOMY

In the study of plain skiagrams of the limbs, the following points should be noted.

1. View of the radiograph.
2. Identification of all bones visible.
3. Normal relations of the bones forming joints and the radiological 'joint space'.
4. The presence of epiphyses in the young bones.

Briefly, such skiagrams are helpful in the diagnosis of the following.

1. Fractures.
2. Dislocations.
3. Diseases.
   • Infective (osteomyelitis),
   • Degenerative (osteoarthritis),
   • Neoplastic (benign and malignant),
   • Deficiency (rickets and scurvy).
4. Developmental defects.
5. The age below 25 years.

HIP

Identify the Following Bones in AP View

1. *Hip bone,* including ilium, pubis, ischium and acetabulum.
2. *Upper end of femur,* including the head, neck, greater trochanter, lesser trochanter, and upper part of shaft.

The *neck-shaft angle* is about 125 degrees in adults, being more in children (140°) and less in females.

In the head, a dense wedge or triangle of cancellous bone is known as *Ward's triangle.* It represents the epiphyseal scar.

Calcar femorale is a dense plate of bone forming a buttress to strengthen the concavity of the neck-shaft angle in front of the lesser trochanter. It transmits weight from the head of femur to the linea aspera.

Cervical torus is a thickened band or ridge of compact bone on the upper part of the neck between the head and the greater trochanter.

3. The *lumbosacral spine* may have been included.

Study the Normal Appearance of the Following Joints

1. *Hip joint:* Normal relation of the head of femur with the acetabulum is indicated by the *Shenton's line,* which is a continuous curve formed by the upper border of obturator foramen and the lower border of the neck of femur (Fig. 14.11).
2. *Pubic symphysis*
3. *Sacroiliac joint.*

Note the Epiphyses and Other Incomplete Ossifications if any, and Determine the Age

The ischiopubic rami fuse by 7–8 years, and the acetabulum is ossified by 17 years.

KNEE

Identify the Following Bones

1. *Lower end of femur,* including the two condyles (Figs 14.12 and 14.13).
2. *Patella* is clearly seen only in the lateral views; in AP views it overlaps the lower end of femur. It lies about 1 cm above the knee joint.

Bilateral separation of the superolateral angles of the patellae is known as *bipartite patella.* The small fragment may be further subdivided

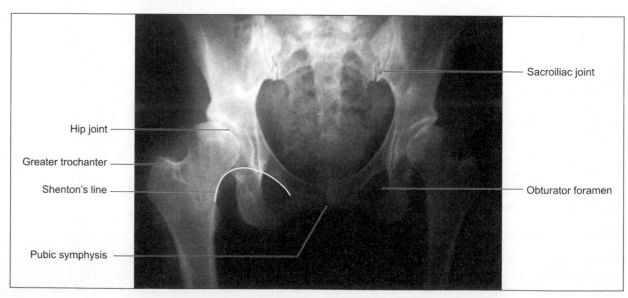

Fig. 14.11: Anteroposterior view of the female pelvis.

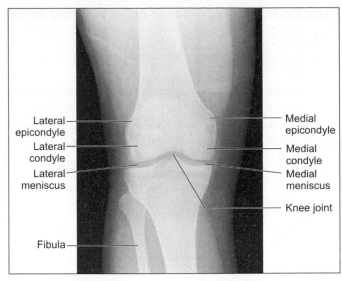

Fig. 14.12: Anteroposterior view of the knee joint.

Labels: Lateral epicondyle, Lateral condyle, Lateral meniscus, Fibula, Medial epicondyle, Medial condyle, Medial meniscus, Knee joint

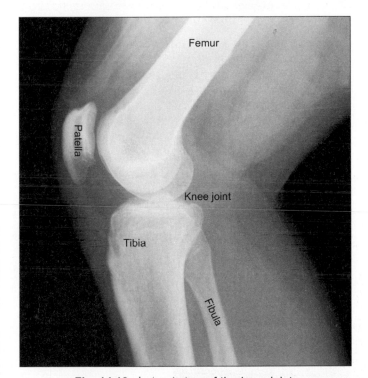

Fig. 14.13: Lateral view of the knee joint.

Labels: Femur, Patella, Knee joint, Tibia, Fibula

to form the multipartite patella. This is due to failure of the ossific centers to fuse.

In *emargination of patella*, its outer margin is concave. The concavity is bounded by a tubercle above and a spine below. This reflects the mode of attachment of the vastus lateralis.

3. *Upper end of tibia*, including the two condyles, intercondylar eminence and tibial tuberosity.

4. *Upper end of fibula*, including the head, neck and upper part of shaft.

5. *Fabella:* It is a small, rounded sesamoid bone in the lateral head of gastrocnemius. It articulates with the posterior surface of the lateral condyle of femur. It measures 1–1.5 cm in diameter, and is present in about 15% individuals. As a rule it is bilateral, and appears at 12–15 years of age.

Study the Normal Appearance of the Following Joints

1. *Knee joint:* The joint space varies inversely with the age. In young adults, it is about 5 mm. It is entirely due to articular cartilage and not due to menisci.

2. *Superior tibiofibular joint.*

Note the Epiphyses if any, and Determine the Age with the Help of Ossification studied

FOOT

Identify the Following Bones

1. *Talus* and *calcaneum* are better seen in lateral view.

2. *Navicular* and *cuboid* are seen clearly in almost all the views (Fig. 14.14).

3. *Cuneiform bones* are seen separately in dorsoplantar views; they overlap each other in a lateral view.

4. *Metatarsals* and *phalanges* are seen separately in dorsoplantar views, but overlap each other in lateral views.

5. Sesamoid and accessory bones should be distinguished from fractures.

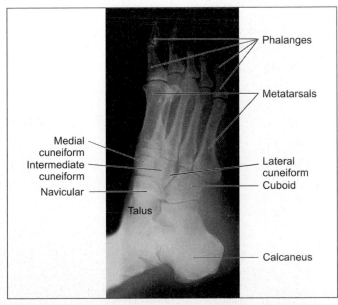

Fig. 14.14: Dorsoplantar view of the ankle and foot.

Labels: Phalanges, Metatarsals, Lateral cuneiform, Cuboid, Medial cuneiform, Intermediate cuneiform, Navicular, Talus, Calcaneus

The common *sesamoids* are found on the plantar surface of the head of first metatarsal bone. They may also be present in the tendons of tibialis anterior, tibialis posterior and peroneus longus.

Accessory bones are separate small pieces of bone which have not fused with the main bone. For example, os trigonum (lateral tubercle of talus) and os vesalianum (tuberosity of fifth metatarsal bone).

Study the Normal Appearance of the Following Joints

1. Ankle joint.
2. Subtalar, talocalcaneonavicular and transverse tarsal joints.
3. Tarsometatarsal, intermetatarsal, metatarsophalangeal, and interphalangeal joints.

Note the epiphyses and other incomplete ossification if any, and determine the age.

Appendix 1

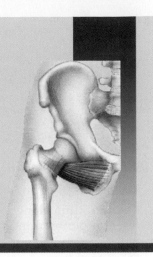

NERVES OF LOWER LIMB

FEMORAL NERVE

Femoral nerve is the nerve of anterior compartment of thigh. Its cutaneous branch, the saphenous nerve extends to the medial side of leg and medial border of foot till the ball of the big toe.

Root value: Dorsal division of ventral rami of L2, L3, L4 segments of spinal cord.

Beginning and course: It emerges at the lateral border of psoas major muscle in abdomen. It passes downwards between psoas major and iliacus muscles. The nerve enters the thigh behind the inguinal ligament, lateral to femoral sheath. It is not a content of femoral sheath (Figs 3.14 and 3.21).

Termination: It ends by dividing into two divisions 4 cm below the inguinal ligament. Both these divisions end in a number of branches.

Branches: In *abdomen*, femoral nerve supplies iliacus muscle. Just above the inguinal ligament, it gives a branch to pectineus muscle, which passes behind the femoral sheath to reach the muscle. Its branches in the thigh are presented in Table A1.1.

OBTURATOR NERVE

Root value: Obturator nerve is a branch of lumbar plexus. It arises from ventral division of ventral rami of L2, L3, L4 segments of spinal cord (Fig. 4.6).

Beginning and course: It emerges on the medial border of psoas major muscle within the abdomen. It crosses the pelvic brim to run downwards and forwards on the lateral wall of pelvis to reach the upper part of obturator foramen.

Termination: It ends by dividing into anterior and posterior divisions.

Anterior division: It passes downwards in front of obturator externus. Then it lies between pectineus and adductor longus anteriorly and adductor brevis posteriorly. It gives muscular, articular and vascular branches.

Posterior division: It pierces the obturator externus and passes behind adductor brevis and in front of adductor magnus. It also ends by giving muscular, articular and vascular branches.

The branches are presented in Table A1.2.

ACCESSORY OBTURATOR NERVE

It is present in 30% subjects.

Root value: Ventral division of ventral rami of L3, L4 nerves.

Table A1.1: Branches of femoral nerve in thigh		
	Superficial division	**Deep division**
Muscular	Sartorius	Vastus medialis Vastus intermedius Vastus lateralis Rectus femoris
Cutaneous	Medial cutaneous nerve of thigh Intermediate cutaneous nerve of thigh	Saphenous for medial side of leg and medial border of foot till ball of big toe
Articular and vascular	Sympathetic fibres to femoral artery	Knee joint from branches to vasti Hip joint from branch to rectus femoris

Table A1.2: Branches of obturator nerve		
	Anterior division	**Posterior division**
Muscular	Pectineus, adductor longus, adductor brevis, gracilis	Obturator externus, adductor magnus (adductor part)
Articular	Hip joint	Knee joint
Vascular and cutaneous	Femoral artery. Medial side of thigh	Popliteal artery

Course: Runs along medial border of psoas major, crosses superior ramus of pubis behind pectineus muscle.

Branches: Deep surface of pectineus, hip joint and communicating branch to anterior division of obturator nerve (Fig. 4.7).

SUPERIOR GLUTEAL NERVE

Root value: L4, L5, S1.

Course: Enters the gluteal region through greater sciatic notch above piriformis muscle. Runs between gluteus medius and gluteus minimus to end in tensor fascia latae.

Branches: It supplies gluteus medius, gluteus minimus and tensor fascia latae (Fig. 5.10).

INFERIOR GLUTEAL NERVE

Root value: L5, S1, S2.

Course: Enters the gluteal region through greater sciatic notch below piriformis muscle (Fig. 5.10).

Branches: It gives a number of branches to the gluteus maximus muscle only. It is the sole supply to the large antigravity, postural muscle with red fibres, responsible for extending the hip joint.

NERVE TO QUADRATUS FEMORIS

Root value: L4, L5, S1.

Branches: It supplies quadratus femoris, inferior gemellus and hip joint.

NERVE TO OBTURATOR INTERNUS

Root value: L5, S1, S2.

Branches: It supplies obturator internus and superior gemellus.

SCIATIC NERVE

Sciatic nerve is the thickest nerve of the body. It is the terminal branch of the lumbosacral plexus.

Root value: Ventral rami of L4, L5, S1, S2, S3. It consists of two parts.

Tibial part: Its root value is ventral division of ventral rami of L4, L5, S1, S2, S3, segments of spinal cord.

Common peroneal part: Its root value is dorsal division of ventral rami of L4, L5, S1, S2 segments of spinal cord.

Course: Sciatic nerve arises in the pelvis. Leaves the pelvis by passing through greater sciatic foramen below the piriformis to enter the gluteal region (Figs 5.10 and 7.6).

In the gluteal region, it lies deep to the gluteus maximus muscle, and crosses superior gemellus, obturator internus, inferior gemellus, quadratus femoris to enter the back of thigh. During its short course, it lies between ischial tuberosity and greater trochanter with a convexity to the lateral side. It gives no branches in the gluteal region.

In the back of thigh, it lies deep to biceps femoris and superficial to adductor magnus.

Termination: It ends by dividing into its two terminal branches in the back of thigh.

Branches: The branches of sciatic nerve are shown in Table A1.3.

TIBIAL NERVE

Root value: Ventral division of ventral rami of L4, L5, S1, S2, S3, segments of spinal cord.

Beginning: It begins as the larger subdivision of sciatic nerve in the back of thigh.

Table A1.3: Branches of sciatic nerve			
	Gluteal region	**Back of thigh; from tibial part**	**From common peroneal part**
Muscular	Nil	Long head of biceps femoris, semitendinosus, semimembranosus, ischial part of adductor magnus	Short head of biceps femoris
Articular	Nil	Hip joint	—
Terminal	Nil	Tibial and common peroneal nerves	—

Course: It has a long course first in the popliteal fossa and then in the back of leg.

Popliteal fossa: The nerve descends vertically in the popliteal fossa from its upper angle to the lower angle. It lies superficial to the popliteal vessels. It continues in the back of leg beyond the distal border of popliteus muscle (Fig. 6.8).

In back of leg: The nerve descends as the neurovascular bundle with posterior tibial vessels. It lies superficial to tibialis posterior and deep to flexor digitorum longus. Lastly it passes deep to the flexor retinaculum of ankle (Fig. 9.3).

Branches: Its branches are shown in Table A1.4.

Termination: The tibial nerve terminates by dividing into medial plantar and lateral plantar nerves as it lies deep to the flexor retinaculum.

COMMON PERONEAL NERVE

This is the smaller terminal branch of sciatic nerve. Its root value is dorsal division of ventral rami of L4, L5, S1, S2 segments of spinal cord.

Beginning: It begins in the back of thigh as a smaller subdivision of the sciatic nerve.

Course: It lies in the upper lateral part of popliteal fossa, along the medial border of biceps femoris muscle. It turns around the lateral surface of fibula. Then it lies in the substance of peroneus longus muscle (Fig. 6.9).

Branches: Its branches are shown in Table A1.5.

Termination: Ends by dividing into two terminal branches, i.e. superficial peroneal and deep peroneal nerves.

DEEP PERONEAL NERVE

The deep peroneal nerve is the nerve of the anterior compartment of the leg and the dorsum of the foot. It corresponds to the posterior interosseous nerve

Table A1.5: Branches of common peroneal nerve in popliteal fossa

Muscular	— Short head of biceps femoris
Cutaneous and vascular (Fig. 9.2)	— Lateral cutaneous nerve of calf — Sural communicating
Articular	— Superior lateral genicular — Inferior lateral genicular — Recurrent genicular
Terminal	— Deep peroneal — Superficial peroneal

of the forearm. This is one of the two terminal branches of the common peroneal nerve given off between the neck of the fibula and the peroneus longus muscle.

Course and relations: The deep peroneal nerve begins on the lateral side of the neck of fibula under cover of the upper fibres of peroneus longus. It enters the anterior compartment of leg by piercing the anterior intermuscular septum. It then pierces the extensor digitorum longus and comes to lie next to the anterior tibial vessels (Fig. 8.12).

In the leg, it accompanies the anterior tibial artery and has similar relations. The nerve lies lateral to the artery in the upper and lower third of the leg, and medial to the artery in the middle one-third.

The nerve ends on the dorsum of the foot, close to the ankle joint, by dividing into the lateral and medial terminal branches (Fig. 8.5).

The lateral terminal branch turns laterally and ends in a pseudoganglion deep to the extensor digitorum brevis. Branches arise from the pseudo-ganglion and supply the extensor digitorum brevis and the tarsal joints (Fig. 8.6).

The medial terminal branch ends by supplying the skin adjoining the first interdigital cleft and the proximal joints of the big toe.

Table A1.4: Branches of tibial nerve

	Popliteal fossa	Back of leg
Muscular	— Medial head of gastrocnemius — Lateral head of gastrocnemius — Plantaris — Soleus — Popliteus. These are given in lower part of fossa	Soleus Flexor digitorum longus Flexor hallucis longus Tibialis posterior
Cutaneous and vascular	Sural nerve. This is given in middle of fossa	Medial calcanean branches and branch to posterior tibial artery
Articular	— Superior medial genicular — Middle genicular — Inferior medial genicular. These are given in upper part of fossa	Ankle joint
Terminal	—	Medial plantar and lateral plantar nerves

Branches and distribution of the deep peroneal nerve:

Muscular branches: The muscular branches supply the following muscles.

1. Muscles of the anterior compartment of the leg. These include:
   (i) Tibialis anterior
   (ii) Extensor hallucis longus
   (iii) Extensor digitorum longus
   (iv) Peroneus tertius.
2. The extensor digitorum brevis (on the dorsum of foot) is supplied by the lateral terminal branch of the deep peroneal nerve.

Cutaneous branches: The lateral terminal branch of the deep peroneal nerve ends by forming the dorsal digital nerves for the adjacent sides of the big toe and second toe (Fig. 8.3).

Articular branches: These are given to the:
(i) Ankle joint
(ii) Tarsal joints
(iii) Tarsometatarsal joint
(iv) Metatarsophalangeal joint of big toe.

SUPERFICIAL PERONEAL NERVE

It is the smaller terminal branch of the common peroneal nerve.

Origin: It arises in the substance of peroneus longus muscle, lateral to the neck of fibula.

Course: It descends in the lateral compartment of leg deep to peroneus longus. Then it lies between peroneus longus and peroneus brevis muscles and lastly between the peronei and extensor digitorum longus.

It pierces the deep fascia in distal one-third of leg and descends to the dorsum of foot.

Branches: It supplies both peroneus longus and peroneus brevis muscles.

It gives cutaneous branches (Fig. 8.3) to most of the dorsum of foot including the digital branches to medial side of big toe, adjacent sides of 2nd and 3rd;

3rd and 4th and 4th and 5th toes. The nail beds are not supplied as these are supplied by medial plantar for medial 3½ and by lateral plantar for lateral 1½ toes. Adjacent sides of big and second toes are supplied by deep peroneal nerve. The medial border of foot is supplied by saphenous and lateral border by sural nerves.

PLANTAR NERVES

The medial and lateral plantar nerves are the terminal branches of the tibial nerve. These nerves begin deep to the flexor retinaculum.

Medial plantar nerve: It is the larger terminal branch of tibial nerve. Its distribution is similar to median nerve of the hand. It lies between abductor hallucis and flexor digitorum brevis and ends by giving muscular, cutaneous and articular branches.

Branches: The branches of medial plantar nerve are shown in Table A1.6.

Lateral plantar nerve: It is the smaller terminal branch of tibial nerve, resembling the ulnar nerve of the hand in its distribution. It runs obliquely between the first and second layers of sole till the tuberosity of fifth metatarsal bone, where it divides into its superficial and deep branches.

Branches: The structures supplied by the trunk, and its two branches are given in Table A1.7.

Table A1.6: Branches of medial plantar nerve

Medial plantar nerve (S2, S3)

Muscular	— Abductor hallucis	: Ist layer
	— Flexor digitorum brevis	: Ist layer
	— First lumbrical	: 2nd layer
	— Flexor hallucis brevis	: 3rd layer
Cutaneous and vascular	— Nail beds of medial 3½ toes — Sympathetic branches to medial plantar artery	
Articular	— Tarsometatarsal, metatarsophalangeal and interphalangeal joints of medial 2/3rd of foot	

Table A1.7: Branches of lateral plantar nerve

	Trunk (S2, S3)	Superficial branch	Deep branch
Muscular	• Abductor digiti minimi: Ist layer • Flexor digitorum accessorius: 2nd layer	• Flexor digiti minimi brevis: 3rd layer • 3rd plantar interosseus: 4th layer • 4th dorsal interosseous: 4th layer	Ist and 2nd plantar interossei: 4th layer 1st, 2nd, 3rd, dorsal interossei: 4th layer 2nd, 3rd, 4th lumbricals: 2nd layer Adductor hallucis: 3rd layer
Cutaneous and vascular	—	Nail beds of lateral 1½ toes Sympathetic branches to lateral plantar artery	—
Articular	Tarsometatarsal	Interphalangeal	Metatarsophalangeal

CLINICAL ANATOMY

- Femoral nerve supplying the quadriceps femoris through L2, L3, L4 segments of spinal cord is tested by doing the 'patellar jerk'. The ligamentum patellae is hit by the hammer and the contraction of the quadriceps is felt and extension of knee is seen (Fig. 3.36).
- Since obturator nerve supplies both the hip and knee joints, pain of one joint may be referred to the other joint.
- The paralysis of left superior gluteal nerve leads to paralysis of left gluteus medius and minimus muscle. During walking when the body is supported on left foot, the right unsupported side of the pelvis droops, causing inability to walk with right foot. This is called positive Trendelenburg's test.
- *Sleeping foot:* Sometimes it happens that one is awake but the foot sleeps. Sciatic nerve lies on quadratus femoris and adductor magnus. Between the two muscles, the nerve lies on the hard femur. So the nerve gets pressed between the femur and the hard edge of table, chair or bed. There is numbness of the lower limb till the foot is hit against the ground a few times. The sensations come back (Fig. 7.6).
- *Injury:* Injury to sciatic nerve leads to paralysis of hamstrings and all muscles of the leg and foot leading to "foot drop" (Fig. 7.11).

- *Sciatica:* Is the name given when there is radiating pain in the back of lower limb. It may be due to slip disc.
- Common peroneal nerve is the commonest nerve to be paralysed. This is injured due to fracture of neck of fibula, 'lathi injury' on the lateral side of knee joint or due to plaster on the leg. In the last case, the nerve gets compressed between hard plaster and neck of fibula. To prevent this cotton must be placed on the upper lateral side of the leg.

The effects of injury are:

Motor loss: To dorsiflexors and evertors of foot. The typical position of the foot is "foot drop"; sensory loss is to the back of leg; lateral side of leg and most of dorsum of foot.

Articular loss to the lateral side of knee joint.

- Paralysis of muscles of the anterior compartment of the leg results in loss of the power of dorsiflexion of the foot. As a result the foot is plantar flexed. The condition is called as "foot drop" (Fig. 8.26).
- The motor and sensory loss in case of injury to the various nerves is shown in Table A1.8.
- Thus most of the muscles of the lower limb are supplied by sciatic nerve except the adductors of thigh and extensors of knee joint.

Table A1.8: Injury to nerves and their effects		
	Motor loss	**Sensory loss**
Femoral nerve	Quadriceps femoris	Anterior side of thigh, medial side of leg till ball of big toe
Sciatic nerve	Hamstring muscles; dorsiflexors and plantar flexors of ankle joint and evertors of foot Foot drop occurs	Back of leg, lateral side of leg, most of dorsum of foot, sole of foot
Common peroneal	Dorsiflexors of ankle, evertors of foot and foot drop occurs	Lateral and anterior sides of leg, most of dorsum of foot, most of digits
Tibial	Plantar flexors of ankle, intrinsic muscles of sole	Skin of sole. Later trophic ulcers develop
Obturator	Adductors of thigh except hamstring part of adductor magnus	Small area on the medial side of thigh
Superior gluteal	Gluteal medius, gluteus minimus and tensor fascia latae	Nil
Inferior gluteal	Gluteus maximus	Nil
Pudendal nerve	Muscles of perineum	Skin of perineum
Deep peroneal	Muscles of anterior compartment of leg	1st interdigital cleft
Superficial peroneal	Peroneus longus and peroneus brevis	Lateral aspect of leg most of dorsum of foot
Medial plantar	Four intrinsic muscles of sole, Table A1.6	Medial 2/3rd of sole and digital nerves to medial 3½ toes, including nail beds
Lateral plantar	Most of intrinsic muscles of sole, Table A1.7	Lateral 1/3rd of sole and digital nerves to lateral 1½ toes, including nail beds

- Arterial occlusive disease of the lower limb: Occlusive disease causes ischaemia of the muscles of lower limb leading to cramp-like pain. The pain disappears with rest but comes back with activity. The condition is called 'intermittent claudication'.

- Palpation of dorsalis pedis artery and posterior tibial artery gives information about peripheral arterial diseases (Fig. 8.14).

- Sympathetic innervation of the arteries: Thoracic 10–12 and L1–L3 segments provide sympathetic innervation to arteries of lower limb. Pregang-lionic fibres relay in the ganglia associated with these segments. Postganglionic fibres reach blood vessels via branches of lumbar and sacral plexuses.

- Femoral artery receives postganglionic fibres from femoral and obturator nerves.

- Arteries of the leg receive postganglionic fibres via the tibial and common peroneal nerves.

- Lumbar sympathectomy for occlusive arterial disease: Sympathectomy, i.e. removal of L2 and L3 ganglia with intervening sympathetic trunk is advised for this condition. This increases the collateral circulation. L1 ganglion is not removed as it is responsible for ejaculation.

- Blood supply to muscles of back of thigh reaches through a rich anastomosis (Fig. A1.1) formed by:
  (a) Superior gluteal artery
  (b) Inferior gluteal artery
  (c) Branches of femoral circumflex arteries
  (d) Perforating arteries
  (e) Branches of popliteal artery.

- Excessive fluid from knee joint can be aspirated by putting in a needle in the joint cavity from its lateral side (Fig. A1.2).

- Serious automobile accident can cause injury to tibial collateral ligament, medial meniscus, anterior cruciate ligament and even fibular collateral ligament (Fig. A1.3).

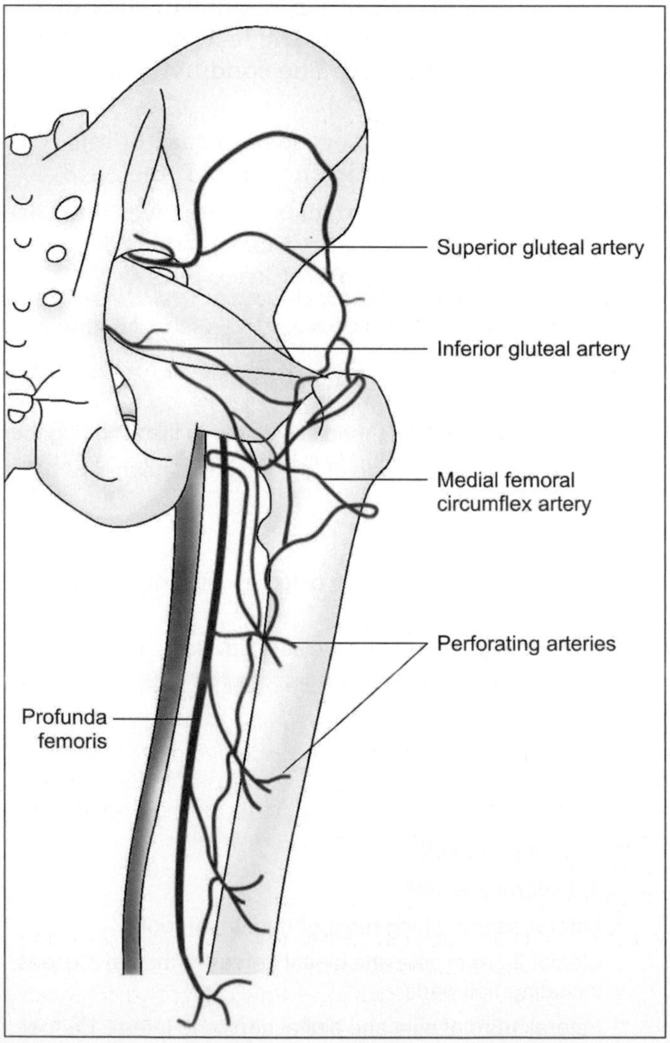

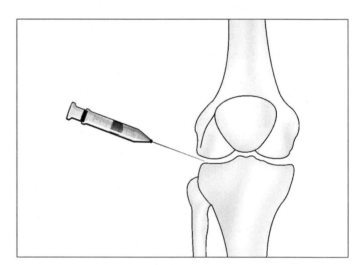

Fig. A1.2: Aspiration of knee joint.

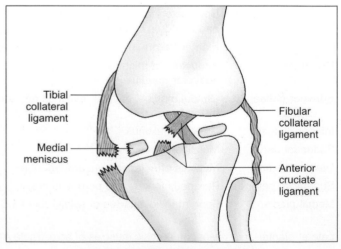

Fig. A1.3: Injury to the knee joint.

Fig. A1.1: Anastomoses on the back of thigh.

Arteries of lower limb

Artery	Beginning, course, termination	Area of distribution
Femoral artery (Fig. 3.14)	It is the continuation of external iliac artery, begins behind the inguinal ligament at the midinguinal point Femoral A. courses through femoral triangle and adductor canal. Then it passes through opening in adductor magnus to continue as the popliteal artery	In femoral triangle femoral artery gives three superficial branches, e.g. superficial external pudendal, superficial epigastric and superficial circumflex iliac, and three deep branches, e.g. profunda femoris, deep external pudendal and muscular branches. In adductor canal, femoral artery gives muscular and descending genicular artery
Superficial external pudendal (Fig. 3.12)	Superficial branch of femoral artery	Supplies skin of external genitalia
Superficial epigastric	Superficial branch of femoral artery	Supplies skin of anterior abdominal wall as it passes towards epigastric region
Superficial circumflex iliac	Superficial branch of femoral artery	Supplies skin over the iliac crest
Profunda femoris	Largest branch of femoral artery which descends posterior to femoral vessels, and ends as the fourth perforating artery	Branches are medial circumflex femoral, lateral circumflex femoral, 1st, 2nd and 3rd perforating. All these branches supply all muscles of thigh and muscles attached to trochanters
Deep external pudendal	Deep branch of femoral artery	Supplies deeper structures in the perineal region
Muscular branches	Deep branch of femoral artery	Supply muscles of thigh
Popliteal artery (Fig. 6.6)	It is the continuation of femoral artery and lies in the popliteal fossa. Popliteal artery ends by dividing into anterior tibial artery and posterior tibial artery at the distal border of popliteus muscle	Gives five genicular, e.g. • Superior medial genicular • Superior lateral genicular • Middle genicular • Inferior medial genicular • Inferior lateral genicular • Cutaneous branches for skin of popliteal fossa • Muscular branches for the muscles of the fossa
Anterior tibial artery (Fig. 8.11)	Smaller terminal branch of popliteal artery reaches the front of leg through an opening in the interosseous membrane. Runs amongst muscles of front of leg till midway between medial and lateral malleoli, where it ends by changing its name to dorsalis pedis artery	Muscular to the muscles of anterior compartment of leg. Cutaneous to the skin of leg. Articular to the knee joint through anterior and posterior tibial recurrent branches. Also to the ankle joint through anterior medial and anterior lateral malleolar branches
Dorsalis pedis artery (Fig. 8.15)	Continuation of anterior tibial artery. Runs along medial side of dorsum of foot to reach proximal end of 1st intermetatarsal space where it enters the sole. In the sole it completes the plantar arch	Two tarsal branches for the intertarsal joints. Arcuate artery runs over the bases of metatarsal bones and gives off 2nd, 3rd and 4th dorsal metatarsal arteries.1st dorsal metatarsal artery gives digital branches to big toe and medial side of 2nd toe
Posterior tibial artery (Fig. 9.10)	It begins as the larger terminal branch of popliteal artery at the distal border of popliteus muscle. It descends down medially between the long flexor muscles to reach midway between medial malleolus and medial tubercle of calcaneus where it ends by dividing into medial plantar and lateral plantar arteries	Peroneal artery is the largest branch. Nutrient artery to tibia. Articular branches to the knee joint and ankle joint. Muscular branches to the neighbouring muscles
Peroneal artery (Fig. 9.10)	Largest branch of popliteal artery given off 2.5 cm below lower border of popliteus	Muscular branches to muscles of posterior and lateral compartments. Cutaneous to skin of leg. Articular to ankle joint. Perforating branch enters the front of leg through a hole in the interosseous membrane to assist the dorsalis pedis artery

Artery	Beginning, course, termination	Area of distribution
Medial plantar artery (Fig. 10.13)	The smaller terminal branch of posterior tibial artery given off under flexor retinaculum. Runs along the medial border of foot and ends by giving digital arteries	Muscular branches to muscles of medial side of foot. Cutaneous branches to medial side of sole and digital branches to medial 3½ digits. Also gives branches to the joints of foot
Lateral plantar artery (Fig. 10.13)	The large terminal branch of posterior tibial artery given off under the flexor retinaculum. It runs laterally between muscles of 1st and 2nd layers of sole till the base of 5th metatarsal bone by becoming continuous with the plantar arch	Muscular branches to muscles of sole, cutaneous branches to skin and fasciae of lateral side of sole
Plantar arch (Fig. 10.11)	It is the direct continuation of lateral plantar artery and is completed medially by dorsalis pedis artery The arch lies between 3rd and 4th layers of muscles of sole. The deep branch of lateral plantar nerve lies in its concavity	Four plantar metatarsal arteries, each of them gives two digital branches for adjacent sides of two digits, including medial side of big toe and lateral side of little toe

CLINICAL TERMS

Policeman's heel: Plantar aponeurosis is attached to posterior tubercle of calcaneus and to all five digits. In plantar fasciatis, there is pain in the heel. Since policeman has to stand for long hours, they often suffer from it.

Dipping gait: Gluteus medius and gluteus minimus support the opposite side of the pelvis, when the foot is raised during walking. If these two muscles get paralysed on right side, walking with left limb becomes difficult, as that limb dips down, while attempting to lift it. Walking with right leg is normal as this leg is supported by the normal left muscles.

Weaver's bottom: Inflammation of the bursa over the ischial tuberosity. Since weavers have to sit for a long time, they suffer from it more often.

Meralgia parasthetica: Lateral cutaneous nerve of thigh may pierce the inguinal ligament and it may get pressed and cause irritation over lateral side of upper thigh (Fig. 3.35).

Housemaid knee: Inflammation of prepatellar bursa (Fig. 2.59).

Clergyman's knee: Inflammation of subcutaneous infrapatellar bursa.

Close-pack position of ankle joint: Dorsiflexed ankle joint when anterior wide trochlear area of talus fits tightly into posterior narrow articular area of lower end of tibia.

Inversion injuries more common than eversion injuries: Inversion is accompanied by plantar-flexion. During plantar flexion the narrow posterior trochlear area of talus lies loosely in the anterior wide articular area of lower end of tibia. So inversion injuries are common.

Fresher's syndrome: Overexertion of the muscles of anterior compartment of leg causes oedema of leg as these are enclosed in tight compartment of deep fascia. This results in pain in the leg. Freshers are compelled to run so it occurs in them.

Sites of intramuscular injections: In upper lateral quadrant of gluteal region into the gluteus medius. Also into the vastus lateralis (Fig. 5.13).

Sites of pulse palpation in lower limb: Femoral artery, popliteal artery, posterior tibial and dorsalis pedis arteries (Figs 3.32, 8.14 and 9.12).

Cut open: A small cut given in great/long saphenous vein to insert a cannula for giving intravenous transfusions. Since position of this vein is constant, anterior to medial malleolus, the great saphenous vein is used for cut-open.

Tarsal tunnel syndrome: The syndrome occurs due to compression of tibial nerve within the fibro-osseous tunnel under the flexor retinaculum of ankle joint. This is associated with pain and parasthesia in the sole of the foot often worse at night (Fig. 9.11).

Injury to medial meniscus: The medial meniscus is more vulnerable to injury than the lateral meniscus, because of its fixity to the capsule and tibial collateral ligament. The lateral meniscus is protected by the popliteus which pulls it backwards so that it is not crushed between the articular surfaces (Fig. 2.52).

Cruciate ligaments: Tear of anterior cruciate ligament leads to abnormal anterior mobility while tear of posterior ligament leads to abnormal posterior mobility of tibia (Fig. 12.35).

Pes planus: Absence or collapse of the arches leads to flat foot (pes planus) (Fig. 13.11).

CLINICOANATOMICAL PROBLEMS

1. A player was kicked hard on the lateral surface of right knee during a hockey game.

Clinicoanatomical problems:
- How do you feel the head of fibula?
- What important structure lies in relation to the neck of fibula?
- What are the effects of injury to the neck of fibula?

Ans. The head of fibula is palpated from the posterior aspect of knee joint. The head of fibula is subcutaneous and lies at the postero-lateral aspect of the knee joint. The neck of fibula lies just beyond the head. The common peroneal nerve winds around the neck of fibula where it divides into superficial peroneal and deep peroneal nerves. In injury to the neck of fibula, common peroneal nerve is usually injured, causing paralysis of the dorsiflexors of foot supplied by deep peroneal nerve and of evertors of foot supplied by the superficial peroneal nerve, resulting in "foot drop" (Fig. 2.42).

2. A 50-year- old woman complained of a swelling in upper medial side of her right thigh, when she coughs.

Clinicoanatomical problems:
- Where is the swelling and why does it appear when she coughs?
- What is the position of the swelling in relation to pubic tubercle?

Ans. The swelling is the femoral hernia which appears at saphenous opening when she coughs due to raised intraabdominal pressure. The swelling is inferolateral to the pubic tubercle. The femoral hernia is more common in females due to larger pelvis, larger femoral canal and smaller femoral vessels.

3. The knee of a football player was flexed at right angle. At this time, his knee was so injured that his tibia got driven forwards.

Clinicoanatomical problems:
- What ligament is injured?
- What are its attachments? What other ligaments can be injured?

Ans. The injured ligament is anterior cruciate ligament. It is attached below to anterior part of intercondylar area of tibia. It is attached above to the medial surface of lateral condyle of femur. This ligament binds the two bones together. With this injury, the menisci and fibular collateral ligament may also be torn.

4. A 60-year-old woman complained of severe pain in the back of her right thigh and leg.

Clinicoanatomical problems:
- Which nerve is involved and what is its root value?
- What is straight leg raising test? If done on this patient, why does it cause pain?

Ans. The nerve involved is sciatic nerve. Its root value is ventral rami of L4, L5, S1, S2, S3, segments of spinal cord. The pain on the back of thigh indicates compression of the roots of sciatic nerve.

Straight leg raising test:

The patient lies supine on the bed. The affected leg is extended at both hip and knee joints. Then it is raised up from the bed by holding the foot. As the nerve is stretched, it causes severe pain.

5. A sportsman, while playing basketball sprained his ankle. He complained of severe pain on the lateral side of his right ankle.

Clinicoanatomical problems:
- What ligament is injured?
- What other ligament could be injured?
- What bone can be fractured?

Ans. His anterior talofibular ligament is torn. The posterior talofibular and calcaneofibular ligaments could be torn. The lower end of fibula could also be fractured.

MULTIPLE CHOICE QUESTIONS

A. Select the best response.

1. Femoral canal.
- (a) Is the lateral compartment containing the femoral artery
- (b) Contains only areolar tissue
- **(c) Is wider in females**
- (d) Is separated from the femoral artery by a fibrous septum

2. Upper two thirds of the line joining midinguinal point to the adductor tubercle represents:
- **(a) Femoral artery**
- (b) Adductor canal
- (c) Femoral nerve
- (d) Profunda femoris artery

3. **All of the following muscles are hybrid except:**
   (a) Pectineus
   (b) Adductor magnus
   (c) Pectoralis major of upper limb
   (d) Quadratus femoris

4. **The following nerve can be rolled against the neck of fibula:**
   (a) Tibial   **(b) Common peroneal**
   (c) Deep peroneal   (d) Superficial peroneal

5. **Which of the following muscles is inserted into lesser trochanter?**
   (a) Vastus medialis   (b) Piriformis
   (c) Gluteus medius   **(d) Psoas major**

6. **Which of the following muscles is not inserted into greater trochanter?**
   (a) Gluteus medius   (b) Gluteus minimus
   (c) Piriformis   **(d) Pectineus**

7. **All of the following muscles are attached to the greater trochanter of femur except:**
   (a) Gluteus maximus (b) Gluteus medius
   (c) Gluteus minimus   (d) Obturator externus

8. **Which of the following is not an action of sartorius?**
   (a) Flexion of leg   (b) Flexion of thigh
   (c) Extension of leg (d) Lateral rotator of thigh

9. **Saphenous opening is located at:**
   (a) Just below pubic tubercle
   (b) Just above pubic tubercle
   (c) Below and lateral to pubic tubercle
   (d) At pubic tubercle

10. **Lateral boundary of femoral canal is formed by:**
    (a) Inguinal ligament   (b) Lacunar ligament
    (c) Femoral nerve   **(d) Femoral vein**

11. **Which of the following is true regarding femoral canal?**
    (a) 5 cm long
    (b) Upper opening is femoral ring
    (c) Content is femoral vein
    (d) Lateral compartment of femoral sheath

12. **Femoral ring is bounded by the following structures except:**
    (a) Femoral artery   (b) Lacunar ligament
    (c) Femoral vein   (d) Inguinal ligament

13. **Obturator nerve innervates all the following muscles except:**
    (a) Adductor longus
    (b) Pectineus

(c) Obturator internus
(d) Obturator externus

14. **Intramuscular injection is given in the following quadrant of the gluteal region:**
    (a) Upper lateral   (b) Upper medial
    (c) Lower medial   (d) Lower lateral

15. **Compression of the following nerve leads to sleeping foot:**
    (a) Sciatic   (b) Femoral
    (c) Tibial   (d) Deep peroneal

16. **Oblique popliteal ligament is the continuation of:**
    (a) Semitendinosus   **(b) Semimembranosus**
    (c) Popliteus   (d) Sartorius

17. **Injury to common peroneal nerve leads to:**
    (a) Foot drop
    (b) Sleeping foot
    (c) Loss of sensation over sole
    (d) Loss of sensation on medial side of leg

18. **Which of the following muscle is known as the peripheral heart:**
    (a) Soleus   (b) Gastrocnemius
    (c) Adductor longus   (d) Tibialis anterior

19. **Which of the following is true regarding popliteus muscle?**
    (a) Locks the knee joint
    (b) Supplied by common peroneal nerve
    (c) Forms the roof of popliteal fossa
    (d) Intracapsular origin

20. **Which of the following structures passes deep to flexor retinaculum of the ankle?**
    (a) Tibialis anterior
    (b) Extensor hallucis longus
    (c) Saphenous vein
    (d) Posterior tibial artery

21. **All the following muscles act both on hip and knee joints except:**
    (a) Rectus femoris
    (b) Sartorius
    (c) Long head of biceps femoris
    (d) Adductor magnus

22. **Unlocking of knee joint is brought about by the action of:**
    (a) Gastrocnemius   (b) Biceps femoris
    (c) Popliteus   (d) Plantaris

23. **Largest synovial joint of the body is:**
    (a) Knee   (b) Hip
    (c) Ankle   (d) Shoulder

24. **Anterior cruciate ligament prevents:**
    (a) Anterior dislocation of femur
    (b) Posterior dislocation of femur
    (c) Anterior dislocation tibia
    (d) Posterior dislocation of tibia

25. **False regarding hip joint is:**
    (a) Lateral rotators supplied by obturator nerve
    (b) Medial rotation by gluteus medius and gluteus minimus
    (c) Flexion by iliopsoas muscle
    (d) Extension by gluteus maximus

B. **Match the following on the left side with their appropriate answers on the right side.**

1. **Types of joints:**
   (a) Hip joint   (i) Saddle
   (b) Ankle joint   (ii) Ball and socket
   (c) Inferior tibiofibular joint   (iii) Syndesmosis
   (d) Calcaneocuboid joint (iv) Hinge

2. **Characteristic features of tarsals:**
   (a) Devoid of any muscular attachments (i) Cuboid
   (b) Forms the prominence of the heel   (ii) Navicular
   (c) Boat-shaped   (iii) Calcaneus
   (d) Has groove on inferior surface for the tendon of peroneus longus (iv) Talus

3. **Muscles and their nerve supply:**
   (a) Rectus femoris   (i) Obturator
   (b) Short head of biceps femoris (ii) Femoral
   (c) Ischial part of adductor magnus (iii) Common peroneal
   (d) Gracilis   (iv) Tibial part of sciatic

4. **Movements at hip joint:**
   (a) Extension   (i) Gluteus medius
   (b) Flexion   (ii) Iliacus
   (c) Abduction   (iii) Obturator internus
   (d) Lateral rotation   (iv) Gluteus maximus

5. **Cutaneous innervation:**
   (a) Medial aspect of leg   (i) Deep peroneal
   (b) Lateral aspect of foot (ii) Superficial peroneal
   (c) Medial aspect of big toe (iii) Saphenous
   (d) Interdigital cleft between 1st and 2nd toes (iv) Sural

C. **For each of the statements or questions below, one or more completions or answers given is/are correct.**

Select
A. If only 1, 2 and 3 are correct
B. If only 1, 3 are correct
C. If only 2, 4 are correct
D. If only 4 is correct
E. If all are correct

1. **The following structure/s pass through the saphenous opening:**
   1. Great saphenous vein
   2. Lymph vessels connecting superficial inguinal lymph nodes with deep inguinal lymph nodes
   3. Superficial epigastric artery
   4. Superficial external pudendal vein

2. **When the neck of femur is fractured:**
   1. There may be avascular necrosis of head of femur
   2. Trendelenburg's test is positive
   3. The distal fragment of the bone is rotated laterally
   4. The affected limb is shortened

3. **The following statement/s is/are true regarding sciatic nerve:**
   1. It reaches gluteal region by passing through greater sciatic foramen above the piriformis muscle
   2. All the muscular branches arise from its lateral side
   3. At the back of the thigh it is crossed by semitendinosus
   4. Tibial nerve is its larger terminal branch

4. **The common peroneal nerve:**
   1. Conveys fibres from the dorsal divisions of ventral rami of L4, L5, S1 and S2
   2. May get injured in the fracture of neck of fibula
   3. Injury leads to foot drop
   4. Injury results in sensory loss on the whole of the dorsum of foot

5. **Popliteus muscle:**
   1. Has intracapsular origin
   2. Pulls the medial meniscus backwards and prevents it from being trapped at the beginning of flexion
   3. Initiates flexion of knee joint by unlocking the locked knee
   4. Is innervated by a branch from the common peroneal nerve

Answers

B. 1. (a) – (ii),   (b) – (iv),   (c) – (iii), (d) – (i)
    3. (a) – (ii),   (b) – (iii),   (c) – (iv), (d) – (i)
    5. (a) – (iii), (b) – (iv),   (c) – (ii), (d) – (i)

    2. (a) – (iv),   (b) – (iii),   (c) – (ii), (d) – (i)
    4. (a) – (iv),   (b) – (ii),   (c) – (i), (d) – (iii)

C. 1. A
    3. D
    5. B

    2. E
    4. A

MNEMONICS

1. ***Attachment on linea aspera***
   I love **B**, **M**r. **B** love **m**e
   From lateral to medial side:
   Vastus **i**ntermedius
   Vastus **l**ateralis
   Short head of **b**iceps femoris
   Adductor **m**agnus
   Adductor **b**revis
   Adductor **l**ongus and pectineus
   Vastus **m**edialis
2. ***Great saphenous vein***
   M, m, m, m, m, m
   M—Medial end of dorsal venous arch
   m—medial marginal vein ends into it
   m—lies anterior to the medial malleolus
   m—crosses medial surface of tibia obliquely
   m—runs behind medial border of tibia to reach behind the knee
   m—runs along medial side of thigh to end in the saphenous opening
3. ***Popliteal fossa***
   Upper part, from medial side to lateral side
   A V N N
   A—Popliteal artery

V—Popliteal vein
N—Tibial nerve
N—Common peroneal nerve
Lower part, from medial side to lateral side
N V A
N—Tibial nerve
V—Popliteal vein
A—Popliteal artery

4. ***Structures under extensor retinaculum of ankle***
   Tall **H**imalayas **a**re **n**ever **d**ry **p**laces
   Tibialis anterior
   Extensor **h**allucis longus
   Anterior tibial artery
   Deep peroneal **n**erve
   Extensor **d**igitorum longus
   Peroneus tertius
5. ***Structures under flexor retinaculum***
   Talented **d**octors **a**re **n**ever **h**ungry
   Tibialis anterior
   Flexor **d**igitorum longus
   Posterior tibial **a**rtery
   Tibial **n**erve
   Flexor **h**allucis longus

FURTHER READING

- Crock HV. An atlas of the arterial supply of the head and neck of femur in man. *Clin orthop* 1980; 152:17–25.
- Eckhoff PG, Kramer RC, Watkins JJ, Alongi CA, Van Gerven DP. Variation in femoral anteversion. *Clin Anat* 1994; 7:72–5.
- Gardner E, Gray DJ. The innervation of the joints of the foot. *Anat Rec* 1968; 161:141–8.
- Gupte CM, Bull AMJ, Thomas RD, Amis AA. A review of the function and biomechanics of the meniscofemoral ligaments. *Arthroscopy* 2003; 19:161–71.
- Jayakumari S, Suri RK, Rath G, Arora S. Accessory tendon and tripartite insertion of pattern of fibularis longus muscle, A case report. *Int J Morphol* 2006; 24: 633–636.
- Joseph J. Movements at the hip joint. *Ann R Coll Surg Eng,* 1975; 56:192–201
- Kakar S, Garg K, Raheja S. Functional anatomy of human foot in relation to dimensions of the sesamoid bones, *Ann Natl Acad Med Sci (India)* 1998; 34 (3): 157–161.
- Neidre A, Macnab I 1983. Anomalies of the lumbosacral nerve roots. *Spine* 8:294–9.
- Raheja S, Choudhry R, Singh P, Tuli A, Kumar H. Morphological description of combined variation of distal attachments of fibulares in a foot. *Surg radiol Anat* 2005; 27: 158–160
- Rajendran K. Mechanism of locking at the knee joint. *J Anat* 1985; 143:189–94.
- Sarrafian SK. *Anatomy of the Foot and Ankle, Descriptive, Topographic, Functional,* 2nd edn. Philadelphia: Lippincott 1993.
- Watanabe M, Takedas S, Ikeuchi H. Atlas of Arthroscopy. Berlin: Springer–Verlag 1979.

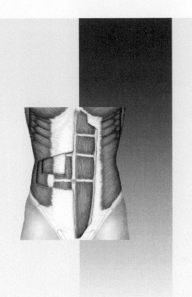

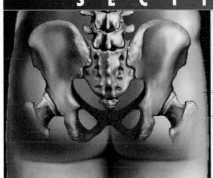

SECTION 2

ABDOMEN AND PELVIS

CHAPTER 15

Introduction to Abdomen and Osteology

The abdomen and pelvis form the single biggest cavity in the body which lodges most parts of digestive system, urinary system and reproductive system, besides the muscles, fasciae, blood vessels, nerves, lymph nodes, and lymphatics. The examination of abdomen is very interesting as it permits inspection, palpation, percussion and auscultation like the thorax. The patient is not really satisfied, unless the abdomen is examined, especially auscultated. Though the abdomen and pelvis lodge so many viscera, there are not many bones, except five lumbar vertebrae and the pelvis. So some of the organs push themselves up and occupy the thoracic cavity and live there happily forever.

The pelvis presents visual differences in the two genders. The female pelvis is lighter, wider and shallower, allowing comfortable delivery of the baby.

INTRODUCTION TO THE ABDOMEN

The abdomen is the lower part of the trunk and lies below the diaphragm. It is divided by the plane of the pelvic inlet into a larger upper part, the abdomen proper, and a smaller lower part, the true or lesser pelvis. The abdomen is bounded to a large extent by muscles, which can easily adjust themselves to periodic changes in the capacity of the abdominal cavity. They can thin out to accommodate distensions of the abdomen imposed by *flatus* or gas, *fat*, *foetus* and *fluid*. The abdomen contains the greater parts of the digestive and urogenital systems. In addition, it also contains the spleen, the suprarenal glands, and numerous lymph nodes, vessels and nerves.

The abdominal wall is made up of the following six layers.

1. *Skin*,
2. *Superficial fascia*,
3. *Muscles* (and bones at places),
4. A continuous layer of fascia, named region-wise as the *diaphragmatic fascia, fascia transver-*

salis; fascia iliaca; anterior layer of thoraco-lumbar fascia, and *pelvic fascia,*

5. *Extraperitoneal connective tissue,* and
6. The *peritoneum* which provides a slippery surface for the movements of the abdominal viscera against one another.

The abdominal cavity is much more extensive than what it appears to be when seen from the outside. It projects upwards deep to the costal margin to reach the diaphragm. It also projects downwards as the pelvic cavity within the bony pelvis. Thus a considerable part of the abdominal cavity is overlapped by the thoracic bony cage above, and by the bony pelvis below.

The *importance of the abdomen* is manifold. To a physician, no examination is ever complete until he/she has thoroughly examined the abdomen of the patient. In fact, the patient, irrespective of his complaints, is never satisfied without an examination of his abdomen. To an obstetrician and gynaecologist, the importance of the abdomen is obvious. The surgeon considers the abdomen as an enigma because in a good proportion of his cases, the cause of abdominal pain, or the nature of an abdominal lump, may not be decided in spite of all possible investigations. Laparotomy, i.e. opening up of the abdomen by a surgeon, may reveal the disease in many obscure cases, but not in all of them. In the course of evolution, adoption of the erect posture by man has necessitated a number of structural modifications in the abdominal wall and pelvis, some of which will be mentioned in the appropriate sections.

OSTEOLOGY

The various bones present in relation to the abdomen are the lumbar vertebrae, the sacrum, and the bony pelvis. These are described below. The lower ribs and costal cartilages are also closely related to the abdominal wall. These have already been considered along with the thorax in Volume 1.

LUMBAR VERTEBRAE

There are five lumbar vertebrae, of which the first four are typical, and the fifth is atypical. A lumbar vertebra is identified by (a) its large size, and (b) the absence of costal facets on the body.

Typical Lumbar Vertebra

1. The *body* is large, and is wider from side to side than from before backwards. The height of the body is slightly greater anteriorly than posteriorly; this difference contributes to the forward convexity of the lumbar spine (Fig. 15.1a and b).
2. The *vertebral foramen* is triangular in shape, and is larger than in the thoracic region; but is smaller than in the cervical region.
3. The *pedicles* are short and strong. They project backwards from the upper part of the body, so that the inferior vertebral notches are much deeper than the superior.
4. The *laminae* are short, thick and broad. They are directed backwards and medially to complete the vertebral foramen posteriorly.

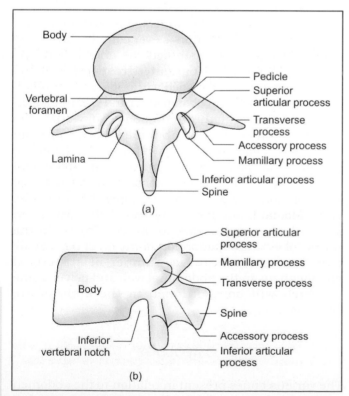

Fig. 15.1: Typical lumbar vertebra: (a) seen from above, and (b) seen from the lateral side.

The overlapping between the laminae of the adjoining vertebrae is minimal.

5. The *spine* forms a vertical quadrilateral plate, directed almost backwards and only slightly downwards. It is thickened along its posterior and inferior borders.
6. The *transverse processes* are thin and tapering, and are directed laterally and slightly backwards. They are homologous with the ribs in the thoracic region. The posteroinferior aspect of the root of each transverse process is marked by a small, rough elevation, the accessory process, which represents the true transverse process of the vertebra. The length of the transverse processes increases from vertebra L1 to L3 and, thereafter, it decreases (Fig. 15.1b).
7. The *superior articular processes* lie farther apart than the inferior. Each process bears a concave facet facing medially and backwards. The posterior border is marked by a rough elevation, the mamillary process.
8. The *inferior articular processes* lie nearer to each other than the superior. Each process bears a convex facet facing laterally and forwards.

Fifth Lumbar Vertebra

1. The most important distinguishing features are as follows.
   (a) The *transverse processes* are thick, short and pyramidal in shape. Their base is attached to the whole thickness of the pedicle and encroaches on the side of the body (Fig. 15.2a).
   (b) The distance between the *inferior articular processes* is equal to or more than the distance between the superior articular processes.
   (c) The *spine* is small, short and rounded at the tip.
2. Other features of the fifth lumbar vertebra are as follows.
   (a) The body is the largest of all lumbar vertebrae. Its anterior surface is much deeper than the posterior surface. This difference is responsible for the creation of the sharp lumbosacral angle.
   (b) The pedicles are directed backwards and laterally.
   (c) The superior articular facets look more backwards than medially, and the inferior articular facets look more forwards than laterally, as compared to other lumbar vertebrae (Fig. 15.2b).

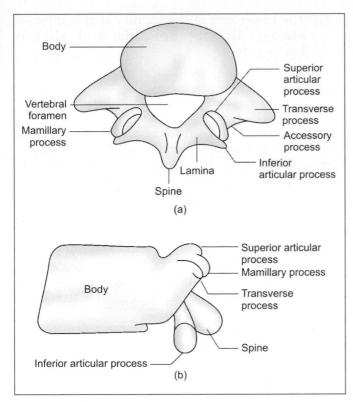

Fig. 15.2: Fifth lumbar vertebra: (a) seen from above, and (b) seen from the lateral side.

Attachments and Some Relations of Lumbar Vertebrae

Body

(a) The upper and lower surfaces provide attachment to *intervertebral discs*.

(b) The upper and lower borders give attachment to the *anterior* and *posterior longitudinal ligaments* in front and behind, respectively.

(c) Lateral to the anterior longitudinal ligament, the *right crus of the diaphragm* is attached to the upper three vertebrae, and the *left crus of the diaphragm* to the upper two vertebrae.

(d) Behind the line of the crura, the upper and lower borders of all the lumbar vertebrae give origin to the psoas major (Fig. 15.3).

(e) Across the constricted part of the body on either side tendinous arches are attached. The lumbar vessels, and the grey ramus communicans from the sympathetic chain, pass deep to each of these arches.

Vertebral Canal

The part of vertebral canal formed by the first and second lumbar vertebrae contains the *conus medullaris*. The part formed by lower three vertebrae contains the *cauda equina*. The canal of all the lumbar vertebrae contains the *spinal meninges*.

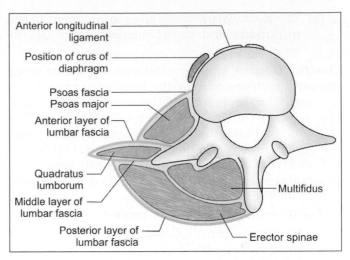

Fig. 15.3: Attachments of the lumbar vertebrae.

Vertebral Arch

The *pedicles* are related above and below to spinal nerves.

The *laminae* provide attachment to the ligamenta flava.

The *spine* provides attachment to:

(a) The posterior layer of the lumbar fascia (Fig. 15.3).

(b) The interspinous and supraspinous ligaments.

(c) The erector spinae, the multifidus and the interspinal muscles.

Transverse processes

(a) The tips of the transverse processes of all lumbar vertebrae give attachment to the *middle layer of the lumbar fascia*. In addition, the tip of the first process gives attachment to the *medial* and *lateral arcuate ligaments*, (Fig. 26.1) and the tip of the fifth process to the *iliolumbar ligament* (Fig. 34.8).

(b) The faint vertical ridge on the anterior surface of each transverse process gives attachment to the *anterior layer of the lumbar fascia*. Medial to the ridge, the anterior surface gives origin to the *psoas major*, and lateral to the ridge to the *quadratus lumborum* (Fig. 15.3).

(c) The posterior surface is covered by deep muscles of the back, and gives origin to the fibres of the *longissimus thoracis*. The *accessory process* gives attachment to the *medial intertransverse muscle*.

(d) The upper and lower borders provide attachment to the *lateral intertransverse muscles*.

Articular processes

(a) The concave articular facets permit some rotation as well as flexion and extension.

(b) The *mamillary process* gives attachment to the multifidus and to the *medial intertransverse muscles.*

Ossification: A lumbar vertebra ossifies from three primary centres—one for the body or centrum and one each for each half of the neural arch. These appear in the third month of foetal life. The two halves of the neural arch fuse with each other, posteriorly during the first year. Fusion of the neural arch with the centrum occurs during the sixth year. The posterolateral parts of the body develop from the centre for the neural arch.

There are seven secondary centres as follows.

1. An upper annular epiphysis for the upper surface of the body.
2. A similar epiphysis for the lower surface of the body.
3, 4. One centre for the tip of each transverse process.
5, 6. One centre for each mamillary process.
7. One centre for the tip of the spine.

Failure of fusion of the two halves of the neural arch results in "spina bifida". Sometimes the body ossifies from two primary centres, and if one centre fails to develop, it results in a "hemivertebra".

THE SACRUM

The sacrum is a large, flattened, triangular bone formed by the fusion of five sacral vertebrae. It forms the posterosuperior part of the bony pelvis, articulating on either side with the corresponding hip bone at the sacroiliac joint. The upper part of the sacrum is massive because it supports the body weight and transmits it to the hip bones. The lower part is free from weight, and therefore tapers rapidly.

Being triangular, the sacrum has a base or upper surface, an apex or lower end, and four surfaces—pelvic, dorsal and right and left lateral. The pelvic surface is smooth and concave. The dorsal surface is irregular and convex. The lateral surface is irregular and partly articular. The sacrum is divided by rows of foramina into:

(a) Median portion, traversed by the sacral canal.
(b) A pair of *lateral masses* formed by fusion of the transverse processes posteriorly, and of the costal elements anteriorly.

When placed in the anatomical position:

(a) The pelvic surface faces downwards and forwards.
(b) The upper surface of the body of the first sacral vertebra slopes forwards at an angle of about 30 degrees.

(c) The upper end of the sacral canal is directed almost directly upwards and slightly backwards.

Features

Base

The base is directed upwards and forwards. It is formed by the upper surface of the first sacral vertebra, and presents features of a typical vertebra in a modified form.

1. The body is lumbar in type. It articulates with vertebra L5 at the *lumbosacral joint*. The projecting anterior margin is called the *sacral promontory*. The surface slopes forwards at an angle of 30 degrees.
2. The vertebral foramen lies behind the body, and leads into the sacral canal. It is triangular in shape.
3. The pedicles are short and are directed backwards and laterally.
4. The laminae are oblique.
5. The spine forms the first spinous tubercle.
6. The superior articular processes project upwards. The facets on them are directed backwards and medially.
7. The transverse processes are highly modified. Each process is massive and fused with the corresponding costal element to form the upper part of the lateral mass of the sacrum (Fig. 15.4).

The base of the lateral mass, forms a broad sloping surface spreading fan wise from the side of the body. It is called the *ala* of the sacrum. The ala is subdivided into a smooth medial part and a rough lateral part.

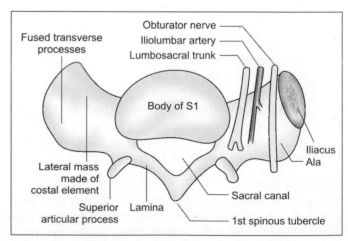

Fig. 15.4: The base of a male sacrum. Relations and attachments of the right ala are shown.

Apex

The apex of the sacrum is formed by the inferior surface of the body of the fifth sacral vertebra. It bears an oval facet for articulation with the coccyx.

Pelvic Surface

This is concave and directed downwards and forwards. The median area is marked by four transverse ridges, which indicate the lines of fusion of the bodies of the five sacral vertebrae. These ridges end on either side at the four pelvic sacral foramina, which communicate with the sacral canal through the intervertebral foramina. The bony bars between the foramina represent the *costal elements*. Lateral to the foramina, the *costal elements* unite with each other and with the transverse processes to form the lateral mass of the sacrum (Fig. 15.5).

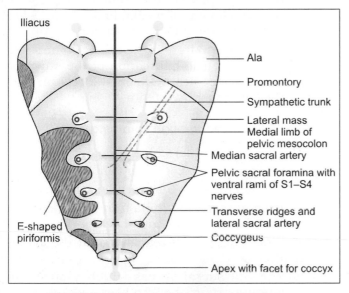

Fig. 15.5: Anterior (pelvic) view of the sacrum

Dorsal Surface

The dorsal surface of the sacrum is rough, irregular and convex, and is directed backwards and upwards.

1. In the median plane, it is marked by the *median sacral crest* which bears 3 to 4 spinous tubercles, representing the fused spines of the upper four sacral vertebrae. Below the 4th tubercle, there is an inverted U-shaped gap in the posterior wall of the sacral canal: this is called the *sacral hiatus*. It results from failure of the laminae of the fifth sacral vertebra to meet posteriorly (Fig. 15.6).

2. Lateral to the median crest, the posterior surface is formed by the fused laminae.

3. Lateral to the laminae and in line with the superior articular process of the first sacral vertebra, there are four articular tubercles, representing the fused articular processes of adjacent vertebrae. The inferior articular processes of the fifth sacral vertebra are free and form the *sacral cornua*, which project downwards at the sides of the sacral hiatus.

4. Lateral to the articular tubercles there are four *dorsal sacral foramina*. They communicate with the sacral canal through the intervertebral foramina.

5. Lateral to the foramina, there is the *lateral sacral* crest on which there are transverse tubercles, representing the fused transverse processes (Fig. 15.6).

Lateral Surface

It is formed by the fused transverse processes and the costal elements of the sacral vertebrae. It is wide above and narrow below. The upper wider part bears an L-shaped *auricular surface* anteriorly, and a

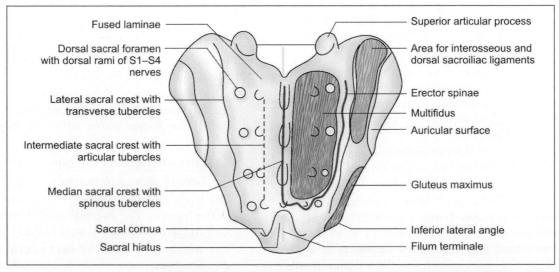

Fig. 15.6: Posterior aspect of the sacrum.

rough, deeply pitted area posteriorly. The auricular surface is formed by the costal elements. It articulates with the auricular surface of the hip bone at the sacroiliac joint. The posterior, roughened and pitted area is formed by the transverse processes.

The abrupt medial bend at the lower end of the lateral surface is called the *inferior lateral angle* of the sacrum.

Sacral Canal

It is formed by the sacral vertebral foramina, and is triangular on cross-section. The upper end of the canal appears oblique, but actually it is directed upwards in the anatomical position. Inferiorly, the canal opens at the sacral hiatus, and laterally it communicates through the intervertebral foramina with the pelvic and dorsal sacral foramina.

The sacral canal contains the spinal meninges. The *filum terminale* and the *subdural* and *subarachnoid spaces* end at the level of the second sacral vertebra. Therefore, the lower sacral nerves and filum terminale pierce the dura and arachnoid at this (S2) level.

Attachments on the Sacrum

1. The anterior and posterior edges of the body of the first sacral vertebra give attachment to the lowest fibres of the anterior and posterior longitudinal ligaments (Figs 15.5 and 15.6). The lamina of this vertebra provide attachment to the *lowest pair of ligamenta flava*.

2. The rough part of the ala gives origin to the *iliacus* anteriorly, and attachment to the lumbosacral ligament posteriorly. The upper part of the *ventral sacroiliac ligament* is attached to its margin (Fig. 15.5).

3. The part of the pelvic surface lateral to the bodies of the middle three pieces of the sacrum gives origin to the *piriformis* (Fig. 15.5). The area extends into the intervals between the pelvic sacral foramina and is E-shaped.

4. The dorsal surface gives origin to the *erector spinae* along a U-shaped line passing over the spinous and transverse tubercles. The area in the concavity of the 'U' gives origin to the *multifidus* (Fig. 15.6).

5. The interosseous sacroiliac ligament is attached to the rough pitted area of the lateral surface, behind the auricular surface (Fig. 15.6).

6. The lower narrow part of the lateral surface, below the auricular surface gives origin to the *gluteus maximus*; attachment to the *sacrotuberous* and *sacrospinous* ligaments; and origin to the *coccygeus*, in that order from behind forwards (Figs 29.2 and 34.7B).

7. The inferior lateral angle gives attachment to the *lateral sacrococcygeal ligament*.

Relations of the Sacrum

1. The smooth part of the ala is related, from medial to lateral side, to the *sympathetic chain*, the *lumbosacral trunk*, the *iliolumbar artery*, and the *obturator nerve*. All these structures are overlapped by the psoas major muscle (Fig. 15.4).

2. The pelvic surface is related to:
   (a) The *median sacral vessels* in the median plane.
   (b) The *sympathetic trunks* along the medial margin of the pelvic foramina.
   (c) The peritoneum in front of the bodies of the upper 2½ pieces, interrupted obliquely by the attachment of medial limb of the *pelvic mesocolon* (Figs 15.5, 18.13 and 18.14).
   (d) The rectum in front of the bodies of the lower 2½ pieces. The bifurcation of the superior rectal artery lies between the rectum and the third sacral vertebra.

Structures Transmitted through Foramina

1. The pelvic sacral foramina transmit:
   (a) The *ventral rami of upper four sacral nerves*.
   (b) The lateral sacral arteries (Fig. 15.5).

2. The dorsal sacral foramina transmit the *dorsal rami of the upper four sacral nerves* (Fig. 15.6).

3. The following structures emerge at the sacral hiatus.
   (a) The *5th sacral nerves* which groove the lateral parts of the fifth sacral vertebra.
   (b) A pair of *coccygeal nerves*.
   (c) Filum terminale which passes to the coccyx.

Sex Differences

The sacrum shows a number of important sexual differences. These are as follows.

1. The relationship of the length and breadth of the sacrum can be expressed quantitatively by using the *sacral index* which is calculated as follows.

$$\frac{\text{Breadth across the base} \times 100}{\text{Length from promontory to apex}}$$

The male sacrum is longer and narrower than in the female. The average sacral index is about 105 in the male and about 115 in the female.

2. The width of the body of first sacral vertebra is greater than that of each ala in the male. In female, the two are equal.

3. The dorsal concavity of auricular surface is less marked in male. In both, the auricular surface extends on to upper three sacral vertebrae.

4. The concavity on the ventral aspect of sacrum is more uniform, and is shallower in males. In females, the concavity is irregular especially between S1 and S2 and between S3 and S4.

5. The sacrovertebral angle is more prominent in the female and the downward direction of the pelvic surface is greater than in the male. The size of pelvic cavity is more in females.

Ossification

The ossification of the sacrum should be regarded as the ossification of five separate vertebrae. However, the upper 3 vertebrae have additional primary centres for the costal bars.

Thus there are 21 primary centres; 5 for the bodies, 10 for the arches, and 6 for the costal bars and 14 secondary centres; 10 for the epiphyses of the bodies, 2 for the auricular surfaces, and 2 for the margins below the auricular surfaces. The primary centres appear between 2nd and 8th week of foetal life, and fuse with each other between 2nd and 8th years of life. The secondary centres appear at puberty and fuse by 25 years.

COCCYX

The coccyx is a small triangular bone formed by fusion of four rudimentary coccygeal vertebrae, which progressively diminish in size from above downwards. The bone is directed downwards and forwards, making a continuous curve with the sacrum.

Features

The first coccygeal piece is the largest. It is commonly found as a separate vertebra. The upper surface of its body forms the base of the coccyx, which articulates with the apex of the sacrum. Projecting upwards from the posterolateral side of the base are the *coccygeal cornua*, which represent the pedicles and superior articular processes. They articulate with the sacral cornua and are connected to them by *intercornual ligaments*. Rudimentary transverse processes project laterally and slightly upwards from the side of the base. They may articulate or fuse with the inferior lateral angle of the sacrum, creating a fifth pair of sacral foramina.

The second, third and fourth coccygeal vertebrae are mere bony nodules which diminish successively in size and are usually fused together.

Attachments

The dorsal surface of the coccyx gives:

(a) Origin to the *gluteus maximus* on either side.

(b) Origin to the *sphincter ani externus* at the tip.

(c) Attachment to the *dorsal sacrococcygeal ligaments* and the *filum terminale* at the first piece.

The pelvic surface:

(a) Provides insertion to the *coccygeus* and to the *levator ani* on either side.

(b) Provides attachment to the ventral sacrococcygeal ligament over the first two pieces.

(c) It is related to the *ganglion impar* and the *glomus coccygeum*. The lateral margins provide attachment to *sacrotuberous* and *sacrospinous* ligaments (Fig. 29.4).

Ossification

The coccyx ossifies from 4 primary centres one for each segment, which appear between 1st and 20th years, and fuse with each other between 20th and 30th years. The coccyx is slightly mobile on the sacrum, but fuses with it late in life.

BONY PELVIS

The bones forming the pelvis, its division into the greater and lesser pelvis, and the important features of the lesser pelvis, including the inlet, outlet and cavity, are described in Chapter 29. Some other important aspects of the pelvis are described here.

Pelvimetry

The importance of the measurements of the pelvis is mainly obstetric, but also forensic and anthropological. Pelvimetry can be done in the following ways.

Pelvimetry on the skeletonized pelves prepared from cadavers.

Clinical pelvimetry on living subjects.

Radiological pelvimetry.

Pelvimetry on Skeletonized Pelves

The relevant diameters are summarized in Table 15.1 and shown in Fig. 15.7.

Clinical Pelvimetry

Pelvic measurements in obstetric cases can be done both externally and internally. External pelvimetry has been mostly given up because of its limited value. It is helpful in diagnosis of gross pelvic contraction.

1. The interspinous diameter, between the outer borders of anterior superior iliac spines, measures 22–25 cm.

2. The intercristal diameter, the widest distance between the outer borders of the iliac crests, measures 25–28 cm.

3. The external conjugate or Baudelocque's diameter, the distance between the tip of the spine of vertebra S5 and the upper border of

Table 15.1: Dimensions of the pelvis in female (Fig. 15.7)

Region	Diameter	Average measurements in cm
I. Pelvic inlet (Fig. 15.7a)	1. *Anteroposterior diameter* (true conjugate), from the midpoint of the sacral promontory to the upper border of the pubic symphysis	11
	2. *Transverse diameter* (maximum)	13
	3. *Oblique diameter*, from one iliopubic eminence to the opposite sacroiliac joint	12
II. Pelvic cavity (Fig. 15.7b)	1. *Anteroposterior diameter*, from midpoint of vertebra S3 to the posterior surface of the pubic symphysis	12
	2. *Transverse diameter*	12
	3. *Oblique diameter*, from the lowest point of one sacroiliac joint to the midpoint of the opposite obturator membrane	12
III. Pelvic outlet (Fig. 15.7c)	1. *Anteroposterior diameter* from the tip of the coccyx to the inferior margin of the pubic symphysis (maximum)	13
	2. *Transverse diameter* (bituberous diameter), between ischial tuberosities	11
	3. *Oblique diameter*, from the midpoint of the sacrotuberous ligament on one side to the junction of the ischiopubic rami on the other side	12

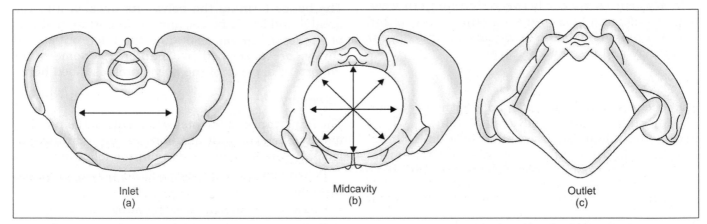

Inlet
(a)

Midcavity
(b)

Outlet
(c)

Fig. 15.7: The bony pelvis: (a) Inlet with longest transverse diameter, (b) cavity with all diameters equal, (c) outlet with longest anteroposterior diameter.

the pubic symphysis, measures not less than 19 cm.

4. The intertuberous diameter, between the lowermost and innermost points on the two ischial tuberosities, measures 10 cm.

5. The anteroposterior diameter of the outlet measures about 13 cm.

6. The posterior sagittal diameter, from the midpoint of the intertuberous diameter to the tip of the coccyx, measures 8–9 cm.

Internal Pelvimetry

It is done by digital examination per vaginum.

1. The diagonal conjugate is the distance between midpoint of promontory and lower border of anterior surface of pubic symphysis. Normally, it is at least 11.5 cm. A rough estimate of the true conjugate is obtained by deducting 1.5 to 2 cm from the diagonal conjugate.

2. The interischial spinous diameter of 9 cm, between the tips of the spines is difficult to assess digitally.

3. In addition, a thorough palpation of the bony pelvis is done to assess the curvature of the sacrum, the mobility of the coccyx, the length of sacrospinous ligament (more than the width of two examining fingers), and the side wall for any tendency to funnelling.

Radiological Pelvimetry

It has become a highly refined technique, but radiation risks impose limitations.

Ultrasound is an extremely useful and safe procedure and has replaced radiological pelvimetry to a great extent.

Morphological Classification of Pelvis

According to Anatomical and Radiological Data

(a) *Gynaecoid type* (41.4%): This is normal female pelvis, the average diameters of which have already been mentioned. The inlet is round or slightly ovoid with transverse diameter placed well forward from the sacrum. The side walls are more vertical than in the android pelvis.

(b) The *android type* (32.5%) resembles a male pelvis.

The inlet is triangular with the greatest transverse diameter placed much nearer the promontory than in the gynaecoid pelvis. The subpubic angle and greater sciatic notches are narrower, so that the cavity is funnel-shaped and the outlet is reduced in all diameters.

(c) The anthropoid type (23.5%) shows resemblance to the pelves of anthropoid apes.

(d) The *platypelloid type* (2.6%) is somewhat opposite to the anthropoid pelvis.

Out of the various types mentioned, only a gynaecoid pelvis permits a normal delivery of the child. The other three represent different types of *contracted pelvis*.

Sex Differences in the Pelvis

The most marked of these differences are due to adaptation of female pelvis for child bearing. Males have stronger muscles, thicker bones and prominent bony markings (Fig. 15.8).

As compared to a male pelvis a female pelvis shows the following differences.

1. The false pelvis is deep in male and shallow in female.
2. Pelvic inlet is heart-shaped in male due to jutting forwards of sacral promontary. In female it is transversely oval.
3. Pelvic cavity is smaller and deeper in male. In female the pelvic cavity is roomier and shallower, i.e. distance between inlet and outlet is shorter.
4. The pelvic outlet is smaller with ischial tuberosities turned inside in male. In female the plevic outlet is bigger with everted ischial tuberosities.
5. Sacrum is longer and narrow in male, while it is shorter and wider in female.
6. Subpubic angle is narrower, i.e. 50°–60° in male. The angle is wider, i.e. 80°–85° in female. This is the most important difference (Fig. 15.8).

Anatomical Position of the Pelvis

When examining an isolated pelvis students generally do not orientate it as it is in the intact body. It can be correctly orientated keeping the following in mind.

In the anatomical position, i.e. with the person standing upright:

1. The anterior superior iliac spines and the pubic symphysis lie in the same vertical plane. A pelvis can be correctly oriented by placing these points against a wall.
2. The pelvic surface of the pubic symphysis faces backwards and upwards.
3. The plane of the pelvic inlet faces forwards and upwards at an angle of 50° to 60° with the horizontal.
4. The plane of the pelvic outlet makes an angle of 15° with the horizontal (Fig. 29.7).
5. The upper end of the sacral canal is directed almost directly upwards.

INTERVERTEBRAL JOINTS

These joints include:

1. The joints between vertebral bodies.
2. The joints between vertebral arches.

The joints between vertebral bodies are *secondary cartilaginous* joints held by the intervertebral discs and two accessory ligaments, the anterior and posterior longitudinal ligaments. Intervertebral disc is described below.

Joints of the vertebral arches are formed by the articular processes of the adjacent vertebrae. These are plane synovial joints, permitting gliding movements. The accessory ligaments include:

(a) Ligamenta flava,
(b) Supraspinous,
(c) Interspinous, and
(d) Intertransverse ligaments.

The lumbar spine permits maximum of extension, considerable amount of flexion and lateral flexion, and least of rotation.

Intervertebral Disc

It is a fibrocartilaginous disc which binds the two adjacent vertebral bodies, from axis or second cervical vertebra to sacrum. Morphologically, it is a segmental structure as opposed to the vertebral body which is intersegmental.

Shape

Its shape corresponds to that of the vertebral bodies between which it is placed.

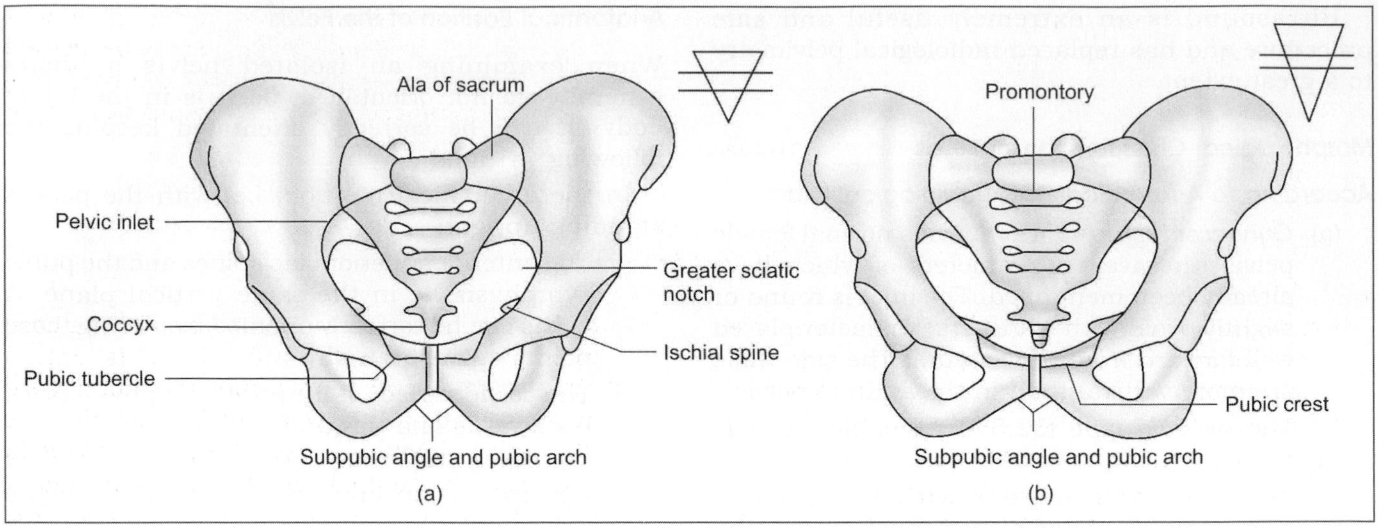

Fig. 15.8: Anterior view of (a) a male pelvis, and (b) a female pelvis.

Thickness

It varies in different regions of the column and in different parts of the same disc. In cervical and *lumbar* regions, the *discs* are *thicker in front* than behind, while in the thoracic region they are of uniform thickness. The discs are thinnest in the upper thoracic and thickest in the lumbar region.

The discs contribute about one-fifth of the length of vertebral column. Such contribution is greater in cervical and lumbar regions than in thoracic region.

Structure

Each disc is made up of the following three parts.

1. *Nucleus pulposus* is the central part of the disc which is soft and gelatinous at birth. Its water content is 90% in newborn and 70% in old age. It is kept under tension and acts as a hydraulic shock-absorber. It represents the remains of the notochord, and contains a few multinucleated notochordal cells during the first decade of life, after which there is a gradual replacement of the mucoid material by fibrocartilage, derived mainly from the cells of annulus fibrosus and partly from the cartilaginous plates covering the upper and lower surfaces of the vertebrae. Thus with advancing age the disc becomes amorphous and difficult to differentiate from the annulus. Its water binding capacity and the elasticity are reduced.

2. *Annulus fibrosus* is the peripheral part of the disc made up of a narrower outer zone of collagenous fibres and a wider inner zone of fibrocartilage. The laminae form incomplete collars which are convex downwards and are connected by strong fibrous bands. They

overlap or dovetail into one another at obtuse angles. The outer collagenous fibres blend with anterior and posterior longitudinal ligaments (Fig. 15.9a and b).

3. *Two cartilaginous plates* lie one above and the other below the nucleus pulposus. Disc gains

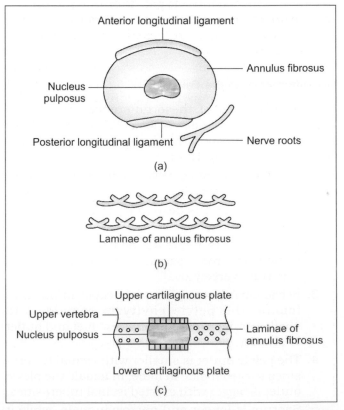

Fig. 15.9: The structure of an intervertebral disc: (a) Superior view showing its relations to the nerve roots and the longitudinal ligaments of vertebral column, (b) arrangement of laminae in the annulus fibrosus, and (c) a vertical section showing three parts of the disc.

its nourishment from the vertebrae by diffusion through these plates (Fig. 15.9c).

Functions

1. Intervertebral discs give shape to the vertebral column.

2. They act as a remarkable series of shock-absorbers or buffers. Each disc may be likened to a "coiled up spring". Should the confining walls be damaged the spring will bulge out at the weak area.

CLINICAL ANATOMY

- The lumbar region is a common site of a number of developmental deformities, causing symptoms ranging from simple backache to serious paralytic manifestations.

Sacralization of the fifth lumbar vertebra

- The *fifth lumbar vertebra* or its transverse process may be fused, on one or both sides, with the sacrum. Sometimes the transverse process may articulate with the ala of the sacrum or with the ilium. This may press on the fifth lumbar nerve.

Spina bifida

- The two halves of the neural arch may fail to fuse leaving a gap in the midline. This is called *spina bifida*. Meninges and spinal cord may herniate out through the gap.

- Protrusion of meninges alone results in the formation of a cystic swelling filled with cerebrospinal fluid. This swelling is called *meningocoele* (Fig. 15.10a). When the spinal cord is also present in the swelling the condition is called *meningomyelocoele* (Fig. 15.10b). The central canal of the herniated part of the cord may be dilated. This condition is called syringomyelocoele. Sometimes the spinal cord may itself be open posteriorly. The condition is then called *myelocoele*. Sometimes a spina bifida is present, but there is no protrusion through it so that there is no swelling on the surface. This is referred to as *spina bifida occulta*.

Spondylolisthesis

- Sometimes the greater part of the fifth lumbar vertebra slips forwards over the sacrum. Normally the tendency to forward slipping is prevented by the fact that the inferior articular processes of the fifth lumbar vertebra lie behind the superior articular processes of the first sacral vertebra. Sometimes, however, the inferior articular processes, spine and laminae of the fifth lumbar vertebra are separate from the rest of the vertebra (due to an anomaly in the mode of ossification). The body of the vertebra can now slip forwards leaving the separated parts behind (Fig. 15.11).

- Spondylolisthesis may be the cause of backache and of pain radiating along the course of the sciatic nerve known as sciatica.

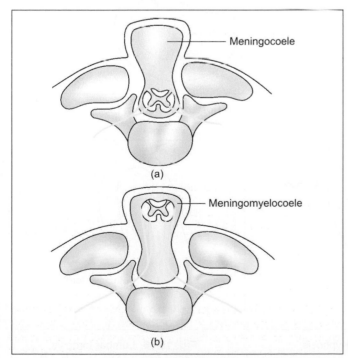

Fig. 15.10: (a) Meningocoele, (b) meningomyelocoele.

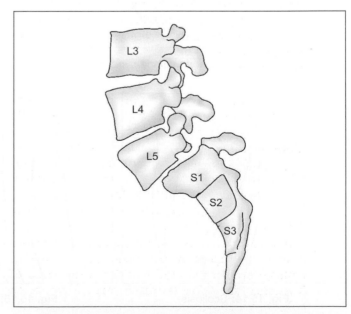

Fig. 15.11: Spondylolisthesis of fifth lumbar vertebra.

Fracture-dislocation

- Fracture-dislocation of lumbar vertebrae results in the *cauda equina syndrome* (Fig. 15.12). It is characterized by:
  - (a) Flaccid paraplegia.
  - (b) Saddle-shaped area of anaesthesia, and analgesia.
  - (c) Sphincter disturbances in the form of incontinence of urine and faeces.
  - (d) Impotence.
- In the young adults, the discs are very strong and cannot be damaged alone. However, after the second decade degenerative changes set in resulting in necrosis, with sequestration of nucleus pulposus, and softening and weakness of the annulus fibrosus. Such a disc is liable to internal or eccentric displacement or external derangements resulting in prolapse due to rupture of annulus fibrosus even after minor strains.
- Cauda equina syndrome described above.

- The unequal tension in the joint in internal derangement leads to muscle spasm and violent pain of acute lumbago.
- Disc prolapse is usually posterolateral (Fig. 15.13). This presses upon the adjacent nerve roots and gives rise to referred pain, such as sciatica. Disc prolapse occurs most commonly in lower lumbar region and is also common in lower cervical region (C5–C7). In sciatica, the pain is increased with rise of pressure in canal (as in sneezing); straight leg raising tests is positive; and the motor effects, with loss of power and reflexes, may follow.
- The spine of thoracic vertebrae may point to one side. The condition is scoliosis (Fig. 15.14).
- There may be projection of the spines posteriorly due to osteoporosis of the bodies of vertebrae leading to kyphosis (Fig. 15.15).
- Anterior convexity of lumbar vertebrae may get exaggerated, leading to "lumbar lordosis" (Fig. 15.16).

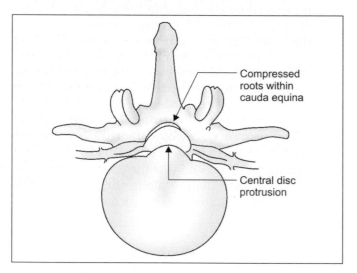

Fig. 15.12: Cauda equina syndrome.

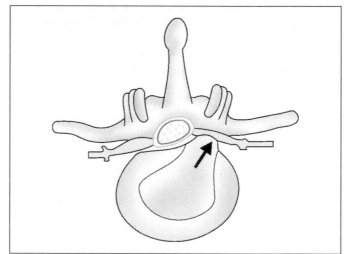

Fig. 15.13: Posterolateral disc prolapse.

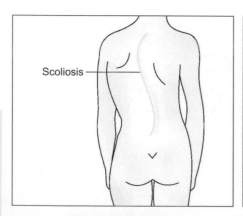

Fig. 15.14: Scoliosis.

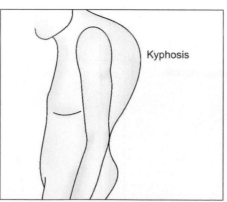

Fig. 15.15: Kyphosis.

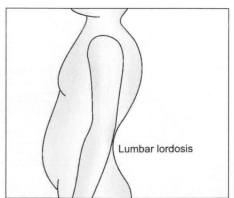

Fig. 15.16: Lumbar lordosis.

CHAPTER 16

Anterior Abdominal Wall

The attachments of the muscles of anterolateral abdominal wall are given in this chapter. The formation and contents of rectus sheath are mentioned. The inguinal canal has been described in detail as its relations are of importance in the reduction/repair of the inguinal hernia.

The heading "anterior abdominal wall" usually includes both the front as well as the side walls of the abdomen and needs to be called anterolateral abdominal wall.

SURFACE LANDMARKS

Before taking up the description of the abdominal wall proper it is desirable to draw attention to some surface landmarks that can be identified in the region.

1. In the anterior median plane, the abdominal wall extends from the *xiphoid process* which

lies at the level of the ninth thoracic vertebra to the pubic symphysis, which lies at the level of the coccyx. Posteriorly and laterally, the vertical extent of the abdominal wall is much less, as it is replaced by the thoracic cage, above and behind; and by the gluteal region, on the posterior aspect of the lower part (Fig. 16.1).

2. The superolateral margins of the anterior abdominal wall are formed by the right and left *costal margins*. Each margin is formed by the seventh, eighth, ninth and tenth costal cartilages. The costal margin reaches its lowest level in the *midaxillary line*. Here the margin is formed by the tenth costal cartilage. The transverse plane passing through the lowest part of the costal margin is called the *subcostal plane*. It passes through the third lumbar vertebra.

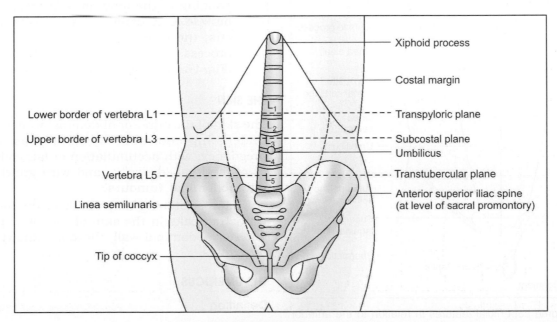

Fig. 16.1: Landmarks of the abdomen.

3. The infrasternal or *subcostal angle* is formed between the right and left costal margins. The xiphoid process lies in a depression at the apex of the infrasternal angle at the level of the ninth thoracic vertebra (Fig. 16.2).

4. The *iliac crest* forms the lower limit of the abdominal wall at the side. The highest point of the iliac crest lies at the level of the fourth lumbar vertebra slightly below the normal level of the umbilicus.

5. The *anterior superior iliac spine* lies at the level of the *sacral promontory.*

6. The *tubercle of the iliac crest* is situated on the outer lip of iliac crest about 5 cm behind the anterior superior iliac spine. The *intertubercular plane* passes through the tubercles. It passes through the fifth lumbar vertebra.

7. The *inguinal ligament* extends from the anterior superior iliac spine to the pubic tubercle. It is convex downwards. It is placed at the junction of the anterior abdominal wall with the front of the thigh.

8. The *spermatic cord* is a soft rounded cord present in the male. It can be felt through the skin as it passes downwards near the medial end of the inguinal ligament to enter the scrotum. It can be picked up between the finger and the thumb. When palpated in this way a firm cord-like structure can be felt within the posterior part of the spermatic cord. This is the ductus deferens.

9. The anterior abdominal wall is divided into right and left halves by a vertical groove. It marks the position of the underlying *linea alba.*

10. A little below the middle of the median furrow there is an irregular depressed or elevated area called the *umbilicus.* It lies at the level of the junction between third and fourth lumbar vertebrae.

11. A few centimeters lateral to the median furrow, the abdominal wall shows a curved vertical groove. Its upper end reaches the costal margin at the tip of the ninth costal cartilage. Inferiorly it reaches the pubic tubercle. This line is called the *linea semilunaris.* It corresponds to the lateral margin of a muscle called the *rectus abdominis.*

12. The *transpyloric plane* is an imaginary transverse plane often referred to in anatomical descriptions. Anteriorly, it passes through the tips of the ninth costal cartilages; and posteriorly, through the lower part of the body of the first lumbar vertebra. This plane lies midway between the suprasternal notch and the pubic symphysis. It is roughly a hand's breadth below the xiphisternal joint.

13. The angle between the last rib and outer border of erector spinae is known as *renal angle.* It overlies the lower part of kidney. The twelfth rib may only be just palpable lateral to erector spinae or may extend for some distance beyond it.

14. *Posterior superior iliac spine* lies about 4 cm lateral to the median plane.

15. Three transverse furrows may be seen crossing the upper part of rectus abdominis, corresponding to the tendinous intersections of the muscle. One usually lies opposite the umbilicus, the other opposite free end of xiphoid process, and the third midway between the two (Fig. 16.12).

THE SKIN

The skin of the anterior abdominal wall is capable of undergoing enormous stretching as is seen in pregnancy, with accumulation of fat, called *obesity* or of fluid called *ascitis,* and with growth of large intraabdominal tumours.

Undue stretching may result in the formation of whitish streaks in the skin of the lower part of the anterior abdominal wall; these are known as *lineae albicantes.*

THE UMBILICUS

Definition

The umbilicus is the normal scar in the anterior

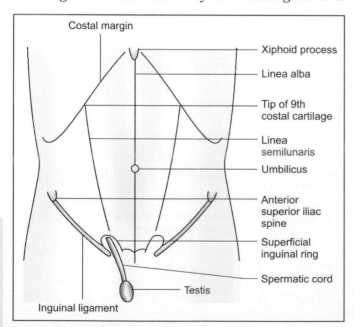

Fig. 16.2: Some superficial features in relation to the anterior abdominal wall.

abdominal wall formed by the remnants of the root of the *umbilical cord.*

The position of the umbilicus is variable. In healthy adults it lies in the anterior median line, at the level of the disc between the third and fourth lumbar vertebrae. It is lower in infants and in persons with a pendulous abdomen.

Apart from its embryological importance there are several facts of interest about the umbilicus. These are:

Anatomical Importance

1. With reference to the lymphatic and venous drainage, the level of the umbilicus is a *watershed.* Lymph and venous blood flow upwards above the plane of the umbilicus; and downwards below this plane. These do not normally cross umbilical plane (Fig. 16.8).
2. The skin around the umbilicus is supplied by segment T10 of the spinal cord (Fig. 16.5).
3. The umbilicus is one of the important sites at which tributaries of the portal vein anastomose with systemic veins (*portocaval anastomoses*). In portal hypertension, these anastomoses open up to form dilated veins radiating from the umbilicus called the *caput medusae.* However, the blood flow in the dilated veins is normal, and does not break the barrier of the water-shed line (Fig. 16.7a).

Embryological Importance

1. Umbilicus is the meeting point of the four (two lateral, head and tail) folds of embryonic plate.
2. This is also the meeting point of three systems, namely the digestive (vitellointestinal duct), the excretory (urachus), and vascular (umbilical vessels).

SUPERFICIAL FASCIA

1. Below the level of the umbilicus, the superficial fascia of the anterior abdominal wall is divided into a superficial fatty layer (*fascia of Camper*) and a deep membranous layer (*fascia of Scarpa*). The various contents of the superficial fascia run between these two layers.

   The *fatty layer* is continuous with the superficial fascia of the adjoining part of the body. In the penis, it is devoid of fat, and in the scrotum it is replaced by the *dartos muscle.*

   The *membranous* layer is continuous below with a similar membranous layer of superficial fascia of the perineum known as Colles' fascia. The attachments of Scarpa's fascia of the abdomen and of Colles' fascia of the perineum

are such that they prevent the passage of extravasated urine due to rupture of urethra backwards into the ischiorectal fossa and downwards into the thigh (Fig. 16.3a). The line of attachment passes over the following.

(a) Holden's line (it begins little lateral to pubic tubercle and extends laterally for 8 cm);
(b) Pubic tubercle;
(c) Body of the pubis and the deep fascia on the adductor longus and the gracilis near their origin;
(d) Margins of the pubic arch; and
(e) The posterior border of the perineal membrane. Above the umbilicus the membranous layer merges with the fatty layer.

2. In the median plane, the membranous layer is thickened to form the *suspensory ligament of the penis or of the clitoris* (Fig. 16.3b).

DISSECTION

Give an incision from xiphoid process till the umbilicus. Make a small circular incision around the umbilicus and extend it till the pubic symphysis. Carry the incision laterally from the umbilicus till the lateral abdominal wall on both sides. Give curved incisions from anterior superior iliac spine to pubic symphysis on either side (Fig. 16.4).

Finally give a horizontal incision across the xiphoid process till the lateral abdominal wall. Carefully reflect the skin in four flaps leaving both the layers of superficial fascia on the anterior abdominal wall.

Make a transverse incision through the entire thickness of the superficial fascia from the anterior superior iliac spine to the median plane. Raise the lower margin of the cut fascia and identify its fatty and membranous layers. Note that the fatty layer is continuous with the fascia of adjoining parts of the body. The membranous layer of anterior abdominal wall is continuous with the similar fascia (Colles' fascia) of the perineum. Note its attachment to pubic arch and posterior margin of *perineal membrane* (inferior fascia of urogenital diaphragm). Locate the *superficial inguinal ring* immediately superolateral to the pubic tubercle. Note the anterior cutaneous branch of the *iliohypogastric nerve* piercing the aponeurosis of the external oblique muscle a short distance superior to the ring. The spermatic cord/round ligament of uterus along with *ilioinguinal nerve* leave the abdomen through the superficial inguinal ring. Identify the external spermatic fascia attaching the spermatic cord to the margins of the ring.

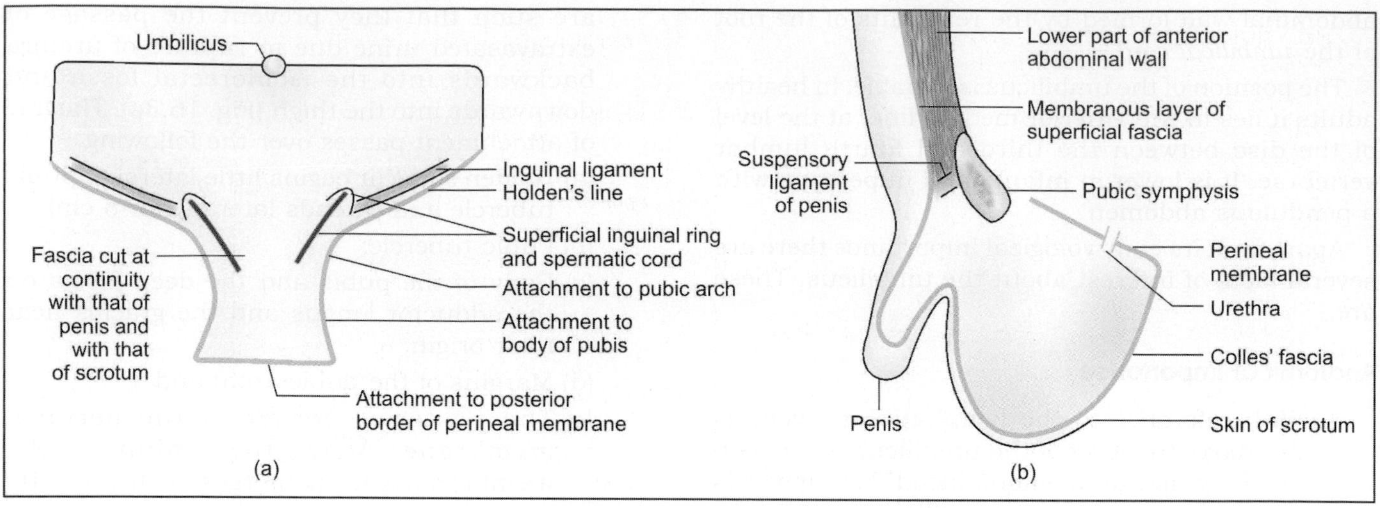

Umbilicus

Inguinal ligament
Holden's line

Superficial inguinal ring
and spermatic cord

Attachment to pubic arch

Fascia cut at
continuity
with that of
penis and
with that
of scrotum

Attachment to
body of pubis

Attachment to posterior
border of perineal membrane

(a)

Lower part of anterior
abdominal wall

Membranous layer of
superficial fascia

Suspensory
ligament
of penis

Pubic symphysis

Perineal
membrane

Urethra

Colles' fascia

Penis

Skin of scrotum

(b)

Fig. 16.3: The extent and attachments of the membranous layer of superficial fascia of the abdomen and perineum in a male. (a) Anterior view, (b) sagittal section.

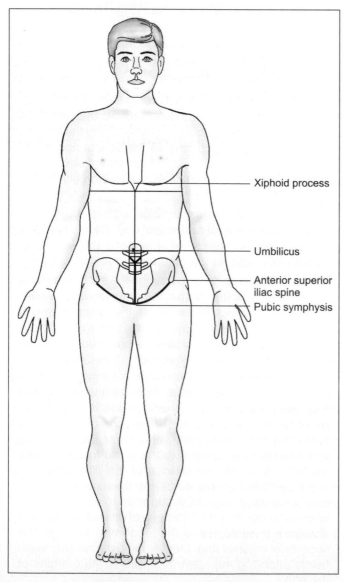

Fig. 16.4: Lines for incisions.

Xiphoid process

Umbilicus

Anterior superior
iliac spine

Pubic symphysis

3. The fascia contains:
   (a) An extremely variable quantity of fat, which tends to accumulate in the lower part of the abdomen after puberty.
   (b) Cutaneous nerves.
   (c) Cutaneous vessels.
   (d) Superficial lymphatics.

Divide the superficial fascia vertically in the median plane and in the line of the posterior axillary fold as far as the iliac crest. Reflect the fascia by blunt dissection from these two cuts and find the anterior and lateral cutaneous branches of the lower intercostal nerves along with respective blood vessels coming out from the anterior and lateral regions of the abdominal wall.

Cutaneous Nerves

The skin of the anterior abdominal wall is supplied by the lower six thoracic nerves and by the first lumbar nerve in the following manner.

The *anterior cutaneous nerves* (seven in number) are derived from the lower five intercostal nerves, the subcostal nerve and the iliohypogastric nerve (L1). T7–T12 nerves enter the abdominal wall directly. They pass between internal oblique and transversus muscle, pierce the posterior lamina of internal oblique aponeurosis to enter rectus sheath. Within the sheath, they pass behind rectus abdominis, then pierce the rectus muscles and the anterior wall of the rectus sheath close to the median plane, divide into medial and lateral branches and supply the skin of the front of the abdomen. They are arranged in serial order; T7 near the xiphoid process, T10 at the level of umbilicus, the iliohypogastric nerve 2.5 cm above the superficial inguinal ring, and others at proportionate distances between them (Fig. 16.5).

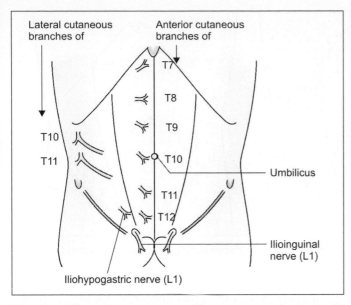

Fig. 16.5: The cutaneous nerves of the anterior abdominal wall.

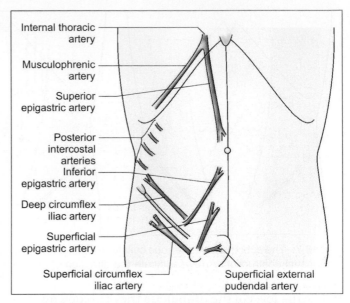

Fig. 16.6: Arteries of the anterior abdominal wall.

Subcostal nerve supplies pyramidalis, iliohypogastric and ilioinguinal *do not* enter rectus sheath. Iliohypogastric becomes cutaneous 2.5 cm above the superficial inguinal ring (Fig. 16.17).

The terminal part of the ilioinguinal nerve emerges through the superficial inguinal ring, pierces the external spermatic fascia and descends to supply the skin of the *external genitalia* and the upper part of the medial side of the thigh.

The lateral cutaneous nerves are two in number and are derived from the lower two intercostal nerves (T10, T11). Each nerve pierces the external intercostal muscle and divides into a large anterior branch and a smaller posterior branch, both of which emerge between the lower *digitations of the external oblique muscle* and supply the skin of the side of the abdomen. The larger anterior branches also supply the external oblique muscle.

The lateral cutaneous branches of the subcostal and iliohypogastric (T12, L1) nerves descend over the iliac crest and supply the skin of the antero-superior part of the gluteal region.

Cutaneous Arteries

1. The *anterior cutaneous arteries* are branches of the *superior* and *inferior epigastric arteries*, and accompany the anterior cutaneous nerves (Fig. 16.6).
2. The *lateral cutaneous arteries* are branches of the lower intercostal arteries, and accompany the lateral cutaneous nerves.
3. These superficial inguinal arteries arise from the femoral artery and supply the skin of the lower part of the abdomen. The *superficial*

epigastric artery runs upwards and medially and supplies the skin up to the umbilicus. The *superficial external pudendal artery* runs medially, passes in front of the spermatic cord, and supplies the skin of the external genitalia and the adjoining part of the lower abdominal wall. The *superficial circumflex iliac artery* runs laterally just below the inguinal ligament and supplies the skin of the abdomen and thigh.

Cutaneous Veins

The veins accompany the arteries. The superficial inguinal veins drain into the great saphenous vein.

When the portal vein, or the superior vena cava, or the inferior vena cava is obstructed the superficial abdominal veins are dilated and provide a collateral circulation. The dilated veins that radiate from the umbilicus are given the name *caput medusae* (Fig. 16.7a). They are seen typically in portal obstruction in which blood flow is upwards above the umbilicus, and downwards below the umbilicus. In vena caval obstructions, the thoracoepigastric veins open up, connecting the great saphenous vein with the axillary vein. In superior vena caval obstruction, the blood in the thoracoepigastric vein flows downwards, breaking the barrier of water-shed line (Fig. 16.7b). In inferior vena caval obstruction, the blood flows upwards, once again crossing the water-shed line (Fig. 16.7c).

Superficial Lymphatics

Lymphatics also pay due respect to the water-shed line. Above the level of the umbilicus the lymphatics run upwards to drain into the *axillary lymph nodes*.

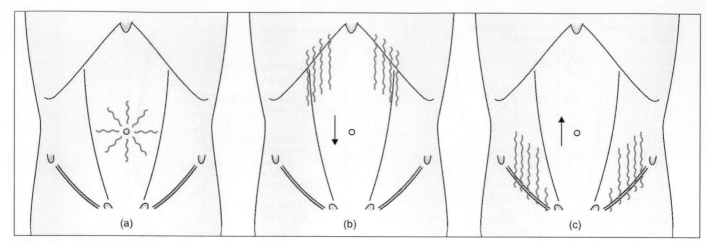

Fig. 16.7: The subcutaneous venous collateral circulation in (a) Portal obstruction; (b) superior vena caval obstruction; and (c) inferior vena caval obstruction. Arrows indicate the direction of blood flow.

Below the level of the umbilicus they run downwards to drain into the *superficial inguinal lymph nodes* (Fig. 16.8).

MUSCLES OF THE ANTERIOR ABDOMINAL WALL

The anterior abdominal wall is made up mainly of muscles. On either side of the midline there are four large muscles. These are the *external oblique*, the *internal oblique*, the *transversus abdominis* and the *rectus abdominis*. Two small muscles, the *cremaster* and the *pyramidalis* are also present. The external oblique, the internal oblique and the transversus abdominis are large flat muscles placed in the anterolateral part of the abdominal wall. Each of

them ends in an extensive aponeurosis that reaches the midline. Here the aponeuroses of the right and left sides decussate to form a median band called the linea alba. The rectus abdominis runs vertically on either side of the linea alba. It is enclosed in a *sheath* formed by the aponeuroses of the flat muscles named above. The various muscles are considered one by one below. The actions of these muscles are described later.

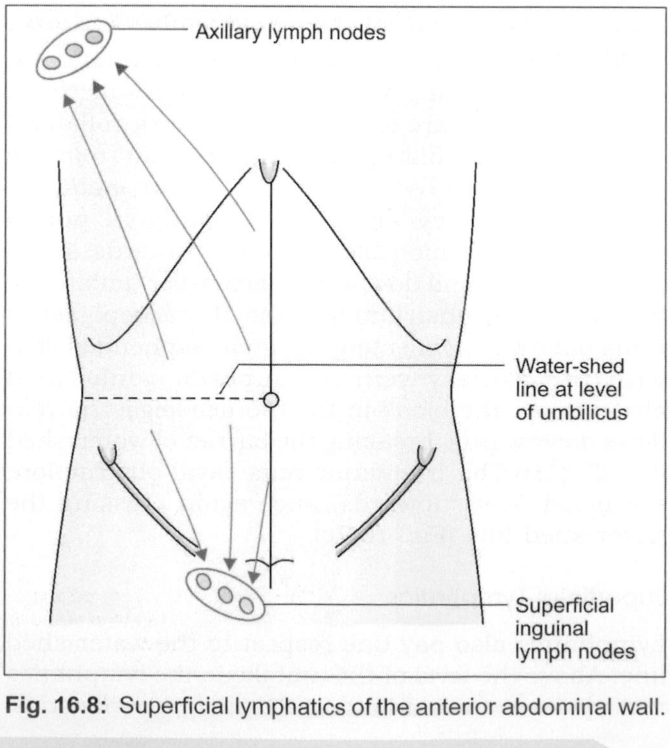

DISSECTION

Identify the origin of the external oblique from the lower eight ribs, and its interdigitations with serratus anterior in the upper part and with latissimus dorsi in the lower part of its origin. Separate 1–6 digitations from the ribs. Cut vertically, through the muscle to the iliac crest posterior to the sixth digitation. Separate the external oblique from the iliac crest in front of this. Try to avoid injury to the lateral cutaneous branches of the subcostal and iliohypogastric nerves which pierce it close to the iliac crest.

Reflect the upper part of the external oblique forwards and expose the deeper internal oblique and its aponeurosis to the line of its fusion with the aponeurosis of the external oblique anterior to rectus abdominis. Just lateral to this line of fusion divide the external oblique aponeurosis vertically till the pubic symphysis. Turn the muscle and aponeurosis inferiorly. This exposes the inferior part of the internal oblique and the lowest portion of aponeurosis of external oblique, i.e. the *inguinal ligament*.

Identify the deep fibres of the inguinal ligament passing posteriorly to the *pecten pubis*. This is the *lacunar ligament* or pectineal part of the inguinal ligament.

Axillary lymph nodes

Water-shed line at level of umbilicus

Superficial inguinal lymph nodes

Fig. 16.8: Superficial lymphatics of the anterior abdominal wall.

External Oblique Muscle

Origin

The muscle arises by eight fleshy slips from the middle of the shaft of the lower eight ribs. The fibres run downwards, forwards and medially (Fig. 16.9).

Insertion

1. Most of the fibres of the muscle end in a broad aponeurosis through which they are inserted from above downwards into the xiphoid process, linea alba, pubic symphysis, pubic crest and the pectineal line of the pubis.
2. The lower fibres of the muscle are inserted directly into the anterior two-thirds of the outer lip of the iliac crest.

Nerve Supply

Lower six thoracic nerves.

Other Points of Interest

1. The upper four slips of origin of the muscle interdigitate with those of the serratus anterior; and the lower four slips with those of the latissimus dorsi.
2. The junction of the muscle fibres with the aponeurosis lies:
   (i) Medial to a vertical line drawn from the ninth costal cartilage in the upper part.
   (ii) Below a line joining the anterior superior iliac spine to the umbilicus. Above the ninth costal cartilage the line curves upwards and medially.
3. Between the anterior superior iliac spine and the pubic tubercle the aponeurosis has a free inferior border that is folded on itself to form the inguinal ligament. The ligament is described in detail later.
4. Between the linea semilunaris and the linea alba, the aponeurosis helps to form the anterior wall of rectus sheath.
5. Just above the pubic crest the aponeurosis of the external oblique muscle presents a triangular aperture called the *superficial inguinal ring.*
6. The muscle has free posterior and upper borders.

Internal Oblique Muscle

Origin

The muscle arises from:
   (a) The lateral two-thirds of the inguinal ligament (Fig. 16.10).
   (b) The anterior two-thirds of the intermediate area of the iliac crest, and
   (c) The thoracolumbar fascia (Fig. 24.11).

From this origin the fibres run upwards, forwards and medially crossing the fibres of the external oblique muscle at right angles.

DISSECTION

Identify internal oblique deep to external oblique muscle. Remove the fascia from the surface of the internal oblique and its aponeurosis. Identify the part of the internal oblique which passes around the spermatic cord. This is the *cremaster muscle.* Trace the fibres of internal oblique into the conjoint tendon. Dissect the *triple* relation of internal oblique to the inguinal canal.

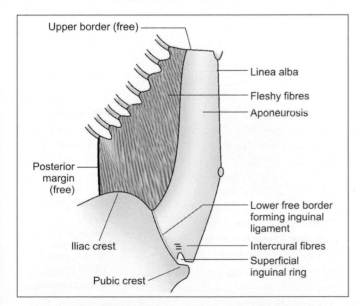

Fig. 16.9: External oblique muscle of the abdomen.

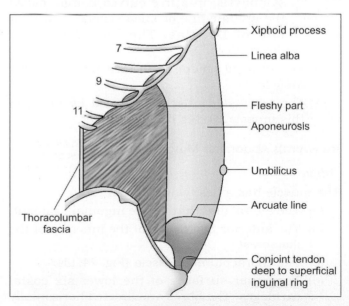

Fig. 16.10: Internal oblique muscle of the abdomen.

Insertion

1. The uppermost fibres are inserted directly into the lower three or four ribs and their cartilages.
2. The greater part of the muscle ends in an aponeurosis through which it is inserted into the seventh, eighth and ninth costal cartilages, the xiphoid process, linea alba, pubic crest and the pectineal line of the pubis (Fig. 16.10). It does not extend beyond the costal margin.

Nerve Supply

Lower six thoracic nerves and the first lumbar nerve.

Other Points of Interest

1. The junction of the muscle fibres with the aponeurosis is roughly at the lateral border of the rectus abdominis.
2. The aponeurosis takes part in the formation of *rectus sheath* as follows. Up to the lateral margin of rectus abdominis the aponeurosis has only one layer. Thereafter, the arrangement of aponeurosis differs in its upper and lower parts.
   (a) Below a level midway between the umbilicus and the pubic symphysis (lower 1/4th of the wall) the aponeurosis remains a single layer. It passes in front of rectus abdominis to reach linea alba. It, thus, takes part in forming the anterior wall of rectus sheath.
   (b) Above this level, i.e. upper 3/4th of the wall, the aponeurosis splits into an anterior lamina that passes medially in front of the rectus abdominis; and a posterior lamina that lies behind the rectus. The posterior lamina ends below, at the level midway between the umbilicus and the pubic symphysis, in a free curved margin called the arcuate line or linea semicircularis, or fold of Douglas. The line is concave downwards.
3. The *conjoint tendon* is formed partly by this muscle.
4. The *cremaster* muscle is formed by fibres of this muscle, and is described later.

Transversus Abdominis Muscle

Origin

The muscle has a fleshy origin from:
   (a) The lateral one-third of the inguinal ligament.
   (b) The anterior two-thirds of the inner lip of the iliac crest.
   (c) The thoracolumbar fascia (Fig. 24.11).
   (d) The inner surfaces of the lower six costal cartilages. The fibres are directed horizontally forwards.

Insertion

The fibres end in a broad aponeurosis which is inserted into the xiphoid process, the linea alba, the pubic crest, and the pectineal line of the pubis (Fig. 16.11).

The lowest fibres of the muscle fuse with the lowest fibres of the internal oblique to form the conjoint tendon.

Nerve Supply

Lower six thoracic nerves, and first lumbar nerve.

Other Points of Interest

1. The aponeurosis of the transversus abdominis takes part in forming the rectus sheath as follows. Above the level of the arcuate line (upper 3/4th) the aponeurosis passes medially behind the rectus abdominis muscle along with the posterior lamina of the internal oblique aponeurosis. The lower edge of this part of the aponeurosis helps to form the *arcuate line*. In the uppermost part, some fleshy fibres of the transversus abdominis may lie behind the rectus abdominis.

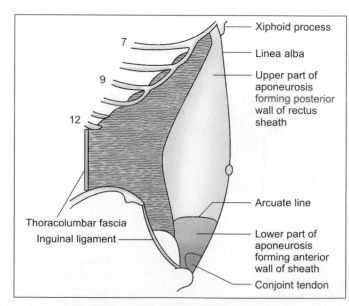

Fig. 16.11: Transversus abdominis muscle.

Below the level of the arcuate line the aponeurosis passes in front of the rectus abdominis and helps to form the anterior wall of the rectus sheath.

2. The *neurovascular plane* of the abdominal wall lies between the *internal oblique* and *transversus muscles*. This plane is continuous with the neurovascular plane of the thoracic wall. Various nerves and vessels run in this plane.

3. The aponeuroses of three flat muscles seem to end in the fibrous raphe—the linea alba. Each aponeurosis is made up of the two laminae, the superficial and deep laminae. The laminae of the two sides interdigitate in a manner that the superficial lamina of one gets continuous with deep lamina of the opposite side and vice versa. This provides enough strength to the anterior abdominal wall.

Rectus Abdominis Muscle

Origin

The muscle arises by two tendinous heads as follows.
(a) *Lateral head* from the lateral part of the pubic crest (Fig. 16.12).
(b) *Medial head* from the anterior pubic ligament.
The fibres run vertically upwards.

Insertion

On the front of the wall of the thorax, along a horizontal line passing laterally from the xiphoid process, and cutting in that order, the 7th, 6th and 5th costal cartilages.

Nerve Supply

Lower six or seven thoracic nerves.

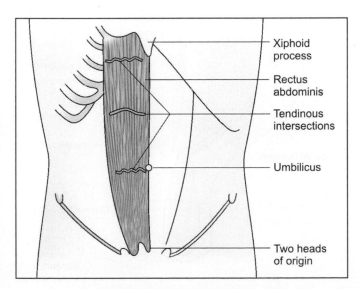

Xiphoid process

Rectus abdominis

Tendinous intersections

Umbilicus

Two heads of origin

Fig. 16.12: Rectus abdominis muscle.

Other Points of Interest

1. The muscle is enclosed in a sheath formed mainly by the aponeuroses of the three flat muscles of the abdominal wall. The sheath is described later.

2. *Tendinous intersections:* These are three transverse fibrous bands which divide the muscle into smaller parts. One lies opposite the umbilicus, the second opposite the free end of the xiphoid process, and the third in between the two. One or two incomplete intersections may be present below the umbilicus. The intersections are actually zigzag in course, traverse only the anterior half of the muscle, and are adherent to the anterior wall of rectus sheath. Embryologically they may represent the segmental origin of muscle, but functionally they make the muscle more powerful by increasing the number of muscle fibres.

Actions of the Main Muscles of the Anterior Abdominal Wall

1. *Support for abdominal viscera:* The abdominal muscles provide a firm but elastic support for the abdominal viscera against gravity. This is chiefly due to the tone of the oblique muscles, especially the internal oblique.

2. *Expulsive acts:* The oblique muscles, assisted by the transversus, can compress the abdominal viscera and thus help in all expulsive acts, like micturition, defaecation, parturition, vomiting, etc. This is one of the most important actions of the abdominal muscles.

3. *Forceful expiratory acts:* The external oblique can markedly depress and compress the lower part of the thorax producing forceful expiration, as in coughing, sneezing, blowing, shouting, etc. This is also an important action of the abdominal muscles.

4. *Movements of the trunk:*
   (a) Flexion of the trunk or lumbar spine is brought about mainly by the rectus abdominis.
   (b) Lateral flexion of the trunk is done by one sided contraction of the oblique muscles.
   (c) Rotation of the trunk is produced by a combined action of the external oblique with the opposite internal oblique.

Inguinal Ligament

1. The inguinal ligament is formed by the lower border of the external oblique aponeurosis which is thickened and folded backwards on

itself. It extends from the anterior superior iliac spine to the pubic tubercle, and lies beneath the fold of the groin. Its lateral half is rounded and oblique. Its medial half is grooved upwards and is more horizontal (Fig. 16.13).

2. *Attachments:*

(a) The fascia lata is attached to the lower border. Traction of this fascia makes the ligament convex downwards.

(b) The upper surface of the ligament gives origin to the internal oblique from its lateral two-thirds, to the transversus abdominis from its lateral one-third, and to the cremaster muscle from its middle part.

3. *Relations:* The upper grooved surface of the medial half of the inguinal ligament forms the floor of the inguinal canal and lodges the spermatic cord or round ligament of the uterus.

4. *Extensions:*

(a) The *pectineal part of the inguinal ligament* or lacunar ligament is triangular. Anteriorly, it is attached to the medial end of the inguinal ligament. Posteriorly, it is attached to the pecten pubis. It is horizontal in position and supports the spermatic cord. The apex is attached to the pubic tubercle. The base is directed laterally. It forms the medial boundary of the femoral ring. It is reinforced by the pectineal fascia and by fibres from the linea alba (Fig. 16.13).

(b) The *pectineal ligament* or *ligament of Cooper* is an extension from the posterior part of the base of the lacunar ligament. It is attached to the pecten pubis. It may be regarded as a thickening in the upper part of the pectineal fascia.

(c) The *reflected part of the inguinal ligament* consists of fibres that pass upwards and medially from the lateral crus of the superficial inguinal ring. It lies behind the superficial inguinal ring and in front of the conjoint tendon. Its fibres interlace with those of the opposite side at the linea alba.

Conjoint Tendon or Falx Inguinalis

The conjoint tendon is formed by fusion of the lowest aponeurotic fibres of the internal oblique and of the transversus muscles, and is attached to the pubic crest and to the medial part of the pecten pubis. Medially, it is continuous with the anterior wall of the rectus sheath. Laterally, it is usually free. Sometimes it may be continuous with an inconstant ligamentous band, named the *interfoveolar ligament,* which connects the lower border of the transversus abdominis to the superior ramus of the pubis. The conjoint tendon strengthens the abdominal wall at the site where it is weakened by the superficial inguinal ring (Fig. 16.10).

The Cremaster Muscle

The cremaster muscle consists of muscle fasciculi embedded in the *cremasteric fascia.* The fasciculi form loops that are attached laterally to the inguinal ligament. Here some fibres may be continuous with the internal oblique or transversus muscles. The medial ends of the loops are attached to the pubic tubercle, the pubic crest or the conjoint tendon (Fig. 16.14).

The muscle is fully developed only in the male. In the female it is represented by a few fibres only.

Along with the intervening connective tissue, the muscle loops to form a sac-like *cremasteric fascia*

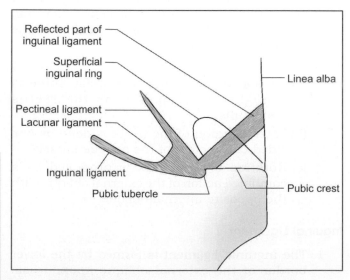

Fig. 16.13: Extensions of the inguinal ligament.

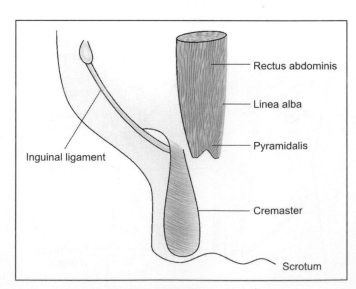

Fig. 16.14: The cremaster and pyramidalis.

around the spermatic cord and testis. It lies deep to the *external spermatic fascia.*

Nerve Supply

Genital branch of the genitofemoral nerve (L1).

Action

The cremaster helps to suspend the testis and can elevate it. The muscle also tends to close the superficial inguinal ring when the intra-abdominal pressure is raised.

Cremasteric Reflex

Upon stroking the skin of the upper part of the medial side of the thigh there is reflex contraction of the cremaster muscle, as evidenced by elevation and retraction of the testis. The reflex is more brisk in children. In upper motor neuron lesions above segment L1, the reflex is lost (Fig. 16.15).

Pyramidalis

This is a small triangular muscle. It is rudimentary in human beings. It arises from the anterior surface of the body of the pubis. Its fibres pass upwards and medially to be inserted into the linea alba (Fig. 16.14).

The muscle is supplied by the subcostal nerve (T12). It is said to be tensor of the linea alba, but the need for such action is not clear.

DEEP NERVES OF THE ANTERIOR ABDOMINAL WALL

The anterior abdominal wall is supplied by the lower six thoracic nerves or lower five intercostal, and subcostal; and by the first lumbar nerve through its iliohypogastric and ilioinguinal branches. These are the nerves which emerge cutaneous nerves. Their deep course is described briefly with the cutaneous nerves in the beginning of this chapter (Figs 16.16 and 16.17).

DEEP ARTERIES OF ANTERIOR ABDOMINAL WALL

The anterior abdominal wall is supplied by:

1. Two large arteries from above, the *superior epigastric* and *musculophrenic.*
2. Two large arteries from below, the *inferior epigastric* and the *deep circumflex iliac.*
3. Small branches of the intercostal, subcostal and lumbar arteries, which accompany the corresponding nerves (Fig. 16.6).

The *superior epigastric artery* is one of the two terminal branches of the internal thoracic artery. It begins in the sixth intercostal space, and enters the abdomen by passing behind the seventh costal cartilage between the costal and xiphoid origins of the diaphragm. It enters the rectus sheath and runs vertically downwards, supplies the rectus muscle, and ends by anastomosing with the inferior epigastric artery (Fig. 16.18). In addition to muscular and cutaneous branches, it gives a *hepatic branch* which runs in the *falciform ligament,* and an anastomotic branch, at the level of the xiphoid process, which anastomoses with the artery of the opposite side.

The *musculophrenic artery* is the other terminal branch of the internal thoracic artery. It runs downwards and laterally behind the seventh costal cartilage, and enters the abdomen by piercing the diaphragm between the seventh and eighth cartilages. It continues downwards and laterally along the deep surface of the diaphragm as far as the tenth intercostal space. It gives branches to the diaphragm, the anterior abdominal wall and the seventh, eighth and ninth intercostal spaces as the anterior intercostal arteries.

The *inferior epigastric artery* arises from the external iliac artery near its lower end just above the inguinal ligament. It runs upwards and medially in the extraperitoneal connective tissue, passes just medial to the deep inguinal ring, pierces the fascia transversalis at the lateral border of the rectus abdominis and enters the rectus sheath by passing in front of the arcuate line (Fig. 16.19). Within the sheath it supplies the rectus muscle and ends by anastomosing with the superior epigastric artery. It gives off the following branches.

(a) A *cremasteric branch* to the spermatic cord, or the artery of the round ligament in females.

(b) A *pubic branch* which anastomoses with the pubic branch of the obturator artery.

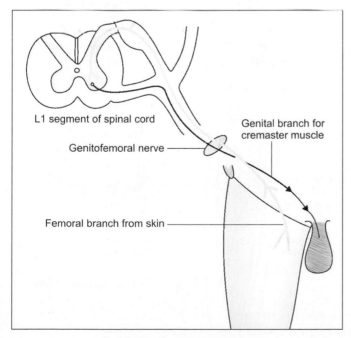

L1 segment of spinal cord

Genitofemoral nerve

Femoral branch from skin

Genital branch for cremaster muscle

Fig. 16.15: Cremasteric reflex.

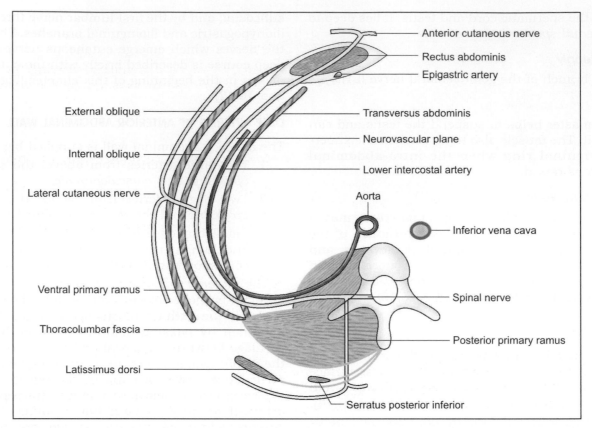

Fig. 16.16: A transverse section through the lumbar region showing the arrangement of the abdominal muscles and the neurovascular plane.

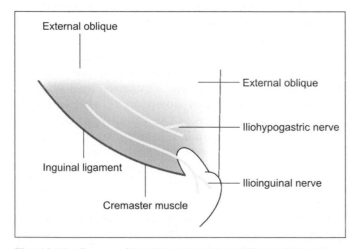

Fig. 16.17: Course of the iliohypogastric and ilioinguinal nerves.

(c) *Muscular* branches to the rectus abdominis.

(d) *Cutaneous* branches to the overlying skin. The pubic branch may replace the obturator artery, and is then known as the *abnormal obturator artery*.

The *deep circumflex iliac artery* is the other branch of the external iliac artery, given off from its lateral side opposite the origin of the inferior epigastric artery. It runs laterally and upwards behind the

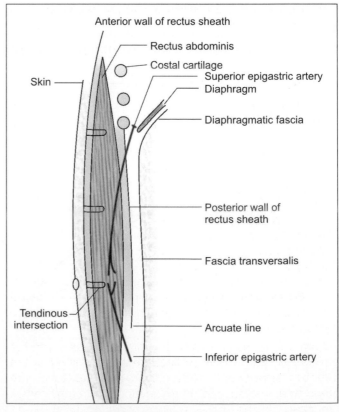

Fig. 16.18: Sagittal section through the rectus sheath.

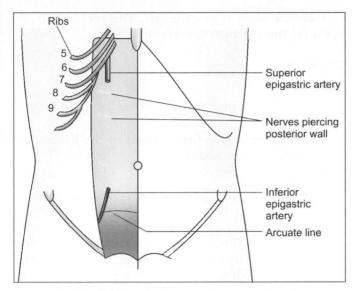

Fig. 16.19: Posterior wall of the rectus sheath.

RECTUS SHEATH

Definition

This is an aponeurotic sheath covering the rectus abdominis. It has two walls, anterior and posterior.

Features

Anterior wall

1. It is complete, covering the muscle from end to end.
2. Its composition is variable as described below.
3. It is firmly adherent to the tendinous intersections of the rectus muscle (Fig. 16.18).

Posterior wall

1. It is incomplete, being deficient above the costal margin and below the arcuate line.
2. Its composition is uniform as described below.
3. It is free from the rectus muscle (Fig. 16.19).

DISSECTION

Strip the peritoneum from the posterior surface of the infraumbilical abdominal wall. Before removing the transversalis fascia from the deep surface of the inguinal ligament pull on the spermatic cord or round ligament of uterus from the anterior surface to confirm the continuity of spermatic cord. *Transversalis fascia* continues as the *internal spermatic fascia* over the spermatic cord.

---

inguinal ligament, pierces the fascia transversalis, and continues along the iliac crest, up to its middle where it pierces the transversus abdominis to enter the interval between the transversus and the internal oblique muscles. At the anterior superior iliac spine it anastomoses with the superior gluteal, the lateral circumflex femoral and superficial circumflex iliac arteries. Just behind the anterior superior iliac spine it gives off an ascending branch which runs upwards in the neurovascular plane.

DISSECTION

Identify the rectus abdominis muscle

At the lateral edge of the rectus abdominis, the aponeurosis of the internal oblique splits to pass partly posterior and partly anterior to the rectus abdominis; the anterior layer fusing with the aponeurosis of external oblique and the posterior layer with that of the transversus abdominis. This is how most of the rectus sheath is formed. Identify the arcuate line midway between umbilicus and pubic symphysis.

Define the origins of the transversus and follow its aponeurosis to fuse with that of the internal oblique, posterior to the rectus abdominis above the arcuate line and anteriorly to the unsplit aponeurosis of internal oblique below the line. See that aponeurosis of all three muscles pass anterior to rectus abdominis below the arcuate line.

Open the rectus sheath by a vertical incision along the middle of the muscle. Reflect the anterior layer of the sheath side ways, cutting its attachments to the tendinous intersections in the anterior part of the rectus muscle. Lift the rectus muscle and identify the 7–11

intercostal and subcostal nerves entering the sheath through its posterior lamina, piercing the muscle and leaving through its anterior wall.

Divide the rectus abdominis transversely at its middle. Identify its attachments and expose the posterior wall of the rectus sheath by reflecting its parts superiorly and inferiorly. Identify and trace the superior and inferior epigastric arteries.

Define the arcuate line on the posterior wall of the rectus sheath.

Identify the *peritoneum*. Divide and reflect it with the anterior abdominal wall. Cut the fold of peritoneum which passes from the median part of the supra-umbilical part of the anterior abdominal wall to the liver known as the *falciform ligament*. This fold contains the *ligamentum teres* of the liver or the *obliterated left umbilical vein* in its free posterior border.

Examine the posterior surface of the reflected anterior abdominal wall. Identify five ill-defined *peritoneal folds* which pass upwards towards the umbilicus. These are *two lateral*, *two medial* and *one median umbilical folds*.

Formation

Details about the formation of the walls are as follows (Fig. 16.20).

Above the costal margin (Fig. 16.20a)

Anterior wall: External oblique aponeurosis.

Posterior wall: It is deficient; the rectus muscle rests directly on the 5th, 6th and 7th costal cartilages.

Between the costal margin and the arcuate line

Anterior wall

1. External oblique aponeurosis.
2. Anterior lamina of the aponeurosis of the internal oblique.

Posterior wall

1. Posterior lamina of the aponeurosis of the internal oblique.
2. Aponeurosis of the transversus muscle (Fig. 16.20b).

Midway between the umbilicus and the pubic symphysis, the posterior wall of the rectus sheath ends in the arcuate line or *linea semicircularis* or *fold of Douglas*. The line is concave downwards.

Below the arcuate line.

Anterior wall: Aponeuroses of all the three flat muscles of the abdomen. The aponeuroses of the transversus and the internal oblique are fused, but the external oblique aponeurosis remains separate (Fig. 16.20c).

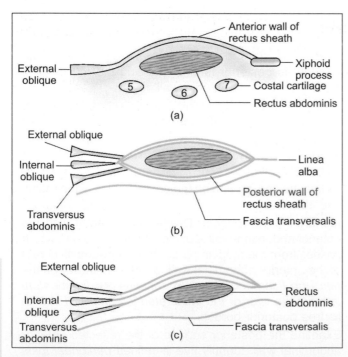

Fig. 16.20: Transverse sections through the rectus abdominis, and its sheath: (a) Above the costal margin, (b) between costal margin and arcuate line, (c) below arcuate line.

Posterior wall: It is deficient. The rectus muscle rests on the fascia transversalis.

Contents

Muscles

1. The *rectus abdominis* is the chief and largest content.
2. The *pyramidalis* lies in front of the lower part of the rectus abdominis.

Arteries

1. The *superior epigastric artery* enters the sheath by passing between the costal and xiphoid origins of the diaphragm. It crosses the upper border of the transversus abdominis behind the seventh costal cartilage. It supplies the rectus abdominis muscle and anastomoses with the inferior epigastric artery (Fig. 16.18).
2. The *inferior epigastric artery* enters the sheath by passing in front of the arcuate line (Fig. 16.19).

Veins

1. The *superior epigastric vein* accompanies its artery and joins the internal thoracic vein.
2. The *inferior epigastric vein* also accompanies its artery and joins the external iliac vein.

Nerves

These are the terminal parts of the lower six thoracic nerves, including the *lower five intercostal nerves* and the *subcostal nerves*.

Functions

1. It checks bowing of rectus muscle during its contraction and thus increases the efficiency of the muscle.
2. It maintains the strength of the anterior abdominal wall.

New Concept of Rectus Sheath

Rectus sheath is formed by decussating fibres from three abdominal muscles of each side. Each forms a bilaminar aponeurosis at their medial borders. Fibres from all three anterior leaves run obliquely upwards, while the posterior fibers run obliquely downwards at right angles to anterior leaves.

Anterior Sheath of Rectus

Both leaves of external oblique aponeurosis and anterior leaf of internal oblique aponeurosis.

Posterior Sheath

Posterior leaf of aponeurosis of internal oblique and both leaves of aponeurosis of transversus abdominis.

Fibres of each layer decussate to the opposite side of the sheath. Fibres also decussate between anterior and posterior sheaths.

The three lateral abdominal muscles may be said to be digastric with a central tendon in the form of linea alba.

Linea alba is a tendinous raphe between xiphoid process above to symphysis pubis and pubic crest below. Above the umbilicus the linea alba is broader. Superficial fibres of linea alba are attached to symphysis pubis, while deep fibres are attached behind rectus abdominis to posterior surface of pubic crest.

THE FASCIA TRANSVERSALIS

Definition

The inner surface of the abdominal muscles is lined by fascia which is separated from peritoneum by extraperitoneal connective tissue. That part of the fascia which lines the inner surface of the transversus abdominis muscle is called the fascia transversalis (Fig. 16.21a).

Extent

Anteriorly, it is adherent to the linea alba above the umbilicus.

Posteriorly, it merges with the anterior layer of the thoracolumbar fascia and is continuous with the renal fascia (Fig. 16.21b).

Superiorly, it is continuous with the diaphragmatic fascia.

Inferiorly,

1. It is attached to the inner lip of the iliac crest and to the lateral half of the inguinal ligament, at both these places it is continuous with the fascia iliaca.

2. Medially, it is attached to the pubic tubercle, the pubic crest and the pectineal line.

3. Part of it is prolonged into the thigh as the anterior wall of the femoral sheath.

Opening of Deep Inguinal Ring

About 1.2 cm above the midinguinal point there is an oval opening in the fascia transversalis. This opening is the deep inguinal ring (Fig. 16.22). The ring lies immediately lateral to the inferior epigastric artery. It transmits the spermatic cord in males, and the round ligament of the uterus in females.

Prolongations

1. A tubular prolongation of the fascia transversalis surrounds the spermatic cord forming the *internal spermatic fascia*.

2. Over the femoral vessels, the fascia transversalis is prolonged into the thigh as the *anterior wall of femoral sheath*.

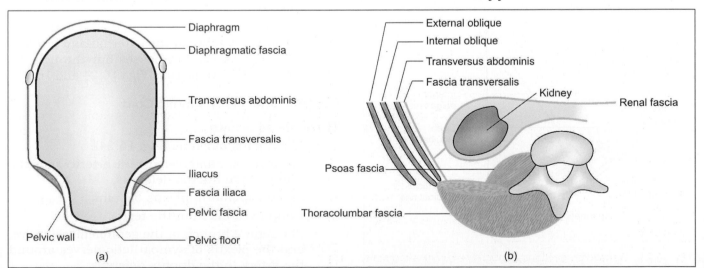

Fig. 16.21: Continuation of the fascia transversalis: (a) Coronal section, (b) transverse section.

Relation to Vessels and Nerves

The main arteries of the abdominal wall and pelvis lie inside the fascia transversalis, while the main nerves are outside. That is why the femoral vessels are inside the femoral sheath, while the femoral nerve is outside the sheath.

INGUINAL CANAL

Definition

This is an oblique passage in the lower part of the anterior abdominal wall, situated just above the medial half of the inguinal ligament.

Length and direction: It is about 4 cm (1.5 inches) long, and is directed downwards, forwards and medially (Fig. 16.22).

The inguinal canal extends from the deep inguinal ring to the superficial inguinal ring. The *deep inguinal ring* is an oval opening in the fascia transversalis, situated 1.2 cm above the midinguinal point, and immediately lateral to the stem of the inferior epigastric artery. The *superficial inguinal ring* is a triangular gap in the external oblique aponeurosis. It is shaped like an obtuse angled triangle. The base of the triangle is formed by the pubic crest. The two sides of the triangle form the lateral or lower and the medial or upper margins of the opening. It is 2.5 cm long and 1.2 cm broad at the base. These margins are referred to as *crura*. At and beyond the apex of the triangle, the two crura are united by intercrural fibres.

Boundaries

The *anterior wall* is formed by the following (Fig. 16.22).

(a) *In its whole extent:*
   (i) Skin

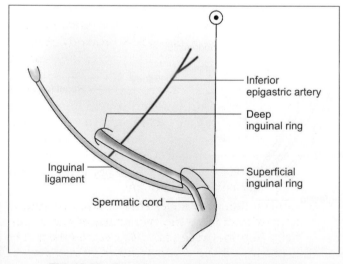

Fig. 16.22: Superficial and deep inguinal rings.

Labels in figure:
- Inferior epigastric artery
- Deep inguinal ring
- Superficial inguinal ring
- Inguinal ligament
- Spermatic cord

   (ii) Superficial fascia
   (iii) External oblique aponeurosis.
(b) *In its lateral one-third:* The fleshy fibres of the internal oblique muscle (Fig. 16.23a).

The *posterior wall* is formed by the following.

(a) *In its whole extent:*
   (i) The fascia transversalis
   (ii) The extraperitoneal tissue
   (iii) The parietal peritoneum.
(b) *In its medial two-thirds:*
   (i) The conjoint tendon
   (ii) At its medial end by the reflected part of the inguinal ligament.
(c) *In its lateral one-third:* By the interfoveolar ligament extending between lower border of transversus abdominis and superior ramus of pubis.

Roof

It is formed by the arched fibres of the internal oblique and transversus abdominis muscles (Fig. 16.23b).

Floor

It is formed by the grooved upper surface of the inguinal ligament; and at the medial end by the lacunar ligament.

Sex Difference

The inguinal canal is larger in males than in females.

Structures Passing through the Canal

1. The *spermatic cord in males*, or the *round ligament of the uterus in females*, enters the inguinal canal through the deep inguinal ring and passes out through the superficial inguinal ring.
2. The ilioinguinal nerve enters the canal through the interval between the external and internal oblique muscles and passes out through the superficial inguinal ring (Figs 16.24 and 16.27).

Constituents of the Spermatic Cord

These are as follows.
1. The ductus deferens (Fig. 16.24).
2. The testicular and cremasteric arteries, and the artery of the ductus deferens.
3. The pampiniform plexus of veins.
4. Lymph vessels from the testis.
5. The genital branch of the genitofemoral nerve, and the plexus of sympathetic nerves around the artery to the ductus deferens.
6. Remains of the processus vaginalis.

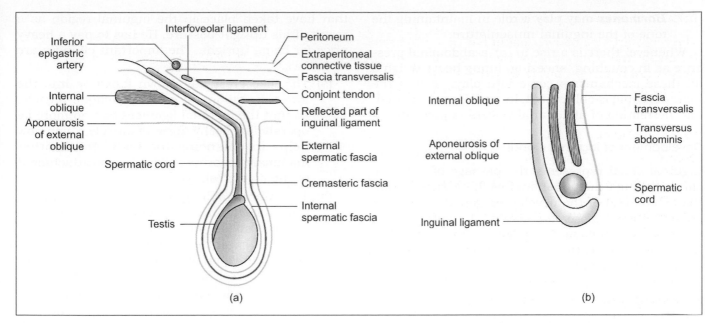

Fig. 16.23: Boundaries of the inguinal canal: (a) Anterior and posterior walls in a horizontal section,(b) the roof and floor in a sagittal section.

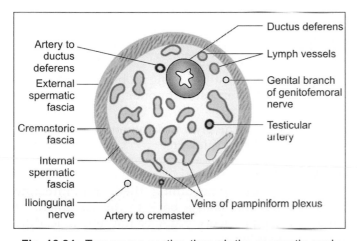

Fig. 16.24: Transverse section through the spermatic cord.

Coverings of Spermatic Cord

From within outwards, these are as follows.

1. The *internal spermatic fascia*, derived from the fascia transversalis; it covers the cord in its whole extent.

2. The *cremasteric fascia* is made up of the muscle loops constituting the cremaster muscle, and the intervening areolar tissue. It is derived from the internal oblique and transversus abdominis muscles, and therefore covers the cord below the level of these muscles.

3. The *external spermatic fascia* is derived from the external oblique aponeurosis. It covers the cord below the superficial inguinal ring.

Mechanism of Inguinal Canal

The presence of the inguinal canal is a cause of weakness in the lower part of the anterior abdominal wall. This weakness is compensated by the following factors.

1. ***Obliquity of the inguinal canal:*** The two inguinal rings do not lie opposite each other. Therefore, when the intra-abdominal pressure rises the anterior and posterior walls of the canal are approximated, thus obliterating the passage. This is known as the flap valve mechanism.

2. **The *superficial inguinal ring is guarded*** from behind by the conjoint tendon and by the reflected part of the inguinal ligament.

3. **The *deep inguinal ring is guarded*** from the front by the fleshy fibres of the internal oblique.

4. ***Shutter mechanism of the internal oblique:*** This muscle has a triple relation to the inguinal canal. It forms the anterior wall, the roof, and the posterior wall of the canal. When it contracts the roof is approximated to the floor, like a shutter. The arching fibres of the transversus also take part in the shutter mechanism.

5. Contraction of the cremaster helps the spermatic cord to plug the superficial inguinal ring (*ball valve mechanism*).

6. Contraction of the external oblique results in approximation of the two crura of the superficial inguinal ring (*slit valve mechanism*). The integrity of the superficial inguinal ring is greatly increased by the intercrural fibres.

7. **Hormones** may play a role in maintaining the tone of the inguinal musculature.

Whenever there is a rise in intra-abdominal pressure as in coughing, sneezing, lifting heavy weights all these mechanisms come into play, so that the inguinal canal is obliterated, its openings are closed, and herniation of abdominal viscera is prevented.

Development of Inguinal Canal

Inguinal canal represents the passage of *gubernaculum* through the abdominal wall; it extends from the caudal end of the developing gonad (in lumbar region) to the *labioscrotal swelling*. In early life, the canal is very short. As the pelvis increases in width, the deep inguinal ring is shifted laterally and the adult dimensions of the canal are attained.

Morphologically

The inguinal hernia peculiarly occurs only in man and not in any other mammal. This predisposition of man to hernia is due to the evolutionary changes that have taken place in the inguinal region as a result of his upright posture. He has to pay a heavy price for being upright. The important changes are as follows.

(a) The iliac crest has grown forwards into the lower digitations of external oblique muscle, so that the inguinal ligament can no more be operated by fleshy fibres of muscle which now helps in balancing the body. In all other mammals, external oblique has no attachment to the iliac crest.

(b) The internal oblique and transversus initially originated from the anterior border of ilium and the sheath of iliopsoas, and acted as a powerful sphincter of the inguinal canal. The shift of their origin to the inguinal ligament and iliac crest has minimised their role.

(c) Due to peculiar growth of hip bones and pelvis, the crural passage (between hip bone and inguinal ligament) in man has become much wider than any other mammal. This predisposes to femoral hernia.

CLINICAL ANATOMY

Hernia

Hernia is a protrusion of any of the abdominal contents through any of its walls. This is called external hernia. At times the intestine or omentum protrudes into the "no entry" zone within the abdominal cavity itself. The condition is called as internal hernia.

Hernia consists of a sac, contents and coverings. Sac is the protrusion of the peritoneum. It comprises a neck, the narrowed part and a body, the bigger part (Fig. 16.25).

Contents are mostly the long mobile, keen to move out, coils of small intestine or omentum or any other viscera.

Coverings are the layers of abdominal wall which are covering the hernial sac.

Complications

Irreducibility: In the beginning, the loop of intestine herniates out but comes back to the abdomen. At times, the loop goes out but does not return, leading to irreducible hernia.

Obstruction: The loop may get narrowed in part, so that contents of the loop cannot move forwards, leading to obstruction.

Strangulation: When the arterial supply is blocked, the loop gets necrosed.

Types of Abdominal Hernia

Internal

In opening of the lesser sac. In paraduodenal recesses.

External

- Umbilical
- Inguinal
- Divarication of recti
- Lumbar
- Femoral
- Epigastric
- Incisional

- **Umbilical hernia:** Congenital umbilical hernia: Due to non-return of midgut loop back to the abdominal cavity (Fig. 16.26).

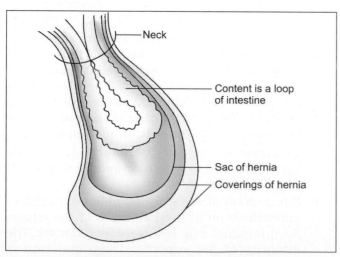

Fig. 16.25: Parts of a hernia.

Neck

Content is a loop of intestine

Sac of hernia

Coverings of hernia

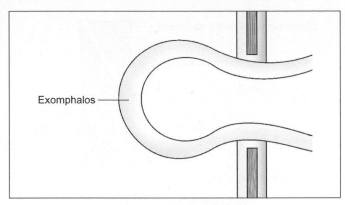

Fig. 16.26: Exomphalos.

Acquired infantile umbilical hernia: Due to weakness of umbilical scar, a part of the gut may be seen protruding out. It disappears as the infant grows (Fig. 16.27).

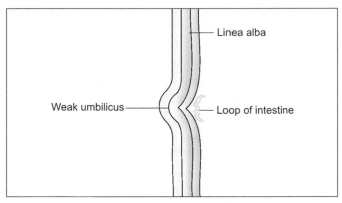

Fig. 16.27: Infantile umbilical hernia.

- ***Paraumbilical hernia:*** Loop of intestine protrude through the linea alba around the region of umbilicus (Fig. 16.28).

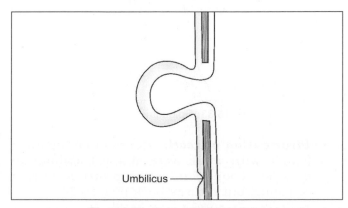

Fig. 16.28: Paraumbilical hernia.

- ***Femoral hernia:*** Occurs more in females, due to larger pelvis, smaller blood vessels and larger femoral canal. Its neck lies below and lateral to the pubic tubercle. Surgery is essential for its treatment (Fig. 16.29). (Also see Chapter 3).

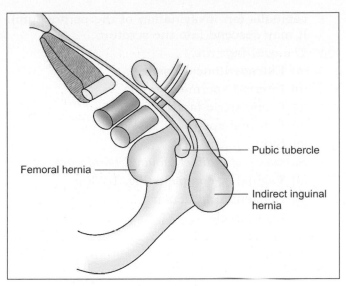

Fig. 16.29: Femoral and inguinal hernia.

- ***Inguinal hernia:*** Protrusion of the loop of intestine through the inguinal wall or inguinal canal is called inguinal hernia (Fig. 16.29).

  When the protrusion occurs through the deep inguinal ring, inguinal canal, superficial inguinal ring into the scrotum, it is called indirect or oblique inguinal hernia.

  It occurs in male infants, children and has a narrow neck of the hernial sac.

  When the protrusion occurs through the weak posterior wall of the inguinal canal, the hernia is a direct inguinal hernia. It occurs in much older men and has a wider neck of hernial sac.

  Differences between indirect and direct hernia are give in Table 16.1.

- ***Indirect or oblique hernia*** occurs due to partial or complete patency of the processus

Table 16.1: Differences between direct and indirect inguinal hernia		
	Direct inguinal hernia	**Indirect inguinal hernia**
1. Aetiology	Weakness of posterior wall of inguinal canal	Preformed sac
2. Precipitating factors	Chronic bronchitis, enlarged prostate	—
3. On standing	Comes out	Does not come out
4. Direction of the sac	It comes out of Hesselbach's triangle	Sac comes through the deep inguinal ring
5. Obstruction	Not common because neck is wide	Common, as neck is narrow
6. Internal ring occlusion test	The swelling is seen	Not seen

vaginalis (an invagination of the peritoneum). It may descend into the scrotum.

The coverings are:

(a) Extraperitoneal tissue

(b) Internal spermatic fascia

(c) Cremasteric fascia

(d) External spermatic fascia

(e) Skin

Subtypes of indirect inguinal hernia are:

(a) Vaginal or complete (Fig. 16.30)

(b) Congenital funicular

(c) Bubonocele

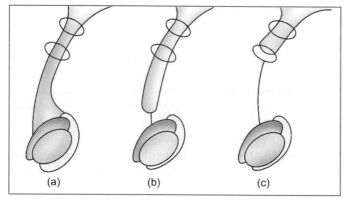

Fig. 16.30: Types of oblique inguinal hernia (a) Complete, (b) funicular, and (c) bubonocele.

- **Direct inguinal hernia** occurs through the posterior wall of the inguinal canal (Fig. 16.31). It occurs through Hesselbach's triangle (Fig. 16.32), bounded by inferior epigastric artery, lateral border of rectus abdominis and inguinal ligament. This area is divided into a medial and lateral parts by the passage of obliterated umbilical artery.

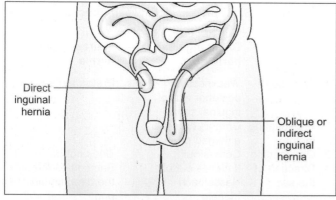

Fig. 16.31: Direct and indirect inguinal hernia.

Coverings of the lateral direct inguinal hernia:

(a) Extraperitoneal tissue

(b) Fascia transversalis

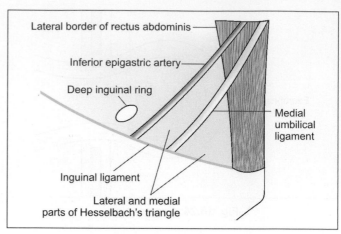

Fig. 16.32: Hesselbach's triangle.

(c) Cremasteric fascia

(d) External spermatic fascia

(e) Skin

Coverings of medial direct inguinal hernia:

(a) Extraperitoneal tissue

(b) Fascia transversalis

(c) Conjoint tendon

(d) External spermatic fascia

(e) Skin

- **Epigastric hernia:** It occurs through the upper part of wide linea alba (Fig. 16.33).

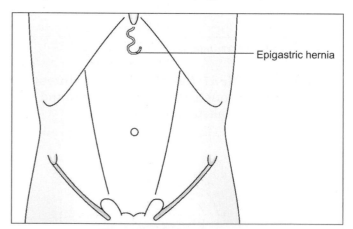

Fig. 16.33: Epigastric hernia.

- **Divarication of recti:** Occurs in multiparous female with weak anterolateral abdominal muscles. Loop of intestine protrude during coughing, but returns back (Fig. 16.34).
- **Incisional hernia:** Occurs through the anterolateral abdominal wall when some incisions were made for the surgery, involving cutting of the spinal nerves.
- **Lumbar hernia:** Occurs through the lumbar triangle in the posterior part of the abdominal wall. It is bounded by the iliac crest, anterior

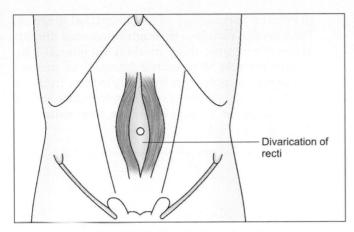

Fig. 16.34: Divarication of recti.

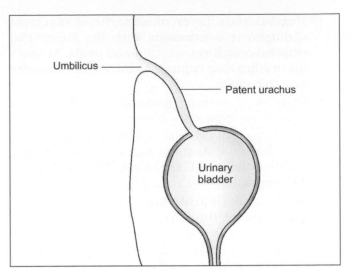

Fig. 16.36: Patent urachus.

border of latissimus dorsi and posterior border of external oblique muscle.

Internal hernia

- Protrusion of loop of intestine within a "no entry" zone of peritoneum.
- Internal hernia mostly occurs in epiploic foramen or opening into the lesser sac or foramen of Winslow. The loop mostly gets strangulated. It may also occur in the "paraduodenal fossac". These are also discussed in Chapter 18.

Others

- Remnants of the vitellointestinal duct may form a tumour at the umbilicus (raspberry red tumour; or cherry red tumour). Persistence of a patent vitellointestinal duct results in a faecal fistula at the umbilicus (Fig. 16.35).

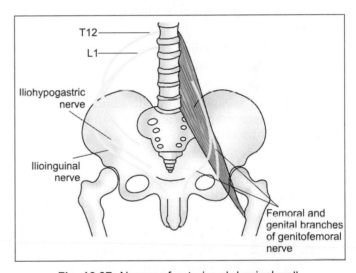

Fig. 16.37: Nerves of anterior abdominal wall.

supply skin, muscles of the abdominal wall and parietal peritoneum. Tubercular infection of lung and pleura may cause radiating pain in the abdominal wall. Peritonitis causes reflex contraction of the abdominal muscles.

- During repair of the wounds of anterior abdominal wall, the nerves T7–T12 need to be anaesthesised along the costal margin. Iliohypogastric and ilioinguinal nerves are anaesthesised by a needle above the anterior superior iliac spine on the spinoumbilical line.
- While examining the abdomen, the knees and hip must be flexed to relax the abdominal muscles.
- Umbilical vessels at birth can be identified at the umbilicus. These are two tortuous umbilical arteries and a single umbilical vein. For some clinical conditions, these vessels need to be catheterized.

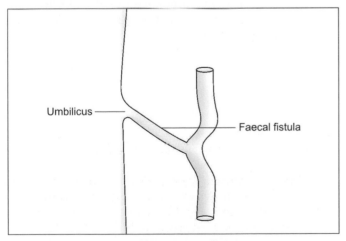

Fig. 16.35: Faecal fistula.

- Persistence of the urachus may form a urinary fistula opening at the umbilicus (Fig. 16.36).
- The nerves of anterior abdominal wall, T7–T12 and L1 supply skin, intercostals muscles and parietal pleura (Fig. 16.37). In addition these

- Membranous layer of superficial fascia of abdomen is continuous with the superficial perineal pouch via scrotum and penis. At times the urethra may rupture and urine extravasates into this space.

- Muscles of anterior abdominal wall contract during the expiratory phase of respiration.

- Due to lack of exercise, the tone of muscles of the anterior abdominal wall decreases leading to protrusion of the wall. This is called visceroptosis.

- Ascitis is a clinical condition, when there is collection of fluid in the peritoneal cavity. Paracentesis is the procedure for removing the fluid. The cannula inserted into the midline will pass through:

  Skin

  Two layers of superficial fascia

  Linea alba

  Fascia transversalis

  Extraperitoneal tissue

  Parietal peritoneum.

- Peritoneal lavage is done to conduct dialysis. The structures penetrated are same as in case of the paracentesis.

- The anterior abdominal wall is punctured for various endoscopic procedures, used for surgeries of gall bladder, vermiform appendix, etc.

- *Supraumbilical median incisions* through the linea alba have several advantages as being bloodless; safety to muscles and nerves but tend to leave a postoperative weakness through which a ventral hernia may develop. *Infraumbilical median incisions* are safer because the close approximation of recti prevents formation of any ventral hernia. *Paramedian incisions* through the rectus sheath are more sound than median incisions. The rectus muscle is *retracted laterally* to protect the nerves supplying it from any injury. In these cases, the subsequent risk of weakness and of incisional or ventral hernia are minimal (Fig. 16.38).

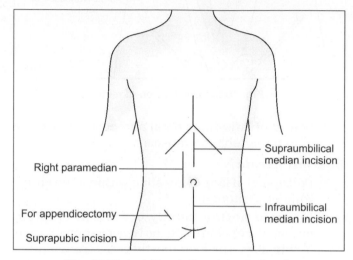

Fig. 16.38: Incisions in the abdominal wall.

- Superior vena cava blockage →backflow in descending order → brachiocephalic → subclavian vein →axillary vein →lateral thoracic vein →thoracoepigastric vein → superficial epigastric vein →great saphenous vein →femoral vein →inferior vena cava → heart (Fig. 16.7b).

- Inferior vena cava blockage blood will backflow in ascending order of the superior vena cava blockage (Fig. 16.7c).

CHAPTER 17

Male External Genital Organs

Male genital organs are situated both outside the pelvic cavity and within the pelvic cavity. As lower temperature is required for *spermatogenesis*, the *testes* are placed outside the pelvic cavity in the scrotal sac. Since urethra serves both the functions of urination and ejaculation, there is only one tube enclosed in the urogenital triangle.

ORGANS INCLUDED

1. Penis,
2. Scrotum,
3. Testes,
4. Epididymis, and
5. Spermatic cords.

The spermatic cord has been described in Chapter 16.

PENIS

The penis is the male organ of copulation. It is made up of: (a) A root or attached portion, and (b) a body or free portion (Fig. 17.1).

Root of Penis

The root of the penis is situated in the *superficial perineal pouch*. It is composed of three masses of erectile tissue, namely the two crura and one bulb. Each *crus* is firmly attached to the margins of the pubic arch, and is covered by the ischiocavernosus. The *bulb* is attached to the perineal membrane in between the two crura. It is covered by the *bulbospongiosus*. Its deep surface is pierced (above its centre) by the urethra, which traverses its substance to reach the corpus spongiosum (located in the body). This part of the urethra within the bulb shows a dilatation in its floor, called the *intrabulbar fossa*.

Body of Penis

The free portion of the penis is completely enveloped by skin. It is continuous with the root in front of the

DISSECTION

From the superficial inguinal ring, make a longitudinal incision downwards through the skin of the anterolateral aspects of the scrotum till its lower part. Reflect the skin alone if possible otherwise reflect skin, *dartos* and the other layers together till the testis enveloped in its *tunica vaginalis* is visualised.

Lift the testis and spermatic cord from the scrotum. Cut through the spermatic cord at the superficial inguinal ring and remove it together with the testis and put it in a tray of water. Incise and reflect the coverings if any, e.g. remains of external spermatic fascia, cremaster muscle, cremasteric fascia and internal spermatic fascia. Separate the various structures of spermatic cord. Feel ductus deferens as the important constituent of spermatic cord. Make a transverse section through the testis to visualise its interior. Identify the *epididymis* capping the superior pole and lateral surface of the testis. The slit-like *sinus of epididymis* formed by tucking-in of the visceral layer of peritoneum between the testis and the epididymis is seen on the anterolateral aspect of the testis.

Cut through and reflect the skin along the *dorsum of the penis* from the symphysis pubis to the end of the *prepuce*. Find the extension of the membranous layer of the superficial fascia of the abdominal wall on to the penis (*fundiform ligament*). The *superficial dorsal vein* of the penis lies in the superficial fascia. Trace it proximally to drain into any of the superficial external pudendal veins of thigh. Deep to this vein is the deep fascia and *suspensory ligament* of the penis. Divide the deep fascia in the same line as the skin incision. Reflect it to see the *deep dorsal vein* with the *dorsal arteries* and *nerves* on each side.

Make a transverse section through the body of the penis, but leave the two parts connected by the skin of urethral surface or ventral surface. Identify two *corpora cavernosa* and single *corpus spongiosum* traversed by the urethra.

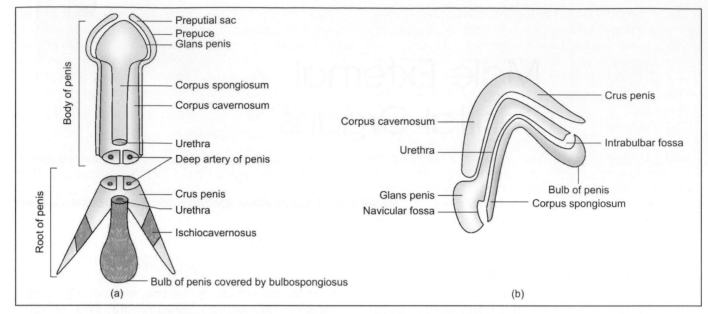

Fig. 17.1: Constituent parts of the penis: (a) Ventral view, (b) sagittal section.

lower part of the pubic symphysis. It is composed of three elongated masses of erectile tissue. During erection of the penis these masses become engorged with blood leading to considerable enlargement. These masses are the right and left corpora cavernosa, and a median corpus spongiosum (Fig. 17.2).

The penis has a ventral surface that faces backwards and downwards, and a dorsal surface that faces forwards and upwards.

The two *corpora cavernosa* are the forward continuations of the crura. They are in close apposition with each other throughout their length. The corpora cavernosa do not reach the end of the penis. Each of them terminates under cover of the *glans penis* in a blunt conical extremity. They are surrounded by a strong fibrous envelope called the *tunica albuginea*. The tunica albuginea has superficial longitudinal fibres enclosing both the corpora, and deep circular fibres that enclose each corpus separately, and also form a median septum.

The *corpus spongiosum* is the forward continuation of the bulb of the penis. Its terminal part is expanded to form a conical enlargement, called the *glans penis*. Throughout its whole length it is traversed by the urethra. Like the corpora, it is also surrounded by a fibrous sheath.

The base of the *glans penis* has a projecting margin, the *corona glandis*, which overhangs an obliquely grooved constriction, known as the *neck of the penis*. Within the glans the urethra shows a dilatation (in its roof) called the *navicular fossa*.

The *skin* covering the penis is very thin and dark in colour. It is loosely connected with the fascial sheath of the organ. At the neck it is folded

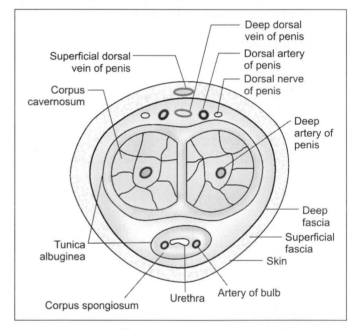

Fig. 17.2: Transverse section through the body of the penis.

to form the *prepuce* or *foreskin* which covers the glans to a varying extent and can be retracted backwards to expose the glans. On the undersurface of the glans there is a median fold of skin called the *frenulum*. The potential space between the glans and the prepuce is known as the *preputial sac*. On the corona glandis and on the neck of the penis there are numerous small preputial or sebaceous glands which secrete a sebaceous material called the *smegma*, which collects in the preputial sac (Fig. 17.1).

The *superficial fascia of the penis* consists of very loosely arranged areolar tissue, completely devoid of fat. It may contain a few muscle fibres. It is continuous with the membranous layer of superficial fascia of the abdomen above and of the perineum below. It contains the superficial dorsal vein of the penis.

The deepest layer of superficial fascia is membranous and is called the *fascia of the penis* or *deep fascia of penis*, or Buck's fascia. It surrounds all three masses of erectile tissue, but does not extend into the glans. Deep to it there are the deep dorsal vein, the dorsal arteries and dorsal nerves of the penis. Proximally, it is continuous with the dartos and with the fascia of the urogenital triangle.

The supports of the body of penis are the following.

1. The *fundiform ligament* which extends downwards from the linea alba and splits to enclose the penis. It lies superficial to the suspensory ligament.
2. The *suspensory ligament* lies deep to the fundiform ligament. It extends from the pubic symphysis and blends below with the fascia on each side of the penis.

Arteries of the Penis

A. The internal pudendal artery gives off three branches which supply the penis.
1. The *deep artery of the penis* runs in the corpus cavernosum. It breaks up into arteries that follow a spiral course and are, therefore, called helicine arteries.
2. The *dorsal artery of the penis* runs on the dorsum, deep to the deep fascia, and supplies the glans penis and the distal part of the corpus spongiosum, the prepuce and the frenulum.
3. The *artery of the bulb of the penis* supplies the bulb and the proximal half of the corpus spongiosum.
B. The femoral artery gives off the *superficial external pudendal artery* which supplies the skin and fasciae of the penis.

Veins of the Penis

The dorsal veins, superficial and deep, are unpaired. Superficial dorsal vein drains the prepuce and penile skin. It runs back in subcutaneous tissue and inclines to right or left, before it opens into one of the external pudenal veins.

Deep dorsal vein lies deep to Buck's fascia. It receives blood from the glans penis and corpora cavernosa penis, and courses back in midline between paired dorsal arteries.

Near the root of the penis, it passes deep to the suspensory ligament and through a gap between the arcuate pubic ligament and anterior margin of perineal membrane, it divides into right and left branches which connect below the symphysis pubis with the internal pudendal veins and ultimately enters the prostatic plexus.

Nerve Supply of the Penis

1. The sensory nerve supply to the penis is derived from the dorsal nerve of the penis and the ilioinguinal nerve. The muscles of the penis are supplied by the *perineal branch of the pudendal nerve.*
2. The autonomic nerves are derived from the pelvic plexus via the *prostatic plexus*. The *sympathetic nerves* are *vasoconstrictor*, and the *parasympathetic* nerves (S2, S3, S4) are *vasodilator*. The autonomic fibres are distributed through the branches of the *pudendal nerve.*

Lymphatic Drainage

Lymphatics from the glans drain into the deep inguinal nodes also called gland of Cloquet. Lymphatics from the rest of the penis drain into the superficial inguinal lymph nodes.

Mechanism of Erection of the Penis

Erection of the penis is a purely vascular phenomenon. The turgidity of the penis during its erection is contributed to by the following factors.

1. Dilatation of the *helicine* arteries pours an increased amount of arterial blood into the *cavernous spaces* of the corpora cavernosa. Blood is also poured in small amount into the corpus spongiosum and into the glans by their arteries. As the spaces within the *erectile tissue* fill up, the penis enlarges.
2. This enlargement presses on the veins preventing outflow of blood through them. Contraction of the ischiocavernosus muscles probably has the same effect.
3. Expansion of the corpora cavernosa, and to a lesser extent of the corpus spongiosum, stretches the deep fascia. This restricts enlargement of the penis. Further flow of blood increases the pressure within the erectile tissue and leads to rigidity of the penis.
4. Erection is controlled by parasympathetic nerves (nervi erigentes, S2, S3, S4).

SCROTUM

The scrotum is a cutaneous bag containing the right

and left testes, the epididymis and the lower parts of the spermatic cords.

1. Externally, the scrotum is divided into right and left parts by a ridge or raphe which is continued forwards on to the undersurface of the penis and backwards along the middle of the perineum to the anus (Fig. 17.3).
2. The left half of the scrotum hangs a little lower than the right, in correspondence with the greater length of the left spermatic cord.
3. Under the influence of cold, and in young and robust persons, the scrotum is short, corrugated and closely applied to the testis. This is due to contraction of the subcutaneous muscle of scrotum, called the *dartos*. However, under the influence of warmth, and in old and debilitated persons, the scrotum is elongated and flaccid due to relaxation of dartos. From this it appears that the dartos muscle helps in regulation of temperature within the scrotum.

Layers of the Scrotum

The scrotum is made up of the following layers from outside inwards (Fig. 17.4).

1. Skin.
2. Dartos muscle which replaces the superficial fascia.
3. The external spermatic fascia.
4. The cremasteric muscle and fascia.
5. The internal spermatic fascia. The dartos muscle is prolonged into a median vertical septum between the two halves of the scrotum.

Blood Supply

The scrotum is supplied by the following arteries: Superficial external pudendal, deep external pudendal, scrotal branches of internal pudendal, and cremasteric branch of inferior epigastric.

Nerve Supply

The anterior one-third of the scrotum is supplied by segment L1 of the spinal cord through the *ilioinguinal nerve* and the *genital branch of the genitofemoral nerve* (Fig. 17.5).

The posterior two-thirds of the scrotum are supplied by *segment S3* of the spinal cord through the *posterior scrotal branches* of the pudendal nerve, and the perineal branch of the *posterior cutaneous nerve of the thigh*. The areas supplied by segments L1 and S3 are separated by the *ventral axial line*.

The dartos muscle is supplied by the *genital branch of the genitofemoral nerve*.

TESTIS

The testis is the male gonad. It is homologous with the ovary of the female.

It is suspended in the scrotum by the spermatic cord. It lies obliquely, so that its upper pole is tilted forwards and medially. The left testis is slightly lower than the right.

The testis is oval in shape, and is compressed from side to side. It is 3.75 cm long, 2.5 cm broad from before backwards, and 1.8 cm thick from side to side. An adult testis weighs about 10 to 15 g.

External Features

The testis has:

1. Two poles or ends, upper and lower.
2. Two borders, anterior and posterior.
3. Two surfaces, medial and lateral (Fig. 17.6).

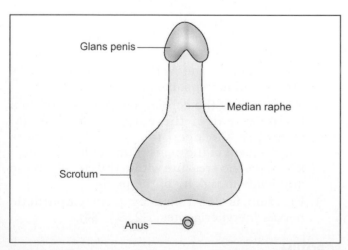

Fig. 17.3: Scrotum and penis viewed from below to show the median raphe.

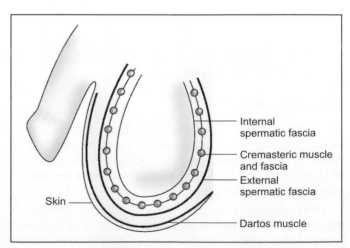

Fig. 17.4: Layers of the scrotum.

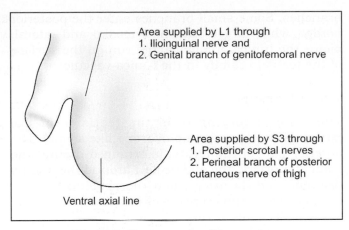

Fig. 17.5: Nerve supply of the scrotum.

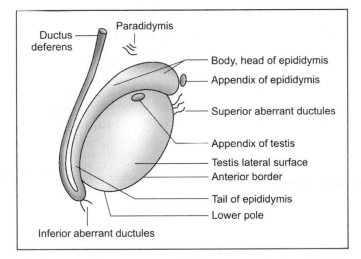

Fig. 17.6: Side view of the testis and epididymis, with the embryonic remnants present in the region.

The *upper* and *lower* poles are convex and smooth. The upper pole provides attachment to the spermatic cord.

The *anterior border* is convex and smooth, and is fully covered by the tunica vaginalis. The *posterior border* is straight, and is only partially covered by the tunica vaginalis. The *epididymis* lies along the lateral part of the posterior border. The lateral part of the epididymis is separated from the testis by an extension of the cavity of the tunica vaginalis. This extension is called the *sinus of epididymis* (Fig. 17.7).

The *medial* and *lateral surfaces* are convex and smooth.

Attached to the upper pole of the testis, there is a small oval body called the *appendix of the testis*. It is a remnant of the *paramesonephric duct*.

Coverings of the Testis

The testis is covered by three coats. From outside inwards, these are the *tunica vaginalis*, the *tunica albuginea* and the *tunica vasculosa* (Fig. 17.7).

The *tunica vaginalis* represents the lower persistent portion of the processus vaginalis. It is invaginated by the testis from behind and, therefore, has a parietal and a visceral layer with a cavity in between. It covers the whole testis, except for its posterior border.

The *tunica albuginea* is a dense, white fibrous coat covering the testis all around. It is covered by the visceral layer of the tunica vaginalis, except posteriorly where the testicular vessels and nerves enter the gland. The posterior border of the tunica

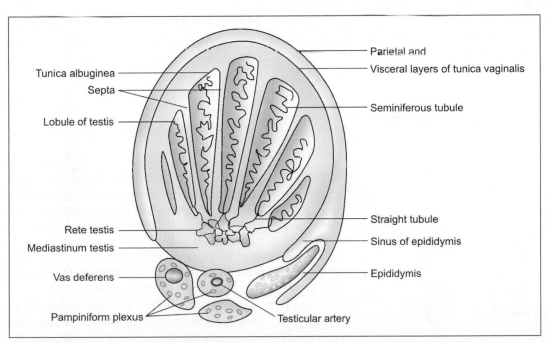

Fig. 17.7: Transverse section through the right testis and surrounding structures.

albuginea is thickened to form an incomplete vertical septum, called the *mediastinum testis*, which is wider above than below. Numerous septa extend from the mediastinum to the inner surface of the tunica albuginea. They incompletely divide the testis into 200 to 300 lobules.

The *tunica vasculosa* is the innermost, vascular coat of the testis lining its lobules.

Structure of the Testis

The glandular part of the testis consists of 200 to 300 lobules. Each lobule contains two to three seminiferous tubules. Each tubule is highly coiled on itself. When stretched out, each tubule measures about 60 cm in length, and is about 0.2 mm in diameter. The tubules are lined by cells which represent stages in the formation of spermatozoa.

The *seminiferous tubules* join together at the apices of the lobules to form 20 to 30 *straight tubules* which enter the mediastinum (Fig. 17.7). Here they anastomose with each other to form a network of tubules, called the *rete testis*. In its turn, the rete testis gives rise to 12 to 30 *efferent ductules* which emerge near the upper pole of the testis and enter the epididymis. Here each tubule becomes highly coiled and forms a lobe of the head of the epididymis. The tubules end in a single duct which is coiled on itself to form the body and tail of the epididymis. It is continuous with the ductus deferens.

Arterial Supply

The *testicular artery* is a branch of the abdominal aorta given off at the level of vertebra L2. It descends on the posterior abdominal wall to reach the deep inguinal ring where it enters the spermatic cord. At the posterior border of the testis, it divides into

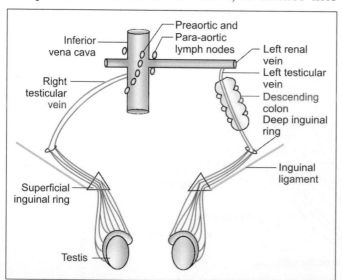

Fig. 17.8: Venous drainage of testis, lymph nodes of testis.

branches. Some small branches enter the posterior border, while larger branches; medial and lateral, pierce the tunica albuginea and run on the surface of the testis to ramify in the tunica vasculosa.

Venous Drainage

The veins emerging from the testis form the *pampiniform plexus* (pampiniform = like a vine). The anterior part of the plexus is arranged around the testicular artery, the middle part around the ductus deferens and its artery, and the posterior part is isolated. The plexus condenses into four veins at the superficial inguinal ring, and into two veins at the deep inguinal ring. These veins accompany the testicular artery. Ultimately one vein is formed which drains into the *inferior vena cava* on the *right side*, and into the *left renal vein* on the *left side* (Fig. 17.8).

Lymphatic Drainage

The lymphatics from the testis ascend along the testicular vessels and drain into the *preaortic* and *paraaortic* groups of lymph nodes at the level of second lumbar vertebra.

Nerve Supply

The testis is supplied by sympathetic nerves arising from segment T10 of the spinal cord. They pass through the renal and aortic plexuses. The nerves are both afferent for testicular sensation and efferent to the blood vessels (vasomotor).

Histology of Seminiferous Tubule

The seminiferous tubule consists of cells arranged in 4–8 layers in fully functioning testis. These cells are of two types, namely:

(a) The spermatogenic cells forming the vast majority.

(b) The supporting/sustentacular or cells of Sertoli.

The spermatogenic cells include spermatogonia, primary spermatocytes, secondary spermatocytes, spermatids and spermatozoa. The cells of Sertoli are tall and columnar in shape extending from the basal lamina to the central lumen. They support and protect the developing germ cells and help in maturation of spermatozoa. Spermatogenesis is controlled by follicle stimulating hormone (FSH) of the anterior pituitary gland.

Interstitial cells or cells of Leydig are found as small clusters in between the seminiferous tubules. They secrete testosterone/androgen (I make man). The activity of Leydig cells is controlled by interstitial cell stimulating hormone (ICSH) of the anterior pituitary gland.

EPIDIDYMIS

The epididymis is an organ made up of highly coiled tube that act as reservoir of spermatozoa.

Parts: Its upper end is called the *head*. The head is enlarged and is connected to the upper pole of the testis by *efferent ductules*. The middle part is called the *body*. The lower part is called the *tail*. The head is made up of highly coiled efferent ductules. The body and tail are made up of a single duct, *the duct of the epididymis* which is highly coiled on itself. At the lower end of the tail this duct becomes continuous with the *ductus deferens* (Figs 17.6 and 17.7).

Vessels and Nerves

The epididymis is supplied by the testicular artery through a branch which anastomoses with and reinforces the tiny artery to the ductus deferens. The venous and lymphatic drainage are similar to those of the testis. Like the testis the epididymis is supplied by sympathetic nerves through the testicular plexus, the fibres of which are derived from segments T11 to L1 of the spinal cord.

HISTOLOGY

The tubules of epididymis are lined by pseudo-stratified columnar epithelium with stereocilia. The tubules are surrounded by connective tissue.

SPERMATIC CORD

See Fig. 16.24.

DEVELOPMENT OF TESTIS

Testis: It is comprised of spermatogenic cells, cells of Sertoli and Leydig's cells.

Spermatogenic series of cells are derived from endoderm of dorsocaudal part of yolk sac, i.e. endoderm.

Cells of Sertoli are derived from epithelial cells, i.e. coelomic epithelium.

Leydig's cells: Mesoderm. There is thick tunica albuginea in the testis and the medulla portion of developing gland predominates.

Descent of the Testis

The testes develop in relation to the developing mesonephros, at the level of segments T10 to T12. Subsequently, they descend to reach the scrotum (Fig. 17.9). Each testis begins to descend during the second month of intrauterine life. It reaches the iliac fossa by the 3rd month, rests at the deep inguinal ring from the 4th to the 6th month, traverses the inguinal canal during the 7th month, reaches the superficial inguinal ring by the 8th month and the bottom of the scrotum by the 9th month. An extension of peritoneal cavity called the *processus vaginalis* precedes the descent of testis into the scrotum, into which the testis invaginates. The

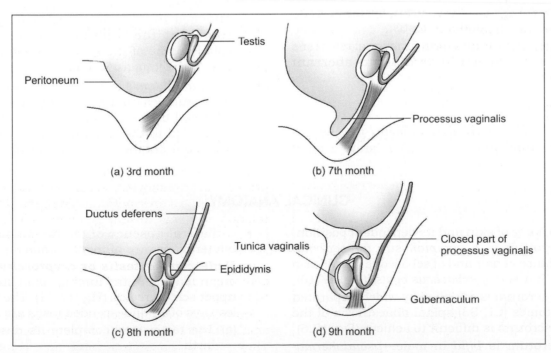

Fig. 17.9: Stages of descent of testis include formation of processus vaginalis.

processus vaginalis closes above the testis. Descent does not occur after one year of age.

The *causes of descent* are not well known. The following factors may help in the process.

1. Hormones including the male sex hormone produced by the testis, and maternal gonadotropins.
2. Differential growth of the body wall.
3. Formation of the gubernaculum: This is a band of loose tissue extending from the lower pole of the testis to the scrotum. It was earlier thought that contraction of this tissue was responsible for descent of the testis, but it is now known that this tissue is not contractile.
4. Intra-abdominal temperature and intra-abdominal pressure may have something to do with descent of the testis.

Development of Ducts

1. The predominant duct in males is the medially placed mesonephric or Wolffian duct. Distally, it opens into the primitive urogenital sinus. Its development and differentiation is affected by Müllerian inhibiting substance, testosterone and dihydrotestosterone.

   Its functional derivatives are:
   • Trigone of urinary bladder
   • Epididymis
   • Ductus deferens
   • Seminal vesicles
   • Ejaculatory duct
2. Paramesonephric duct forms vestigeal component, the appendix of testis.
3. Mesonephric tubules form functional rete testis and vestigeal paradidymis and aberrant ductules.

External Genitalia

As early as 3rd week of development, the mesenchymal cells from *primitive streak* migrate around the *cloacal membrane*. These form raised *cloacal folds*. Cranially the folds fuse to form *genital tubercle*.

During 6th week of development cloacal folds are divided into *urethral folds* anteriorly and *anal folds* posteriorly. Lateral to urethral folds a pair of swellings, the *genital swellings* appear.

Genital swellings form the scrotum. Genital tubercle elongates to form the *phallus*. Urethral folds get pulled forwards to form lateral wall of *urethral groove* extending on inferior aspect of phallus. Lining of groove forms *urethral plate* and is endodermal in origin. Urethral folds close over the urethral plate to form most of the penile urethra.

Urethra in the glans penis is formed by invagination of *ectodermal cells* into the glans. The ectodermal urethra gets continuous with the endodermal urethra.

Embryological Remnants Present in Relation to the Testis

These are as follows (Fig. 17.6). Their importance is that they may sometimes form cysts:

1. The *appendix of the testis*.
2. The *appendix of the epididymis* or pedunculated hydatid of Morgagni is a small rounded pedunculated body attached to the head of the epididymis. It represents the cranial end of the mesonephric duct.
3. The *superior aberrant ductules* are attached to the testis cranial to the efferent ductules. They represent the upper mesonephric tubules.
4. The *inferior aberrant ductules*, one or two, are attached to the tail of the epididymis, and represent the intermediate mesonephric tubules. One of them which is more constant may be as long as 25 cm.
5. The *paradidymis* or organ of Giraldes consists of free tubules lying in the spermatic cord above the head of the epididymis. They are neither connected to the testis nor to the epididymis, and represent the caudal mesonephric tubules.

CLINICAL ANATOMY

• Due to laxity of skin and its dependent position, the scrotum is a *common site for oedema*. Abundance of hair and of sebaceous glands also makes it a *site of sebaceous cysts* (Fig. 17.10).
• As the scrotum is supplied by widely separated dermatomes (L1, S3) spinal anaesthesia of the whole scrotum is difficult to achieve (Fig. 17.5).
• The scrotum is *bifid* in male—*pseudohermaphroditism*.

• Unilateral absence of testis—*monorchism* or bilateral absence of testis—*anorchism*.
• ***Undescended testis or cryptorchidism:*** The organ may lie in the lumbar, iliac, inguinal, or upper scrotal region (Fig. 17.11). The important features of an undescended testis are as follows.
  (a) The testis may complete its descent after birth.
  (b) Spermatogenesis may fail to occur in it.

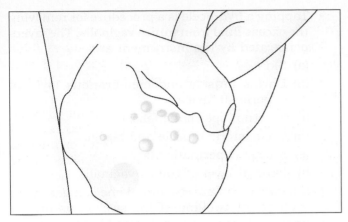

Fig. 17.10: Sebaceous cysts in the scrotum.

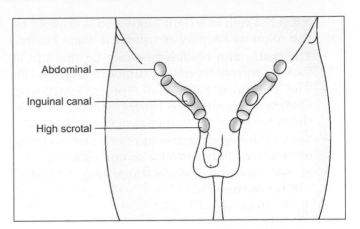

Fig. 17.11: Bilateral undescended testes.

(c) A malignant tumour is more prone to develop in it.

(d) The condition can be surgically corrected.

- *Ectopic testis*: The testis may occupy an abnormal position due to deviation from the normal route of descent. It may be under the skin of the lower part of the abdomen, under the skin of the front of the thigh, in the femoral canal, under the skin of the penis, and in the perineum behind the scrotum (Fig. 17.12). The important features of an ectopic testis are as follows.

(a) The testis is usually fully developed.

(b) It is usually accompanied by indirect inguinal hernia.

(c) It may be divorced from the epididymis which may lie in the scrotum.

- *Hermaphroditism* or intersex is a condition in which an individual shows some features of a male and some of a female. In true hermaphroditism, both testis and ovary are present. In pseudohermaphroditism, the gonad is of one sex while the external or internal genitalia are of the opposite sex.

- *Hydrocoele* is a condition in which fluid accumulates in the processus vaginalis (Fig. 17.13). The various types of hydrocoele are as follows.

(a) *Vaginal*, in tunica vaginalis.

(b) *Infantile*, when the processus vaginalis is closed at the deep inguinal ring.

(c) *Congenital*, when the entire processus vaginalis is patent and communicates with the peritoneal cavity.

(d) *Encysted*, when the middle part of the processus is patent.

- *Varicocoele* is produced by dilatation of the pampiniform plexus on veins (Fig. 17.14). It is usually left-sided; possibly because the left testicular vein is longer than the right, enters the

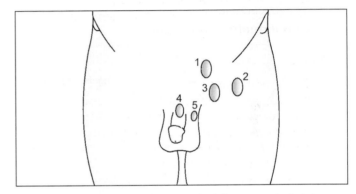

Fig. 17.12: Positions of ectopic testis 1. Lower part of abdomen, 2. front of thigh, 3. femoral canal, 4. skin of penis, and 5. behind the scrotum.

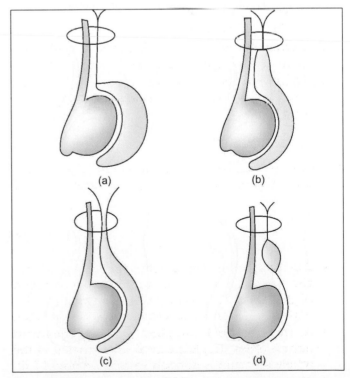

Fig. 17.13: Types of hydrocoele (a) Vaginal, (b) infantile, (c) congenital, and (d) encysted.

left renal vein at a right angle and is crossed by the colon which may compress it when loaded.

- The testis and epididymis may be the site of various infections and of tumours (Fig. 17.15).
- The common causes of epididymitis and epididymoorchitis are tuberculosis, filariasis, the gonococcal and other pyogenic infections.
- Testis may be palpated to check any nodules, or any irregularity or size or consistency.
- Some common abnormalities (Fig. 17.15) of scrotal contents are:
  - (a) Tumour of the testis
  - (b) Hydrocoele
  - (c) Epididymitis
  - (d) Varicocoele
  - (e) Spermatocoele

- Tapping a hydrocele is a procedure for removing the excess fluid from tunica vaginalis. The layers penetrated by the instrument are:
  - (a) Skin.
  - (b) Dartos muscle and membranous layer of superficial fasica.
  - (c) External spermatic fascia.
  - (d) Cremasteric muscle and fascia.
  - (e) Internal spermatic fascia.
  - (f) Parietal layer of tunica vaginalis.
- If a swelling is purely scrotal one can get above the level of swelling. If the swelling is due to inguinal hernia, it is not possible to get above the swelling (Fig. 17.16).
- Epididymis is felt along the upper pole and posterior border of the testis (Fig. 17.17).

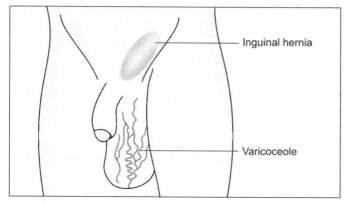

Fig. 17.14: Varicocoele with inguinal hernia.

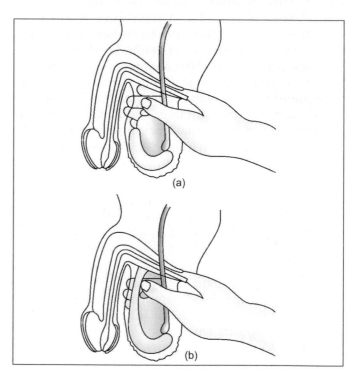

Fig. 17.16: (a) Scrotal swelling (b) inguinal hernia.

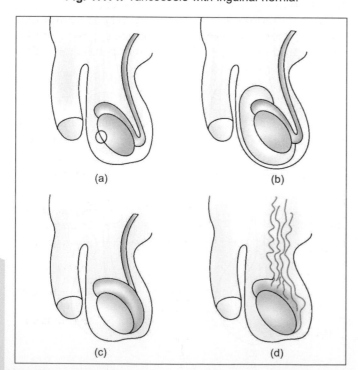

Fig. 17.15: (a) Tumour of the testis, (b) hydrocoele, (c) epididymitis and (d) varicocoele.

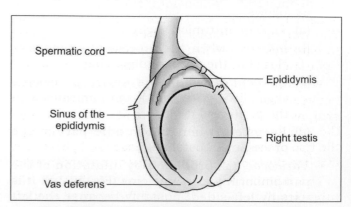

Fig. 17.17: Epididymis and sinus of the epididymis.

CHAPTER 18

Abdominal Cavity and Peritoneum

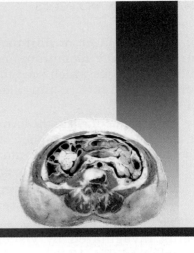

Abdominal cavity is the largest cavity. It encloses the peritoneal cavity between its parietal and visceral layers. Parietal layer clings to the wall of parieties while visceral layer is intimately adherent to viscera concerned. So their vascular supply and nerve supply are same as the parieties and viscera respectively.

There are very lengthy organs in the peritoneal cavity. These had to be disciplined with limited movements for proper functioning of the gut in particular and the body in general. Infections involving the parietal peritoneum impart protective "board-like rigidity" to the abdominal wall. Referred pain from the viscera to a distant area is due to somatic and sympathetic nerves reaching the same spinal segment.

The abdominal cavity is an extensive space which extends upwards, deep to the costal margin, into the concavity of the diaphragm; and projects downwards and backwards into the bony pelvis as the pelvic cavity. Thus a considerable part of the abdominal cavity is overlapped by the thoracic cage above, and the bony pelvis below.

NINE REGIONS OF ABDOMEN

For the purpose of describing the location of viscera, the abdomen is divided into nine regions by four imaginary planes, two horizontal and two vertical. The horizontal planes are the transpyloric and transtubercular planes. The vertical planes are the right lateral and the left lateral planes (Fig. 18.1).

The *transpyloric plane* of Addison passes midway between the suprasternal notch and the pubic symphysis. It lies roughly a hand's breadth below the xiphisternal joint. Anteriorly, it passes through the tips of the ninth costal cartilage; and posteriorly through the body of vertebra L1 near its lower border.

The *transtubercular plane* passes through the tubercles of the iliac crest and the body of vertebra L5 near its upper border.

The *right* and *left lateral planes* correspond to the midclavicular or mammary lines. Each of these vertical planes passes through the midinguinal point and crosses the tip of the ninth costal cartilage.

The nine regions marked out in this way are arranged in three vertical zones, median, right and left. From above downwards, the median regions are *epigastric, umbilical* and *hypogastric*. The right and left regions, in the same order, are *hypochondriac, lumbar* and *iliac*.

Position of many organs is shown in Fig. 19.2. Liver chiefly occupies the right hypochondrium. Stomach and spleen occupy the left hypochondrium. Duodenum lies in relation to posterior abdominal wall (Fig. 20.2). Coils of jejunum and ileum fill up the umbilical, lumbar and iliac regions.

Large intestine lies at the periphery of abdominal cavity, caecum, ascending colon on right side, descending colon on left side and transverse colon across the cavity.

PERITONEUM

The peritoneum is a large serous membrane lining the abdominal cavity. Histologically, it is composed

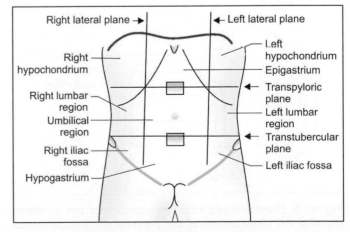

Fig. 18.1: Regions of the abdomen.

of an outer layer of fibrous tissue, which gives strength to the membrane and an inner layer of mesothelial cells which secrete a serous fluid which lubricates the surface, thus allowing free movements of viscera.

The peritoneum is in the form of a closed sac which is invaginated by a number of viscera. As a result the peritoneum is divided into:
1. An outer or parietal layer.
2. An inner or visceral layer; and folds of peritoneum by which the viscera are suspended.

The peritoneum which is a simple cavity, before being invaginated by viscera becomes highly complicated (Fig. 18.2).

Parietal Peritoneum

1. It lines the inner surface of the abdominal and pelvic walls and the lower surface of the diaphragm. It is loosely attached to the walls by extraperitoneal connective tissue and can, therefore, be easily stripped.
2. Embryologically, it is derived from the somatopleuric layer of the lateral plate mesoderm.
3. Its blood supply and nerve supply are the same as those of the overlying body wall. Because of the somatic innervation, parietal peritoneum is *pain-sensitive*.

Visceral Peritoneum

1. It lines the outer surface of the viscera, to which it is firmly adherent and cannot be stripped. In fact it forms a part and parcel of the viscera.
2. Embryologically, it is derived from the splanchnopleuric layer of the lateral plate mesoderm.
3. Its blood supply and nerve supply are the same as those of the underlying viscera. Because of the autonomic innervation, visceral peritoneum evokes pain when viscera is stretched, ischaemic or distended.

Folds of Peritoneum

1. Many organs within the abdomen are suspended by folds of peritoneum. Such organs are mobile. The degree and direction of mobility are governed by the size and direction of the peritoneal fold. Other organs are fixed and immobile. They rest directly on the posterior abdominal wall, and may be covered by peritoneum on one side. Such organs are said to be *retroperitoneal*. Some organs are suspended by peritoneal folds in early embryonic life, but later become retroperitoneal (Fig. 18.3).
2. Apart from allowing mobility, the peritoneal folds provide pathways for passage of vessels, nerves and lymphatics.
3. Peritoneal folds are given various names:
   (i) In general, the name of the fold is made up of the prefix 'mes' or 'meso' followed by the name of the organ, e.g. the fold suspending the small intestine or *enteron* is called the *mesentery*; and a fold suspending part of the colon is called *mesocolon*.
   (ii) Large peritoneal folds attached to the stomach are called *omenta* singular of which is *omentum* which means cover.
   (iii) In many situations, double-layered folds of peritoneum connect organs to the abdominal wall or to each other. Such folds are called *ligaments*. These may be named after the structures they connect. For example, the gastrosplenic ligament connects the stomach to the spleen. Other folds are named according to their shape, e.g. the triangular ligaments of the liver.

Some of the larger peritoneal folds are considered in this chapter, while others are considered along with the organs concerned.

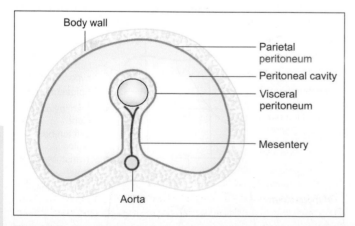

Fig. 18.2: Diagrammatic transverse section of the abdomen showing the arrangement of the peritoneum. The peritoneal cavity is actually a potential space and not so spacious as shown.

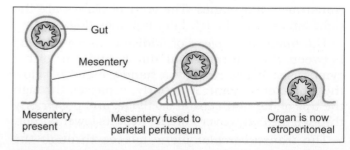

Fig. 18.3: Scheme to show how a loop of gut may lose its mesentery.

Peritoneal Cavity

The viscera which invaginate the peritoneal cavity completely fill it so that the cavity is reduced to a potential space separating adjacent layers of peritoneum. Between these layers there is a thin film of serous fluid secreted by the mesothelial cells. This fluid performs a lubricating function and allows free movement of one peritoneal surface over another. Under abnormal circumstances there may be collection of fluid called *ascites*, or of blood called *haemoperitoneum*, or of air called *pneumoperitoneum* within the peritoneal cavity.

The peritoneal cavity is divided broadly into two parts. The main, larger part is known as the *greater sac*, and the smaller part, situated behind the stomach, the lesser omentum and the liver, is known as the *lesser sac*. The two sacs communicate with each other through the epiploic foramen or foramen of Winslow or opening into the lesser sac.

Small pockets or recesses of the peritoneal cavity may be separated from the main cavity by small folds of peritoneum. These peritoneal recesses or fossae are of clinical importance. Internal hernia may take place into these recesses.

Sex Differences

In the male, the peritoneum is a closed sac lined by mesothelium or flattened epithelium. The female peritoneum has the following distinguishing features.

1. The peritoneal cavity communicates with the exterior through the uterine tubes.
2. The peritoneum covering the ovaries is lined by cubical epithelium.
3. The peritoneum covering the fimbria is lined by columnar ciliated epithelium

Functions of Peritoneum

1. *Movements of viscera:* The chief function of the peritoneum is to provide a slippery surface for free movements of abdominal viscera. This permits peristaltic movements of the stomach and intestine, abdominal movements during respiration and periodic changes in the capacity of hollow viscera associated with their filling and evacuation. The efficiency of the intestines is greatly increased as a result of the wide range of mobility that is possible because the intestines are suspended by large folds of peritoneum.
2. *Protection of viscera:* The peritoneum contains various phagocytic cells which guard against infection. Lymphocytes present in normal peritoneal fluid provide both cellular and humoral immunological defence mechanisms.

The greater omentum has the power to move towards sites of infection and to seal them thus preventing spread of infection. For this reason the greater omentum is often designated as the "policeman of the abdomen".

3. *Absorption and dialysis:* The mesothelium acts as a semipermeable membrane across which fluids and small molecules of various solutes can pass. Thus, the peritoneum can absorb fluid effusions from the peritoneal cavity. Water and crystalloids are absorbed directly into the blood capillaries, whereas colloids pass into lymphatics with the aid of phagocytes. The greater absorptive power of the upper abdomen or subphrenic area is due to its larger surface area and because respiratory movements aid absorption.

Therapeutically, considerable volumes of fluid can be administered through the peritoneal route. Conversely, metabolites, like urea, can be removed from the blood by artificially circula-ting fluid through the peritoneal cavity. This procedure is called peritoneal dialysis.

4. *Healing power and adhesions:* The mesothelial cells of the peritoneum can transform into fibroblasts which promote healing of wounds. They may also form abnormal adhesions causing obstruction in hollow organs.
5. *Storage of fat:* Peritoneal folds are capable of storing large amounts of fat, particularly in obese persons.

PERITONEAL FOLDS

The folds can be best understood by recapitulating the embryology of the gut. The developing gut is divisible into three parts, foregut, midgut and hindgut. Each part has its own artery which is a ventral branch of the abdominal aorta. The coeliac artery supplies the foregut; the superior mesenteric artery supplies the midgut; and the inferior mesenteric artery supplies the hindgut (Fig. 18.4).

Apart from some other structures the *foregut* forms the oesophagus, the stomach, and the upper part of the duodenum up to the opening of the common bile duct. The midgut forms the rest of the duodenum, the jejunum, the ileum, the appendix, the caecum, the ascending colon, and the right two-thirds of the transverse colon. The *hindgut* forms the left one-third of the transverse colon, the descending colon, the sigmoid colon, proximal upper part of the rectum. The anorectal canal forms distal part of rectum and the upper part of the anal canal up to the pectinate line.

The abdominal part of the foregut is suspended by mesenteries both ventrally and dorsally. The

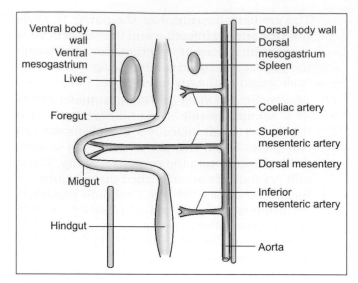

Fig. 18.4: Three parts of the primitive gut with their arteries.

ventral mesentery of the foregut is called the ventral mesogastrium, and the dorsal mesentery is called dorsal mesogastrium (*gastrium*-stomach) (Fig. 18.5).

The *ventral mesogastrium* becomes divided by the developing liver into a ventral part and a dorsal part. The ventral part forms the ligaments of the liver, namely:

(a) The falciform ligament,

(b) The right and left triangular ligaments, and

(c) The superior and inferior layers of the coronary ligament.

The dorsal part of the ventral mesogastrium forms the lesser omentum.

The fate of the *dorsal mesogastrium* is as follows.

1. The greater or caudal part of the dorsal mesogastrium becomes greatly elongated and forms the greater omentum.

2. The spleen develops in relation to the cranial part of the dorsal mesogastrium, and divides it into dorsal and ventral parts. The ventral part forms the gastrosplenic ligament while the dorsal part forms the lienorenal ligament.

3. The cranial most part of the dorsal meso-gastrium forms the gastrophrenic ligament.

The *midgut* and *hindgut* have only a dorsal mesentery, which forms the mesentery of jejunum and ileum, the mesoappendix, the transverse mesocolon and the sigmoid mesocolon. The mesenteries of the duodenum, the ascending colon, the descending colon and the rectum are lost during development (Fig. 18.6).

Greater Omentum

The greater omentum is a large fold of peritoneum which hangs down from the greater curvature of the

Expose the extensive abdominal cavity.

Identify the parietal peritoneum, adherent to the parieties or walls of the abdominal cavity. Trace it from the walls to form various double-layered folds which spread out to enclose the viscera as the visceral peritoneum.

Identify and lift up the greater omentum. See its continuity with the stomach above and the transverse colon fused with its posterior surface a short distance inferior to the stomach.

Cut through the anterior layers of the greater omentum 2–3 cm inferior to the arteries to open the lower part of the omental bursa sufficiently to admit a hand. Explore the bursa.

Pull the liver superiorly and lift its inferior margin anteriorly to expose the lesser omentum. Examine the right free margin of lesser omentum, containing the bile duct, hepatic artery and portal vein. This free margin forms the anterior boundary of the opening into the lesser sac, i.e. epiploic foramen. The posterior boundary is the inferior vena cava. Superior to opening into the lesser sac is the caudate process of liver and inferiorly is the first part of duodenum.

Remove the anterior layer of peritoneum from the lesser omentum along the lesser curvature of the stomach. Find and trace the left gastric vessels along the lesser curvature of stomach. Trace the oesophageal branches to the oesophagus.

Trace the right gastric artery to the proper hepatic artery and the vein to the portal vein. Expose the proper hepatic artery and trace its branches to the porta hepatis.

Trace the cystic duct from the gall bladder. Follow the common hepatic duct to the porta hepatis and the bile duct till it passes posterior to the duodenum.

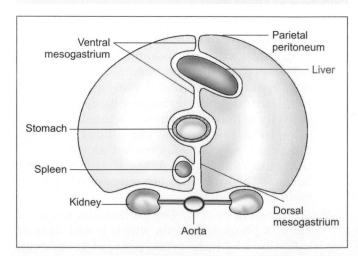

Fig. 18.5: Transverse section through the embryonic foregut showing the ventral and dorsal mesogastria and their divisions.

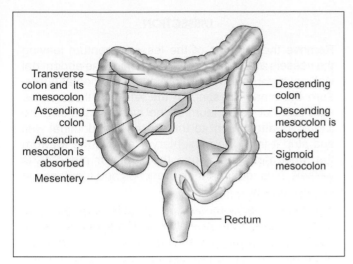

Fig. 18.6: Anterior view of the small and large intestines showing the parts of the dorsal mesentery that persist and other parts which are absorbed.

stomach like an apron and covers the loops of intestines to a varying extent. It is made up of four layers of peritoneum all of which are fused together to form a thin fenestrated membrane containing variable quantities of fat and small arteries and veins (Figs 18.7 and 18.8).

Attachments

The anterior two layers descend from the greater curvature of the stomach to a variable extent, and fold upon themselves to form the posterior two layers which ascend to the anterior surface of the head, and the anterior border of the body of the pancreas.

The folding of the omentum is such that the first layer becomes the fourth layer and the second layer becomes the third layer. In its upper part, the fourth layer is partially fused to the anterior surface of the transverse colon and of the transverse mesocolon. The part of the peritoneal cavity called the lesser sac between the second and third layers gets obliterated, except for about 2.5 cm below the greater curvature of the stomach.

Contents

1. The right and left gastroepiploic vessels anastomose with each other in the interval between the first two layers of the greater omentum a little below the greater curvature of the stomach.
2. It is often laden with fat.

Functions

1. It is a storehouse of fat.
2. It protects the peritoneal cavity against infection because of the presence of macrophages in it. Collections of macrophages form small, dense patches, known as *milky spots*, which are visible to the naked eye.
3. It also limits the spread of infection by moving to the site of infection and sealing it off from the surrounding areas. On this account, the greater omentum is also known as the *policeman of the abdomen*.

The greater omentum forms a partition between the supracolic and infracolic compartments of the greater sac.

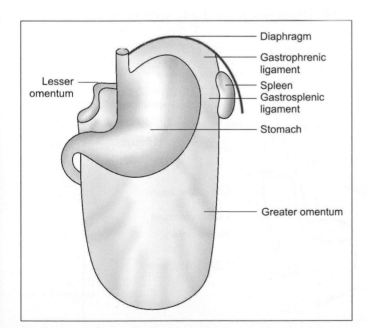

Fig. 18.7: Anterior view of the peritoneal folds attached to the greater and lesser curvatures of the stomach.

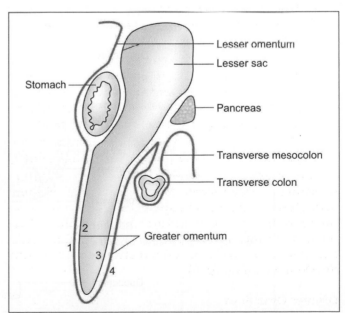

Fig. 18.8: Left view of a sagittal section of the abdomen showing the greater and lesser omenta and the transverse mesocolon.

Lesser Omentum

This is a fold of peritoneum which extends from the lesser curvature of the stomach and the first 2 cm of the duodenum to the liver. The portion of the lesser omentum between the stomach and the liver is called the *hepatogastric ligament*, and the portion between the duodenum and the liver is called the *hepato-duodenal ligament*. Behind the lesser omentum there lies a part of the lesser sac. The lesser omentum has a free right margin behind which there is the epiploic foramen. The greater and lesser sacs communicate through this foramen.

Attachments

Inferiorly, the lesser omentum is attached to the lesser curvature of the stomach and to the upper border of the first 2 cm of the duodenum. Superiorly, it is attached to the liver, the line of attachment being in the form of an inverted 'L'. The vertical limb of the 'L' is attached to the bottom of the fissure for the ligamentum venosum, and the horizontal limb to the margins of the porta hepatis (Fig. 18.9).

Contents

The right free margin of the lesser omentum contains:

    (a) The hepatic artery proper;

    (b) The portal vein;

    (c) The bile duct;

    (d) Lymph nodes and lymphatics; and

    (e) The hepatic plexus of nerves, all enclosed in a perivascular fibrous sheath.

Along the lesser curvature of the stomach and along the upper border of the adjoining part of the duodenum it contains:

DISSECTION

Remove the remains of the lesser omentum leaving the vessels and duct intact and examine the abdominal wall posterior to the omentum and the omental bursa. Turn the small intestine to the left. Cut through the right layer of peritoneum of the mesentery along the line of its attachment to the posterior abdominal wall and strip it from the mesentery. Remove the fat from the mesentery to expose the superior mesenteric vessels in its root and their branches and tributaries in the mesentery.

Trace the superior mesenteric vessels proximally and distally. Dissect the branches to the jejunum, ileum, caecum, appendix, ascending colon, right two-thirds of transverse colon, the distal part of duodenum and pancreas.

Turn the small intestine and its mesentery to the right. Remove the peritoneum and fat on the posterior abdominal wall between the mesentery and descending colon to expose the inferior mesenteric vessels and the autonomic nerves and lymph nodes associated with them.

Turn the caecum upwards and uncover the structures posterior to it. Trace the three taeniae on the external surface of the colon and cranial to the root of the vermiform appendix.

    (a) The right gastric vessels;

    (b) The left gastric vessels;

    (c) The gastric group of lymph nodes and lymphatics; and

    (d) Branches from the gastric nerves (Fig. 18.9).

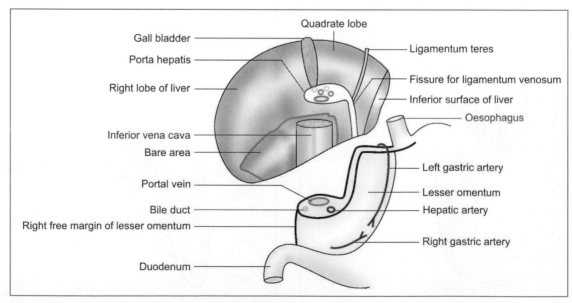

Fig. 18.9: The attachments and contents of the lesser omentum. The liver has been turned upwards so that its posteroinferior surface can be seen.

Mesentery

The mesentery of the small intestine or mesentery proper is a broad, fan-shaped fold of peritoneum which suspends the coils of jejunum and ileum from the posterior abdominal wall (Fig. 18.10).

Border

The *attached border*, or *root of the mesentery*, is 15 cm long, and is directed obliquely downwards and to the right. It extends from the duodenojejunal flexure on the left side of vertebra L2 to the upper part of right sacroiliac joint. It crosses the following.

1. The third part of the duodenum where the superior mesenteric vessels enter into it;
2. The abdominal aorta;
3. The inferior vena cava;
4. The right ureter; and
5. The right psoas major.

The free or *intestinal border* is 6 metres long, and is thrown into pleats. It is attached to the gut, forming its visceral peritoneum or serous coat.

The *breadth* of the mesentery is maximum and is about 20 cm in the central part, but gradually diminishes towards both the ends.

Distribution of Fat

Fat is most abundant in the lower part of the mesentery, extending from the root to the intestinal border. The upper part of the mesentery contains less fat, which tends to accumulate near the root. Near the intestinal border it leaves oval or circular fat-free, translucent areas, or *windows*.

Contents

The contents of the mesentery are:

1. Jejunal and ileal branches of the superior mesenteric artery;
2. Accompanying veins;
3. Autonomic nerve plexuses;
4. Lymphatics or lacteals;
5. 100–200 lymph nodes; and
6. Connective tissue with fat.

Mesoappendix

It is a small, triangular fold of peritoneum which suspends the vermiform appendix from the posterior surface of the lower end of the mesentery close to the ileocaecal junction. Usually the fold extends up to the tip of the appendix, but sometimes it fails to reach the distal one-third or so. It contains vessels, nerves, lymph nodes and lymphatics of the appendix (Fig. 18.11).

Transverse Mesocolon

This is a broad fold of peritoneum which suspends the transverse colon from the upper part of the posterior abdominal wall (Figs 18.6 and 18.8).

Attachments

The root of the transverse mesocolon is attached to the anterior surface of the head, and the anterior border of the body of the pancreas. The line of attachment is horizontal with an upward inclination towards the left (Fig. 18.12).

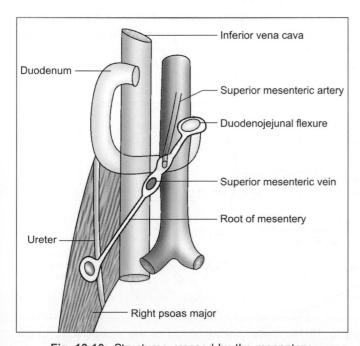

Fig. 18.10: Structures crossed by the mesentery.

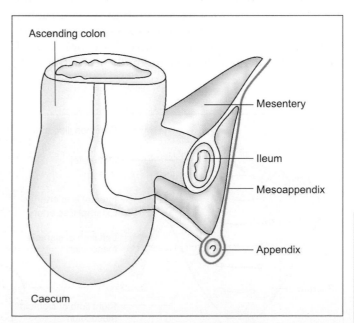

Fig. 18.11: The attachment of the mesoappendix to the posterior (left) surface of the lower end of the mesentery.

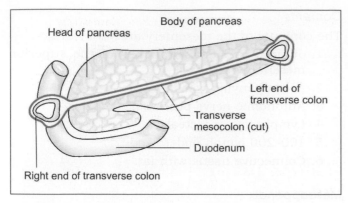

Fig. 18.12: Attachment of the root of the transverse mesocolon.

Expose the anterior border of the pancreas and define the attachments of the transverse mesocolon. Trace the duodenum from the pylorus to the duodenojejunal flexure.

Contents

It contains the middle colic vessels; the nerves, lymph nodes and lymphatics of the transverse colon.

Sigmoid Mesocolon

This is a triangular fold of peritoneum which suspends the sigmoid colon from the pelvic wall (Fig. 18.6).

Attachment

The root is shaped like an inverted 'V'. Its apex lies over the left ureter at the termination of the left common iliac artery. The left limb of 'V' is attached along the upper half of the left external iliac artery; and the right limb to the posterior pelvic wall extending downwards and medially from the apex

to the median plane at the level of vertebra S3 (Figs 18.13 and 18.14).

Contents

The sigmoid vessels in the left limb, superior rectal vessels in the right limb and the nerves, lymph nodes and lymphatics of the sigmoid colon.

DISSECTION

Trace the fold of peritoneum from the upper half of left external iliac artery to the termination of left common iliac artery and then downwards till the third piece of sacrum.

REFLECTION OF PERITONEUM ON THE LIVER

From Fig. 18.5 it can be seen that on reaching the liver, the peritoneum forming the two layers of the lesser omentum passes on to the surface of the liver. After lining the surfaces of the liver this peritoneum is reflected on to the diaphragm and to the anterior abdominal wall in the form of a number of ligaments. These are the falciform ligament, the left triangular ligament, the coronary ligaments and the right triangular ligament. They are shown in Figs 18.15 and 18.16. The falciform ligament is described below. The other ligaments are described later along with the liver.

The *falciform ligament* is a sickle-shaped fold of peritoneum which connects the anterosuperior surface of the liver to the anterior abdominal wall and to the undersurface of the diaphragm. This fold is raised by the ligamentum teres of the liver. The ligamentum teres extends from the umbilicus to the inferior border and inferior surface of the liver. It joins the left branch of the portal vein at the left end of the porta hepatis opposite the ligamentum venosum.

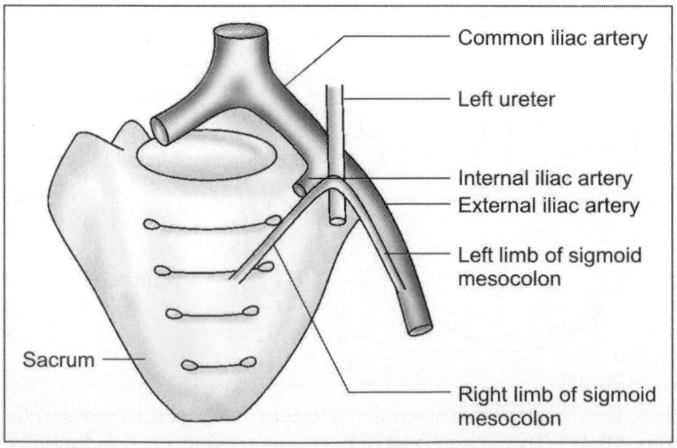

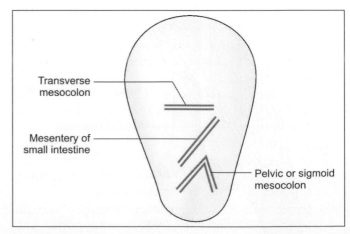

Fig. 18.13: Attachment of the root of the sigmoid mesocolon.

Fig. 18.14: Mode of attachment of the mesenteries to the posterior abdominal wall.

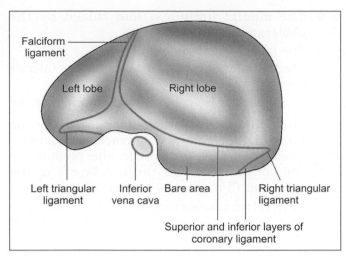

Fig. 18.15: Reflections of peritoneum on the liver. Superior aspect.

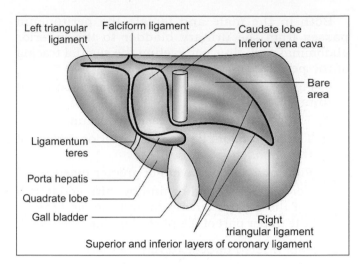

Fig. 18.16: Reflection of peritoneum on the liver. Posterior aspect.

Peritoneal Cavity

The layout of the greater sac can be studied by tracing the peritoneum both vertically and horizontally.

Vertical Tracing

1. Peritoneum lining the anterior abdominal wall and diaphragm, layer 1 (Fig. 18.17a).
2. Peritoneum lining upper part of posterior abdominal wall and diaphragm, layer 3.
3. Layers 1 and 3 enclose most of the liver. The two layers get reflected at porta hepatis to form the lesser omentum.
4. Lesser omentum encloses the stomach and two layers pass downwards covering the intestines, where these fold upon themselves. First layer becomes fourth layer and second layer becomes the third layer.
5. Third and fourth layers enclose transverse colon to continue as transverse mesocolon.
6. Third layer lines the structures in the upper part of posterior abdominal wall.
7. The fourth layer passes around the small intestine to form the mesentery of small intestine.
8. Peritoneum lines the structures in the posterior abdominal wall and descends into the true pelvis in front of the rectum. The subsequent tracing is different in the male and in the female.
9. In the male (Fig. 18.17a), the peritoneum passes from the front of rectum to the urinary bladder, forming rectovesical pouch.
10. In the female, it passes from the front of rectum to the uterus forming rectouterine pouch and from the uterus to the urinary bladder forming the vesicouterine pouch (Fig. 18.17b).

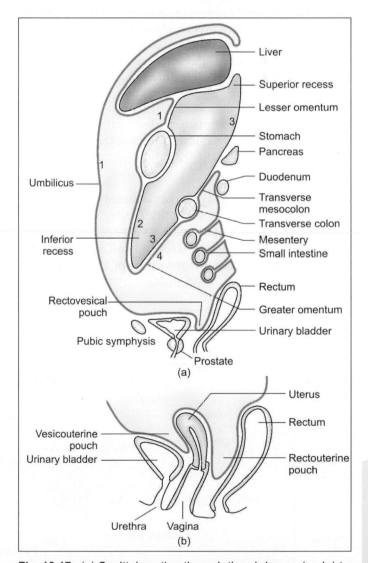

Fig. 18.17: (a) Sagittal section through the abdomen (male) to show the reflections of peritoneum, (b) sagittal section through a female pelvis showing the peritoneal reflections.

Both in the male and female the peritoneum passes from the urinary bladder to the anterior abdominal wall, thus completing the sagittal tracing of the peritoneum.

In Fig. 18.17 note that the lesser sac is bounded in front by:

1. The posterior layer of lesser omentum.
2. The peritoneum lining the posterior surface of the stomach.
3. First and second layers of greater omentum.

Lesser sac is bounded behind by third and fourth layers of the greater omentum and the peritoneum lining the upper part of the posterior abdominal wall.

Horizontal Tracing above Transverse Colon

Falciform ligament from the anterior abdominal wall encloses the liver. At porta hepatis it forms lesser omentum which encloses the stomach. The two layers pass to left towards spleen as gastrosplenic ligament. At the hilum, the two layers of gastrosplenic ligament diverge. The anterior layer encloses the spleen, forms one layer of lienorenal ligament, covers left kidney and continues to line the structures in the anterior abdominal wall (Fig. 18.18). The posterior layer forms the other layer of lienorenal ligament and lines the structures in the posterior abdominal wall. The two layers get reflected as falciform ligament on the liver.

Horizontal Tracing below the Level of the Transverse Colon

On the back of the anterior abdominal wall we see a number of peritoneal folds, and fossae. Starting from the median plane these are as follows (Fig. 18.19).

1. The median umbilical fold raised by the median umbilical ligament (remnant of the urachus).
2. The medial inguinal fossa.

3. The medial umbilical fold raised by the obliterated umbilical artery.
4. The lateral inguinal fossa.
5. The lateral umbilical fold raised by the inferior epigastric vessels.
6. The femoral fossa overlying the femoral septum.

Further laterally the peritoneum passes over the lateral part of abdominal wall to reach the posterior abdominal wall. Near the middle, the peritoneum becomes continuous with the two layers of the mesentery and thus reaches the small intestine.

At this level we also see the greater omentum made up of four layers. It lies between the intestines and the anterior abdominal wall.

Horizontal Tracing of Peritoneum in the Lesser Pelvis (Male)

In Fig. 18.20 note the following.

1. The rectovesical pouch;
2. The pararectal fossae;
3. The sacrogenital folds forming the lateral limit of the rectovesical pouch;
4. The pararectal fossae;
5. The paravesical fossae. The sigmoid colon and mesocolon are present, but are not shown in the diagram.

Horizontal Tracing of Peritoneum in the Lesser Pelvis (Female)

In Fig. 18.21 note the following.

1. The uterus and the broad ligaments form a transverse partition across the pelvis.
2. The pararectal and paravesical fossae.
3. The rectouterine pouch.

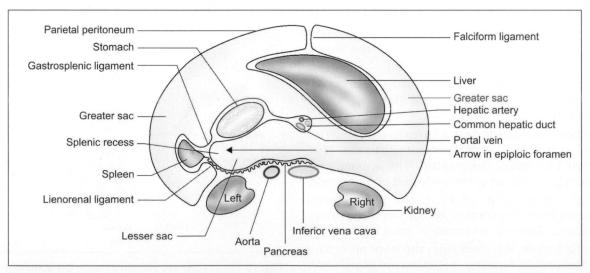

Fig. 18.18: Horizontal section through the supracolic compartment of the abdomen showing the horizontal disposition of the peritoneum.

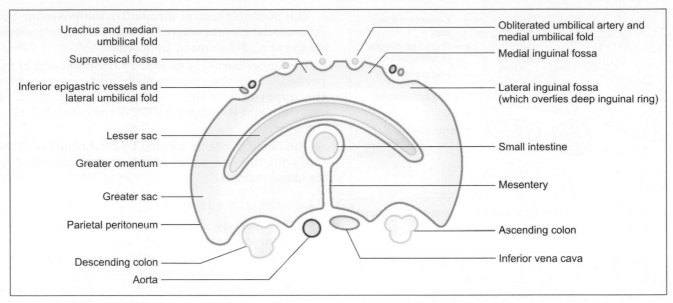

Fig. 18.19: Horizontal section through infracolic compartment of the abdomen showing the horizontal disposition of the peritoneum.

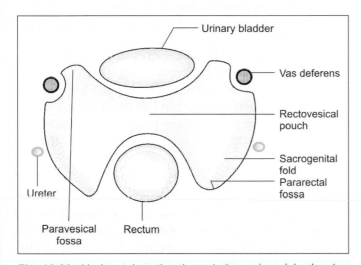

Fig. 18.20: Horizontal section through the male pelvis showing the horizontal disposition of the peritoneum.

4. The mesovarium by which the ovary is suspended from the posterior (or superior) layer of the broad ligament.

Epiploic Foramen

Synonyms: Foramen of Winslow, aditus or opening to the lesser sac. This is a vertical slit-like opening through which the lesser sac communicates with the greater sac.

The foramen is situated behind the right free margin of the lesser omentum at the level of the 12th thoracic vertebra.

Boundaries

Anteriorly: Right free margin of the lesser omentum containing the portal vein, proper hepatic artery, and the common hepatic duct (Fig. 18.22).

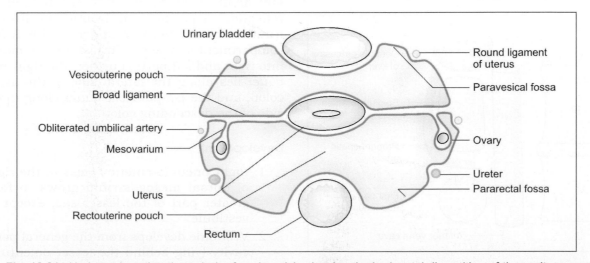

Fig. 18.21: Horizontal section through the female pelvis showing the horizontal disposition of the peritoneum.

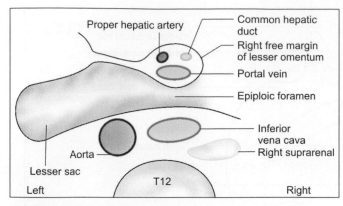

Fig. 18.22: Epiploic foramen as seen in a transverse section at the level of the twelfth thoracic vertebra.

Posteriorly: The inferior vena cava, the right suprarenal gland and T12 vertebra.

Superiorly: Caudate process of the liver.

Inferiorly: First part of the duodenum and the horizontal part of the hepatic artery (Fig. 18.23).

Lesser Sac or Omental Bursa

This is a large recess of the peritoneal cavity behind the stomach, the lesser omentum and the caudate lobe of the liver. It is closed all around, except in the upper part of its right border where it communicates with the greater sac through the epiploic foramen (Figs 18.17 and 18.18).

Boundaries

The *anterior wall* is formed by:
1. The caudate lobe of the liver.
2. The lesser omentum.
3. The stomach.
4. The anterior two layers of the greater omentum (Fig. 18.17).

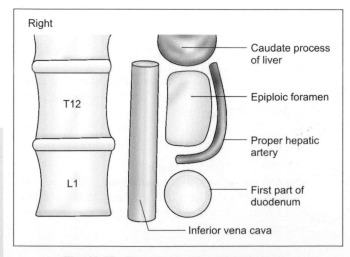

Fig. 18.23: Boundaries of epiploic foramen.

The *posterior wall* is formed by the posterior two layers of the greater omentum (Fig. 18.24), transverse mesocolon, duodenum, pancreas.

The *upper border* is formed by the reflection of the peritoneum to the diaphragm from the oesophagus, the upper end of the fissure for the ligamentum venosum and the upper border of the caudate lobe of the liver.

The *lower border* is formed by continuation of the 2nd with the 3rd layers of the greater omentum at its lower margin.

Subdivision of the Lesser Sac

1. The downward and forward course of the common hepatic artery raises a sickle-shaped fold of peritoneum from the posterior wall; this is known as the *right gastropancreatic fold.* Similarly, the upwards course of the left gastric artery raises another similar fold, called the *left gastropancreatic fold.* These folds divide the lesser sac into a superior and an inferior recess.

2. The *superior recess* of the lesser sac lies behind the lesser omentum and the liver. The portion behind the lesser omentum is also known as the *vestibule* of the lesser sac.

3. The *inferior recess* of the lesser sac lies behind the stomach and within the greater omentum.

4. The *splenic recess* of the lesser sac lies between the gastrosplenic and lienorenal ligaments (Fig. 18.18).

SPECIAL REGIONS OF THE PERITONEAL CAVITY

From a surgical point of view the peritoneal cavity has two main parts, the abdomen proper and the pelvic cavity. The abdominal cavity is divided by the transverse colon and the transverse mesocolon into the *supracolic* and *infracolic compartments.* The supracolic compartment is subdivided by the reflection of peritoneum around the liver into a number of *subphrenic spaces.* The infracolic compartment is also subdivided, by the mesentery, into right and left parts. Further, the right *paracolic gutter* lies along the lateral side of the ascending colon, and the *left paracolic gutter* along the lateral side of the descending colon.

Development

1. Right pneumo-enteric recess in the right wall of dorsal mesogastrium grows to form the greater part of the lesser sac, except for the vestibule.

2. Vestibule develops from the general peritoneal cavity lying behind the lesser omentum after the rotation of stomach.

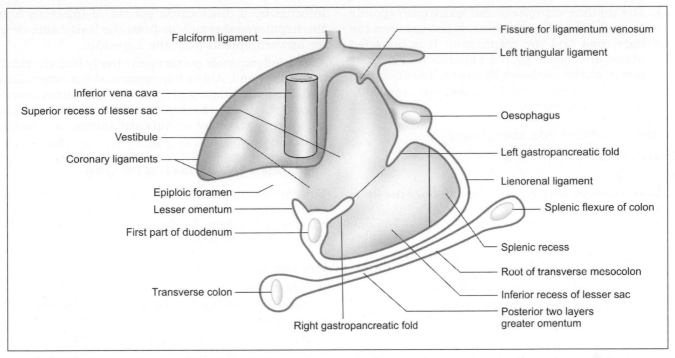

Fig. 18.24: Lesser sac seen after removal of its anterior wall.

Subphrenic Spaces/Supracolic Compartment

Subphrenic spaces are present just below the diaphragm in relation to the liver (Fig. 18.25).

Classification

The *intraperitoneal spaces* are:
1. The left anterior space
2. The left posterior space
3. The right anterior space
4. The right posterior space.

The *extraperitoneal spaces* include:
1. The right extraperitoneal space
2. The left extraperitoneal space
3. Midline extraperitoneal space is the name given to bare area of liver.

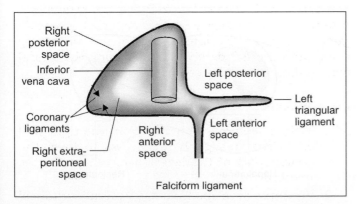

Fig. 18.25: Subphrenic spaces shown in relation to the peritoneal reflections on the liver.

Some details of these spaces are as follows.

1. The *left anterior space* or the left subphrenic space lies between the left lobe of the liver and the diaphragm, in front of the left triangular ligament. Inferiorly, it extends to the front of the lesser omentum and of the stomach. Towards the left it reaches the spleen. As abscess may form in this space following operations on the stomach, the spleen, the splenic flexure of the colon, and the tail of the pancreas.

2. The *left posterior space* or the left subhepatic space is merely the lesser sac which has already been described.

3. The *right anterior space* or right subphrenic space lies between the right lobe of the liver and the diaphragm, in front of the superior layer of the coronary ligament and of the right triangular ligament. Infection may spread to this space from the gall bladder, or the vermiform appendix; or may follow operations on the upper abdomen.

4. The *right posterior space* or right subhepatic space is also called the hepatorenal pouch of Morison. It is described below.

5. The *left extraperitoneal space* lies around the left suprarenal gland and the upper pole of the left kidney. This is the site for a left perinephric abscess.

6. Right extraperitoneal space lies around upper pole of right kidney.

7. The midline *extraperitoneal space* corresponds to the bare area of the liver. It lies between the bare area and the diaphragm. It is bounded above and below by the superior and inferior layers of the coronary ligament. Infection can spread to this space from the liver, resulting in liver abscess.

Hepatorenal Pouch (Morison's Pouch)

Boundaries

Anteriorly:
1. The inferior surface of the right lobe of the liver.
2. The gall bladder.

Posteriorly:
1. The right suprarenal gland
2. The upper part of the right kidney
3. The second part of the duodenum
4. The hepatic flexure of the colon
5. The transverse mesocolon
6. A part of the head of the pancreas.
   Superiorly: The inferior layer of the coronary ligament. *Inferiorly:* It opens into the general peritoneal cavity (Fig. 18.26).

Infracolic Compartments of Peritoneal Cavity

The *right infracolic compartment* lies between the ascending colon and the mesentery, below the transverse mesocolon. It is triangular in shape with its apex directed downwards.

The *left infracolic compartment* lies between the descending colon and the mesentery. It is also triangular with its apex directed upwards. Inferiorly, it opens freely into the pelvis.

Paracolic Gutters

The *right paracolic gutter* opens freely into the hepatorenal pouch at its upper end. It may be infected by a downwards spread of infection from the hepatorenal pouch or from the lesser sac, or by an upward spread from the appendix.

The *left paracolic gutter* opens freely into the pelvis at its lower end. Above it is separated from the spleen and from the lienorenal space by the phrenicocolic ligament. It may be infected from the supracolic compartment, or by an upward spread of infection from the pelvis.

Rectouterine Pouch (Pouch of Douglas)

This is the most dependent part of the peritoneal cavity when the body is in the upright position. In the supine position, it is the most dependent part of the pelvic cavity (Fig. 18.27).

Boundaries

It is bounded:

Anteriorly, by the uterus and the posterior fornix of the vagina.

Posteriorly, by the rectum (Fig. 18.28).

Inferiorly (floor) by the rectovaginal fold of peritoneum.

PERITONEAL FOSSAE (RECESSES)

These are small pockets of the peritoneal cavity enclosed by small, inconstant folds of peritoneum. They commonly occur at the transitional zones between the absorbed and unabsorbed parts of the mesentery. These are best observed in foetuses, and are mostly obliterated in adults. Sometimes they persist to form potential sites for internal hernia and their strangulation.

Classification

Lesser Sac

The lesser sac is the largest recess. It is always present, and has been described earlier.

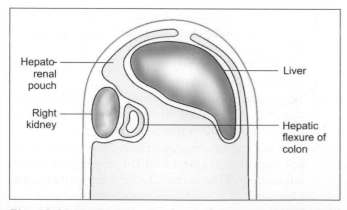

Fig. 18.26: Left view of a sagittal section through the hepatorenal pouch.

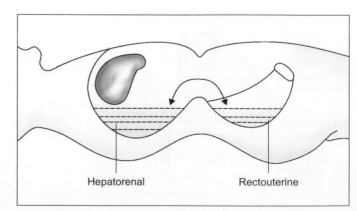

Fig. 18.27: Morison's or hepatorenal pouch with rectouterine or Douglas pouch.

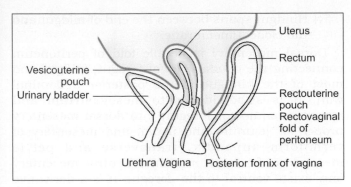

Fig. 18.28: Left view of a sagittal section through the rectouterine pouch.

Duodenal Fossae or Recesses

1. The *superior duodenal recess* is present in about 50% of subjects. It is situated at the level of vertebra L2. It is about 2 cm deep. Its orifice looks downwards (Fig. 18.29).

2. The *inferior duodenal recess* is present in about 75% of subjects. It is situated at the level of vertebra L3. It is about 3 cm deep. Its orifice looks upwards.

3. The *paraduodenal recess* is present in about 20% of subjects. The inferior mesenteric vein lies in the free edge of the peritoneal fold. Its orifice looks to the right.

4. The *retroduodenal recess* is present occasionally. It is the largest of the duodenal recesses. It is 8 to 10 cm deep. Its orifice looks to the left.

5. The *duodenojejunal* or *mesocolic recess* is present in about 20% of subjects. It is about 3 cm deep. Its orifice looks downwards and to the right.

6. The *mesenterico-parietal fossa* of Waldeyer is present in about 1% of subjects. It lies behind the upper part of the mesentery. Its orifice looks to the left. The superior mesenteric vessels lie in the fold of peritoneum covering this fossa.

Caecal Fossae

1. The *superior ileocaecal recess* is quite commonly present. It is formed by a vascular fold present between the ileum and the ascending colon. Its orifice looks downwards and to the left (Fig. 18.30).

2. The *inferior ileocaecal recess* is covered by the bloodless fold of Treves. The orifice of the recess looks downwards and to the left.

3. The *retrocaecal recess* lies behind the caecum. It often contains the appendix. Its orifice looks downwards.

The Intersigmoid Recess

This recess is constantly present in the foetus and in early infancy, but may disappear with age. It lies behind the apex of the sigmoid mesocolon. Its orifice looks downwards (Fig. 18.31).

DEVELOPMENT

The primitive gut is formed by incorporation of secondary yolk sac into the embryo. The gut is divided into the following.

(i) Pharyngeal gut (from buccopharyngeal membrane to tracheobronchial diverticulum). Its derivatives have been dealt in Vol. 3.

(ii) Foregut situated caudal to pharyngeal gut till the origin of hepatic bud.

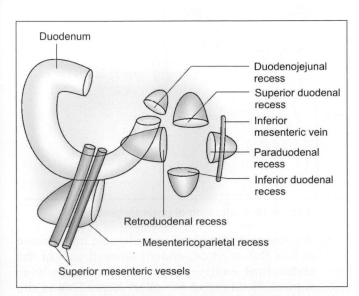

Fig. 18.29: Duodenal recesses of peritoneum.

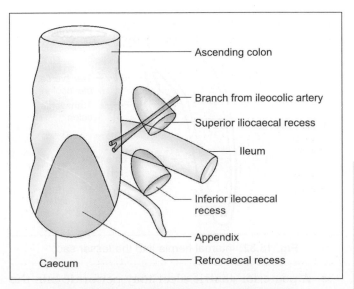

Fig. 18.30: Caecal recesses of peritoneum.

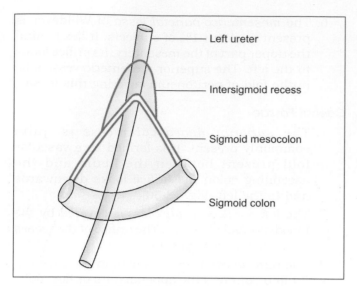

Fig. 18.31: Intersigmoid recess of peritoneum.

(iii) Midgut extends from origin to hepatic bud downwards. Its terminal point is the junction of right two-thirds and left one-third of transverse colon of adult. It communicates with the yolk sac.

(iv) Hindgut spans between the end of midgut and the cloacal membrane.

Dorsal mesentery is double fold of peritoneum connecting the caudal part of foregut, midgut and most of the hindgut to the posterior abdominal wall. It is subdivided into mesogastrium and mesoduodenum for foregut, into dorsal mesentery proper for jejunum and ileum; and mesentery of vermiform appendix, transverse and pelvic mesocolons for large intestine. Ventral mesentery only exists ventral to the foregut. It is a derivative of the septum transversum.

Derivatives of ventral mesogastrium:

Lesser omentum

Falciform ligament

Coronary ligaments

Triangular ligaments

Derivatives of dorsal mesogastrium:

Greater omentum

Lienorenal ligament

Gastrophrenic ligament

Gastrosplenic ligament

CLINICAL ANATOMY

• Strangulated internal hernia into the lesser sac through epiploic foramen is approached through the greater omentum because the epiploic foramen cannot be enlarged due to the presence of important structures all around it (Fig. 18.32).

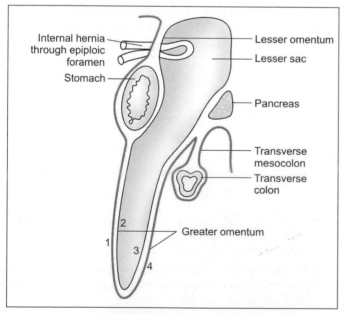

Fig. 18.32: Internal hernia into the lesser sac.

• A posterior gastric ulcer may perforate into the lesser sac. The leaking fluid passes out through epiploic foramen to reach the hepatorenal pouch. Sometimes in these cases the epiploic foramen is closed by adhesions. Then the lesser sac becomes distended, and can be drained by a tube passed through the lesser omentum (Fig. 18.33).

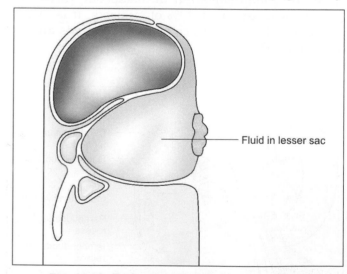

Fig. 18.33: Perforation of posterior gastric ulcer.

• Hepatorenal space is of considerable importance as it is the most dependent (lowest) part of the abdominal cavity proper when the body is supine. Fluids tend to collect here. This is the commonest site of a subphrenic abscess, which may be caused by spread of infection from the gall bladder, the appendix, or other organs in the region (Fig. 18.27).

- The floor of the retouterine pouch is 5.5 cm from the anus, and can be easily felt with a finger passed through the rectum or the vagina. The corresponding rectovesical pouch in males lies 7.5 cm above the anus (Fig. 18.17).

- Being the most dependent part of the peritoneal cavity, pus tends to collect here.

- The pouch can be drained either through the rectum or through the posterior fornix of the vagina (Fig. 18.34).

- Collection of free fluid in the peritoneal cavity is known as *ascites*. Common causes of ascites are cirrhosis of the liver, tuberculous peritonitis, congestive heart failure, and malignant infiltration of the peritoneum. Veins also get prominent in cirrhosis of liver (Fig. 18.35).

- Fluid in the abdomen may be removed by puncturing the abdominal wall either in the median plane midway between the umbilicus and pubic symphysis, or at a point just above the anterior superior iliac spine. The procedure is called *paracentesis*. Urinary bladder must be emptied before the procedure (Fig. 18.36).

- Inflammation of the peritoneum is called *peritonitis*. It may be localized when a subjacent organ is infected; or may be generalized. The latter is a very serious condition.

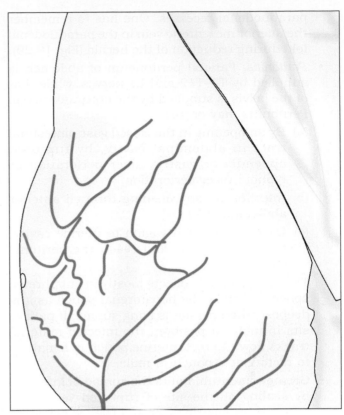

Fig. 18.35: Ascites with prominent veins.

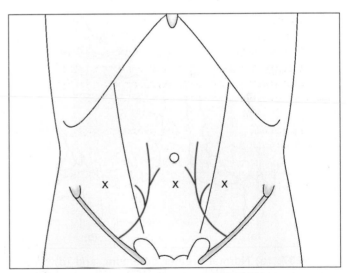

Fig. 18.36: x sites for paracentesis.

- The presence of air in the peritoneal cavity is called *pneumoperitoneum*. It may occur after perforation of the stomach or intestines.

- *Laparoscopy* is the examination of the peritoneal cavity under direct vision using an instrument called *laparoscope*.

- Opening up the abdominal cavity by a surgeon is called *laparotomy*.

- *Internal hernia:* May occur in the opening of lesser sac. It may also occur in between

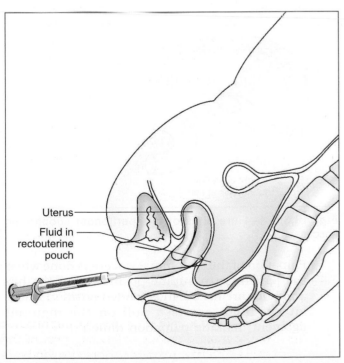

Uterus

Fluid in rectouterine pouch

Fig. 18.34: Fluid in rectouterine pouch being drained through posterior fornix of vagina.

paraduodenal recesses. One has to remember the inferior mesenteric vein in the paraduodenal fold during reduction of the hernia (Fig. 18.29).

- *Peritonitis:* Parietal peritoneum of abdomen is supplied by T7–T12 and L1 nerves, while that of the pelvis is supplied by the obturator nerve. Peritonitis may occur:

(a) By an opening in the closed gastrointestinal tract in abdominal cavity, by ruptured appendix or gastric ulcer perforation or typhoid ulcer perforation.

(b) Infection by any opening through anterior abdominal wall.

(c) Infection through vagina to uterine cavity, to fallopian tube and reach the peritonel cavity.

The infected fluid collects mostly in subphrenic space especially the hepatorenal pouch as it is deepest when person is lying supine. If patient sits in inclined position, the infected material tracks down to rectouterine pouch in female or to rectovesical pouch in male.

- Greater omentum limits the spread of infection by sealing off the site of ruptured vermiform appendix or gastric ulcer and tries to delay the onset of peritonitis (Fig. 18.37).

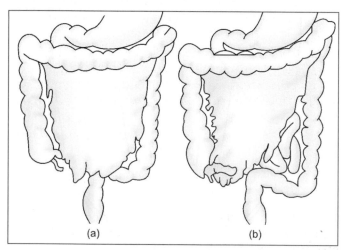

Fig. 18.37: (a) Normal greater omentum, and (b) greater omentum in appendicitis.

- Inflammation of parietal peritoneum causes localized severe pain and rebound tenderness on removing the fingers.
- Peritoneal dialysis is done in case of renal failure. The procedure removes the urea, etc. as it diffuses through blood vessels into the peritoneal cavity.

- *Hepatorenal pouch:* Being the most dependent part of peritoneal cavity, pus tends to collect here unless appropriate physiotherapy and regular postural changes are implemented.
- Pain of foregut derived structuers is felt in the epigastric area.
- Pain of midgut derived structures is felt in the periumbilical area (Fig. 18.38).

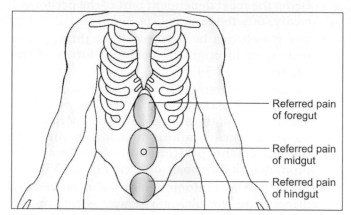

Fig. 18.38: Referred pain from the gut-derived structures.

- Pain of hindgut derived structures is felt in the suprapubic area.
- Intraperitoneal subphrenic spaces may get distended by collection of pus. These are called subphrenic abscesses (Fig. 18.39).

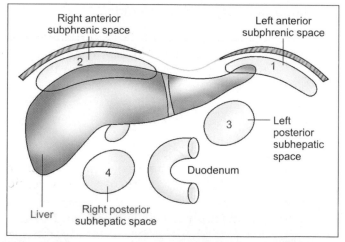

Fig. 18.39: 1–4 are sites of intraperitoneal subphrenic abscesses.

- Palpation of the abdominal viscera is done when the patient is in supine position, and the hip and knee are flexed. In extended position fascia lata of thigh exerts a pull on the inguinal ligament, making palpation difficult.

Abdominal Part of Oesophagus and Stomach

Only about one centimetre of oesophagus lies in the abdominal cavity. It acquires great importance as it is a site of portosystemic anastomoses. Stomach is the chief organ in the epigastric and left hypochondriac regions. Its lesser curvature bears the brunt of all fluids which are too hot or too cold, including the insults by the alcoholic beverages.

ABDOMINAL PART OF OESOPHAGUS

1. The abdominal part of the oesophagus is only about 1.25 cm long.
2. It enters the abdomen through the oesophageal opening of the diaphragm situated at the level of vertebra T10, slightly to the left of the median plane.
3. The oesophageal opening also transmits the anterior and posterior gastric nerves, the oesophageal branches of the left gastric artery and the accompanying veins.
4. These veins drain partly into portal and partly into systemic circulation. Veins accompanying left gastric vein drain into portal vein. Others drain into hemiazygos, in thoracic cavity, and continue into vena azygos and superior vena cava. So it is a site of portosystemic anastomosis.
5. The oesophagus runs downwards and to the left in front of the left crus of the diaphragm and of the inferior surface of the left lobe of the liver, and ends by opening into the cardiac end of the stomach at the level of vertebra T11, about 2.5 cm to the left of the median plane. Its right border is continuous with the lesser curvature of the stomach, but the left border is separated from the fundus of the stomach by the cardiac notch. Peritoneum covers the oesophagus only anteriorly and on the left side.
6. Anterior gastric nerve contains mainly the left vagal fibres, and the posterior gastric nerve mainly the right vagal fibres. Each gastric nerve is represented by one or two trunks and combines a few sympathetic fibres from the greater splanchnic nerve.

HISTOLOGY

Mucous membrane—Epithelial lining is stratified squamous nonkeratinised in nature. Lamina propria consists of loose connective tissue with papillae.

Muscularis mucosae is distinct in lower part and formed by longitudinal muscle fibres.

Submucosa contains mucus secreting oesophageal glands.

Muscularis externa is composed of striated muscle in upper third, mixed type in middle third and smooth muscles in lower third. Outer layer comprises longitudinal coat and inner circular coat of muscle fibres.

Adventitia is the connective tissue with capillaries.

STOMACH

Synonyms

The stomach is also called the gaster or venter from which we have the adjective gastric applied to structures related to the organ.

Definition

The stomach is a muscular bag forming the widest and most distensible part of the digestive tube. It is connected above to the lower end of the oesophagus, and below to the duodenum. It acts as a reservoir of food and helps in digestion of carbohydrates, proteins and fats.

Location

The stomach lies obliquely in the upper and left part of the abdomen, occupying the epigastric, umbilical

Identify the stomach and trace it towards the abdominal part of oesophagus. Clean this part of oesophagus. Note various parts of stomach, e.g. cardiac end, fundus, body and pyloric parts. Trace the right and left gastric arteries along the lesser curvature and right and left gastroepiploic arteries along the greater curvature.

Tie two ligatures each at the lowest part of oesophagus and the pylorus. Remove the stomach by cutting between two upper ligatures through the oesophagus, left gastric artery, gastrophrenic ligament; and by cutting the pylorus between the lower two ligatures. Free the stomach from the adherent peritoneum if any and put it in a tray for further dissection.

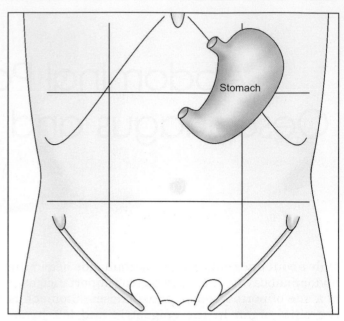

Fig. 19.1: Location of the stomach.

and left hypochondriac regions. Most of it lies under cover of the left costal margin and the ribs (Fig. 19.1).

Shape and Position

The shape of the stomach depends upon the degree of its distension and that of the surrounding viscera, e.g. the colon. When empty, the stomach is somewhat J-shaped (vertical) (Fig. 19.2); when partially distended, it becomes pyriform in shape. In obese persons, it is more horizontal. The shape of the stomach can be studied in the living by radiographic examination after giving a barium meal (Fig. 36.1).

Size

The stomach is a very distensible organ. It is about 25 cm long, and the mean capacity is one ounce (30 ml) at birth, one litre (1000 ml) at puberty, and 1½ to 2 litres or more in adults.

External Features

The stomach has two orifices or openings, two curvatures or borders, and two surfaces (Fig. 19.3).

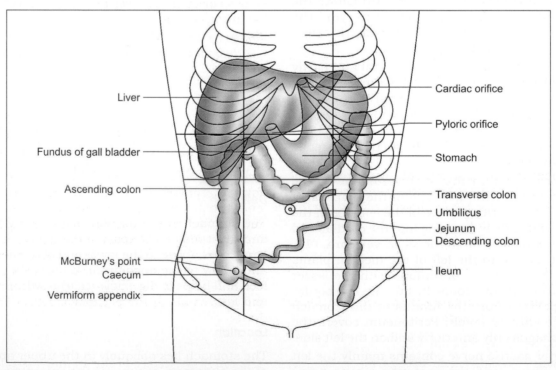

Fig. 19.2: Position of some abdominal organs.

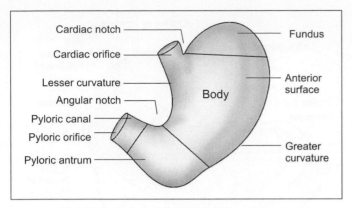

Fig. 19.3: External features of the stomach.

Two Orifices

The *cardiac orifice* is joined by the lower end of the oesophagus. It lies behind the left 7th costal cartilage 2.5 cm from its junction with the sternum, at the level of vertebra T11. There is physiological evidence of sphincteric action at this site, but a sphincter cannot be demonstrated anatomically.

The *pyloric orifice* opens into the duodenum. In an empty stomach and in the supine position, it lies 1.2 cm to the right of median plane, at the level of lower border of vertebra L1 or transpyloric plane. Its position is indicated on the surface of the stomach:

(a) By a circular groove (*pyloric constriction*) produced by the underlying pyloric sphincter or pylorus (*pylorus* = gate guard) which feels like a large firm nodule.

(b) By the *prepyloric vein* which lies in front of the constriction.

Two Curvatures

The *lesser curvature* is concave and forms the right border of the stomach. It provides attachment to the lesser omentum. The most dependent part of the curvature is marked by the *angular notch* or incisura angularis.

The *greater curvature* is convex and forms the left border of the stomach. It provides attachment to the greater omentum, the gastrosplenic ligament and the gastrophrenic ligament. At its upper end the greater curvature presents the *cardiac notch* which separates it from the oesophagus.

Two Surfaces

The *anterior* or *anterosuperior surface* faces forwards and upwards.

The *posterior* or *posteroinferior surface* faces backwards and downwards.

Two Parts Subdivided into Four

The stomach is divided into two parts. 1. Cardiac and 2. Pyloric by a line drawn downwards and to the left from the incisura angularis. The larger, cardiac part is further subdivided into the fundus and body, and the smaller, pyloric part is subdivided into the pyloric antrum and pyloric canal (Fig. 19.3).

Cardiac

(a) The *fundus of the stomach* is the upper convex dome-shaped part situated above a horizontal line drawn at the level of the cardiac orifice. It is commonly distended with gas which is seen clearly in radiographic examination under the left dome of the diaphragm.

(b) The *body of the stomach* lies between the fundus and the pyloric antrum. It can be distended enormously along the greater curvature. The gastric glands distributed in the fundus and body of stomach, contain all three types of secretory cells, namely:

  (i) The mucous cells.

  (ii) The chief, peptic or zymogenic cells which secrete the digestive enzymes.

  (iii) The parietal or oxyntic cells which secrete HCl.

Pyloric

(a) The *pyloric antrum* is separated from the pyloric canal by an inconstant sulcus, sulcus intermedius present on the greater curvature. It is about 7.5 cm long. The pyloric glands are richest in mucous cells.

(b) The *pyloric canal* is about 2.5 cm long. It is narrow and tubular. At its right end it terminates at the pylorus.

Relations of Stomach

Peritoneal Relations

The stomach is lined by peritoneum on both its surfaces. At the lesser curvature the layers of peritoneum lining the anterior and posterior surfaces meet and become continuous with the *lesser omentum*. Along the greater part of the greater curvature the two layers meet to form the *greater omentum*. Near the fundus the two layers meet to form the gastrosplenic ligament. Near the cardiac end the peritoneum on the posterior surface is reflected on to the diaphragm as the *gastrophrenic ligament* (Fig. 18.7). Cranial to this ligament a small part of the posterior surface of the stomach is in direct contact with the diaphragm (left crus). This is the bare area of the stomach. The greater and lesser curvatures along the peritoneal reflections are also bare.

Visceral Relations

The anterior surface of the stomach is related to the liver, the diaphragm, and the anterior abdominal

DISSECTION

Open the stomach along the lesser curvature and examine the mucous membrane with a hand lens. Then strip the mucous membrane from one part and expose the internal muscle coat. Dissect the muscle coat, e.g. outer longitudinal, middle circular and inner oblique muscle fibres. Feel thickened pyloric sphincter. Incise the beginning of duodenum and examine the duodenal and pyloric aspects of the pyloric sphincter.

wall. The areas of the stomach related to these structures are shown in Fig. 19.4. The diaphragm separates the stomach from the left pleura, the pericardium, and the sixth to ninth ribs. The costal cartilages are separated from the stomach by the transversus abdominis. Gastric nerves and vessels ramify deep to the peritoneum.

The posterior surface of the stomach is related to structures forming the stomach bed, *all of which are separated from the stomach by the cavity of the lesser sac.* These structures are:

1. Diaphragm.
2. Left kidney.
3. Left suprarenal gland.
4. Pancreas.
5. Transverse mesocolon.
6. Splenic flexure of the colon.
7. Splenic artery (Fig. 19.5). Sometimes the spleen is also included in the stomach bed, but it is separated from the stomach by the cavity of the greater sac (and not of the lesser sac). Gastric nerves and vessels ramify deep to the peritoneum (Figs 18.8, 18.17a and 18.18).

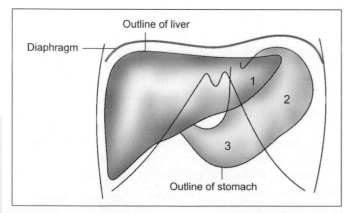

Fig. 19.4: Anterior relations of stomach. Area 1 is covered by the liver; area 2 by the diaphragm; and area 3 by the anterior abdominal wall.

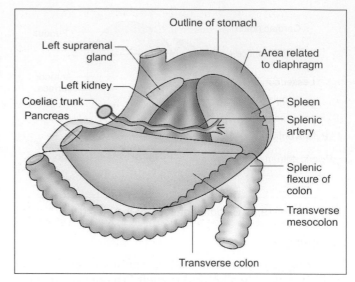

Fig. 19.5: The stomach bed.

Interior of Stomach

The stomach has to be opened to see its internal structure.

1. The *mucosa* of an empty stomach is thrown into folds termed as gastric rugae. The rugae are longitudinal along the lesser curvature and are irregular elsewhere. The rugae are flattened in a distended stomach. On the mucosal surface there are numerous small depressions that can be seen with a hand lens. These are the gastric pits. The gastric glands open into these pits.

   The part of the lumen of the stomach that lies along the lesser curvature, and has longitudinal rugae, is called the gastric canal or magenstrasse. This canal allows rapid passage of swallowed liquids along the lesser curvature directly to the lower part before it spreads to the other part of stomach.

   Thus lesser curvature bears maximum insult of the swallowed liquids, which makes it vulnerable to peptic ulcer. *So, beware of your drinks.*

2. *Submucous coat* is made of connective tissue, arterioles and nerve plexus.

3. *Muscle coat* is arranged as under:
   (i) Longitudinal fibres are most superficial, mainly along the curvatures.
   (ii) Inner circular fibres encircle the body and are thickened at pylorus to form pyloric sphincter.
   (iii) The deepest layer consists of oblique fibres which loop over the cardiac notch. Some fibres spread in the fundus and body of stomach. Rest form a well-developed ridge on each side of the lesser curvature. These

fibres on contraction form "gastric canal" for the passage of fluids.

4. *Serous coat* consists of the peritoneal covering.

Blood Supply

The stomach is supplied along the lesser curvature by:

1. The left gastric artery, a branch of the coeliac trunk.
2. The right gastric artery, a branch of the proper hepatic artery.
3. Along the greater curvature it is supplied by the right gastroepiploic artery, a branch of the gastroduodenal.
4. The left gastroepiploic artery, a branch of the splenic.
5. Fundus is supplied by 5 to 7 short gastric arteries, which are also branches of the splenic artery (Fig. 19.6).

The veins of the stomach drain into the portal, superior mesenteric and splenic veins.

Right and left gastric drain in the portal vein. Right gastroepiploic ends in superior mesenteric vein; while left gastroepiploic and short gastric veins terminate in splenic vein.

Lymphatic Drainage

The stomach can be divided into four lymphatic territories as shown in Fig. 19.7. The drainage of these areas is as follows.

Area (a) of Fig. 19.7, i.e. upper part of left 1/3rd drains into the pancreaticosplenic nodes lying along the splenic artery, i.e. on the back of the stomach. Lymph vessels from these nodes travel along the splenic artery to reach the coeliac nodes.

Area (b), i.e. right 2/3rd drains into the left gastric nodes lying along the artery of the same name. These nodes also drain the abdominal part of the oesophagus. Lymph from these nodes drains into the coeliac nodes.

Area (c), i.e lower part of left 1/3rd drains into the right gastroepiploic nodes that lie along the artery of the same name. Lymph vessels arising in these nodes drain into the subpyloric nodes which lie in the angle between the first and second parts of the duodenum. From here the lymph is drained further into the hepatic nodes that lie along the hepatic artery; and finally into the coeliac nodes.

Lymph from *area* (d), i.e. pyloric part drains in different directions into the pyloric, hepatic, and left gastric nodes, and passes from all these nodes to the coeliac nodes.

Note that lymph from all areas of the stomach ultimately reaches the coeliac nodes. From here it passes through the intestinal lymph trunk to reach the cisterna chyli.

Nerve Supply

The stomach is supplied by sympathetic and parasympathetic nerves. The *sympathetic nerves* are derived from thoracic six to ten segments of the spinal cord, via the greater splanchnic nerves, and coeliac and hepatic plexuses. They travel along the arteries supplying the stomach. These nerves are:

(a) Vasomotor.
(b) Motor to the pyloric sphincter, but inhibitory to the rest of the gastric musculature.
(c) The chief pathway for pain sensations from the stomach.

The *parasympathetic nerves* are derived from the vagi, through the oesophageal plexus and gastric

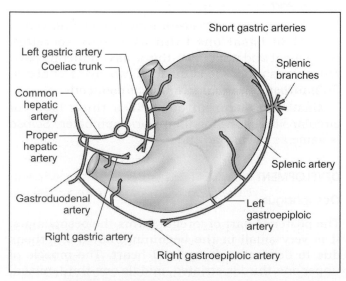

Fig. 19.6: Arteries supplying the stomach.

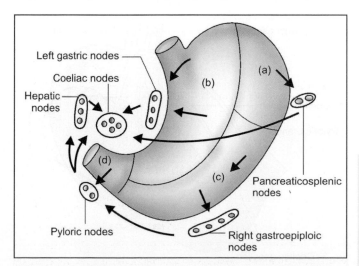

Fig. 19.7: Lymphatic drainage of the stomach. Note the manner in which the organ is subdivided into different territories.

nerves. The anterior gastric nerve (made up of one or two trunks) contains mainly the left vagal fibres, and the posterior gastric nerve (again made up of one to two trunks) contains mainly the right vagal fibres. The *anterior gastric nerve* divides into:

(a) A number of gastric branches for the anterior surface of the fundus and body of the stomach.

(b) Two pyloric branches, one for the pyloric antrum and another for the pylorus.

The *posterior gastric nerve* divides into:

(a) Smaller, gastric branches for the posterior surface of the fundus, the body and the pyloric antrum.

(b) Larger, coeliac branches for the coeliac plexus. Parasympathetic nerves are motor and secretomotor to the stomach. Their stimulation causes increased motility of the stomach and secretion of gastric juice rich in pepsin and HCl (Fig. 19.8).

Functions

1. The stomach acts primarily as a reservoir of food.
2. By its peristaltic movements it softens and mixes the food with the gastric juice.
3. The gastric glands produce the gastric juice which contains enzymes that play an important role in digestion of food.
4. The gastric glands also produce hydrochloric acid which destroys many organisms present in food and drink.
5. The lining cells of the stomach produce abundant mucus which protects the gastric mucosa against the corrosive action of hydrochloric acid.

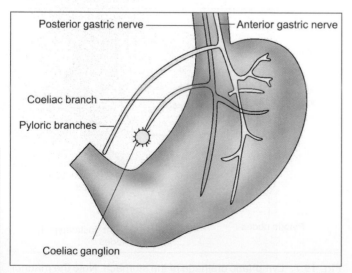

Fig. 19.8: Nerve supply of the stomach.

6. Some substances like alcohol, water, salt and few drugs are absorbed in the stomach.
7. Stomach produces the "intrinsic factor" of Castle which helps in the absorption of vitamin B12.

HISTOLOGY OF STOMACH

At the cardiac end of stomach the stratified epithelium of oesophagus *abruptly* changes to simple columnar epithelium of stomach.

Cardiac End

Mucous membrane: The epithelium is simple columnar with small tubular glands. Lower half of the gland is secretory and upper half is the conducting part. Muscularis mucosae consists of smooth muscle fibres.

Submucosa: It consists of loose connective tissue with Meissner's plexus.

Muscularis externa: It is made of outer longitudinal and inner circular layer including the myenteric plexus of nerves.

Serosa: It is lined by single layer of squamous cells.

Fundus and Body of Stomach

Mucous membrane: It contains tall simple tubular gastric glands. Upper one-third is conducting, while lower two-thirds is secretory. The various cell types seen in the gland are chief or zymogenic, oxyntic or parietal and mucous neck cells.

Muscularis mucosae and *submucosa* are same.

Muscularis externa: It contains an additional innermost oblique coat of muscle fibres.

Serosa is same as of cardiac end.

Pyloric Part

Mucous membrane: There are pyloric glands which consist of basal one-third as mucus secretory component and upper two-thirds as conducting part. Muscularis mucosae is made of two layers of fibres. Submucosa is same as in the cardiac end.

Muscularis externa comprises thick layer of circular fibres forming the pyloric sphincter. *Serosa* is same as of cardiac end.

DEVELOPMENT

Oesophagus

The posterior part of foregut forms the oesophagus. It is very small in the beginning, but it lengthens due to descent of lungs and heart. The muscle of upper one-third is striated, middle one-third, mixed, and lower one-third smooth. Nerve supply to upper two-thirds is from vagus and to lower one-third is from autonomic plexus. Epithelium of oesophagus is endodermal and rest of the layers are from splanchnic mesoderm.

Stomach

The caudal part of foregut shows a fusiform dilatation with anterior and posterior borders and left and right surfaces. This is the stomach. It rotates 90° clockwise, so that left surface faces anteriorly. Even

the original posterior border of stomach grows faster, forming the greater curvature.

The stomach also rotates along anteroposterior axis, so that distal or pyloric part moves to right and proximal or cardiac part moves to left side.

The 90° rotation of stomach along the vertical axis pulls the dorsal mesogastrium to the left side creating the lessor sac or omental bursa.

Spleen appears as mesodermal condensation in the left leaf of dorsal mesogastrium.

CLINICAL ANATOMY

- The lower end of the oesophagus is one of the important sites for portosystemic anastomosis. In portal hypertension, the anastomosis opens and forms venous dilatations called *oesophageal varices*. Their rupture causes severe and dangerous haematemesis (Fig. 19.9).

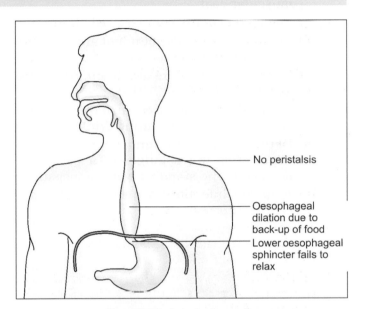

Fig. 19.10: Achalasia cardia

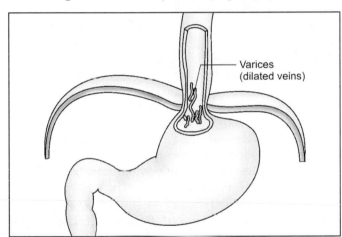

Fig. 19.9: Oesophageal varices at the lower end of oesophagus.

- Normally the lower end of the oesophagus remains closed and dilates only during the passage of food. However, due to neuromuscular incoordination it may fail to dilate leading to difficulty in passage of food or dysphagia. The condition is known as *achalasia cardia*. Marked dilatation of the oesophagus may occur due to collection of food in it (Fig. 19.10).
- The lower end of the oesophagus is also prone to inflammation or ulceration by regurgitation of acid from the stomach. It is the commonest site of oesophageal carcinoma. Next site is the middle third of oesophagus (Fig. 19.11).
- Gastric pain is felt in the epigastrium because the stomach is supplied from segments T6 to T10 of the spinal cord, which also supply the upper part of the abdominal wall. Pain is produced either by spasm of muscle, or by over-

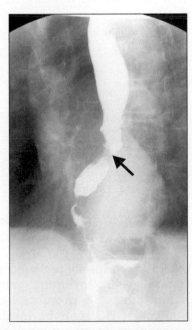

Fig. 19.11: Cancer of the middle third of oesophagus.

distension. Ulcer pain is attributed to local spasm due to irritation (Fig. 18.38).

- *Peptic ulcer* can occur in the sites of pepsin and hydrochloric acid, namely the stomach, first part of duodenum, lower end of oesophagus and Meckel's diverticulum.

Gastric ulcer occurs typically along the lesser curvature (Fig. 19.12). This is possibly due to the following peculiarities of lesser curvature.

(a) It is homologous with the gastric trough of ruminants.

(b) Mucosa is not freely movable over the muscular coat.

(c) The epithelium is comparatively thin.

(d) Blood supply is less abundant and there are fewer anastomoses.

(e) Nerve supply is more abundant, with large ganglia.

(f) Because of the gastric canal, it receives most of the insult from irritating drinks.

(g) Being shorter in length the wave of contraction stays longer at a particular point, viz., the standing wave of incisura.

(h) *H. pylori* infection is also an important causative factor.

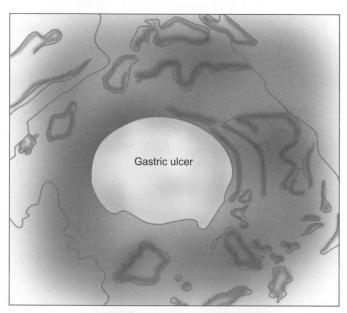

Fig. 19.12: Gastric ulcer.

Gastric ulcers are common in people who are always in "hurry", mostly "worry" about incidents and eat "spicy curry".

Gastric ulcer is notoriously resistant to healing and persists for years together, causing great degree of morbidity. To promote healing the irritating effect of HCl can be minimised by antacids, partial gastrectomy, or vagotomy.

- *Gastric carcinoma* is common and occurs along the greater curvature. On this account the lymphatic drainage of stomach assumes importance. Metastasis can occur through the thoracic duct to the left supraclavicular lymph node (Troisier's sign). These lymph nodes are called as "signal nodes".

- *Pyloric obstruction* can be congenital or acquired. It causes visible peristalsis in the epigastrium, and vomiting after meals.

- Hiatal hernia occurring through the oesophageal opening and can be rolling or para-oesophageal and sliding (Fig. 19.13).

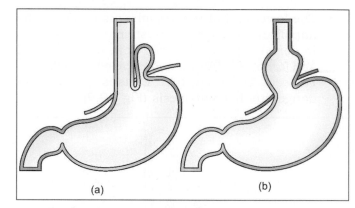

Fig. 19.13: Hiatal hernia (a) Rolling and (b) sliding.

- *Barrett's oesophagus:* Squamous epithelium of lower oesophagus may be replaced by columnar epithelium in certain clinical conditions. The abnormal type of epithelium present in oesophagus is referred as Barrett's epithelium.

- *Tracheo-oesophageal fistula:* At times the separation of trachea and oesophagus may not be complete. Proximal segment ends in a blind pouch and distal segment communicates with trachea (Fig. 19.14).

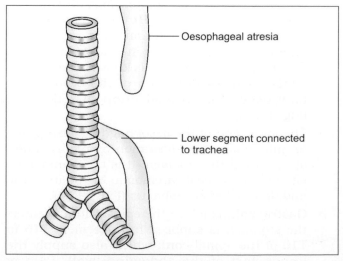

Fig. 19.14: Tracheo-oesophageal fistula.

CHAPTER 20

Small and Large Intestines

The intestine, which is the longest part of the digestive tube, is divided into long, less distensible, small intestine, and shorter, more distensible large intestine. Food has to be digested, metabolised and stored for expulsion in the intestines. Intestines suffer from bacterial infection like typhoid, tuberculosis; parasitic infection, like roundworm, tape worm, etc. in addition to diarrhoea and dysentery. Good and healthy eating habits definitely prevent some of these conditions. The proximal one and a half parts of duodenum, including liver, gall bladder and pancreas, develop from foregut. The distal two and a half parts of duodenum, jejunum, ileum, caecum, appendix, ascending colon and right two-thirds of transverse colon develop from midgut. Lastly, the left one-third of transverse colon, descending colon, pelvic colon and proximal part of rectum develop from hind gut.

SMALL INTESTINE

The small intestine extends from the pylorus to the ileocaecal junction. It is about 6 m long. The length is greater in males than in females, and greater in cadavers, due to loss of tone than in the living. It is divided into:

(a) An upper, fixed part, called the duodenum, which measures about 25 cm in length; and

(b) A lower, mobile part, forming a very long convoluted tube.

The upper two-fifths of the mobile intestine are known as the jejunum, and the lower three-fifths are known as the ileum. The structure of the small intestine is adapted for digestion and absorption.

RELEVANT FEATURES

Large Surface Area

For absorption of digested food a very large surface area is required. This is achieved by:

(a) The great length of the intestine.

(b) The presence of circular folds of mucous membrane, villi and microvilli.

The *circular folds of mucous membrane, plicae circulares,* or *valves of Kerkring* form complete or incomplete circles. These folds are permanent, and are not obliterated by distension. They begin in the second part of the duodenum, and become large and closely set below the level of the major duodenal papilla. They continue to be closely set in the proximal half of the jejunum, but diminish progressively in size and number in the distal half of the jejunum and in the proximal half of the ileum. They are almost absent in the distal half of the ileum. Apart from increasing the surface area for absorption, the circular folds facilitate absorption by slowing down the passage of intestinal contents.

The *intestinal villi* are finger-like projections of mucous membrane, just visible to the naked eye. They give the surface of the intestinal mucosa a velvety appearance. They are large and numerous in the duodenum and jejunum, but are smaller and fewer in the ileum. They vary in density from 10 to 40 per square millimetre, and are about 1 to 2 mm long. They increase the surface area of the small intestine about eight times.

Each villus is covered by a layer of absorptive columnar cells. The surface of these cells has a striated border which is seen, under the electron microscope to be made of *microvilli*.

Intestinal Glands or Crypts of Lieberkuhn

These are simple tubular glands distributed over the entire mucous membrane of the jejunum and ileum. They open by small circular apertures on the surface of mucous membrane between the villi. They secrete digestive enzymes and mucus. The epithelial cells deep in the crypts show a high level of mitotic activity. The proliferated cells gradually move towards the surface, to be shed from the tips of the villi. In this way, the complete epithelial lining of the intestine is replaced every two to four days.

The duodenal glands or Brunner's glands lie in the submucosa. These are small, compound tubulo-acinar glands which secrete mucus.

Lymphatic Follicles

The mucous membrane of the small intestine contains two types of lymphatic follicles. The *solitary lymphatic follicles* are 1 to 2 mm in diameter, and are distributed throughout the small and large intestines. The *aggregated lymphatic follicles* or *Peyer's patches* form circular or oval patches, varying in length from 2 to 10 cm and containing 10 to over 200 follicles. They are largest and most numerous in the ileum, and are small, circular and fewer in the distal jejunum. They are placed lengthwise along the antimesenteric border of the intestine. Peyer's patches are ulcerated in *typhoid fever*, forming oval ulcers with their long axes along the long axis of the bowel.

Both the solitary and aggregated lymphatic follicles are most numerous at puberty, but there-after diminish in size and number, although they may persist up to old age.

Each villus has a central lymph vessel called a *lacteal*. Lymph from lacteals drains into plexuses in the walls of the gut and from there to regional lymph nodes.

Arterial Supply

The *arterial supply* to jejunum and ileum is derived from the jejunal and ileal branches of the superior mesenteric artery. The *vasa recta* are distributed alternately to the opposite surfaces of the gut. They run between the serous and muscular coats, and give off numerous branches which supply and pierce the muscular coat and form a plexus in the submucosa. From this plexus, minute branches pass to the glands and villi. The anastomosis between the terminal intestinal branches is poor (Fig. 21.9).

Lymphatics

The *lymphatics* (lacteals) have a circular course in the walls of the intestine. Tuberculous ulcers and subsequent strictures are due to involvement of these lymphatics. Large lymphatic vessels formed at the mesenteric border pass to the mesenteric lymph nodes.

Nerve Supply

The *nerve supply* of the small intestine is sympathetic (T9 to T11) as well as parasympathetic (vagus), both of which pass through the coeliac and superior mesenteric plexuses. The nerves form the *myenteric plexus* of Auerbach, containing parasym-pathetic ganglia between circular and longitudinal muscle coats. Fibres from this plexus form the *submucous plexus* of Meissner which also contains parasympathetic ganglia. Sympathetic nerves are motor to the sphincters and to the muscularis mucosae, and inhibitory for peristaltic movements. The parasympathetic nerves stimulate peristalsis, but inhibit the sphincters. The nerve plexuses and neurotransmitters of the gut are quite complex. These are now called the *enteric nervous system*.

Function

The *function* of the small intestine comprises *digestion* and *absorption* of the digested contents from the fluid.

The parts of the small intestine are considered one by one.

DUODENUM

Term

The term *duodenum* is a Latin corruption of the Greek word, *dudekadaktulos*, meaning twelve fingers.

Definition and Location

The duodenum is the shortest, widest and most fixed part of the small intestine. It extends from the pylorus to duodenojejunal flexure. It is curved around the head of pancreas in the form of letter 'C'. The duodenum lies above the level of umbilicus, opposite first, second and third lumbar vertebrae.

Length and Parts

Duodenum is 25 cm long and is divided into the following four parts (Figs 20.2 and 20.3).

1. First or superior part, 5 cm long.

DISSECTION

Examine the C-shaped duodenum and head of pancreas lying in its concavity (Fig. 20.1). Cut through the lower wall of the first part extending the cut on medial wall of second and upper wall of third part of duodenum to see its interior. Carefully look for the longitudinal fold on the posteromedial wall below the middle of second part. The longitudinal fold is often covered by a circular fold containing orifice of the major duodenal papilla draining both the bile and pancreatic ducts. Identify and dissect the structures related to all the four parts of the duodenum.

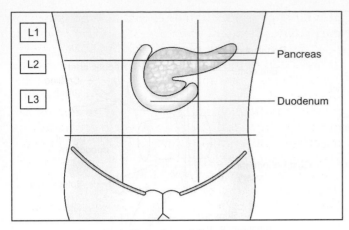

Fig. 20.1: Location of the duodenum.

2. Second or descending part, 7.5 cm long.
3. Third or horizontal part, 10 cm long.
4. Fourth or ascending part, 2.5 cm long.

Peritoneal Relations

The duodenum is mostly retroperitoneal and fixed, except at its two ends where it is suspended by folds of peritoneum, and is, therefore, mobile. Anteriorly, the duodenum is only partly covered with peritoneum.

First Part

The first part begins at the pylorus, and passes backwards, upwards and to the right to meet the second part at the superior duodenal flexure. Its relations are as follows.

Peritoneal relations

1. The proximal 2.5 cm is movable. It is attached to the lesser omentum above, and to the greater omentum below.
2. The distal 2.5 cm is fixed. It is retroperitoneal.

It is covered with peritoneum only on its anterior aspect.

Visceral Relations

Anteriorly: Quadrate lobe of liver, and gall bladder (Fig. 20.4a).

Posteriorly: Gastroduodenal artery, bile duct and portal vein (Fig. 20.4b).

Superiorly: Epiploic foramen (Fig. 20.4a).

Inferiorly: Head and neck of the pancreas.

Second Part

Course

This part is about 7.5 cm long. It begins at the superior duodenal flexure, passes downwards to reach the lower border of the third lumbar vertebra, where it curves towards the left at the inferior duodenal flexure, to become continuous with the third part. Its relations are as follows.

Peritoneal Relations

It is retroperitoneal and fixed. Its anterior surface is covered with peritoneum, except near the middle, where it is directly related to the colon.

Visceral relations

Anteriorly:
(a) Right lobe of the liver
(b) Transverse colon
(c) Root of the transverse mesocolon
(d) Small intestine (Fig. 20.5a).

Posteriorly:
(a) Anterior surface of the right kidney near the medial border
(b) Right renal vessels
(c) Right edge of the inferior vena cava
(d) Right psoas major (Fig. 20.5b).

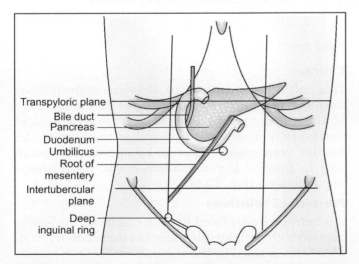

Fig. 20.2: Position of duodenum, pancreas, root of mesentery.

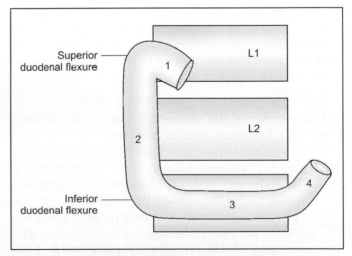

Fig. 20.3: Parts of the duodenum.

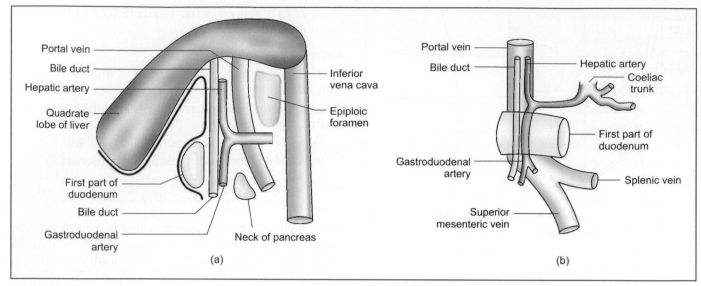

Fig. 20.4: Relations of the first part of the duodenum: (a) Sagittal section viewed from the left side, (b) posterior relations.

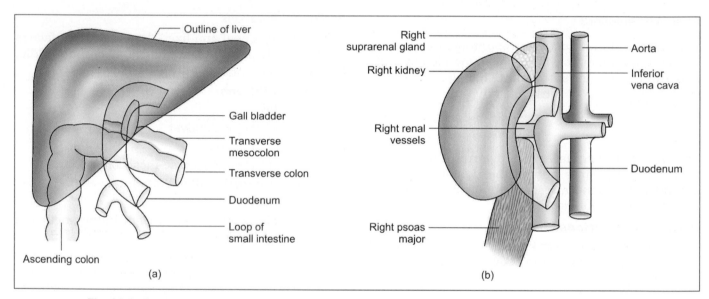

Fig. 20.5: Relations of the second part of the duodenum: (a) Anterior relations, (b) posterior relations.

Medially:

(a) Head of the pancreas

(b) The bile duct (Fig. 20.2).

Laterally: Right colic flexure (Fig. 20.5a).

The interior of the second part of the duodenum shows the following special features.

1. The *major duodenal papilla* is an elevation present posteromedially, 8 to 10 cm distal to the pylorus. The hepatopancreatic ampulla opens at the summit of the papilla.

2. The *minor duodenal papilla* is present 6 to 8 cm distal to the pylorus, and presents the opening of the accessory pancreatic duct (Fig. 23.16).

Third Part

Course

This part is about 10 cm long. It begins at the inferior duodenal flexure, on the right side of the lower border of the third lumbar vertebra. It passes almost horizontally and slightly upwards in front of the inferior vena cava, and ends by joining the fourth part in front of the abdominal aorta. Its relations are as follows (Fig. 20.6).

Peritoneal relations

It is retroperitoneal and fixed. Its anterior surface is covered with peritoneum, except in the median plane, where it is crossed by the superior mesenteric vessels and by the root of the mesentery.

Visceral relations

Anteriorly:

(a) Superior mesenteric vessels

(b) Root of mesentery (Fig. 20.6a).

Posteriorly:

(a) Right ureter

(b) Right psoas major

(c) Right testicular or ovarian vessels

(d) Inferior vena cava

(e) Abdominal aorta with origin of inferior mesenteric artery (Fig. 20.6b).

Superiorly: Head of the pancreas with uncinate process (Fig. 20.1).

Inferiorly: Coils of jejunum (Fig. 20.5a).

Fourth Part

Course

This part is 2.5 cm long. It runs upwards on or immediately to the left of the aorta, up to the upper border of the second lumbar vertebra, where it turns forwards to become continuous with the jejunum at the duodenojejunal flexure. Its relations are as follows.

Peritoneal relations

It is mostly retroperitoneal, and covered with peritoneum only anteriorly. The terminal part is suspended by the uppermost part of the mesentery, and is mobile.

Visceral relations

Anteriorly:

(a) Transverse colon,

(b) Transverse mesocolon,

(c) Lesser sac, and

(d) Stomach.

Posteriorly:

(a) Left sympathetic chain,

(b) Left renal artery,

(c) Left gonadal artery, and

(d) Inferior mesenteric vein (Figs 18.29 and 20.7).

To the right: Attachment of the upper part of the root of the mesentery (Fig. 20.6).

To the left:

(a) Left kidney and

(b) Left ureter.

Superiorly: Body of pancreas (Fig. 20.2).

Suspensory Muscle of Duodenum or Ligament of Treitz

This is a fibromuscular band which suspends and supports the duodenojejunal flexure. It arises from

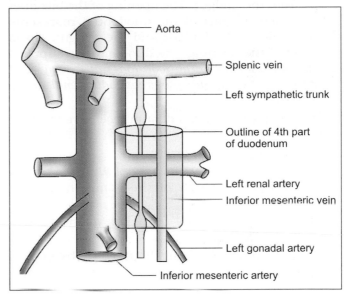

Fig. 20.7: Posterior relations of the fourth part of the duodenum.

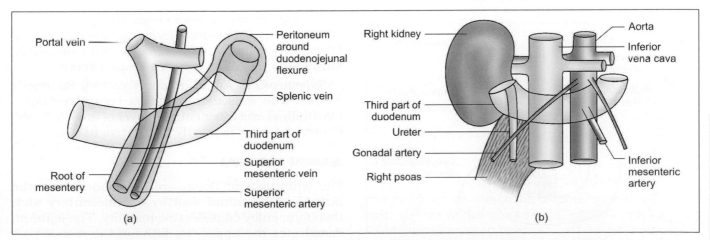

Fig. 20.6: Relations of the third part of the duodenum: (a) Anterior relations, (b) posterior relations.

the right crus of the diaphragm, close to the right side of the oesophagus, passes downwards behind the pancreas, and is attached to the posterior surface of the duodenojejunal flexure and the third and fourth parts of the duodenum (Fig. 20.8).

It is made up of:

(a) Stripped muscle fibres in its upper part

(b) Elastic fibres in its middle part

(c) Plain muscle fibres in its lower part.

Normally its contraction increases the angle of the duodenojejunal flexure. Sometimes it is attached only to the flexure, and then its contraction may narrow the angle of the flexure, causing partial obstruction of the gut.

Arterial Supply

The duodenum develops partly from the foregut and partly from the midgut. The opening of the bile duct into the second part of the duodenum represents the junction of the foregut and the midgut. Up to the level of the opening, the duodenum is supplied by the *superior pancreaticoduodenal artery*, and below it by the *inferior pancreaticoduodenal artery* (Fig. 20.9).

The first part of the duodenum receives additional supply from:

(a) The right gastric artery.

(b) The supraduodenal artery of Wilkie, which is usually a branch of the common hepatic artery.

(c) The retroduodenal branches of the gastroduodenal artery.

(d) Some branches from the right gastroepiploic artery.

Venous Drainage

The veins of the duodenum drain into the splenic, superior mesenteric and portal veins.

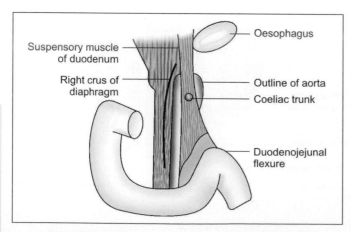

Fig. 20.8: Suspensory muscle of the duodenum.

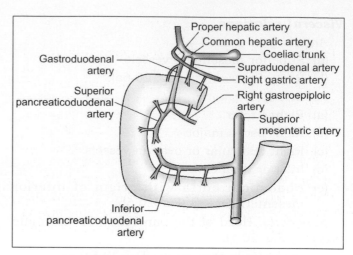

Fig. 20.9: Arterial supply of the duodenum.

Lymphatic Drainage

Most of the lymph vessels from the duodenum end in the pancreaticoduodenal nodes present along the inside of the curve of the duodenum, i.e. at the junction of the pancreas and the duodenum. From here the lymph passes partly to the hepatic nodes, and through them to the coeliac nodes; and partly to the superior mesenteric nodes and ultimately via intestinal lymph trunk into the cisterna chyli. Some vessels from the first part of the duodenum drain into the pyloric nodes, and through them to the hepatic nodes. Some vessels drain into the hepatic nodes directly. All the lymph reaching the hepatic nodes drains into the coeliac nodes.

Nerve Supply

Sympathetic nerves from thoracic ninth and tenth spinal segments and parasympathetic nerves from the vagus, pass through the coeliac plexus and reach the duodenum along its arteries.

Histology

Mucous membrane: Shows evaginations in the form of *villi* and invaginations to form *crypts of Lieberkuhn.* Lining of villi is of columnar cells with microvilli. Muscularis mucosae comprises two layers.

Submucosa is full of mucus-secreting Brunner's glands. The *muscularis externa* comprises outer longitudinal and inner circular layer of muscle fibres. Outermost layer is mostly connective tissue.

JEJUNUM AND ILEUM

The jejunum and ileum are suspended from the posterior abdominal wall by the mesentery and, therefore, enjoy considerable mobility. The jejunum constitutes the upper two-fifths of the mobile part of the small intestine, while the ileum constitutes the lower three-fifths. The jejunum begins at the duodenojejunal flexure. The ileum terminates at the ileocaecal junction. The structure and functions of the jejunum and ileum correspond to the general description of the small intestine. The differences between the jejunum and the ileum are given in Table 20.1.

Blood Supply

The jejunum and ileum are supplied by branches from the superior mesenteric artery, and are drained by corresponding veins.

Lymphatic Drainage

Lymph from lacteals drains into plexuses in the wall of the gut. From there it passes into lymphatic vessels in the mesentery. Passing through numerous lymph nodes present in the mesentery, and along the superior mesenteric artery, it ultimately drains into nodes present in front of the aorta at the origin of the superior mesenteric artery.

Nerve Supply

Sympathetic nerves are from T9–T11 segments and parasympathetic is from vagus.

Histology

Jejunum

The *villi* here are tongue-shaped. No mucous glands or aggregated lymphoid follicles are present in the *submucosa*. *Muscularis externa* is same as in duodenum. Outermost is the serous layer.

Ileum

The *villi* are few, thin and finger-like. Collection of lymphocytes in the form of *Peyer's patches* in lamina propria extending into submucosa is a characteristic feature.

Rest is same as above.

Meckel's Diverticulum (Diverticulum Ilei)

Meckel's diverticulum is the persistent proximal part of the vitellointestinal duct which is present in the embryo, and which normally disappears during the 6th week of intrauterine life. Some points of interest about it are as follows (Fig. 20.10).

1. It occurs in 2% subjects.
2. Usually it is 2 inches or 5 cm long.
3. It is situated about 2 feet or 60 cm proximal to the ileocaecal valve, attached to antimesenteric border of the ileum.
4. Its calibre is equal to that of the ileum.

Table 20.1: Differences between jejunum and ileum

Feature	Jejunum	Ileum
1. Location	Occupies upper and left parts of the intestinal area	Occupies lower and right parts of the intestinal area
2. Walls	Thicker and more vascular	Thinner and less vascular
3. Lumen	Wider and often empty	Narrower and often loaded
4. Mesentery	(a) Windows present (b) Fat less abundant (c) Arterial arcades, 1 or 2 (d) Vasa recta longer and fewer	(a) No windows (b) Fat more abundant (c) Arterial arcades, 3 or 6 (d) Vasa recta shorter and more numerous
5. Circular mucosal folds	Larger and more closely set	Smaller and sparse
6. Villi	Large, thick (leaf-like) and more abundant	Shorter, thinner (finger-like) and less abundant
7. Peyer's patches	Absent	Present
8. Solitary lymphatic follicles	Fewer	More numerous

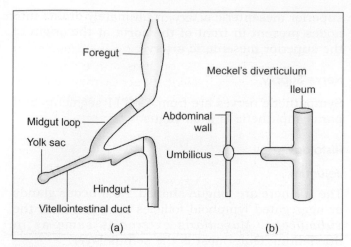

Fig. 20.10: Meckel's diverticulum: (a) Vitellointestinal duct in an early embryo; and (b) Meckel's diverticulum, the proximal persistent part of the vitellointestinal duct.

5. Its apex may be free or may be attached to the umbilicus, to the mesentery, or to any other abdominal structure by a fibrous band.

LARGE INTESTINE

The large intestine extends from the ileocaecal junction to the anus. It is about 1.5 m long, and is divided into the caecum, the ascending colon, the transverse colon, the descending colon, the sigmoid colon, the rectum and the anal canal. In the angle between the caecum and the terminal part of the ileum there is a narrow diverticulum called the vermiform appendix.

The general structure of large intestine is considered first followed by its parts one by one.

The structure of the large intestine is adapted for storage of matter reaching it from the small

DISSECTION

Locate the various parts of large intestine beginning from caecum, vermiform appendix, ascending, transverse, descending and sigmoid colons and ending with the rectum and anal canal. Identify the taenia, haustration and appendices epiploicae. Trace the taenia from the root of the vermiform appendix through the ascending to the transverse colon and note the change in their respective positions.

Caecum: Turn the caecum upwards and identify its posterior relations.

Incise the lateral wall of the caecum and locate the ileocaecal orifice and its associated valve. Below the ileocaecal valve identify the orifice of the vermiform appendix.

intestines, and for absorption of fluid and solutes from it. The epithelium is absorptive (columnar), but *villi are absent.* Adequate lubrication for passage of its contents is provided by numerous goblet cells scattered in the crypts as well as on the surface of the mucous membrane. The presence of numerous solitary lymphatic follicles provides protection against bacteria present in the lumen of the intestine.

Relevant Features

The relevant features of the large intestine are as follows.

1. The large intestine is *wider in calibre* than the small intestine. The calibre is greatest at its commencement, and gradually diminishes towards the rectum where it is dilated to form the rectal ampulla just above the anal canal.

2. The greater part of the large intestine is *fixed*, except for the appendix, the transverse colon and the sigmoid colon.

3. The longitudinal muscle coat forms only a thin layer in this part of the gut. The greater part of it forms three ribbon-like bands, called the *taeniae coli.* Proximally the taeniae converge at the base of the appendix, and distally they spread out on the terminal part of the sigmoid colon to become continuous with the longitudinal muscle coat of the rectum. In the caecum, the ascending colon and the descending colon the positions of taeniae are anterior or taenia libera; posteromedial or taenia mesocolica and posterolateral or taenia omentalis but in the transverse colon the corresponding positions of taenia are inferior, posterior and superior.

   One taenia, *taenia libera,* is placed anteriorly in the caecum, ascending, descending and sigmoid colon, but is placed inferiorly in the transverse colon.

   Second taenia, *taenia mesocolica* is present on the posteromedial surface of caecum, ascending, descending and sigmoid colon, but is placed posteriorly on transverse colon at the site of attachment of the transverse mesocolon.

   Third taenia, *taenia omentalis,* is situated posterolaterally in caecum, ascending, descending and sigmoid colon, but is situated on the anterosuperior surface of transverse colon where layers three and four of greater omentum meet the transverse colon. This change in position is due to twist in transverse colon.

4. Since the taeniae are shorter than the circular muscle coat, the colon is *puckered* and *sacculated.*

5. Small bags of peritoneum filled with fat, and called the *appendices epiploicae*, are scattered over the surface of the large intestine, except for the appendix, the caecum and the rectum. These are most numerous on the sides of the sigmoid colon and on the posterior surface of the transverse colon.

The differences between the small and large intestine are summarised in Table 20.2.

6. The *blood supply* to the colon is derived from the marginal artery (Fig. 21.12). Terminal branches from the marginal artery are distributed to the intestine as long and short vessels, *vasa longa* and *vasa brevia*. The long arteries divide into anterior and posterior branches close to the mesocolic taenia to pass between the serous and muscular coats and reach the amesocolic taeniae. They gradually pierce the muscular coat and reach the submucosa. The anastomosis between the two amesocolic taeniae is extremely poor. So longitudinal incisions should be made along this line.

Short branches arise either from the marginal artery or from the long branches, and the majority of them at once sink into the bowel wall at the mesocolic border. The short and long branches together thus provide the mesocolic region of the wall with abundant blood supply. It is only the amesocolic region which has scanty blood supply.

Subserous coat of long branches is intimately related to appendices epiploicae, to which they contribute branches. During removal of these appendages care must be taken not to pull on them in order to avoid traction on the subjacent vessel.

Bowel wall is weakened where it is pierced by the vessels and at the sites of attachment of appendices epiploicae. Mucosa may herniate in these situations causing diverticulosis, with associated dangers of diverticulitis, fibrosis and stricture.

7. *Lymph* from the large intestine passes through four sets of lymph nodes.
   (a) *Epicolic lymph nodes,* lying on the wall of the gut (Fig. 20.18).
   (b) *Paracolic nodes*, on the medial side of the ascending and descending colon and near the mesocolic border of the transverse and sigmoid colon.
   (c) *Intermediate nodes*, on the main branches of the vessels.
   (d) *Terminal nodes*, on the superior and inferior mesenteric vessels.

In carcinoma of the colon, the related paracolic and intermediate lymph nodes have to be removed. Their removal is possible only after the ligature of the main branch of the superior or inferior mesenteric artery along which the involved lymph nodes lie. It is necessary, therefore, to remove a large segment of the bowel than is actually required by the extent of the disease, in order to avoid gangrene as a result of interference with the blood supply. It is always wise to remove the whole portion of the bowel supplied by the ligated vessel.

8. The *nerve supply* of the large intestine, barring the lower half of the anal canal, is both

Table 20.2: Differences between the small intestine and the large intestine

Feature	Small intestine	Large intestine
1. Appendices epiploicae	Absent	Present
2. Taeniae coli	Absent	Present
3. Sacculations	Absent	Present
4. Distensibility	Less	More
5. Fixity	Greater part is freely mobile	Greater part is fixed
6. Villi	Present	Absent
7. Transverse mucosal folds	Permanent	Obliterated when longitudinal muscle coat relaxes
8. Peyer's patches	Present in ileum	Absent
9. Common site for	(a) Intestinal worms (b) Typhoid (c) Tuberculosis	(a) *Entamoeba histolytica* (b) Dysentery organisms (c) Carcinoma
10. Effects of infection and irritation	Diarrhoea	Dysentery

sympathetic and parasympathetic. The midgut territory receives its sympathetic supply from the coeliac and superior mesenteric ganglia (T11 to L1), and its parasympathetic supply from the vagus. Both types of nerves are distributed to the gut through the superior mesenteric plexus.

The hindgut territory receives its sympathetic supply from the lumbar sympathetic chain (L1, L2), and its parasympathetic supply from the pelvic splanchnic nerve (*nervi erigentes*), both via the superior hypogastric and inferior mesenteric plexuses. Some parasympathetic fibres reach the colon along the posterior abdominal wall. The ultimate distribution of nerves in the gut is similar to that in the wall of the small intestine.

The parasympathetic nerves are motor to the large intestine and inhibitory to the internal anal sphincter. The sympathetic nerves are largely vasomotor, but also motor to the internal anal sphincter, and inhibitory to colon. Pain impulses from the gut up to the descending colon travel through the sympathetic nerves, and from the sigmoid colon and rectum through the pelvic splanchnic nerves.

Functions of Colon

The functions of the colon are as follows.
  (a) Lubrication of faeces by mucus.
  (b) Absorption of the water, salts and the other solutes.
  (c) Bacterial flora of colon synthesises vitamin B.
  (d) Mucoid secretion of colon is rich in antibodies of IgA group, which protect it from invasion by microorganisms.
  (e) The microvilli (apical tufts) of some columnar cells serve a sensory function.

CAECUM

Caecum is a large blind sac forming the commencement of the large intestine. It is situated in the right iliac fossa, above the lateral half of inguinal ligament. It communicates superiorly with ascending colon, medially at the level of caecocolic junction with ileum, and posteromedially with the appendix (Fig. 20.11).

Dimensions

It is 6 cm long and 7.5 cm broad. It is one of those organs of the body that have greater width than the length. The other examples are the prostate, pons and pituitary.

Relations

Anterior: Coils of intestine and anterior abdominal wall.

Posterior:
  (a) *Muscles:* Right psoas and iliacus (Fig. 20.12).
  (b) *Nerves:* Genitofemoral, femoral and lateral cutaneous nerve of thigh (all of the right side).
  (c) *Vessels:* Testicular or ovarian.
  (d) Appendix in the retrocaecal recess.

Types

The caecum and appendix develop from the caecal bud arising from the postarterial segment of the midgut loop. The proximal part of the bud dilates to form the caecum. The distal part remains narrow to form the appendix. Thus initially the appendix arises from the apex of the caecum. However, due to rapid growth of the lateral wall of the caecum, the attachment of the appendix shifts medially.

Developmental arrest in the shift of the appendix forms the basis of the types of caeca.

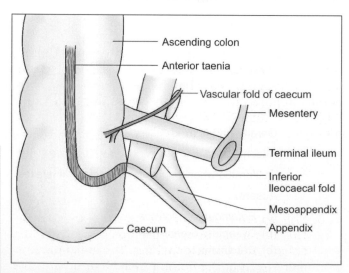

Fig. 20.11: Anterior view of the ileocaecal region.

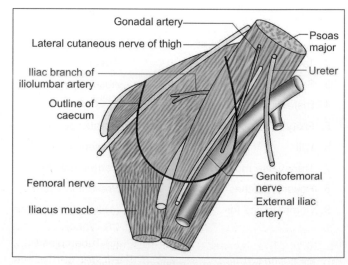

Fig. 20.12: Relations of caecum.

1. *Conical type* (13%), where the appendix arises from the apex of the caecum (Fig. 20.13a).
2. *Intermediate type* (9%), where the right and left caecal pouches are equal in size, and the appendix arises from a depression between them (Fig. 20.13b).
3. *Ampullary type* (78%), where the right caecal pouch is much larger than left, and appendix arises from the medial side (Fig. 20.13c).

It was seen that caecum is mobile in 20% subjects, more often in females than in males.

Vessels and Nerves

The arterial supply of the caecum is derived from the caecal branches of the ileocolic artery. The veins drain into the superior mesenteric vein. The nerve supply is same as that of the midgut (thoracic 11 to lumbar 1; parasympathetic, vagus).

Ileocaecal Valve

The lower end of the ileum opens on the postero-medial aspect of the caecocolic junction. The ileocaecal opening is guarded by the ileocaecal valve (Fig. 20.14).

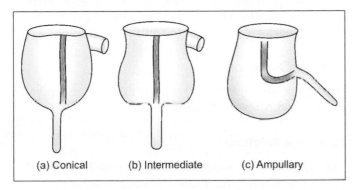

(a) Conical (b) Intermediate (c) Ampullary

Fig. 20.13: Different forms of the caecum.

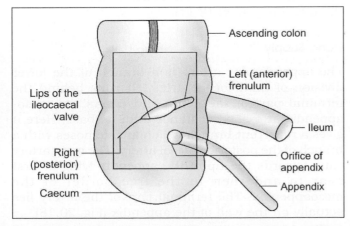

Ascending colon
Left (anterior) frenulum
Lips of the ileocaecal valve
Ileum
Right (posterior) frenulum
Orifice of appendix
Caecum
Appendix

Fig. 20.14: The ileocaecal valve seen after removal of the anterior walls of the caecum and of the lower part of the ascending colon.

Structure

The valve has two lips and two frenula.

1. The *upper lip* is horizontal and lies at the ileocolic junction.
2. The *lower lip* is longer and concave, and lies at the ileocaecal junction.

The two *frenula* are formed by the fusion of the lips at the ends of the aperture. These are the left or anterior and the right or posterior frenula. The left end of the aperture is rounded, and the right end narrow and pointed.

Control and Mechanism

1. The valve is actively closed by sympathetic nerves, which cause tonic contraction of the ileocaecal sphincter.
2. It is mechanically closed by distension of the caecum.

Functions

1. It prevents reflux from caecum to ileum.
2. It regulates the passage of ileal contents into the caecum, and prevents them from passing too quickly.

VERMIFORM APPENDIX

This is a worm-like diverticulum arising from the posteromedial wall, of the caecum, about 2 cm below the ileocaccal orifice (Fig. 20.11).

Dimensions

The length varies from 2 to 20 cm with an average of 9 cm. It is longer in children than in adults. The diameter is about 5 mm. The lumen is quite narrow and may be obliterated after mid-adult life.

Positions

The appendix lies in the right iliac fossa. Although the base of the appendix is fixed, the tip can point in any direction, as described below. The positions are often compared to those of the hour hand of a clock (Figs 20.15 and 20.16).

1. The appendix may pass upwards and to the right. This is paracolic or 11 O'clock position.
2. It may lie behind the caecum or colon, known as retrocaecal or 12 O'clock position. This is the commonest position of appendix, about 65%.
3. The appendix may pass upwards and to the left. It points towards the spleen. This is the splenic or 2 O'clock position. The appendix may lie in front of the ileum (preileal) or behind the ileum (postileal).

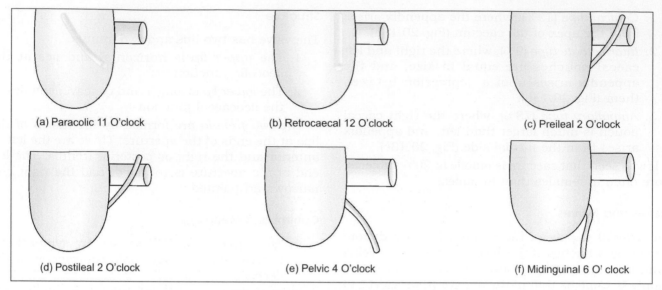

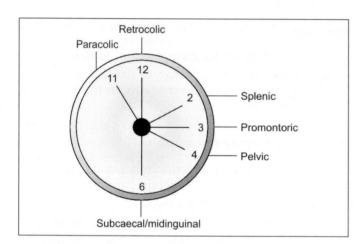

(a) Paracolic 11 O'clock

(b) Retrocaecal 12 O'clock

(c) Preileal 2 O'clock

(d) Postileal 2 O'clock

(e) Pelvic 4 O'clock

(f) Midinguinal 6 O' clock

Fig. 20.15: Positions of the appendix.

Fig. 20.16: Positions of the appendix according to the clock.

4. It may pass horizontally to the left (as if pointing to the sacral promontory called promontoric or 3 O'clock position.

5. It may descend into the pelvis called pelvic or 4 O'clock position. This is the second most common position about 30%.

6. It may lie below the caecum (subcaecal) and may point towards the inguinal ligament called as midinguinal or 6 O'clock position.

Appendicular Orifice

1. The appendicular orifice situated on the posteromedial aspect of the caecum 2 cm below the ileocaecal orifice.

2. The appendicular orifice is occasionally guarded by an indistinct semilunar fold of the mucous membrane, known as the *valve of Gerlach.*

3. The orifice is marked on the surface by a point situated 2 cm below the junction of transtubercular and right lateral planes (Fig. 20.17a).

4. McBurney's point is the site of maximum tenderness in appendicitis. The point lies at the junction of lateral one-third and medial two-thirds of line joining the right anterior superior iliac spine to umbilicus (Fig. 20.17b).

Lumen of Appendix

It is quite small and may be partially or completely obliterated after mid-adult life.

Peritoneal Relations

The appendix is suspended by a small, triangular fold of peritoneum, called the mesoappendix, or appendicular mesentery. The fold passes upwards behind the ileum, and is attached to the left layer of the mesentery (Fig. 18.11).

Blood Supply

The appendicular artery is a branch of the lower division of the ileocolic artery. It runs behind the terminal part of the ileum and enters the mesoappendix at a short distance from its base. Here it gives a recurrent branch which anastomoses with a branch of the posterior caecal artery. The main artery runs towards the tip of the appendix lying at first near to and then in the free border of the mesoappendix. The terminal part of the artery lies actually on the wall of the appendix (Fig. 20.18).

Blood from the appendix is drained by the appendicular, ileocolic and superior mesenteric veins, to the portal vein.

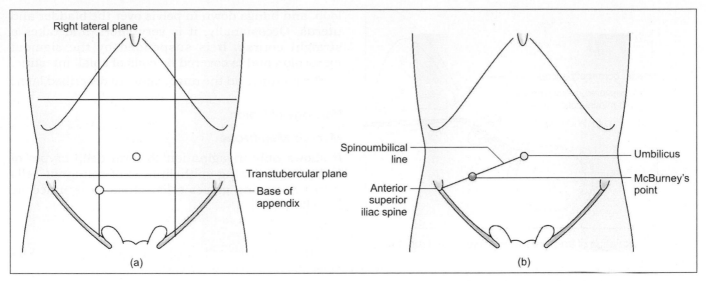

Fig. 20.17: Position of the appendix: (a) The base of the appendix is marked by a point 2 cm below the junction of the transtubercular and right lateral planes, and (b) McBurney's point is the site of maximum tenderness in acute appendicitis.

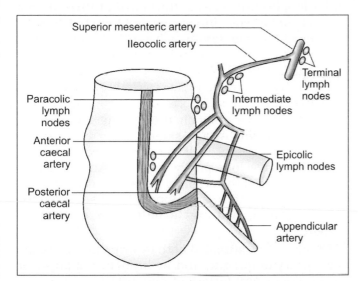

Fig. 20.18: Arterial supply of caecum and appendix. Various groups of lymph nodes are also seen.

Nerve Supply

Sympathetic nerves are derived from thoracic nine and ten segments through the coeliac plexus. Parasympathetic nerves are derived from the vagus. Referred pain of appendix is felt at umbilicus, similar to that of small intestine and testis.

Lymphatic Drainage

Most of the lymphatics pass directly to the ileocolic nodes, but a few of them pass indirectly through the appendicular nodes situated in the meso-appendix.

Histology

The lumen of appendix is very narrow. There are *no villi*. The epithelium invaginates to form crypts of Lieberkuhn. Muscularis mucosae is ill defined.

Submucosa reveals many lymphoid masses. That ·is why it is called the *abdominal tonsil*. *Muscularis externa* comprises two layers. Outermost is the serous layer.

ASCENDING COLON

Ascending colon is about 12.5 cm long and extends from the caecum to the inferior surface of the right lobe of the liver. Here it bends to the left to form the right colic flexure. It is covered by peritoneum on three sides.

Anteriorly, it is related to the coils of small intestine, the right edge of the greater omentum, and the anterior abdominal wall. *Posteriorly*, it is related to the iliacus, the quadratus lumborum, the transversus abdominis, the lateral cutaneous, ilioinguinal, and iliohypogastric nerves and the right kidney.

RIGHT COLIC FLEXURE (HEPATIC FLEXURE)

Right colic flexure lies at the junction of the ascending colon and transverse colon. Here the colon bends forwards, downwards and to the left. The flexure lies on the lower part of right kidney. Antero-superiorly, it is related to the colic impression on inferior surface of the right lobe of liver (Fig. 20.5a).

TRANSVERSE COLON

Transverse colon is about 50 cm long and extend across the abdomen from the right colic flexure to the left colic flexure. Actually it is not transverse, but hangs low as a loop to a variable extent. It is suspended by the transverse mesocolon attached to the anterior border of pancreas, and has a wide range of mobility (Fig. 20.19).

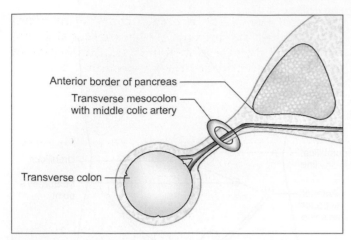

Fig. 20.19: Relation of transverse mesocolon to anterior border of pancreas.

Anteriorly, it is related to the greater omentum and to the anterior abdominal wall. *Posteriorly*, it is related to the second part of the duodenum, the head of the pancreas, and to coils of small intestine.

LEFT COLIC FLEXURE (SPLENIC FLEXURE)

Left colic flexure lies at the junction of the transverse colon and the descending colon. Here the colon bends downwards, and backwards. The flexure lies on the lower part of the left kidney and diaphragm, behind the stomach, and below the anterior end of the spleen (Fig. 23.7). The flexure is attached to the eleventh rib (in the midaxillary line) by a horizontal fold of peritoneum, called the *phrenicocolic ligament*. This ligament supports the spleen and forms a partial upper limit of the left paracolic gutter.

DESCENDING COLON

Descending colon is about 25 cm long and extends from the left colic flexure to the sigmoid colon. It runs vertically up to the iliac crest, and then inclines medially on the iliacus and psoas major to reach the pelvic brim, where it is continuous with the sigmoid colon. The descending colon is narrower than the ascending colon.

Anteriorly, it is related to the coils of small intestine. *Posteriorly*, it is related to the transversus abdominis, the quadratus lumborum, the iliacus and psoas muscles; the iliohypogastric, ilioinguinal, lateral cutaneous, femoral and genitofemoral nerves; the gonadal and external iliac vessels (Fig. 27.2).

SIGMOID COLON (PELVIC COLON)

Sigmoid colon is about 37.5 cm long, and extends from the pelvic brim to the third piece of the sacrum, where it becomes the rectum. It forms a sinuous loop, and hangs down in pelvis over the bladder and uterus. Occasionally, it is very short, and takes a straight course. It is suspended by the sigmoid mesocolon and is covered by coils of small intestine.

The rectum and the anal canal are described later.

Histology of Colon

Mucous Membrane

It shows only invagination to form deep crypts of Lieberkuhn. Lining epithelium is of columnar cells with intervening goblet cells. Muscularis mucosae is well defined.

Submucosa

Contains solitary lymphoid follicles with the Meissner's plexus of nerves.

Muscularis Externa

Outer longitudinal coat is thickened at three places to form taenia coli. Inner coat is of circular fibres. *Outermost layer* is serous/adventitia.

Development

Duodenum

During rotation of stomach, the C-shaped duodenum falls to the right. At the same time it lies against posterior abdominal wall and gets retroperitoneal. Duodenum develops partly from foregut and partly from midgut. Till the origin of hepatic bud it develops from foregut, i.e. first and upper half of second part. The remaining two and a half parts arise from midgut.

Duodenum is supplied both by branches of coeliac axis (artery of foregut) and by branches of superior mesenteric artery (artery of midgut).

Midgut

It gives rise to the part of duodenum distal to the opening of bile duct, jejunum, ileum, caecum, vermiform appendix, ascending colon, hepatic flexure and right two-thirds of transverse colon.

Midgut is in the form of primary intestinal loop. At the apex of the loop it is connected to the yolk sac and grows very rapidly during 6th week, so much so that it protrudes into the umbilical cord. This is called *physiological herniation*. After an interval of 4 weeks, i.e. at 10th week it returns back into the enlarged abdominal cavity. During this herniation and return the midgut loop rotates by 270° in a counter clockwise direction.

Hindgut

Its cranial part gives rise to left one-third of transverse colon, descending colon, pelvic colon, proximal part of rectum. The distal part of hindgut is dilated to form the cloaca, which gets separated by urorectal septum into a posterior part—the anorectal canal and an anterior part—the primitive urogenital sinus. The anorectal canal forms distal part of rectum and proximal part of anal canal. Distal part of anal canal is formed from an invagination of surface ectoderm called the proctodeum.

CLINICAL ANATOMY

- In the skiagrams taken after giving a barium meal, the first part of the duodenum is seen as a triangular shadow called the duodenal cap (Fig. 20.20).

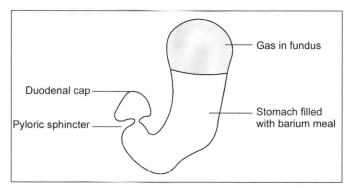

Fig. 20.20: Line drawing of radiograph of the stomach after barium meal.

- The first part of the duodenum is one of the commonest sites for peptic ulcer, possibly because of direct exposure of this part to the acidic contents reaching it from the stomach (Fig. 20.20).

  The patient is usually an over busy young person with a tense temperament. The ulcer pain located at the right half of epigastrium is relieved by meals and reappears on an empty stomach.

- The first part of duodenum is overlapped by the liver and gall bladder, either of which may become adherent to, or even ulcerated by a duodenal ulcer. Other clinically important relations of duodenum are the right kidney and transverse colon (Fig. 20.5).

- Duodenal diverticula are fairly frequent. They are seen along its concave border, generally at points where arteries enter the duodenal wall.

- Congenital stenosis and obstruction of the second part of the duodenum may occur at the site of the opening of the bile duct. Other causes of obstruction are:

  (a) An annular pancreas.

  (b) Pressure by the superior mesenteric artery (Fig. 20.21).

  (c) Contraction of the suspensory muscle of the duodenum.

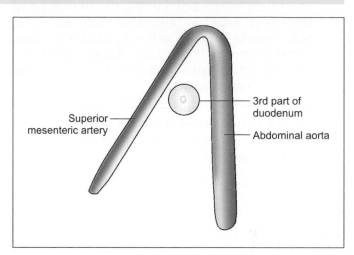

Fig. 20.21: Obstruction of third part of the duodenum between the two arteries.

- Meckel's diverticulum may cause intestinal obstruction (Fig. 20.10).

- Occasionally it may have small regions of gastric mucosa.

- Acute inflammation of the diverticulum may produce symptoms that resemble those of appendicitis.

- It may be involved in other diseases similar to those of the intestine.

- Caecum is commonly involved in:

  (a) Amoebiasis, causing amoebic dysentery.

  (b) Intestinal tuberculosis (ileocaecal tuberculosis) and carcinoma.

  (c) Inflammation of caecum is known as caecitis or typhlitis.

- Inflammation of the appendix is known as appendicitis. In this condition, it is usually necessary to remove the appendix. The operation for removal of the appendix is called *appen-dicectomy*. Some anatomical facts relevant to the diagnosis and treatment of appendicitis are as follows.

- Pain caused by appendicitis is first felt in the region of the umbilicus. This is referred pain. Note the fact that both the appendix and the umbilicus are innervated by segment T10 of the spinal cord; appendix by sympathetic fibres and umbilicus by somatic fibres. With increasing inflammation pain is felt in the right iliac fossa.

This is caused by involvement of the parietal peritoneum of the region (remember that parietal peritoneum is sensitive to pain, but visceral peritoneum is not).

- *McBurney's point* is the site of maximum tenderness in appendicitis. The point lies at the junction of the lateral one-third and the medial two-thirds of the line joining the umbilicus to the right anterior superior iliac spine. It corresponds, roughly, to the position of the base of the appendix (Fig. 20.22). Examination of a case of acute appendicitis reveals following physical signs.

  (a) Hyperaesthesia in the right iliac fossa

  (b) Tenderness at McBurney's point

  (c) Muscle guard and rebound tenderness over the appendix.

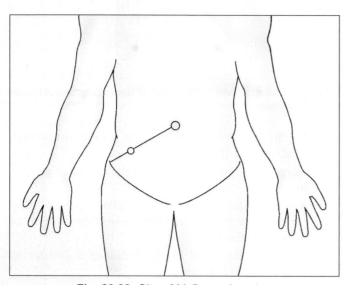

Fig. 20.22: Site of McBurney's point.

- When the appendix is retrocaecal, extension of the hip joint may cause pain because the appendix is disturbed by stretching of the psoas major muscle (Fig. 20.23).

- In pelvic appendicitis pain may be felt when the thigh is flexed and medially rotated, because the obturator internus is stretched.

- *Appendicular dyspepsia:* Chronic appendicitis produces dyspepsia resembling disease of stomach, duodenum or gall bladder. It is due to passage of infected lymph to the subpyloric nodes which cause irritation of pylorus. There is history of earlier acute appendicitis.

- Large intestine can be directly viewed by a procedure called colonoscopy (Fig. 20.24).

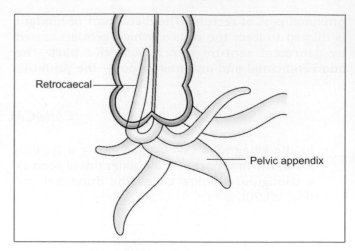

Fig. 20.23: Positions of appendix.

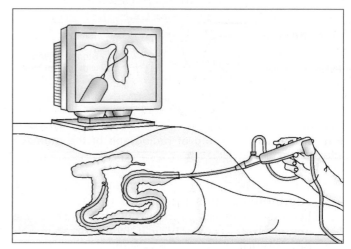

Fig. 20.24: Colonoscopy.

- Diverticulum is a small evagination of mucous membrane of colon at the entry point of the arteries. Its inflammation is called diverticulitis (Fig. 20.25).

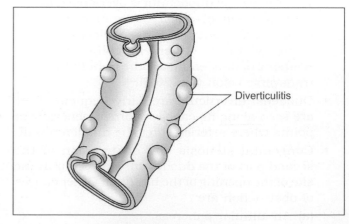

Fig. 20.25: Diverticulitis.

Large Blood Vessels of the Gut

The three ventral branches of the abdominal aorta are coeliac trunk, superior mesenteric and inferior mesenteric arteries. These are the arteries of the foregut, midgut and hindgut, respectively. There is anastomoses between the branches of these three main arteries.

Portal vein, laden with the products of absorption of carbohydrate and proteins, enters the gateway of liver and deposits them in liver for timely utilisation. Tributaries of portal vein also anastomose with the tributaries of superior vena cava and those of the inferior vena cava. These are called portosystemic anastomoses. Liver cellular disease leading to fibrosis causes disturbance and obstruction in portal vein circulation. In such cases these anastomoses open up to bring the portal blood into the systemic circulation. These anastomoses at sites like umbilicus, lower end of oesophagus and in anal canal produce distinct clinical symptoms.

In this chapter we will consider the coeliac trunk, the superior and inferior mesenteric vessels, and the portal vein.

COELIAC TRUNK

The coeliac trunk is the artery of the foregut (Figs 21.1 and 21.2). It supplies all derivatives of the foregut that lie in the abdomen namely:

1. The lower end of the oesophagus, the stomach and upper part of the duodenum up to the opening of the common bile duct.
2. Liver
3. Spleen
4. Greater part of the pancreas.

Origin and Length

The coeliac trunk arises from the front of the abdominal aorta just below the aortic opening of the diaphragm at the level of the disc between vertebrae

thoracic twelve and first lumbar. The trunk is only about 1.25 cm long. It ends by dividing into its three terminal branches, namely the left gastric, hepatic and splenic arteries (Figs 21.3, 21.4 and 21.5).

Relations

1. It is surrounded by the coeliac plexus of nerves (Fig. 27.4).
2. Anteriorly, it is related to the lesser sac and to the lesser omentum (Fig. 21.2).
3. To its right, there are the right crus of the diaphragm, the right coeliac ganglion and the caudate process of the liver.
4. To its left, there are the left crus of the diaphragm, the left coeliac ganglion and the cardiac end of the stomach.
5. Inferiorly, it is related to the body of the pancreas and to the splenic vein (Fig. 21.2).

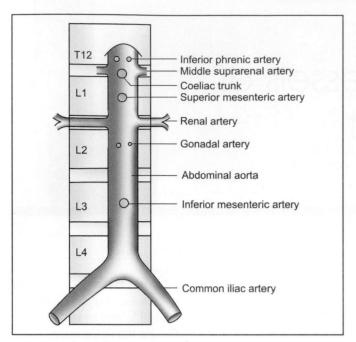

Fig. 21.1: Ventral and lateral branches of the abdominal aorta with their levels of origin.

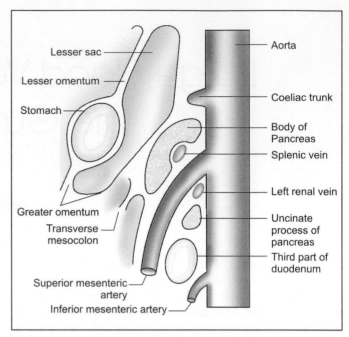

Fig. 21.2: Left view of a sagittal section through the abdominal aorta showing the origin of its three ventral branches.

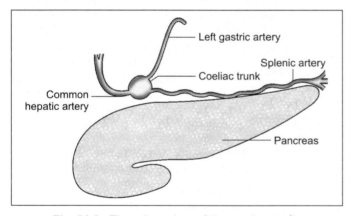

Fig. 21.3: Three branches of the coeliac trunk.

Branches

Left Gastric Artery

The *left gastric artery* is the smallest of the three branches of the coeliac trunk. It runs upwards to the left behind the lesser sac to reach the cardiac end of the stomach where it turns forwards and enters the lesser omentum to run downwards along the lesser curvature of the stomach. It ends by anastomosing with the right gastric artery.

It gives off:

(a) Two or three *oesophageal branches* at the cardiac end of the stomach.

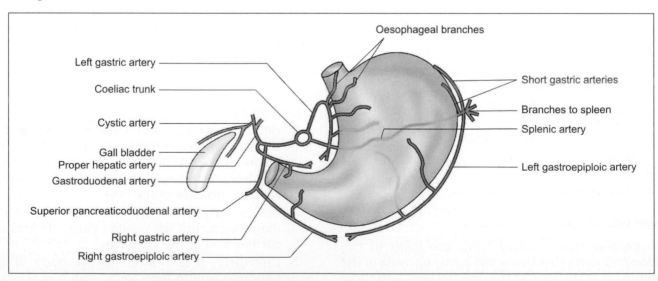

Fig. 21.4: Arteries arising from the branches of the coeliac trunk.

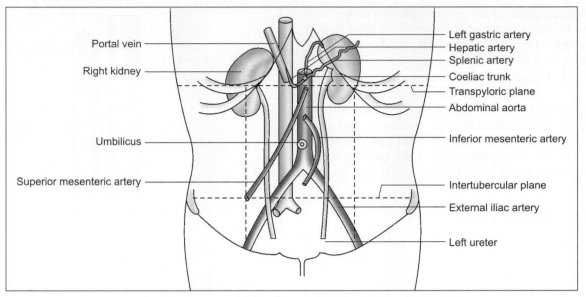

Fig. 21.5: Position of various blood vessels and kidneys.

(b) Numerous *gastric branches* along the lesser curvature of the stomach (Fig. 21.4).

Common Hepatic Artery

The *common hepatic artery* runs downwards, forwards and to the right, behind the lesser sac to reach the upper border of the duodenum. Here it enters the lesser omentum. It then run upwards in the right free margin of the lesser omentum, in front of the portal vein, and to the left of the bile duct (Figs 20.4 and 21.3). Reaching the porta hepatis it terminates by dividing into right and left hepatic branches.

Branches

(a) The *gastroduodenal artery* is a large branch which arises at the upper border of the first part of the duodenum. The part of the hepatic artery till the origin of the gastroduodenal artery is called the *common hepatic artery*. The part distal to it is the *proper hepatic artery*.

The gastroduodenal artery runs downwards behind the first part of the duodenum and divides at its lower border into the right gastroepiploic and superior pancreaticoduodenal arteries.

The *right gastroepiploic artery* enters the greater omentum, follows the greater curvature of the stomach, and anastomoses with the left gastroepiploic artery.

The *superior pancreaticoduodenal artery* (often represented by two arteries anterior and posterior) runs downwards in the pancreaticoduodenal groove, and ends by anastomosing with the inferior pancreaticoduodenal artery, a branch of the superior mesenteric.

(b) The *right gastric artery* is a small branch which arises from the proper hepatic artery close to the gastroduodenal artery. It runs to the left along the lesser curvature and ends by anastomosing with the left gastric artery.

(c) The *cystic artery* is a branch of the right hepatic artery. It passes behind the common hepatic and cystic ducts to reach the upper surface of the neck of the gall bladder where it divides into superficial and deep branches for the inferior and superior surfaces of the gall bladder, respectively.

Splenic Artery

The *splenic artery* is the largest branch of the coeliac trunk. It runs horizontally to the left along the upper border of the pancreas behind the lesser sac. It crosses the left suprarenal gland and the upper part of the left kidney to enter the lienorenal ligament, through which it reaches the hilum of spleen where it divides into 5 to 7 splenic branches (Figs 19.5, 21.3 and 21.4).

Branches

It gives off the following branches.

(a) Numerous *pancreatic branches* which supply the body and tail of the pancreas. One of the branches to the body of the pancreas is large and is known as the *arteria pancreatica magna*. Another large branch to the tail is known as the *arteria caudae pancreatis*. These large arteries anastomose (on the back of the pancreas) with the left branch of a *dorsal artery* which may arise from one of the following arteries: superior mesenteric, middle colic, hepatic, or coeliac.

(b) Five to seven *short gastric arteries* arise from the terminal part of the splenic artery, run in the gastrosplenic ligament, and supply the fundus of the stomach.

(c) The *left gastroepiploic artery* also arises from the terminal part of the splenic artery, runs downwards in the greater omentum, follows the greater curvature of the stomach, and ends by anastomosing with the right gastroepiploic artery. As the name suggests the gastroepiploic arteries supply both the stomach and greater omentum.

SUPERIOR MESENTERIC ARTERY

The superior mesenteric artery is the artery of the midgut. It supplies all derivatives of the midgut, namely:

1. Lower part of the duodenum below the opening of the bile duct.
2. Jejunum
3. Ileum
4. Appendix
5. Caecum
6. Ascending colon
7. Right two-thirds of the transverse colon
8. Lower half of the head of the pancreas (Figs 21.2 and 21.3).

Origin, Course and Termination

The superior mesenteric artery arises from the front of the abdominal aorta, behind the body of the pancreas, at the level of vertebra L1, one centimeter below the coeliac trunk (Fig. 21.6). It runs downwards and to the right, forming a curve with its convexity towards the left.

At its origin it lies first behind the body of the pancreas and then in front of the uncinate process. Next it crosses the third part of the duodenum, enters the root of mesentery, and runs between its two layers. It terminates in the right iliac fossa by anastomosing with a branch of the ileocolic artery.

Relations

Above the Root of the Mesentery

(a) *Anteriorly*, it is related to the body of the pancreas and to the splenic vein.
(b) *Posteriorly*, to the aorta, the left renal vein, the uncinate process and the third part of the duodenum (Fig. 21.7).

Within the Root of the Mesentery

It *crosses* the inferior vena cava, and the right psoas. Throughout its course it is accompanied by the

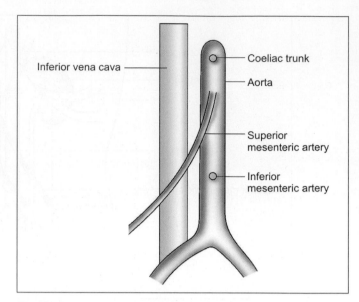

Fig. 21.6: Anterior view of the course of the superior mesenteric artery.

superior mesenteric vein which lies on its right side. The artery is surrounded by the superior mesenteric plexus of nerves.

Branches

The superior mesenteric artery gives off five sets of branches both from its right and left sides. Those arising from its right side are:

1. Inferior pancreaticoduodenal
2. Middle colic
3. Right colic
4. Ileocolic.

Those arising from its left side are 12–15 jejunal and ileal branches (Fig. 21.8).

Inferior Pancreaticoduodenal Artery

Inferior pancreaticoduodenal artery arises from the superior mesenteric artery at the upper border of the third part of the duodenum. The artery soon divides into anterior and posterior branches which run in the pancreaticoduodenal groove, supply the head of the pancreas and the duodenum, and ends by anastomosing with the superior pancreaticoduodenal artery.

Middle Colic Artery

Middle colic artery arises from the right side of the superior mesenteric artery just below the pancreas. It runs downwards and forwards in the transverse mesocolon. It divides into a right branch, which anastomoses with the right colic artery, and a left branch, which anastomoses with the left colic artery. Further branches arising from these, form arcades and supply the transverse colon.

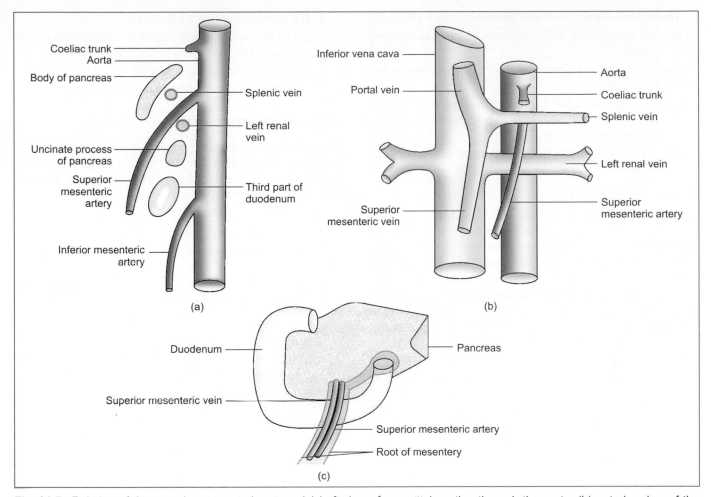

Fig. 21.7: Relation of the superior mesenteric artery. (a) Left view of a sagittal section through the aorta, (b) anterior view of the vessel after removal of the duodenum and pancreas, and (c) anterior view of the vessel with the duodenum and pancreas in place.

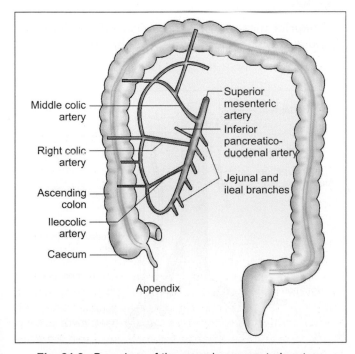

Fig. 21.8: Branches of the superior mesenteric artery.

Right Colic Artery

Right colic artery arises near the middle of the concavity of the superior mesenteric artery. It passes to the right behind the peritoneum, and at the upper part of the ascending colon it divides into a descending branch, which anastomoses with the ileocolic artery, and an ascending branch, which anastomoses with the middle colic artery. The branches form arch, from the convexity of which smaller branches are distributed to the upper two thirds of the ascending colon and the right flexure of the colon.

Ileocolic Artery

Ileocolic artery arises from the right side of the superior mesenteric artery. It runs downwards and to the right, and divides into superior and inferior branches. The superior branch anastomoses with the right colic artery, and the inferior branch anastomoses with the termination of the superior mesenteric artery.

The inferior branch of the ileocolic artery gives off:

(a) An ascending colic branch to the ascending colon.

(b) Anterior and posterior caecal branches to the caecum.

(c) An appendicular branch which passes behind the ileum and reaches the appendix through its mesentery (Fig. 20.18).

(d) The ileal branch to the terminal portion of the ileum.

Jejunal and Ileal Branches

Jejunal and ileal branches are about 12 to 15 in number and arise from the left side of the superior mesenteric artery. They run between the two layers of the mesentery towards the gut. They anastomose with one another to form arterial arcades which give off straight branches or vasa recta to the gut. These branches supply the jejunum (Fig. 21.9a) and most of ileum (Fig. 21.9b). The terminal part of the ileum is supplied by the ileocolic artery.

On passing from jejunum to ileum, the number of arterial arcades increases from one to as many as five. The vasa recta are longer and less numerous in the jejunum than in the ileum. These are distributed alternately to opposite surfaces of the gut, and the neighbouring vessels do not anastomose with one another.

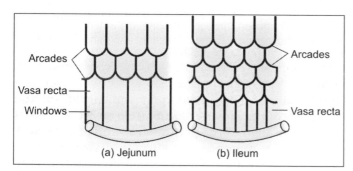

Fig. 21.9: Arterial arcades and vasa recta.

SUPERIOR MESENTERIC VEIN

1. Superior mesenteric vein is a large vein which drains blood from the small intestine, the appendix, the caecum, the ascending colon and the transverse colon.

2. It begins in the right iliac fossa by the union of tributaries from the ileocaecal region. It accompanies the superior mesenteric artery. The vein lies on the right side of the artery. It terminates, behind the neck of the pancreas, by joining the splenic vein to form the portal vein.

3. Its *tributaries* are as follows.

(a) Veins corresponding to the branches of the superior mesenteric artery.

(b) Right gastroepiploic vein.

(c) Inferior pancreaticoduodenal vein.

INFERIOR MESENTERIC ARTERY

The inferior mesenteric artery is the artery of the hindgut. It supplies the parts of the gut that are derivatives of the hindgut and posterior part of cloaca, the anorectal canal, namely:

1. The left one-third of the transverse colon

2. The descending colon

3. The sigmoid colon

4. The rectum

5. The upper part of the anal canal, above the anal valves.

Origin

Inferior mesenteric artery arises from the front of the abdominal aorta behind the third part of the duodenum, at the level of third lumbar vertebra, and 3 to 4 cm above the bifurcation of the aorta.

Course and Termination

It runs downwards and to the left, behind the peritoneum, crosses the common iliac artery medial to the left ureter, and continues in the sigmoid mesocolon as the superior rectal artery (Fig. 21.10).

Branches

The inferior mesenteric artery gives off the left colic, sigmoid and superior rectal branches (Fig. 21.11).

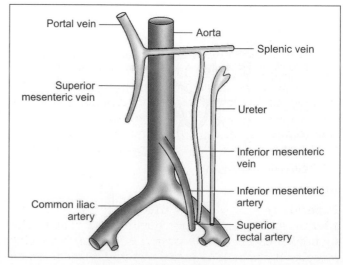

Fig. 21.10: Course of the inferior mesenteric vessels.

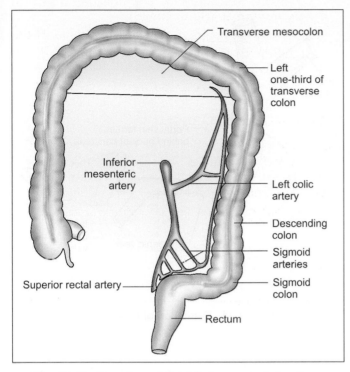

Fig. 21.11: Branches of the inferior mesenteric artery.

Left Colic Artery

Left colic artery is the first branch of the inferior mesenteric artery. It runs upwards and to the left, behind the peritoneum of the posterior wall of the left infracolic compartment and after a variable course divides into an ascending and a descending branch. The ascending branch enters the transverse mesocolon and anastomoses with the middle colic artery. The descending branch anastomoses with the highest sigmoid artery. They form a part of the marginal artery from which branches are distributed to the left one-third of the transverse colon and to the descending colon (Fig. 21.11).

Sigmoid Arteries

Sigmoid arteries are 2 to 4 in number. They pass downwards and to the left, and anastomose with each other to form the lower part of the marginal artery. The uppermost branch anastomoses with the descending branch of the left colic artery, whereas the lowest sigmoid artery sends a branch to anastomose with the superior rectal artery. They supply the descending colon in the iliac fossa and the sigmoid colon.

Superior Rectal Artery

Superior rectal artery is the continuation of the inferior mesenteric artery beyond the root of the sigmoid mesocolon, i.e. over the left common iliac vessels. It descends in the sigmoid mesocolon to reach the rectum. Opposite third sacral vertebra it

divides into right and left branches which descend one on each side of the rectum. They pierce the muscular coat of the rectum and divide into several branches, which anastomose with one another at the level of the anal sphincter to form loops around the lower end of the rectum. These branches communicate with the middle and inferior rectal arteries in the submucosa of the anal canal (Fig. 21.11).

INFERIOR MESENTERIC VEIN

1. The inferior mesenteric vein drains blood from the rectum, the anal canal, the sigmoid colon and the descending colon.
2. It begins as the *superior rectal vein* from the upper part of the internal rectal venous plexus. In the plexus it communicates with the middle and inferior rectal veins. The superior rectal vein crosses the left common iliac vessels medial to the left ureter and continues upwards as the inferior mesenteric vein. This vein lies lateral to the inferior mesenteric artery. The vein ascends behind the peritoneum, passes lateral to the duodenojejunal flexure and behind the body of the pancreas. It opens into the splenic vein (Fig. 21.10).
3. Its *tributaries* correspond to the branches of the inferior mesenteric artery.

MARGINAL ARTERY

Marginal artery was described by Von Haller in 1803 and its present name was given by Sudeck in 1907. The marginal artery is an arterial arcade situated along the concavity of the colon. It is formed by anastomoses between the main arteries supplying the colon, namely the ileocolic, right colic, middle colic, left colic and sigmoid arteries. It lies at a distance of 2.5 to 3.8 cm from the colon. It is closest to the colon in its descending and sigmoid parts. Vasa recta arise from the marginal artery and supply the colon (Fig. 21.12).

The marginal artery is capable of supplying the colon even in the absence of one of the main feeding trunks. This fact is utilized in surgery. However, at the junctional points between the main vessels, there may be variations in the competence of the anastomoses.

PORTAL VEIN

Portal vein is a large vein which collects blood from:
(a) The abdominal part of the alimentary tract
(b) The gall bladder
(c) The pancreas
(d) The spleen, and conveys it to the liver. In the liver, the portal vein breaks up into sinusoids

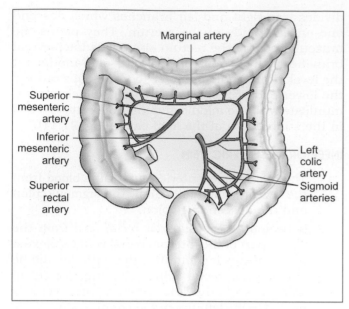

Fig. 21.12: The marginal artery.

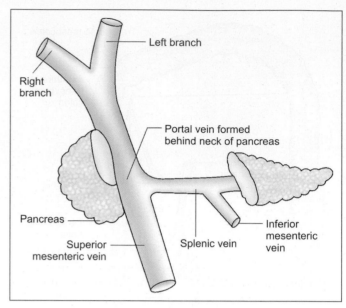

Fig. 21.14: Formation of portal vein.

which are drained by the hepatic veins to the inferior vena cava (Figs 21.13 and 21.14).

It is called the portal vein because its main tributary, the superior mesenteric vein, begins in one set of capillaries (in the gut) and the portal vein ends in another set of capillaries in the liver.

Formation

The portal vein is about 8 cm long. It is formed by the union of the superior mesenteric and splenic veins behind the neck of the pancreas at the level of second lumbar vertebra. Inferior mesenteric vein drains into splenic vein.

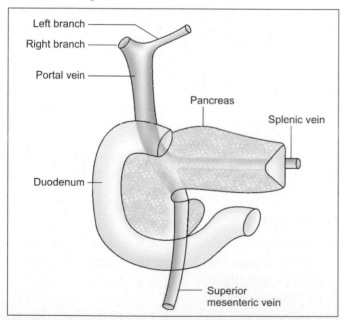

Fig. 21.13: Formation and course of the portal vein.

Course

It runs upwards and a little to the right, first behind the neck of the pancreas, next behind the first part of the duodenum, and lastly in the right free margin of the lesser omentum.

The blood flow in portal vein is slow. Blood of superior mesenteric vein drains into right lobe. Blood of splenic and inferior mesenteric vein drains into left lobe. This is called "streamline flow".

The portal vein can thus be divided into infra-duodenal, retroduodenal and supraduodenal parts.

Termination

The vein ends at the right end of the porta hepatis by dividing into right and left branches which enter the liver.

Relations

Infraduodenal Part

Anteriorly: Neck of pancreas.

Posteriorly: Inferior vena cava (Figs 20.4 and 21.15).

Retroduodenal Part

Anteriorly:

(a) First part of duodenum

(b) Bile duct

(c) Gastroduodenal artery.

Posteriorly: Inferior vena cava (Fig. 20.4).

Supraduodenal Part

Anteriorly:

(a) Hepatic artery

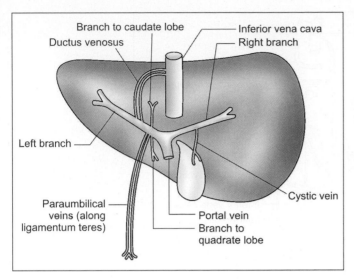

Fig. 21.15: The portal vein, its communications and branches.

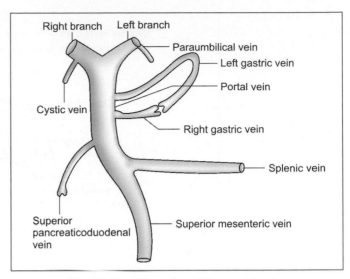

Fig. 21.16: Tributaries of the portal vein.

(b) Bile duct (within free margin of the lesser omentum).

Posteriorly: Inferior vena cava, separated by epiploic foramen (Fig. 18.9).

Branches of Portal Vein

1. The *right branch* is shorter and wider than the left branch. After receiving the cystic vein, it enters the right lobe of the liver (Fig. 21.16).

2. The left branch is longer and narrower than the right branch. It traverses the porta hepatis from its right end to the left end, and furnishes branches to the caudate and quadrate lobes. Just before entering the left lobe of the liver, it receives:
   (a) Paraumbilical veins along the ligamentum teres.
   (b) Ligamentum venosum.

Intrahepatic Course

After entering the liver, each branch divides and redivides along with the hepatic artery to end ultimately in the hepatic sinusoids, where the portal venous blood mixes with the hepatic arterial blood.

Tributaries

Portal vein receives the following veins.
   (i) Splenic
   (ii) Superior mesenteric
   (iii) Left gastric
   (iv) Right gastric
   (v) Superior pancreaticoduodenal
   (vi) Cystic
   (vii) Paraumbilical veins (Fig. 21.16).

The left gastric vein accompanies the corresponding artery. At the cardiac end of the stomach it receives a few oesophageal veins. The right gastric vein accompanies the corresponding artery. It receives the prepyloric vein.

The paraumbilical veins are small veins that run in the falciform ligament, along the ligamentum teres, and establish anastomoses between the veins of the anterior abdominal wall present around the umbilicus and the portal vein.

PORTOSYSTEMIC COMMUNICATIONS (PORTOCAVAL ANASTOMOSES)

These communications form important routes of collateral circulation in portal obstruction. The following are the important sites of portosystemic communications.

1. ***Umbilicus:*** The left branch of the portal vein anastomoses with the veins of the anterior abdominal wall (systemic) through the paraumbilical veins (Fig. 21.17). In portal obstruction the veins around the umbilicus enlarge forming the *caput medusae* (Fig. 16.7a).

2. ***Lower end of oesophagus:*** Oesophageal tributaries of the left gastric vein (portal) anastomose with the oesophageal tributaries of the accessory hemiazygos vein (systemic).

3. ***Anal canal:*** The superior rectal vein (portal) anastomoses with the middle and inferior rectal veins (systemic) as shown in Figs 21.17 and 21.18.

4. ***Bare area of the liver:*** Hepatic venules (portal) anastomose with the phrenic and intercostal veins (systemic).

5. ***Posterior abdominal wall:*** Veins of retroperitoneal organs, like the duodenum, the

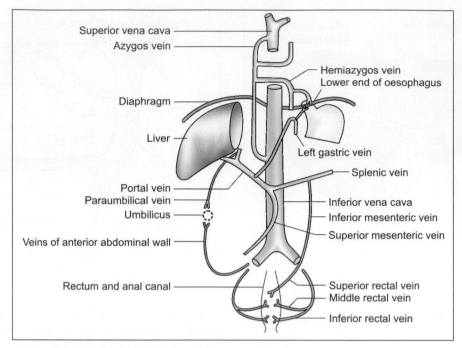

Fig. 21.17: Important sites of communication of portal and systemic veins: 1. Lower end of oesophagus, 2. around umbilicus 3. anal canal.

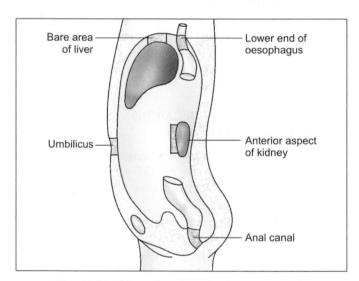

Fig. 21.18: Sites of portosystemic anastomosis.

ascending colon and the descending colon (portal) anastomose with the retroperitoneal veins of the abdominal wall and of the renal capsule (systemic).

6. *Liver:* Rarely, the ductus venosus remains patent and connects the left branch of the portal vein directly to the inferior vena cava.

DEVELOPMENT

Portal vein develops from the following sources.

1. Infraduodenal part, from a part of the left vitelline vein distal to the dorsal anastomosis.
2. Retroduodenal part, from the dorsal anastomosis between the two vitelline veins.
3. Supraduodenal part, from the cranial part of the right vitelline vein.

CLINICAL ANATOMY

- Acquired diverticula of small intestine are more common in upper jejunum. They occur on the side of the mesenteric border at the site of the entry of the vasa recta. Vulnerability of jejunum is due to relative weakness or occasional absence of the longitudinal muscle coat (Fig. 20.25).
- Sudden occlusion of the superior mesenteric artery, vein or both may occur due to embolism or thrombosis. It is usually followed by a rapidly spreading form of intestinal obstruction due to

the haemorrhagic infarction of the involved gut.
- *Portal pressure:* Normal pressure in the portal vein is about 5–15 mm Hg. It is usually measured by splenic puncture and recording the intrasplenic pressure.
- *Portal hypertension* (pressure above 40 mm Hg): It can be caused by the following.
  (a) Cirrhosis of liver, in which the vascular bed of liver is markedly obliterated.

(b) Banti's disease

(c) Thrombosis of portal vein.

The effects of portal hypertension are as follows.

(a) Congestive splenomegaly

(b) Ascites

(c) Collateral circulation through the porto-systemic communications. It forms

   (i) Caput medusae around the umbilicus, which is of diagnostic value to the clinician (Fig. 16.7a).

   (ii) Oesophageal varices at the lower end of oesophagus which may rupture and cause dangerous or even fatal haematemesis (Fig. 19.9).

   (iii) Haemorrhoids in the anal canal may be responsible for repeated bleeding per rectum (Fig. 33.9).

In cases of cirrhosis of liver, sometimes a shunt operation is done, where one of the main portal channels (splenic, superior mesenteric, or portal vein) is directly anastomosed with either inferior vena cava or the left renal vein (Fig. 21.19). But the greatest hazard of such an operation is the hepatic coma, possibly due to toxic effects of ammonia on brain. Normally, the ammonia absorbed from intestines is deaminated in the liver, but after the shunt operation, it passes as such in the general circulation.

- Superior mesenteric artery crosses third part of duodenum (Fig. 20.21). This part of duodenum may get obstructed as it lies between abdominal aorta and superior mesenteric artery. Duodenum behaves like a nut between the two tongs formed by these two arteries.

- Since the blood flow in portal vein is slow, and streamlined, the toxic infective substances absorbed from small intestine pass via the superior mesenteric vein into the right lobe of liver leading to toxic changes or amoebic abscess in right lobe. The lack of amino acids, etc. which are absorbed via the inferior mesenteric vein affect the left lobe, leading to its fibrosis or cirrhosis (Fig. 21.20).

Inferior mesenteric vein lies in the free margin of paraduodenal fold before draining into splenic vein. In case of strangulated internal hernia in

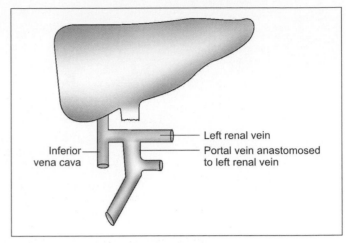

Fig. 21.19: Shunt operation between left renal vein and portal vein.

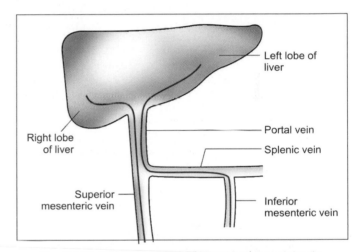

Fig. 21.20: Streamline flow of blood in the portal vein.

duodenojejunal recess these folds may be cut to enlarge the space. One needs to remember that inferior mesenteric vein (not the artery) lies in the fold, and it needs to be ligated (Fig. 18.29).

- The lower end oesophagus is one of the sites of portocaval anastomoses. Some oesophageal veins drain into left gastric vein and then into portal vein. Other oesophageal veins drain into hemiazygos and then into vena azygos and superior vena cava. In liver cirrhosis portal vein presssure is raised, leading to oesophageal varices, which may rupture leading to haematemesis (Fig. 19.9).

Extrahepatic Biliary Apparatus

The components of extrahepatic biliary apparatus are important from clinical aspects. Since gall bladder concentrates the bile and stores it, it is vulnerable for gall stones. These small but usually numerous stones cause referred pain and other problems. There is a lot of variation in the pattern of ducts and their termination and in their arterial supply as well. These need to be revised before surgery is undertaken in this area.

INTRODUCTION

The biliary apparatus collects bile from the liver, stores it in the gall bladder, and transmits it to the 2nd part of duodenum. The apparatus consists of:

1. Right and left hepatic ducts,
2. Common hepatic duct,
3. Gall bladder,
4. Cystic duct, and
5. Bile duct (Fig. 22.1).

HEPATIC DUCTS

The right and left hepatic ducts emerge at the porta hepatis from the right and left lobes of the liver. The arrangement of structures at the porta hepatis from behind forwards is:

(i) Branches of the portal vein,

DISSECTION

Locate the porta hepatis on the inferior surface of liver. Look for two hepatic ducts there. Follow them till these join to form common hepatic duct. Identify cystic duct and usually green-coloured gall bladder.

See the point of junction of cystic duct with common hepatic duct and the formation of bile duct. Trace the bile duct in relation to the duodenum. Its opening has been seen in dissection of the duodenum. Trace the cystic artery supplying gall bladder, cystic duct, hepatic ducts and upper part of bile duct.

(ii) Hepatic artery, and
(iii) Hepatic ducts (Fig. 22.2).

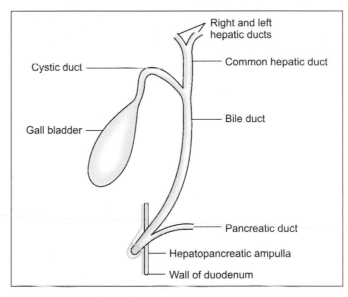

Fig. 22.1: Parts of the biliary apparatus.

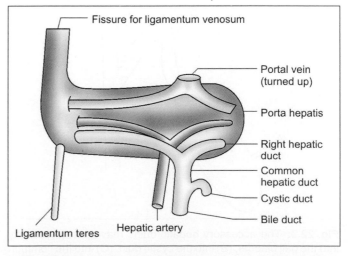

Fig. 22.2: Arrangement of structures in the porta hepatis.

Common Hepatic Duct

It is formed by the union of the right and left hepatic ducts near the right end of the porta hepatis. It runs downwards for about 3 cm and is joined on its right side at an acute angle by the cystic duct to form the bile duct.

Accessory hepatic ducts are present in about 15% of subjects. They usually issue from the right lobe of the liver, and terminate either in the gall bladder, or in the common hepatic duct anywhere in its course, or even in the upper part of the bile duct (Fig. 22.3).

They are responsible for oozing of bile from the wound after cholecystectomy. Therefore, it is always better to use a drain to avoid retention of bile in the depths of the wound.

GALL BLADDER

Gall bladder is a pear-shaped reservoir of bile situated in a fossa on the inferior surface of the right lobe of the liver. The fossa for the gall bladder extends from the right end of the porta hepatis to the inferior border of the liver (Figs 22.1 and 22.4).

Dimensions and Capacity

The gall bladder is 7 to 10 cm long, 3 cm broad at its widest part, and about 30 to 50 ml in capacity.

Parts

The gall bladder is divided into:
1. The fundus,
2. The body, and
3. The neck.

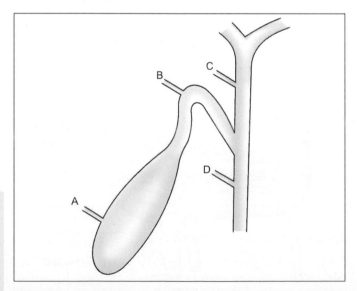

Fig. 22.3: The accessory hepatic ducts may open (A) directly into the gall bladder, (B) into the cystic duct, (C) into the common hepatic duct, or (D) into the bile duct.

The *fundus* projects beyond the inferior border of the liver, in the angle between the lateral border of the right rectus abdominis and the ninth costal cartilage. It is entirely surrounded by peritoneum, and is related anteriorly to the anterior abdominal wall, and posteriorly to the beginning of the transverse colon.

The *body* lies in the fossa for the gall bladder on the liver. The upper narrow end of the body is continuous with the neck at the right end of the porta hepatis. The superior surface of the body is devoid of peritoneum, and is adherent to the liver. The inferior surface is covered with peritoneum, and is related to the beginning of the transverse colon and to the first and second parts of the duodenum (Fig. 22.5).

The *neck* is the narrow upper end of the gall bladder. It is situated near the right end of the porta hepatis. It first curves anterosuperiorly and then posteroinferiorly to become continuous with the cystic duct. Its junction with the cystic duct is marked by a constriction.

Superiorly, the neck is attached to the liver by areolar tissue in which the cystic vessels are embedded. Inferiorly, it is related to the first part of the duodenum. The mucous membrane of the neck is folded spirally to prevent any obstruction to the inflow or outflow of bile. The posteromedial wall of the neck is dilated outwards to form a pouch called the Hartmann's pouch which is directed downwards and backwards. Gall stones may lodge in this pouch.

Cystic Duct

Cystic duct is about 3 to 4 cm long. It begins at the neck of the gall bladder, runs downwards, backwards and to the left, and ends by joining the common hepatic duct at an acute angle to form the bile duct. The mucous membrane of the cystic duct forms a series of 5 to 12 crescentic folds, arranged spirally to form the so-called *spiral valve* of Heister. This is not a true valve (Fig. 22.6).

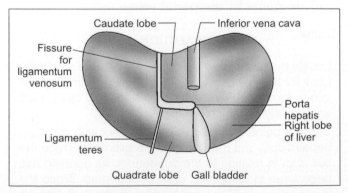

Fig. 22.4: Location of the gall bladder on the inferior surface of the right lobe of the liver.

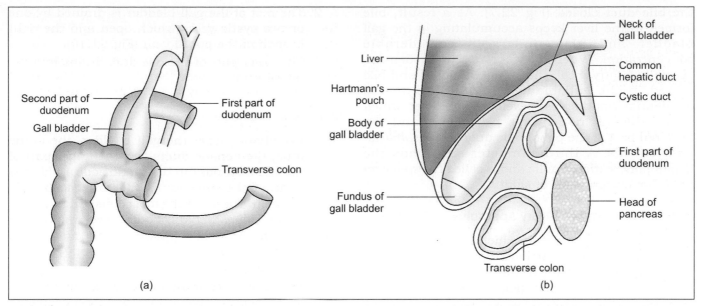

Fig. 22.5: Relations of the gall bladder: (a) Anterior view after removal of the liver, and (b) left view of sagittal section through the gall bladder fossa.

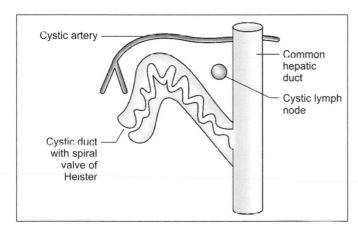

Fig. 22.6: The spiral valve of the cystic duct.

Bile Duct

Bile duct is formed by the union of the cystic and common hepatic ducts near the porta hepatis. It is 8 cm long and has a diameter of about 6 mm.

Course

The bile duct runs downwards and backwards, first in the free margin of the lesser omentum, *supra-duodenal part*; then behind the first part of the duodenum the *retroduodenal part*; and lastly behind, or embedded in, the head of pancreas *infraduodenal part*. Near the middle of the left side of the second part of the duodenum it comes in contact with the pancreatic duct and accompanies it through the wall of the duodenum, the *intraduodenal part*. The course of the duct through the duodenal wall is very oblique. Within the wall the two ducts usually unite to form

the *hepatopancreatic ampulla*, or *ampulla of Vater*. The distal constricted end of the ampulla opens at the summit of the major duodenal papilla 8 to 10 cm distal to the pylorus.

Relations

A. Supraduodenal Part

Supraduodenal part in the free margin of lesser omentum.

1. Anteriorly: Liver.
2. Posteriorly: Portal vein and epiploic foramen.
3. To the left: Hepatic artery (Fig. 22.2).

B. Retroduodenal Part

1. Anteriorly: First part of duodenum (Fig. 22.5).
2. Posteriorly: Inferior vena cava.
3. To the left: Gastroduodenal artery.

C. Infraduodenal Part

1. Anteriorly: A groove in the upper and lateral parts of the posterior surface of the head of the pancreas.
2. Posteriorly: Inferior vena cava.

D. Intraduodenal Part

Sphincters Related to the Bile and Pancreatic Ducts

The terminal part of the bile duct is surrounded just above its junction with the pancreatic duct by a ring of smooth muscle that forms the *sphincter choledochus* (*choledochus* = bile duct). This sphincter is always present. It normally keeps the lower end of the bile duct closed (Fig. 22.7). As a result, bile formed in the liver keeps accumulating in the gall bladder and also undergoes considerable concentration. When food enters the duodenum, specially a fatty meal, the sphincter opens and bile stored in the gall bladder is poured into the duodenum. Another less developed sphincter, which is usually but not always present around the terminal part of the pancreatic duct is the *sphincter pancreaticus*. A third sphincter surrounds the hepatopancreatic ampulla and is called the *sphincter ampullae* or sphincter of Oddi.

Arteries Supplying the Biliary Apparatus

1. The cystic artery is the chief source of the blood supply, and is distributed to the gall bladder, the cystic duct, the hepatic ducts and the upper part of the bile duct (Fig. 22.8).
2. Several branches from the posterior superior pancreaticoduodenal artery supply the lower part of the bile duct.
3. The right hepatic artery forms a minor source of supply to the middle part of the bile duct.

The *cystic artery* usually arises from the right hepatic artery, passes behind the common hepatic and cystic ducts, and reaches the upper surface of the neck of the gall bladder, where it divides into superficial and deep branches.

Venous Drainage

1. The superior surface of the gall bladder is drained by veins which enter the liver through the fossa for the gall bladder and join tributaries of hepatic veins.

2. The rest of the gall bladder is drained by one or two cystic veins which open into the right branch of the portal vein (Fig. 21.16).
3. The lower part of the bile duct drains into the portal vein.

Lymphatic Drainage

1. Lymphatics from the gall bladder, the cystic duct, the hepatic ducts and the upper part of the bile duct pass to the cystic node and to the node of the anterior border of the epiploic foramen. These are the most constant members of the upper hepatic nodes. The cystic node lies in the angle between the cystic and common hepatic ducts; it is constantly enlarged in cholecystitis.
2. The lower part of the bile duct drains into the lower hepatic and upper pancreaticosplenic nodes.

Nerve Supply

The *cystic plexus* of nerves, supplying the territory of the cystic artery, is derived from the hepatic plexus, which receives fibres from the coeliac plexus, the left and right vagi and the *right phrenic nerves*. The lower part of the bile duct is supplied by the nerve plexus over the superior pancreaticoduodenal artery.

Parasympathetic nerves are motor to the musculature of the gall bladder and bile ducts, but inhibitory to the sphincters. *Sympathetic nerves* from thoracic seven to nine are vasomotor and motor to the sphincters.

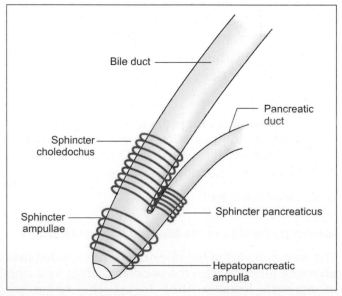

Fig. 22.7: Sphincters in the region of the junction of the bile duct and the main pancreatic duct with the duodenum.

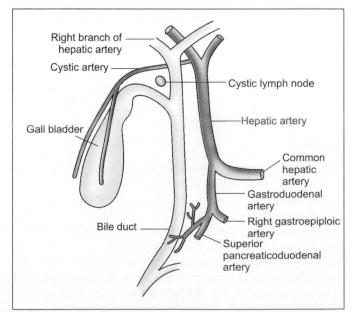

Fig. 22.8: Blood supply of the gall bladder and bile ducts.

Pain from the gall bladder may travel along the vagus, the sympathetic nerves, or along the phrenic nerves. It may be referred to different sites through these nerves as follows.

1. Through vagus to the stomach (epigastrium).
2. Through the sympathetic nerves to the inferior angle of the right scapula. Lateral horn of thoracic 7 segment of spinal cord gives sympathetic fibres to coeliac ganglion through greater splanchnic nerve. T7 segment receives pain fibres from skin over inferior angle of scapula. So visceral pain is referred to somatic area.
3. Through the phrenic nerve to the right shoulder (C4 gives fibres to phrenic nerve and supraclavicular nerves).

Functions of Gall Bladder

1. Storage of bile, and its release into the duodenum when required.
2. Absorption of water, and concentration of bile. Bile may be concentrated as much as ten times.
3. The normal gall bladder also absorbs small amounts of a loose bile salt-cholesterol compound. When the gall bladder is inflamed, the concentration function becomes abnormal and the bile salts alone are absorbed leaving cholesterol behind. Bile salts have a powerful solvent action on cholesterol which tends to

be precipitated. This can lead to the formation of the gall stones.

4. It regulates pressure in the biliary system by appropriate dilatation or contraction. Thus the normal, choledochoduodenal mechanism is maintained.

Histology

Mucous membrane: It is projected to form folds. Epithelium consists of a single layer of tall columnar cells. Lamina propria contains loose connective tissue.

The fibromuscular coat: It consists of smooth muscle fibres and collagen fibres which rests on an outer fibroareolar coat.

Development

Hepatic bud arises from the endoderm of caudal part of foregut. The bud elongates cranially. It gives rise to a small bud on its right side. This is called *pars cystica* and the main part is *pars hepatica. Pars cystica* forms the gall bladder and the cystic duct, which drains into the common hepatic duct (CHD). Pars hepatica forms CHD and divides into right and left hepatic ducts. These ducts reach *septum transversum* and proliferate to form the *hepatic parenchyma.* The entire epithelium is endodermal and other layers are of splanchnic origin.

CLINICAL ANATOMY

- *Humoral control of the gall bladder:* The gall bladder contracts when food rich in fat enters the duodenum. The fat causes certain cells in duodenum to liberate a hormone called *cholecystokinin-pancreozymin.* The hormone is carried to the gall bladder and causes its contraction. It also causes dilatation of the sphincters.
- Gall bladder function can be investigated by ultrasound.
- Inflammation of the gall bladder is called *cholecystitis.* The patient complains of pain over the right hypochondrium radiating to the inferior angle of the right scapula, or to right shoulder. When a finger is placed just below the costal margin, at the tip of the 9th costal cartilage, the patient feels sharp pain on inspiration. He winces with a "catch" in his breath. This is referred to as *Murphy's sign* (Fig. 22.9).
- Stones may form in the gall bladder. The condition is called *cholelithiasis* (Fig. 22.10).

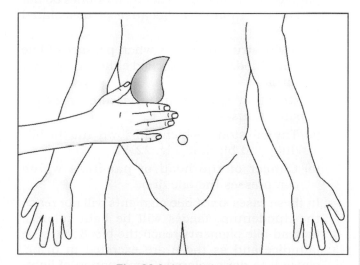

Fig. 22.9: Murphy's sign.

They typically occur in fat, fertile, female of forty (but also in males). The stones are responsible for the time to time spasmodic pain called biliary colic. In these cases, Murphy's sign is of great

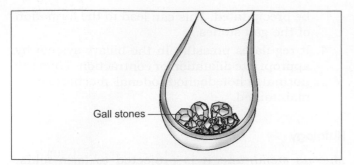

Fig. 22.10: Gall stones.

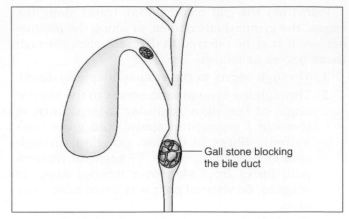

Fig. 22.11: Gall stones blocking the bile duct.

diagnostic value. Gall stones never develop in dog, cat, sheep, rabbit because of high fatty acid content of their bile. Stones are common in man, ox and hog because of low fatty acid in them. They can give rise to severe spasmodic pain which is called *biliary colic.*

- The region of the gall bladder is frequently operated upon. It is, therefore, necessary for the surgeon to be aware of the numerous variations that may exist in the extrahepatic biliary apparatus, and in the related blood vessels. The operation for removal of the gall bladder is called *cholecystectomy.*
- The most significant lesions of typhoid fever occur in lymphoid tissue, bone marrow and gall bladder. Gall bladder is invariably infected in these cases, and the carrier state may be due to persistence of typhoid bacilli in this organ.
- *Courvoisier's law:* Dilatation of the gall bladder occurs only in extrinsic obstruction of the bile duct like pressure by carcinoma of head of pancreas. Intrinsic obstruction by stones do not cause any dilatation because of associated fibrosis.
- Biliary obstruction arises when passage of bile into the duodenum is blocked either completely or partially.

Obstruction may be intrahepatic or extra-hepatic. Causes are:

(a) The gall stones which slip down into the bile duct and block it (Fig. 22.11).

(b) Cancer of the head of pancreas which compresses the bile duct.

In these cases since bile pigments will not reach the duodenum, faeces will be light-colored. Instead bile pigments reach the blood, causing jaundice and as these are excreted in urine, cause it to dark-colored. Combination of light-colored stools with dark-colored urine implies obstructive jaundice. If it is associated with episodes of pain, it is likely to be due to gall stones. If it is associated with loss of weight

etc., it is likely to be due to cancer of head of pancreas.

- *Calot's triangle:* Triangular space formed by cystic duct, common hepatic duct and segment-V of right hemiliver forms Calot's triangle. This space contains cystic artery, cystic lymph node and autonomic fibres reaching the gall bladder.
- Bile duct can be assessed from the duodenum by a procedure—endoscopic retrograde cholangiography.
- *Referred pain:* Pain of stretch of CBD or gall bladder is referred to epigastrium. It is also referred to right shoulder and inferior angle of right scapula (Fig. 22.12).

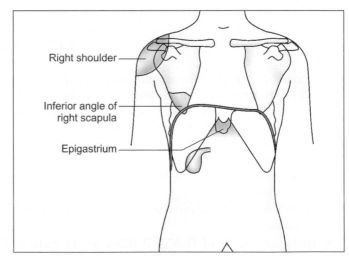

Fig. 22.12: Sites of referred pain due to stretch of bile duct or gall stone.

- Gall bladder is related to duodenum. The gall stones may penetrate wall of gall bladder and duodenum to get into the lumen of duodenum. These stones travel through the coils of small intestine and may block the narrow ileocaecal junction leading to intestinal obstruction.

CHAPTER 23

Spleen, Pancreas and Liver

Synonyms: Lien (Latin); *splen* (Greek).

INTRODUCTION

Spleen is a lymphatic organ connected to the blood vascular system. It acts as a filter for blood and plays an important role in the immune responses of the body.

SPLEEN

Location

The spleen is a wedge-shaped organ lying mainly in the left hypochondrium, and partly in the epigastrium. It is wedged in between the fundus of the stomach and the diaphragm. The spleen is tetrahedral in shape (Figs 23.1 and 23.2).

The spleen is soft, highly vascular and dark purple in colour. The size and weight of the spleen are markedly variable. On an average the spleen is 1 inch or 2.5 cm thick, 3 inches or 7.5 cm broad, 5 inches or 12.5 cm long, **7** ounces in weight, and is related to 9th to 11th ribs. The odd numbers 1, 3, 5, 7, 9, 11. Normally, the spleen is not palpable.

DISSECTION

Locate the spleen situated deep in the left hypochondrium. The gastrophrenic ligament has already been cut during removal of stomach. Now cut through the posteriorly placed lienorenal ligament taking care of the splenic vessels contained therein. See the close relation of spleen to the left costodiaphragmatic recess and the left lung.

Identify the viscera related to the spleen, e.g. stomach, tail of pancreas, left kidney and splenic flexure of colon. Trace the branches of splenic artery into the substance of spleen as far as possible. Cut the phrenicocolic ligament of peritoneum and deliver the spleen from the abdominal cavity.

Position (Axis of Spleen)

The spleen lies obliquely along the long axis of the 10th rib. Thus it is directed downwards, forwards and laterally, making an angle of about 45 degrees with the horizontal plane (Fig. 23.3).

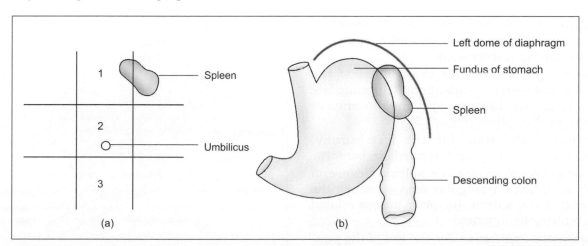

Fig. 23.1: Location of the spleen: (a) In relation to the nine regions of the abdomen; and (b) in relation to the fundus of the stomach and the diaphragm. 1 Epigastrium; 2 Umbilical region; and 3 Hypogastrium.

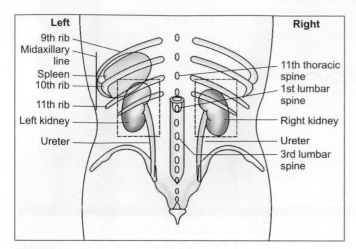

Fig. 23.2: Position of spleen, kidney and ureter from the posterior aspect.

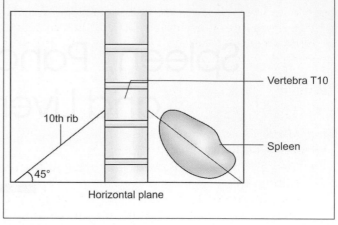

Fig. 23.3: The axis of the spleen corresponds to the long axis of the 10th rib of the left side; it makes an angle of about 45° with the horizontal plane.

External Features

The spleen has two ends, three borders and two surfaces (Figs 23.4 and 23.5).

Two Ends

The *anterior end* is expanded and is more like a border. It is directed downwards and forwards, and reaches the midaxillary line.

The *posterior end* is rounded. It is directed upwards, backwards and medially, and rests on the upper pole of the left kidney.

Three Borders

The *superior border* is characteristically notched near the anterior end.

The *inferior border* is rounded.

The *intermediate border* is also rounded and is directed to the right.

Two Surfaces

The *diaphragmatic surface* is convex and smooth.

The *visceral surface* is concave and irregular. It bears the following impressions.

The *gastric impression*, for the fundus of the stomach, lies between the superior and intermediate borders. It is the largest and most concave impression on the spleen (Fig. 23.5).

The *renal impression,* for the left kidney, lies between the inferior and intermediate borders.

The *colic impressions,* for the splenic flexure of the colon, occupies a triangular area adjoining the anterior end of the spleen. Its lower part is related to the phrenicocolic ligament.

The *pancreatic impression,* for the tail of the pancreas, lies between the hilum and the colic impression.

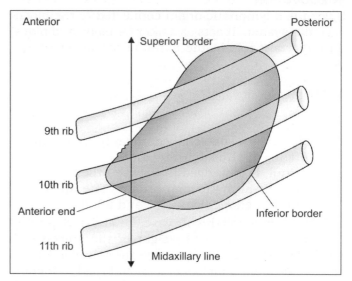

Fig. 23.4: Position of spleen in relation to left 9th–11th ribs—diaphragmatic surface.

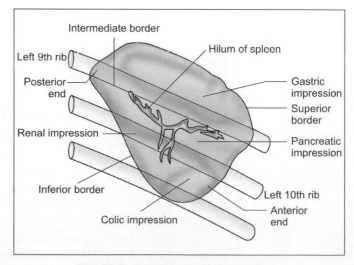

Fig. 23.5: Relation of visceral surface.

The *hilum* lies on the inferomedial part of the gastric impression along the long axis of the spleen. It transmits the splenic vessels and nerves, and provides attachment to the gastrosplenic and lienorenal ligaments.

Relations

Peritoneal Relations

The spleen is surrounded by peritoneum, and is suspended by following ligaments.

1. The *gastrosplenic ligament* extends from the hilum of the spleen to the greater curvature of the stomach. It contains the short gastric vessels and associated lymphatics and sympathetic nerves (Figs 18.18 and 23.6).
2. The *lienorenal ligament* extends from the hilum of the spleen to the anterior surface of the left kidney. It contains the tail of the pancreas, the splenic vessels, and associated pancreaticosplenic lymph nodes, lymphatics and sympathetic nerves.
3. The *phrenicocolic ligament* is not attached to the spleen, but supports its anterior end. It is a horizontal fold of peritoneum extending from the splenic flexure of colon to the diaphragm opposite the 11th rib in the midaxillary line. It limits the upper end of the left paracolic gutter.

Visceral Relations

Visceral surface

The visceral surface is related to the fundus of the stomach, the anterior surface of the left kidney, the splenic flexure of the colon and the tail of the pancreas (Fig. 23.7).

Diaphragmatic surface

The diaphragmatic surface is related to the diaphragm which separates the spleen from the costodiaphragmatic recess of pleura, lung and 9th, 10th and 11th ribs of the left side (Fig. 23.8).

Arterial Supply

The spleen is supplied by the splenic artery which is the largest branch of the coeliac trunk. The artery is tortuous in its course to allow for movements of the spleen. It passes through the lienorenal ligament to reach the hilum of the spleen where it divides into five or more branches. These branches enter the spleen to supply it.

Within the spleen it divides repeatedly to form successfully the straight vessels called penicilli, ellipsoids and arterial capillaries. Further course of the blood is controversial. According to *closed* theory of splenic circulation, the capillaries are continuous with the venous sinusoids that lie in the red pulp; the sinusoids join together to form veins.

However, according to *open* theory of splenic circulation, the capillaries end by opening into the red pulp from where the blood enters the sinusoids through their walls.

Still others believe in a *compromise* theory, where the circulation is *open* in distended spleen and *closed* in contracted spleen. The splenic circulation is adapted for the mechanism of separation and storage of the red blood cells.

On the basis of its blood supply, the spleen is said to have superior and inferior *vascular segments*. The two segments are separated by an avascular plane. Each segment may be subdivided into one to two disc-like middle segments and a cap-like pole segment. Apart from its terminal branches, the splenic artery gives off:

(i) Numerous branches to the pancreas;

(ii) 5 to 7 short gastric branches, and

(iii) The left gastroepiploic artery (Fig. 19.6).

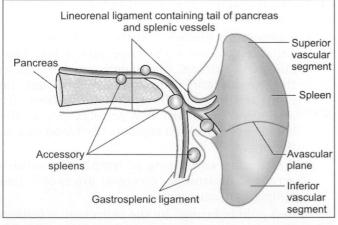

Fig. 23.6: Peritoneal ligaments attached to the spleen, and common sites of accessory spleen.

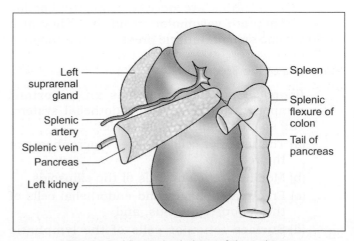

Fig. 23.7: Visceral relations of the spleen.

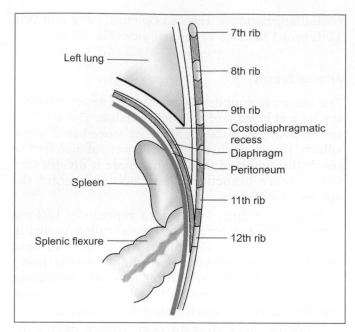

Fig. 23.8: Relations of diaphragmatic surface.

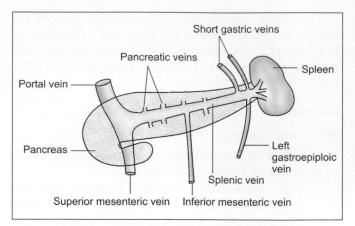

Fig. 23.9: Splenic vein and tributaries.

Venous Drainage

The splenic vein is formed at the hilum of the spleen. It runs a straight course behind the pancreas. It joins the superior mesenteric vein behind the neck of the pancreas to form the portal vein. Its tributaries are the short gastric, left gastroepiploic, pancreatic and inferior mesenteric veins (Fig. 23.9).

Lymphatic Drainage

Splenic tissue proper has no lymphatics. A few lymphatics arise from the connective tissue of the capsule and trabeculae and drain into the *pancreaticosplenic* lymph nodes situated along the splenic artery.

Nerve Supply

Sympathetic fibres are derived from the coeliac plexus. They are vasomotor in nature. They also supply some smooth muscle present in the capsule.

Functions of the Spleen

1. *Phagocytosis:* The spleen is an important component of the reticuloendothelial system. The splenic phagocytes include:
   (a) The reticular cells and free macrophages of the red pulp.
   (b) Modified reticular cells of the ellipsoids.
   (c) Free macrophages and endothelial cells of the venous sinusoids, and
   (d) Surface reticular cells of the lymphatic follicle. The phagocytes present in the organ

remove cell debris and old and effete RBCs, other blood cells and microorganisms, and thus filter the blood. Phagocytosis of circulating antigens initiates humoral and cellular immune responses.

2. *Haemopoiesis:* The spleen is an important haemopoietic organ during foetal life. Lymphopoiesis continues throughout life. The lymphocytes manufactured in it take part in immune responses of the body.

   In the adult spleen, haemopoiesis can restart in certain diseases, like chronic myeloid leukaemia and myelosclerosis.

3. *Immune responses:* Under antigenic stimulation, there occurs increased lymphopoiesis for cellular responses, and increased formation of plasma cells for the humoral responses.

4. *Storage of RBCs:* Red blood cells can be stored in the spleen and released into the circulation when needed. This function is better marked in animals than in man.

Histology

Histologically, spleen is made up of the following four component parts.

1. Supporting fibroelastic tissue, forming the capsule, coarse trabeculae and a fine reticulum. In human, the smooth muscle cells in the capsule and trabeculae are few, and the contraction and distension of spleen are attributed to constriction or relaxation of the blood vessels, which regulate the blood flow in the organ.

2. White pulp consisting of lymphatic nodules arranged around an eccentric arteriole called Malpighian corpuscle.

3. Red pulp is formed by the collection of cells in the interstices of reticulum, in between the sinusoids. The cell population includes:

(a) All types of lymphocytes (small, medium and large),

(b) All three types of blood cells (RBC, WBC and platelets), and

(c) The fixed and free macrophages. Lymphocytes are freely transformed into plasma cells which can produce large amounts of antibodies, immunoglobulins.

4. Vascular system transverses the organ and permeates it thoroughly.

Development

Spleen develops the mesoderm in the cephalic part of dorsal mesogastrium, from its left layer, during sixth week of intrauterine life, into a number of nodules which soon fuse to form a lobulated spleen. Notching of the superior border of the adult spleen is an evidence of its multiple origin. These nodules which fail to fuse, form accessory spleens. Fig. 23.6 shows the usual sites of accessory spleens.

Accessory Spleens or Spleniculi

These may be found:

(a) In the derivatives of the dorsal mesogastrium, i.e. gastrosplenic ligament, lienorenal ligament, gastrophrenic ligament and greater omentum.

(b) In the broad ligament of the uterus.

(c) In the spermatic cord.

PANCREAS

The pancreas (*pan* = all; *kreas* = flesh) is a gland that is partly exocrine and partly endocrine. The exocrine part secretes the digestive pancreatic juice; and the endocrine part secretes hormones, e.g. insulin. It is soft, lobulated and elongated organ.

Location

The pancreas lies more or less transversely across the posterior abdominal wall, at the level of first and second lumbar vertebrae.

Size and Shape

It is J-shaped or retort-shaped, set obliquely. The bowl of the retort represents its head, and the stem of the retort, its neck, body and tail. It is about 15–20 cm long, 2.5–3.8 cm broad and 1.2–1.8 cm thick and weighs about 90 g.

The pancreas is divided (from right to left) into head, neck, body and the tail. The head is enlarged and lies within the concavity of the duodenum. The tail reaches the hilum of the spleen (Figs 23.10 and 23.11). The entire organ lies posterior to the stomach

Identify the pancreas—a retroperitoneal organ lying transversely across the posterior abdominal wall. Head is easily identifiable in the concavity of duodenum. Uncinate process of the head is the part behind the upper part of superior mesenteric artery. Portal vein is formed behind its neck. Rest of the part extending to the left is its body and tail reaching till the hilum of spleen. Turn the descending part of the duodenum and the head of the pancreas to the left. Look for the posterior pancreaticoduodenal vessels and the bile duct on the head of the pancreas.

Expose the structures posterior to pancreas.

Turn the tail and body of the pancreas to the right stripping the splenic artery and vein from its posterior surface and identify the vessels passing to the gland from them.

On the posterior surface of the pancreas, make a cut into the gland parallel to and close to the superior and inferior margins of the body. Pick away the lobules of the gland between the cuts to expose the greyish white duct and the interlobular ducts draining into the main duct.

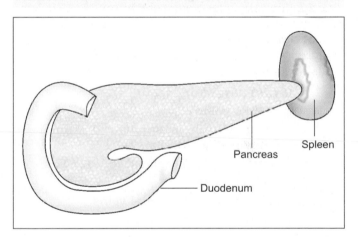

Fig. 23.10: Location of the pancreas.

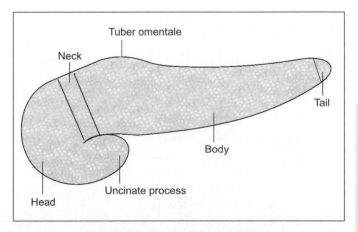

Fig. 23.11: Parts of the pancreas.

separated from it by the lesser sac (Figs 18.17 and 18.18).

Head of the Pancreas

Head is the enlarged flattened right end of pancreas, situated within the curve of the duodenum.

External Features

The head has three *borders,* superior, inferior and right lateral; two *surfaces,* anterior and posterior; and one *process,* called the uncinate process, which projects from the lower and left part of the head towards the left.

Relations

Three borders

The *superior border* is overlapped by the first part of the duodenum and is related to the superior pancreaticoduodenal artery (Fig. 23.12). The *inferior border* is related to the third part of the duodenum and to the inferior pancreaticoduodenal artery. The *right lateral border* is related to the second part of the duodenum, the terminal part of the bile duct and the anastomosis between the two pancreatico-duodenal arteries (Fig. 23.17).

Two Surfaces

The *anterior surface* is related, from above downwards, to:

1. The first part of duodenum.
2. Transverse colon.
3. Jejunum which is separated from it by peritoneum (Fig. 23.12a).

The *posterior surface* is related to:

1. Inferior vena cava.
2. Terminal parts of the renal veins.
3. Right crus of the diaphragm.

4. Bile duct which runs downwards and to the right and is often embedded in the substance of pancreas (Fig. 23.12b).

Uncinate process

It is related anteriorly to the superior mesenteric vessels, and posteriorly to the aorta.

Neck of the Pancreas

This is the slightly constricted part of the pancreas between its head and body. It is directed forwards, upwards and to the left. It has two surfaces, anterior and posterior.

Relations

The *anterior surface* is related to: (1) The peritoneum covering the posterior wall of the lesser sac, and (2) the pylorus (Fig. 23.13a).

The *posterior surface* is related to the termination of the superior mesenteric vein and the beginning of the portal vein (Fig. 23.13b).

Body of the Pancreas

The body of the pancreas is elongated. It extends from its neck to the tail. It passes towards the left with a slight upward and backward inclination.

External Features

It is triangular on cross-section, and has three *borders* (anterior, superior and inferior). A part of the body projects upwards beyond the rest of the superior border, a little to the left of the neck. This projection is known as the *tuber omentale.*

Relations

Three borders

The *anterior border* provides attachment to the root of the transverse mesocolon. The *superior border* is

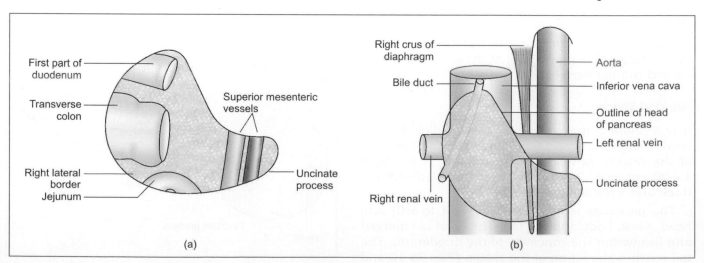

Fig. 23.12: (a) Anterior, and (b) posterior relations of the head of the pancreas.

related to coeliac trunk over the tuber omentale, the hepatic artery to the right, and the splenic artery to the left (Fig. 21.3). The *inferior border* is related to the superior mesenteric vessels at its right end (Fig. 23.14).

Three surfaces

The *anterior surface* is concave and is directed forwards and upwards. It is covered by peritoneum, and is related to the lesser sac and to the stomach.

The *posterior surface* is devoid of peritoneum, and is related to:

1. The aorta with the origin of the superior mesenteric artery.
2. Left crus of the diaphragm.
3. Left suprarenal gland.
4. Left kidney.
5. Left renal vessels.
6. Splenic vein (Fig. 23.15).

The *inferior surface* is covered by peritoneum, and is related to the duodenojejunal flexure, coils of jejunum and the left colic flexure (Fig. 23.14).

Tail of the Pancreas

This is the left end of the pancreas. It lies in the lienorenal ligament together with the splenic vessels. It comes into contact with the lower part of the gastric surface of the spleen (Fig. 23.6).

Ducts of the Pancreas

The exocrine pancreas is drained by two ducts, main and accessory (Fig. 23.16).

1. The *main pancreatic duct* of Wirsung lies near the posterior surface of the pancreas and is recognised easily by its white colour. It begins at the tail; runs towards the right through the body; and bends at the neck to run downwards, backwards and to the right in the head.
2. Its lumen is about 3 mm in diameter.
3. It receives many small tributaries which join it at right angles to its long axis forming what has been described as a *herring bone pattern*.
4. Within the head of the pancreas the pancreatic duct is related to the bile duct which lies on its

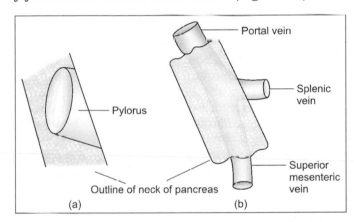

Fig. 23.13: Relations of the neck of the pancreas: (a) Anterior relations, (b) posterior relations.

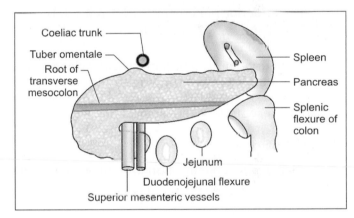

Fig. 23.14: Anterior and inferior relations of the body of the pancreas.

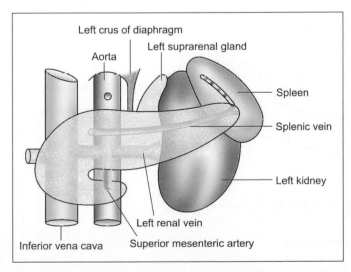

Fig. 23.15: Posterior relations of the body of the pancreas.

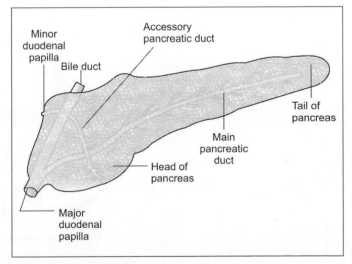

Fig. 23.16: The pancreatic ducts.

right side. The two ducts enter the wall of the second part of the duodenum, and join to form the *hepatopancreatic ampulla* of Vater which opens by a narrow mouth on the summit of the *major duodenal papilla*, 8 to 10 cm distal to the pylorus.

5. The *accessory pancreatic duct of Santorini* begins in the lower part of the head, crosses the front of the main duct with which it communicates and opens into the duodenum at the minor duodenal papilla. The papilla of accessory pancreatic duct is situated 6 to 8 cm distal to the pylorus. The opening of the accessory duct lies cranial and ventral to that of the main duct. The two ducts remind the double origin of pancreas from the ventral and dorsal pancreatic buds.

Arterial Supply

The pancreas is supplied:
1. Mainly by pancreatic branches of the splenic artery,
2. The superior pancreaticoduodenal artery, and
3. The inferior pancreaticoduodenal artery (Fig. 23.17).

Like the duodenum the pancreas develops at the junction of the foregut and midgut, and is supplied by branches derived from both the coeliac and superior mesenteric arteries.

Venous Drainage

Veins drain into splenic, superior mesenteric and portal veins (Fig. 23.18).

Lymphatic Drainage

Lymphatics follow the arteries and drain into the pancreaticosplenic, coeliac and superior mesenteric groups of lymph nodes.

Nerve Supply

The vagus or parasympathetic and splanchnic sympathetic nerves supply the pancreas through the plexuses around its arteries.

Sympathetic nerves are vasomotor. Parasympathetic nerves control pancreatic secretion. Secretion is also influenced by the hormone cholecystokinin produced by cells in the duodenal epithelium. The pancreatic juice contains various enzymes that help in the digestion of proteins, carbohydrates and fats.

Functions

1. *Digestive:* Pancreatic juice contains many digestive enzymes of which the important ones are as follows. Trypsin breaks down proteins to lower peptides. Amylase hydrolyses starch and glycogen to disaccharides. Lipase breaks down fat into fatty acids and glycerol.
2. *Endocrine:* Carbohydrates are the immediate source of energy. Insulin helps in utilizations of sugar in the cells. Deficiency of insulin results in hyperglycaemia. The disease is called *diabetes mellitus.* There appears to be poverty in plenty.
3. *Pancreatic juice:* It provides appropriate alkaline medium (pH 8) for the activity of the pancreatic enzymes.

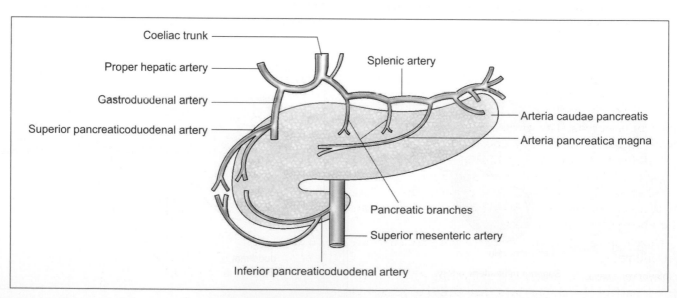

Fig. 23.17: Arterial supply of the pancreas.

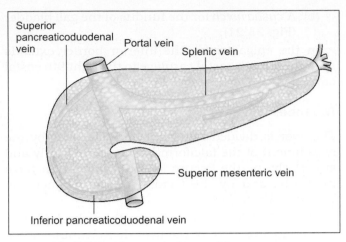

Fig. 23.18: Venous drainage of the pancreas.

Histology

1. The exocrine part is a serous gland, made up of tubular acini lined by pyramidal cells with basal round nuclei, containing zymogen granules. It secretes the digestive pancreatic juice.

2. The endocrine part of pancreas is made up of microscopic elements called the pancreatic islets of Langerhans. These are small isolated masses of cells distributed throughout the pancreas. They are most numerous in the tail. The islets have various types of cells the most important of which are the *beta cells* which are granular and basophilic, forming about 80% of the cell population. They produce insulin. Other types of cells are *alpha cells* with subtype A1 and A2. These are granular and acidophilic and form about 20% of the cell population. A1 cells belong to enterochromaffin group and secrete pancreatic gastrin and serotonin. A2 cells secrete glucagon.

Development

It arises as a larger dorsal bud and a smaller ventral bud. These soon fuse to form the pancreas. Ventral bud forms uncinate process and an inferior part of head of pancreas. The dorsal bud forms part of the head, whole of neck, body and tail of pancreas.

The duct of ventral bud taps the duct of dorsal pancreatic bud near its neck and opens into the duodenum as the main pancreatic duct. The proximal part of duct of dorsal pancreatic bud forms the accessory pancreatic duct.

Developmental anomalies of the pancreas include the following.

(a) An *annular pancreas* encircling the second part of the duodenum. An annular pancreas may be the cause of duodenal obstruction.

(b) *Accessory pancreatic tissue* may be present at various sites. These include the wall of the duodenum, the jejunum, the ileum, or of Meckel's diverticulum.

(c) *Inversion of pancreatic ducts:* In this condition, the accessory duct is larger than the main duct, and the main drainage of the pancreas is through the minor duodenal papilla.

LIVER

The liver is a large, solid, gland situated in the right upper quadrant of the abdominal cavity. In the living subject, the liver is reddish brown in colour, soft in consistency, and very friable. It weighs about 1600 g in males and about 1300 g in females.

Location

The liver occupies the whole of the right hypochondrium, the greater part of the epigastrium, and extends into the left hypochondrium reaching up to the left lateral line. From the above it will be obvious that most of the liver is covered by ribs and costal cartilages, except in the upper part of the epigastrium where it is in contact with the anterior abdominal wall (Fig. 23.19).

The liver is the largest gland in the body. It secretes bile and performs various other metabolic functions.

The liver is also called the 'hepar' from which we have the adjective 'hepatic' applied to many structures connected with the organ.

External Features

The liver is wedge-shaped. It resembles a four-sided pyramid laid on one side (Fig. 23.20).

Five Surfaces

It has five surfaces. These are:

1. Anterior,

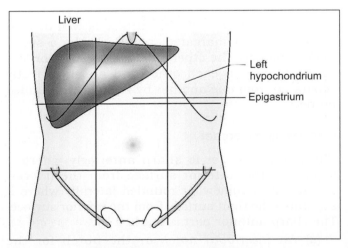

Fig. 23.19: Location of the liver.

DISSECTION

Pull the liver downwards and divide the anterior layers of the coronary and left triangular ligaments.

Identify the inferior vena cava between the liver and the diaphragm and separate the liver downwards from inferior vena cava. If the inferior vena cava happens to be deeply buried in the liver, divide it and remove a segment with the liver.

Expose the structures in the porta hepatis and follow them to their entry into the liver. Identify the viscera related to the inferior surface of the liver and see their demarcations on the liver. Explore the extent of right and left pleural cavities and pericardium related to the superior and anterior surfaces of liver, though separated from it by the diaphragm.

Cut the structures close to the porta hepatis and separate all the peritoneal ligaments and folds of the liver. Remove the liver from the body. Identify its various borders, surfaces, lobes.

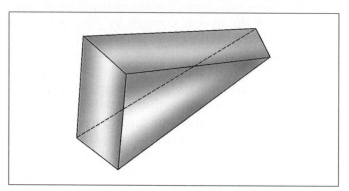

Fig. 23.20: Comparison of the orientation of the surfaces of the liver to those of a four-sided pyramid.

2. Posterior,
3. Superior,
4. Inferior, and
5. Right.

Out of these the inferior surface is well defined because it is demarcated, anteriorly, by a sharp inferior border. The other surfaces are more or less continuous with each other and are imperfectly separated from one another by ill-defined, rounded borders.

One Prominent Border

The *inferior border* is sharp anteriorly where it separates the anterior surface from the inferior surface. It is somewhat rounded laterally where it separates the right surface from the inferior surface. The sharp anterior part is marked by:

(a) An *interlobar notch* or the notch for the ligamentum teres.

(b) A *cystic notch* for the fundus of the gall bladder (Fig. 23.21).

In the epigastrium, the inferior border extends from the left 8th costal cartilage to the right 9th costal cartilage.

Two Lobes

The liver is divided into right and left lobes by the attachment of the falciform ligament anteriorly and superiorly; by the fissure for the ligamentum teres inferiorly; and by the fissure for the ligamentum venosum posteriorly.

The *right lobe* is much larger than the left lobe, and forms five sixth of the liver. It contributes to all the five surfaces of the liver, and presents the caudate and quadrate lobes.

The *caudate lobe* is situated on the posterior surface. It is bounded on the right by the groove for the inferior vena cava, on the left by the fissure for the ligamentum venosum, and inferiorly by the porta hepatis. Above it is continuous with the superior surface. Below and to the right, just behind the porta hepatis, it is connected to the right lobe of the liver by the *caudate process* (Fig. 23.22). Below and to the left it presents a small rounded elevation called the *papillary process*.

The *quadrate lobe* is situated on the inferior surface, and is rectangular in shape. It is bounded anteriorly by the inferior border, posteriorly by the porta hepatis, on the right by the fossa for the gall bladder, and on the left by the fissure for the ligamentum teres (Fig. 23.23).

The *porta hepatis* is a deep, transverse fissure about 5 cm long, situated on the inferior surface of the right lobe of the liver. It lies between the caudate lobe above and the quadrate lobe below and in front. The portal vein, the hepatic artery and the hepatic plexus of nerves enter the liver through the porta hepatis, while the right and left hepatic ducts and a

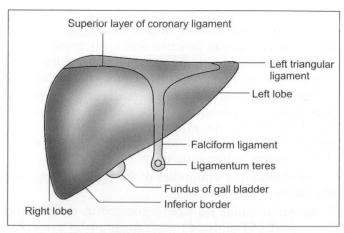

Fig. 23.21: Liver seen from the front.

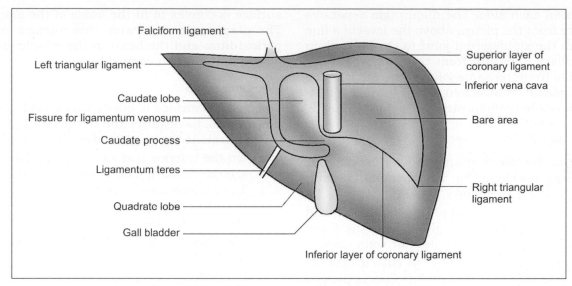

Fig. 23.22: Liver seen from behind.

few lymphatics leave it. The relations within the porta hepatis are from behind forwards the portal vein, the hepatic artery and the hepatic ducts. The lips of the porta hepatis provide attachment to the lesser omentum (Fig. 23.23).

The *left lobe* of the liver is much smaller than the right lobe and forms only one-sixth of the liver. It is flattened from above downwards. Near the fissure for the ligamentum venosum, its inferior surface presents a rounded elevation, called the omental tuberosity or tuber omentale.

Relations

Peritoneal Relations

Most of the liver is covered by peritoneum. The areas not covered by peritoneum are as follows.

(a) A triangular *bare area*, on the posterior surface of the right lobe, limited by the upper and lower layers of the coronary ligament and by the right triangular ligament.

(b) The *groove for the inferior vena cava*, on the posterior surface of the right lobe of the liver, between the caudate lobe and the bare area.

(c) The *fossa for the gall bladder* which lies on the inferior surface of the right lobe to the right of the quadrate lobe.

(d) The *coronary ligament* having superior and inferior layers, which enclose the bare area of the liver; and

(e) The *lesser omentum* (Figs 23.22 and 23.23).

Visceral Relations

Anterior Surface

The anterior surface is triangular and slightly convex. It is related to the xiphoid process and to the anterior abdominal wall in the median plane; and to

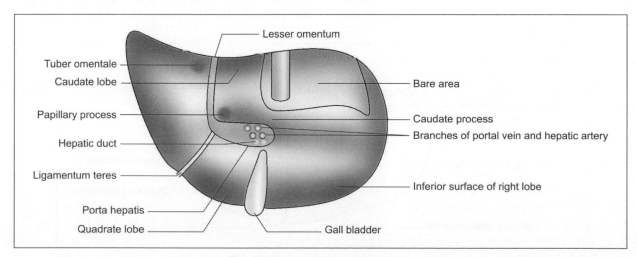

Fig. 23.23: Liver seen from below.

diaphragm on each side. The diaphragm separates this surface from the pleura above the level of a line drawn from the xiphisternal joint to the 10th rib in the midaxillary line; and from the lung above the level of a line from the same joint to the 8th rib. The falciform ligament is attached to this surface a little to the right of the median plane.

Posterior Surface

The posterior surface is triangular. Its middle part shows a deep concavity for the vertebral column. Other relations are as follows.

1. The *bare area* is related to the diaphragm; and to the right suprarenal gland near the lower end of the groove for the inferior vena cava.

2. The *groove for the inferior vena cava* lodges the upper part of the vessel, and its floor is pierced by the hepatic veins.

3. The *caudate lobe* lies in the superior recess of the lesser sac. It is related to the crura of the diaphragm above the aortic opening, to the right inferior phrenic artery, and to the coeliac trunk.

4. The *fissure for the ligamentum venosum* is very deep and extends to the front of the caudate lobe. It contains two layers of the lesser omentum. The ligamentum venosum lies on its floor. The ligamentum venosum is a remnant of the ductus venosus of foetal life; it is connected below to the left branch of the portal vein, and above to the left hepatic vein near its entry into the inferior vena cava (Fig. 23.22).

5. The *posterior surface of the left lobe* is marked by the oesophageal impression.

Superior Surface

The superior surface is quadrilateral and shows a concavity in the middle. This is the cardiac impression. On each side of the impression the surface is convex to fit the dome of the diaphragm. The diaphragm separates this surface from the pericardium and the heart in the middle; and from pleura and lung on each side.

Inferior Surface

The inferior surface is quadrilateral and is directed downwards, backwards and to the left. It is marked by impressions for neighbouring viscera as follows.

1. On the inferior surface of the left lobe there is a large concave *gastric impression* (Fig. 23.24). The left lobe also bears a raised area that comes in contact with the lesser omentum: it is called the *omental tuberosity*.

2. The *fissure for the ligamentum teres* passes from the inferior border to the left end of the porta hepatis. The ligamentum teres represents the obliterated left umbilical vein.

3. The *quadrate lobe* is related to the lesser omentum, the pylorus, and the first part of the duodenum. When the stomach is empty the quadrate lobe is related to the first part of the duodenum and to a part of the transverse colon.

4. The *fossa for the gall bladder* lies to the right of the quadrate lobe (Fig. 23.23).

5. To the right of this fossa the inferior surface of the right lobe bears the *colic impression* for the hepatic flexure of the colon, the renal impression for the right kidney, and the duodenal impression for the second part of the duodenum.

Right Surface

The right surface is quadrilateral and convex. It is related to the diaphragm opposite the 7th to 11th ribs in the midaxillary line. It is separated by the diaphragm from the pleura up to the 10th rib, and from the lung up to the 8th rib. Thus, the upper one-third of the surface is related to the diaphragm, the pleura and the lung; the middle one-third, to

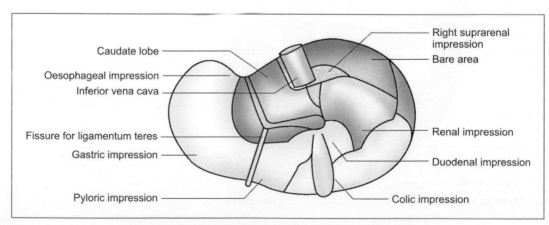

Fig. 23.24: Relations of the inferior surface of the liver.

the diaphragm and the costodiaphragmatic recess of the pleura; and the lower one-third to the diaphragm alone.

Blood Supply

The liver receives 20% of its blood supply through the hepatic artery, and 80% through the portal vein. Before entering the liver, both the hepatic artery and the portal vein divide into right and left branches. Within the liver, they redivide to form segmental vessels which further divide to form interlobular vessels which run in the portal canals. Further ramifications of the interlobular branches open into the hepatic sinusoids. Thus the hepatic arterial blood mixes with the portal venous blood in the sinusoids. There are no anastomoses between adjoining hepatic arterial territories and hence each branch is an end artery.

Venous Drainage

Hepatic sinusoids drain into interlobular veins, which join to form sublobular veins. These in turn unite to form the hepatic veins which drain directly into the inferior vena cava. These veins provide great support to the liver, besides the intra-abdominal pressure.

The *hepatic veins* are arranged in two groups, upper and lower. The *upper group* consists of three large veins right, left and middle, which emerge through the upper part of the groove for the inferior vena cava, and open directly into the vena cava. The *lower group* consists of a variable number of small veins from the right lobe and the caudate lobe which emerge through the lower part of the caval groove and open into the vena cava.

Microscopically the tributaries of hepatic veins, i.e. central veins are seen as separate channels from those of the portal radicles.

Lymphatic Drainage

The superficial lymphatics of the liver run on the surface of the organ beneath the peritoneum, and terminate in caval, hepatic, paracardial and coeliac lymph nodes. Some vessels from the coronary ligament may directly join the thoracic duct.

The deep lymphatics end partly in the nodes around the end of the inferior vena cava, and partly in the hepatic nodes.

Nerve Supply

The liver receives its nerve supply from the hepatic plexus which contains both sympathetic and parasympathetic or vagal fibres. Nerves also reach the liver through its various peritoneal ligaments.

Hepatic Segments

On the basis of the intrahepatic distribution of the hepatic artery, the portal vein and the biliary ducts, the liver can be divided into the right and left functional lobes. These do not correspond to the anatomical lobes of the liver. The physiological lobes are separated by a plane passing on the antero-superior surface along a line joining the cystic notch to the groove for the inferior vena cava. On the inferior surface the plane passes through the fossa for the gall bladder; and on the posterior surface it passes through the middle of the caudate lobe (Fig. 23.25).

The right lobe is subdivided into anterior and posterior segments, and the left lobe into medial and lateral segments. Thus there are four segments in the liver.

1. Right anterior,
2. Right posterior,
3. Left lateral, and
4. Left medial.

Some authorities further subdivide each of these segments into the upper and the lower parts (Fig. 23.26).

The hepatic segments are of surgical importance. The hepatic veins tend to be intersegmental in their course.

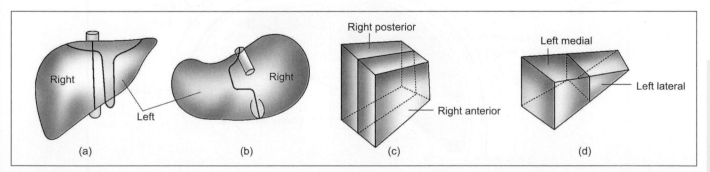

Fig. 23.25: The segments (physiological lobes) of the liver. (a) Anterior aspect, (b) inferior aspect, (c) scheme of the right lobe, and (d) scheme of the left lobe.

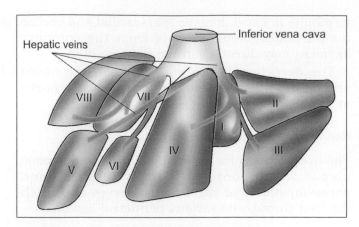

Fig. 23.26: The segments of liver.

Functions

1. *Metabolism* of carbohydrates, fats and proteins;
2. *Synthesis* of bile and prothrombin;
3. *Excretion* of drugs, toxins, poisons, cholesterol, bile pigments and heavy metals;
4. *Protective* by conjugation, destruction, phagocytosis, antibody formation and excretion; and
5. *Storage* of glycogen, iron, fat, vitamin A and D.

Histology

Liver is covered by Glisson's capsule. In the pig there are hexagonal lobules with portal radicles at 3–5 corners. Each radicle contains bile ductule, branch each of portal vein and hepatic artery. Central vein lies in the centre and all around the central vein are the hepatocytes in form of laminae. On one side of the lamina is the sinusoid and on the other side is a bile canaliculus. Portal lobule seen in human is triangular in shape with three central veins at the sides and portal tract in the centre. The liver acinus is defined as the liver parenchyma around a preterminal branch of hepatic arteriole between two adjacent central veins. The liver acinus is the functional unit of liver. Blood reaches the acinus via branches of portal vein and hepatic artery to open into the sinusoids to reach the central vein. On the other hand, the flow of bile is along bile canaliculi, bile ductules and the interlobular bile ducts. Hepatocytes in zone I close to preterminal branch are better supplied by oxygen, nutrients and toxins. The liver cells in zone III close to central veins are relatively hypoxic while cells in zone II are intermediate in oxygen supply. Histology of the liver can be studied by liver biopsy (Fig. 23.27).

Development

From the caudal end of foregut, an endodermal hepatic bud arises during 3rd week of development. The bud elongates cranially. It gives rise to a small bud on its right side. This is called pars cystica and the main part is pars hepatica. Pars cystica forms the gall bladder and the cystic duct which drains into common hepatic duct (CHD).

The epithelial cells of pars hepatica proliferate to form the parenchyma. These cells mix up with umbilical and vitelline veins to form hepatic sinusoids.

Kupffer's cells and blood cells are formed from the mesoderm of septum transversum.

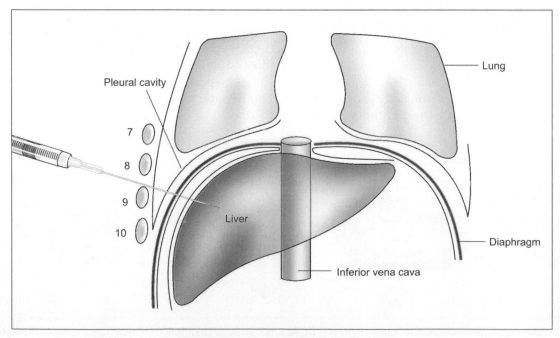

Fig. 23.27: Procedure for liver biopsy.

CLINICAL ANATOMY

Spleen

- *Palpation of the spleen:* A normal spleen is not palpable. An enlarged spleen can be felt under the left costal margin during inspiration. Palpation is assisted by turning the patient to his right side. Note that the spleen becomes palpable only after it has enlarged to about twice its normal size.
- *Splenomegaly:* Enlargement of the spleen is called *splenomegaly* (Fig. 23.28). It may occur in a number of diseases. Sometimes the spleen becomes very large. It then projects towards the right iliac fossa in the direction of the axis of the tenth rib.

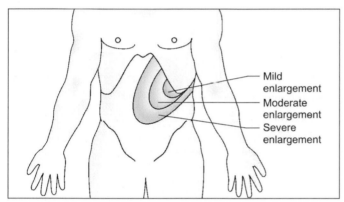

Fig. 23.28: Stages of enlargement of spleen towards right iliac fossa.

- *Splenectomy:* Surgical removal of the spleen is called *splenectomy* (Fig. 23.29). During this operation damage to the tail of the pancreas has to be carefully avoided, as the tail of pancreas is very rich in islets of Langerhans. Spleen has 2 pedicles, gastrosplenic and lienorenal. Their contents are separated carefully before the ligaments are cut.

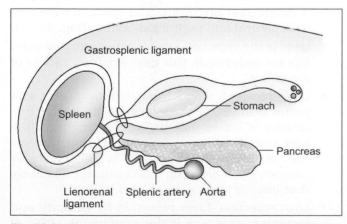

Fig. 23.29: Two pedicles of spleen to be cut during splenectomy.

- *Splenic puncture:* Spleen can be punctured through the 8th or 9th intercostal space in the midaxillary line using a lumbar puncture needle. When enlarged, it can be punctured through the mid axillary line. To avoid laceration of spleen, the patient must hold his breath during the procedure (Fig. 23.8).

  Intrasplenic pressure is an indirect record of the portal pressure. Splenic venography reveals and confirms the enlarged portosystemic communications in cases of portal hypertension.

- *Splenic infarction:* The smaller branches of splenic artery are end arteries. Their obstruction (embolism) therefore, results in splenic infarction which causes referred pain in the left shoulder (Kehr's sign) (Fig. 23.30).

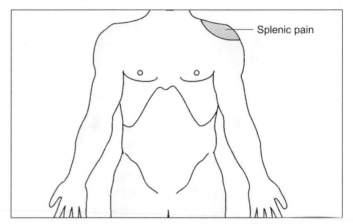

Fig. 23.30: Referred pain of spleen to left shoulder.

- Spleen is in danger of trauma to the left lower thoracic cage especially 9, 10, 11th ribs. A ruptured spleen may cause severe haemorrhage, as it has a rich blood supply.
- *Referred pain:* Pain of splenic tissue is poorly localised. It is also referred to the epigastrium. Stretch of the splenic capsule produces localized pain in the posterior left upper quadrant (hypochondrium).
- *Spleen:* If there is a small tear in the spleen, it can be sutured with catgut and the greater omentum can be wrapped round.
- *Partial splenectomy:* Since there are segmental branches of the splenic artery, only one segment can be removed according to the state of spleen.
- After splenectomy, spleen can be cut into small pieces and these can be implanted within the greater omentum. Because of vascularization, spleen survives and does its function of producing the antibodies.

Pancreas

- Deficiency of insulin causes the disease *diabetes mellitus.*
- Deficiency of pancreatic enzymes causes digestive disturbances.
- *Carcinoma* is common in the head of the pancreas. Pressure over the posteriorly placed bile duct leads to persistent obstructive jaundice. It may press upon the portal vein, causing ascites; or may involve the stomach, causing pyloric obstruction (Fig. 23.16).
- Acute pancreatitis is a serious disease. It may be a complication of mumps.
- Pancreatic cyst presents as a large fixed tumour in the upper part of abdomen along the median plane. They are often symptomless.
- Pancreatic pain is felt in the back as well as in the front of abdomen.
- Pancreatitis results in collection of fluid in the lesser sac—a pseudocyst of pancreas.
- Annular pancreas is a developmental anomaly where a ring of pancreatic tissue surrounds and obstructs the duodenum.
- *Pain from pancreatitis:* This pain is poorly localized. Pain is referred to epigastrium. Pain is also referred to posterior paravertebral region and around the lower thoracic vertebrae, due to inflammation of soft tissues of retroperitoneum. Their afferents are being sent through lower intercostal nerves.
- *Pancreatitis:* It may be primary or may be due to gall stones in the common bile duct.
- Superior mesenteric vessels are lying behind body of pancreas and in front of its uncinate process (Fig. 23.14). Pancreatitis may cause inflammatory aneurysm of the artery and/or thrombosis of the vein.
- Since pancreas has profuse blood supply, it is prone to hemorrhage (Fig. 23.17). Blood can appear in the flanks or in the groins. It may also enter bare area of liver to run forward in the falciform ligament and reach around umbilicus.
- Acute pancreatitis may cause gastric stasis and vomiting. The autonomic supply to midgut may be affected resulting in paralytic ileus.
- Sometimes fluid resulting from pancreatic inflammation may collect in the lesser sac of peritoneum, called as pseudocyst. It needs to be drained.
- *Pancreas resection:* It is a difficult and complicated procedure. Only resection of its head and neck is possible.

Liver

- In the infrasternal angle, the liver is readily accessible to examination on percussion, though it is *normally not palpable* due to the normal tone of the recti muscles and the softness of the liver. Normally in the median plane the inferior border of the liver lies on the transpyloric plane, about a hand's breadth below the xiphisternal joint. In women and children this border usually lies at a slightly lower level and tends to project downwards for a short distance below the right costal margin. It enlarges towards right iliac fossa (Fig. 23.31). Spleen also enlarges towards right iliac fossa.

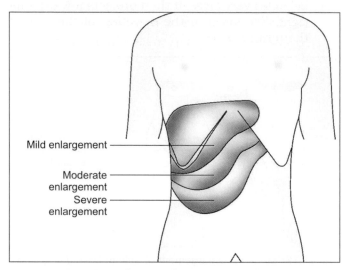

Mild enlargement

Moderate enlargement

Severe enlargement

Fig. 23.31: Stages of enlargement of liver.

- Inflammation of the liver is referred to as *hepatitis*. It may be infective hepatitis or amoebic hepatitis.
- Under certain conditions, e.g. malnutrition, liver tissue undergoes fibrosis and shrinks. This is called *cirrhosis* of the liver.
- Liver biopsy needs to be done in certain clinical conditions. Liver biopsy needle is passed through right 8th intercostal space. It traverses both pleural and peritoneal cavities (Fig. 23.27).
- Liver is the common site of metastatic tumours. The secondaries in this case are from cancer of the colon.
- Liver receives blood from hepatic artery and portal vein. Both these vessels lie in the free margin of lesser omentum. Bleeding from the liver can be stopped by compressing the free edge of lesser omentum. This is called Pringles manoeuvre. If bleeding still continues it is likely that inferior vena cava is also injured.
- *Liver resection:* Liver resection for primary and secondary tumours is done commonly. 80% of

liver mass can be removed safely. Liver can regrow to its original size within 6–12 months after resection. Major resections follow the planes between segments and are anatomical.

- *Liver transplantation:* It can be done in patients with end stage liver disease. The implant of the graft requires an inferior caval anastomoses, followed by anastomosis of the portal vein. Finally the arterial and biliary anastomoses are performed.
- Sometimes a right hemiliver comprising segments V to segments VIII can be removed from a healthy donor and transplanted into the needy patient.
- Transjugular intraparenchymal portosystemic shunt (TIPS) for portal hypertension.

In severe portal hypertension, balloon catheters are introduced from internal jugular vein → superior vena cava →inferior vena cava → hepatic veins →liver tissue →portal vein branch.

- Liver cirrhosis causes "caput medusae" at the umbilicus (Fig. 23.32).

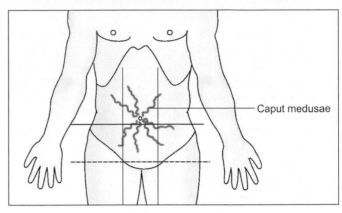

Fig. 23.32: Caput medusae

Kidney and Ureter

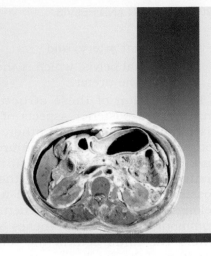

The kidneys are kept in position by renal fascia, perirenal fat and pararenal fat. If the fat is lost drastically, as in dieting, the support of the kidneys is lost and these may descend down, leading to *kinking of the ureter*. So the loss of weight must be slow and steady. Kidneys are also liable to *stone formation*. The renal stones mostly have calcium and are easily seen on plain radiographs of the abdomen.

Kidney also gets affected by toxins of a particular type of bacteria responsible for pharyngitis. The condition is called *acute glomerulonephritis*.

The closely packed structure and numerous functions of the kidney illustrate the beautiful workmanship of our *Creator*. It not only applies to the kidney but to each and every part of our body.

KIDNEYS

Synonyms

The kidneys are also called *renes* from which we have the derivative *renal*; and *nephros* from which we have the terms *nephron, nephritis*, etc.

Definition

Kidneys are a pair of excretory organs situated on the posterior abdominal wall, one on each side of the vertebral column, behind the peritoneum. They remove waste products of metabolism and excess of water and salts from the blood, and maintain its pH.

External Features

Each kidney is bean-shaped. It has upper and lower poles, medial and lateral borders, and anterior and posterior surfaces.

Two Poles of the Kidney

The upper pole is broad and is in close contact with the corresponding suprarenal gland. The lower pole is pointed.

DISSECTION

Remove the fat and fascia from the anterior surface of left and right kidneys and suprarenal glands. Find left suprarenal vein and left testicular or ovarian vein and trace both to left renal vein. Follow this vein from the left kidney to inferior vena cava and note its tributaries. Displace the vein and expose left renal artery, follow its branches to the left suprarenal gland and ureter. Follow the ureter in abdomen.

Identify the structures related to the anterior surface of both the kidneys. Turn the left kidney medially to expose its posterior surface and that of its vessels and the ureter and identify the muscles, vessels and nerves which are posterior to them. Carry out the same dissection on the right side. Note that the right testicular or ovarian and suprarenal veins drain directly into the inferior vena cava. Cut through the convex border of the kidney till the hilus. Look at its interior. Identify the cortex, pyramids, calyces. Follow the ureters in the renal pelvis, in the abdomen, in the pelvic cavity and finally through the wall of urinary bladder.

Two Surfaces

The anterior surface is said to be irregular and the posterior surface flat, but it is often difficult to recognize the anterior and posterior aspects of the kidney by looking at the surfaces. The proper way to do this is to examine the structures present in the hilum as described below.

Two Borders

The lateral border is convex. The medial border is concave. Its middle part shows a depression, the hilus or hilum.

Hilum

The following structures are seen in the hilum from anterior to posterior side.

1. The renal vein

2. The renal artery, and

3. The renal pelvis, which is the expanded upper end of the ureter.

Examination of these structures enables the anterior and posterior aspects of the kidney to be distinguished from each other. As the pelvis is continuous inferiorly with the ureter, the superior and inferior poles of the kidney can also be distinguished by examining the hilum. So it is possible to determine the side to which a kidney belongs by examining the structures in the hilum. Commonly, one of the branches of the renal artery enters the hilus behind the renal pelvis, and a tributary of the renal vein may be found in the same plane.

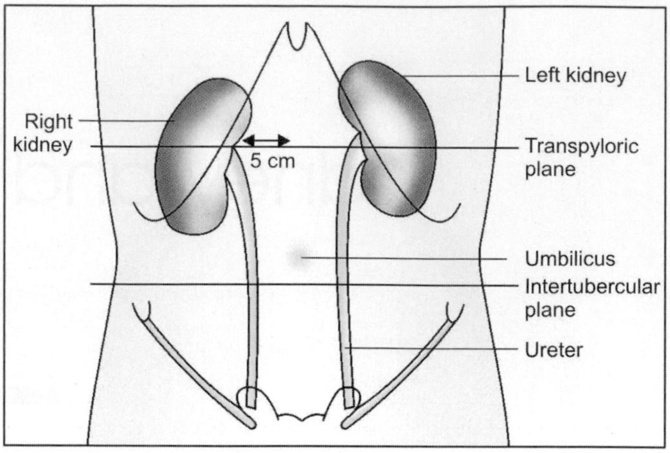

Location

The kidneys occupy the epigastric, hypochondriac, lumbar and umbilical regions (Fig. 24.1). Vertically they extend from the upper border of twelfth thoracic vertebra to the centre of the body of third lumbar vertebra. The right kidney is slightly lower than the left, and the left kidney is a little nearer to the median plane than the right.

The transpyloric plane passes through the upper part of the hilus of the right kidney, and through the lower part of the hilus of the left kidney.

Shape, Size, Weight and Orientation

Each kidney is about 11 cm long, 6 cm broad, and 3 cm thick. The left kidney is a little longer and narrower than the right kidney. On an average the kidney weighs 150 g in males and 135 g in females. The kidneys are reddish brown in colour.

The long axis of the kidney is directed downwards and laterally, so that the upper poles are nearer to the median plane than the lower poles (Fig. 24.2). The transverse axis is directed laterally and backwards.

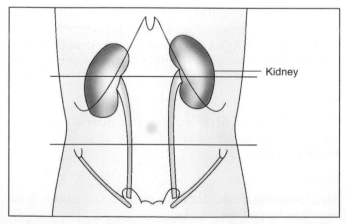

Fig. 24.1: Location of the kidneys.

Fig. 24.2: Position of kidneys from anterior aspect.

In the foetus the kidney is lobulated and is made up of about 12 lobules. After birth the lobules gradually fuse, so that in adults the kidney is uniformly smooth. However, the evidence of foetal lobulation may persist.

Relations of the Kidneys

The kidneys are retroperitoneal organs and are only partly covered by peritoneum anteriorly.

Relations Common to the Two Kidneys

1. The upper pole of each kidney is related to the corresponding suprarenal gland. The lower poles lie about 2.5 cm above the iliac crests.

2. The medial border of each kidney is related to:

   (i) The suprarenal gland, above the hilus, and

   (ii) To the ureter below the hilus (Fig. 24.3).

3. Posterior relations: The posterior surfaces of both kidneys are related to the following.

   (i) Diaphragm

   (ii) Medial and lateral arcuate ligaments

   (iii) Psoas major

   (iv) Quadratus lumborum

   (v) Transversus abdominis

   (vi) Subcostal vessels; and

   (vii) Subcostal, iliohypogastric and ilioinguinal nerves (Fig. 24.4).

   In addition, the right kidney is related to twelfth rib, and the left kidney to eleventh and twelfth ribs (Fig. 24.5).

4. The structures related to the hilum have been described earlier.

Other Relations of the Right Kidney

Anterior relations

1. Right suprarenal gland

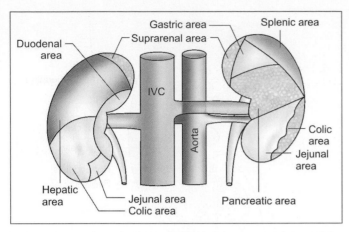

Fig. 24.3: Anterior relations of the kidneys. Areas covered by peritoneum are shaded.

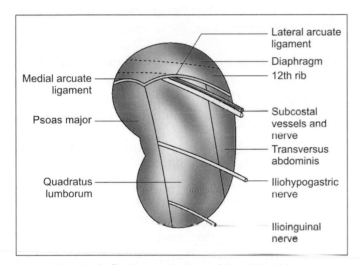

Fig. 24.4: Posterior relations of the right kidney.

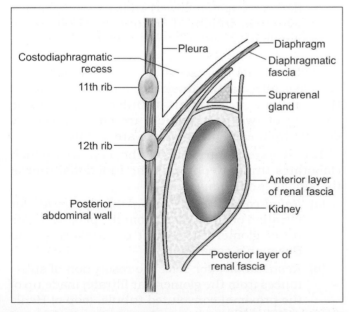

Fig. 24.5: Vertical section through the posterior abdominal wall showing the relationship of the pleura to the kidney.

2. Liver
3. Second part of duodenum
4. Hepatic flexure of colon
5. Small intestine. Out of these the hepatic and intestinal surfaces are covered by peritoneum.

The lateral border of the right kidney is related to the right lobe of the liver and to the hepatic flexure of the colon (Fig. 24.3).

Other Relations of the Left Kidney

Anterior relations

1. Left suprarenal gland
2. Spleen
3. Stomach
4. Pancreas
5. Splenic vessels
6. Splenic flexure and descending colon
7. Jejunum.

Out of these the gastric, splenic and jejunal surfaces are covered by peritoneum.

The lateral border of the left kidney is related to the spleen and to the descending colon.

Capsules or Coverings of Kidney

The Fibrous Capsule

This is a thin membrane which closely invests the kidney and lines the renal sinus. Normally it can be easily stripped off from the kidney, but in certain diseases it becomes adherent and cannot be stripped (Fig. 24.6).

Perirenal or Perinephric Fat

This is a layer of adipose tissue lying outside the fibrous capsule. It is thickest at the borders of the kidney and fills up the extra space in the renal sinus.

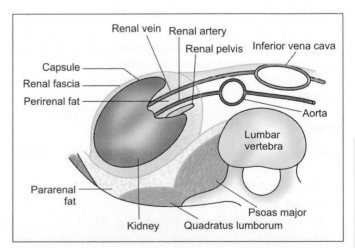

Fig. 24.6: Transverse section through the lumbar region showing the capsules of the kidney.

The perirenal fascia was originally described as being made up of two separate layers.

Posterior layer was called fascia of Zuckerkandall and anterior layer as fascia of Gerota.

These two fasciae fused laterally to form lateral conal fascia. According to this view, lateral conal fascia continued anterolaterally behind colon to blend with parietal peritoneum.

But lately it has been seen that the fascia is not made up of fused fasciae, but of a single multi-laminated structure which is fused posteromedially with muscular fasciae of psoas major and quadratus lumborum muscles.

The fascia then extends anteromedially behind the kidney as bilaminated sheet, which divides at a variable point into thin layer which courses around the front of kidney as anterior perirenal fascia and a thicker posterior layer which continues antero-laterally as the lateral conal fascia.

It was believed earlier that above the suprarenal gland the anterior and posterior perirenal fasciae fuse with each other and then get fused to the diaphragmatic fascia, but research presently demonstrates that superior aspect of perirenal space is "open" and is in continuity to the bare area of liver on the right side and with subphrenic extraperitoneal space on the left side.

On the right side at the level of upper pole of kidney anterior fascia blends with inferior coronary layer and bare area of liver.

On the left side, anterior layer fuses with gastrophrenic ligament.

Posterior layer on both right and left sides fuses with fasciae of muscles of posterior abdominal wall, i.e. psoas major and quadratus lumborum as well as with fascia on the inferior aspect of thoraco-abdominal diaphragm.

Pararenal or Paranephric Body (Fat)

It consists of a variable amount of fat lying outside the renal fascia. It is more abundant posteriorly and towards the lower pole of the kidney. It fills up the paravertebral gutter and forms a cushion for the kidney.

Structure

Naked eye examination of a coronal section of the kidney shows:

(a) An outer, reddish brown cortex.

(b) An inner, pale medulla.

(c) A space, the renal sinus (Fig. 24.7).

The *renal medulla* is made up of about 10 conical masses, called the *renal pyramids*. Their apices form the *renal papillae* which indent the minor calyces.

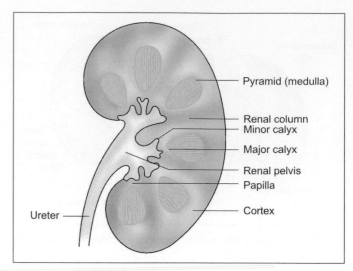

Fig. 24.7: A coronal section through the kidney showing the naked eye structure.

The *renal cortex* is divisible into two parts.

(a) *Cortical arches* or *cortical lobules*, which form caps over the bases of the pyramids.

(b) Renal columns, which dip in between the pyramids.

Each pyramid along with the overlying cortical arch forms a lobe of the kidney.

The *renal sinus* is a space that extends into the kidney from the hilus. It contains:

(a) Branches of the renal artery.

(b) Tributaries of the renal vein.

(c) The renal pelvis. The pelvis divides into 2 to 3 major calyces, and these in their turn divide into 7 to 13 minor calyces. Each minor calyx (*kalyx* = cup of a flower) ends in an expansion which is indented by one to three renal papillae.

Histology

Histologically, each kidney is composed of one to three million uriniferous tubules. Each tubule consists of two parts which are embryologically distinct from each other. These are as follows.

The secretory part, called the *nephron,* which elaborates urine. Nephron is the functional unit of the kidney, and comprises:

(a) *Renal corpuscle* or *Malpighian corpuscle,* (for filtration of substances from the plasma) made up of glomerulus (a tuft of capillaries) and Bowman's capsule.

(b) *Renal tubule,* (for selective resorption of subs-tances from the glomerular filtrate) made up of the proximal convoluted tubule, loop of Henle with its descending and ascending limbs, and the distal convoluted tubule (Fig. 24.8).

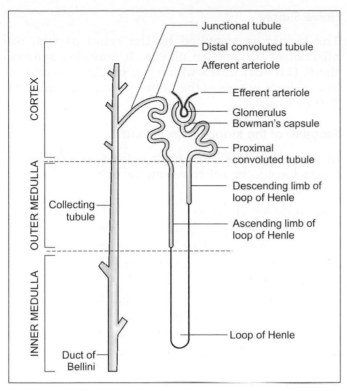

Fig. 24.8: Placement of the uriniferous tubule in various zones of kidney.

The *collecting tubule* begins as a junctional tubule from the distal convoluted tubule. Many tubules unite together to form the ducts of Bellini which open into the minor calyces through the renal papillae.

Juxtaglomerular apparatus is formed at the vascular pole of glomerulus which is intimately related to its own ascending limb of the Henle's loop near the distal convoluted tubule. The apparatus consists of:

(a) *Macula densa,* formed by altered cells of the tubule.

(b) *Juxtaglomerular cells,* formed by the epithelioid cells in the media of the afferent arteriole.

(c) *Some* agranular cells between macula densa and the glomerulus proper.

Arterial Supply

There is one *renal artery* on each side, arising from the abdominal aorta.

At or near the hilus the renal artery divides into anterior and posterior divisions. Further branching of these divisions gives rise to segmental arteries each of which supplies one vascular segment. Five such segments are described. These are:

1. Apical
2. Upper
3. Middle
4. Lower
5. Posterior (Fig. 24.9).

The segmental arteries are end arteries, so that the vascular segments are independent units.

Each segmental artery divides into *lobar arteries,* usually one for each pyramid. Each lobar artery divides into 2–3 *interlobar arteries* which run on each side of the pyramid. At the corticomedullary junction, the interlobar arteries divide dichotomously into *arcuate arteries* which arch over the bases of the pyramids, at right angles to the interlobar arteries. The arcuate arteries give off *interlobular arteries* which run radially into the cortical substance at right angles to the arcuate arteries. The arcuate arteries do not anastomose with their neighbours but finally turn up into the cortex as additional interlobular arteries. The interlobular arteries do not anastomose with their neighbours, and, therefore, are end arteries (Fig. 24.10).

Afferent glomerular arterioles are derived mostly as side branches from interlobular arteries.

The *efferent glomerular arteriole,* from most of the glomeruli, divides soon to form the *peritubular capillary plexus* around the proximal and distal convoluted tubules. Since blood passes through two

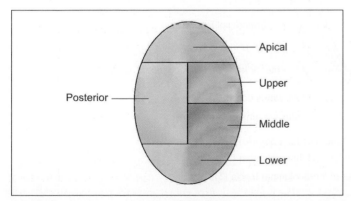

Fig. 24.9: Vascular segments of the kidney as seen in a sagittal section.

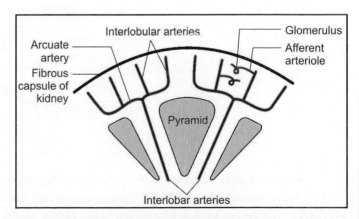

Fig. 24.10: Arrangement of the arteries in the kidney.

sets of capillaries, glomerulus and peritubular plexus, it forms the *renal portal circulation.*

Arterial supply of the medulla is derived mostly from the efferent *arterioles of the juxtamedullary glomeruli,* and partly from a number of *aglomerular arterioles.* Each arteriole dips into renal pyramid, breaks up into 1–2 dozen of *descending vasa recta* which run into the outer part of medulla. These break up to form capillary plexus in the inner part of pyramids, closely related to the loops of Henle and the collecting ducts. At the venous end the plexus gives rise to *ascending vasa recta* which return blood to interlobular or arcuate veins. In the outer part of medulla, the close relation between the descending vasa recta, the venules, and the medullary portion of renal tubules and ducts provides the structural basis for the countercurrent exchange and multiplier system.

Venous Drainage

The venous end of the peritubular capillary plexus gives rise to *interlobular veins* which run along the corresponding arteries. The interlobular veins drain into the *arcuate veins,* which in their turn open into the *interlobar veins.* These emerge at the renal sinus and join to form the *renal vein* which drains into the inferior vena cava.

The venous end of the capillary plexus along the vasa recta gives rise to veins which drain into the arcuate veins.

Lymphatic Drainage

The lymphatics of the kidney drain into the lateral aortic nodes located at the level of origin of the renal arteries (L2).

Nerve Supply

The kidney is supplied by the renal plexus, an offshoot of the coeliac plexus. It contains sympathetic (T10–L1) fibres which are chiefly vasomotor. The afferent nerves of the kidney belong to segments T10 to T12.

Exposure of the Kidney from Behind

In exposing the kidney from behind, the following layers have to be reflected one by one.
1. Skin
2. Superficial fascia
3. Posterior layer of thoracolumbar fascia with latissimus dorsi and serratus posterior inferior
4. Erector spinae, which can be removed for convenience
5. Middle layer of thoracolumbar fascia
6. Quadratus lumborum
7. Anterior layer of thoracolumbar fascia in which the related nerves are embedded (Fig. 24.11).

Histology

The cortex of kidney shows cut sections of glomeruli, many sections of proximal convoluted tubule, some sections of distal convoluted tubule few collecting ducts. Section through the pyramid of the medulla shows light staining collecting ducts, sections of loop of Henle, thick and thin segments of descending and ascending limbs, capillaries and connective tissue.

URETERS

The ureters are a pair of narrow, thick-walled

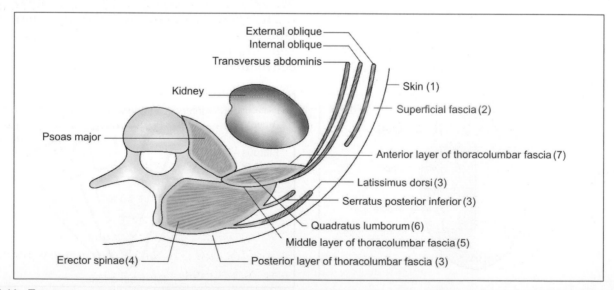

Fig. 24.11: Transverse section through the upper lumbar region showing the layers of thoracolumbar fascia encountered during exposure of the kidney from behind.

muscular tubes which convey urine from the kidneys to the urinary bladder (Fig. 24.12).

They lie deep to the peritoneum, closely applied to the posterior abdominal wall in the upper part, and to the lateral pelvic wall in the lower part.

Dimensions

Each ureter is about 25 cm (10 in.) long, of which the upper half (5 in.) lies in the abdomen, and the lower half (5 in.) in the pelvis. It measures about 3 mm in diameter, but it is slightly constricted at five places.

Course

The ureter begins within the renal sinus as a funnel-shaped dilatation, called the *renal pelvis*. The pelvis issues from the hilus of the kidney, descends along its medial margin, or partly behind it. Gradually it narrows till the lower end of the kidney where it becomes the ureter proper.

The ureter passes downwards and slightly medially on the psoas major muscle, and enters the pelvis by crossing in front of the termination of the common iliac artery (Fig. 24.13).

In the lesser or true pelvis the ureter at first runs downwards, and slightly backwards and laterally, following the anterior margin of the greater sciatic notch. Opposite the ischial spine it turns forwards and medially to reach the base of the urinary bladder.

Normal Constrictions

The ureter is slightly constricted at five places.

1. At the pelviureteric junction.
2. At the brim of the lesser pelvis.
3. Point of crossing of ureter by ductus deferens or broad ligament of uterus.

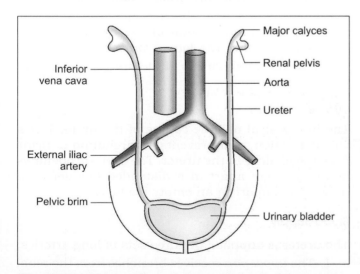

Fig. 24.12: The location of the ureters on the posterior abdominal and lateral pelvic walls.

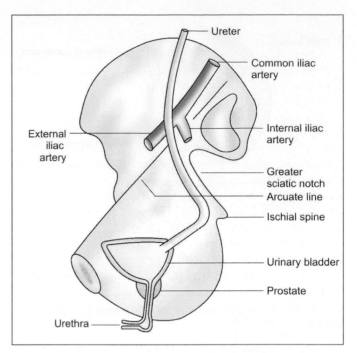

Fig. 24.13: General course of the ureter in the pelvis.

4. During its oblique passage through the bladder wall.
5. At its opening in lateral angle of trigone.

Relations

Renal Pelvis

In the renal sinus, branches of renal vessels lie both in front and behind it.

Outside the Kidney

Anteriorly: On the *right side*, there are the renal vessels and the second part of the duodenum. On the *left side*, there are the renal vessels, the pancreas, the peritoneum and the jejunum (Fig. 24.3).

Posteriorly: Psoas major muscle (Fig. 24.4).

Abdominal Part of Ureter

Anteriorly

On the *right side*, the ureter is related to:

1. Third part of the duodenum (Fig. 24.14)
2. Peritoneum
3. Right colic vessels
4. Ileocolic vessels
5. Gonadal vessels
6. Root of the mesentery
7. Terminal part of the ileum.

On the *left side* (Fig. 24.15) the ureter is related to:

1. Peritoneum
2. Gonadal artery
3. Left colic vessels

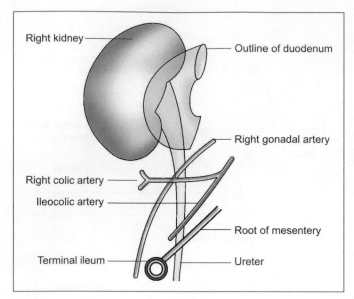

Fig. 24.14: Anterior relations of the abdominal part of the right ureter.

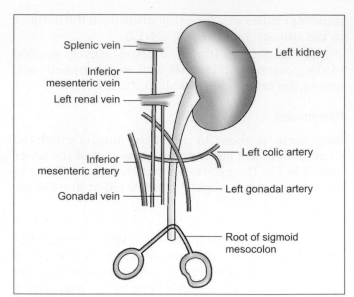

Fig. 24.15: Anterior relations of the abdominal part of the left ureter.

4. Sigmoid colon
5. Sigmoid mesocolon.

Posteriorly

The ureter lies on
1. Psoas major
2. Tips of transverse processes (Fig. 36.3)
3. Genitofemoral nerve.

Medially

On the *right side* there is the inferior vena cava; on the *left side*, there is the left gonadal vein, and still further medially, the inferior mesenteric vein.

Pelvic Part of Ureter

In its downward course:

Posteriorly

1. Internal iliac artery
2. Commencement of the anterior trunk of the internal iliac artery
3. Internal iliac vein
4. Lumbosacral trunk
5. Sacroiliac joint (Fig. 24.16).

Laterally

1. Fascia covering the obturator internus,
2. Superior vesical artery
3. Obturator nerve
4. Obturator artery
5. Obturator vein
6. Inferior vesical vein
7. Middle rectal artery
8. In the female, it forms the posterior boundary of the ovarian fossa.

In its forward course:

In males

1. *Ductus deferens* crosses the ureter superiorly from lateral to medial side.
2. *Seminal vesicle* lies below and behind the ureter (Fig. 24.17).
3. Vesical veins surround the terminal part of ureter.

In females

1. The ureter lies in the extraperitoneal connective tissue in the lower and medial part of the *broad ligament of the uterus* (Fig. 24.18).
2. *Uterine artery* lies first above and in front of the ureter for a distance of about 2.5 cm and then crosses it superiorly from lateral to medial side.
3. The ureter lies about 2 cm lateral to the *supravaginal portion of the cervix*. It runs slightly above the *lateral fornix of the vagina*.
4. The terminal portion of the ureter lies anterior to the *vagina*.

Intravesical Part

The intravesical oblique course of the ureter has a valvular action, and prevents regurgitation of urine from the bladder to the ureter. The ureteric openings lie about 5 cm apart in a distended bladder, and only 2.5 cm apart in an empty bladder.

Blood Supply

The ureter is supplied by three sets of long arteries:
1. The *upper part* receives branches from the renal artery. It may also receive branches from the gonadal, or colic vessels.

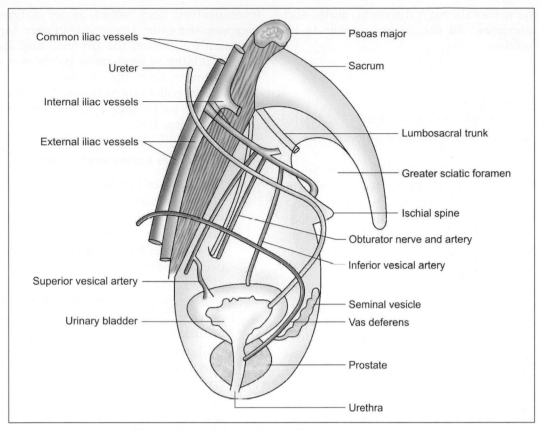

Fig. 24.16: Relations of the pelvic part of the ureter.

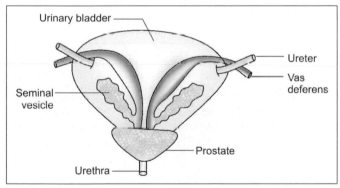

Fig. 24.17: Posterior view of the male urinary bladder showing the relations of the ureter to the vas deferens and the seminal vesicle.

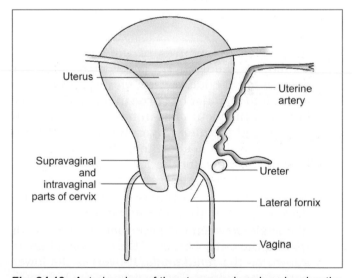

Fig. 24.18: Anterior view of the uterus and vagina showing the relation of the ureter to the uterine artery, the cervix of the uterus, and the vagina.

2. The *middle part* receives branches from the aorta. It may also receive branches from the gonadal, or iliac vessels.

3. The *pelvic part* is supplied by branches from the vesical, middle rectal, or uterine vessels. The arteries to the ureter lie closely attached to peritoneum. They divide into ascending and descending branches which first form a plexus on the surface of the ureter, and then supply it.

In about 10% of cases, the middle part of the ureter is supplied only by minute twigs from the peritoneal vessels. In another 2% of cases although there are several long arteries to the middle part, the upper and lower parts are supplied by short vessels.

Nerve Supply

The ureter is supplied by sympathetic from T10–L1 segments and parasympathetic from S2–S4 nerves.

They reach the ureter through the renal, aortic and hypogastric plexuses. All the nerves appear to be sensory in function.

Histology

Ureter is composed of:

(i) The innermost mucous membrane.

(ii) Middle layer of well developed smooth muscle layer.

(iii) Outer tunica adventitia. The epithelial lining is of transitional epithelium. Muscle coat in upper two-thirds has inner longitudinal and outer circular fibres. Lower one-third comprises an additional outer longitudinal layer. Connective tissue forms the outer layer.

Development of Kidney and Ureter

Kidney develops from metanephros, though pronephros and mesonephros appear to disappear. Only the duct of mesonephros, the mesonephric duct persists. Thus the nephrons of the kidney arise from the metanephros. Parts of nephron formed are Bowman's capsule, proximal convoluted tubule, loop of Henle, distal convoluted tubule. Tuft of capillaries form the glomeruli. Collecting part of kidney develops from ureteric bud, which is an outgrowth of the mesonephric duct. Ureteric bud gets capped by the metanephric tissue, the ureteric bud forms ureter. Soon it dilates to form renal pelvis and divides and subdivides to form major and minor calyces and 1–3 million collecting tubules. Kidney starts developing in the sacral region, then it ascends to occupy its lumbar position.

Anomalies of the Kidney and Ureter

1. Nonunion of the secretory and collecting parts of the kidney results in the formation of *congenital polycystic kidney.*

2. Fusion of the lower poles may occur, resulting in a *horseshoe kidney.* In these cases the ureters pass anterior to the isthmus of the kidney.

3. The early *pelvic position* of the kidney may persist. The renal artery then arises from the common iliac artery.

4. Unilateral *aplasia* or *hypoplasia* of the kidney may occur. Sometimes both kidneys may lie on any one side of the body.

5. The ureteric bud may divide into two, forming double ureter partly or completely.

CLINICAL ANATOMY

- In surgical exposures of the kidney, when sometimes the 12th rib is resected for easier delivery of the kidney, *danger of opening the pleural cavity* must be borne in mind. The lower border of the pleura lies in front of the 12th rib and behind the diaphragm. When the 12th rib is absent or is too short to be felt, the 11th rib may be mistaken for the 12th, and the chances of opening the pleural cavity are greatly increased. Lithotripsy has replaced conventional method to some degree.

- The angle between the lower border of the 12th rib and the outer border of the erector spinae is known as the *renal angle.* It overlies the lower part of the kidney. Tenderness in the kidney is elicited by applying pressure over this angle, with the thumb (Fig. 24.19).

- Blood from a ruptured kidney or pus in a perinephric abscess first distends the renal fascia, then forces its way within the renal fascia downwards into the pelvis. It cannot cross to opposite side because of the fascial septum and midline attachment of the renal fascia.

- Kidney is palpated bimanually, with one hand placed in front and the other hand behind

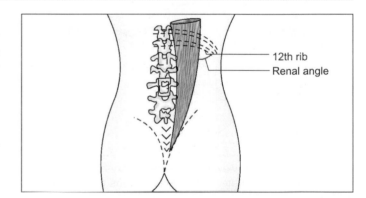

Fig. 24.19: Renal angle.

the flank. When enlarged, the lower pole of kidney becomes palpable on deep inspiration (Fig. 24.20).

A floating kidney can move up and down within the renal fascia, but not from side to side.

- The common diseases of kidney are nephritis, pyelonephritis, tuberculosis of kidney, renal stones and tumours.

Common manifestations of a kidney disease are renal oedema and hypertension. Raised blood urea indicates suppressed kidney function and

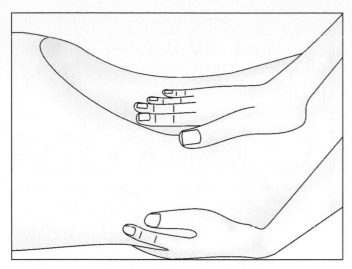

Fig. 24.20: Bimanual palpation of the kidney.

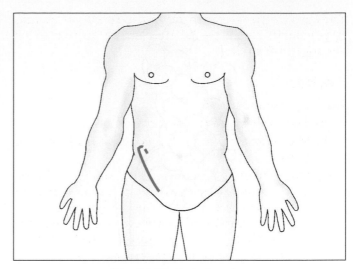

Fig. 24.22: Ureteric colic.

renal failure. Kidney transplantation can be done in selected cases (Fig. 24.21).

- *Ureteric colic:* This term is used for severe pain due to a ureteric stone or calculus which causes spasm of thc urctcr. Thc pain starts in thc loin and radiates down the groin, the scrotum or the labium majus and the inner side of the thigh. Note that the pain is referred to the cutaneous areas innervated by segments, mainly T11 to L2, which also supply the ureter (Fig. 24.22).

- *Ureteric stone:* A ureteric stone is liable to become impacted at one of the sites of normal cons-triction of the ureter, e.g. pelviureteric junction, brim of the pelvis and intravesical course (Fig. 24.23).

- One common congenital condition of kidney is polycystic kidney which leads to hypertension (Fig. 24.24).

- In cases of chronic renal failure dialysis needs to be done. It can be done as peritoneal dialysis (Fig. 24.25) or haemodialysis (Fig. 24.26).

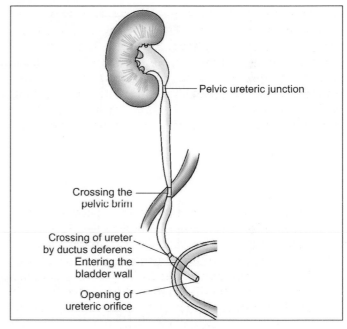

Pelvic ureteric junction

Crossing the pelvic brim

Crossing of ureter by ductus deferens

Entering the bladder wall

Opening of ureteric orifice

Fig. 24.23: Ureteric colic.

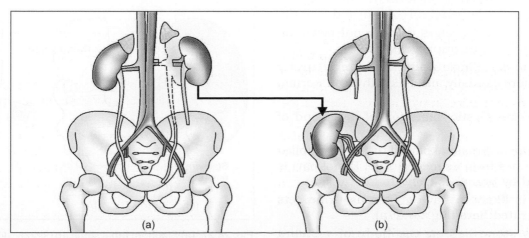

Fig. 24.21: (a) Donor's left kidney transplanted as (b) recipient's right kidney.

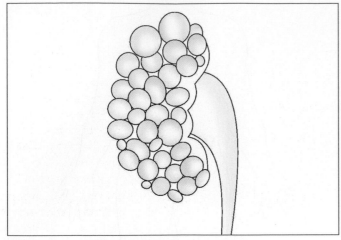

Fig. 24.24: Polycystic kidney.

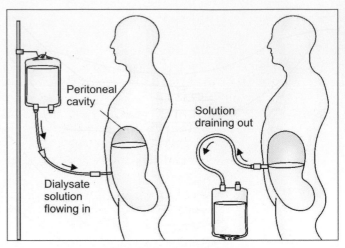

Fig. 24.25: Peritoneal dialysis.

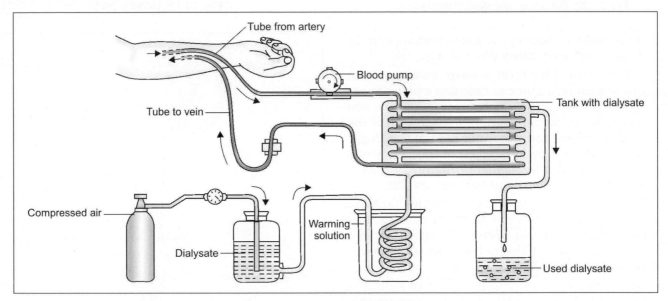

Fig. 24.26: Haemodialysis .

- The kidneys are likely to be injured due to penetrating injuries to lower thoracic cage. These may also be injured by kicks in the renal angle—angle between the vertebral column and 12th rib.
- *Duplex ureter:* 2 ureters drain renal pelvis on one side called as duplex system.
- *Ectopic ureter:* Single ureter and longer ureter insert more caudally and medially than normal one.
- *Ureteroceles:* Cystic dilatation of lower end of ureter.
- *Blood supply:* Proximal part of ureter is supplied by branches from its medial side. Distal part is supplied by branches from its lateral side.
- Kidney is likely to have stones as urine gets concentrated here (Fig. 24.27a).
- Kidneys stone lies on the body of vertebra (Fig. 24.27b).

- Gall stones lie anterior to body of vertebra (Fig. 24.27c).

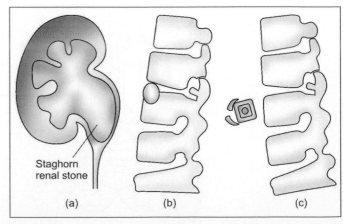

Fig. 24.27: (a) Staghorn renal stone, (b) kidney stone on the body of vertebra, and (c) gall stone anterior to the vertebra.

Suprarenal Gland and Chromaffin System

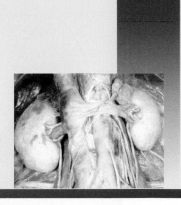

The suprarenal or adrenal glands are endocrine glands subjected to hyper- or hypofunctioning. Lack of secretion of the cortical part leads to Addison's disease. Excessive secretion causes retention of salts and fluids.

Tumour of adrenal medulla or pheochromocytoma causes persistent severe hypertension.

SUPRARENAL GLANDS

The suprarenal glands are a pair of important endocrine glands situated on the posterior abdominal wall over the upper pole of the kidneys behind the peritoneum (Fig. 25.1). They are made up of two parts.

(a) An outer cortex of mesodermal origin, which secretes a number of steroid hormones.

(b) An inner medulla of neural crest origin, which is made up of chromaffin cells and secretes adrenalin and noradrenalin or catecholamines.

Location

Each gland lies in the epigastrium, at the upper pole of the kidney, in front of the crus of the diaphragm,

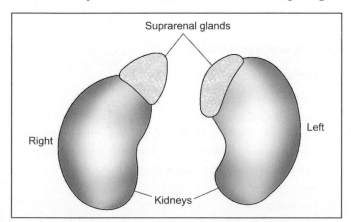

Fig. 25.1: The suprarenal glands.

DISSECTION

Locate the suprarenal glands situated along the upper pole and medial border of the two kidneys. Identify the structures related to the right and left suprarenal glands.

opposite the vertebral end of the 11th intercostal space and the 12th rib.

Size, Shape and Weight

Each gland measures 50 mm in height, 30 mm in breadth and 10 mm in thickness. It is approximately one-third of the kidney at birth and about one-thirtieth of it in adults. It weighs about 5 g, the medulla forming one-tenth of the gland. Right suprarenal is triangular or pyramidal in shape and the left is semilunar in shape.

Sheaths

The suprarenal glands are immediately surrounded by areolar tissue containing considerable amount of fat.

Outside the fatty sheath, there is the perirenal fascia. Between the two layers lies the suprarenal gland (Fig. 25.2). The two layers are not fused above the suprarenal. The perirenal space is open and is in continuity with bare area of liver on the right side and with subphrenic extraperitoneal space on the left side.

The gland is separated from the kidney by a septum.

RIGHT SUPRARENAL GLAND

The right suprarenal gland is triangular to pyramidal in shape. It has:

1. An apex
2. A base
3. Two surfaces—anterior and posterior.

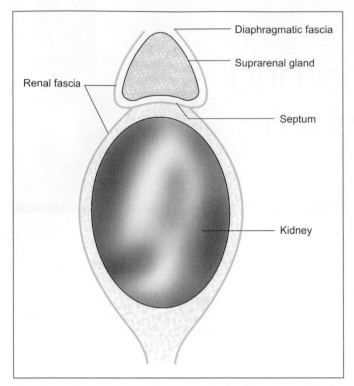

Fig. 25.2: The kidney and suprarenal glands enclosed in the renal fascia with a septum intervening.

Structure

Naked eye examination of a cross-section of the suprarenal gland shows an outer part, called the *cortex*, which forms the main mass of the gland, and a thin inner part, called the *medulla*, which forms only about one-tenth of the gland. The two parts are absolutely distinct from each other structurally, functionally and developmentally.

The cortex is composed of three zones.

1. The outer, zona glomerulosa which produces mineralocorticoids that affect electrolyte and water balance of the body.
2. The middle, zona fasciculata which produces glucocorticoids.
3. The inner, zona reticularis which produces sex hormones. The medulla is composed of chromaffin cells that secrete adrenalin and noradrenalin. Zona glomerulosa contains groups of arches of columnar cells; zona fasciculata contains cells arranged in vertical columns. The cells are light stained. Zona reticularis contains anastomosing cords of cells. Medulla contains cells in groups with lots of capillaries. Autonomic ganglion cells are also seen.

Arterial Supply

Each gland is supplied by:

1. The *superior suprarenal artery*, a branch of the inferior phrenic artery.
2. The *middle suprarenal artery*, a branch of the abdominal aorta.
3. The *inferior suprarenal artery*, a branch of the renal artery (Fig. 25.4).

Venous Drainage

Each gland is drained by one vein (Fig. 25.5). The right suprarenal vein drains into the inferior vena cava, and the left suprarenal vein into the left renal vein.

4. Three borders—anterior, medial and lateral (Fig. 25.3a and d).

LEFT SUPRARENAL GLAND

The *left gland* is semilunar. It has:

1. Two ends, upper—narrow end and lower, rounded end.
2. Two borders—medial convex and lateral concave.
3. Two surfaces—anterior and posterior (Fig. 25.3b and c).

Comparison of right and left suprarenal glands is given in Table 25.1.

Table 25.1: Comparison of right and left suprarenal glands		
	Right suprarenal gland	**Left suprarenal gland**
Shape:	Pyramidal	Semilunar
Parts and relations:	Apex: Bare area of liver	Upper end: Close to spleen
	Base: Upper pole of right kidney	Lower end: Presents hilum, left vein emerges from here
Anterior surface:	Inferior vena cava, bare area of liver	Cardiac end of stomach, pancreas with splenic artery
Posterior surface:	Right crus of diaphragm, right kidney	Left crus of diaphragm, left kidney
Anterior border:	Presents hilum, right vein emerges	—
Medial border:	Coeliac ganglion	Coeliac ganglion
Lateral border:	Liver	Stomach

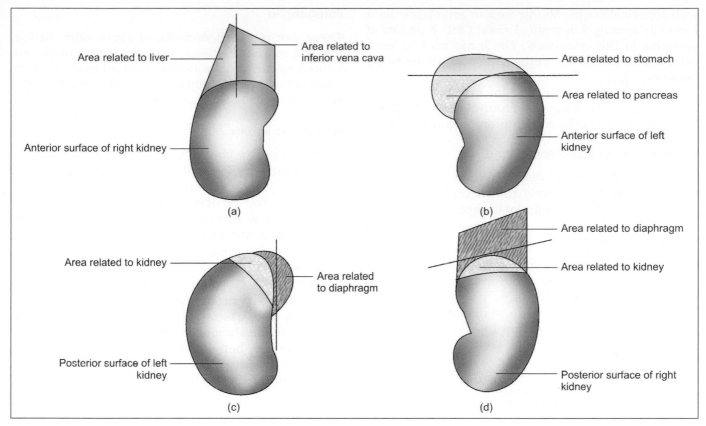

Fig. 25.3: Relations of the suprarenal glands. (a) Anterior view of right suprarenal gland, (b) anterior view of left suprarenal gland, (c) posterior view of left suprarenal gland, and (d) posterior view of right suprarenal gland.

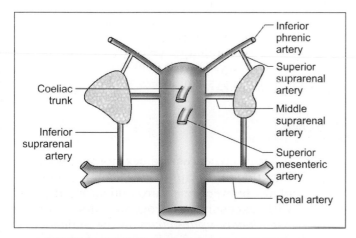

Fig. 25.4: Arterial supply of the suprarenal glands.

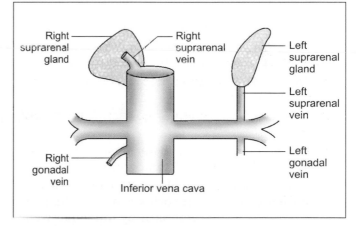

Fig. 25.5: Venous drainage of the suprarenal glands.

Lymphatic Drainage

Lymphatics from the suprarenal glands drain into the lateral aortic nodes.

Nerve Supply

The suprarenal medulla has a rich nerve supply through myelinated *preganglionic* sympathetic fibres. The chromaffin cells in it are considered homologous with postganglionic sympathetic neurons.

Accessory Suprarenal Glands

These are small masses of cortical tissue often found in the areolar tissue around the main glands and sometimes in the spermatic cord, the epididymis, and the broad ligament of the uterus.

Histology

Cortex: It consists of three zones. Outer zone is zona glomerulosa which contains groups of columnar cells with spherical nuclei. Middle zone or zona fasciculata has cells arranged in vertical rows. Cells have lots of vacuoles in the cytoplasm. The inner zone or zona reticularis contains cells in an anastomosing network. These cells are less vacuolated.

Medulla: It is composed of chromaffin cells, arranged in small groups, surrounded by capillaries. In between these cells are autonomic ganglion cells.

Development of Suprarenal Gland

The cortex of the gland develops from mesoderm of coelomic epithelium while the medulla is derived from the neural crest cells (neuroectoderm).

CHROMAFFIN SYSTEM

Chromaffin system is made up of cells which have an affinity for certain salt of chromic acid. Such cells are called chromaffin cells or pheochromocytes. These are situated close to sympathetic ganglia because both of them develop from the cells of the neural crest. Chromaffin cells secrete adrenalin and noradrenalin. This system includes the following groups of cells.

1. Suprarenal medulla (described above).
2. Paraganglia.
3. Para-aortic bodies.
4. Coccygeal body.
5. Small masses of chromaffin cells scattered irregularly amongst ganglia of sympathetic chain, splanchnic nerves, autonomic plexuses, and may be closely related to various organs like heart, liver, kidney, ureter, prostate, epididymis, etc.

Paraganglia

These are rounded nodules of chromaffin tissue, about 2 mm in diameter, situated inside or closely related to the ganglia of the sympathetic chain. In adults they are generally represented by microscopic remnants only.

Para-aortic Bodies

Two para-aortic bodies, each about 1 cm long, lie on each side of the origin of the inferior mesenteric artery. They are connected together above the artery to form an inverted horseshoe, or an H-shaped body. They develop during foetal life, attain their maximum size in the first three years of life, and gradually atrophy to disappear by the age of 14 years. The chromaffin cells of the para-aortic bodies secrete noradrenalin.

Other small chromaffin bodies are found in the foetus in all parts of the prevertebral sympathetic plexuses of the abdomen and pelvis. They reach their maximum size between the 5th and 8th months of foetal life. In adults, they can be made out only in the vicinity of the coeliac and superior mesenteric arteries.

Coccygeal Body (Glomus Coccygeum)

Also known as glomus coccygeum, it is a small oval body about 2.5 cm in diameter situated in front of the coccyx. It is closely connected to the termination of the median sacral artery and to the ganglion impar. It is made up of epithelioid cells grouped around a sinusoidal capillary. Thus it does not clearly belong to the chromaffin system.

CLINICAL ANATOMY

- Suprarenal gland can be *demonstrated radiologically* by computerised tomography (CT scan).
- Insufficiency of cortical secretion due to atrophy or tuberculosis of the cortex results in *Addison's disease.* It is characterized by muscular weakness, low blood pressure, anaemia, pigmentation of skin and terminal circulatory and renal failure.
- Excessive cortical secretion due to hyperplasia of the cortex may produce various effects.
  - (a) In adults, hyperglucocorticism causes *Cushing's syndrome,* which is characterized by obesity, hirsutism, diabetes and hypogonadism.
  - (b) In women, excessive androgens may cause *masculinization (virilism).*
  - (c) In men, excessive oestrogens may cause *feminization* and breast enlargement.
  - (d) In children, excessive sex hormones cause *adrenogenital syndrome,* cortical hyperplasia between the third and fourth months with excessive androgens causes *female pseudohermaphroditism;* in the male foetus, it causes excessive development of external genital organs.
- Bilateral removal of adrenal glands (*adrenalectomy*) is done as a treatment of some advanced and inoperable cases of disseminated carcinoma of the breast and prostate which do not respond to radiotherapy and which are considered to be dependent on hormonal control.
- Tumours of the suprarenal medulla (*pheochromocytoma*) cause attacks of hypertension associated with palpitation, headache, excessive sweating and pallor of skin.

CHAPTER 26

Diaphragm

The diaphragm, while separating the thoracic and abdominal cavities, gives passage to a number of structures passing in both the directions. It is the chief muscle of quiet respiration. Since it develops in the region of the neck, it continues to be innervated by the same loyal nerve despite its descent to a much lower level.

During inspiration, the central tendon is pulled by the contracting muscle fibres, so that inferior vena caval opening is enlarged helping in venous return to the heart. This venous blood is pumped to the lungs. The air also gets into the lungs during this phase of inspiration. So both the venous blood in the capillaries and air in the alveoli *come close by* in the lung tissue, separated by the lining of the alveoli. The exchange of gases takes place, carbon dioxide is expelled in expiration and purified blood is returned to the left atrium.

Definition

The diaphragm is a dome-shaped muscle forming the partition between the thoracic and abdominal cavities. It is the chief muscle of respiration.

Muscle fibres form the periphery of the partition. They arise from circumference of the thoracic outlet and are inserted into a central tendon (Fig. 26.1).

Origin

The muscle fibres may be grouped into three parts, sternal, costal and lumbar.

The *sternal part* arises by two fleshy slips from the back of the xiphoid process.

The *costal part* arises from the inner surfaces of the cartilages and the adjacent parts of the lower six ribs on each side, interdigitating with the transversus abdominis.

The *lumbar part* arises from the medial and lateral lumbocostal arches and from the lumbar vertebrae by right and left *crura*.

(a) The *medial lumbocostal arch* or medial arcuate ligament is a tendinous arch in the fascia covering the upper part of the psoas major. Medially, it is attached to the side of the body of vertebra L1 and is continuous with the lateral margin of the corresponding crus. Laterally, it is attached to the front of the transverse process of vertebra L1 (Fig. 15.3).

(b) The *lateral lumbocostal arch* or lateral arcuate ligament is a tendinous arch in the fascia covering the upper part of the quadratus lumborum. It is attached medially to the front of the transverse process of vertebra L1, and laterally to the lower border of the 12th rib.

(c) The *right crus* is larger and stronger than the left crus, because it has to pull down the liver during each inspiration. It arises from the anterolateral surfaces of the bodies of the upper three lumbar vertebrae and the intervening intervertebral discs.

(d) The *left crus* arises from the corresponding parts of the upper two lumbar vertebrae. The medial margins of the two crura form a tendinous arc across the front of the aorta, called the *median arcuate ligament*.

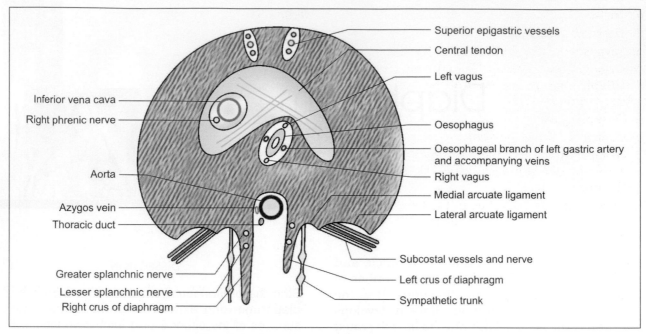

Fig. 26.1: The diaphragm as seen from below.

Muscle Fibres

1. From the circumferential origin described above, the fibres arch upwards and inwards to form the right and left domes. The right dome is higher than the left dome (Fig. 26.2a and b). In full expiration, it reaches the level of the fourth intercostal space. The left dome reaches the fifth rib. The central tendon lies at the level of the lower end of the sternum at 6th costal cartilage. The downward concavity of the dome is occupied by the liver on the right side and by the fundus of the stomach on the left side.

2. The medial fibres of the right crus run upwards and to the left, and encircle the oesophagus.

3. In general, all fibres converge towards the central tendon for their insertion (Fig. 26.2c).

Insertion

The *central tendon* of the diaphragm lies below the pericardium and is fused to the latter. The tendon is *trilobar* in shape, made up of three leaflets. The middle leaflet is triangular in shape with its apex directed towards the xiphoid process. The right and left leaflets are tongue-shaped and curve laterally and backwards, the left being a little narrower than the right. The central area consists of four well-marked *diagonal bands* which fan out from a central point of decussation located in front of the opening for the oesophagus (Fig. 26.1).

Openings in the Diaphragm

Large or Main Openings in the Diaphragm

The *aortic opening* is osseoaponeurotic. It lies at lower border of the 12th thoracic vertebra. It transmits:

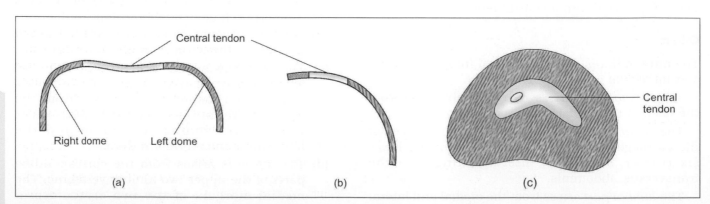

Fig. 26.2: Shape of the diaphragm: (a) Anteroposterior view shows the right and left domes, (b) in left lateral view, it resembles an inverted J, and (c) in superior view, it is kidney-shaped.

(i) Aorta

(ii) Thoracic duct

(iii) Azygos vein (Fig. 26.3).

The *oesophageal opening* lies in the muscular part of the diaphragm, at the level of the 10th thoracic vertebra. It transmits:

(i) Oesophagus

(ii) Gastric or vagus nerves

(iii) Oesophageal branches of the left gastric artery, with some oesophageal veins that accompany the arteries.

The *vena caval opening* lies in the central tendon of the diaphragm at the level of the 8th thoracic vertebra. It transmits:

(i) The inferior vena cava

(ii) Branches of the right phrenic nerve.

Small Openings in the Diaphragm

(a) Each crus of the diaphragm is pierced by the greater and lesser splanchnic nerves. The left crus is pierced in addition by the hemiazygos vein.

(b) The sympathetic chain passes from the thorax to the abdomen behind the medial arcuate ligament or medial lumbocostal arch.

(c) The subcostal nerve and vessels pass behind the lateral arcuate ligament or lateral lumbocostal arch (Fig. 26.1).

(d) The superior epigastric vessels and some lymphatics pass between the xiphoid process and 7th costal cartilage origins of the diaphragm. This gap is known as Larry's space or foramen of Morgagni.

(e) The musculophrenic vessels pierce the diaphragm at the level of 9th costal cartilage.

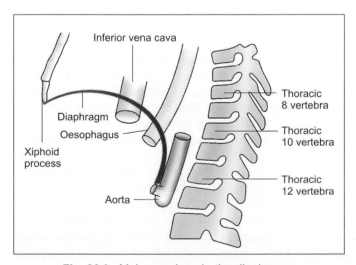

Fig. 26.3: Main openings in the diaphragm.

Relations

Superiorly

1. Pleurae, and
2. Pericardium.

Inferiorly

1. Peritoneum,
2. Liver,
3. Fundus of the stomach,
4. Spleen,
5. Kidneys, and
6. Suprarenals.

Nerve Supply

Motor

The phrenic nerves are the sole motor nerves to the diaphragm (ventral rami C3, **C4**, C5).

Sensory

The phrenic nerves are sensory to the central part, and the lower six thoracic nerves are sensory to the peripheral part of the diaphragm.

In addition to the diaphragm, the phrenic nerves also supply sensory fibres to the mediastinal and diaphragmatic pleurae, the fibrous pericardium, the parietal layer of serous pericardium, and the part of the parietal peritoneum lying below the central part of the diaphragm. Through its communications with the phrenic branches of the coeliac plexus, the phrenic nerve is also distributed to the falciform and coronary ligaments of the liver, the inferior vena cava, the suprarenal glands, and the *gall bladder*.

Actions

1. The diaphragm is the *principal muscle of inspiration*. On contraction, the diaphragm descends increasing the vertical diameter of the thorax. The excursion of the diaphragm is about 1.5 cm during quiet breathing. In deep inspiration, it may be from 6 to 10 cm.

2. The diaphragm acts in all *expulsive acts* to give additional power to each effort. Thus before sneezing, coughing, laughing, crying, vomiting, micturition, defaecation, or parturition, a deep inspiration takes place. This is followed by closure of the glottis and powerful contraction of the trunk muscles.

3. The sphincteric action in lower end of oesophagus is due to the contraction of the intrinsic muscle in the lower 2 cm of the oesophagus.

The position of the diaphragm in the thorax depends upon three main factors. These are as follows.

1. The elastic recoil of lung tissue tends to pull the diaphragm upwards.
2. On lying down, the pressure exerted by the abdominal viscera pushes the diaphragm upwards. On standing or sitting, the viscera tend to pull the diaphragm downwards.
3. While standing, the muscles in the abdominal wall contract increasing the intra-abdominal pressure. This pressure tends to push the diaphragm upwards. In sitting or lying down, the muscles are relaxed (Ref. Chapter 13, Vol.1).

Because of these factors the level of the diaphragm is highest in the supine position, lowest while sitting, and intermediate while standing. The higher position of the diaphragm, the greater respiratory excursion.

Development

Diaphragm develops from the following sources.

1. Septum transversum forms the central tendon.
2. Pleuroperitoneal membranes form the dorsal paired portion.
3. Lateral thoracic wall contributes to the circumferential portion of the diaphragm.
4. Dorsal mesentery of oesophagus forms the dorsal unpaired portion.

CLINICAL ANATOMY

- *Hiccough* or *hiccup* is the result of spasmodic contraction of the diaphragm. It may be:
  (a) Peripheral, due to local irritation of the diaphragm or its nerve.
  (b) Central, due to irritation of the hiccough centre in the medulla. Uraemia is an important cause of hiccough.
- *Shoulder tip pain:* Irritation of the diaphragm may cause referred pain in the shoulder because the phrenic and supraclavicular nerves have the same root values (C3, **C4**, C5) (Figs 22.12 and 23.30).
- *Unilateral paralysis of the diaphragm*, due to a lesion of the phrenic nerve anywhere in its long course, is a common occurrence. The paralysed side moves opposite to the normal side, i.e. paradoxical movements. This can be seen both clinically and fluoroscopically.
- *Eventration* is a condition in which diaphragm is pushed upwards due to a congenital defect in the musculature of its left half which is represented only by a fibrous membrane containing a few scattered muscle fibres.
- *Diaphragmatic hernia* may be congenital or acquired:
  Congenital Hernia
  (a) *Retrosternal hernia:* It occurs through the space between the xiphoid and costal origins of the diaphragm, or foramen of Morgagni, or space of Larrey. It is more common on the right side and lies between the pericardium and the right pleura. Usually it causes no symptoms (Fig. 26.4).
  (b) *Posterolateral hernia:* This is by far the commonest type of congenital diaphragmatic hernia. It occurs through the pleuroperitoneal hiatus or *foramen of Bochdalek*

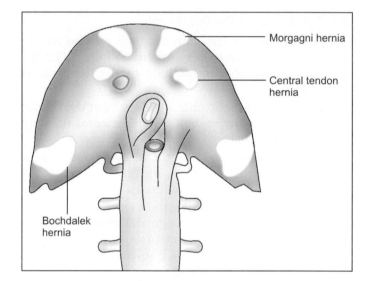

Fig. 26.4: Sites of diaphragmatic hernia.

situated at the periphery of the diaphragm in the region of attachments to the 10th and 11th ribs. It is more common on the left side. There is a free communication between the pleural and peritoneal cavities. Such a hernia may cause death of the infant within a few hours of birth due to acute respiratory distress caused by abdominal viscera filling the left chest. This hernia requires operation in the first few hours of life.

(c) *Posterior hernia:* This is due to failure of development of the posterior part of the diaphragm. One or both crus may be absent. The aorta and oesophagus lie in the gap, but there is no hernial sac.

(d) *Central hernia:* It is rare, left-sided, and is supposed to be the result of rupture of the foetal membranous diaphragm in the region of the left dome.

Acquired Hernia

(a) *Traumatic hernia:* It is due to bullet injuries of the diaphragm.

(b) *Hiatal hernia:* It may be congenital or acquired.

- A *congenital hiatal hernia* is due to persistence of an embryonic peritoneal process in the posterior mediastinum in front of the cardiac end of the stomach. The stomach can 'roll' upwards until it lies upside down in the posterior mediastinum. It is, therefore, called a rolling type of hernia. It is a rare type of hernia where the normal relationship of the cardio-oesophageal junction to the diaphragm is undisturbed, and, therefore, the mechanics of the cardio-oesophageal junction usually remains unaltered (Fig. 26.5a).

- An *acquired hiatal hernia* or sliding type (Fig. 26.5b) is the commonest of all internal hernia. It is due to weakness of the phrenico-oesophageal membrane which is formed by the reflection of diaphragmatic fascia to the lower end of the oesophagus. It is often caused by obesity, or by operation in this area. The cardiac end can slide up through the hiatus. In this way the valvular mechanism at the cardio-

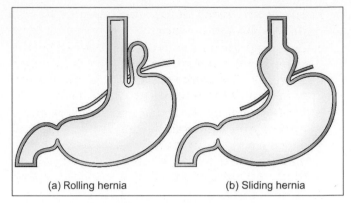

(a) Rolling hernia   (b) Sliding hernia

Fig. 26.5: Types of hiatal hernia.

oesophageal junction is disturbed causing reflux of gastric contents into the oesophagus.

- *Diaphragmatic hernia:* Summary.

(a) *Congenital:* Retrosternal, posterolateral, posterior and central.

(b) *Acquired:*

  (i) Traumatic

  (ii) Hiatal

    – Congenital hiatal rolling hernia

    – Acquired hiatal sliding hernia (commonest).

Posterior Abdominal Wall

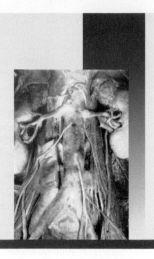

Posterior abdominal wall is muscular and supports not only the retroperitoneal organs like kidney, ureter, duodenum but all the other organs and vessels, etc. of the biggest cavity of the body.

It contains the lumbar plexus, and part of the course of its branches. In addition, both the sympathetic and parasympathetic components of autonomic nervous system are visible here. The sympathetic is unsympathetic to gastrointestinal tract. It is seen in the form of coeliac, superior and inferior mesenteric plexuses.

INTRODUCTION

Posterior abdominal wall includes the study of the following structures.

1. Abdominal aorta.
2. Inferior vena cava.
3. Abdominal parts of the azygos and hemiazygos veins.
4. Lymph nodes of posterior abdominal wall and cisterna chyli.
5. Muscles of the posterior abdominal wall and thoracolumbar fascia.
6. Nerves of the posterior abdominal wall including lumbar plexus and the abdominal part of autonomic nervous system.

ABDOMINAL AORTA

The abdominal aorta begins in the midline at the aortic opening of the diaphragm, opposite the lower border of vertebra T12. It runs downwards and slightly to the left in front of the lumbar vertebrae, and ends in front of the lower part of the body of vertebra L4, about 1.25 cm to the left of the median plane, by dividing into the right and left common iliac arteries (Fig. 27.1). Due to the forward convexity of the lumbar vertebral column, aortic pulsations can be felt in the region of the umbilicus, particularly in slim persons.

DISSECTION

Expose the centrally placed abdominal aorta and inferior vena cava to the right of aorta. Trace the ventral, lateral, posterior and terminal branches of abdominal aorta and the respective tributaries of inferior vena cava. Remove the big lymph nodes present in the posterior abdominal wall.

Identify the muscles of the posterior abdominal wall by removing their fascial coverings. These are psoas major, quadratus lumborum, and iliacus. Avoid injury to the vessels and nerves related to the muscles.

Detach psoas major from the intervertebral discs and vertebral bodies and trace the lumbar vessels and the rami communicans posteriorly deep to the tendinous arches from which psoas major arises. Dissect the genitofemoral nerve only on the anterior surface of psoas major.

Trace the various branches of lumbar plexus, e.g. iliohypogastric, ilioinguinal, lateral cutaneous nerve of thigh and femoral nerve. These exit from the lateral border of psoas major. Identify obturator and lumbosacral trunk seen on the medial aspect of the muscle.

Locate the lumbar part of the right and left sympathetic chains. Trace their branches into the coeliac and superior mesenteric plexuses of nerves in addition to giving rami communicans to the lumbar spinal nerves.

Relations

Anteriorly

From above downwards, the aorta is related to:

1. Coeliac and aortic plexuses.
2. Body of the pancreas, with the splenic vein embedded in its posterior surface (Fig. 23.15).
3. Third part of the duodenum (Fig. 21.2).

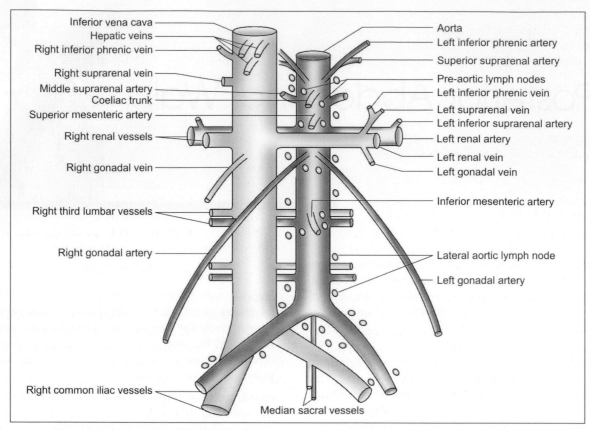

Fig. 27.1: The abdominal aorta, inferior vena cava and associated lymph nodes.

Posteriorly

The aorta is related to:

1. The bodies of upper four lumbar vertebrae and the corresponding intervertebral discs (Fig. 21.1).
2. Anterior longitudinal ligament.

To the right side of the aorta there are:

1. Inferior vena cava.
2. Right crus of the diaphragm.
3. Cisterna chyli and the azygos vein in the upper part.

To the left side of the aorta there are from above downwards:

1. Left crus of the diaphragm.
2. Pancreas.
3. Fourth part of the duodenum.

Branches

The branches of the abdominal aorta are classified as given below (Fig. 27.1).

Ventral branches, which develop from ventral splanchnic or vitelline arteries and supply the gut. These are as follows.

1. Coeliac trunk (Chapter 21) gives left gastric, common hepatic and splenic branches.

2. Superior mesenteric artery (Chapter 21) gives inferior pancreaticoduodenal, middle colic, right colic, ileocolic and 12–15 jejunal and ileal branches.
3. Inferior mesenteric artery (Chapter 21) gives left colic, sigmoid arteries and continues as superior rectal.

Lateral branches, which develop from the lateral splanchnic or mesonephric arteries and supply the viscera derived from the intermediate mesoderm. These are the right and left:

1. Inferior phrenic arteries.
2. Middle suprarenal arteries.
3. Renal arteries.
4. Testicular or ovarian arteries.

Dorsal branches represent the somatic intersegmental arteries and are distributed to the body wall. These are the:

1. Lumbar arteries—four pairs.
2. Median sacral artery—unpaired.

Terminal branches are a pair of common iliac arteries. They supply the pelvis and lower limbs.

Inferior Phrenic Arteries

Inferior phrenic arteries arise from the aorta just above the coeliac trunk. Each artery runs upwards and laterally on the corresponding crus of the diaphragm, medial to the suprarenal gland. Each artery gives off two to three superior suprarenal arteries, and is then distributed to the diaphragm.

Middle Suprarenal Arteries

Middle suprarenal arteries arise at the level of the superior mesenteric artery. Each passes laterally and slightly upwards over the corresponding crus of the diaphragm, to reach the gland (Fig. 25.4).

Renal Arteries

Renal arteries are large arteries which arise from the abdominal aorta just below the level of origin of the superior mesenteric artery. The *right renal artery* passes laterally behind the inferior vena cava to reach the hilum of the right kidney. The *left renal artery* runs behind the left renal vein, the splenic vein. Each artery gives off the inferior suprarenal and ureteral branches, and is then distributed to the kidney (Fig. 24.3).

Gonadal; Testicular or Ovarian Arteries

Gonadal arteries are small and arise from the front of the aorta a little below the origin of the renal arteries. Each artery runs downwards and slightly laterally on the psoas major. On the right side the artery crosses in front of the inferior vena cava, the ureter and the genitofemoral nerve. It passes deep to the ileum. On the left side the artery crosses in front of the ureter and the genitofemoral nerve; and passes deep to the colon.

The *testicular artery* joins the spermatic cord at the deep inguinal ring, and traverses the inguinal canal. Within the cord, it lies anterior to the ductus deferens. At the upper pole of the testis, it breaks up into branches which supply the testis and the epididymis.

The *ovarian artery* crosses the external iliac vessels at the pelvic brim to enter the suspensory or infundibulopelvic ligament of the ovary. It thus enters the broad ligament and runs below the uterine tube to reach the ovary through the mesovarium. The artery gives a branch which continues medially to anastomose with the uterine artery, and supplies twigs to the uterine tube and to the pelvic part of the ureter (Fig. 31.4).

Lumbar Arteries

Four pairs of lumbar arteries arise from the aorta opposite the bodies of the upper four lumbar vertebrae. The small, fifth pair is usually represented by the lumbar branches of the iliolumbar arteries.

The upper four lumbar arteries run across the sides of the bodies of the upper four lumbar vertebrae, passing deep to the crura (upper arteries only) deep to the psoas major and the quadratus lumborum, to end in small branches between the transversus and internal oblique muscles. Each artery gives off a dorsal branch, which arises at the root of the transverse process. The dorsal branch gives off a spinal branch to the vertebral canal, and then runs backwards to supply the muscles and skin of the back.

Median Sacral Artery

Median sacral artery represents the continuation of the primitive dorsal aorta. It arises from the back of the aorta just above the bifurcation of the latter, and runs downwards to end in front of the coccyx. It supplies the rectum, and anastomoses with the iliolumbar and lateral sacral arteries.

Common Iliac Arteries

Course

These are the terminal branches of the abdominal aorta, beginning in front of vertebra L4, 1.25 cm to the left of the median plane. On each side it passes downwards and laterally and ends in front of the sacroiliac joint, at the level of the lumbosacral intervertebral disc, by dividing into the external and internal iliac arteries.

The *right common iliac artery* passes in front of the commencement of the inferior vena cava. The right common iliac vein is posterior to the vena cava above, and medial to it below.

The *left common iliac artery* is shorter than the right artery. It is crossed at its middle by the inferior mesenteric vessels. The left common iliac vein is medial to it. The structures lying on the left ala of the sacrum are deep to it.

INFERIOR VENA CAVA

The inferior vena cava is formed by the union of the right and left common iliac veins on the right side of the body of vertebra L5. It ascends in front of the vertebral column, on the right side of the aorta, grooves the posterior surface of the liver, pierces the central tendon of the diaphragm at the level of vertebra T8, and opens into the lower and posterior part of the right atrium (Fig. 26.1).

Relations

Anteriorly

From above downwards, inferior vena cava is related to:

1. Posterior surface of the liver.
2. Epiploic foramen (Fig. 18.22).
3. First part of the duodenum and the portal vein.

4. Head of the pancreas along with the bile duct.
5. Third part of duodenum (Fig. 20.6b).

Posteriorly

Above, the right crus of the diaphragm is separated from the inferior vena cava by the right renal artery, the right coeliac ganglion, and the medial part of the right suprarenal gland. Below, it is related to the right sympathetic chain and to the medial border of the right psoas.

Tributaries

1. The *common iliac veins* formed by the union of the external and internal iliac veins unite to form the inferior vena cava. Each vein receives an iliolumbar vein. The median sacral vein joins the left common iliac vein.

2. The *third* and *fourth lumbar veins* run along with the corresponding arteries and open into the posterior aspect of the inferior vena cava. The veins of the left side cross behind the aorta to reach the vena cava.

   The first and second lumbar veins end in the ascending lumbar vein, on the right side, or the hemiazygos vein on the left side.

   The ascending lumbar vein is an anastomotic channel which connects the lateral sacral, iliolumbar, and the subcostal veins. It lies within the psoas muscle, in front of the roots of the transverse processes of the lumbar vertebrae. On joining the subcostal vein it forms the azygos vein on the right side, and the hemiazygos vein on the left side.

3. The *right testicular* or *ovarian vein* opens into the inferior vena cava just below the entrance of the renal veins. The left gonadal vein drains into the left renal vein.

4. The *renal veins* join the inferior vena cava just below the transpyloric plane. Each renal vein lies in front of the corresponding artery. The right vein is shorter than the left and lies behind the second part of the duodenum. The left vein crosses in front of the aorta, and lies behind the pancreas and the splenic vein. It receives the left suprarenal and gonadal veins.

5. The *right suprarenal vein* is extremely short. It emerges from the hilum of the gland and soon opens into the inferior vena cava. The left suprarenal vein opens into the left renal vein.

6. The *hepatic veins* are three large and many small veins which open directly into the anterior surface of the inferior vena cava just before it pierces the diaphragm. These act as important support of liver.

ABDOMINAL PARTS OF AZYGOS AND HEMIAZYGOS VEINS

These veins usually begin in the abdomen. The *azygos vein* may arise from the posterior surface of the inferior vena cava near the renal veins; may be formed by the union of the right ascending lumbar vein and the right subcostal vein. It enters the thorax by passing through the aortic opening of the diaphragm.

The *hemiazygos vein* is the mirror image of the lower part of the azygos vein. It may arise from the posterior surface of the left renal vein, or may be formed by the union of the left ascending lumbar vein and the left subcostal vein. It enters the thorax by piercing the left crus of the diaphragm.

LYMPH NODES OF POSTERIOR ABDOMINAL WALL

These are the external iliac, common iliac and lumbar or aortic nodes.

The *external iliac nodes* 8 to 10 lie along the external iliac vessels, being lateral, medial and anterior to them. They receive afferents from:

1. Inguinal lymph nodes
2. Deeper layers of the infraumbilical part of the abdominal wall
3. Adductor region of the thigh
4. Glans penis or clitoris
5. Membranous urethra
6. Prostate
7. Fundus of the urinary bladder
8. Cervix uteri
9. Part of the vagina. Their efferents pass to common iliac nodes. The inferior epigastric and circumflex iliac nodes are outlying members of the external iliac group.

The *common iliac nodes*, 4 to 6 in number lie along the common iliac artery and below the bifurcation of the aorta in front of vertebra L5 or in front of the sacral promontory. They receive afferents from the external and internal iliac nodes, and send their efferents to the lateral aortic nodes.

The *lumbar* or *aortic nodes* are divided into preaortic, lateral aortic groups. The *preaortic nodes* lie directly anterior to the abdominal aorta, and are divisible into coeliac, superior mesenteric and inferior mesenteric groups. They receive afferents from intermediate nodes associated with the subdiaphragmatic part of the gastrointestinal tract, the liver, the pancreas and the spleen. Their efferents form the *intestinal trunks* which enter the cisterna chyli.

The *lateral aortic nodes* lie on each side of the abdominal aorta. They receive afferents from the structures supplied by the lateral and dorsal branches of the aorta and form the common iliac nodes. Their efferents form a *lumbar trunk* on each side, both of which terminate in the cisterna chyli.

Cisterna Chyli

This is an elongated lymphatic sac, about 5 to 7 cm long. It is situated in front of the first and second lumbar vertebrae, immediately to the right of the abdominal aorta. It is overlapped by the right crus of the diaphragm. Its upper end is continuous with the thoracic duct. It is joined by the right and left lumbar and intestinal lymph trunks.

The lumbar trunks arise from the lateral aortic nodes, and bring lymph from the lower limbs, the pelvic wall and viscera, the kidneys, the suprarenal glands, the testes or ovaries, and the deeper parts of the abdominal wall. The intestinal trunks bring lymph from the stomach, the intestine, the pancreas, the spleen, and the anteroinferior part of the liver.

The cisterna chyli may be replaced by anastomotic channels between the two lumbar trunks, or by dilatations of the lumbar trunks which join to form the thoracic duct. The intestinal trunks may thus join the cisterna chyli, the lumbar trunks, or the thoracic duct.

MUSCLES OF THE POSTERIOR ABDOMINAL WALL

These are the psoas major, the psoas minor, the iliacus and the quadratus lumborum. Their attach-

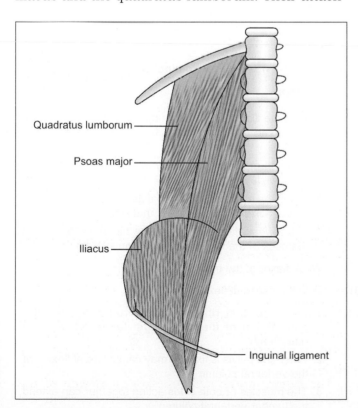

Quadratus lumborum
Psoas major
Iliacus
Inguinal ligament

Fig. 27.2: Muscles of the posterior abdominal wall.

ments are given in Table 27.1 and their nerve supply and actions in Table 27.2. Some additional facts about the psoas major are given below (Fig. 27.2).

Relations of the Psoas Major

In the Posterior Mediastinum

The uppermost part of the psoas major lies in the posterior mediastinum, and is related anteriorly to the diaphragm and pleura.

In the Abdomen

Its *anterolateral surface* is related to:
1. Medial lumbocostal arch or medial arcuate ligament and psoas fascia (Fig. 24.4).
2. Peritoneum and extraperitoneal connective tissue.
3. Kidney and ureter (Fig. 24.6).
4. Renal and gonadal vessels.
5. Genitofemoral nerve.
6. Psoas minor.
7. Inferior vena cava and the terminal ileum on the right side.
8. Colon on the left side.

The *posterior surface* is related to:
1. Transverse processes of lumbar vertebrae.
2. Lumbar plexus lies in substance of the muscle.

The *medial surface* is related to:
1. Bodies of the lumbar vertebrae.
2. Lumbar vessels.

The *medial (anterior) margin* is related to:
1. Sympathetic chain.
2. Aortic lymph nodes.
3. Inferior vena cava on the right side.
4. Aorta on the left side.
5. External iliac vessels along the pelvic brim.

In the Thigh

Anteriorly: Femoral artery and fascia lata.

Posteriorly: Capsule of hip joint separated by a bursa.

Medially: Pectineus and femoral vein.

Laterally: Femoral nerve and iliacus (Chapter 3).

Thoracolumbar Fascia (Lumbar Fascia)

Lumbar fascia is the fascia enclosing the deep muscles of the back (Fig. 24.11). It is made up of three layers—posterior, middle and anterior. The posterior layer is thickest and the anterior layer thinnest.

Extent

The posterior layer covers the loin and is continued upwards on the back of the thorax and neck. The

Table 27.1: Attachments of muscles of the posterior abdominal wall

Muscle	Origin	Insertion
1. **Psoas major** This is a fusiform muscle placed on the side of the lumbar spine and along the brim of the pelvis. The psoas and the iliacus are together known as the iliopsoas, due to their common insertion and actions	(a) From anterior surfaces and lower borders of transverse process of all lumbar vertebrae (Fig. 2.8) (b) By 5 slips, one each from the bodies of two adjacent vertebrae and their intervertebral discs, from vertebrae, T12 to L5 (c) From 4 tendinous arches extending across the constricted parts of the bodies of lumbar vertebrae, between the preceding slips. The origin is a continuous one from the lower border of T12 to upper border of L5	The muscle passes behind the inguinal ligament and in front of the hip joint to enter the thigh. It ends in a tendon which receives the fibres of the iliacus on its lateral side. It is then inserted into the tip and medial part of the anterior surface of the lesser trochanter of the femur
2. **Psoas minor** This is a small muscle which lies in front of the psoas major. It is frequently absent	Sides of the bodies of vertebrae T12 and L1 and the disc between them	The muscle ends in a long, flat tendon which is inserted into the pecten pubis and the iliopubic eminence
3. **Iliacus** This is a triangular muscle	(a) Upper 2/3rd of iliac fossa (Fig. 2.9) (b) Inner lip of the iliac crest and the ventral sacroiliac and iliolumbar ligaments (c) Upper surface of the lateral part of the sacrum	Lateral part of anterior surface of the lesser trochanter. The insertion extends for 2.5 cm below the trochanter
4. **Quadratus lumborum** This is a quadrate muscle lying in the lumbar region. Its origin lies below and the insertion is above	(a) Transverse process of vertebra L5 (b) Iliolumbar ligament (c) Adjoining 5 cm of the inner lip of the iliac crest (Fig. 2.3)	(a) Transverse processes of upper 4 lumbar vertebrae (b) Medial half of the lower border and anterior surface of the 12th rib

Table 27.2: Nerve supply and actions of muscles of the posterior abdominal wall

Muscle	Nerve supply	Actions
1. **Psoas major**	Branches from the roots of spinal nerve L2, L3 and sometimes L4.	1. With the iliacus, it acts as a powerful flexor of the hip, joint as in raising the trunk from recumbent to sitting posture 2. Helps in maintaining stability at the hip. Balances the trunk while sitting 3. When the muscle of one side acts alone it brings about lateral flexion of the trunk on that side 4. It is a weak medial rotator of the hip. After fracture of the neck of the femur the limb rotates laterally
2. **Psoas minor**	Branches from spinal nerve L1	Weak flexor of the trunk
3. **Iliacus**	Branches from femoral nerve (L2, 3)	With the psoas, it flexes the hip joint
4. **Quadratus lumborum**	Ventral rami of spinal nerves T12 to L4	1. Fixes the last rib during inspiration so that the contraction of the diaphragm takes place more effectively 2. When the pelvis is fixed, it may cause lateral flexion of the vertebral column 3. The muscles of both sides acting together can extend the lumbar vertebral column

middle and anterior layers are confined to the lumbar region.

Attachments

Posterior layer

Medially, the posterior layer is attached to the tips of the lumbar and sacral spines and the interspinous ligaments. *Laterally,* it blends with the middle layer at the lateral border of the erector spinae. *Superiorly,* it continues on to the back of the thorax where it is attached to the vertebral spines and the angles of the ribs. *Inferiorly,* it is attached to the posterior one-fourth of the outer lip of the iliac crest.

Middle layer

Medially, the middle layer is attached to the tips of the lumbar transverse processes and the inter-transverse ligaments. *Laterally,* it blends with the anterior layer at the lateral border of the quadratus lumborum. *Superiorly,* it is attached to the lower border of the 12th rib and to the lumbocostal ligament. *Inferiorly,* it is attached to the posterior part of the intermediate area of the iliac crest.

Anterior layer

Medially, the anterior layer is attached to the vertical ridges on the anterior surface of the lumbar transverse processes. *Laterally,* it blends with the middle layer at the lateral border of the quadratus lumborum. *Superiorly,* it forms the lateral arcuate ligament, extending from the tip of the first lumbar transverse process to the 12th rib. *Inferiorly,* it is attached to the inner lip of the iliac crest and the iliolumbar ligament (Fig. 24.11).

NERVES OF THE POSTERIOR ABDOMINAL WALL

Lumbar Plexus

The lumbar plexus lies in the posterior part of the substance of the psoas major muscle. It is formed by the ventral rami of the upper four lumbar nerves (Fig. 3.3). The first lumbar nerve receives a contribution from the subcostal nerve, and the fourth lumbar nerve gives a contribution to the lumbosacral trunk; which takes part in the formation of the sacral plexus. The branches of the lumbar plexus are summarized.

Iliohypogastric Nerve (L1)

The *iliohypogastric nerve* (L1) emerges at the lateral border of the psoas, runs downwards and laterally in front of the quadratus lumborum, and behind the kidney and colon, pierces the transversus abdominis a little above the iliac crest, and runs in the abdominal wall supplying the anterolateral muscles.

Ilioinguinal Nerve (L1)

The *ilioinguinal nerve* (L1) has the same course as the iliohypogastric nerve, but on a slightly lower level. It exits through superficial inguinal ring.

Genitofemoral Nerve

The *genitofemoral nerve* (L1, L2 ventral divisions) emerges on the anterior surface of the psoas muscle near its medial border and runs downwards in front of the muscle. Near the deep inguinal ring it divides into femoral and genital branches. The *femoral branch* passes through the arterial compartment of the femoral sheath and is distributed to the skin of the upper part of the front of the thigh. The *genital branch* pierces the psoas sheath and enters the inguinal canal through the deep inguinal ring. In the male, it supplies the cremaster muscle, and in the female, it gives sensory branches to the round ligament of the uterus and to the skin of the labium majus (Fig. 16.15).

Lateral Cutaneous Nerve of the Thigh

The *lateral cutaneous nerve of the thigh* (L2, L3; dorsal divisions) emerges at the lateral border of the psoas, runs downwards and laterally across the right iliac fossa, over the iliacus and reaches the anterior superior iliac spine. Here it enters the thigh by passing behind the lateral end of the inguinal ligament (Fig. 3.3).

Femoral Nerve

The *femoral nerve* (L2, L3, L4; dorsal divisions) emerges at the lateral border of the psoas below the iliac crest, and runs downwards and slightly laterally in the furrow between the psoas and iliacus. It lies under cover of the fascia iliaca. It passes deep to the inguinal ligament to enter the thigh lying on the lateral side of the femoral sheath. Before entering the thigh it supplies the iliacus. In thigh it supplies quadriceps femoris and sartorius (Fig. 3.21).

Obturator Nerve

The *obturator nerve* (L2, L3, L4; ventral divisions) emerges on the medial side of the psoas muscle and runs forwards and downwards on the pelvic wall, below the pelvic brim. Near its commencement it is crossed by the internal iliac vessels and the ureter. It enters the thigh by passing through the obturator canal. It supplies 3 adductor muscles, obturator externus and gracilis (Fig. 4.6).

Lumbosacral Trunk

The *lumbosacral trunk* (L4, L5; ventral rami) is formed by union of the descending branch of nerve L4 with nerve L5. It enters the lesser pelvis by passing over and grooving the lateral part of the ala of the sacrum, posterior to the common iliac vessels and the medial part of the psoas. It is related medially to the sympathetic chain; and laterally to the iliolumbar artery and the obturator nerve (Fig. 15.4). In the pelvis, it takes part in the formation of the sacral plexus.

Abdominal Part of the Autonomic Nervous System

The abdomen is supplied by both sympathetic and parasympathetic nerves. The *sympathetic nerves* are derived from two sources.

1. The lumbar sympathetic trunk supplies somatic branches to the lower abdominal wall and the lower limb; and visceral branches for the pelvic organs (Fig. 27.3).
2. The coeliac plexus, formed by splanchnic nerves from the thorax, supplies all the abdominal organs, including the gonads.

The *parasympathetic nerves* are also derived from two sources.

1. The vagus joins the coeliac plexus.
2. The pelvic splanchnic nerves join the inferior hypogastric plexus.

Lumbar Sympathetic Chain

This is ganglionated chain situated on either side of the bodies of the lumbar vertebrae containing five ganglia.

The lumbar sympathetic chain is continuous with the thoracic part deep to the medial arcuate ligament. It runs vertically downwards along the medial margin of the psoas major, and across the lumbar vessels. On the right side, it is overlapped by the inferior vena cava, and on the left by the lateral aortic lymph nodes.

The lumbar chain ends by becoming continuous with the sacral part of the sympathetic chain behind the common iliac vessels.

The anterior primary rami of the first and second lumbar nerves send white rami communicans to the corresponding ganglia.

Branches

Lateral

All the five lumbar nerves receive grey rami communicans from the corresponding lumbar ganglia. The grey rami carry fibres which are distributed to the lower abdominal wall and to the lower limb (Fig. 27.4).

Medial

The lumbar splanchnic nerves are generally four in number. The upper two join the coeliac and aortic plexuses, and the lower two join the superior hypogastric plexus.

Coeliac Ganglia and Coeliac Plexus

The *coeliac ganglion* (Fig. 27.5) is the largest ganglion in the body, situated one on each side of the coeliac trunk. Each ganglion is irregular in shape and is usually divided into a larger upper part which receives the greater splanchnic nerve, and a smaller lower part; aorticorenal ganglion which receives the lesser splanchnic nerve.

The *coeliac plexus* or solar plexus (Fig. 27.5) is closely related to the coeliac ganglion. The plexus is situated on the aorta around the coeliac trunk and

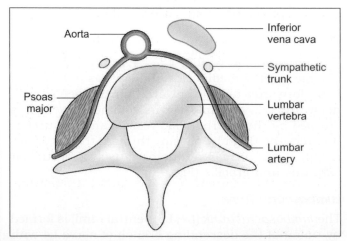

Fig. 27.3: Transverse section through the lumbar region showing location of the lumbar sympathetic chain.

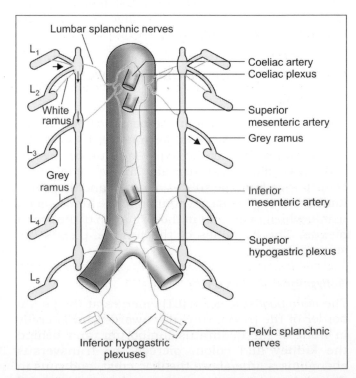

Fig. 27.4: The lumbar sympathetic chain and its branches. L = lumbar spinal nerves; and G = lumbar sympathetic ganglia.

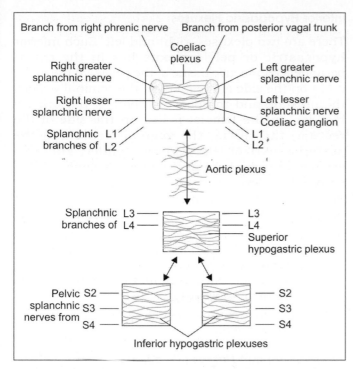

Fig. 27.5: Scheme to show the connections of the coeliac, superior hypogastric and inferior hypogastric plexuses.

around the root of the superior mesenteric artery. The plexus extends on to the crura of the diaphragm. It is overlapped by the inferior vena cava and by the pancreas. The fibres making up the plexus are as follows.

1. Preganglionic sympathetic fibres reach it through the greater and lesser splanchnic nerves.
2. Postganglionic sympathetic fibres arising in the coeliac ganglion.
3. Preganglionic vagal fibres are derived from the posterior vagal trunk containing fibres from both the right and left vagal nerves. The fibres from the right vagus predominate.
4. Sensory fibres from the diaphragm reach the coeliac plexus along the inferior phrenic arteries.

Branches

The coeliac plexus forms a number of secondary plexuses which surround branches of the aorta.

1. The *phrenic plexus* passes along the inferior phrenic artery to the suprarenal gland. The right phrenic plexus contains a right phrenic ganglion.
2. The *hepatic plexus* is distributed to the liver, the gall bladder and the bile ducts.
3. The *left gastric plexus* passes to the stomach.

4. The *splenic plexus* supplies the vessels and smooth muscle of the spleen.
5. The *suprarenal plexus* contains *preganglionic fibres*, that end in relation to the chromaffin cells of the suprarenal gland. These cells are homologous with postganglionic sympathetic neurons.
6. The *renal plexus* is formed by filaments from the coeliac plexus, the aorticorenal ganglion, the lowest thoracic splanchnic nerve, the first lumbar splanchnic nerve and the aortic plexus. It supplies the kidney and the upper part of the ureter.
7. The *testicular plexus* supplies the testis, the epididymis and the vas deferens.
8. The *ovarian plexus* supplies the ovary and the uterine tube.
9. The *superior mesenteric plexus* contains a superior mesenteric ganglion, and supplies the territory of the superior mesenteric artery.
10. The *abdominal aortic plexus* or intermesenteric plexus is formed by the coeliac plexus and filaments from the first and second lumbar splanchnic nerves. It is situated on the sides and the front of the aorta, between the origins of the superior and inferior mesenteric arteries. Actually it is made up of four to twelve intermesenteric nerves connected by oblique filaments. It is continuous above with the coeliac plexus and below with the superior hypogastric plexus. Its branches form parts of the testicular, inferior mesenteric, iliac and superior hypogastric plexuses, and supply the inferior vena cava.

The *inferior mesenteric plexus* is formed chiefly by fibres from the aortic plexus. It is distributed to the territory of the inferior mesenteric artery.

Superior Hypogastric Plexus (Presacral Nerve)

The superior hypogastric plexus lies in front of the bifurcation of the abdominal aorta, the left common iliac vein, the median sacral vessels, the body of fifth lumbar vertebra, the promontory of the sacrum, and between the two common iliac arteries. Though it is often called the presacral nerve, it is neither a single nerve nor presacral in position. The plexus lies more towards the left, and contains scattered nerve cells (Fig. 27.6).

The plexus is formed by fibres from the following sources.

Sympathetic Nerves

1. Descending fibres from the aortic plexus.
2. Third and fourth lumbar splanchnic nerves.

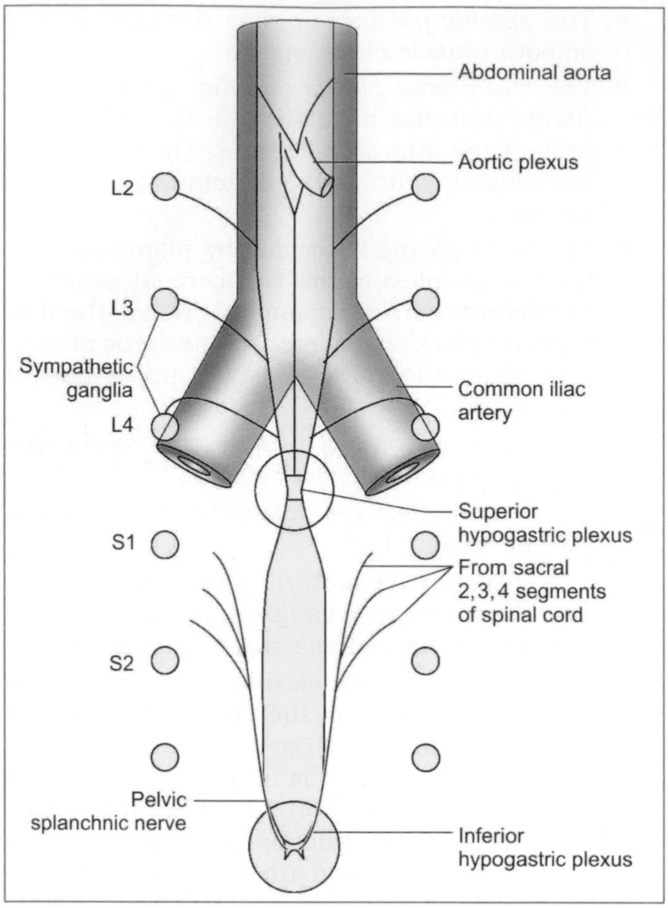

Fig. 27.6: Formation of plexuses.

Inferior Hypogastric Plexuses

There are two plexuses, right and left. Each inferior hypogastric or pelvic plexus lies in the extraperitoneal connective tissue of the pelvis. In the male, it lies on the side of the rectum, the seminal vesicle, the prostate and the posterior part of the urinary bladder. In the female, it lies on the side of the rectum, the cervix, the vaginal fornix and the posterior part of the urinary bladder; and also extends into the base of the broad ligament of the uterus. The plexus contains numerous small ganglia. The fibres forming the inferior hypogastric plexuses are as follows.

Sympathetic Nerves (T10 to L2)

1. These are chiefly derived from the hypogastric nerve which is represented either by a single nerve or by a plexus.
2. A few sympathetic fibres come from sympathetic ganglia.

Parasympathetic Nerves (S2, S3, S4)

These are derived from the pelvic splanchnic nerves. They relay in the walls of the viscera supplied.

Branches

Branches from the inferior hypogastric plexus are distributed to the pelvic viscera and some abdominal viscera, either directly or along the branches of the internal iliac artery.

Parasympathetic Nerves

Fibres from the pelvic splanchnic nerves reach it through the inferior hypogastric plexus. Usually these fibres ascend through the left part of the superior hypogastric plexus, cross the sigmoid and left colic vessels, and are distributed along the vessels as well as independently to the derivatives of the hindgut.

Branches

1. Inferiorly, the plexus divides into the right and left hypogastric nerves which descend into the pelvis and form the two inferior hypogastric plexuses.
2. Superiorly, the hypogastric plexus also gives off branches to the ureteric, testicular or ovarian, and the common iliac plexuses.

Parasympathetic System

As already noted the parasympathetic supply of the abdomen proper, minus hindgut comes from the vagi, and of the pelvis and hindgut from the pelvic splanchnic nerves or nervi erigentes (S2, S3, S4). These fibres are distributed through the coeliac and inferior hypogastric plexuses.

Functional Considerations

In general, the *sympathetic nerves* are vasomotor, motor to sphincters, inhibitory to peristalsis, and sensory to all the viscera supplied. The *parasympathetic nerves*, on the other hand, are motor and secretomotor to the gut and the glands associated with it.

CLINICAL ANATOMY

- *Thrombosis* in the inferior vena cava causes oedema of the legs and back. The collateral venous circulation between the superior and inferior venae cavae is established through the superficial or deep veins, or both. The participating superficial veins include the epigastric, circumflex iliac, lateral thoracic, thoracoepigastric, internal thoracic, posterior intercostal, external pudendal and lumbo-vertebral veins (Fig. 27.7). The deep veins are the azygos, hemiazygos and lumbar veins. The vertebral venous plexus may also provide an effective collateral circulation between the two venae cavae.

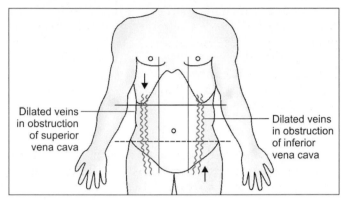

Fig. 27.7: Dilated veins in obstruction of superior vena cava and inferior vena cava.

- The inferior vena cava may sometimes be duplicated below the level of the renal veins.
- *Psoas abscess:* The psoas is enclosed in the psoas sheath, a part of the lumbar fascia. Pus from tubercular infection of the thoracic and lumbar vertebrae may track down through the sheath into the thigh, producing a soft swelling in the femoral triangle (Fig. 27.8).

The typical posture of a laterally rotated lower limb following fracture of the neck of the femur is produced by contraction of the psoas muscle.

- *Visceral pain:* Viscera are insensitive to cutting, crushing or burning. However, visceral pain is caused by:

(a) Excessive distension

(b) Spasmodic contraction of smooth muscle

(c) Ischaemia.

The pain felt in the region of the viscus itself is known as true visceral pain. It is poorly localized and is dull or heavy. Pain arising in viscera may also be felt in the skin or other somatic tissues, supplied by somatic nerves arising from the same spinal segment. This kind of pain is called *referred pain*. If the inflammation spreads from a diseased viscus to the parietal peritoneum it causes *local somatic pain* in the overlying body wall (Fig. 27.9).

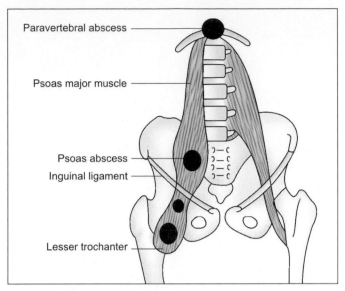

Fig. 27.8: Positions of psoas abscesses.

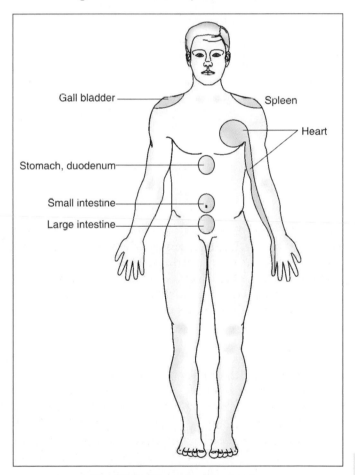

Fig. 27.9: Sites of referred pain.

CHAPTER 28

Perineum

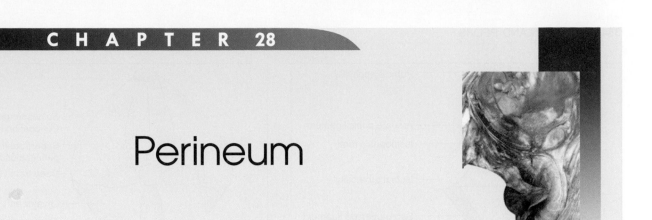

The perineum is the lowest part of the trunk. In males there are two openings, one of the gastro-intestinal system and the other being the common opening of urinary and genital system. In females there are three separate openings, one each of the gastrointestinal, genital and urinary systems. The perineal body supports the reproductive system. Its injury without repair, may lead to prolapse of the uterus. Pudendal nerve supplies muscles, skin, mucous membrane of both anal and urogenital triangles. Pudendum means "to be ashamed of". So far it is the most covered area of the body.

Perineum is the region at the lower end of the trunk, in the interval between the two thighs. The external genitalia are located, in the perineum. The perineum forms the lower division of the pelvis that lies below the pelvic diaphragm, formed by the levator ani and coccygeus, and fills in the pelvic outlet or inferior aperture of the pelvis.

Superficial Boundaries

Anteriorly: The scrotum in males, and the mons pubis in females (Figs 28.1 and 28.2).

Posteriorly: The buttocks.

On each side: The upper part of the medial side of the thigh.

Deep Boundaries of the Perineum

The deep boundaries of the perineum are the same as those of the pelvic outlet.

Anteriorly: Upper part of the pubic arch and the arcuate or inferior pubic ligament (Fig. 28.3).

Posteriorly: Tip of the coccyx.

On each side:

(i) Conjoined ischiopubic rami.

(ii) Ischial tuberosity.

(iii) Sacrotuberous ligament.

Divisions of the Perineum

A transverse line joining the anterior parts of the ischial tuberosities, and passing immediately anterior to the anus, divides the perineum into two triangular areas, a posterior, *anal region* or triangle, and an anterior, *urogenital region* or triangle (Fig. 28.3).

The *anal region* contains the termination of the anal canal in the median plane and an ischioanal fossa on each side.

Urogenital region contains the external urogenital organs. In males, the urethra enclosed in the root of penis, partly hidden anteriorly by the scrotum; and in females, the female external genital organs.

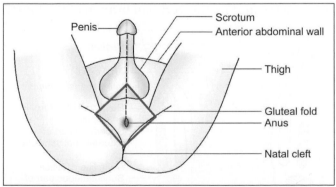

Fig. 28.1: The male perineum. Green lines indicate the outlines of pelvic outlet.

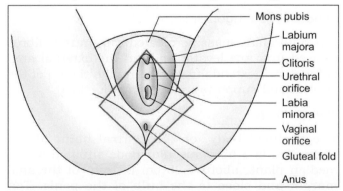

Fig. 28.2: The female perineum. Green lines indicate the position of pelvic outlet.

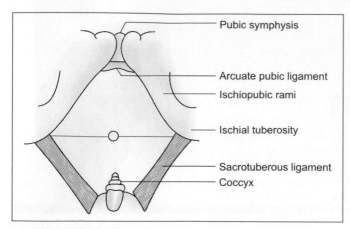

Fig. 28.3: Boundaries of perineum. Green line shows the division of perineum into urogenital and anal regions.

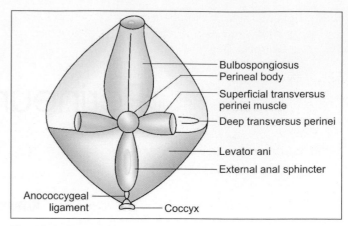

Fig. 28.4: Perineal body and the anococcygeal ligament in male.

In the urogenital region, there are the superficial perineal space or pouch and the deep perineal space or pouch.

The chief neurovascular bundle of the perineum occupies a fascial tunnel, the *pudendal canal*, and contains the pudendal nerve and the internal pudendal vessels. The pudendal canal lies in the lateral wall of the ischioanal fossa.

ANAL REGION

Cutaneous Innervation

The *inferior rectal nerve* (S2, S3, S4) supplies the skin around the anus and over the ischioanal fossa. The *perineal branch of the fourth sacral nerve* supplies the skin posterior to the anus.

Superficial Fascia

It contains a large amount of fat which fills the ischioanal fossa.

Deep Fascia

It is formed by the inferior fascia of the pelvic diaphragm and the fascia covering the obturator internus below the attachment of the levator ani.

Anococcygeal Ligament

It is a fibrofatty mass permeated with muscle fibres derived from the levator ani and the external anal sphincter. It extends from the anus to the tip of the coccyx, and supports the rectum (Fig. 28.4).

Perineal Body

The perineal body, or the central point of the perineum, is a fibromuscular node situated in the median plane, about 1.25 cm in front of the anal margin and close to the bulb of the penis. Ten muscles of the perineum converge and interlace in the perineal body.

Two unpaired:
- External anal sphincter.
- Fibres of longitudinal muscle coat of anal canal.

Paired:
- Bulbospongiosus.
- Superficial and deep transversus perenei.
- Levator ani.

All these converge and interlace in the perineal body. Nine are visible in Fig. 28.4. Last one is unstripped fibres of longitudinal muscle coat of the anal canal.

The perineal body is very important in the female for support of the pelvic organs. Sphincter urethro-vaginalis is also attached here. It may be damaged during parturition or childbirth. This may result in prolapse of the urinary bladder, the uterus, the ovaries and even of the rectum.

External Anal Sphincter

Anal canal is surrounded in its upper three-fourths by the internal anal sphincter which ends below at the level of white line of Hilton (Fig. 28.5).

The external anal sphincter surrounds the whole length of the anal canal. It is supplied by the inferior rectal nerve and by the perineal branch of the fourth

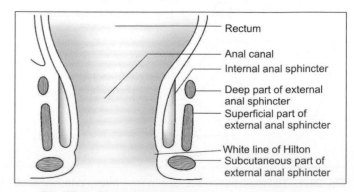

Fig. 28.5: The external and internal anal sphincters.

sacral nerve. It is under voluntary control and keeps the anus and anal canal closed. It is described in detail in Chapter 33.

ISCHIOANAL FOSSA

The ischioanal fossa is a wedge-shaped space situated one on each side of the anal canal below the pelvic diaphragm. Its base is directed downwards, towards the surface. The apex is directed upwards.

Dimensions

Length (anteroposteriorly), 5 cm; width (side to side), 2.5 cm; and depth (vertically), 5 to 6.2 cm.

Boundaries

The *base* is formed by the skin.

The *apex* is formed by the line where the obturator fascia meets the inferior fascia of the pelvic diaphragm or anal fascia. The line corresponds to the origin of the levator ani from the lateral pelvic wall.

Anteriorly, the fossa is limited by the posterior border of the perineal membrane (but for the anterior recess of the fossa) (Fig. 28.6).

Posteriorly, the fossa reaches.

(a) Lower border of the gluteus maximus.

(b) Sacrotuberous ligament.

The *lateral wall* is vertical, and is formed by:

(a) Obturator internus with the obturator fascia.

(b) Medial surface of the ischial tuberosity, below the attachment of obturator fascia (Fig. 28.7).

The *medial wall* slopes upwards and laterally, and is formed by:

(a) The external anal sphincter, with the fascia covering it in the lower part.

(b) The levator ani with the anal fascia in the upper part (Fig. 28.7).

Recesses

These are narrow extensions of the fossa beyond its boundaries.

1. The *anterior recess* extends forwards above the perineal membrane, reaching almost up to the posterior surface of the body of the pubis. It is closely related to the prostate or the vagina.

2. The *posterior recess* is smaller than the anterior. It extends deep to sacrotuberous ligament.

3. The horseshoe recess connects the two ischio-anal fossae behind the anal canal (Fig. 28.8).

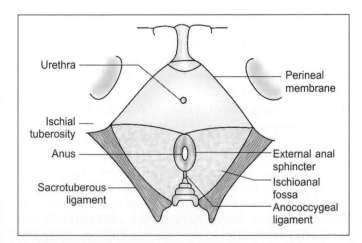

Fig. 28.6: Surface view of the ischioanal fossa, and perineal membrane.

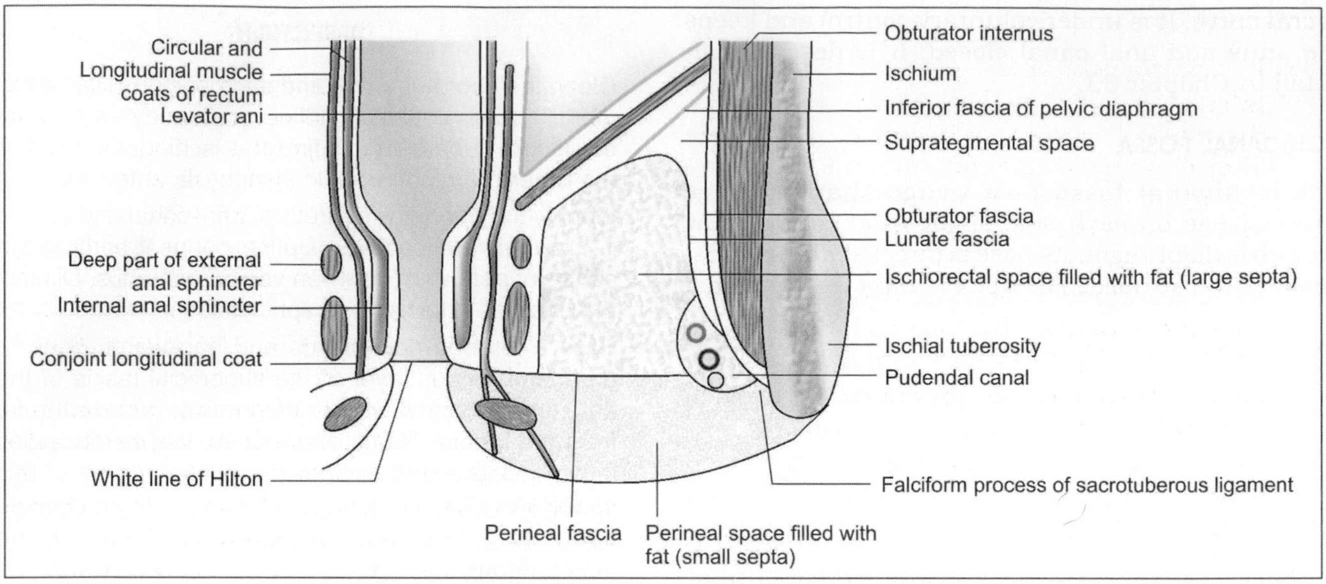

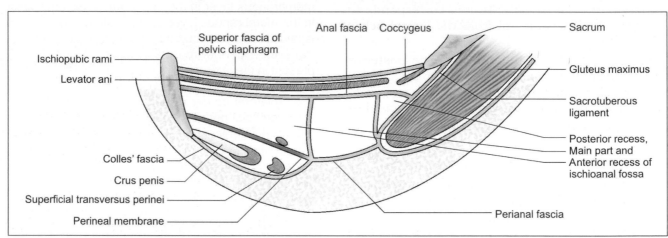

Fig. 28.7: Coronal section through the ischioanal fossa.

Fig. 28.8: Parasagittal section through the ischioanal fossa, showing its recesses.

Spaces and Canals of the Fossa

The arrangement of the fascia in this region forms the following spaces.

Perianal Space

The perianal fascia is in the form of a septum that passes laterally from the lower end of the longitudinal coat of the anal canal. It extends medially from the white line of Hilton to the pudendal canal laterally. It separates a shallow subcutaneous *perianal space* from the deep *ischioanal space*. The fat in the perianal space is tightly arranged in small loculi formed by complete septa. The infections of this space are, therefore, very painful due to the tension caused by swelling.

Ischioanal Space

This is large and deep. The fat in this space is loosely arranged in large loculi formed by incomplete delicate septa. The infections of this space are, therefore, least painful because swelling can occur without tension (Fig. 28.7).

The *lunate fascia* arches over the ischioanal fat. It begins laterally at the pudendal canal and merges medially with the fascia covering the deep part of the external anal sphincter. The fascia divides the ischioanal space into:

(a) *Suprategmental space*, above the fascia.

(b) *Tegmental space*, below the fascia.

Pudendal Canal

This is a fascial canal in the lateral wall of the ischioanal fossa, enclosing the pudendal nerve and internal pudendal vessels. The fascia of the canal is fused with the lower part of the obturator fascia laterally, with the lunate fascia above, with the perianal fascia medially, and with the falciform process of the sacrotuberous ligament below.

Contents of Ischioanal Fossa

1. Ischiorectal pad of fat.
2. Inferior rectal nerve and vessels. They pass through the fossa from lateral to medial side. They arch upwards above the fat (Fig. 28.9) to supply mucous membrane, external sphincter and the skin around the anus.
3. Pudendal canal with its contents. This canal lies along the lateral wall of the fossa.
4. Posterior scrotal or posterior labial (in females) nerves and vessels. They cross the anterolateral part of the fossa and enter the urogenital triangle.
5. Perineal branch of the fourth sacral (S4) nerve. It enters the posterior angle of the fossa and runs over the levator ani to the external anal sphincter.
6. Perforating cutaneous branches of nerves S2, S3. They appear at the lower border of the gluteus maximus, in the posterior part of the fossa.

UROGENITAL REGION

The anterior division of the perineum is the urogenital region. It contains the superficial and deep perineal spaces or pouches.

Cutaneous Innervation

(a) *Dorsal nerve of penis* or of clitoris. It supplies the skin of the penis or clitoris, except at its root (Figs 28.10 and 28.11).

(b) *Ilioinguinal nerve* and *genital branch of the genitofemoral nerve.* These supply the skin of the *anterior one-third* of the scrotum or labium majus and the root of the penis.

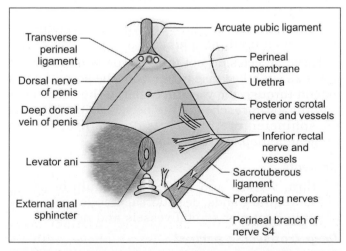

Fig. 28.9: Surface view of the ischiorectal fossa, showing its contents.

Transverse perineal ligament
Dorsal nerve of penis
Deep dorsal vein of penis
Levator ani
External anal sphincter
Arcuate pubic ligament
Perineal membrane
Urethra
Posterior scrotal nerve and vessels
Inferior rectal nerve and vessels
Sacrotuberous ligament
Perforating nerves
Perineal branch of nerve S4

(c) *Perineal branch of posterior cutaneous nerve of thigh:* It supplies the skin of the lateral part of the urogenital region and the lateral part of the *posterior two-thirds* of the scrotum or of the labium majus.

(d) *Posterior scrotal or labial nerves:* These supply the skin of the medial part of the urogenital region including the labium minus in females and the medial part of the posterior two-thirds of the scrotum or labium majus.

(e) The mucous membrane of urethra is supplied by the *perineal branch of the pudendal nerve.*

Superficial Fascia

It is made up of two layers as in the lower part of the anterior abdominal wall. The superficial *fatty layer* is continuous with the superficial fascia of the surrounding regions. The deep *membranous layer* or Colles' fascia is attached posteriorly to the posterior border of perineal membrane, and on each side to pubic arch below the crus penis. Anteriorly, it is continuous with the fascia of the scrotum containing the dartos, fascia of the penis, and with the membranous layer of the superficial fascia of the anterior abdominal wall or fascia of Scarpa.

Deep Fascia

It is also made up of one layer that lines the deep perineal space inferiorly.

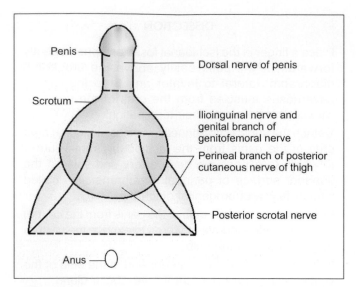

Fig. 28.10: Cutaneous innervation of the male perineum.

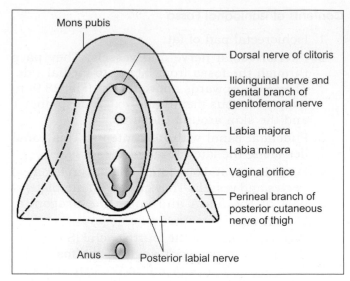

Fig. 28.11: Cutaneous innervation of the female perineum.

This fascia of the urogenital diaphragm is thick. It is also called the perineal membrane.

MALE UROGENITAL REGION

The urogenital region is bounded posteriorly by the interischial line which usually overlies the posterior border of the transverse perinei muscles. Anteriorly and laterally, it is bounded by symphysis pubis and ischiopubic rami.

Urogenital region extends superficially to encompass the scrotum and root of penis.

Urogenital region is divided into two parts by strong perineal membrane.

Above it: Deep perineal space.

Below it: Superficial perineal space.

Deep Perineal Space

Previous view: Space between superior fascia of urogenital diaphragm and perineal membrane that contained urethra and urethral sphincter.

Present view: Now the urethral sphincter is known to be contained inside the urethra itself (within). The urogenital diaphragm does not exist. The space is thin and open above (Fig. 28.12).

Boundaries

Deep aspect: Endopelvic fascia of pelvic floor.

Superficial aspect: Perineal membrane. Between these two fascial layers lie deep transverse perinei; superficial to the proximal urethral sphincter mechanism and pubourethralis (Fig. 28.17).

The previous view was that sphincter urethrae extended between the two ischiopubic rami and was pierced by urethra and (vagina in females) but as of

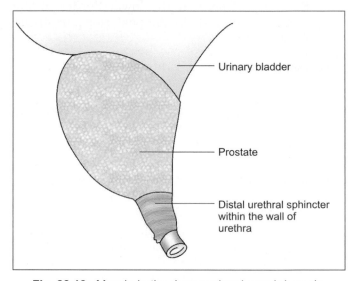

Fig. 28.12: Muscle in the deep perineal pouch in male.

now the sphincter urethrae lies within wall of urethra as proximal urethral sphincter.

These muscles do not form a true diaphragmatic sheet as such because fibres from the several parts extend through the visceral outlet in the pelvic floor into the lower reaches of the pelvic cavity. (There is no sphincter urethrae outside urethra. So, no urogenital diaphragm exists).

Contents

Urethra, vessels and nerve to the bulb of penis, bulbourethral glands, deep dorsal vessels and nerves of penis, posterior scrotal vessels and nerves.

Deep transverse perinei

It forms an incomplete sheet of skeletal muscle extending across the urogenital triangle from the medial aspects of the ischiopubic rami. Posteriorly, the sheet is attached to perineal body where its fibres decussate with those of opposite side.

Anteriorly, the muscles are deficient and the visceral structures pass across the endopelvic fascia and the perineal membrane. Some fibres pass to the deep part of external anal sphincter posteriorly and sphincter urethrae (contained within the urethra).

Together with superficial transverse perinei the muscles act to tether the perineal body in median plane. The muscle gives dynamic support for pelvic viscera.

Supplied by perineal branches of pudenal nerve and vessels.

Distal urethral sphincter mechanism

Consists of intrinsic striated and smooth muscles of urethra and the pubourethralis component of levator ani which surrounds the urethra at the point of maximum concentration of those muscles. It surrounds the membranous urethra in the male.

Smooth muscle fibres also reach up to the lowest part of the neck of the bladder and between the two, fibres lie on the surface of prostate.

Bulk of fibres surround the membranous urethra. There are circularly disposed striated muscle fibres called *rhabdosphincter* which forms main part of distal urethral sphincter mechanism (Fig. 28.17). Some fibres are attached to inner surface of the ischiopubic ramus, *forming compressor urethrae*.

Perineal Membrane

Perineal membrane is almost triangular membrane:
- Laterally attached to periosteum of ischiopubic rami.
- Apex attached to arcuate ligament of pubis, where the membrane is attached to this arcuate ligament of pubis, it is particularly thick and is called *transverse perineal ligament.*
- Posterior border is fused to deep parts of perineal body and is continuous with the fascia over deep transerve perinei.

Perineal membrane (Fig. 28.13) is crossed by or pierced by:
- Urethra 2–3 cm behind the inferior border of pubic symphysis.
- Artery to the bulb of penis.
- Duct of bulbourethral gland.
- Muscular branches.
- Deep artery of the penis, urethral artery.
- Dorsal artery and dorsal nerves of penis.
- Posterior scrotal vessels and nerves, anterior to transverse perinei.

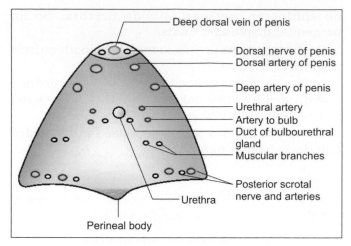

Fig. 28.13: Structures piercing the perineal membrane (male).

Superficial perineal space is given in Table 28.1.

FEMALE UROGENITAL REGION

The urogenital region is bounded by the interischial line which usually overlies the posterior border of the transverse perinei muscles.

Anteriorly and laterally, it is bounded by symphysis pubis and ischiopubic rami.

In the female, urogenital region extends to the labia majora and mons pubis.

Urogenital region is divided into two parts by perineal membrane.

Above it: Deep perineal space.

Below it: Superficial perineal space.

Deep Perineal Space

Previous view: Space between urogential diaphragm and perineal membrane that contained urethra and urethral sphincter.

Present view: Now the urethral sphincter is known to be contained inside the urethra itself (within). The urogential diaphragm does not exist. It is thin space, open above.

Boundaries

Superficial aspect: Perineal membrane. On the deep aspect of perineal membrane lie deep transverse perenei; superficial to compressor urethrae and sphincter urethrovaginalis.

Previous view was that sphincter urethrae extended between the two ischiopubic rami and was pierced by urethra and vagina but as of now the sphincter urethrae lies within urethra.

These muscles do not form a true diaphragmatic sheet as such because fibres from the several parts extend through the visceral outlet in the pelvic floor into the lower reaches of the pelvic cavity. (There is no sphincter urethrae outside urethra. So no urogenital diaphragm exists).

Deep transverse perinei is mainly smooth muscle in female.

In female perineal membrane is less well defined and divided into two halves by urethra and vagina so that it forms triangle on two sides.

The pubourethral ligament links the two sides anteriorly behind pubic arch.

Contents

Urethra, vagina, deep dorsal vessels and nerves of clitoris, posterior labial vessels and nerves.

Distal urethral sphincter mechanism

Consists of intrinsic smooth muscle, intrinsic skeletal muscle. This is anatomically separate from the pubourethralis component of levator ani.

The sphincter mechanism surrounds more than the middle third of urethra. It blends above with the smooth muscle of bladder neck and below with the smooth muscle of lower urethra and vagina. Skeletal muscle fibres are circularly disposed, called *rhabdosphincter*. This forms main part of external urethral sphincter.

Action

Compresses the urethra, particularly when bladder contains fluid. It contracts to expel the final drops of urine.

Nerve supply

Perineal branch of pudendal nerve and pelvic splanchnic nerves.

Extensions of the muscles are:

Compressor urethrae

Compressor urethrae arises from ischiopubic rami of each side by a small tendon. Fibres pass anteriorly to meet their counterparts in a flat band which lies anterior to urethra. A variable number of these fibres pass medially to reach the lower wall of vagina. Sphincter urethrae is within the wall of urethra (Fig. 28.14).

Sphincter urethrovaginalis

Sphincter urethrovaginalis arises from perineal body. Its fibres pass forwards on either side of urethra and vagina to meet their counterparts in a flat band, anterior to urethra below compressor urethrae.

Actions

Direction of the fibres of compressor urethrae and sphincter urethrovaginalis suggest that these produce elongation as well as compression of the membranous urethra and thus aid continence in females. Both are supplied by perineal nerve.

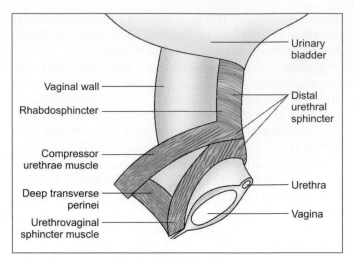

Fig. 28.14: Muscles in the deep perineal pouch in female.

Perineal Membrane

Perineal membrane (Fig. 28.15) is crossed/pierced by:

- Urethra, 2–3 cm behind the inferior border of pubic symphysis.
- Vagina (centrally), behind urethra.
- Deep artery of clitoris.
- Dorsal vessels and nerves of clitoris.
- Artery to bulb of vestibule.
- Muscular branches.
- Posterior labial vessels and nerves, anterior to transverse perinei.

Superficial perineal space is given in Table 28.1.

FEMALE EXTERNAL GENITAL ORGANS/PUDENDUM OR VULVA *(Fig. 28.16)*

Pudendum includes:
1. Mons pubis
2. Labia majora
3. Labia minora.

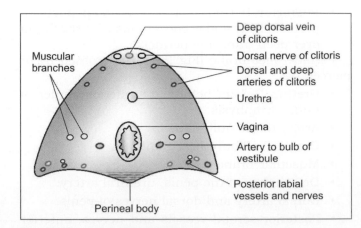

Fig. 28.15: Structures piercing the perineal membrane (female).

Table 28.1: The superficial perineal space

Features	Male	Female
Definition	This is the superficial space of the urogenital region situated superficial to the perineal membrane	Same
Boundaries		
(a) Superficial	Colles' fascia	Same
(b) Deep	Perineal membrane	Same
(c) On each side	Ischiopubic rami	Same
(d) Posteriorly	Closed by the fusion of perineal membrane with Colles' fascia.	Same
(e) Anteriorly	Open and continuous with the spaces of the scrotum, penis and the anterior abdominal wall	Open and continuous with the spaces of the clitoris and the anterior abdominal wall
Contents	Root of penis, made up of two corpora cavernosa and one corpus spongiosum traversed by the urethra (Fig. 28.17)	Body of clitoris, made up only of two corpora cavernosa *separated by an incomplete septum. The corpus* spongiosum *is absent.* Urethral orifice lies 2 cm behind the clitoris. Vaginal orifice just behind urethral orifice. Two bulbs of vestibule are there, one on each side of these two orifices. These unite and get attached to the glans clitoridis (Fig. 28.18)
Muscles on each side	(a) Ischiocavernosus covering the corpora cavernosa of penis (Fig. 28.19) (b) Bulbospongiosus covering corpus spongiosum; both are united by a median raphe (c) Superficial transversus perinei	(a) Ischiocavernosus covering the corpora cavernosa of clitoris (Fig. 28.20) (b) Bulbospongiosus covering bulb of vestibule. These remain separated to give passage to urethra and vagina (c) Superficial transversus perinei
Nerves	(a) Three sets of branches from perineal nerve namely posterior scrotal nerve, branch to bulb and muscular branches (b) Long perineal nerve from posterior cutaneous nerve of thigh	(a) Three sets of branches from perineal nerve namely posterior labial nerve, branch to bulb of vestibule and muscular branches (b) Same
Vessels	(a) Two branches of perineal artery namely, the posterior scrotal and transverse perineal (b) Four branches from the artery of penis namely, artery to the bulb of penis, urethral artery, deep and dorsal arteries of penis	(a) Two branches of perineal artery namely posterior labial and transverse perineal (b) Four branches from the artery of clitoris, namely artery to bulb of vestibule, urethral artery, deep and dorsal arteries of clitoris
Glands and ducts	Only the ducts of bulbourethral glands	Greater vestibular glands and their ducts

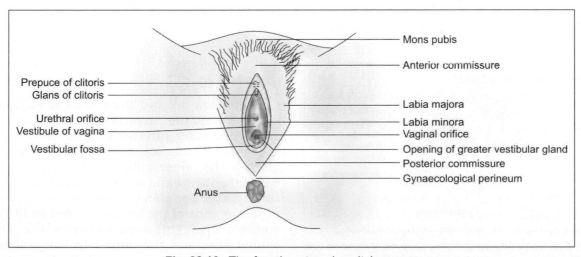

Fig. 28.16: The female external genital organs.

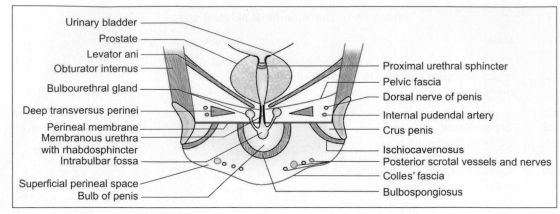

Fig. 28.17: Coronal section through the urogenital region of the male perineum.

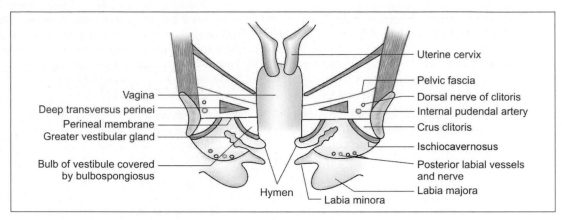

Fig. 28.18: Coronal section through the urogenital region of the female perineum.

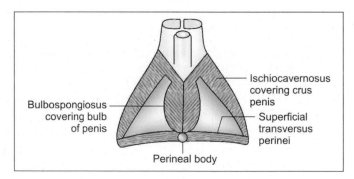

Fig. 28.19: Superficial muscles of the male perineum.

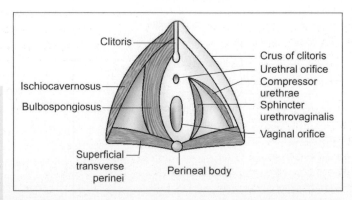

Fig. 28.20: Female perineum showing superficial muscles (left half) and deep perineal muscles on right half.

4. Clitoris.
5. Vestibule of the vagina.
6. Bulbs of the vestibule.
7. Greater vestibular glands.

Mons Pubis

Mons pubis is a rounded eminence present in front of the pubic symphysis. It is formed by accumulation of subcutaneous fat. It is covered with pubic hair. The hair bearing area has a nearly horizontal upper limit.

Labia Majora

Labia majora are two thick folds of skin enclosing fat. They form the lateral boundaries of the *pudendal cleft*. Their outer surfaces are covered with hair, and the inner surfaces are studded with large sebaceous glands. The larger anterior ends are connected to each other below the mons pubis to form the *anterior commissure*. The skin connecting the less prominent posterior ends of the labia is known as the *posterior commissure*. The area between the posterior commissure and the anus which is about 2.5 cm long constitutes the *gynaecological perineum*.

Labia Minora

Labia minora are two thin folds of skin, which lie within the pudendal cleft. Anteriorly, each labium minus splits into two layers; the upper layer joins the corresponding layer of the opposite side to form the *prepuce of the clitoris*. Similarly the lower layers of the two sides join to form the *frenulum of the clitoris*. Posteriorly, the two labia minora meet to form the *frenulum of the labia minora*. The inner surface of the labia minora contains numerous sebaceous glands.

Clitoris

The clitoris is an erectile organ, homologous with the penis. However, *it is not traversed by urethra*. It lies in the anterior part of pudendal cleft. The body of clitoris is made up of two *corpora cavernosa* enclosed in a fibrous sheath and partly separated by an incomplete *pectiniform septum*. *A corpus spongiosum is absent.* Each corpus cavernosum is attached to the ischiopubic rami. The down-turned free end of clitoris is formed by a rounded tubercle, *glans clitoridis*, which caps the free ends of corpora. The glans is made up of erectile tissue continuous posteriorly with the commissural venous plexus uniting right and left bulbs of vestibule called *bulbar commissure*. The surface of glans is highly sensitive and plays an important role in sexual responses.

Vestibule of the Vagina

Vestibule of the vagina is space between two labia minora. It presents the following features.

1. The *urethral orifice* lies about 2.5 cm behind the clitoris and just in front of the vaginal orifice.
2. *Vaginal orifice* or *introitus* lies in the posterior part of the vestibule, and is partly closed, in the virgin, by a thin membrane called the *hymen*. In married women, the hymen is represented by rounded tags of tissue called the carunculae hymenales.
3. *Orifices of the ducts of greater vestibular glands* lie one on each side of vaginal orifice, between the hymen and labium minus (Fig. 28.19).
4. Numerous *lesser vestibular* or *mucous glands* open on the surface of vestibule.
5. The posterior part of vestibule between vaginal orifice and frenulum of labia minora forms a shallow depression known as *vestibular fossa*.

Bulbs of the Vestibule

Bulbs of the vestibule are two oval bodies of erectile tissue that correspond to the two halves of the bulb of the penis. The bulbs lie on either side of the vaginal and urethral orifices, superficial to the perineal membrane. The tapering anterior ends of the bulbs are united in front of the urethra by a venous plexus, called the *bulbar commissure*. The expanded posterior ends of the bulbs partly overlap the greater vestibular glands.

Greater Vestibular Glands of Bartholin

Greater vestibular glands are homologous with the bulbourethral glands of Cowper in the male. These lie in the superficial perineal space. Each gland has a long duct about 2 cm long which opens at the side of the hymen, between the hymen and the labium minus.

PERINEAL SPACES/POUCHES

The arrangement of the superficial and deep fasciae in the urogenital region results in the formation of two triangular spaces, the superficial and deep perineal spaces or pouches (Figs 28.17 and 28.18).

The boundaries and contents of these spaces are summarised in Tables 28.1, 28.2 and 28.3.

Muscles of the Urogenital Region

These muscles are arranged in superficial and deep, groups. The superficial muscles are the ischio-cavernosus, the bulbospongiosus and the superficial transversus perinei, described in Table 28.3. The deep muscles are the distal urethral sphincter mechanism, sphincter urethrae with extensions and the deep transversus perinei (described earlier).

PUDENDAL CANAL

This is a fascial tunnel present in the lateral wall of the ischioanal fossa, just above the sacrotuberous ligament. It transmits the pudendal nerve and the internal pudendal vessels.

The canal extends from the lesser sciatic notch to the posterior border of the perineal membrane.

Formation

The pudendal canal is a space between obturator fascia and the lunate fascia. Others believe that it is formed by splitting of the obturator fascia (Fig. 28.7).

Contents

1. *Pudendal nerve* (S2, S3, S4): In the posterior part of the canal, pudendal nerve gives off the inferior rectal nerve and then soon divides into a larger perineal nerve and a smaller dorsal nerve of penis.

Table 28.2: Deep perineal space

Features	Male	Female
Definition	This is the thin space of the urogenital region situated deep to the perineal membrane Contributes to pelvic floor	Same
Boundaries		
(a) Superficial	Perineal membrane (Fig. 28.20)	Same
(b) Deep	Open above	Same
(c) On each side	Ischiopubic rami	Same
(d) Anteriorly	Gap between perineal membrane and inferior pubic ligament	Same
Contents		
1. Tubes	Part of urethra	Parts of urethra and vagina
2. Muscles	(a) Sphincter urethrae or distal urethral sphincter within the wall of urethra (b) Deep transversus perinei. Mainly skeletal muscle	(a) Sphincter urethrae within the wall of urethra (b) Same attachment. Mainly smooth muscle (c) Compressor urethrae (d) Sphincter urethrovaginalis
3. Nerves on each side	(a) Dorsal nerve of penis (b) Muscular branches from perineal nerve	(a) Dorsal nerve of clitoris (b) Muscular branches from perineal nerve
4. Vessels	(a) Artery of penis (b) Stems of origin of four branches namely, artery to the bulb of penis, urethral artery, deep and dorsal arteries of penis	(a) Artery of clitoris (b) Stems of origin of four branches namely artery to bulb of vestibule, urethral artery, deep and dorsal arteries of clitoris
5. Glands	Bulbourethral glands	No glands

Table 28.3: The superficial perineal muscles

Muscles	Origin	Fibres	Insertion	Nerve supply	Actions
1. *Ischiocavernosus* It covers the crus penis or crus clitoridis; smaller in females	(a) Medial surface of ischial ramus behind the crus (b) Posterior part of perineal membrane	Fibres run forwards and spiral over the crus	Inserted by an aponeurosis into the sides and undersurface of the anterior part of the crus	Perineal branch of pudendal nerve	It helps in maintaining erection of the penis by compressing the crus Causes erection of clitoris in female
2. *Bulbospongiosus* It covers the bulb of penis and the two muscles are united by a median raphe In females, it covers the bulb of vestibule and the two muscles are separated by the vagina and urethra	(a) Perineal body (b) Median raphe over the bulb of penis	Posterior fibres embrace the posterior end of the bulb Middle fibres embrace the corpus spongiosum Anterior fibres embrace the entire body of penis	(a) Posterior *fibres,* into the perineal membrane (b) Middle fibres embrace the bulb and corpus spongiosum, and the raphe on their upper surface (c) Anterior fibres are inserted into the raphe on the dorsal surface of the penis	Perineal branch of pudendal nerve	1. Helps in ejecting the last drops of urine at the end of micturition 2. Middle fibres assist in the erection of the corpus spongiosum penis by compressing the bulb 3. Anterior fibres also help in the erection of penis by compressing the deep dorsal vein of penis In females it acts as sphincter of vagina and assists in erection of clitoris
3. *Superficial transversus perinei* Narrow slip running transversely in front of anus on either side	Medial surface of the root of ischial ramus	Fibres run medially	Inserted into the perineal body where it interlaces with other converging muscles	Perineal branch of pudendal nerve	Steadies the perineal body

2. *Internal pudendal artery*: This artery gives off the inferior rectal artery in the posterior part of the canal. In the anterior part of the canal, the artery divides into the perineal artery and the artery of penis. Vein accompanies the artery.

Pudendal Nerve

Pudendal nerve is the chief nerve of the perineum and of the external genitalia. It is accompanied by the internal pudendal vessels.

Origin

Pudendal nerve arises from the sacral plexus in the pelvis. It is derived from spinal nerves S2, S3, S4.

Course

It originates in the pelvis, enters gluteal region through greater sciatic notch, leaves it through lesser sciatic notch to enter the pudenal canal in the lateral wall of ischioanal fossa. It terminates by dividing into branches.

Relations

1. *In the pelvis*, the pudendal nerve descends in front of the piriformis deep to its fascia. It leaves the pelvis, to enter the gluteal region, by passing through the lower part of the greater sciatic foramen, between the piriformis and the coccygeus, medial to internal pudendal vessels.
2. *In the gluteal region*, the pudendal nerve crosses the apex of the sacrospinous ligament, under cover of gluteus maximus. Here it lies medial to the internal pudendal vessels which cross the ischial spine. Accompanying these vessels, the nerve leaves the gluteal region by passing through the lesser sciatic foramen, and enters the pudendal canal.
3. *In the pudendal canal*, the neurovascular bundle lies in the lateral wall of the ischioanal fossa (Fig. 28.21).

Branches

In the posterior part of the pudendal canal the pudendal nerve gives off the inferior rectal nerve, and then divides into two terminal branches, the perineal nerve and the dorsal nerve of the penis or clitoris (Fig. 28.22).

The *inferior rectal nerve* pierces the medial wall of the pudendal canal, crosses the ischioanal fossa from lateral to medial side, and supplies the external anal sphincter, the skin around the anus, and the lining of the anal canal below the pectinate line.

The *perineal nerve* is the larger terminal branch of the pudendal nerve. It runs forwards below the

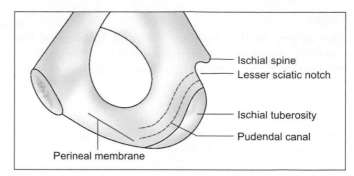

Fig. 28.21: Inner surface of the right hip bone showing the position of pudendal canal.

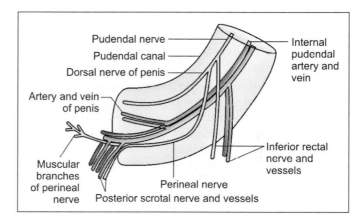

Fig. 28.22: Contents of pudendal canal.

internal pudendal vessels, and terminates by dividing into:
  (a) Medial and lateral *posterior scrotal* or labial nerves.
  (b) *Muscular branches* to the urogenital muscles, and to anterior parts of external anal sphincter and the levator ani. The nerve to the bulbospongiosus also gives off the nerve to bulb which supplies corpus spongiosum, penis and the urethra.

The *dorsal nerve of the penis* or *clitoris* is the smaller terminal branch of the pudendal nerve. It runs forwards first in the pudendal canal above the internal pudendal vessels; and then in the deep perineal space between these vessels and the pubic arch. Next it passes through the lateral part of the oval gap between the apex of the perineal membrane and the arcuate pubic ligament, runs on the dorsum of the penis or clitoris, and ends in the glans penis or glans clitoridis. It supplies the skin of the body of the penis or clitoris and of the glans.

Internal Pudendal Artery

This is the chief artery of the perineum and of the external genital organs. It is smaller in females than in males.

Origin

The artery is the smaller terminal branch of the anterior division of the internal iliac artery, given off in the pelvis; the larger branch is the inferior gluteal.

Course

The course of internal pudendal artery is similar to the course of pudendal nerve.

Relations

In the pelvis, the artery runs downwards in front of the piriformis, the sacral plexus and the inferior gluteal artery. It leaves the pelvis by piercing the parietal pelvic fascia and passing through the greater sciatic foramen, below the piriformis, thus entering the gluteal region.

In the gluteal region, the artery crosses the dorsal aspect of the tip of the ischial spine, under cover of the gluteus maximus. Here it lies between the pudendal nerve medially and the nerve to the obturator internus laterally. It leaves the gluteal region by passing through the lesser sciatic foramen, and thus enters the pudendal canal.

In the pudendal canal, the artery runs downwards and forwards in the lateral wall of the ischioanal fossa, about 4 cm above the lower margin of the ischial tuberosity. Here it is related to the dorsal nerve above and the perineal nerve below. The artery gives off the inferior rectal artery in the posterior part of the canal, and the perineal artery in the anterior part. The internal pudendal artery continues into the deep perineal space as the artery of the penis or of the clitoris (Fig. 28.22).

In the deep perineal space, the artery of the penis or clitoris which is continuation of internal pudendal artery, runs forwards close to the side of pubic arch, medial to the dorsal nerve of penis or of clitoris. The artery ends a little behind the arcuate pubic ligament by dividing into the deep and dorsal arteries of penis or of the clitoris (Fig. 28.23).

Branches

1. The *inferior rectal artery* arises near the posterior end of the pudendal canal, and accompanies the nerve of the same name. The artery supplies the skin and muscles and mucous membrane of the anal region, and anastomoses with the superior and middle rectal arteries (Fig. 28.23).

2. The *perineal artery* arises near the anterior end of the pudendal canal, and pierces the base of the perineal membrane to reach the superficial perineal space. Here it divides into the *transverse perineal* and the *posterior scrotal* or *posterior labial* branches.

3. The *artery of the penis* or *the clitoris* runs in the deep perineal space and gives off:

   (a) Artery to the bulb.

   (b) Urethral artery.

   (c) Deep artery of the penis or the clitoris.

   (d) Dorsal artery of the penis or the clitoris.

   All of them pierce the perineal membrane and reach the superficial perineal space. The *artery to the bulb* supplies the bulb of the penis or bulb of vestibule and the posterior part of the urethra or only the urethra. The *urethral artery* supplies the corpus spongiosum and the anterior part of the urethra. The *deep artery of the penis* or *the clitoris* traverses and supplies the crus and the corpus cavernosum. The *dorsal artery of the penis* or *the clitoris* supplies the skin and fasciae of the body of the penis and of the glans or the glans clitoridis.

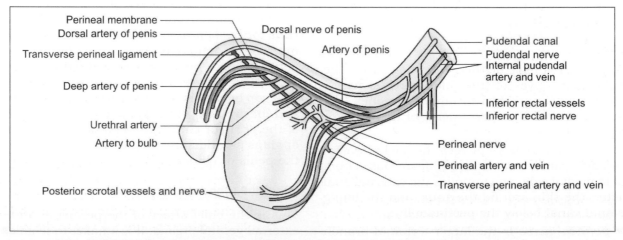

Fig. 28.23: Course and distribution of the pudendal nerve, and of the internal pudendal artery.

Internal Pudendal Vein

The tributaries of internal pudendal vein follow the branches of the internal pudendal artery. The vein drains into internal iliac vein.

Histology of Body of Penis/Clitoris

Penis consists of two corpora cavernosa containing the deep artery of the penis and a single corpora spongiosum with the urethra. All three erectile masses contain spaces or caverns. The spaces are larger in corpora cavernosa and smaller in corpus spongiosum. These three corpora are covered by fasciae and skin. In the deep fascia lie deep dorsal vein of penis, two dorsal arteries and two dorsal nerves of penis. The superficial dorsal vein of the penis lies in the superficial fascia.

Clitoris comprises two corpora covernosa only. *Corpus spongiosum is absent.* The two erectile masses contain caverns or spaces.

CLINICAL ANATOMY

- The two ischioanal fossae allow distention of the rectum and anal canal during passage of faeces.
- Both the perianal and ischioanal spaces are common sites of abscesses (Fig. 28.24).

  Sometimes an abscess may burst into the anal canal or rectum internally, and on to the surface of the perineum externally. In this way an ischioanal type of *anorectal fistula* or *fistula in ano* may be produced. The most common site of the internal opening is in the floor of one of the anal crypts. If the abscess bursts only externally, and healing does not follow an *external sinus* is produced. Through the horseshoe recess a unilateral abscess may become bilateral.
- The ischioanal fat acts as a cushion-like support to the rectum and anal canal. Loss of this fat in debilitating diseases like diarrhoea in children may result in *prolapse of the rectum.*
- The occasional gap between the tendinous origin of levator ani and the obturator fascia is known as *hiatus of Schwalbe.* Rarely pelvic organs may herniate through this gap into the ischioanal fossa, resulting in an *ischioanal hernia.*
- The pudendal nerve supplies sensory branches to the lower of the vagina, through the inferior rectal and posterior labial branches. Therefore, in vaginal operations, general anaesthesia can be replaced by a *pudendal nerve block.* The nerve is infiltrated near the ischial spine by a needle passed through the vaginal wall and then guided by a finger (Fig. 28.25).

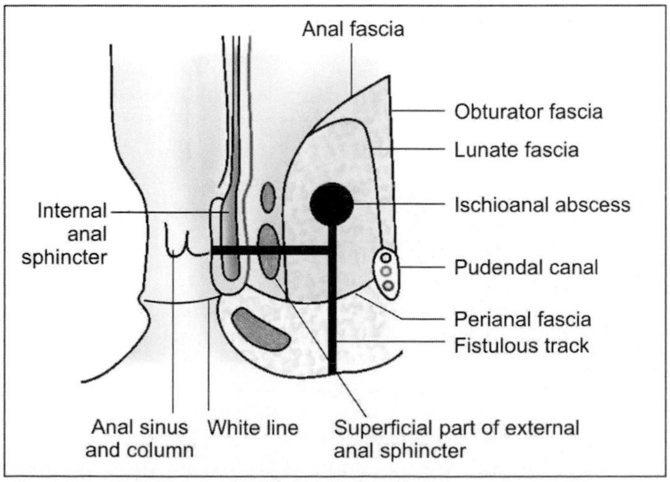

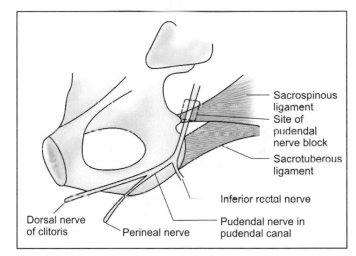

Fig. 28.25: Pudendal nerve block.

- *The membranous part of the male urethra* is the narrowest and least dilatable part of the urethra. In inexperienced hands, it is likely to be ruptured during instrumentation. The urethra can also rupture in accidental injuries.
- Rupture of the urethra leads to extravasation of urine, which may be superficial or deep. In *superficial extravasation,* the urine spreads downwards deep to the membranous layer of the superficial fascia. It first fills the superficial perineal space; and then the scrotum, the penis and the lower part of the anterior abdominal wall. It is prevented from going to the ischioanal fossa or the thigh by the firm attachment of the

Fig. 28.24: Ischiorectal type of fistula in ano. Internally it usually opens into one of anal crypts. The track traverses the superficial parts of external anal sphincter and lower part of internal anal sphincter. A blind sinus lies high up in the ischiorectal fossa.

membranous layer of superficial fascia to their boundaries (Fig. 28.26).

In *deep extravasation*, the urine spreads upwards into the extraperitoneal space of the pelvis around bladder and prostate into the anterior abdominal wall (Fig. 28.27).

- The cutaneous nerves of perineum are derived from the sacral nerves (S2, S3, S4). These segments also supply parasympathetic fibres to the pelvic organs. Diseases of these organs may, therefore, cause *referred pain* in the perineum.

- *Perineal body* is one of chief supports of pelvic organs, like uterus. Damage to the perineal body often leads to *prolapse of the uterus* and of other pelvic organs.

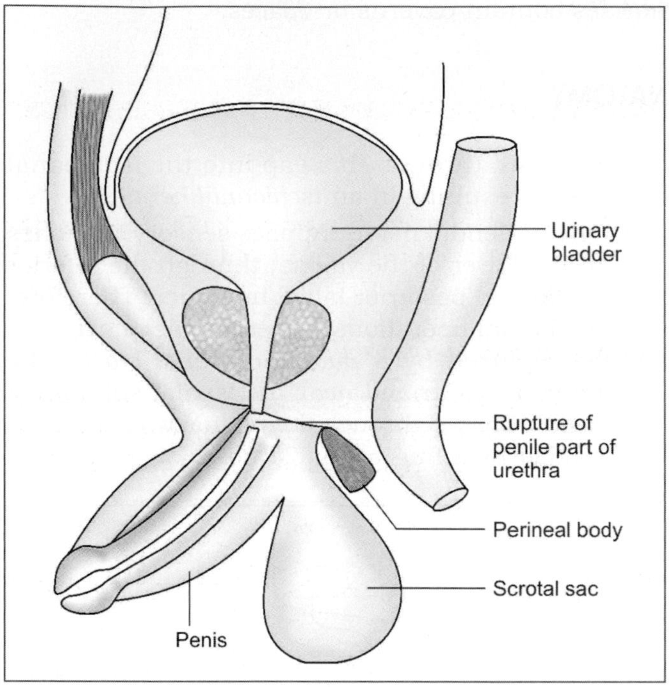

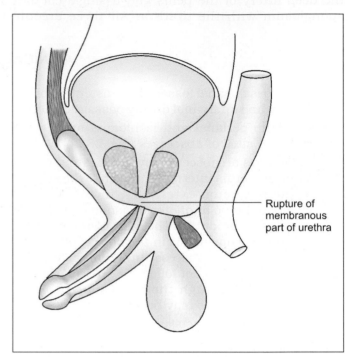

Fig. 28.26: Extravasation of urine due to rupture of penile urethra.

Fig. 28.27: Extravasation of urine due to rupture of membranous urethra.

Preliminary Consideration of Boundaries and Contents of Pelvis

Pelvis is formed by articulation of each of the two hip bones with the sacrum behind and with each other in front. The greater pelvis is comfortably occupied by the abdominal viscera, leaving only the lesser pelvis for the pelvic viscera. Urinary bladder lies behind pubic symphysis; rectum and anal canal are close to the sacrum and coccyx. The middle space left is for the genital organs. Many structures cross the brim of the pelvis, i.e. curved line extending around the pelvis at the junction of greater and lesser pelves (linea terminalis).

The bony pelvis is formed by *four bones* united at *four joints*. The bones are the two hip bones in front and on the sides, and the sacrum and coccyx behind. The joints are the two sacroiliac joints, the pubic symphysis and the sacrococcygeal joint.

The pelvis is divided by the plane of the *pelvic inlet* or pelvic brim, or superior aperture of the pelvis into two parts.

(a) Upper part is known as greater or *false pelvis*.

(b) Lower part is known as the *lesser* or *true pelvis*. The plane of the pelvic inlet passes from the sacral promontory to the upper margin of the pubic symphysis. The *greater* or *false pelvis* includes the two iliac fossae, and forms a part of the posterior abdominal wall. The *lesser* or *true pelvis* contains the pelvic viscera.

LESSER PELVIS

Pelvic Walls

The pelvic walls are made up of bones, ligaments and muscles.

Bony Walls

These are formed:

(a) *Anteriorly* by the pubic symphysis and bodies of the pubic bones.

(b) *Posteriorly* by the sacrum and coccyx.

(c) *On each side* by the two rami of the pubis, the ischium with its ramus, and the lower part of the ilium (Fig. 29.1).

Ligaments and Membranes

1. *Obturator membrane* closes the greater part of the obturator foramen, and completes the lower part of the lateral wall of the pelvis (Fig. 29.2).

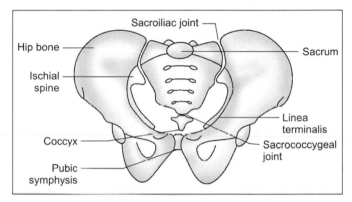

Fig. 29.1: Anterior view of the male pelvis.

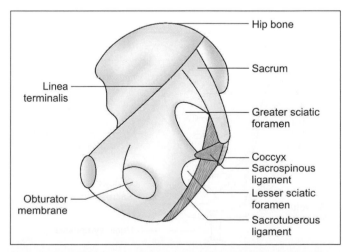

Fig. 29.2: Pelvic bones and ligaments seen from the medial side.

2. *Sacrotuberous* ligament and *sacrospinous* ligaments bridge the gap between the hip bone and the sacrum, and convert the greater and lesser sciatic notches into the foramina of the same name (Fig. 29.3).

Muscles

1. The *obturator internus* with its fascia reinforces the lateral wall of the pelvis from the inside.
2. The *piriformis* with its fascia forms the posterior wall of the pelvis. It also helps in filling the gap of the greater sciatic foramen (Figs 29.4 and 29.5).

Pelvic Inlet: Superior Aperture of Pelvis

The pelvic inlet is an oblique plane, making an angle of 50 to 60 degrees with the horizontal. It is *bounded posteriorly* by the sacral promontory, *anteriorly* by the upper margin of the pubic symphysis, and on *each side* by the linea terminalis. The linea terminalis includes the anterior margin of the ala of the sacrum, the arcuate line or lower part of the medial border of the ilium, the pectineal line of the pubis or pecten pubis, and the pubic crest.

The pelvic inlet is heart-shaped *in the male*, and is widest in its posterior part. *In the female*, it is oval, and is widest more anteriorly than in the male. Posteriorly, the inlet is indented by the sacral promontory, more so in the male than in the female (Fig. 29.6).

Pelvic Outlet: Inferior Aperture of Pelvis

The pelvic outlet is *bounded anteriorly* by the arcuate or inferior pubic ligament; *posteriorly* by the coccyx; and *on each side* by the ischiopubic rami or side of the pubic arch, the ischial tuberosities and the sacrotuberous ligaments. The posterior part of the outlet is formed by the coccyx and the sacro-tuberous ligaments. It is mobile on the sacrum, and the sacrum itself is slightly mobile at the sacroiliac joints (Fig. 29.7).

The pubic arch is formed by the ischiopubic rami of the two sides and by the lower margin of the pubic symphysis which is rounded off by the arcuate pubic ligament (Fig. 28.3).

Pelvic Floor

The pelvic floor is formed by the pelvic diaphragm which consists of the levator ani and the coccygeus (Chapter 34). It resembles a hammock, or a gutter because it slopes from either side towards the median plane where it is traversed by the urethra and the anal canal, and also by the vagina in the female. The pelvic diaphragm separates the perineum below from the pelvis above.

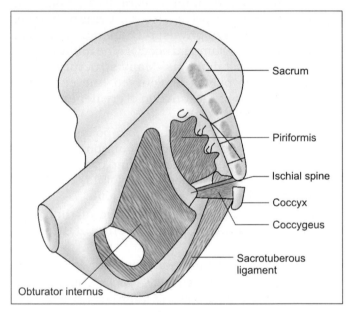

Fig. 29.4: Muscles of the pelvic wall seen from the medial side.

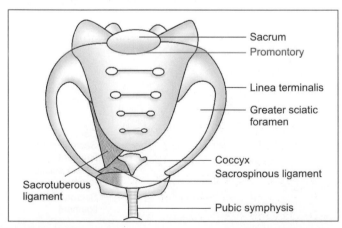

Fig. 29.3: Bones and ligaments of pelvis seen from the front.

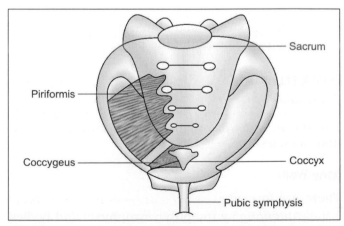

Fig. 29.5: Muscles of the posterior part of the pelvic wall seen from the front.

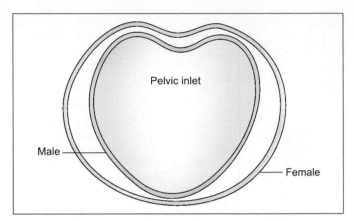

Fig. 29.6: Shape of pelvic inlet in the male, and in the female.

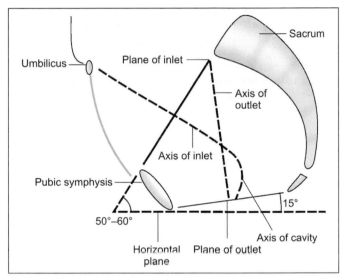

Fig. 29.7: Sagittal section of the pelvis showing the planes of its inlet and outlet and their axes. The axis of the pelvic cavity is J-shaped.

The muscles of the true pelvis, its blood vessels and nerves are considered in Chapter 34.

Pelvic Cavity

The pelvic cavity is continuous above with the abdominal cavity at the pelvic brim, and is limited below by the pelvic diaphragm. The cavity is curved in such a way that it is first directed downwards and backwards, and then downwards and forwards (J-shaped) as shown in Fig. 29.8. It has unequal walls, measuring only about 5 cm anteriorly and 15 cm posteriorly. The cavity is more roomy or larger in the female than in the male.

Contents

1. Sigmoid colon and rectum occupy the posterior part of the pelvis.
2. Urinary bladder lies anteriorly. The prostate lies below the neck of urinary bladder.

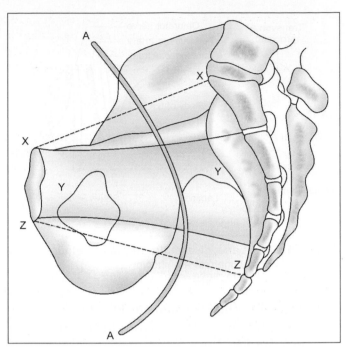

Fig. 29.8: Side view of bony female pelvis. AA—Axis of pelvic cavity. XX—Plane of inlet. YY—Zone of cavity. ZZ—Plane of outlet.

3. In between the bladder and rectum, there is a transverse septum or *genital septum* made up of connective tissue. In the male, the septum is small. It contains the ductus deferens, the seminal vesicle and the ureter on each side.

In the female, the septum is large, and contains the uterus, the uterine tubes, the round ligament of the uterus, the ligaments of the ovary, ovaries, the vagina and the ureters.

These contents are considered in detail in the chapters that follow.

Structures Crossing the Pelvic Inlet/Brim of the Pelvis

From posterior median plane sweeping laterally and anteriorly:

1. Median sacral vessels (Fig. 29.10).
2. Sympathetic trunk.
3. Lumbosacral trunk (Fig. 29.9).
4. Iliolumbar artery.
5. Obturator nerve.
6. Internal iliac vessels (Figs 24.16 and 34.1)
7. Medial limb of sigmoid mesocolon with superior rectal vessels—left side only (Fig. 29.10).
8. Ureter (Figs 24.13 and 30.3).
9. Sigmoid colon—on left side only.
10. Ovarian vessels in female.
11. Ductus deferens in male/round ligament of uterus in female (Fig. 32.2).

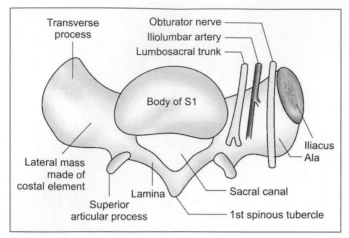

Fig. 29.9: The base of a male sacrum. Relations and attachments of the right ala are shown.

12. Lateral umbilical ligament (Fig. 29.11).
13. Median umbilical ligament or urachus (Fig. 29.11).
14. Lymphatics.
15. Autonomic nerve plexuses.
16. Coils of intestine.
17. Pregnant uterus.
18. Full urinary bladder.

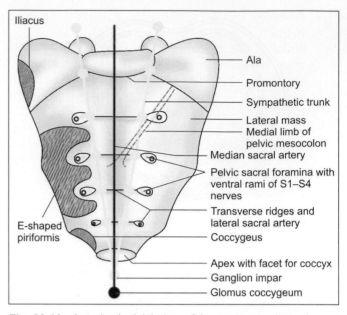

Fig. 29.10: Anterior (pelvic) view of the sacrum and attachment of sigmoid mesocolon.

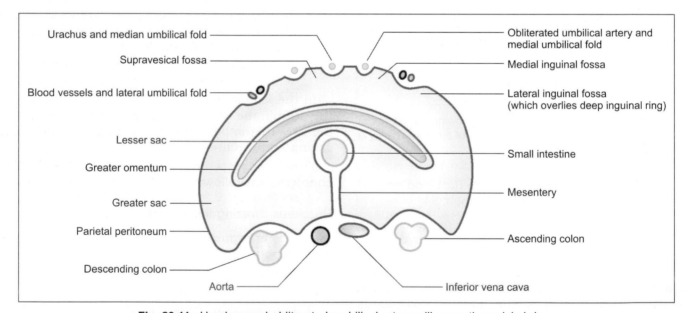

Fig. 29.11: Urachus and obliterated umbilical artery will cross the pelvic brim.

CLINICAL ANATOMY

- The pelvis is a basin with its various walls and many openings. The posterior wall contains 5 pairs of anterior sacral foramina. The greater and lesser sciatic notches are converted into foramina of the same name with the help of sacrotuberous and sacrospinous ligaments. Greater sciatic foramen is the "doorway" of the gluteal region. Pudendal nerve enters the region through the greater sciatic notch and quickly leaves it through lesser sciatic notch to enter the perineum. The lateral wall contains obturator foramen for the passage of obturator nerve which supplies adductors of the hip joint.

- Fracture may occur in the true (ring-like) pelvis. If fracture is at one point, the fracture will be stable. In athletes, anterior superior iliac spine may be pulled off by forcible contraction of sartorius. Similarly anterior inferior iliac spine or ischial tuberosity may get **avulsed** by the contraction of their attached muscles.

- Pelvic floor formed by two gutter-shaped levator ani muscles supports the pelvic viscera, especially during raised intra-abdominal pressure. The foetal head travels in the axis of pelvic cavity (Fig. 29.12).

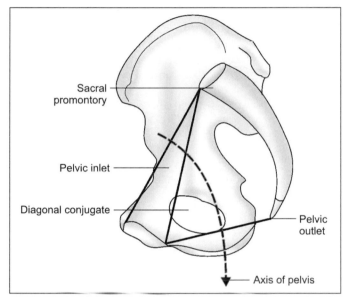

Fig. 29.12: Axis of pelvis.

During second stage of labor, the head of the baby on reaching the pelvic floor rotates from earlier transverse position to the anteroposterior position. The occiput moves downwards and forwards and reaches below the 80°–85° angled pubic arch. Then the head passes through the anterior hiatus of the levator ani to reach the perineum and then deliver. Sometimes episiotomy is given to enlarge the perineum (Fig. 29.13).

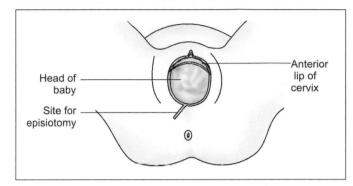

Fig. 29.13: Head of the delivering baby seen at the perineum. Site of episiotomy is also seen.

- Injury to pelvic floor which mostly occurs during vaginal delivery, may cause uterine, vaginal or even rectal prolapse (Fig. 29.14).

- Appendicitis occurring due to pelvic position of the appendix may irritate the obturator nerve leading to referred pain in the medial side of thigh (Figs 20.16 and 20.17).

- Inflammation of ovaries may cause referred pain in the medial side of thigh due to irritation of the obturator nerve (Fig. 30.1).

- The 2nd to 4th sacral nerves and coccygeal nerve can be anaesthesised by the anaesthetic agent put into the sacral canal. It is called caudal anaesthesia and is used in obstetrics practice.

- Pain in the sacroiliac joint is felt on pressing the posterior superior iliac spine present in a dimple on the lower back (Fig. 5.1).

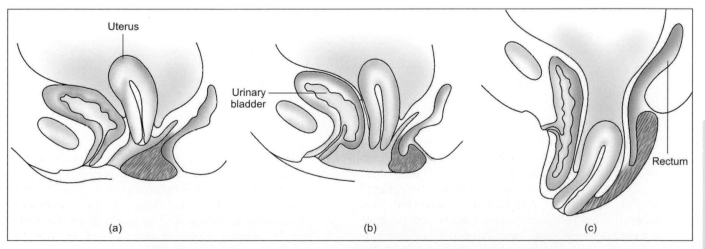

Fig. 29.14: Injury to pelvic floor with different degrees of prolapse of uterus.

CHAPTER 30

Urinary Bladder and Urethra

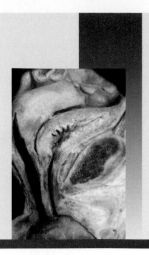

URINARY BLADDER

Urinary bladder is the temporary store house of urine which gets emptied through the urethra. The external urethral sphincter is the sphincter urethrae which is placed proximally in the wall of urethra, and not at the terminal part of the urethra. In the case of pylorus or anal canal, the sphincters are placed at their terminal ends.

The male urethra subserving the functions of urination and ejaculation, i.e. expulsion of semen is 18–20 cm long with curvatures and comprises preprostatic, prostatic, membranous and longest anterior bulbar and penile parts.

The female urethra is for urination only and is 4 cm long. The cathetarisation if required is much easier in the female than in the male.

The urinary bladder is a muscular reservoir of urine, which lies in the anterior part of the pelvic cavity. The detrusor muscle of urinary bladder is arranged in whorls and spirals and is adapted for mass contraction rather than peristalsis.

Size, Shape and Position

The bladder varies in its size, shape and position according to the amount of urine it contains.

When empty, it lies entirely within the pelvis; but as it fills it expands and extends upwards into the abdominal cavity, reaching up to the umbilicus or even higher.

External Features

An *empty bladder is tetrahedral* in shape and has:
  (a) *Apex*, directed forwards.
  (b) *Base* or fundus, directed backwards.
  (c) *Neck*, which is the lowest and most fixed part of the bladder.
  (d) *Three surfaces*, superior, and right and left inferolateral.

DISSECTION

Clean and define the muscles, membranes and ligaments in the pelvic cavity.

Identify the peritoneum on the superior surface of the bladder situated just behind the pubic symphysis. Identify and follow the median umbilical ligament from the apex of bladder. Define the surfaces, blunt borders and the openings in the urinary bladder.

In the male, trace the ductus deferens and ureter to the base of the bladder on both sides. Pull the bladder medially and identify the structures on its lateral surface, e.g. the levator ani, obturator vessels and nerve, superior vesical branch of umbilical artery and the obliterated umbilical artery.

Make the incision through the bladder wall along the junction of the superior and inferolateral surface on both sides. Extend these incisions till the lateral extremities of the base. Fold the superior wall of the bladder to be able to visualise its interior.

In the male, make a median section through the penis, opening the entire length of the spongy part of the urethra. Examine the internal structure of the urethra.

  (e) *Four borders*, two lateral, one anterior and one posterior (Figs 30.1 and 30.2).

A *full bladder is ovoid* in shape and has:
  (a) *An apex*, directed upwards towards the umbilicus.
  (b) *A neck*, directed downwards.
  (c) *Two surfaces*, anterior and posterior.

Relations

  1. The *apex* is connected to the umbilicus by the median umbilical ligament which represents the obliterated embryonic urachus (Fig. 30.1).
  2. *Base:*
     (a) *In the female*, it is related to the uterine cervix and to the vagina (Fig. 31.15).

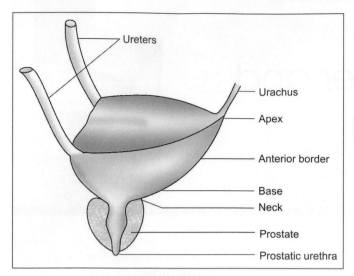

Fig. 30.1: The shape of the urinary bladder.

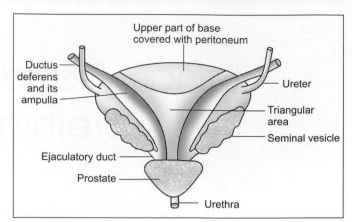

Fig. 30.3: Posterior view of a male urinary bladder and its relations to the genital ducts and glands.

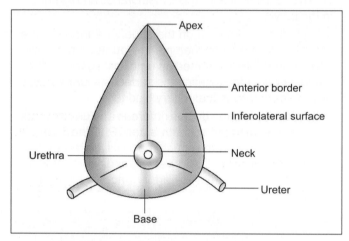

Fig. 30.2: Urinary bladder seen from below.

(b) *In the male*, the upper part of the base is separated from the rectum by the rectovesical pouch (Fig. 18.17a) and the contained coils of intestine; and the lower part is related to the seminal vesicles and the terminations of the vas deferens. The triangular area between the two deferent ducts is separated from the rectum by the rectovesical fascia of Denonvilliers (Fig. 30.3).

3. The *neck* is the lowest and most fixed part of the bladder. It lies 3 to 4 cm behind the lower part of the pubic symphysis, a little above the plane of the pelvic outlet. It is pierced by the internal urethral orifice.

(a) *In males*, smooth muscle bundles surround the bladder neck and preprostatic urethra. These are arranged as distinct circular collar with its own distinct adrenergic innervations. This is the preprostatic

sphincter and is devoid of parasympathetic cholinergic nerves. It is part of proximal urethral sphincter mechanism.

(b) *In females*, neck is related to the pelvic fascia which surrounds the upper part of the urethra.

In infants, the bladder lies at a higher level. The internal urethral orifice lies at the level of the superior border of the pubic symphysis. It gradually descends to reach the adult position after puberty.

4. *Superior surface:*

(a) *In males*, it is completely covered by peritoneum, and is in contact with the sigmoid colon and coils of the terminal ileum (Fig. 18.17a).

(b) *In females*, peritoneum covers the greater part of the superior surface, except for a small area near the posterior border, which is related to the supravaginal part of the uterine cervix. The peritoneum from the superior surface is reflected to the isthmus of the uterus to form the vesicouterine pouch (Fig. 18.17b).

5. *Inferolateral surfaces:* These are devoid of peritoneum, and are separated from each other anteriorly by the anterior border, and from the superior surface by the lateral borders.

(a) *In the male*, each surface is related to the pubis, the puboprostatic ligaments, the retropubic fat, the levator ani and the obturator internus (Fig. 30.4).

(b) *In the female*, the relations are same, except that the puboprostatic ligaments are replaced by the pubovesical ligaments.

As the bladder fills, the inferolateral surfaces form the anterior surface of the distended bladder, which is covered by peritoneum only in its upper part. The

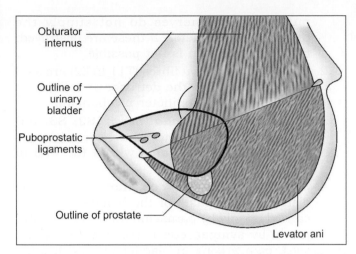

Fig. 30.4: Medial view of the lower part of the pelvic wall and the pelvic diaphragm. The urinary bladder has been superimposed to show relations of its inferolateral surface.

lower part comes into direct contact with the anterior abdominal wall, there being no intervening peritoneum. This part can be approached surgically without entering the peritoneal cavity.

Ligaments of the Bladder

True Ligaments

These are condensations of pelvic fascia around the neck and base of the bladder. They are continuous with the fascia on the superior surface of the levator ani.

1. The *lateral true ligament* of the bladder extends from the side of the bladder to the tendinous arch of the pelvic fascia (Fig. 30.5).
2. The *lateral puboprostatic ligament* is directed medially and backwards. It extends from the anterior end of the tendinous arch of the pelvic fascia to the upper part of the prostatic sheath (Fig. 32.6).
3. The *medial puboprostatic ligament* is directed downwards and backwards. It extends from the back of the pubic bone (near the pubic symphysis) to the prostatic sheath. The ligaments of the two sides form the floor of the retropubic space (Fig. 32.6).

   In females, bands similar to the puboprostatic ligaments are known as the *pubovesical ligaments*. They end around the neck of the bladder (Fig. 30.5).
4. The *median umbilical ligament* is the remnant of the urachus (Fig. 30.1).
5. The *posterior ligament* of the bladder is directed backwards and upwards along the vesical plexus of veins. It extends on each side from the base of bladder to the wall of pelvis (Fig. 30.5).

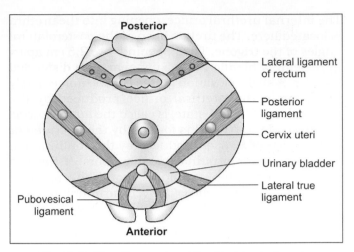

Fig. 30.5: True ligaments of the bladder in female.

False Ligaments

These are peritoneal folds, which do not form any support to the bladder. They include:

1. Median umbilical fold.
2. Medial umbilical fold.
3. Lateral false ligament, formed by peritoneum of the paravesical fossa.
4. Posterior false ligament formed by peritoneum of the sacrogenital folds (Figs 18.19 and 18.20).

Interior of the Bladder

It can be examined by cystoscopy, at operation or at autopsy.

In an empty bladder, the greater part of the mucosa shows irregular folds due to its loose attachment to the muscular coat (Fig. 30.6).

In a small triangular area over the lower part of the base of the bladder, the mucosa is smooth due to its firm attachment to the muscular coat. This area is known as the *trigone* of the bladder. The apex of the trigone is directed downwards and forwards.

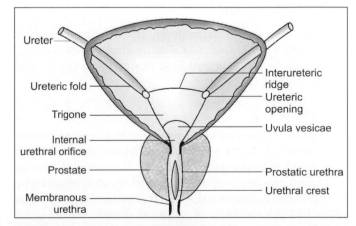

Fig. 30.6: Coronal section through the bladder and prostate to show the interior of the bladder.

The internal urethral orifice, opening into the urethra is located here. The ureters open at the posterolateral angles of the trigone. Their openings are 2.5 cm apart in the empty bladder, and 5 cm apart in a distended bladder. A slight elevation on the trigone immediately posterior to the urethral orifice produced by the median lobe of the prostate, is called the *uvula vesicae*. The base of the trigone is formed by the *interureteric ridge* or *bar of Mercier* produced by the continuation of the inner longitudinal muscle coats of the two ureters. The ridge extends beyond the ureteric openings as the *ureteric folds* over the interstitial part of the ureters.

Capacity of the Bladder

The mean capacity of the bladder in an adult male is 220 ml, varying from 120 to 320 ml. Filling beyond 220 ml causes a desire to micturate, and the bladder is usually emptied when filled to about 250 to 300 ml. Filling up to 500 ml may be tolerated, but beyond this it becomes painful. Referred pain is felt in the lower part of the anterior abdominal wall, perineum and penis (T11 to L2; S2 to S4).

Arterial Supply

1. The main supply comes from the superior and inferior vesical arteries, branches of anterior trunk of the internal iliac artery (Fig. 34.1).
2. Additional supply is derived from the obturator, and inferior gluteal arteries; and in females from the uterine and vaginal arteries instead of inferior vesical.

Venous Drainage

Lying on the inferolateral surfaces of the bladder there is a vesical venous plexus. Veins from this plexus pass backwards in the posterior ligaments of the bladder, and drain into the internal iliac veins.

Lymphatic Drainage

Most of the lymphatics from the urinary bladder terminate in the external iliac nodes. A few vessels may pass to the internal iliac nodes or to the lateral aortic nodes.

Nerve Supply

The urinary bladder is supplied by the vesical plexus of nerves which is made up of fibres derived from the inferior hypogastric plexus. The vesical plexus contains both sympathetic and parasympathetic components, each of which contains motor or efferent and sensory or afferent fibres.

1. *Parasympathetic efferent* fibres or nervi erigentes, S2, S3, S4 are motor to the detrusor muscle. These nerves do not supply the preprostatic sphincter. If these are destroyed, normal micturition is not possible.
2. *Sympathetic efferent* fibres (T11 to L2) are said to be inhibitory to the detrusor and motor to the preprostatic sphincter mechanism.
3. The somatic, *pudendal nerve* (S2, S3, S4) supplies the sphincter urethrae which is voluntary and is situated within the wall of urethra.
4. *Sensory nerves:* Pain sensations, caused by distension or spasm of the bladder wall, are carried mainly by parasympathetic nerves and partly by sympathetic nerves. In the spinal cord, pain arising in bladder passes through the *lateral spinothalamic tract*, and awareness of bladder distension is mediated through the *posterior columns. Bilateral anterolateral cordotomy*, therefore, selectively abolishes pain without affecting the awareness of bladder distension and the desire to micturate.

MALE URETHRA

Male urethra is 18–20 cm long that extends from the internal urethral orifice in the urinary bladder to the external opening (meatus) at the end of the penis.

Considered in two parts:

1. Relatively short posterior urethra which is 4 cm long lies in the pelvis proximal to corpus spongiosum and is acted upon by urogenital sphincter mechanisms and also acts as a conduit.

   Posterior urethra
   - Preprostatic segment (Fig. 30.7).
   - Prostatic segment.
   - Membranous segment.

2. Relatively long anterior urethra which is 16 cm long within the perineum (proximally) and penis (distally). It is surrounded by corpus spongiosum and is functionally a conduit.

   Anterior urethra
   - Bulbar urethral proximal component surrounded by bulbospongiosus. Entirely within perineum (Fig. 30.8).
   - Pendulous/penile component that continues to the tip of penis.

In flaccid penis, urethra as a whole represents double curve except during the passage of fluid along it. The urethral canal is a mere slit.

In transverse section:
- The urethral slit is crescentic or transversely arched in prostatic part.
- In the preprostatic and membranous part it is stellate.

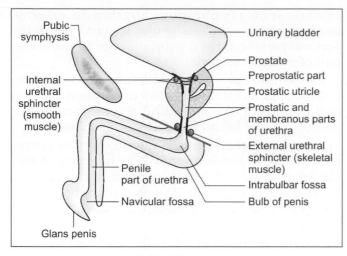

Fig. 30.7: Left view of a sagittal section through the male urethra showing its subdivisions.

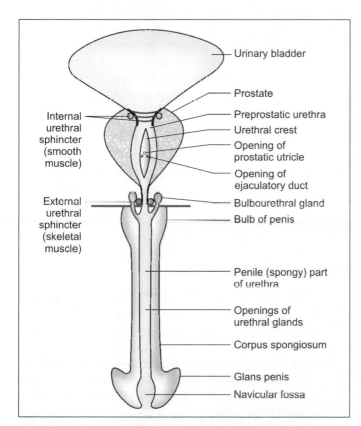

Fig. 30.8: Anterior view of the male urethra straightened and cut open.

- In bulbar and penile portions it is transverse.
- In external urethral orifice it is sagittal.

Passage of urine through different shapes of urethra causes it to flow in a continuous stream. Since it is passing under pressure, stream falls a little away from the body. Males can urinate standing without wetting themselves. Sorry, females cannot.

Posterior Part

Preprostatic Part

1–1.5 cm in length. It extends almost vertically from bladder neck to verumontanum (superior aspect) in prostatic urethra.

The preprostatic part is surrounded by proximal urethral sphincter mechanism (proximal).

Proximal urethral sphincter mechanism

In addition to the smooth muscle bundles which run in continuity from the bladder neck down to the prostatic urethra and distinct from the smooth muscle within the prostate, smooth muscle bundles, surround the bladder neck and preprostatic urethra. They are arranged as distinct circular collar which has its own distinct adrenergic innervations.

The bundles which form this preprostatic sphincter are small in size compared with the muscle bundles of detrusor and are separated by a relatively larger connective tissue component rich in elastic fibres.

It is also different in that unlike detrusor and rest of urethral smooth muscle (common to both sexes), the preprostatic sphincter is almost totally devoid of parasympathetic cholinergic nerves.

Contraction of preprostatic urethra serves to prevent retrograde flow of ejaculate through proximal urethra into bladder.

It may maintain continence when external sphincter has been damaged. It is extensively disrupted in vast majority of men with:

(a) Bladder neck surgery.

(b) Transurethral resection of prostate.

So retrograde ejaculation occurs in such patients.

Prostatic Part

3–4 cm in length. It tunnels through the substance of prostate closer to anterior than the posterior surface of gland. Emerging from the prostate slightly anterior to the apex (most inferior part), urethra turns inferiorly as it passes through the prostate making an angle of 35°.

Throughout its length, the posterior wall has a midline ridge called as urethral crest. This crest projects into the lumen causing the lumen to appear crescentic in transverse section.

On each side of crest are shallow depression called prostatic sinus, the floor of which is perforated by orifices of 15–20 ducts (prostatic ducts).

There is an elevation called verumontanum (colliculus seminalis) at about middle of urethral crest. It contains slit-like orifice of prostatic utricle.

On both side of or just within this orifice are the two small openings of the ejaculatory ducts.

Prostatic utricle

It is a cul-de-sac 6 mm long, which runs upwards and backwards in the substance of prostate behind its median lobe. The walls are composed of fibrous tissue, muscle fibres and mucous membrane. The mucous membrane is pitted by the openings of numerous small glands. It develops from paramesonephric ducts or urogenital sinus and is thought to be homologous with the vagina of female.

So vagina masculine is also a name for this prostatic utricle.

Lowermost part of prostatic urethra is fixed by puboprostatic ligaments and is, therefore, immobile.

Membranous Part

1.5 cm and shortest, least dilatable and with the exception of external orifice is the narrowest section of urethra. Descends with a slight ventral concavity from the prostate to bulb of penis, passing through the perineal membrane. 2.5 cm posteroinferior to pubic symphysis.

Wall of membranous urethra, i.e. part of distal urethral sphincter mechanism

Its muscle coat is separated from epithelium by narrow layer of fibroelastic connective tissue. Muscle coat consists of relatively thin layer of bundles of smooth muscle, which are continuous proximally with those of prostatic urethra and a prominent outer layer of circularly oriented striated muscle fibres (rhabdosphincter) which form external urethral spincter.

External sphincter represents points of highest intraurethral pressure in the normal, contracted state.

Intrinsic striated muscle is made of fibres of very small diameter, devoid of muscle spindles physiologically being slow twitch type, unlike pelvic floor with heterogenous mixture of slow and fast twitch type of larger diameter. So slow twitch fibres of sphincter are capable of sustained contraction over long period of time and contribute to tone that closes the urethra and maintains urinary continence.

So several components of distal urethral sphincter mechanism are:
 (i) Urethral smooth muscle.
 (ii) Urethral striated muscle (of rhabdosphincter). It is most important component as it is capable of sustained contractions.
 (iii) Pubourethral part of levator ani, important to resist surges of intra-abdominal pressure (on coughing or exercise).

Anterior Part

Anterior or spongiosus part lies in corpus spongiosum and is 16 cm long when penis is flaccid. It extends from membranous urethra to external urethral orifice on glans penis. It starts below the perineal membrane at a point anterior to the lowest part of pubic symphysis.

Part of anterior urethra which is surrounded by bulbospongiosus is called *bulbar urethra* and is widest part of urethra. Bulbourethral glands open in this section 2.5 cm below the perineal membrane.

From here, when penis is flaccid, urethra curves downwards as *penile urethra*. It is narrow and slit-like when empty and has diameter of 6 mm when passing urine. It is dilated at its termination within the glans penis and dilatation is called "navicular fossa".

External urethral orifice is the narrowest part of urethra and is a sagittal slit, 6 mm long, bounded on each side by a small labium.

Epithelium of urethra, particularly in bulbar and distal penile segment presents orifice of numerous small glands and follicles situated in the submucous tissue called urethral glands. It contains a number of small pit-like receses, or lacunae of varying size whose orifice are directed forwards.

One lacuna larger than the rest is *lacuna magna* which is situated on the roof of navicular fossa.

Why Preprostatic Part of Urethra?

Simple mucus-secreting glands lie in the tissue around the preprostatic urethra and surrounded by the preprostatic sphincter. These simple glands are similar to those in the female urethra and are unlike the glands of prostate. So, it is better not to include this part within prostatic part of urethra.

TRAUMATIC INJURY TO URETHRA

Injured by a fall-astride (or straddle) results in injury to bulbar urethra in the perineum (Fig. 28.26).

Extravasation of urine occurs but is prevented from going:
 (a) Posteriorly as the perineal membrane and the membranous layer of superficial fascia are continuous with the fascia around superficial transverse perinei.
 (b) Laterally by ischial and pubic rami.
 (c) Above to lesser pelvis by intact perineal membrane. So, extravasated urine goes anteriorly into the loose connective tissue of scrotum and penis and then to anterior abdominal wall.

Vascular Supply and Innervation

Arteries

 (a) Urethral artery arises from internal pudendal artery just below perineal membrane and travels through corpus spongiosum to reach glans penis.

(b) Dorsal penile artery via circumflex branches on each side.

Veins

Anterior urethra →dorsal vein of penis →internal pudendal vein which drains into prostatic venous plexus.

Posterior urethra →prostatic and vesical venous plexus →internal iliac veins.

Lymphatic

(a) Prostatic urethra →internal iliac.
(b) Membranous urethra →internal iliac.
(c) Anterior urethra →accompany that of glans →deep inguinal.

Innervation

Prostatic plexus supplies the smooth muscle of prostate and prostatic urethra. Greater cavernous nerves are sympathetic to preprostatic sphincter during ejaculation. Parasympathetic nerves are from 2nd–4th sacral segments.

Nerve supply of rhabdosphincter is controversial but is said to be by neurons in Onuf's nucleus situated in sacral 2 segment of spinal cord via perineal branch of pudendal nerve.

FEMALE URETHRA

Only 4 cm long and 6 mm in diameter. It begins at the internal urethral orifice of bladder, approximately opposite middle of the pubic symphysis and runs anteroinferiorly behind the symphysis pubis, embedded in anterior wall of vagina. It crosses the perineal membrane and ends at external urethral orifice as an anteroposterior slit with rather prominent margins situated directly anterior to the opening of vagina and 2.5 cm behind glans clitoridis.

Except during passage of urine anterior and posterior wall of canal possesses a ridge which is termed urethral crest. Many small mucous urethral glands and minute pit-like receses or lacunae open into urethra. On each side, near the lower end of urethra, a number of these glands are grouped and open into a duct, named paraurethral duct.

Each paraurethral duct runs down in the submucous tissue and ends in a small aperture on the lateral margins of external urethral orifice.

Arteries

Superior vesical and vaginal arteries.

Veins

Venous plexus around urethra →vesical venous plexus →internal pudendal vein.

Lymphatic

Internal and external iliac nodes.

Innervation

Parasympathetic preganglionic fibres from 2nd–4th sacral segments of spinal cord. These run through pelvic splanchnic nerves and synapse in vesical venous plexus. Postganglionic fibres reach smooth muscles.

Somatic fibres from same segments (S2–S4) to striated muscles but through pelvic splanchnic nerves that do not synapse in vesical plexus.

Sensory fibres in pelvic splanchnic nerves reach to 2nd–4th sacral segments of spinal cord. Postganglionic sympathetic fibres arise from plexus around the vaginal arteries.

Walls of Urethra

Wall has outer muscle coat and inner mucosa that lines the lumen and is continuous with that of bladder.

Muscle coat: Outer sheath of striated muscle external urethral sphincter or distal sphincter mechanism together with smooth muscle.

Female external urethral sphincter is anatomically separate from the adjacent periurethral striated muscle of the anterior pelvic floor, i.e. pubourethralis part of levator ani.

The sphincter form a sleeve which is thickest anteriorly in the middle one third of urethra, and is relatively deficient posteriorly. The striated muscle extends into the anterior wall of both proximal and distal thirds of urethra, but is deficient posteriorly. Muscle cells forming external urethral sphincter are all small diameter slow twitch fibres.

Smooth muscle coat (inner) extends throughout the length of urethra. A few circularly arranged muscle fibres occur in the outer aspect of non striated muscle layer which are oblique or longitudinally oriented and these intermingle with striated muscle fibres forming inner parts of external urethral sphincter.

Proximally, the urethral smooth muscle extends as far as the neck of bladder where it is replaced by detrusor smooth muscle. But this region in the females *lacks* well-defined circular smooth muscle components comparable to the ***preprostatic sphincter*** of male.

Distally, urethral smooth muscle terminate in subcutaneous adipose tissue around external urethral meatus.

Smooth muscle of female urethra receives an extensive presumptive cholinergic nerve supply, but few noradrenengic fibres.

In the absence of an anatomical sphincter, competence of female bladder neck and proximal urethra is unlikely to be totally dependent on smooth muscle activity and is probably related to support provided by ligamentous structure which surround them.

Longitudinal orientation and the innervation of muscles suggests that urethral smooth muscle in female is active during micturition and serves to shorten and widen urethral lumen.

Micturition

1. Initially the bladder fills without much rise in the intravesical pressure. This is due to adjustment of bladder tone.
2. When the quantity of urine exceeds 220 cc, the intravesical pressure rises. This stimulates sensory nerves and produces a desire to micturate. If this is neglected, rhythmic reflex contractions of the detrusor muscle start, which become more and more powerful as the quantity of urine increases. This gives a feeling of fullness of the bladder, and later on becomes painful. The voluntary holding of urine is due to contraction of the sphincter urethrae and of the perineal muscles, with coincident inhibition of the detrusor muscle.
3. Micturition is initiated by the following successive events.
   (a) First there is relaxation of perineal muscles, except the distal urethral sphincter and contraction of the abdominal muscles.
   (b) This is followed by firm contraction of the detrusor and relaxation of the proximal urethral sphincter mechanism.
   (c) Lastly, distal urethral sphincter mechanism relaxes, and the flow of urine begins.
4. The bladder is emptied by the contraction of the detrusor muscle. Emptying is assisted by the contraction of abdominal muscles.
5. When urination is complete, the detrusor muscle relaxes, the proximal urethral sphincter mechanism contracts, and finally the distal urethral sphincter mechanism contracts. In the male, the last drops of urine are expelled from the bulbar portion of the urethra by contraction of the bulbospongiosus.

Histology of Urinary Bladder

The epithelium of urinary bladder is of transitional variety. The luminal cells are well-defined squamous cells with prominent nuclei. The middle layers are pear-shaped cells and the basal layer is of short columnar cells. The muscle coat is admixture of longitudinal, circular and oblique layers. Outermost layer is the serous or adventitial coat.

Development of Urinary Bladder and Urethra

Cloaca is divided by the *urorectal septum* into posterior *anorectal canal* and anterior *primitive urogenital sinus*. The cranial and largest part of primitive urogenital sinus called the *vesicourethral canal* forms most of the urinary bladder. It is connected with the *allantois*. The lumen of allantois gets obliterated to form *urachus* connecting the apex of the bladder to the umbilicus. This ligament is the *median umbilical ligament*. *Trigone* of bladder is formed by the absorption of *mesonephric ducts* and is mesodermal in origin. With time, the mesodermal lining is replaced by endodermal epithelium. So the epithelium is wholly endodermal, while muscles are of splanchnic origin.

1. Vesicourethral canal formed by endoderm forms the anterior wall of prostatic urethra above the opening of prostatic utricle.
2. Absorbed portions of the mesonephric ducts, i.e. mesoderm forms posterior wall of prostatic urethra above the opening of prostatic utricle.
3. Definitive urogenital sinus formed by endoderm forms the lower part of prostatic urethra and the membranous urethra.
4. Urethral plate or endoderm forms most of the anterior part of urethra.
5. Surface epithelium of glans penis or ectoderm forms the terminal portion of penile urethra.

Congenital Anomalies

Ectopia vesicae is a developmental anomaly characterised by the absence of infraumbilical part of anterior abdominal wall, pubic bones and the anterior wall of urinary bladder. The umbilicus is absent and epispadias is usually associated. The trigone of bladder bulges in the pubic area, on which the two ureters open. The periphery of the mucosa is continuous with the skin.

CLINICAL ANATOMY

- A distended bladder may be *ruptured* by injuries of the lower abdominal wall. The peritoneum may or may not be involved.

- Chronic obstruction to the outflow of urine by an enlarged prostate causes hypertrophy of bladder leading to trabeculated bladder.

- The interior of the bladder can be examined in the living by *cystoscope* (Fig. 30.9).

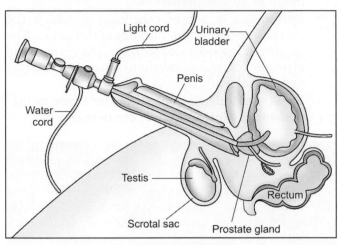

Fig. 30.9: Cystoscopy.

- In the operation of *suprapubic cystotomy,* the bladder is distended with about 300 ml of fluid. As a result the anterior aspect of the bladder comes into direct contact with the anterior abdominal wall, and can be approached without entering the peritoneal cavity.
- *Emptying of bladder:* Emptying of the bladder is essentially a reflex function, involving the motor and sensory pathways. Voluntary control over this reflex is exerted through upper motor neurons, and as long as one pyramidal tract is functioning normally, control of the bladder remains normal. Acute injury to the cervical/ thoracic segments of spinal cord leads to a state of spinal shock. The muscle of the bladder is relaxed, the sphincter vesicae contracted, but sphincter urethrae relaxed. The bladder distends and urine dribbles.

  After a few days, the bladder starts contracting reflexly. When it is full, it contracts every 2–4 hours. This is "automatic reflex bladder" (Fig. 30.10).

  Damage to the sacral segments of spinal cord situated in lower thoracic and lumbar one vertebra results in "autonomous bladder". The bladder wall is flaccid and its capacity is greatly increased. It just fills to capacity and overflows. So there is continuous dribbling (Fig. 30.11).
- *Catheterization of bladder:* In some cases, the patient is unable to pass urine leading to retention of urine. In such cases a rubber tube called a *catheter* is passed into the bladder through the urethra. While passing a catheter one has to remember the normal curvatures of the urethra. It has also to be remembered that the lacunae are directed forwards, and may

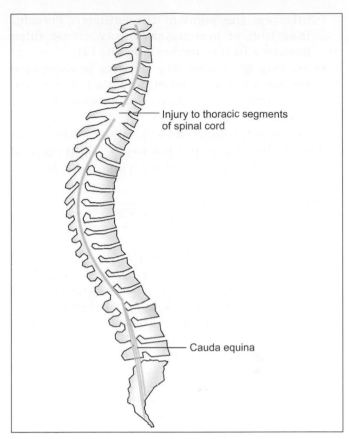

Fig. 30.10: Injury to thoracic segments of spinal cord.

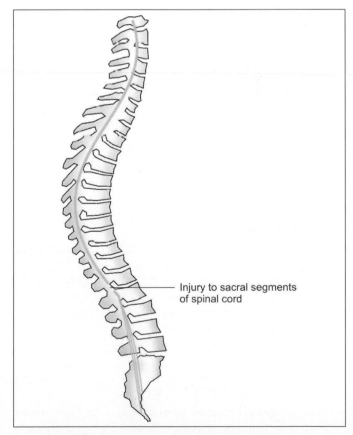

Fig. 30.11: Injury to sacral segments of spinal cord.

intercept the point of the catheter. Forceful insertion of instruments may create false passages in the urethra (Fig. 30.12).

- *Rupture of urethra:* The urethra is commonly ruptured beneath the pubis by a fall astride a sharp object. This causes extravasation of urine (Figs 28.26 and 28.27).
- Infection of the urethra is called *urethritis.*
- A constriction of the urethra is called *stricture* of the urethra. It is usually a result of infection.

- *Hypospadias* is a common anomaly in which the urethra opens on the undersurface of the penis or in the perineum.
- *Epispadias* is a rare condition in which the urethra opens on the dorsum of the penis. The condition is associated with ectopia vesicae and absence of infraumbilical part of anterior abdominal wall.
- Urinary bladder is one of sites for stone formation as concentrated urine lies here (Fig. 30.13).

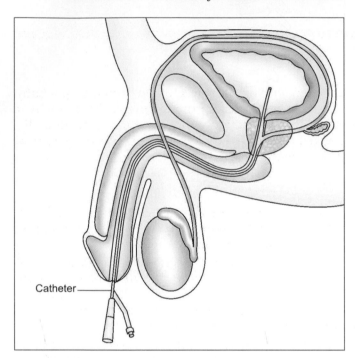

Fig. 30.12: Catheterisation of urinary bladder in male.

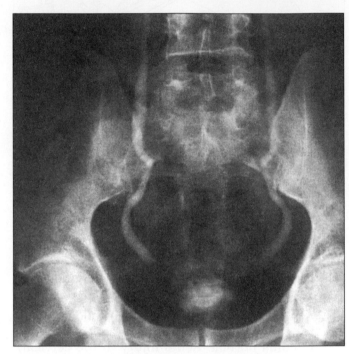

Fig. 30.13: Stone in urinary bladder.

CHAPTER 31

Female Reproductive Organs

The internal genital organs in female are located in pelvis. The sex gland or ovary is comfortably located in the lateral pelvic wall and can withstand the body temperature during oogenesis. Its counterpart, the testis in the male which needs lower temperature for spermatogenesis is made to hang outside the abdominal cavity. Fallopian tube connects the ovary with the uterus and carries the secondary oocyte in the hope of getting it fertilized, to be nurtured in the muscular organ, the uterus for a period of nine months.

The process of parturition, i.e. normal delivery of the baby, is a miracle of nature and is believed only after watching the agonising process. The love and affection which a mother gives in bringing up a baby is insurmountable and unimaginable. That is why it is said, "Since God could not be everywhere, He created Mothers". We thrive in this world because of these angel moms.

INTRODUCTION

Female reproductive organs include external and internal genital organs. The external genital organs have been described in Chapter 28.

The internal genital organs comprise a pair of ovaries, a pair of uterine/fallopian tubes, single uterus and vagina. The ovaries are homologous to the testes of males but lie within the pelvis. The ovaries are much smaller than the testes.

Identify the broad ligament attaching uterus to the lateral pelvic wall and note various structures present in its borders and surfaces.

OVARIES

The ovaries are the female gonads. The female gametes, called oocytes, are formed in them.

Situation

Each ovary lies in the ovarian fossa on the lateral pelvic wall. The ovarian fossa is bounded:

(a) *Anteriorly* by the obliterated umbilical artery.

(b) *Posteriorly* by the ureter and the internal iliac artery (Fig. 31.1).

Position

The position of the ovary is variable. In nulliparous women, its long axis is nearly vertical, so that the ovary is usually described as having an upper pole and a lower pole. However, in multiparous women, the long axis becomes horizontal; so that the upper pole points laterally and the lower pole medially (Fig. 31.2).

DISSECTION

Cut through the pubic symphysis with a knife in the median plane and extend the incision into the urethra. Make a median dorsal cut with a saw through the fourth and fifth lumbar vertebrae, the sacrum and coccyx to meet the knife. Cut through the soft tissues.

Separate the two halves of the pelvis and examine the cut surface of all the tissues.

Locate the ovary on the lateral wall of pelvis in the female cadaver. Identify the ovarian vessels in the infundibulopelvic ligament and trace these to the ovary and uterine tube. Follow, the ovarian artery till its anastomosis with the uterine artery.

Identify the uterus and follow the peritoneum on its superior and inferior surfaces which is thus free to move. Trace the uterus downwards till the supravaginal part of cervix which is attached to the lateral pelvic wall by transverse cervical ligaments and to the sacrum by uterosacral ligaments.

The vaginal part of cervix is surrounded on all sides by fornices of the vagina. The posterior fornix is the deepest. These can be felt by putting index and middle fingers through the vagina.

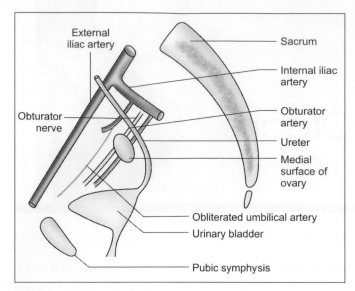

Fig. 31.1: Medial view of the boundaries of the ovarian fossa as seen in a sagittal section.

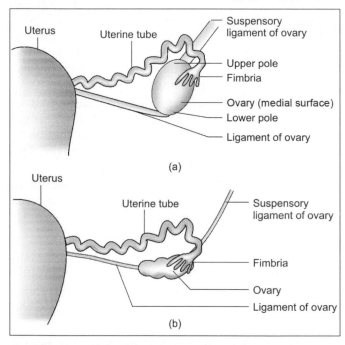

Fig. 31.2: Positions of the ovary. (a) It is vertical in nullipara; and (b) horizontal in multipara (after one or more deliveries) due to the pull by the pregnant uterus. The surface of the ovary is smooth before puberty, but puckered after puberty due to the scars of ovulation.

External Features

In young girls, *before the onset of ovulation*, the ovaries have a smooth surfaces which are greyish pink in colour. *After puberty*, the surface becomes uneven and the colour changes from pink to grey.

Each ovary has *two poles* or *extremities*, the upper or tubal pole, and the lower or uterine pole; *two borders*, the anterior or mesovarian border, and the

posterior or free border; and *two surfaces*, lateral and medial.

Relations

Peritoneal Relations

The ovary is almost entirely covered with peritoneum, except along the mesovarian or anterior border where the two layers of the covering peritoneum are reflected on to the posterior layer of the broad ligament of the uterus. The ovary is connected to the posterior layer of the broad ligament by a short fold of peritoneum, called the *mesovarium* (Fig. 31.3). The squamous epithelium of the mesovarium is continuous with the cubical epithelium of the ovary. The mesovarium transmits the vessels and nerves to and from the ovary (Fig. 18.21).

The lateral part of the broad ligament of uterus, extending from the infundibulum of the uterine tube and the upper pole of the ovary, to the external iliac vessels, forms a distinct fold known as *suspensory ligament of the ovary* or *infundibulopelvic ligament*. It contains the ovarian vessels and nerves (Fig. 31.4).

Visceral Relations

1. *Upper or tubal pole:* It is broader than the lower pole, and is related to the uterine tube and the external iliac vein. The right ovary may be related to the appendix if the latter is pelvic in position. The ovarian fimbria and the suspensory ligament of the ovary are attached to the upper pole of the ovary (Fig. 31.2).

2. *Lower or uterine pole:* It is narrower than the upper pole and is related to the pelvic floor. It

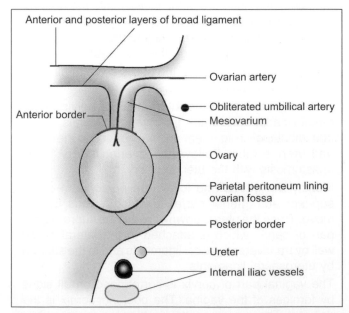

Fig. 31.3: Superior view of a horizontal section through the right ovarian fossa and the lateral part of the broad ligament.

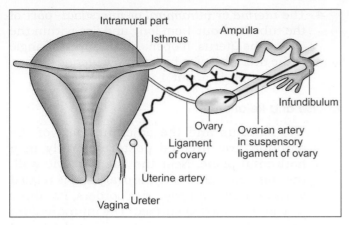

Fig. 31.4: The subdivisions, relations and blood supply of the uterine tube.

is connected, by the ligament of the ovary, to the lateral angle of the uterus, posteroinferior to the attachment of the uterine tube. The ligament lies between the two layers of the broad ligament of the uterus and contains some smooth muscle fibres (Fig. 31.7).

3. *Anterior or mesovarian border:* It is straight and is related to the uterine tube and the obliterated umbilical artery. It is attached to the back of the broad ligament of the uterus by the mesovarium, and forms the *hilus* of the ovary.

4. *Posterior or free border:* It is convex and is related to the uterine tube and the ureter.

5. *Lateral surface:* It is related to the ovarian fossa which is lined by parietal peritoneum. This peritoneum separates the ovary from the obturator vessels and nerve (Fig. 31.1).

6. *Medial surface:* It is largely covered by the uterine tube. The peritoneal recess between the mesosalpinx and this surface is known as the *ovarian bursa.*

Only the lower pole and lateral surfaces are not related to utrine tube, remaining two borders, upper pole and medial surface are related to the tube.

Arterial Supply

1. The *ovarian artery* arises from the abdominal aorta just below the renal artery. It descends over the posterior abdominal wall and enters the suspensory ligament of the ovary. It sends branches to the ovary through the meso-varium, and continues medially through the broad ligament of the uterus to anastomose with the uterine artery (Fig. 31.4). In addition to ovary, the ovarian artery also supplies the uterine tube, the side of uterus and the ureter.

2. The uterine artery gives some branches which reach the ovary through the mesovarium.

Venous Drainage

The veins emerge at the hilus and form a pampiniform plexus around the artery. The plexus condenses into a single ovarian vein near the pelvic inlet. This vein ascends on the posterior abdominal wall and drains into the *inferior vena cava* on the right side and into the *left renal vein* on the left side.

Lymphatic Drainage

The lymphatics from the ovary communicate with the lymphatics from the uterine tube and fundus of the uterus. They ascend along the ovarian vessels to drain into the lateral aortic and preaortic nodes.

Nerve Supply

The ovarian plexus, derived from the renal, aortic and hypogastric plexuses, accompanies the ovarian artery. It contains both sympathetic and parasympathetic nerves. Sympathetic nerves (T10, T11) are afferent for pain as well as efferent or vasomotor. Parasympathetic nerves (S2, S3, S4) are vasodilator.

Functions

1. *Production of oocytes:* During reproductive life of about 30 years (from puberty to menopause), the ovaries produce alternately one oocyte per month (per ovarian cycle of 28 days).

   Liberation of ovum from the ovary is called *ovulation.* It occurs on or about the 14th day of the 28-day menstrual cycle. Variations in the length of menstrual cycle are due to variations in the preovulatory phase; the postovulatory phase is constant.

   An oocyte is viable (capable of being fertilized) for about 12–24 hours.

2. *Production of hormones:*
   (a) *Oestrogen* is secreted by the follicular and paraluteal cells.
   (b) *Progesterone* by the luteal cells.

Histology

Histologically, the ovary is made up of the following parts from without inwards.

1. *Germinal epithelium* of cubical cells, derived from peritoneum.
2. *Tunica albuginea* is a thin layer of connective tissue.
3. The *cortex* contains *ovarian follicles* at various stages of development. Each follicle contains one oocyte. One follicle matures every month and sheds an oocyte. Total of 400 oocytes are ovulated in the reproductive life.

Liberation of an oocyte from the ovary is called *ovulation*. It occurs on or about the 14th day of a 28-day menstrual cycle. After the oocyte is liberated the Graafian follicle is converted into a structure called the *corpus luteum*.

4. The hormone oestrogen is secreted by follicular cells of ovarian follicles. Another hormone, progesterone, is produced by the corpus luteum.

5. Medulla is richly vascular connective tissue, containing vessels, nerves and lymphatics.

UTERINE TUBES

Synonym

The uterine tubes are also called *fallopian tubes/ salpinx*.

Definition

They are tortuous ducts which convey oocyte from the ovary to the uterus. Spermatozoa introduced into the vagina pass up into the uterus, and from there into the uterine tubes. Fertilization usually takes place in the lateral part of the tube.

Situation

These are situated in the free upper margin of the broad ligament of uterus.

Dimensions

Each uterine tube is about 10 cm long. At the lateral end, the uterine tube opens into the peritoneal cavity through its *abdominal ostium*. This ostium is about 3 mm in diameter.

Subdivisions

1. The lateral end of the uterine tube is shaped like a funnel and is, therefore, called the *infundibulum*. It bears a number of finger-like processes called *fimbriae* and is, therefore, called the *fimbriated end*. One of the fimbriae is longer than the others and is attached to the tubal pole of the ovary. It is known as the *ovarian fimbria* (Fig. 31.2).

2. The part of the uterine tube medial to the infundibulum is called the *ampulla*. It is thin-walled, dilated and tortuous, and forms approximately the lateral two-thirds or 6 to 7 cm of the tube. It arches over the upper pole of the ovary. The ampulla is about 4 mm in diameter.

3. The *isthmus* succeeds the ampulla. It is narrow, rounded and cord-like, and forms approximately the medial one-third or 2 to 3 cm of the tube.

4. The *uterine* or *intramural* or *interstitial* part of the tube is about 1 cm long and lies within the wall of the uterus. It opens at the superior angle of the uterine cavity by a narrow *uterine ostium*. This ostium is about 1 mm in diameter.

Course and Relations

1. The isthmus and the adjoining part of the ampulla are directed posterolaterally in a horizontal plane. Near the lateral pelvic wall, the ampulla arches over the ovary and is related to its anterior and posterior borders, its upper pole and its medial surface. The infundibulum projects beyond the free margin of the broad ligament.

2. The uterine tube lies in the upper free margin of the broad ligament of the uterus. The part of the broad ligament between the attachment of the mesovarium and the uterine tube is known as the *mesosalpinx* (Fig. 31.6). It contains the termination of the uterine and ovarian vessels and the epoophoron.

Blood Supply

The *uterine artery* supplies approximately the medial two-thirds, and the ovarian artery supplies the lateral one-third, of the tube. The *veins* run parallel with the arteries and drain into the pampiniform plexus of the ovary and into the uterine veins (Fig. 31.4).

Lymphatic Drainage

Most of the tubal lymphatics join the lymphatics from the ovary and drain with them into the *lateral aortic* and *preaortic nodes*. The lymphatics from the isthmus accompany the round ligament of the uterus and drain into the *superficial inguinal nodes*.

Nerve Supply

The uterine tubes are supplied by both the sympathetic and parasympathetic nerves running along the uterine and ovarian arteries.

1. The *sympathetic nerves* from T10 to L2 segments are derived from the hypogastric plexuses. They contain both visceral afferent and efferent fibres. The latter are vasomotor and perhaps stimulate tubal peristalsis. However, peristalsis is mainly under hormonal control.

2. *Parasympathetic nerves* are derived from the vagus for the lateral half of the tube and from the pelvic splanchnic nerves from S2, S3, S4 for the medial half. They inhibit peristalsis and produce vasodilatation.

Histology

Uterine tube is made up of the following coats.

1. An outer *serous coat,* derived from peritoneum.
2. The middle *muscular coat,* which is thick in the isthmus and thin in the ampulla. The circular muscle coat is thickest in the isthmus and acts as a sphincter which delays the progress of the zygote towards the uterus until it is sufficiently mature for implantation.
3. The inner *mucous membrane,* which is lined by the ciliated columnar epithelium mixed with the non-ciliated secretory cells or peg cells. The mucous membrane is thrown into *complicated folds* which fill up the lumen of the tube. In the isthmus, there are only 3–6 primary folds and the cilia tend to disappear. But in the ampulla, the folds are more complex and exhibit the secondary and even tertiary folds.

UTERUS

Synonym

In layman's language, the uterus is called the womb. It is also called *hystera,* on which word hysterectomy is based.

Definition

Uterus is a child-bearing organ in females, situated in the pelvis between bladder and rectum. Though hollow, it is thick walled and firm, and can be palpated bimanually during a PV (per vaginum) examination.

It is the organ which protects and provides nutrition to a fertilized ovum, enabling it to grow into a fully formed foetus. At the time of childbirth or parturition contractions of muscle in the wall of the organ result in expulsion of the foetus from the uterus.

Size and Shape

The uterus is pyriform in shape. It is about 7.5 cm long, 5 cm broad, and 2.5 cm thick. It weighs 30 to 40 grams. It is divisible into an upper expanded part called the *body* and a lower cylindrical part called the *cervix.* The junction of these two parts is marked by a circular constriction. The body forms the upper two-thirds of the organ, and the cervix forms the lower one-third.

Normal Position and Angulation

Normally, the long axis of the uterus forms an angle of about 90 degrees with the long axis of the vagina. The angle is open forwards. The forward bending of the uterus relative to the vagina is called *anteversion.*

The uterus is also slightly flexed on itself: this is referred to as *anteflexion.* The angle of anteflexion is 125 degree (Fig. 31.5).

Roughly, the long axis of the uterus corresponds to the axis of the pelvic inlet, and the axis of the vagina to the axis of the pelvic cavity and of the pelvic outlet (Fig. 29.7).

Communications

Superiorly, the uterus communicates on each side with the uterine tube, and inferiorly, with the vagina.

BODY OF UTERUS

The body has:

(a) A fundus.
(b) Two surfaces, anterior or vesical and posterior or intestinal.
(c) Two lateral borders.

The *fundus* is formed by the free upper end of the uterus. Fundus lies above the openings of the uterine tubes. It is convex like a dome. It is covered with peritoneum and is directed forward when the bladder is empty. The fertilized oocyte is usually implanted in the posterior wall of the fundus (Fig. 31.6).

The *anterior* or *vesical surface* is flat and related to the urinary bladder. It is covered with peritoneum and forms the posterior or superior wall of the uterovesical pouch.

The *posterior* or *intestinal surface* is convex and is related to coils of the terminal ileum and to the sigmoid colon. It is covered with peritoneum and forms the anterior wall of the rectouterine pouch (Figs 18.17 and 18.21).

Each *lateral border* is rounded and convex. It provides attachment to the broad ligament of the uterus which connects it to the lateral pelvic wall. The uterine tube opens into the uterus at the upper

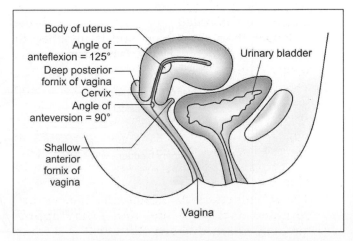

Fig. 31.5: Angulations of the uterus and vagina, and their axes.

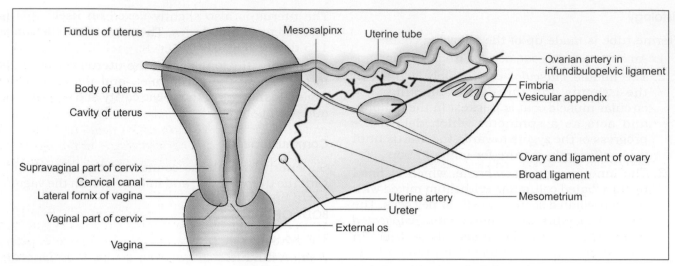

Fig. 31.6: Posterosuperior view of the uterus and the right broad ligament.

end of this border. This end of the border gives attachment to the round ligament of the uterus, anteroinferior to the tube; and to the ligament of the ovary posteroinferior to the tube. The uterine artery ascends along the lateral border of the uterus between the two layers of the broad ligament (Figs 31.7 and 31.8).

In sagittal section, the cavity of the body of the uterus is seen as a mere slit because the uterus is compressed anteroposteriorly. In coronal section, the cavity is seen to be triangular in shape, the apex being directed downwards. At the apex, the cavity becomes continuous with the canal of the cervix. The junction is called the *internal os*. The supero-lateral angles of the cavity receive the openings of the right and left uterine tubes (Fig. 31.6).

Cervix of Uterus

The cervix is the lower, cylindrical part of the uterus. It is less mobile than the body. It is about 2.5 cm long, and is slightly wider in the middle than at either end. The lower part of the cervix projects into the anterior wall of the vagina which divides it into supravaginal and vaginal parts.

The *supravaginal part of the cervix* is related:

(a) Anteriorly to the bladder.

(b) Posteriorly to the rectouterine pouch, containing coils of intestine and to the rectum (Fig. 18.17b).

(c) On each side, to the ureter and to the uterine artery, embedded in parametrium. The fibrofatty tissue between the two layers of the

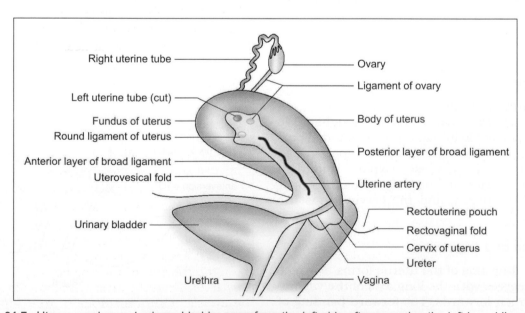

Fig. 31.7: Uterus, vagina and urinary bladder seen from the left side after removing the left broad ligament.

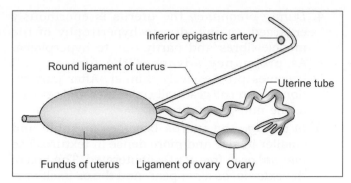

Fig. 31.8: Fundus of the uterus seen from above.

broad ligament and below it, is called the *parametrium*. It is most abundant near the cervix and vagina.

The *vaginal part* of the cervix projects into the anterior wall of the vagina. The spaces between it and the vaginal wall are called the vaginal fornices. The cervical canal opens into the vagina by an opening called the *external os*. In a nulliparous woman, i.e. a woman who has not borne children, the external os is small and circular (Fig. 31.6). However, in multiparous women, the external os is bounded by anterior and posterior lips, both of which are in contact with the posterior wall of the vagina.

The *cervical canal,* i.e. the cavity of the cervix is fusiform in shape. It communicates above with the cavity of the body of the uterus, through the *internal os,* and below with the vaginal cavity through the *external os.* The canal is flattened from before backwards so that it comes to have anterior and posterior walls. These walls show mucosal folds which resemble the branches of a tree called the *arbor vitae uteri.* The folds in the anterior and posterior walls interlock with each other and close the canal.

Ligaments of Uterus

Peritoneal Ligaments

These are mere peritoneal folds which do not provide any support to the uterus.

1. The *anterior ligament* consists of the utero-vesical fold of peritoneum.
2. The *posterior ligament* consists of the rectovaginal fold of peritoneum (Fig. 31.7).
3. The right and left *broad ligaments* are folds of peritoneum which attach the uterus to the lateral pelvic wall. When the bladder is full, the ligament has anterior and posterior surfaces, and upper, lower, medial and lateral borders. The upper border is free. The anterior and posterior layers of peritoneum forming the ligament become continuous here. The lateral and inferior borders of the ligament are

attached to the corresponding parts of the pelvic wall. The medial border is attached to the lateral margin of the uterus (Fig. 18.21).

Some names given to subdivisions of the broad ligament may now be noted. The ovary is attached to the posterior layers of the ligament through the *mesovarium* (Fig. 31.3). The ligament of the ovary passes from the lower pole of the ovary to the lateral angle of the uterus. The part of the broad ligament lying between the uterine tube and the ovarian ligament of ovary is called the *mesosalpinx*, while the part below the ligament of ovary is called the *mesometrium*. The part of the broad ligament that stretches from the upper pole of the ovary and the infundibulum of the uterine tube to the lateral pelvic wall is called the *suspensory ligament of the ovary* or the *infundibulopelvic ligament* (Fig. 31.6).

The broad ligament contains the following structures.

1. The uterine tube (Figs 31.6 and 31.7).
2. The round ligament of the uterus.
3. The ligament of the ovary.
4. Uterine vessels near its attachment to the uterus (Fig. 31.4).
5. Ovarian vessels in the infundibulopelvic ligament.
6. The uterovaginal and ovarian nerve plexuses.
7. Epoophoron.
8. Paroophoron.
9. Some lymph nodes and lymph vessels.
10. Dense connective tissue or parametrium present on the sides of the uterus.

Fibromuscular Ligaments

The fibromuscular ligaments are:

1. Round ligaments of the uterus.
2. Transverse cervical ligaments
3. Uterosacral ligaments.

These are described separately under the heading of "supports" of uterus.

Arterial Supply

The uterus is supplied:

1. Chiefly by the two uterine arteries which are markedly enlarged during pregnancy.
2. Partly by the ovarian arteries.

The *uterine artery* is a branch of the anterior division of the internal iliac artery. It first runs medially towards the cervix, crossing the ureter above the lateral fornix of the vagina and 2 cm lateral to the cervix. Then the artery ascends along the side of the uterus, with a tortuous course. Finally, it runs laterally towards the hilus of the ovary, and ends by anastomosing with the ovarian artery. The tortuosity of the artery permits expansion of the uterus during pregnancy (Fig. 31.4). Apart from the uterus, the artery also gives branches to:

1. Vagina.
2. Medial two-thirds of the uterine tube.
3. Ovary.
4. Ureter.
5. To structures present in the broad ligament (Fig. 31.6).

Venous Drainage

The veins form a plexus along the lateral border of the uterus. The plexus drains through the uterine, ovarian and vaginal veins into the internal iliac veins.

Lymphatic Drainage

Lymphatics of the uterus begin at three inter-communicating networks, endometrial, myometrial and subperitoneal. These plexuses drain into lymphatics on the side of the uterus. Of these, the *upper lymphatics* from the fundus and upper part of the body drain mainly into the aortic nodes, and only partly to the superficial inguinal nodes along the round ligament of the uterus. The *lower lymphatics* from the cervix drain into the external iliac, internal iliac and sacral nodes. The *middle lymphatics* from the lower part of body drain into the external iliac nodes.

Nerve Supply

The uterus is richly supplied by both sympathetic and parasympathetic nerves, through the inferior hypogastric and ovarian plexuses. Sympathetic nerves from T12, L1 segment of spinal cord produce uterine contraction and vasoconstriction. The parasympathetic nerves (S2, S3, S4) produce uterine inhibition and vasodilatation. However, these effects are complicated by the pronounced effects of hormones on the genital tract.

Pain sensation from the body of the uterus pass along the sympathetic nerves, and from the cervix, along the parasympathetic nerves.

Age and Reproductive Changes

1. *In foetal life* the cervix is larger than the body which projects a little above the pelvic brim.
2. *At puberty* the uterus enlarges and descends to the adult position. The arbor vitae uteri also appear.
3. *During menstruation* the uterus is slightly enlarged and becomes more vascular. The lips of the *external os* are swollen.
4. *During pregnancy* the uterus is enormously enlarged, mainly due to hypertrophy of the muscle fibres and partly due to hyperplasia. As pregnancy advances the uterine wall becomes progressively thinner. After parturition the uterus gradually involutes and returns to the non-pregnant size.
5. *In old age* the uterus becomes atrophic and smaller in size and more dense in texture. The *internal os* is frequently obliterated. The lips of the *external os* disappear, and the os itself may be obliterated.

Supports of the Uterus

The uterus is a mobile organ which undergoes extensive changes in size and shape during the reproductive period of life. It is supported and prevented from sagging down by a number of factors which are chiefly muscular and fibromuscular.

Primary Supports

Muscular or Active Supports

1. Pelvic diaphragm.
2. Perineal body.
3. Distal urethral sphincter mechanism.

Fibromuscular or Mechanical Supports

1. Uterine axis.
2. Pubocervical ligaments.
3. Transverse cervical ligaments of Mackenrodt.
4. Uterosacral ligaments.
5. Round ligaments of uterus.

Secondary Supports

These are of doubtful value and are formed by peritoneal ligaments.

1. Broad ligaments (Fig. 31.6).
2. Uterovesical fold of peritoneum (Fig. 31.7).
3. Rectovaginal or rectouterine fold of peritoneum (Figs 31.7 and 31.15).

Role of Individual Supports

Pelvic Diaphragm

The pelvic diaphragm (Fig. 31.9) supports the pelvic viscera and resists any rise in the intra-abdominal pressure. The pubococcygeus part of the levator ani is partly inserted into the perineal body between the vagina and the rectum. Some of these fibres also form a supporting sling and a sphincter for the vagina, and so indirectly for the uterus and the urinary bladder. If the pubococcygeus is torn during parturition, the support to the vagina is lost, and the latter tends to sink into the vestibule along with the uterus, thus causing *prolapse* of the uterus. The efficacy of the levator ani as a support is also lost when the perineal muscles are torn. They normally fix the perineal body, and make it an anchor for the levator ani (Fig. 31.9).

Perineal Body

It is a fibromuscular node to which ten muscles are attached. It acts as an anchor for the pelvic diaphragm, and thus maintains the integrity of the pelvic floor. The muscles are two superficial transversus, two deep transversus perinei, two pubococcygeus part of levator ani, two bulbo-spongiosus and single sphincter ani externus and unstripped fibres of longitudinal muscle coat of the anal canal (Fig. 28.4).

Distal Urethral Sphincter Mechanism

The urogenital diaphragm does not exist as sphincter urethrae is within the wall of the urethra. Distal urethral sphincter mechanism exists. In addition there is compressor urethrae and sphincter urethrae vaginalis. Since these are inserted into vagina, they support the uterus indirectly.

Uterine Axis

The anteverted position of the uterus itself prevents the organ from sagging down through the vagina. Any rise in intra-abdominal pressure tends to push the uterus against the bladder and pubic symphysis, which further accentuates anteversion. The angle of anteversion is maintained by the uterosacral and round ligaments (Figs 31.10 and 31.11).

Pubocervical Ligaments

These ligaments connect the cervix to the posterior surface of pubis. They are derived from the endopelvic fascia, and correspond to the medial and lateral puboprostatic ligaments in the male (Fig. 31.12).

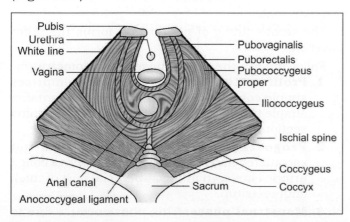

Fig. 31.9: Superior view of the pelvic diaphragm (the levator ani and coccygeus).

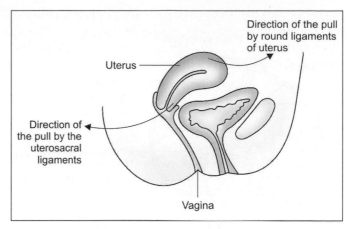

Fig. 31.10: Anteversion of the uterus is maintained by the couple of forces provided by the pull of the uterosacral ligament and the round ligament of the uterus.

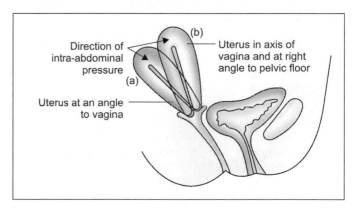

Fig. 31.11: (a) No chance of prolapse of uterus, (b) Chance of prolapse of uterus.

Transverse Cervical Ligaments of Mackenrodt

These are also known by various other names like lateral cervical ligaments; cardinal ligaments; paracervical ligaments; retinacula uterine sustent-aculum of Bonny (Figs 31.12 and 31.13).

These are fan-shaped condensations of the endopelvic fascia on each side of the cervix above the levator ani and around the uterine vessels. They connect the lateral aspects of the cervix and of the upper vaginal wall to the lateral pelvic wall, about 2.5 cm ventral to the ischial spine. They form a 'hammock' that supports the uterus.

Uterosacral Ligaments

These are also condensations of the endopelvic fascia. They connect the cervix to the periosteum of the sacrum (S2, S3) and are enclosed within rectouterine folds of peritoneum (which form the lateral boundaries of the rectouterine pouch). The uterosacral ligaments keep the cervix braced backwards against the forward pull of the round ligaments. The two ligaments form a couple that maintains the uterine axis (Figs 31.12a and 31.14).

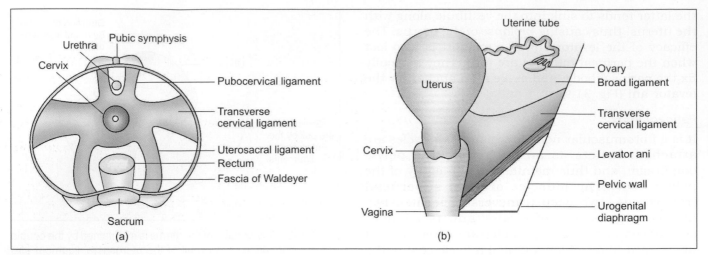

Fig. 31.12: Condensation of pelvic fascia forming the supports of the pelvic organs. (a) Superior view of the ligamentous supports of the uterus and rectum, (b) coronal view of the right cardinal ligament.

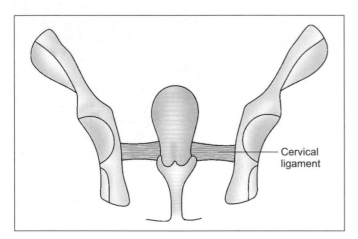

Fig. 31.13: Cervical ligaments supporting the uterus.

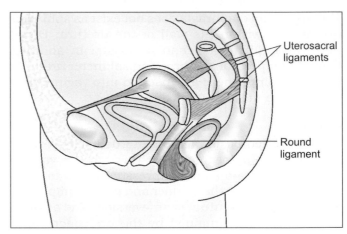

Fig. 31.14: Uterosacral and round ligaments supporting the uterus.

Round Ligaments of Uterus

The round ligaments are two fibromuscular flat bands, 10 to 12 cm long, which lie between the two layers of the broad ligament, anteroinferior to the uterine tube. Each ligament begins at the lateral angle of the uterus, runs forwards and laterally, passes through the deep inguinal ring, traverses the inguinal canal and merges with the areolar tissue of the labium majus after breaking up into thin filaments. In the inguinal canal, it is accompanied by a process of peritoneum during foetal life. If it persists after birth, it is known in females as the *canal of Nuck*. The round ligament keeps the fundus pulled forwards and maintains the angle of anteversion against the backward pull of the uterosacral ligaments (Figs 31.7, 31.8 and 31.10).

Histology

The mucous membrane is called the endometrium, which undergoes cyclic changes in three phases in one menstrual cycle.

Myometrium is thickest layer made of an outer and an inner longitudinal coats and middle thick circular coat.

The serous lining of peritoneum forms the outer covering.

Following are the three phases of endometrium.
1. **Proliferative phase:** The lining comprises simple columnar epithelium. Stroma contains simple tubular glands. Its deeper part contains sections of coiled arteries.

2. **Progestational phase:** The glands get sacculated and tortuous. The sections of coiled arteries are seen in the superficial part of thick endometrium.

3. **Menstrual phase:** This phase occurs due to decline of both the hormones. The endometrium becomes ischaemic and starts being shed. The

vessel wall gets necrosed and blood enters the stroma and menstrual flow starts.

VAGINA

Synonym

Kolpos = Vagina (use of the terms colposcopy, colpotomy and colporrhaphy).

Definitions

The vagina is a fibromuscular canal, forming the female copulatory organ. The term 'vagina' means a sheath.

Extent and Situation

The vagina extends from the vulva to the uterus, and is situated behind the bladder and the urethra, and in front of the rectum and anal canal.

Direction

In the erect posture, the vagina is directed upwards and backwards. Long axis of uterus forms an angle of 90° with long axis of vagina.

Size and Shape

The anterior wall of the vagina is about 8 cm long and the posterior wall about 10 cm long.

The *diameter* of the vagina gradually increases from below upwards. The upper end or vault is roughly 5 cm twice the size of the lower end (2.5 cm). However, it is quite distensible and allows passage of the head of the foetus during delivery (Fig. 31.10).

The *lumen* is circular at the upper end because of the protrusion of the cervix into it. Below the cervix, the anterior and posterior walls are in contact with each other, so that the lumen is a transverse slit in the middle part, and is H-shaped in the lower part.

In the virgin, the lower end of the vagina is partially closed by a thin annular fold of mucous membrane called the *hymen*. In married women the hymen is represented by rounded elevations around the vaginal orifice, the *caruncular hymenales*.

Fornices of Vagina

The interior of the upper end of the vagina or vaginal vault is in the form of a circular groove that surrounds the protruding cervix. The groove becomes progressively deeper from before backwards and is arbitrarily divided into four parts called the vaginal fornices. The *anterior fornix* lies in front of the cervix and is shallowest. The *posterior fornix* lies behind the cervix and is deepest. The *lateral fornices* lie one on each side of the cervix (Figs 31.5 and 31.6).

Relations

Anterior Wall

1. Upper half is related to the base of the bladder.
2. Lower half to the urethra (Fig. 31.15).

Posterior Wall

1. Upper one-fourth is separated from the rectum by the rectouterine pouch.
2. Middle two-fourths are separated from the rectum by loose connective tissue.
3. Lower one-fourth is separated from the anal canal by the perineal body and the muscles attached to it.

Lateral Walls

On each side:
1. Upper one-third is related to the transverse cervical ligament of pelvic fascia in which are embedded a network of vaginal veins, and the *ureter gets crossed by the uterine artery.*
2. Middle one-third is related to the pubo-coccygeus part of the levator ani.
3. Lower one-third pierces the perineal membrane, below which it is related to the bulb of the vestibule, the bulbospongiosus and the duct of greater vestibular gland of Bartholin (Figs 31.16, 31.17 and 28.19).

Arterial Supply

The vagina is a very vascular organ, and is supplied by the following arteries.

1. The main artery supplying it is the vaginal branch of the internal iliac artery.
2. In addition, the upper part is supplied by the cervicovaginal branch of the uterine artery (Fig. 31.17). The lower part is by the middle rectal and internal pudendal arteries.

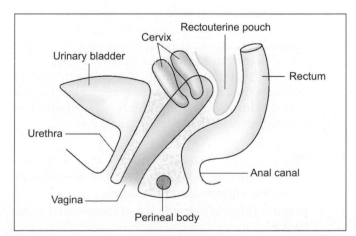

Fig. 31.15: Vagina and some related structures as seen in sagittal section.

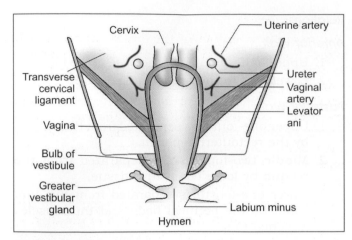

Fig. 31.16: Vagina and some related structures as seen in coronal section.

Branches of these arteries anastomose to form anterior and posterior midline vessels called the *vaginal azygos arteries*.

Venous Drainage

The rich vaginal venous plexus drains into the internal iliac veins through the vaginal veins which accompany the vaginal arteries.

Lymphatic Drainage

Lymphatics from the upper one-third of the vagina drain into the external iliac nodes; from the middle one-third into the internal iliac nodes; and from the lower one-third into the medial group of superficial inguinal nodes.

Nerve Supply

1. The lower one-third of the vagina is pain sensitive and is supplied by the pudendal nerve through the inferior rectal and posterior labial branches of the perineal nerve.
2. The upper two-thirds of the vagina are pain insensitive and are supplied by sympathetic L1, L2 and parasympathetic segments S2 to S4. Nerves are derived from the inferior hypogastric and uterovaginal plexuses. Sympathetic nerves are vasoconstrictor and parasympathetic nerves vasodilator. The fibres which accompany the vaginal arteries form the vaginal nerves.

Histology

1. Mucous membrane is lined by nonkeratinised stratified squamous epithelium.
2. Lamina propria is made up of loose connective tissue.
3. Muscle coat consists of an outer longitudinal and an inner circular layer.

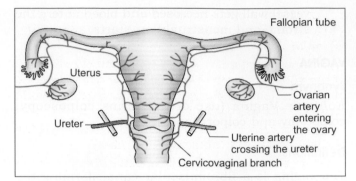

Fig. 31.17: Arterial supply of vagina by the uterine artery.

4. The outer fibrous coat is the usual connective tissue.

There are no glands in the vaginal mucosa. It is kept moist by the cervical glands from above and the greater vestibular glands from below. The vaginal fluid is acidic in nature because of the fermentation of glycogen (in vaginal cells) by the Doderlein's bacilli.

Ureter in Female Pelvis

As ureter lies anterior to internal iliac artery and immediately behind ovary it forms the posterior boundary of the ovarian fossa. It descends down till ischial spine. Then it courses anteromedially towards urinary bladder.

In its anteromedial part, ureter is related to the uterine artery, cervix and vaginal fornices. Ureter lies in endopelvic fascia in inferomedial part of broad ligament of uterus, where it may be damaged.

In the broad ligament, uterine artery is anterosuperior to ureter by 2.5 cm and then crosses the ureter to ascend along lateral side of the uterus.

Ureter runs forwards slightly above the lateral fornix of vagina and is 2 cm lateral to supravaginal part of cervix. It then turns medially towards urinary bladder and is apposed to vagina.

Left ureter to often more close to vagina, as uterus is slightly on the right side and vagina is on the left side of median plane.

One has to be careful of ureter, especially during ligation of the uterine artery. Ureter exhibits peristaltic movements and can be identified easily.

DEVELOPMENT OF FEMALE REPRODUCTIVE SYSTEM

Female reproductive system comprises two ovaries and

1. Genital ducts
2. External genitalia

Ovary

Sex of the embryo is determined at the time of fertilization.

The chromosomal complement in female is 'XX'. Various components of ovary are germs cells, follicular cells and the stromal cells.

Germ cells get migrated from the dorsocaudal end of the yolk sac. Follicular cells are derived from the epithelial cells of the coelomic epithelium, while stromal cells are derived from mesoderm.

There is no tunica albuginea in the ovary and the cortical part of the gonad predominates.

Ovary descends down till the pelvis. Its descent is interrupted due to the presence of the single uterus, which divides the gubernaculum into ligament of ovary and round ligament of uterus.

Ducts

In female, Müllerian or paramesonephric duct predominates. This duct is situated lateral to mesonephric duct. It opens caudally into definitive urogenital sinus. Müllerian duct proliferates due to both presence of oestrogens and absence of testosterone and Mullerian inhibiting substance. Müllerian duct forms all four parts of fallopian tube. The distal part of the two ducts fuse to form the single uterovaginal canal which gives rise to uterus with its fundus, body and cervix parts.

Wolffian duct or mesonephric duct forms the trigone of urinary bladder as functional component. Duct of Gartner is its vestigial component.

Mesonephric Tubules

These only form vestigial elements in female. These are epoophoron, paroophoron and aberrant ductules.

Vestigial Remnants Present in the Broad Ligament

Epoophoron

It consists of 10 to 15 parallel tubules situated in the lateral part of the mesosalpinx between the ovary and the uterine tube. The tubules end in a longitudinal duct. These tubules represent cranial mesonephric tubules while the duct is a remnant of the mesonephric duct.

Paroophoron

It consists of a few very short rudimentary tubules situated in the broad ligament between the ovary and uterus. These represent caudal mesonephric tubules which are not attached to the mesonephric duct.

Duct of gartner

Occasionally, the duct of the epoophoron is much larger than usual and is called the *duct of Gartner*. It can be traced first along the uterine tube, and then along the lateral margin of the uterus up to the level of the *internal os*. Further down it runs through the cervix and the lateral wall of the vagina, and ends near the free margin of the hymen. It represents the mesonephric duct. It may form a cyst in the anterior or lateral wall of the vagina.

Vesicular appendix

Occasionally, one or two pedunculated cysts are found attached to the fimbriated end of the uterine tube. These are called the *vesicular appendices* or *paramesonephric appendices*. These are believed to develop from the cranial end of the paramesonephric duct.

Vagina

As the fused Müllerian or paramesonephric ducts which form the uterovaginal canal open into the definitive urogenital sinus, the endoderm bulges to form the Müllerian tubercle. Uterovaginal canal forms upper 1/3rd of vagina.

Endoderm on either side of Mullerian tubercle proliferates to form two sinovaginal bulbs which fuse to form vaginal plate. The vaginal plate surrounds the caudal end of the uterovaginal canal.

Soon there is canalisation of the vaginal plate to form lower 2/3rd of vagina and vaginal fornices. It opens through an endodermal partial septum—the hymen in the definitive urogenital sinus.

External Genitalia

Mesenchymal cells migrate around cloacal membrane to form cloacal folds. These folds fuse ventrally to form genital tubercle.

Cloacal folds get divided into urethral folds anteriorly and anal folds posteriorly. This occurs at the same time that the cloacal membrane gets divided into urogenital membrane and anal membrane.

Lateral to urethral folds another pair of folds, the genital folds, make their appearance.

Genital tubercle forms clitoris; urethral folds form labia minora, genital swellings form labia majora, urogenital membrane gets ruptured to form the vestibule.

CLINICAL ANATOMY

- *Determination of ovulation:* In cases of sterility, the ovulation can be determined by repeated ultrasonography.

- *Prolapse of ovaries:* Ovaries are frequently displaced to the pouch of Douglas where they can be palpated by a PV or per vaginum examination.

- *Ovarian cysts:* The developmental arrest of the ovarian follicles may result in the formation of one or more small ovarian cysts.

  Multiple small theca lutein cysts involve both the ovaries in cases with *Stein-Leventhal syndrome.* The syndrome is characterized by mild hirsutism, deep voice, secondary amenorrhoea, and cystic enlargement of both the ovaries.

- *Carcinoma of ovary* is common, and accounts for 15% of all cancers and 20% of gynaecological cancers.

- Ovaries are the commonest site in the abdomen for endometriosis. The endometrial cysts in the ovary are called the *chocolate cysts.*

- *Salpingitis:* Inflammation of the uterine tube is called salpingitis (Salpinx-trumpet or tube).

- *Sterility:* Inability to have a child is called sterility. The most common cause of sterility in the female is tubal blockage which may be congenital, or caused by infection. Patency of the tube can be investigated by:

  (a) *Insufflation test* or *Rubin's test.* Normally, air pushed into the uterus passes through the tubes and leaks into the peritoneal cavity. This leakage produces a hissing or bubbling sound which can be auscultated over the iliac fossae.

  (b) *Hysterosalpingography* is a radiological technique by which the cavity of the uterus and the lumina of the tubes can be visualized, after injecting a radiopaque oily dye into the uterus (Fig. 31.18).

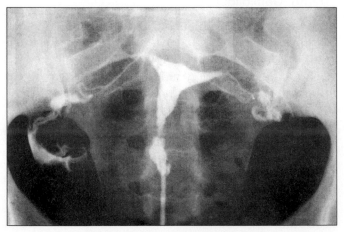

Fig. 31.18: Hysterosalpingogram.

- *Tubal pregnancy:* Sometimes the fertilized ovum instead of reaching the uterus adheres to the walls of the uterine tube and starts developing there. This is known as *tubal pregnancy.* The enlarging embryo may lead to rupture of tube.

- *Tubectomy:* For purposes of family planning a woman can be sterilized by removing a segment of the uterine tube on both sides. This can be done by laproscopy (Fig. 31.19) and through an incision in abdominal wall (Fig. 31.20).

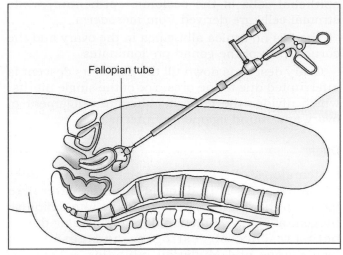

Fallopian tube

Fig. 31.19: Laparoscopic sterilisation.

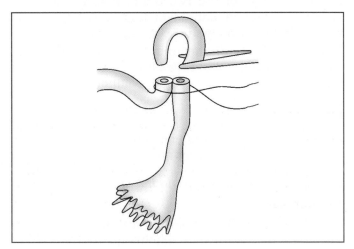

Fig. 31.20: Abdominal sterilisation.

- *Transport of ovum:* The initial phase of transport of ovum is chiefly due to tubal contractions. After ovulation, however, the contractions diminish, and the ciliary movements create an effective stream of lymph towards the uterus which assists in the transport of ovum in the lumen of the tube over the mucosal ridges.

- *Vaginal Examination*

  (a) *Inspection:* Vagina is first inspected at the introitus by separating the labia minora with the left hand. Next the speculum examination is done to inspect the cervix and vaginal vault, and to take the vaginal swab.

  (b) *Palpation* of the pelvic organs can be done by a per vaginum (PV) digital examination

(Fig. 31.21). With the examining fingers one can feel:

– *Anteriorly,* the urethra, bladder and pubic symphysis;
– *Posteriorly,* the rectum and pouch of Douglas;
– *Laterally,* the ovary, tube, lateral pelvic wall, thickened ligaments, and ureters; and
– *Superiorly,* the cervix.

Bimanual (abdominovaginal) examination helps in the assessment of the size and position of the uterus, enlargements of the ovaries and tubes, and the other pelvic masses.

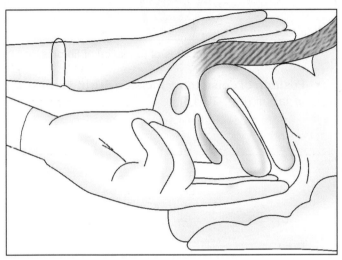

Fig. 31.21: Bimanual examination of the female internal genital organs.

• *Vaginal lacerations:* Traumatic lacerations of vagina are common, and may be caused by forcible coitus (rape) during childbirth, or by accidents. This may give rise to profuse bleeding.

• *Vaginitis:* It is common before puberty and after menopause because of the thin delicate epithelium. In adults, the resistant squamous epithelium prevents the infection. Vaginitis is commonly caused by the trichomonas, monilial and gonococcal infections. It causes leucorrhoea or white discharge.

• *Prolapse:* Prolapse of the anterior wall of vagina drags the bladder (cystocoele) and urethra (urethrocoele); the posterior wall drags the rectum (rectocoele) (Fig. 31.22).

Weakness of supports of uterus can give rise to different degrees of prolapse (Fig. 29.14).

Similarly, trauma to the anterior and posterior walls of vagina can cause the vesicovaginal, urethrovaginal and rectovaginal fistulae.

• *Neoplasms:* Primary new growths of vagina, like the infections, are uncommon. However,

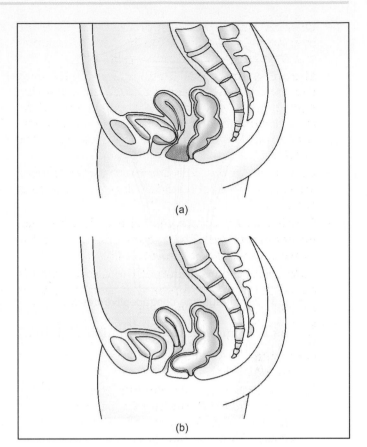

Fig. 31.22: (a) Cystocoele, and (b) rectocoele.

secondary involvement of vagina by the cancer cervix is very common.

• *Colpotomy and colporrhaphy:* Posterior colpotomy is done to drain the pus from the pouch of Douglas (Fig. 31.23).

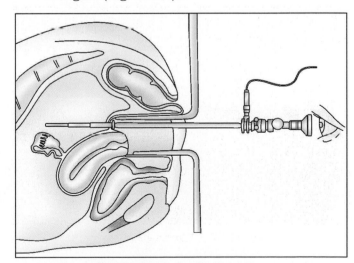

Fig. 31.23: Posterior colpotomy.

• Intrauterine contraceptive device is used to prevent implantation of fertilised oocyte (Fig. 31.24).

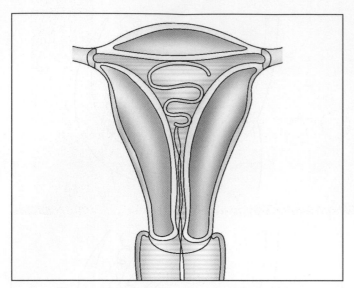

Fig. 31.24: Intrauterine contraceptive device.

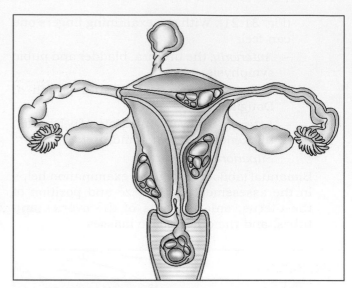

Fig. 31.25: Common sites of formation of fibroids.

- Uterus is common site of formation of fibroids (Fig. 31.25).

- Position of episiotomy incision during 2nd stage of labor (Fig. 29.13).

Male Reproductive Organs

INTRODUCTION

The delicate gonads of the male lie outside the abdominal cavity as these cannot withstand the temperature of the abdominal cavity. The epididymis carrying the spermatozoa starts from the testis and continues as the vas deferens. The vas deferens after a course in the scrotum enters the anterior abdominal wall, crosses the pelvic brim to enter the anterior part of pelvic cavity.

Seminal vesicles are placed at the base of urinary bladder. The duct of seminal vesicle unites with vas deferens to form the ejaculatory duct which opens into the prostatic urethra.

Prostate is an important gland; for its secretions help in maturation of the sperms. It undergoes a lot of changes from birth to old age and is very vulnerable to malignant changes. Cancer prostate can metastasise even to cranial cavity as the prostatic venous plexus communicates with the quiet but dangerous vertebral venous plexus.

The male reproductive organs include the external and internal genitalia. The external genitalia are the penis and the scrotum. The internal genitalia on each side are the epididymis, the ductus deferens, the seminal vesicle, the ejaculatory ducts, the prostate, and the male urethra.

The external genitalia, the testis and the epididymis have been described in Chapter 17, and the male urethra in Chapter 30. The remaining structures are considered below.

DUCTUS DEFERENS

Synonyms

The *ductus deferens* is also called the *vas deferens* or the *deferent duct*.

Definition

The ductus deferens is a thick-walled, muscular tube which transmits spermatozoa from the

DISSECTION

The ductus deferens has been seen till the deep inguinal ring in the anterior abdominal wall. Follow it from there as it hooks round the lateral side of inferior epigastric artery to pass backwards and medially across the external iliac vessels to enter into the lesser pelvis. There it crosses the ureter and lies on the posterior surface of urinary bladder medial to the seminal vesicle. Separate the ductus from the adjacent seminal vesicle and trace these till the base of the prostate gland.

Follow the deep dorsal vein of the penis and its two divisions into the prostatic venous plexus situated in the angle between the bladder and the prostate. Feel the thickened puboprostatic ligaments. Feel the firm prostate lying just at the neck of the urinary bladder.

Identify the levator prostatae muscle lying inferolateral to the prostate. This is identifiable by pulling both the bladder and prostate medially. The first part of urethra traverses the prostate. Cut through the anterior one third of the gland to expose the prostatic urethra.

epididymis to the ejaculatory duct. It feels cord-like at the upper lateral part of scrotum. Ductus deferens has a narrow lumen except at the terminal dilated part called the ampulla.

Length

The ductus deferens is about 45 cm long when straightened.

Location and Course

In its course, the vas lies successively:

1. Within the scrotum along the posterior border of the testis.
2. In the inguinal canal as part of the spermatic cord (Fig. 32.1).

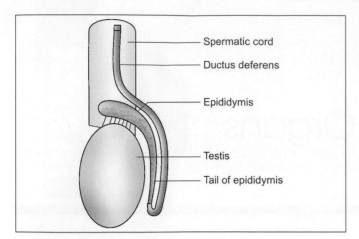

Fig. 32.1: Schematic diagram to show the relationship of the ductus deferens to the testis and the spermatic cord.

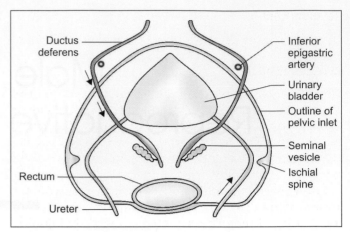

Fig. 32.2: Schematic diagram to show the course of the ductus deferens.

3. In the greater pelvis.
4. In the lesser pelvis.

Course and Relations

1. The ductus deferens begins as a continuation of the tail of the epididymis.
2. *Along the posterior border of the testis:* At first it is very tortuous, but gradually straightens as it ascends along the posterior border of the testis, medial to the epididymis.
3. *In the spermatic cord:* The ductus deferens lies vertically in posterior part of spermatic cord. It runs upwards to the superficial inguinal ring, and then traverses the inguinal canal. In the vertical part of its course, it can be felt as a cord-like structure within the spermatic cord.
4. *In the greater pelvis:* At the deep inguinal ring it leaves the spermatic cord, and hooks round the lateral side of the inferior epigastric artery. It then passes backwards and medially, across the external iliac vessels, and enters the lesser pelvis (Fig. 32.2).
5. *In the lesser pelvis:* The ductus deferens runs downwards and backwards on the lateral pelvic wall, deep to the peritoneum. Here it crosses the obliterated umbilical artery, the obturator nerve and vessels, and the vesical vessels. It then crosses the ureter, and bends medially at right angles, to enter the sacrogenital fold of peritoneum. Reaching the base of the urinary bladder the ductus runs downwards and forwards medial to the seminal vesicle. Here it approaches the opposite duct and reaches the base of the prostate (Fig. 32.3).

At the base of the prostate, the ductus deferens is joined at an acute angle by the duct of the seminal vesicle to form the ejaculatory duct.

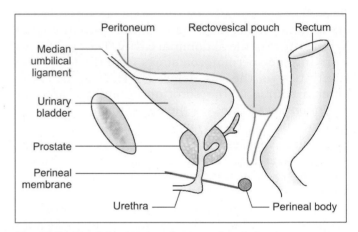

Fig. 32.3: Prostate gland and some related structures as seen in sagittal section.

The part of the ductus lying behind the base of the bladder, is dilated and tortuous, and is known as the ampulla (Fig. 30.3).

Arterial Supply

The artery to the ductus deferens usually arises from one of the terminal branches of the superior vesical artery; but occasionally it arises from the inferior vesical artery. It accompanies the ductus to testis, where it anastomoses with the testicular artery.

Venous Drainage

Veins from the ductus join the vesical venous plexus which opens into the internal iliac vein.

Histology

The lining epithelium of vas deferens is of pseudo-stratified ciliated type. The underlying lamina propria contains elastic fibres. The muscle coat is in three layers, middle is circular and outer and inner layers are of longitudinal type. Adventitia is made of thin connective tissue layer with fine nerves and arterioles.

Development

Ductus deferens develops from the mesonephric duct.

SEMINAL VESICLES

These are two lobulated sacs, situated between the bladder and rectum. Each vesicle is about 5 cm long, and is directed upwards and laterally. The lower narrow end forms the duct of the seminal vesicle which joins the ductus deferens to form the ejaculatory duct (Fig. 30.3).

The seminal vesicles do not form a reservoir for spermatozoa. Their secretion forms a large part of the seminal fluid. The secretion is slightly alkaline and contains fructose and a coagulating enzyme called the vesiculase.

PROSTATE

The prostate is an accessory gland of the male reproductive system. The secretions of this gland add bulk to the seminal fluid along with those of the seminal vesicles and the bulbourethral glands. The prostate is firm in consistency. Its firmness is due to the presence of a dense fibromuscular stroma in which the glandular elements are embedded. In the female the prostate is represented by the paraurethral glands of Skene.

Situation

The prostate lies in the lesser pelvis, below the neck of the urinary bladder, behind the lower part of the pubic symphysis and the upper part of the pubic arch, and in front of the ampulla of the rectum (Figs 32.3 and 32.4).

Shape, Size and Weight

It resembles an inverted cone, measuring about 4 cm transversely at the base, i.e. width 3 cm vertically, i.e. length, and 2 cm anteroposteriorly or thickness. It weighs about 8 g.

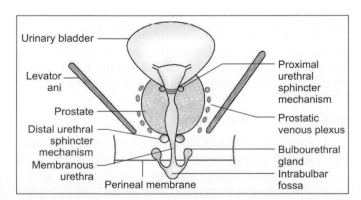

Fig. 32.4: Prostate and some related structures as seen in a coronal section.

Gross Features

The prostate comprises an apex directed downwards; a base; four surfaces, anterior, posterior and two inferolateral.

Apex

The *apex* is directed downwards surrounds the junction of prostatic and membranous parts of posterior urethra. It is separated from the anal canal by the perineal body (Fig. 32.3).

Base

The *base* is directed upwards, and is structurally continuous with the neck of the bladder. The junction is marked by a circular groove which lodges venules of the vesical and prostatic plexuses.

Surfaces

The *anterior surface* is narrow and convex from side to side. It lies 2 cm behind the pubic symphysis, with retropubic fat intervening. Its upper part is connected to the pubic bones by the puboprostatic ligaments. The lower end of this surface is pierced by the urethra. The lower end of urethra emerges from this surface anterosuperior to the apex of gland. This surface is composed of fibrous tissue.

The *posterior surface* is triangular in shape. It is flattened from side to side and convex from above downwards. It is separated from the rectum by the fascia of Denonvilliers which is the obliterated rectovesical pouch of peritoneum. Near its upper border it is pierced on each side of the median plane by the ejaculatory duct. This surface lies 4 cm from the anus, and can be easily palpated on digital examination through the rectum (Fig. 32.5).

The *inferolateral surfaces* are related to the side walls of pelvis. The anterior fibres of the levator ani enclose the gland in pubourethral sling. They are separated from the muscle by a plexus of veins embedded in its sheath (Fig. 32.4).

Zones of the Prostate

According to McNeal, the gland is divided into:

(a) The peripheral zone forms 70% of glandular tissue. It is situated posteriorly and is cancer vulnerable.

(b) Central zone constitutes 25% of glandular tissue situated posterior to urethral lumen and above the ejaculatory ducts. The two zones are like an egg in its egg-cup. The central zone is not involved in disease and is of Wolfian duct origin.

(c) There is a periurethral transition zone (5%) from which benign prostatic hyperplasia

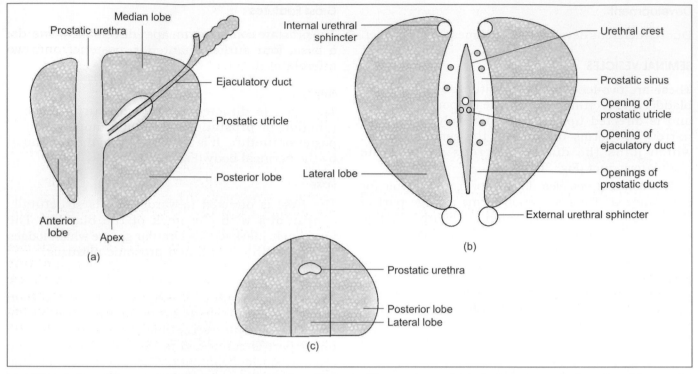

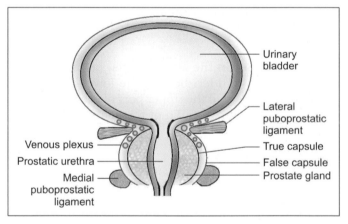

Fig. 32.5: Lobes of the prostate gland as seen in sections through different planes. (a) Left view of a sagittal section, (b) posterior half of a coronal section, and (c) horizontal section. The prostatic utricle, ejaculatory duct and the prostatic urethra are also seen.

arises. The central zone and transition zone constitute "central gland".

In the preprostatic part of prostate and bladder neck there is proximal urethral sphincter mechanism that subserves sexual function of closing during ejaculation. If this sphincter gets resected, retrograde ejaculation occurs.

Distal urethral sphincter mechanism is seen at the junction of prostatic and membranous parts of urethra. It is horseshoe shaped, with most of the bulk lying anteriorly. It is distinct from muscle of pelvic floor.

The prostate gland was described as having five lobes initially. As of now, the glandular tissue is divided into three lobes, two lateral and one median.

Capsules and Ligaments of Prostate

True capsule

It is formed by condensation of the peripheral part of the gland. It is fibromuscular in structure and is continuous with stroma of the gland. It contains no venous plexus (Fig. 32.6).

False Capsule

It lies outside the true capsule and is derived from the endopelvic fascia. *Anteriorly,* it is continuous with the puboprostatic ligaments. On each side, the prostatic venous plexus is embedded in it. *Posteriorly,* it is avascular, and is formed by the rectovesical fascia of Denonvilliers.

Fig. 32.6: Ligaments and venous plexus of prostate gland.

A pair of medial puboprostatic and a pair of lateral puboprostatic ligaments extend from the false capsule to the back of pubic bone. The medial pair lie near the apex while lateral pair is close to the base. These four ligaments support the gland (Fig. 32.6).

Structures within the Prostate

1. Prostatic urethra traverses the gland vertically at the junction of its anterior one-third with the posterior two-thirds.

2. The prostatic utricle is a blind sac directed upwards and backwards. It opens at the middle of the urethral crest.

3. The ejaculatory ducts pass downwards and forwards, and open into the prostatic urethra on each side of the opening of the prostatic utricle (Fig. 32.5).

Structural Zones of the Prostate

Histological sections of the prostate do not show the lobar pattern of the organ. Instead there are two well-defined concentric zones separated by an ill-defined irregular capsule. The zones are absent anteriorly (Fig. 32.7).

The *outer larger zone* is composed of large branched glands, the ducts of which curve backwards and open mainly into the prostatic sinuses. This zone is frequently the site of carcinoma.

The *inner smaller zone* is composed of submucosal glands opening in the prostatic sinuses, and a group of short, simple mucosal glands surrounding the upper part of the urethra. These zones are typically prone to *benign hypertrophy*.

Blood Supply

The prostate is supplied by branches from the inferior vesical, middle rectal and internal pudendal arteries. Branches of these arteries form a large outer or subcapsular plexus, and a small inner or periurethral plexus. The greater part of the gland is supplied by the subcapsular plexus.

The *veins* form a rich plexus around the sides and base of the gland. The plexus communicates with the vesical plexus and with the internal pudendal vein, and drains into the vesical and internal iliac veins. Valveless communications exist between the prostatic and vertebral venous plexuses through which prostatic carcinoma can spread to the vertebral column and to the skull.

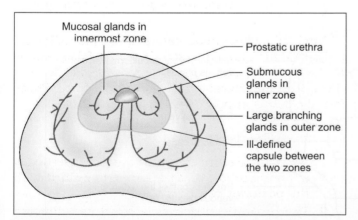

Fig. 32.7: Horizontal section through the prostate gland showing the histological zones and the glands in them.

Labels: Mucosal glands in innermost zone — Prostatic urethra — Submucous glands in inner zone — Large branching glands in outer zone — Ill-defined capsule between the two zones

Lymphatic Drainage

Lymphatics from the prostate drain chiefly into the internal iliac and sacral nodes; and partly into the external iliac nodes.

Nerve Supply

The prostatic plexus of nerves is derived from the lower part of the inferior hypogastric plexus. It contains thick nerves and numerous large ganglia. In addition to the prostate and structures within it, the plexus also supplies the seminal vesicles, the corpora cavernosa, the corpus spongiosum, the membranous and penile parts of the urethra, and the bulbourethral glands.

The prostate is supplied by both sympathetic and parasympathetic nerves. The gland contains numerous end-organs, impulses from which are relayed to the lower three lumbar and upper sacral segments. Secretions of the prostate are produced and discharged after stimulation of both the parasympathetic and sympathetic nerves.

Age Changes in Prostate

1. *At birth* the prostate is small in size, and is made up mainly of stroma in which a simple duct system is embedded. During the first 6 weeks after birth the epithelium of the ducts and of the prostatic utricle undergoes hyperplasia and squamous metaplasia, under the stimulation of maternal oestrogens. Thereafter, up to the age of 9 years changes are negligible. Between 9 and 14 years, the duct system becomes more elaborate by formation of side buds, and the gland slowly increases in size.

2. *At puberty* the male hormones bring about rapid changes in the gland. In about one year it becomes double its prepubertal size due to rapid growth of the follicles and condensation and reduction of the stroma.

3. *From 20 to 30 years* there occurs marked proliferation of the glandular elements with infolding of the glandular epithelium into the lumen of the follicles, making them irregular.

4. *From 30 to 45 years* the size of the prostate remains constant, and involution starts. The epithelial infoldings gradually disappear and amyloid bodies increase in number.

5. *After 45 to 50 years* the prostate is either enlarged called the benign hypertrophy or reduced in size called the senile atrophy.

Histology

Prostate is a fibromuscular glandular organ. The stroma comprises collagen fibres and smooth fibres.

The columnar epithelium of acini is folded. The lumen may contain small colloid masses called amyloid bodies. The prostatic urethra, lined by transitional epithelium may also be seen.

Development

Prostate develops from a series of *endodermal buds* from the lining of primitive urethra and the adjacent portion of urogenital sinus, during first 3 months of intrauterine life. The surrounding *mesenchyme* condenses to form the stroma of the gland. Prostatic utricle develops in the region of Müllerian tubercle similar to uterus or vagina in females. The central zone of glandular tissue is of wolfian duct system.

VERTEBRAL SYSTEM OF VEINS

Synonym: Batson's plexus (Batson, 1957).

The vertebral venous plexus assumes importance in cases of:

1. Carcinoma of prostate causing secondaries in the vertebral column and the skull.
2. Chronic empyema causing brain abscess by septic emboli.

Anatomy of Batson's Plexus

Vertebral venous system is made up of a valveless, complicated network of veins with a longitudinal pattern. It runs parallel to and anastomoses with the superior and inferior venae cavae. This network has three intercommunicating subdivisions (Fig. 32.8).

1. *Epidural plexus* lies in vertebral canal outside the dura mater. The plexus consists of a postcentral and a prelaminar portion. Each portion is drained by two vessels. It drains the structures in the vertebral canal, and is itself drained at regular intervals by segmental veins (vertebral, posterior intercostal, lumbar and lateral sacral).
2. *Plexus within the vertebral bodies:* It drains backwards into the epidural plexus, and antero-laterally into the external vertebral plexus.
3. *External vertebral venous plexus:* It consists of anterior vessels in front of the vertebral bodies, and the posterior vessels on the back of vertebral arches and adjacent muscles. It is drained by segmental veins.

Suboccipital plexus of veins is a part of the external plexus. It lies on and in the suboccipital triangle. It receives the occipital veins of scalp, is connected with the transverse sinus by emissary veins, and drains into the subclavian veins.

Communications and Implications

The vertebral system of veins communicates:

1. Above with the intracranial venous sinuses.
2. Below with the pelvic veins, portal vein, and caval system of veins.

The veins are valveless and the blood can flow in them in either direction. An increase in intrathoracic or intra-abdominal pressure, such as is brought about by coughing and straining, may cause blood to flow in the plexus away from the heart, either upwards or downwards. Such periodic changes in venous pressure are clinically important because they make possible the spread of tumours or infections. For example, cells from pelvic, abdominal, thoracic and breast tumours may enter the venous system, and may ultimately lodge in the vertebrae, the spinal cord, skull, or brain.

The common primary sites causing secondaries in vertebrae are the breast, prostate, and kidney. Vertebral tuberculosis is similarly explained.

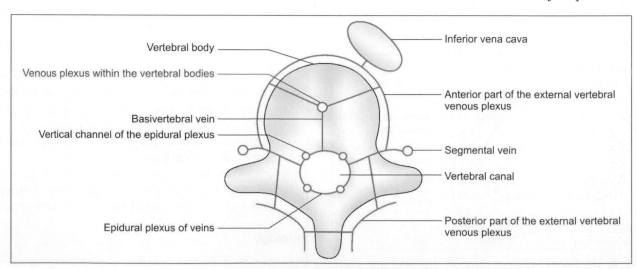

Fig. 32.8: The vertebral system of veins.

CLINICAL ANATOMY

- *Vasectomy* or removing part of the vas deferens is one of the commonest operations being done for purposes of family planning. It is a minor operation which is done under local anaesthesia. A median incision is made in the upper part of the scrotum, just below the penis. Through this incision both the deferent ducts are operated. A short segment of each duct is excised, and the cut ends are ligated. The operation is reversible, and recanalisation can be done if required (Fig. 32.9).

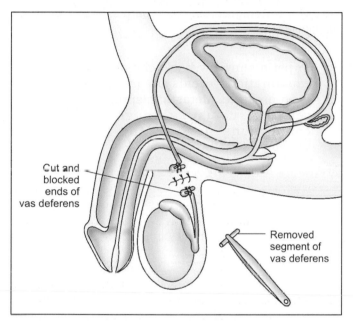

Fig. 32.9: Vasectomy.

After vasectomy, the testes continue to produce the hormones normally to maintain the male characteristics. The hormones pass out through the veins. Sperms are present in a few ejaculations after vasectomy, as it is an emptying process. Newly formed sperms are destroyed in the epididymis and are removed by phagocytosis.

- *Senile enlargement of prostate:* After 50 years of age the prostate is often enlarged due to benign hypertrophy or due to the formation of an adenoma. This causes retention of urine due to distortion of the urethra. Enlargement of the median lobe not only projects into bladder, but forms a sort of valve over the internal urethral orifice, so that more patient strains, more it obstructs the passage. Urine passes when the patient relaxes.

Digital examination of the rectum is very helpful in the diagnosis of an enlarged prostate

(Fig. 32.10). Removal of such a prostate called *prostatectomy* relieves the urinary obstruction. During removal, the enlarged gland is enucleated, leaving behind both the capsules and venous plexus between them. The prostate can be removed through bladder (transvesical), through prostatic capsule (retropubic), or through perineum and fascia of Denonvilliers (perineal approach) or through urethra (TUR–transurethral resection) (Fig. 32.11).

- Inflammation of the prostate is referred to as *prostatitis*. It may be acute or chronic. Acute prostatitis is secondary to gonococcal urethritis and chronic prostatitis may be secondary to tuberculous infection of epididymis, seminal vesicles and the bladder.

- Different zones of the prostate gland are seen in Fig. 32.12.

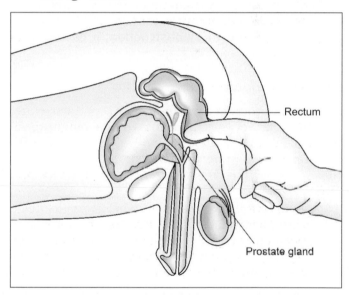

Fig. 32.10: Digital examination of the rectum.

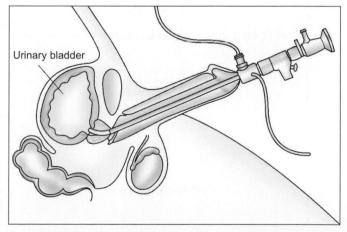

Fig. 32.11: Transurethral resection of prostate gland.

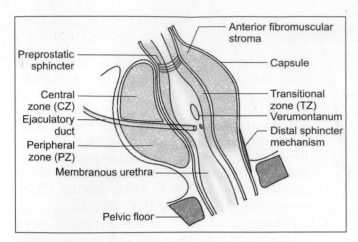

Fig. 32.12: Different zones of the prostate gland, e.g. central zone (CZ), peripheral zone (PZ) and transitional zone (TZ).

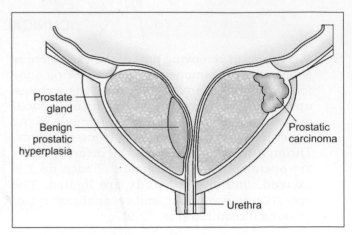

Fig. 32.13: Benign prostatic hyperplasia and prostatic carcinoma.

- Benign prostatic hyperplasia occurs in periurethral zone. Carcinoma of prostate occurs in perpheral zone (Fig. 32.13).
- The prostate is a common site of carcinoma. It usually occurs after the age of 55 years. In addition to urinary obstruction, it causes pain in perineum, low backache or sciatica. Rectal examination reveals an irregular hard and fixed prostate. Metastatic spread occurs to the vertebral column through the valveless connections between the prostatic and vertebral venous plexuses.

CHAPTER 33

Rectum and Anal Canal

The lowest part of the gastrointestinal tract is formed by the rectum and anal canal. Useful components of the food are absorbed and waste material is expelled from the anus; which is the external opening of the anal canal seen in the perineum. Anal canal is heavily guarded by the sphincters and is subjected to many maladies. Balanced food at proper timing decreases these maladies.

RECTUM

The rectum is the distal part of the large gut. It is placed between the sigmoid colon above and the anal canal below. Distension of the rectum causes the desire to defaecate.

The rectum in man is not straight as the name implies. In fact it is curved in an anteroposterior direction and also from side to side. The three cardinal features of the large intestine, e.g. sacculations, appendices epiploicae and taeniae are absent in the rectum.

Situation

The rectum is situated in the posterior part of the lesser pelvis, in front of the lower three pieces of the sacrum and the coccyx.

Extent

The rectum *begins* as a continuation of the sigmoid colon at the level of third sacral vertebra. The rectosigmoid junction is indicated by the lower end of the sigmoid mesocolon. The rectum *ends* by becoming continuous with the anal canal at the anorectal junction. The junction lies 2 to 3 cm in front of and a little below the tip of the coccyx. In males the junction corresponds to the apex of the prostate.

Dimensions

The rectum is 12 cm long. In the upper part it has the same diameter of 4 cm as that of the sigmoid

colon, but in the lower part it is dilated to form the *rectal ampulla*.

Course and Direction

In its course, the rectum runs first downwards and backwards, then downwards, and finally downwards and forwards (Fig. 33.1).

The beginning and the end of the rectum lie in the median plane, but it shows two types of curvatures in its course.

Two anteroposterior curves:

1. The sacral flexure of the rectum follows the concavity of the sacrum and coccyx.
2. The perineal flexure of the rectum is the backward bend at the anorectal junction (Fig. 33.2).

Three lateral curves:

1. The upper lateral curve of rectum is convex to the right.
2. The middle lateral curve is convex to the left and is most prominent.
3. The lower lateral curve is convex to the right.

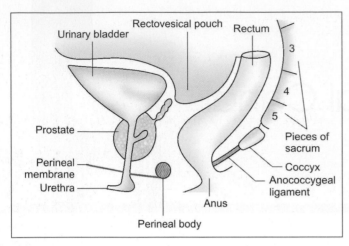

Fig. 33.1: Sagittal section through the male pelvis showing the location of the rectum and some of its anterior and posterior relations.

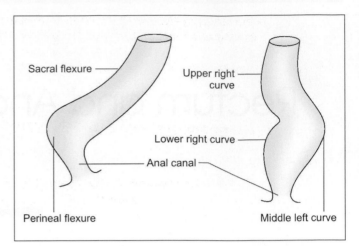

Fig. 33.2: Curvatures of the rectum, (a) Anteroposterior curves, and (b) side to side (lateral) curves.

Relations

Peritoneal Relations

1. The upper one-third of the rectum is covered with peritoneum in front and on the sides.
2. The middle one-third is covered only in front.
3. The lower one-third, which is dilated to form the ampulla, is devoid of peritoneum, and lies below the rectovesical pouch in males and below the rectouterine pouch in females. The distance between the anus and the floor of the pouch is 7.5 cm in males but only 5.5 cm in females (Fig. 33.3).

Visceral Relations

Anteriorly in males

1. The upper two-thirds of the rectum are related to the rectovesical pouch with coils of intestine and sigmoid colon.

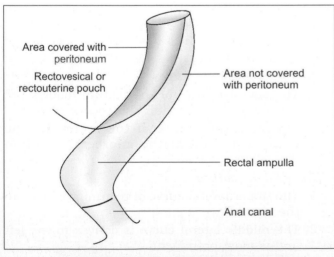

Fig. 33.3: Peritoneal relations of the rectum.

2. The lower one-third of the rectum is related to the base of the urinary bladder, the terminal parts of the ureters, the seminal vesicles, the deferent ducts and the prostate (Fig. 30.3).

Anteriorly in females

1. The upper two-thirds of the rectum are related to the rectouterine pouch with coils of intestine and sigmoid colon. The pouch separates the rectum from the uterus, and from the upper part of the vagina.
2. The lower one-third of the rectum is related to the lower part of the vagina (Figs 18.17b and 31.15).

Posteriorly

The relations are the same in the male and female. They are as follows.

1. Lower three pieces of the sacrum, the coccyx and the anococcygeal ligament.
2. Piriformis, the coccygeus and the levator ani.
3. The median sacral, the superior rectal and the lower lateral sacral vessels.
4. The sympathetic chain with the ganglion impar; the anterior primary rami of S3, S4, S5, Co1 and the pelvic splanchnic nerves; lymph nodes, lymphatics and fat (Fig. 33.4).

Mucosal Folds

The mucous membrane of an empty rectum shows two types of folds, longitudinal and transverse.

The *longitudinal folds* are transitory. They are present in the lower part of an empty rectum, and are obliterated by distension.

The *transverse* or *horizontal folds* or Houston's valves or plicae transversales are permanent and most marked when the rectum is distended.

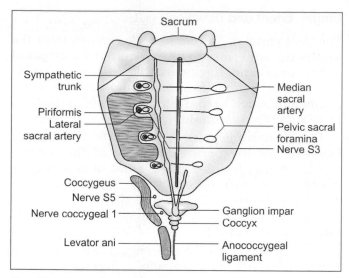

Fig. 33.4: Posterior relations of the rectum (below the level of the middle of the third piece of the sacrum).

1. The *upper fold* lies near the upper end of the rectum, and projects from the right or the left wall. Sometimes it may encircle and partially constrict the lumen.
2. The *middle fold,* the largest and most constant, lies at the upper end of the rectal ampulla, and projects from the anterior and right walls.
3. The *lowest fold* which is inconstant lies 2.5 cm below the middle fold, and projects from the left wall (Fig. 33.5).

Functional Parts of Rectum

The rectum has two developmental parts. The upper part related to the peritoneum develops from the hindgut and lies above the middle fold of the rectum. The lower part devoid of peritoneum develops from the cloaca and lies below the middle fold.

Functionally, the sigmoid colon is the faecal reservoir and the whole of the rectum is empty in normal individuals, being sensitive to distension. Passage of faeces into the rectum, therefore, causes the desire to defaecate.

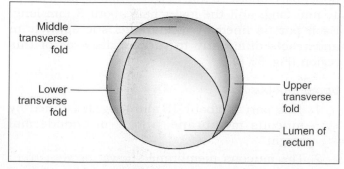

Fig. 33.5: Superior view of the transverse mucosal folds of the rectum.

Arterial Supply

1. *Superior rectal artery:* This is the chief artery of the rectum. It is the continuation of the inferior mesenteric artery at the pelvic brim, medial to the left ureter. It lies in medial limb of pelvic mesocolon (Fig. 15.5) and divides opposite the third sacral vertebra into right and left branches which run on each side of the rectum. Each branch breaks up at the middle of the rectum into several small branches which pierce the muscular coats and run in the anal columns up to the anal valves where they form looped anastomoses (Fig. 21.11).
2. *Middle rectal arteries:* These supply only the superficial coats of the lower rectum. They arise from the anterior division of the internal iliac artery, run in the lateral ligaments of rectum, and supply the muscle coats of the lower part of the rectum (Fig. 34.1). Their anastomoses with the adjacent arteries are poor.
3. *Median sacral artery:* This is a small branch arising from the back of the aorta near its lower end. It descends in the median plane and supplies the posterior wall of the anorectal junction (Figs 27.1 and 33.4).

Venous Drainage

1. *Superior rectal vein:* The tributaries of this vein begin in the anal canal, from the internal rectal venous plexus, in the form of about three veins of considerable size. They pass upwards in the rectal submucosa, pierce the muscular coat about 7.5 cm above the anus and unite to form the superior rectal vein which continues upwards as the inferior mesenteric vein to end in the splenic vein (Fig. 23.9).
2. *Middle rectal vein:* They drain, chiefly, the muscular walls of the rectal ampulla, and open into the internal iliac veins.
3. Median sacral vein joins left common iliac vein.

Lymphatic Drainage

1. Lymphatics from more than the *upper half* of the rectum pass along the superior rectal vessels to the inferior mesenteric nodes after passing through the pararectal and sigmoid nodes.
2. Lymphatics from the *lower half* of the rectum pass along the middle rectal vessels to the internal iliac nodes.

Nerve Supply

The rectum is supplied by both sympathetic (L1, L2) and parasympathetic (S2, S3, S4) nerves through the superior rectal or inferior mesenteric and inferior hypogastric plexuses.

Sympathetic nerves are vasoconstrictor, inhibitory to the rectal musculature and motor to the internal sphincter. Parasympathetic nerves are motor to the musculature of the rectum and inhibitory to the internal sphincter.

Sensations of distension of the rectum pass through the parasympathetic nerves, while pain sensations are carried by both the sympathetic and parasympathetic nerves.

Supports of Rectum

1. Pelvic floor formed by levator ani muscles.
2. *Fascia of Waldeyer:* It attaches the lower part of the rectal ampulla to the sacrum. It is formed by condensation of the pelvic fascia behind the rectum. It encloses the superior rectal vessels and lymphatics.
3. *Lateral ligaments of the rectum:* They are formed by condensation of the pelvic fascia on each side of the rectum. They enclose the middle rectal vessels, and branches of the pelvic plexuses, and attach the rectum to the posterolateral walls of the lesser pelvis.
4. *Rectovesical fascia of Denonvilliers:* It extends from the rectum behind to the seminal vesicles and prostate in front.
5. The *pelvic peritoneum* and the related *vascular pedicles* also help in keeping the rectum in position.
6. Perineal body with its muscles.

ANAL CANAL

The anal canal is the terminal part of the large intestine.

Situation

Anal canal is situated below the level of the pelvic diaphragm. It lies in the anal triangle of perineum in between the right and left ischioanal fossae, which allow its expansion during passage of the faeces. The sacculations and taeniae are absent here also.

DISSECTION

Identify the relations of the anal canal in both male and female. Examine the lining of the anal canal. Strip the mucous membrane and skin from a sector of the anal canal. Identify the thickened part of the circular muscle layer forming the internal sphincter of the anus. Locate the external anal sphincter with its parts, partly overlapping the internal sphincter.

Length, Extent and Direction

The anal canal is 3.8 cm long. It extends from the anorectal junction to the anus. It is directed downwards and backwards. The anal canal is surrounded by inner involuntary and outer voluntary sphincters which keep the lumen closed in the form of an anteroposterior slit.

The *anorectal junction* is marked by the forward convexity of the perineal flexure of the rectum (Fig. 33.2) and lies 2–3 cm in front of and slightly below the tip of the coccyx. Here the ampulla of the rectum suddenly narrows and pierces the pelvic diaphragm. In males it corresponds to the level of the apex of the prostate.

The *anus* is the surface opening of the anal canal, situated about 4 cm below and in front of the tip of the coccyx in the cleft between the two buttocks. The surrounding skin is pigmented and thrown into radiating folds, and contains a ring of large apocrine glands.

Relations of the Anal Canal

Anteriorly

  (a) In both sexes: perineal body.
  (b) In males: membranous urethra and bulb of penis.
  (c) In females: lower end of the vagina (Fig. 31.15).

Posteriorly

1. Anococcygeal ligament.
2. Tip of the coccyx (Fig. 28.6).

Laterally: Ischioanal fossae (Fig. 28.6).

All round: Anal canal is surrounded by the sphincter muscles, the tone of which keeps the canal closed.

Interior of the Anal Canal

The interior of the anal canal shows many important features and can be divided into three parts: the upper part, about 15 mm long; the middle part, about 15 mm long; and the lower part about 8 mm long. Each part is lined by a characteristic epithelium and reacts differently to various diseases of this region (Fig. 33.6).

Upper Mucous Part

1. This part is about 15 mm long. It is lined by mucous membrane, and is of endodermal origin.
2. The mucous membrane shows:
    (a) 6 to 10 vertical folds; these folds are called the *anal columns* of Morgagni.

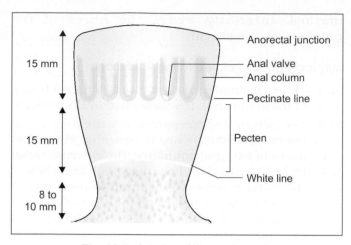

Fig. 33.6: Interior of the anal canal.

(b) The lower ends of the anal columns are united to each other by short transverse folds of mucous membrane; these folds are called the *anal valves*.

(c) Above each valve there is a depression in the mucosa which is called the *anal sinus*.

(d) The anal valves together form a transverse line that runs all round the anal canal. This is the *pectinate line*. It is situated opposite the middle of internal anal sphincter, the junction of ectodermal and endodermal parts. Occasionally the anal valves show epithelial projections called *anal papillae*. These papillae are remnants of the embryonic anal membrane.

Middle Part or Transitional Zone or Pecten

1. The next 15 mm or so of the anal canal is also lined by mucous membrane, but anal columns are not present here. The mucosa has a bluish appearance because of a dense venous plexus that lies between it and the muscle coat. The mucosa is less mobile than in the upper part of the anal canal. This region is referred to as the *pecten* or *transitional zone*. The lower limit of the pecten often has a whitish appearance because of which it is referred to as the *white line of Hilton*. Hilton's line is situated at the level of the interval between the subcutaneous part of external anal sphincter and the lower border of internal anal sphincter.

2. It marks the lower limit of pecten or stratified squamous epithelium which is thin, pale and glossy and is devoid of sweat glands.

Lower Cutaneous Part

It is about 8 mm long and is lined by true skin containing sweat and sebaceous glands. The epithelium of the lower part resembles that of true skin in which sebaceous and sweat glands are present.

Musculature of the Anal Canal

Anal Sphincters

The *internal anal sphincter* is involuntary in nature. It is formed by the thickened circular muscle coat of this part of the gut. It surrounds the upper three-fourths, i.e. 30 mm of the anal canal extending from the upper end of the canal to the white line of Hilton.

The *external anal sphincter* is under voluntary control. It is made up of a striated muscle and is supplied by the inferior rectal nerve and the perineal branch of the fourth sacral nerve. It surrounds the whole length of the anal canal and has three parts, subcutaneous, superficial and deep.

Contrary to earlier view, the external anal sphincter forms a single functional and anatomic entity. Uppermost fibres blend with fibres of puborectalis. Anteriorly some fibres decussate with superficial transverse perinei muscle and posterior fibres get attached to anococcygeal raphe (Fig. 33.7).

Middle fibres surround lower part of internal anal sphincter. These are attached to perineal body anteriorly and to coccyx via anococcygeal ligament posteriorly. Some fibres of each side decussate to form a commissure in the midline.

Lower fibres lie below the level of internal anal sphincter and are separated from anal epithelium by submucosa.

In males transverse perinei and bulbospongiosus end in central point of perineum, so that there is a surgical plane of cleavage between urogenital triangle and anal canal.

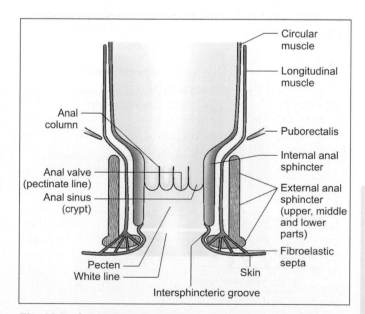

Fig. 33.7: Coronal section through the wall of the anal canal.

In females, the puborectalis is separate from external anal sphincter. Its anterior portion is thinner and shorter.

In addition, in females, transverse perinei and bulbospongiosus fuse with external anal sphincter in lower part of perineum.

Conjoint Longitudinal Coat

It is formed by fusion of the puborectalis with the longitudinal muscle coat of the rectum at the anorectal junction. It lies between the external and internal sphincters. When traced downwards it becomes fibroelastic and at the level of the white line it breaks up into a number of fibroelastic septa which spread out fan wise, pierce the subcutaneous part of the external sphincter, and are attached to the skin around the anus. The most lateral of these septa forms the perianal fascia. The most medial septum forms, the *anal intermuscular septum*, which is attached to the white line. In addition, some strands pass obliquely through the internal sphincter and end in the submucosa below the anal valves (Fig. 33.8).

Anorectal Ring

This is a muscular ring present at the anorectal junction. It is formed by the fusion of the puborectalis, uppermost fibres of external sphincter and the internal sphincter. It is easily felt by a finger in the anal canal. Surgical division of this ring results in rectal incontinence. The ring is less marked anteriorly where the fibres of the puborectalis are absent.

Surgical Spaces Related to the Anal Canal

1. The *ischioanal space* or fossa lies on each side of the anal canal. It is described in Chapter 28.
2. The *perianal space* surrounds the anal canal below the white line. It contains the lower fibres of external sphincter, the external rectal venous plexus, and the terminal branches of the inferior rectal vessels and nerves. Pus in this space tends to spread to the anal canal at the white line or to the surface of the perineal skin rather than to the ischioanal space.
3. The *submucous space* of the canal lies above the white line between the mucous membrane and the internal sphincter. It contains the internal rectal venous plexus and lymphatics.

Arterial Supply

1. The part of the anal canal above the pectinate line is supplied by the superior rectal artery.
2. The part below the pectinate line is supplied by the inferior rectal artery.

Venous Drainage

1. The *internal rectal venous plexus* or haemorrhoidal plexus lies in the submucosa of the anal canal. It drains mainly into the superior rectal vein, but communicates freely with the external plexus and thus with the middle and inferior rectal veins. The internal plexus is, therefore, an important site of communication between the portal and systemic veins. The internal plexus is in the form of a series of dilated pouches connected by transverse branches around the anal canal.

   Veins present in the three anal columns situated at 3, 7 and 11 O'clock positions as seen in the lithotomy position are large and constitute potential sites for the formation of primary internal piles (Fig. 33.9).
2. The *external rectal venous plexus* lies outside the muscular coat of the rectum and anal canal, and communicates freely with the internal plexus. The lower part of the external plexus is drained by the inferior rectal vein into the internal pudendal vein; the middle part by the middle rectal vein into the internal iliac vein; and the upper part by the superior rectal vein which continues as the inferior mesenteric vein.
3. The *anal veins* are arranged radially around the anal margin. They communicate with the

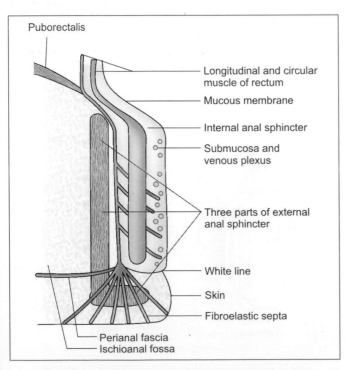

Puborectalis

— Longitudinal and circular muscle of rectum

— Mucous membrane

— Internal anal sphincter

— Submucosa and venous plexus

— Three parts of external anal sphincter

— White line

— Skin

— Fibroelastic septa

— Perianal fascia
— Ischioanal fossa

Fig. 33.8: Coronal section through the anal canal.

internal rectal plexus and with the inferior rectal veins. Excessive straining during the defaecation may rupture one of these veins, forming a subcutaneous perianal haematoma known as external piles.

Lymphatic Drainage

Lymph vessels from the part above the pectinate line, drain with those of the rectum into the internal iliac nodes.

Vessels from the part below the pectinate line drain into the medial group of the superficial inguinal nodes.

Nerve Supply

1. *Above the pectinate line*, the anal canal is supplied by autonomic nerves, both sympathetic (inferior hypogastric plexus; L1, L2) and parasympathetic (pelvic splanchnic, S2, S3, S4). Pain sensations are carried by both of them.
2. *Below the pectinate line*, it is supplied by somatic (inferior rectal, S2, S3, S4) nerves.
3. *Sphincters:* The internal sphincter is caused to contract by sympathetic nerves and is relaxed by parasympathetic nerves. The external sphincter is supplied by the inferior rectal nerve and by the perineal branch of the fourth sacral nerve.

Histology

Rectum: The mucous membrane of rectum has many large folds. The epithelium and crypts contain abundant goblet cells. Submucosa contains plexus of nerves and capillaries. Muscularis externa is of uniform thickness. Serosa is seen in upper part and adventitia in lower part.

Anal canal: The epithelium lining of upper 15 mm is simple or stratified columnar; while that of middle 15 mm is stratified squamous without any sweat gland or sebaceous gland or hair follicle. The epithelium of lowest 8 mm resembles that of true skin with sweat and sebaceous glands and hair follicles.

The thick inner circular layer covers the upper three-fourths of anal canal to form the internal anal sphincter. The outer longitudinal layer is a thin layer. Outside these smooth muscle layers is the striated external anal sphincter.

Development

Rectum

The distal part of hindgut known as cloaca is divided by urorectal septum into primitive anorectal canal posteriorly and vesicourethral canal anteriorly. Primitive anorectal canal forms the lower part of rectum and proximal part of anal canal. Its distal part of anal canal is formed by the proctodeum.

Upper part of rectum, i.e. part above the middle fold of rectum, develops from endoderm of hindgut. This part is related to peritoneum. Lower part, below the middle fold, is formed from the dorsal part of the cloaca. It is devoid of peritoneum.

Anal Canal

Upper 15 mm develops from the primitive anorectal canal. Lower part below the pectinate line (lower 15 + 8 mm) is formed from ectodermal invagination, i.e. proctodeum. Non-continuity of the two parts results in imperforate anus.

CLINICAL ANATOMY

- Digital per rectum (PR) examination: In PR examination the finger enters anal canal before reaching lower end of rectum (Fig. 33.9).

  In a normal person, the following structures can be palpated by a finger passed per rectum.

  In males (Fig. 33.10):
  1. Posterior surface of prostate.
  2. Seminal vesicles.
  3. Vasa deferentia.

  In females (Fig. 33.11):
  1. Perineal body.
  2. Cervix.
  3. Occasionally the ovaries.

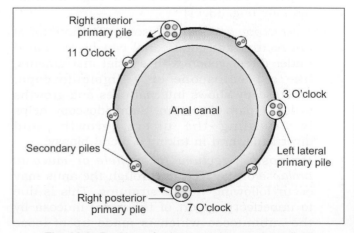

Fig. 33.9: Position of primary and secondary piles.

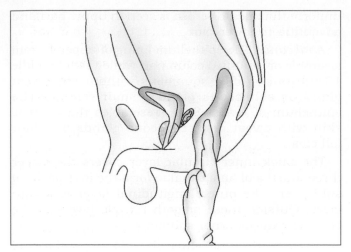

Fig. 33.10: Digital per rectum examination in male.

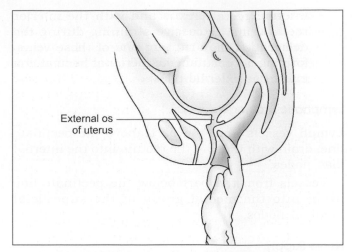

Fig. 33.11: Digital per rectum examination in female.

In both sexes:

1. Anorectal ring.
2. Coccyx and sacrum.
3. Ischioanal fossae and ischial spines.

In patients, a PR examination can help in the palpation of following abnormalities.

(a) Within the lumen: Faecal impaction and foreign bodies.

(b) In the rectal wall: Rectal growths and strictures, and thrombosed piles.

(c) Outside the rectal wall: In males, the enlargements of prostate, seminal vesicles and bulbourethral glands, and stone in membranous urethra; in females, enlargements of uterus, tubes and ovaries, and abnormalities in the pouch of Douglas; and in both sexes, the distended bladder, lower ureteric stones, and tumours of the bony pelvis.

During parturition the dilatation of cervix is commonly assessed through the rectal wall to avoid infection by repeated vaginal examinations (Fig. 33.11).

- *Proctoscopy and sigmoidoscopy:* The interior of the rectum and anal canal can be examined under direct vision with special instruments, like a proctoscope or a sigmoidoscope. Proctoscopy shows internal piles and growths in lower part of rectum. Sigmoidoscopy helps in revealing the ulcers, growths and diverticula, and in taking a rectal biopsy.

- *Prolapse of rectum: Incomplete* or *mucosal prolapse* of the rectum through the anus may occur following violent straining. This is due to imperfect support of the rectal mucosa by the submucosa which is made up of loose areolar tissue.

Complete prolapse or *procidentia* is the condition in which the whole thickness of the rectal wall protrudes through the anus. The contributory factors in its causation are:

(a) Laxity of the pelvic floor.

(b) Excessively deep rectovesical or rectouterine pouch.

(c) Inadequate fixation of the rectum in its presacral bed.

- *Neurological disturbances of the rectum:* In spite of the identical innervation of the rectum and bladder, the rectal involvement in nervous lesions is less severe than that of the bladder. After sacral denervation of the rectum the peripheral nervous plexus controls the automatic evacuation of the rectum. This reflex activity is more massive and complete when sacral innervation is intact, e.g. complete cord lesion above the sacral region. However, due to weak musculature of the rectum and sparing of the tone of the external sphincter by transverse lesions of the cord, rectal disturbances tend to cause constipation, although complete lesions may cause reflex defaecation.

- *Carcinoma of rectum:* It is quite common, and is generally situated at the rectosigmoid junction (constricting type), or in the ampulla (proliferating type). It causes bleeding per rectum from an indurated raised ulcer. The condition is surgically treated by an abdominoperineal excision in which the anus, anal canal and rectum with their fascial sheaths, and a varying amount of distal colon along with its mesentery containing the lymph nodes are removed en bloc, and a permanent colostomy in the left iliac fossa is done with the proximal cut end of the colon.

- *Piles/haemorrhoids: Internal piles* or true piles are saccular dilatations of the internal rectal venous plexus. They occur above the pectinate line and are, therefore, painless. They bleed profusely during straining at stool. The *primary piles* occur in 3, 7 and 11 O'clock positions of the anal wall when viewed in the lithotomy position. They are formed by enlargement of the three main radicles of the superior rectal vein which lie in the anal columns, which occupy the left lateral, right posterior, and right anterior positions (Fig. 33.9). Varicosities in other positions of the lumen are called *secondary piles*. The various *factors* responsible for causing of internal piles are:

(a) Poor support to veins from the surrounding loose connective tissue, so that the veins are less capable of resisting increased blood pressure;

(b) Absence of valves in the superior rectal and portal veins;

(c) Compression of the veins at the sites where they pierce the muscular coat of the rectum; and

(d) Direct transmission of the increased portal pressure at the portosystemic communications. For these reasons the development of piles is favoured by constipation, prolonged standing, excessive straining at stool, and portal hypertension.

External piles or false piles occur below the pectinate line and are, therefore, very painful. They do not bleed on straining at stool.

- *Fissure in ano:* Anal fissure is caused by the rupture of one of the anal valves, usually by the passage of dry hard stool in a constipated person. Each valve is lined with mucous membrane above, and with skin below. Because of the involvement of skin the condition is extremely painful and is associated with marked spasm of the anal sphincters.

- *Fistula in ano:* A fistula is an abnormal epithelialised track connecting two cavities, or one cavity with the exterior (Fig. 28.24).

  Fistula in ano is caused by spontaneous rupture of an abscess around the anus or may follow surgical drainage of the abscess. Most of these abscesses are formed by the small vestigial glands opening into the anal sinuses. Such an anorectal abscess tends to track in various directions and may open medially into the anal sinus, laterally into the ischioanal fossa, inferiorly at the surface, and superiorly into the rectum. A fistula can also be caused by an ischioanal or a pelvirectal abscess. The fistula is said to be complete when it opens both internally into the lumen of the gut and externally at the surface.

- *Rectal continence:* Rectal continence depends solely on the anorectal ring. Damage to the ring results in rectal incontinence. The surgeon has to carefully protect the anorectal ring in operating on the region.

- More severe malformations of the anorectal region include the following.

  (a) Anal stenosis.

  (b) Anal agenesis with or without a fistula.

  (c) Anorectal agenesis with or without a fistula. Most of the anorectal malformations are caused by abnormal partitioning of the cloaca by the urorectal septum.

Walls of Pelvis

All the pelvic viscera, i.e. terminal parts of digestive and urinary system; and components of genital system are located in the pelvis. These organs are provided due protection and nutrition by the bones, muscles, fascia, blood vessels, lymphatics and nerves of the pelvis. The posterior superior iliac spine seen as a dimple (mostly covered) lies opposite the middle of the sacroiliac joint.

Contents: In this chapter the vessels, nerves, muscles, fascia, and joints of the pelvis will be considered.

VESSELS OF THE PELVIS

INTERNAL ILIAC ARTERY

The internal iliac artery is the smaller terminal branch of the common iliac artery. It is 3.75 cm long. It supplies:

1. Pelvic organs except those supplied by the superior rectal, ovarian and median sacral arteries.
2. Perineum.
3. Greater part of the gluteal region.
4. Iliac fossa.

In the foetus, internal iliac artery is double the size of the external iliac artery because it transmits blood to the placenta through the umbilical artery. The umbilical artery with the internal iliac then forms the direct continuation of the common iliac artery. After birth the proximal part of umbilical artery persists to form the first part of superior vesical artery, and the rest of it degenerates into a fibrous cord, the medial umbilical ligament.

Course and Relations

The internal iliac artery begins in front of the sacroiliac joint, at the level of the intervertebral disc between the fifth lumbar vertebra and the sacrum.

DISSECTION

Remove the viscera from the pelvic wall and the pelvic cavity. Trace the internal iliac artery and its two divisions. Follow the branches of each of its divisions to the position of the viscera and the parieties. Remove the veins and venous plexuses as these obstruct the view of the arteries. Clean the hypogastric plexus.

Here it lies medial to the psoas major muscle. The artery runs downwards and backwards, and ends near the upper margin of the greater sciatic notch, by dividing into anterior and posterior divisions or trunks (Fig. 34.1).

The artery is related: A*nteriorly* to the ureter, and in females to the ovary and the lateral end of the uterine tube; *posteriorly* to the internal iliac vein, the lumbosacral trunk and the sacroiliac joint; *laterally* to the external iliac vein and to the obturator nerve; and *medially* to the peritoneum and to a few tributaries of the internal iliac vein.

Branches

Branches of Anterior Division

In the male, it gives off six branches.

1. Superior vesical.
2. Obturator.
3. Middle rectal.
4. Inferior vesical.
5. Inferior gluteal.
6. Internal pudendal. The last two are the terminal branches.

In the female, it gives off seven branches. The inferior vesical artery is replaced by the vaginal artery. The uterine artery is the seventh branch.

Branches of Posterior Division

It gives off:

1. Iliolumbar.

419

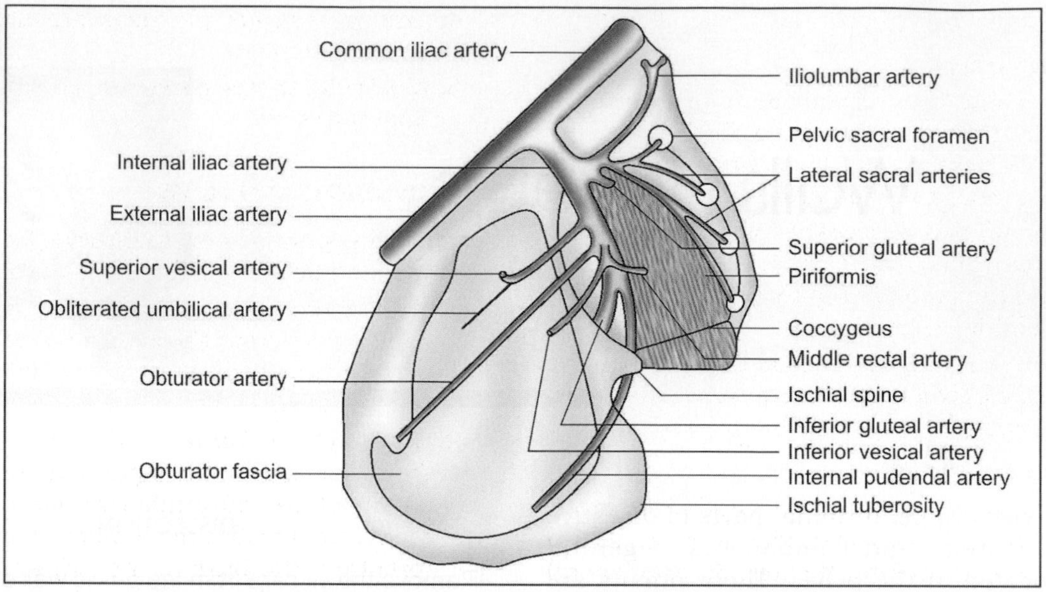

Fig. 34.1: Branches of the right internal iliac artery in a male.

2. Two lateral sacral.

3. Superior gluteal arteries.

Branches of Anterior Division

1. Superior vesical artery

The proximal 2.5 cm or so of the superior vesical artery represents the persistent part of the umbilical artery. It supplies many branches to the upper part of the urinary bladder. One of these branches gives off the artery to the ductus deferens.

2. Obturator artery

It runs forwards and downwards on the obturator fascia below the obturator nerve and above the obturator vein (NAV). Medially, it is crossed by the ureter and the ductus deferens, and is covered with peritoneum. It passes through the obturator foramen to leave the pelvis and enter the thigh. In the pelvis it gives off :

(a) Iliac branches to the iliac fossa.

(b) A vesical branch to the urinary bladder.

(c) A pubic branch to the peritoneum on the back of the pubis, which anastomoses with the pubic branch of the inferior epigastric artery and with its fellow of the opposite side.

3. Middle rectal artery

It is characterized by three features.

(a) It is often absent, especially in females.

(b) Very little of its blood goes to the rectum, and that too goes only to its muscle coats.

(c) Most of its blood goes to the prostate and seminal vesicles.

4. Inferior vesical artery

It supplies the trigone of the bladder, the prostate, the seminal vesicles, and the lower part of the ureter.

5. Inferior gluteal artery

It is the largest branch of the anterior division of the internal iliac artery. It is the axial artery of the lower limb. It supplies chiefly the buttock and the back of the thigh. In the pelvis, it runs downwards in front of the sacral plexus and piriformis. Next, it pierces the parietal pelvic fascia, passes below the first sacral nerve and then between the piriformis and the coccygeus, and enters the gluteal region through the lower part of the greater sciatic foramen. In the pelvis, it supplies:

(a) Muscular branches to nearby muscles.

(b) Vesical branches to the base of the bladder, the seminal vesicles and the prostate.

6. Internal pudendal artery

It is the smaller terminal branch of the anterior division of the internal iliac artery. It supplies the perineum and external genitalia. Its branches are inferior rectal, perineal, artery to bulb, urethra, deep and dorsal arteries. It is described in Chapter 28.

7. Vaginal artery

It corresponds to the inferior vesical artery of the male, and supplies the vagina, the bulb of the vestibule, the base of the urinary bladder, and the adjacent part of the rectum.

8. Uterine artery

It has a tortuous course. Crosses the ureter 2 cm lateral to cervix. Runs along side of uterus. Supplies vagina, cervix uterus, fallopian tube.

Branches of Posterior Division

1. Iliolumbar artery

It runs upwards in front of the sacroiliac joint and lumbosacral trunk, and behind the obturator nerve and external iliac vessels (Fig. 15.6). Behind the psoas major, it divides into the lumbar and iliac branches.

The *lumbar branch* represents the fifth lumbar artery, and supplies the psoas, the quadratus lumborum and the erector spinae. Its spinal branch supplies the cauda equina.

The *iliac branch* supplies the iliac fossa and the iliacus. It participates in the anastomoses around the anterior superior iliac spine.

2. Lateral sacral arteries

These are usually two in number, upper and lower. They run downwards and medially over the sacral nerves. Their branches enter the four anterior sacral foramina to supply the contents of the sacral canal. Their terminations pass out through the posterior sacral foramina and supply the muscles and skin on the back of the sacrum.

3. Superior gluteal artery

It runs backwards, pierces the pelvic fascia, passes above the first sacral nerve, and leaves the pelvis through the greater sciatic foramen above the piriformis. It supplies gluteus maximus muscle. Also takes part in anastomoses around anterior superior iliac spine and in trochanteric anastomoses to supply nearby muscles and overlying skin. For further course see Chapter 5.

INTERNAL ILIAC VEIN

It ascends posteromedial to the internal iliac artery, and joins the external iliac vein to form the common iliac vein at the pelvic brim, in front of the lower part of the sacroiliac joint. Its tributaries correspond with the branches of the artery, except for the iliolumbar vein which joins the common iliac vein. The tributaries are as follows.

Veins arising in and outside the pelvic Wall

1. Superior gluteal is the largest tributary,
2. Inferior gluteal,
3. Internal pudendal,
4. Obturator, and
5. Lateral sacral veins.

   Veins arising from the plexuses of pelvic viscera:

1. Rectal venous plexus is drained by the superior, middle and inferior rectal veins.
2. Prostatic venous plexus is drained into the vesical and internal iliac veins.
3. Vesical venous plexus is drained by the vesical veins.
4. Uterine venous plexuses are drained by the uterine veins.
5. Vaginal venous plexuses are drained by the vaginal veins.

LYMPH NODES OF THE PELVIS

The pelvic lymphatics drain into the following lymph nodes, which lie along the vessels of the same name.

1. The *common iliac nodes* 4 to 6 receive lymphatics from the external and internal iliac nodes, and send their efferents to the lateral aortic nodes.
2. The *external iliac nodes* 8 to 10 receive lymphatics from the inguinal nodes, the deeper layers of the infraumbilical part of the anterior abdominal wall, the membranous urethra, the prostate, the base of the urinary bladder, the uterine cervix, and part of the vagina. Their efferents pass to the common iliac nodes. The *inferior epigastric* and *circumflex iliac nodes* are outlying members of this group.
3. The *internal iliac nodes* receive lymphatics from all the pelvic viscera, the deeper parts of the perineum, and muscles of the buttocks and of the back of the thigh. Their efferents pass to the common iliac nodes. The sacral and obturator nodes are outlying members of this group.

NERVES OF THE PELVIS

The nerves of the pelvis include:

1. Lumbosacral plexus,
2. Coccygeal plexus, and
3. Pelvic splanchnic nerves.

LUMBOSACRAL PLEXUS

Formation

The lumbosacral plexus is formed by the lumbosacral trunk and the ventral rami of the first to third sacral nerves, and part of the fourth sacral nerve (Figs 7.4 and 34.2).

The *lumbosacral trunk* is formed by the descending branch of the ventral ramus of nerve L4 and the whole of L5. The trunk descends over the ala of the sacrum, crosses the pelvic brim in front of the sacroiliac joint, and joins nerve S1.

Nerves S1 and S2 are large. The other sacral nerves become progressively smaller in size.

Relations

1. The lumbosacral trunk and ramus S1 are separated from each other by the superior

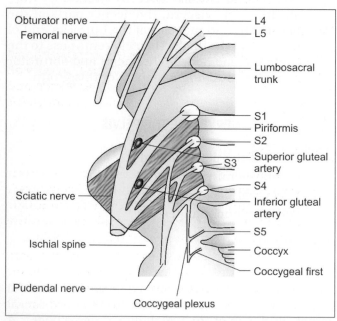

Fig. 34.2: Anterior view of the right sacral and coccygeal plexuses.

gluteal vessels. Both lie in front of the sacroiliac joint before passing on to the surface of the piriformis. Thus both may be involved in pathological conditions of the joint.

2. Ramus S1 is separated from ramus S2 by the inferior gluteal vessels.

3. Rami S2, S3 and a part of S4 lie between the anterior surface of the piriformis and the pelvic fascia.

4. The main plexus lies in front of the piriformis deep to the pelvic fascia, and behind the internal iliac vessels and the ureter (Fig. 34.4).

Layout of Connections and Branches

1. Each ventral ramus receives a *grey ramus communicans* from the sympathetic chain at the anterior sacral foramen.

2. Before uniting to form the plexus, the ventral rami give off:

    (a) Twigs to the piriformis (S1, S2).

    (b) Twigs to the levator ani, the coccygeus and the sphincter ani externus (S4).

    (c) Pelvic splanchnic nerves (S2, S3, S4).

3. The plexus gives rise to two main branches namely, the sciatic and pudendal nerves, concerned respectively with locomotion and reproduction.

4. As in other plexuses, the rami tend to divide into ventral and dorsal divisions which supply the corresponding aspects of the lower limb and trunk. In general, the *dorsal divisions* supply the extensors and the abductors, and the *ventral divisions* supply the flexors and the adductors, of the limb.

Branches

Branches derived from both dorsal and ventral divisions are as follows.

1. *Sciatic nerve:* The common peroneal nerve component arises from dorsal divisions of L4, L5, S1, S2. It supplies evertors of foot and dorsiflexors of ankle joint. The tibial nerve component arises from ventral divisions of L4, L5, S1, S2, S3. It supplies the hamstring muscles, all muscles of calf and intrinsic muscles of the sole. This nerve is described in Chapter 7.

2. *Posterior cutaneous nerve of thigh:* Dorsal divisions of S1, S2 and ventral divisions of S2, S3 (Chapter 7).

Branches from Dorsal Divisions

1. Superior gluteal nerve: L4, L5, S1 (Chapter 7).

2. Inferior gluteal nerve: L5, S1, S2 (Chapter 7).

3. Nerve to piriformis: S1, S2.

4. Perforating cutaneous nerve: S2, S3.

Branches from Ventral Division

1. Nerve to quadratus femoris: L4, L5, S1.

2. Nerve to obturator internus: L5, S1, S2.

3. Pudendal nerve: S2, S3, S4. Supplies sphincter ani externus and all muscles in urogenital triangle.

4. Muscular branches to the levator ani, the coccygeus and the sphincter ani externus, including perineal branch of nerve S4.
5. Pelvic splanchnic nerves: S2, S3, S4.

Muscular Branches

Nerves to the levator ani or iliococcygeus part and the coccygeus or ischiococcygeus arise from nerve S4 and enter their pelvic surfaces. The nerve to the middle part of the sphincter ani externus is called the *perineal branch of the fourth sacral nerve*. It runs forwards on the coccygeus and reaches the ischioanal fossa by passing between the coccygeus and the levator ani. In addition to the lower end of external sphincter, it supplies the skin between the anus and the coccyx.

COCCYGEAL PLEXUS

1. It is formed by the ventral rami of spinal nerves S4 (descending branch), S5 and the coccygeal nerve (Fig. 34.2).
2. The three nerves join on the pelvic surface of the coccygeus to form a small plexus known as the coccygeal plexus.
3. The plexus gives off the anococcygeal nerves, which pierce the sacrotuberous ligament and supply the skin in the region of the coccyx.

PELVIC AUTONOMIC NERVES

Pelvic Sympathetic System

The pelvic part of the sympathetic chain runs downwards and slightly medially over the body of sacrum, and then along the medial margins of the anterior sacral foramina. The two chains unite in front of the coccyx to form a small *ganglion impar*. The chain bears four sacral ganglia on each side and the single ganglion impar in the central part.

The *branches* of the chain are:
1. Grey rami communicans to all sacral and coccygeal ventral rami.
2. Branches to the inferior hypogastric plexus from the upper ganglia.
3. Branches to the median sacral artery from the lower ganglia.
4. Branches to the rectum from the lower ganglia.
5. Branches to the glomus coccygeum (Chapter 27) from the ganglion impar.

The *inferior hypogastric plexus* (Chapter 27) one on each side of the rectum and other pelvic viscera is formed by the corresponding hypogastric nerve from the superior hypogastric plexus; branches from the upper ganglia of the sacral sympathetic chain; and the pelvic splanchnic nerves. Branches of the plexus accompany the visceral branches of the internal iliac artery; and are named:
1. Rectal plexus,
2. Vesical plexus,
3. Prostatic plexus, and
4. Uterovaginal plexus.

Pelvic Splanchnic Nerves

Nervi Erigentes

The nervi erigentes represent the sacral outflow of the parasympathetic nervous system. The nerves arise as fine filaments from the ventral rami of S2, S3 and S4. They join the inferior hypogastric plexus and are distributed to the pelvic organs. Some parasympathetic fibres ascend with the hypogastric nerve to the superior hypogastric plexus and thence to the inferior mesenteric plexus. Others ascend independently and directly to the part of the colon derived from the hindgut.

PELVIC FASCIA AND MUSCLES

PELVIC FASCIA

The pelvic fascia is distributed in the extraperitoneal space of the pelvis. It covers the lateral pelvic wall and the pelvic floor called *parietal pelvic fascia*; and also surrounds the pelvic viscera called *visceral pelvic fascia*.

Principles Governing its Distribution

1. The fascia is dense and membranous over nonexpansile structures, e.g. lateral pelvic wall, but is only loosely arranged over expansile structures, e.g. viscera, and over mobile structures, e.g. the pelvic floor (Fig. 34.3).
2. As a rule the fascia does not extend over bare bones; at the margins of the muscles it fuses with the periosteum. In this respect, the fascia of Waldeyer is an exception, which extends from the sacrum to the ampulla of rectum.

Parietal Fascia of the Lateral Pelvic Wall

1. The fascia covering the muscles of the lateral pelvic wall is condensed to form thick and strong membranes. It is closely adherent to the walls of the pelvic cavity. It is attached along a line from iliopectineal line to the inferior border of pubic bone.
2. The fascia covering the obturator internus is called the *obturator fascia*. It shows a linear thickening or tendinous arch for the origin of the levator ani. Below this origin it is closely

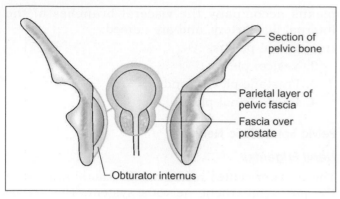

Fig. 34.3: Pelvic fascia.

related to the lunate fascia and to the pudendal canal.

3. The *fascia covering the piriformis* is thin. The nerves over the piriformis, i.e. the sacral plexuses lie external to the pelvic fascia and, therefore, do not pierce the fascia while passing out of the pelvis. The gluteal vessels, on the other hand, lie internal to the pelvic fascia and, therefore, have to pierce the fascia while passing out of the pelvis (Fig. 34.4).

Parietal Fascia of the Pelvic Floor

1. The pelvic fascia covers both the surfaces of the pelvic diaphragm, forming the superior and inferior layers. The inferior fascia is also known as the anal fascia.

2. In general, the fascia of the pelvic floor is loosely arranged between the peritoneum and the pelvic floor, forming a dead space for distension of the bladder, the rectum, the uterus and the vagina. Because of the loose nature of the fascia infections can spread rapidly within it.

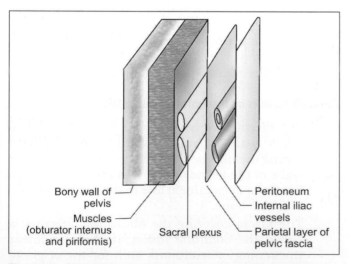

Fig. 34.4: Arrangement of structures on the walls of true pelvis.

3. However, the fascia is condensed at places to form fibromuscular ligaments which support the pelvic viscera. The various ligaments are dealt with individual viscera including the prostate, bladder, uterus and the rectum.

Visceral Pelvic Fascia

This fascia surrounds the extraperitoneal parts of the pelvic viscera. It is loose and cellular around distensible organs like bladder, rectum and vagina, but is dense around non-distensible organs, like the prostate. The visceral layer is attached along a line extending from the middle of back of pubis to the ischial spine.

PELVIC MUSCLES

The pelvic muscles include two groups.

1. Piriformis and obturator internus, which are short lateral rotators of the hip joint and are described with the muscles of the lower limb.

2. Levator ani and coccygeus, which with the corresponding muscles of the opposite side, form the pelvic diaphragm. The diaphragm separates the pelvis from the perineum (Fig. 34.5).

The levator ani and coccygeus may be regarded as one morphological entity, divisible from before backwards into the pubococcygeus, the iliococcygeus

---

DISSECTION

Muscles of lesser pelvis

Identify the origin of piriformis from the ventral surface of the sacrum. Trace it through the greater sciatic foramen to its insertion into the upper border of greater trochanter of femur.

Feel the ischial spine and trace the fibres of coccygeus and levator ani that arise from it. Trace the origin of levator ani from thickened fascia, i.e. tendinous arch over the middle of obturator internus muscle till the back of body of the pubis.

Note that the right and left sheet like levator ani muscles are united and the muscles are inserted into central perineal tendon or perineal body, anal canal, anococcygeal ligament.

Detach the origin of levator ani from obturator fascia. While removing obturator fascia identify pudendal canal with its contents in the lower part of the fascia.

Trace the tendon of obturator internus muscle. This tendon along with superior and inferior gemelli muscles leaves through the lesser sciatic foramen to be inserted into the medial surface of greater trochanter of femur.

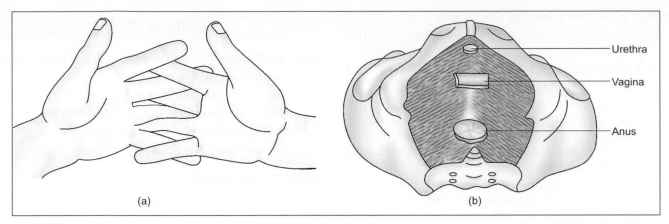

Fig. 34.5: (a) Interlocking hands represent the interlacing fibres of two levator ani muscles, (b) openings in the pelvic diaphragm (formed by the levator ani muscles).

and the ischiococcygeus or coccygeus. They have a continuous linear origin from the pelvic surface of the body of the pubis, the obturator fascia or white line or tendinous arch and the ischial spine. The muscle fibres slope downwards and backwards to the midline, making a gutter-shaped pelvic floor. These muscles are described below.

The Levator Ani

The muscle is divisible into a pubococcygeus part and an iliococcygeus part (Fig. 34.6).

Pubococcygeus Part

1. The anterior fibres of this part arise from the medial part of the pelvic surface of the body of the pubis. In the male these fibres closely surround the prostate and constitute the *levator prostatae*. In the female these fibres surround the vagina and form the *sphincter vaginae*. Both in the male and female the anterior fibres are inserted into the perineal body.
2. The middle fibres constitute the puborectalis. These arise from the lateral part of the pelvic surface of the body of the pubis. They partly form a loop or sling around the anorectal junction; and are partly continuous with the longitudinal muscle coat of the rectum.
3. The posterior fibres of the pubococcygeus arise from the anterior half of the white line on the obturator fascia. These get attached to anococcygeal ligament and tip of coccyx.

Iliococcygeus Part

The fibres of this part arise from:
(a) The posterior half of the white line on the obturator fascia.
(b) The pelvic surface of the ischial spine. They are inserted into the anococcygeal ligament

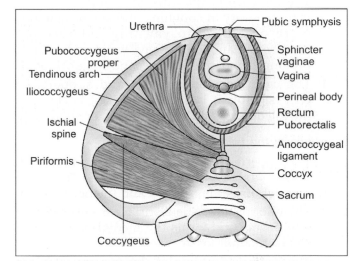

Fig. 34.6: The levator ani, the coccygeus and the piriformis in a female.

and into the side of the last two pieces of coccyx.

Coccygeus

This muscle represents the posterior or ischio-coccygeus part of the pelvic diaphragm. It is triangular in shape. It is partly muscular and partly tendinous.

Its fibres arise from:
(a) The pelvic surface of the ischial spine.
(b) The sacrospinous ligament. It is inserted into the side of the coccyx, and into the fifth sacral vertebra.

Nerve Supply

The levator ani is supplied by:
1. A branch from the fourth sacral nerve.
2. A branch either from the inferior rectal nerve.

The coccygeus is supplied by a branch derived from the fourth and fifth sacral nerves.

Actions of Levators Ani and Coccygeus

1. The levatores ani and coccygeus close the posterior part of the pelvic outlet.
2. The levators ani fix the perineal body and support the pelvic viscera.
3. During coughing, sneezing, lifting and other muscular efforts, the levators ani and coccygei counteract or resist increased intra-abdominal pressure and help to maintain continence of the bladder and the rectum.

   In micturition, defaecation and parturition, a particular pelvic outlet is open, but contraction of fibres around other openings resists increased intra-abdominal pressure and prevents any prolapse through the pelvic floor. The increase in the intra-abdominal pressure is momentary in coughing and sneezing and is more prolonged in yawning, micturition, defaecation and lifting heavy weights. It is most prolonged and intense in second stage of labour.
4. The coccygei pull forwards and support the coccyx, after it has been pressed backwards during defaecation or parturition or childbirth.

Relations of the Levator Ani

1. The superior or pelvic surface is covered with pelvic fascia which separates it from the bladder, prostate, rectum and the peritoneum.
2. The inferior or perineal surface is covered with anal fascia and forms the medial boundary of the ischioanal fossa.
3. The anterior borders of the two muscles are separated by a triangular space for the passage of the urethra and the vagina.
4. The posterior border is free and lies against the anterior margin of coccygeus (Fig. 34.6).

Morphology of Pelvic Diaphragm

1. In lower mammals, both the pubococcygeus and the iliococcygeus are inserted only into the coccygeal vertebrae and are responsible for movements of the tail. With the disappearance of the tail during evolution, the muscles have been modified to form the pelvic diaphragm which supports the viscera. Such support became necessary with the adoption of the erect posture by man.
2. In lower mammals, the levator ani arises from the pelvic brim. In man, the origin has shifted down to the side wall of the pelvis.
3. The coccygeus muscle corresponds exactly with the sacrospinous ligament, which is a degenerated part of the aponeurosis of this muscle. The two are inversely proportional in their development.

Parts included: The following parts are considered.
1. Lumbosacral joints,
2. Sacrococcygeal and intercoccygeal joints,
3. Sacroiliac joints with vertebropelvic ligaments,
4. Pubic symphysis; followed by
5. The mechanism of pelvis.

LUMBOSACRAL JOINTS

1. The joints and ligaments between the fifth lumbar vertebra and the base of the sacrum are similar to those between any two typical vertebrae. The lumbosacral disc is very thick, and is thickest anteriorly.
2. The stability of the fifth lumbar vertebra on the sacrum is further increased by:
   (a) The widely spaced articular processes.
   (b) Strong *iliolumbar ligament* which extends from the stout transverse process of the fifth lumbar vertebra to the iliac crest. The ligament fans out inferiorly to be attached to the lateral part of the ala of the sacrum as the lumbosacral ligament.
3. The body of the fifth lumbar vertebra makes an angle of about 120 degrees opens backwards with the sacrum. This is the lumbosacral or sacrovertebral angle, and opens backwards.
4. This region is subject to a number of variations which give rise to symptoms of backache. These are:
   (a) Sacralization of the fifth lumbar vertebra.
   (b) Lumbralization of the first sacral vertebra.
   (c) Spina bifida.
   (d) Spondylolisthesis, etc.

SACROCOCCYGEAL AND INTERCOCCYGEAL JOINTS

The *sacrococcygeal joint* is a secondary cartilaginous joint between the apex of the sacrum and the base of the coccyx. The bones are united by:

DISSECTION

Joints

Remove the remains of any muscle of the back or thoracolumbar fascia. Identify the iliolumbar and dorsal sacroiliac ligaments. Remove the dorsal sacroiliac ligament to identify the deeply placed interosseous sacroiliac ligaments. Divide this interosseous ligament and open the joint from the posterior aspect.

Define the attachments of ventral sacroiliac ligament. Cut through this thin ligament to open the sacroiliac joint.

(a) A thin intervertebral disc.

(b) Ventral sacrococcygeal ligament corresponding to the anterior longitudinal ligament.

(c) Deep dorsal sacrococcygeal ligament corresponding to the posterior longitudinal ligament.

(d) Superficial dorsal sacrococcygeal ligament, completing the lower part of the sacral canal.

(e) Lateral sacrococcygeal ligament corresponding to the intertransverse ligament and completing the foramen for the fifth sacral nerve.

(f) Intercornual ligament, connecting the cornua of the sacrum and the coccyx. In old age the joint is obliterated and the ligaments are ossified. Sometimes the joint is synovial, and the coccyx is freely mobile.

The *intercoccygeal joints* are present only in young subjects. Fusion of the segments begins at the age of 20 years and is complete by about 30 years.

SACROILIAC JOINT

Type

This is a synovial joint of the plane variety. The articular surfaces are flat in infants; but in adults show interlocking irregularities which discourage movements at this joint.

Articular Surface

The joint is formed between:

1. Auricular surface of the sacrum, which is covered with fibrocartilage.

2. Auricular surface of the ilium, which is covered with hyaline cartilage (Fig. 34.7).

Ligaments

1. The *fibrous capsule* is attached close to the margins of the articular surfaces. It is lined by synovial membrane (Fig. 34.8).

2. The *ventral sacroiliac ligament* is a thickening of the anterior and inferior parts of the fibrous capsule. Its lower part is attached to the preauricular sulcus.

3. The *interosseous sacroiliac ligament* is massive and very strong, forming the chief bond of union between the sacrum and the ilium. It connects the wide, rough areas adjoining the concave margins of the auricular surfaces, and is covered by the dorsal sacroiliac ligament.

4. The dorsal sacroiliac ligament covers the interosseous sacroiliac ligament, from which it is separated by the dorsal rami of the sacral spinal nerves and vessels. It consists of:

(a) Short transverse fibres or *short posterior sacroiliac ligament* passing from the ilium to the transverse tubercles of the first two sacral pieces.

(b) A long, more vertical, band or *long posterior sacroiliac ligament* passing from the posterior superior iliac spine to the transverse tubercles of the third and fourth sacral pieces; it is continuous laterally with medial edge of the sacrotuberous ligament.

5. The *vertebropelvic ligaments* include the iliolumbar, sacrotuberous and sacrospinous ligaments. These are accessory ligaments to the sacroiliac joint and are important in maintaining its stability.

(a) The *iliolumbar ligament* is a strong, triangular ligament, extending from the

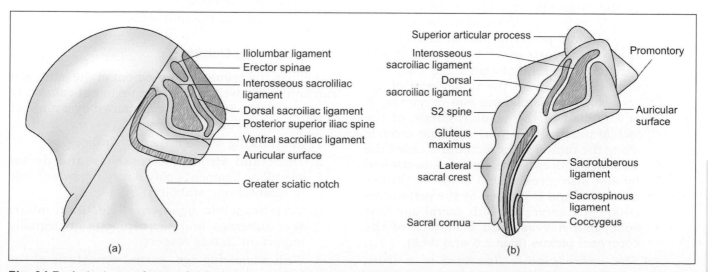

Fig. 34.7: Articular surfaces of the right sacroiliac joint. (a) Medial view of the upper part of the right hip bone, and (b) right lateral view of the sacrum.

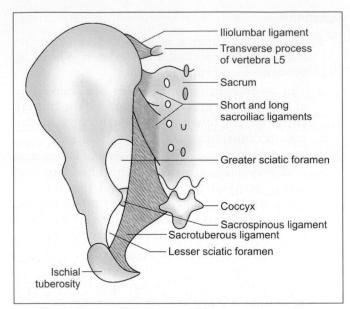

Fig. 34.8: Ligaments of the pelvis as seen from behind.

thick transverse process of the fifth lumbar vertebra to the posterior part of the inner lip of the iliac crest. It is continuous with the middle and anterior layers of the thoracolumbar fascia and gives partial origin to the quadratus lumborum. It is covered anteriorly by the psoas, and posteriorly by the erector spinae. It prevents anteroinferior slipping of the fifth lumbar vertebra under the influence of body weight, and also prevents forward movement at the sacroiliac joint (Fig. 34.7).

(b) The *sacrotuberous ligament* is a long and strong band which forms parts of the boundaries of the pelvic outlet and of the sciatic foramina. Its superomedial end or base is wide. It is attached to the posterior superior and posterior inferior iliac spines, the lower transverse tubercles of the sacrum, the lateral margin of the lower part of the sacrum and the upper part of the coccyx. The inferolateral end is narrow. It is attached to the medial margin of the ischial tuberosity. A part of it that extends along the ramus of the ischium is called the falciform process. The ligament is covered by and also gives partial origin to gluteus maximus, and is pierced by the perforating cutaneous nerve, the fifth sacral and first coccygeal nerves, and branches of the coccygeal plexus (Figs 2.6 and 34.8).

(c) The *sacrospinous ligament* is a thin, triangular ligament, which lies deep to sacrotuberous ligament, and separates the

greater and lesser sciatic foramina. Its base is attached to the lateral margins of the last piece of the sacrum and to the coccyx and its apex to the ischial spine. Its pelvic surface is covered by and also gives origin to the coccygeus. Morphologically, the ligament is a degenerated part of the coccygeus (Fig. 34.8).

The sacrotuberous and sacrospinous ligaments bind the sacrum to the ischium. They oppose upward tilting of the lower end of the sacrum and therefore, downward tilting of its upper end under body weight.

Relations

Posteriorly

1. Joint is covered by the erector spinae, the gluteus maximus and the sacrotuberous ligament.
2. Dimple overlying the posterior superior iliac spine lies opposite the middle of joint (Fig. 5.1).

Abdominal Surface

1. It is covered by the psoas and iliacus (Fig. 2.8).
2. Deep to the psoas, the joint is crossed by the iliolumbar vessels and the obturator nerve (Fig. 15.6).
3. Femoral nerve is separated from the joint by the iliacus muscle.

The *pelvic surface* is related to:

1. Lumbosacral trunk and the posterior division of the internal iliac artery.
2. Internal iliac vein and the anterior division of the internal iliac artery.
3. Superior gluteal vessels and the first sacral nerve (Fig. 34.2).
4. Upper part of the piriformis.

Factors providing Stability

Stability is the primary requirement of the joint as it transmits body weight from the vertebral column to the lower limbs. Stability is maintained by a number of factors which are as follows.

1. Interlocking of the articular surfaces.
2. Thick and strong interosseous and dorsal sacroiliac ligaments play a very important role in maintaining stability.
3. Vertebropelvic ligaments, i.e. iliolumbar, sacrotuberous and sacrospinous are equally important in this respect.
4. With advancing age, partial synostosis of the joint takes place which further reduces movements.

Blood Supply

Sacroiliac joint is supplied by twigs from all the three branches of posterior division of internal iliac artery, i.e. iliolumbar, lateral sacral and superior gluteal arteries.

Nerve Supply

The joint is supplied by the following nerves.
1. Superior gluteal.
2. Ventral rami and the lateral branches of dorsal rami of the first and second sacral nerves.

Movements

During flexion and extension of the trunk, stooping and straightening, i.e. the sacroiliac joint permits a small amount of *anteroposterior rotatory movement* around a transverse axis passing 5 to 10 cm vertically below the sacral promontory. This little movement serves the important function of *absorbing the shocks* of jumping and bearing of loads. The range of movement is increased temporarily in pregnancy in which all the ligaments of the pelvis become loose, under the influence of hormones, to facilitate delivery of the foetus.

PUBIC SYMPHYSIS

This is a secondary cartilaginous joint between the bodies of the right and left pubic bones. Each articular surface is covered with a thin layer of hyaline cartilage. The fibrocartilaginous disc is reinforced by surrounding ligamentous fibres. The fibres are thickest inferiorly where they form the *arcuate pubic ligament*. Anteriorly, the fibres form the *anterior pubic ligament*.

The pubic symphysis permits slight movement between the hip bones, which helps in absorbing

shocks. The range of movement is increased during pregnancy.

THE MECHANISM OF PELVIS

The most important mechanical function of the pelvis is to transmit the weight of trunk to the lower limb. The weight passes mainly through the alae of sacrum and through the thick part of hip bone lying between sacroiliac joint and acetabulum.

Theoretically, the weight falling on the lumbosacral joint is divided into two components.

(a) *One component of the force* is expanded in trying to drive the sacrum downwards and backwards between the iliac bones. This is resisted by the ligaments of pubic symphysis.

(b) *Second component of the force* tries to push the upper end of sacrum downwards and forwards towards the pelvic cavity. This is resisted by the middle segment of the sacroiliac joint, where the auricular surface of the sacrum is wider posteriorly, i.e. wedge-shaped and is concave for interlocking with the reciprocal surface of the ilium.

Because of the poor wedging and poor locking of the articular surfaces in the anterior and posterior segments of the sacroiliac joint, the sacrum is forced to rotate under the influence of body weight. In this rotation, the anterior segment is tilted downwards and the posterior segment upwards. The downward tilt of the anterior segment is prevented chiefly by the dorsal and interosseous sacroiliac ligaments; and the upward tilt of the posterior segment is prevented chiefly by the sacrotuberous and sacrospinous ligaments.

During all these movements the separation of iliac bones is resisted by sacroiliac and iliolumbar ligaments, and the ligaments of pubic symphysis.

CLINICAL ANATOMY

- The muscles of the pelvic floor may be injured during parturition. When the perineal body is torn, and has not been repaired satisfactorily, the contraction of anterior fibres of the levator ani increases the normal gap in the pelvic floor, instead of decreasing it. This results in abnormalities like cystocoele (Fig. 31.22a), or prolapse of the uterus (Fig. 29.14).
- The lumbosacral trunk (L4, L5) and the ventral ramus of nerve S1 cross the pelvic surface of the joint and may be involved in disease of the joint, causing pain in the area of their (Fig. 15.4)

distribution below the knee. L4 supplies medial aspect of leg and sole. S1 supplies lateral aspect of sole (Fig. 34.9).
- During pregnancy the pelvic joints and ligaments are relaxed, so that the range of movement is increased and locking mechanism becomes less efficient. This naturally puts greater strain on the ligaments. The *sacroiliac strain* thus produced may persist even after pregnancy.

After childbirth the ligaments are tightened up again, so that the locking mechanism returns to its original efficiency. Sometimes locking

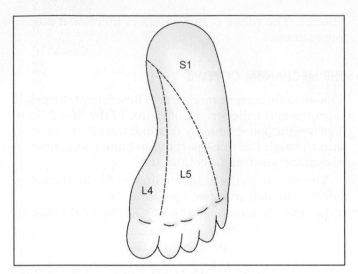

Fig. 34.9: Dermatomes of the sole.

occurs in the rotated position of the hip bones adopted during pregnancy. This results in *subluxation* of the joint, causing low backache due to strain on ligaments.

• The *diseases of the lumbosacral and sacroiliac joints can be differentiated* by the following tests.

(a) In lumbosacral lesions, the tenderness is present over the spines and above the dimple of posterior superior iliac spine (over the iliolumbar ligament); in sacroiliac lesions, the tenderness is located inferomedial to the dimple (over the posterior sacroiliac ligament) (Fig. 34.10).

(b) In lumbosacral disease, the movements of vertebral column are restricted in all directions; in sacroiliac disease, the movements are free, except for extreme forward bending, when the tension on hamstrings causes backward rotation of the hip bones, opposite to that of sacrum, producing pain in a diseased joint.

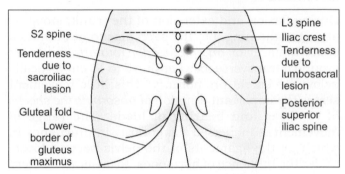

Fig. 34.10: Sites of tenderness in lumbosacral and sacroiliac lesions.

Surface Marking of Abdomen and Pelvis

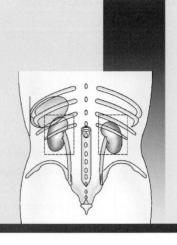

PLANES AND REGIONS OF THE ABDOMEN

Two horizontal (transpyloric and transtubercular) and two vertical (right and left lateral) planes divide the abdomen into nine regions (Fig. 35.1). These are described in Chapter 18.

SURFACE MARKING

Viscera

Spleen

(a) It is marked on the left side of the back, with its long axis corresponding with that of the 10th rib.

(b) The upper border corresponds to the upper border of the 9th rib, and the lower border to the lower border of the 11th rib (Fig. 35.2).

(c) The medial end lies 4 to 5 cm from the midline; and the lateral end on the midaxillary line.

Stomach

(a) *Cardiac orifice:* It is marked by two short parallel lines 2 cm apart, directed downwards and to the left on 7th costal cartilage, 2.5 cm to the left of median plane (Fig. 35.3).

(b) *Pyloric orifice:* It is marked by two short parallel lines 2 cm apart, directed upwards and to the right, on transpyloric plane, 1.2 cm to the right of the median plane.

(c) *Lesser curvature:* It is marked by joining the right margin of the cardiac orifice with upper margin of the pyloric orifice by a J-shaped curved line. The lowest point of this line reaches a little below the transpyloric plane.

(d) *Fundus:* This is marked by a line convex upwards drawn from the left margin of the cardiac orifice to highest point in the left 5th intercostal space just below the nipple.

(e) *Greater curvature:* This is marked by a curved line convex to the left and downwards, drawn from the fundus to the lower margin of the pyloric orifice. It cuts the left costal margin between the tips of the 9th and 10th costal cartilages and extends down to the subcostal plane, i.e. level of lumbar 3 vertebra.

Fig. 35.1: Surface marking of regions of the abdomen.

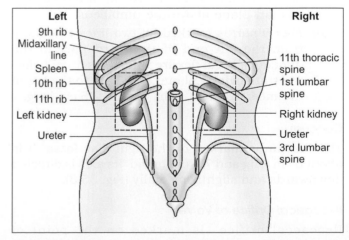

Fig. 35.2: Position of spleen, kidney and ureter from the posterior aspect.

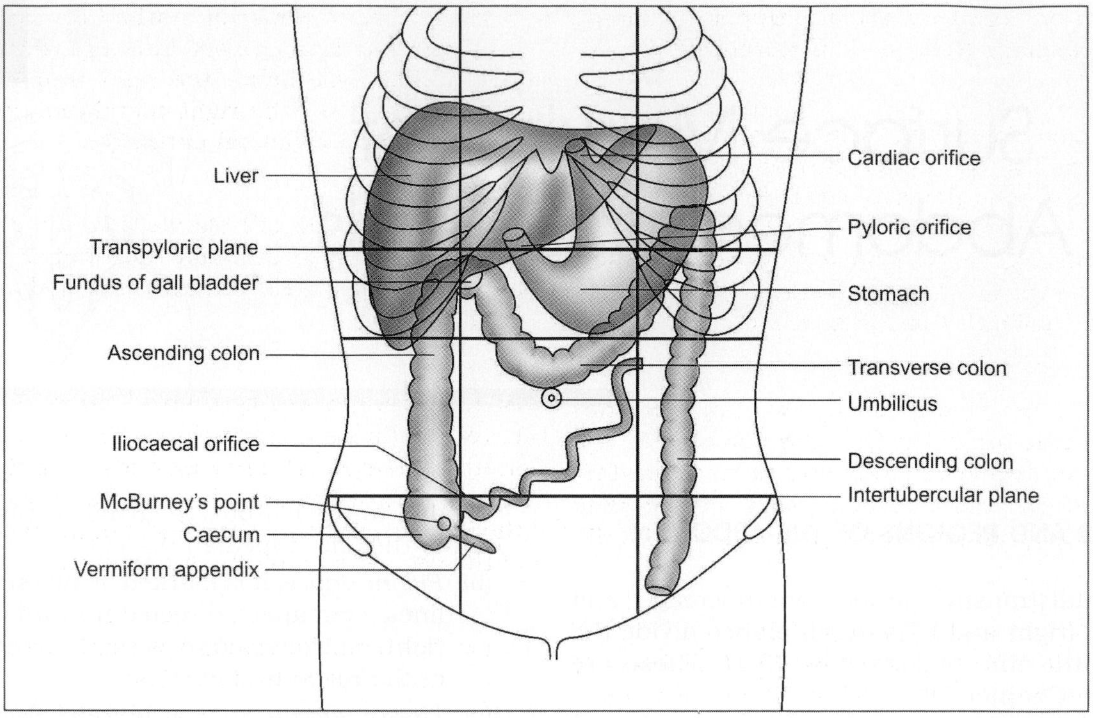

Fig. 35.3: Surface marking of some abdominal organs.

Duodenum

The duodenum is 2.5 cm wide, and lies above the umbilicus. Its four parts are marked in the following way.

(a) *First part* is marked by two parallel lines 2.5 cm apart extending from the pyloric orifice upwards and to the right for 2.5 cm (Fig. 35.4).

(b) *Second part* is marked by similar lines on the right lateral vertical plane extending from the end of the first part downwards for 7.5 cm.

(c) *Third part* is marked by two transverse parallel lines 2.5 cm apart on the subcostal plane, extending from the lower end of the second part towards the left for 10 cm. It crosses the median plane above the umbilicus.

(d) *Fourth part* is marked by two lines extending from the left end of the third part to the duodenojejunal flexure which lies 1 cm below the transpyloric plane, and 3 cm to the left of the median plane. This part is 2.5 cm long.

Caecum

The caecum is marked in the right iliac fossa. It is about 6 cm long and 7.5 cm broad. Its axis is directed downwards and slightly medially (Fig. 35.3).

Ileocaecal Orifice or Valve

Ileocaecal orifice is marked on the point of intersection of the right lateral and transtubercular planes (Fig. 35.3).

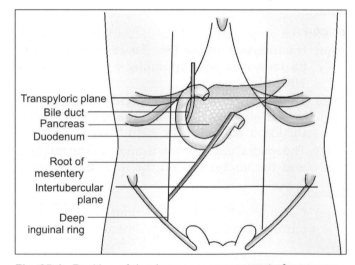

Fig. 35.4: Position of duodenum, pancreas, root of mesentery.

Appendix

(a) The *appendicular orifice* is marked at a point 2 cm below the ileocaecal orifice (Fig. 35.3).

(b) The *appendix* is marked by two parallel lines 1 cm apart and 7 to 10 cm long, extending from the appendicular orifice usually upwards behind the caecum. However, the position of the appendix is highly variable.

Ascending Colon

Ascending colon is marked by two parallel lines 5 cm apart, immediately to the right of the right lateral vertical plane, from the level of the transtubercular plane (upper end of caecum) to the upper part of the 9th costal cartilage (right colic flexure) (Fig. 35.3).

Transverse Colon

Transverse colon is marked by two parallel lines 5 cm apart. It begins at the upper part of the 9th costal cartilage (right colic flexure), runs downwards and medially to the umbilicus, and then upwards and laterally, crossing the transpyloric plane and also the left lateral vertical plane, to end at the 8th costal cartilage (left colic flexure) (Fig. 35.3).

Descending Colon

Descending colon is marked by two parallel lines 2.5 cm apart. It begins at the 8th costal cartilage (left colic flexure), runs downward immediately lateral to the left lateral vertical plane, and ends at the fold of the groin (inguinal ligament) (Fig. 35.3).

Rectum and Anal Canal

Rectum and anal canal are marked on the back by drawing two lines joining the posterior superior iliac spines to the anus. The lower parts of these lines (from 1 cm below the second sacral spine) represent the rectum and anal canal.

Liver

In surface projection the liver is triangular in shape when seen from the front (Fig. 35.3).

(a) The *upper border* is marked by joining the following points.
  1. First point in the left 5th intercostal space 9 cm from the median plane.
  2. Second point at the xiphisternal joint.
  3. Third point at the upper border of the right 5th costal cartilage in the right lateral vertical plane.
  4. Fourth point at the 6th rib in midaxillary line.
  5. Fifth point at the inferior angle of right scapula.
  6. Sixth point at the 8th thoracic spine.

(b) The *lower border* is marked by a curved line joining the following points.
  1. First point in the left 5th intercostal space 9 cm from the median plane.
  2. Second point at the tip of the 8th costal cartilage on the left costal margin.
  3. Third point at the transpyloric plane in the midline.
  4. Fourth point at the tip of the 9th costal cartilage on the right costal margin.
  5. Fifth point 1 cm below the right costal margin at the tip of 10th costal cartilage.
  6. Sixth point at the 11th thoracic spine.

(c) The *right border* is marked on the front by a curved line convex laterally, drawn from a point little below the right nipple to a point 1 cm below the right costal margin at the tip of the 10th costal cartilage.

Gall Bladder

The fundus of the gall bladder (Fig. 35.3) is marked at the right angle between the right costal margin and the outer border of the rectus abdominis (linea semilunaris).

Bile Duct

Bile duct is marked by a line 7.5 cm long. The line is vertical in its upper half and inclines to the right in its lower half. The line extends from a point 5 cm above the transpyloric plane and 2 cm to the right of the median plane, to the middle of the medial border of the second part of the duodenum.

Pancreas

(a) The *head* is marked within the concavity of the duodenum (Fig. 35.4).
(b) The *neck* passes upwards and to the left behind the pylorus in the transpyloric plane.
(c) The *body* is marked by two parallel lines 3 cm apart, drawn upwards and to the left for 10 cm from the neck, occupying the upper two-thirds of the space between the transpyloric and subcostal planes.

Kidney

The kidney measures 11 × 5 cm. It can be marked both on the back as well on the front.

On the back, it is marked within *Morris' parallelogram* which is drawn in the following way. Two horizontal lines are drawn, one at the level of the 11th thoracic spine and the other at the level of the 3rd lumbar spine (Fig. 35.2).

On the front, the bean-shaped kidney is marked with following specifications.

1. On the right side the *centre of the hilum* lies 5 cm from the median plane a little below the transpyloric plane; and on the left side it lies 5 cm from the median plane a little above the transpyloric plane, just medial to the tip of the 9th costal cartilage.
2. The *upper pole* lies 4 to 5 cm from the midline, half way between the xiphisternum and the transpyloric plane (right one, a little lower).
3. The *lower pole* lies 6 to 7 cm from the midline on the right side at the umbilical plane and on the left side at subcostal plane (Fig. 35.5).

Ureter

The ureter can also be marked both on the front as well as on the back.

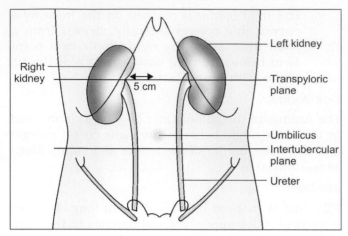

Fig. 35.5: Surface marking of kidneys from anterior aspect.

(a) *On the front,* it is marked by a line running downwards and slightly medially from the tip of the 9th costal cartilage to the pubic tubercle. The upper 5 cm of this line represents the renal pelvis (Fig. 35.5).

(b) *On the back,* it is marked by a line running vertically upwards from the posterior superior iliac spine to the level of the second lumbar spine. The lower end of the renal hilum lies at this level (Fig. 35.2).

Vessels

Abdominal Aorta

Abdominal aorta is marked by two parallel lines 2 cm apart, extending from a point 2.5 cm above the transpyloric plane in the median plane to a point 1.2 cm below and to the left of the umbilicus (level of vertebra L4).

Common Iliac Artery

Common iliac artery is represented by the upper one-third of a broad line drawn from the lower end of the abdominal aorta to the midinguinal point.

External Iliac Artery

External iliac artery is represented by the lower two-thirds of a line drawn from the lower end of the abdominal aorta to the midinguinal point.

Coeliac Trunk and its Branches

The coeliac trunk is marked as a point 1 cm below the beginning of the abdominal aorta (Fig. 35.6).

The *left gastric artery* is marked by a line passing from the coeliac artery upwards and to the left towards the cardiac end of the stomach.

The *splenic artery* is marked by a broad line passing from the coeliac artery towards the left and slightly upwards for about 10 cm.

The *common hepatic artery* is marked by a line passing from the coeliac artery towards the right and slightly downwards for 2.5 cm, and then vertically upwards for 3 cm as proper hepatic artery.

Superior Mesenteric Artery

Superior mesenteric artery is marked by a curved line convex to the left, extending from the abdominal aorta just above the transpyloric plane to the point of intersection of the transtubercular and right lateral planes.

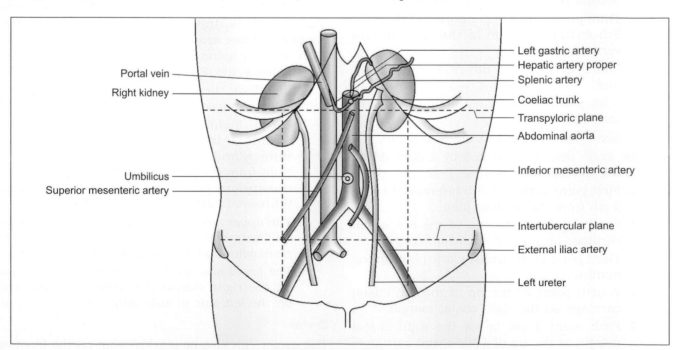

Fig. 35.6: Surface marking of various blood vessels and kidneys.

Inferior Mesenteric Artery

Inferior mesenteric artery is marked by a curved line slightly convex to the left, extending from the abdominal aorta 4 cm below the transpyloric plane to a point 4 cm below the umbilicus, and about the same distance to the left of median plane (Fig. 35.6).

Inferior Vena Cava

Inferior vena cava is marked by two vertical parallel lines 2.5 cm apart, a little to the right of the median plane. It extends from a point just below the transtubercular plane to the sternal end of the right 6th costal cartilage.

Portal Vein

Portal vein is marked by a broad line extending from a point on the transpyloric plane 1.2 cm to the right of the median plane upwards and to the right for about 8 cm (Fig. 35.6).

Miscellaneous

Inguinal Canal

Inguinal canal is marked by two parallel lines 1 cm apart and about 3.7 cm long, above the medial half of the inguinal ligament, extending from the deep to the superficial inguinal ring (see below).

The *deep inguinal ring* is marked 1 cm above the midinguinal point, as a vertical oval ring (Fig. 35.7).

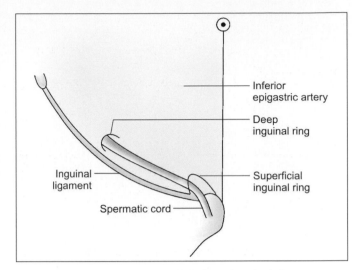

Fig. 35.7: Superficial and deep inguinal rings.

The *superficial inguinal ring* is marked immediately above the pubic tubercle as a triangle with its centre 1 cm above and lateral to the pubic tubercle.

Root of Mesentery

Root of mesentery is marked by two parallel lines close together, extending from the duodenojejunal flexure to the junction to the right lateral and transtubercular planes. The duodenojejunal flexure lies 1 cm below the transpyloric plane and 3 cm to the left of the median plane (Fig. 35.4).

CHAPTER 36

Radiological and Imaging Procedures

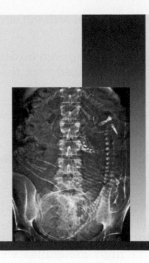

The common radiological methods used for the study or investigation of abdomen include the following.

1. Plain radiography.
2. Barium studies for the gastrointestinal tract.
3. Ultrasonography for the gall bladder, cystic duct and common bile duct, pancreas, kidneys, spleen, abdominal vessels, uterus, ovaries and prostate.
4. Hysterosalpingography for uterus and fallopian tubes (Fig. 31.18).
5. Aortography and selective angiography for coeliac, superior and inferior mesenteric vessels, iliac vessels and renal vessels.

PLAIN SKIAGRAM OF ABDOMEN

Nomenclature

Anteroposterior plain skiagram of the abdomen has been variously named, as the straight film, survey film, scout and KUB film. When done in a case of acute abdomen, it is often called a straight film. A scout film is obtained before taking a contrast radiograph. A KUB film is taken primarily for examining the kidney, ureter, and urinary bladder, for which the acronym KUB stands.

Preparation

In cases of emergency, requiring urgent surgical intervention, a straight film is taken without any preparation. However, in chronic conditions it is better to prepare the patient to obtain a clear and good picture. The object of preparation is to make the gastrointestinal tract as empty as possible, free from food in the stomach and from gases and faecal matter in the intestines. This may be achieved by:

(a) Using for 3 days antiflatulents, like enzyme preparations, charcoal tablets and laxatives.

(b) Avoiding oral feeds for about 12 hours before the investigation. Constipated subjects may require an enema to empty their bowels.

In a picture taken without any preparation, the shadows of the gases and faecal matter may completely mask the significant findings.

Reading of Skiagram

The plain skiagram of the abdomen can be studied systematically in the following way.

Bony Shadows

The picture shows:

(a) The lower ribs.
(b) Lumbar vertebrae.
(c) Upper parts of the hip bones.
(d) Sacrum with the sacroiliac joints.

However, the whole of the pelvis may have been included in the exposure. The bony shadows are used as landmarks for the assessment of the position of viscera and of existing abnormalities. Any variation in the ribs and vertebrae, if present, may be noted.

Soft Tissue Shadows

The faint shadows of the following structures may be seen.

(a) Domes of the diaphragm.
(b) Psoas major.
(c) Kidney, made visible by the perirenal fat.
(d) Liver, beneath the right dome of diaphragm.
(e) The spleen.

Gas Shadows

Gas shadows are seen as black shadows because gases are radiolucent.

(a) Gas in the fundus of stomach appears as a large bubble under the left dome of diaphragm.

(b) The scattered intestinal gas shadows are often intermixed with the shadows of faecal matter.

Abnormal Shadows

Various abnormal shadows may be seen in different diseases.

ALIMENTARY CANAL: BARIUM STUDIES

Contrast Medium

The alimentary canal can be visualized and examined radiologically by using a suspension of barium sulphate in water. Barium is radiopaque because of its high molecular weight. Barium sulphate is absolutely harmless to the body and is not absorbed from the gastrointestinal tract. Barium sulphate is not soluble in water, and can make only a suspension or emulsion in it.

Principle Involved

The passage of barium through the lumen outlines the mucosal patterns, which can be examined under a screen (fluoroscopy) or radiographed on a film.

Barium Meal Examination

Preparation

The subject is instructed not to eat or drink anything during 6 hours before the examination.

Administration of Contrast Medium

The patient is made to drink 300 to 400 cc (10 to 15 oz.) of a 5% barium sulphate suspension in water, and then examined under fluoroscopy. Thus, the entire alimentary canal can be examined by following the barium and taking successive radiographs. The stomach and duodenum are visualized immediately after the barium drink (Fig. 36.1). The medium reaches the ileocaecal region in 3 to 4 hours, the hepatic flexure of the colon in about 6 hours, the splenic flexure of the colon in about 9 hours, the descending colon in 11 hours, and the sigmoid colon in about 16 hours. It is usually evacuated in 16 to 24 hours. However, some barium may persist in the large intestine for several days.

Stomach

As barium enters the stomach, it tends to form a triangular mass below the air in the fundus. It then descends in a narrow stream (canalization) to the pyloric part of the stomach. In addition, the shape, curvatures, peristaltic waves, and the rate of emptying, of the stomach can also be studied.

Duodenum

The beginning of the first part of duodenum shows a well-formed *duodenal cap* produced by poorly

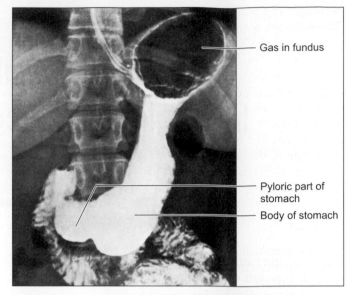

Gas in fundus

Pyloric part of stomach

Body of stomach

Fig. 36.1: Barium meal.

developed circular folds of mucous membrane and protruding pylorus into it. The rest of the duodenum has a characteristic feathery or floccular appearance due to the presence of well-developed circular folds.

Jejunum and Ileum

The greater part of the small intestine presents a feathery or floccular appearance due to the presence of transverse mucosal folds and their rapid movements. However, the terminal part of the ileum is comparatively narrow and shows a homogeneous shadow of barium.

Large Intestine

It is identified by its smooth outline marked by characteristic haustra or sacculations which are most prominent in the proximal part and may disappear in the distal part. Acute curvatures at the flexures cause superimposition of the shadows. Occasionally, the appendix may also be visible. Diseases of the large intestine are better examined by barium enema which gives a better filling.

Barium Enema

Preparation

(a) A mild laxative is given on two nights before the examination.

(b) A plain warm water enema on the morning of the examination.

Contrast Medium

About 2 litres of barium sulphate suspension are slowly introduced through the anus, from a can kept at a height of 2 to 4 feet. The enema is stopped when the barium starts flowing into the terminal ileum through the ileocaecal valve (as seen under the fluoroscopic screen).

Appearance

The rectum and sigmoid colon appear much dilated, and the colon shows characteristic haustrations. The outline of the colon and the haustra may be accentuated by the double-contrast method in which the barium is evacuated and air is injected through the anus to distend the colon. In the background of air, the barium still lining the mucosa makes it clearly visible (Fig. 36.2).

PYELOGRAPHY

Pyelography (urography) is a radiological method by which the urinary tract is visualized. The radiograph thus obtained is called a *pyelogram*. It can be done in two ways depending on the route of administration of the radiopaque dye. When the dye is injected intravenously, it is called the *excretory* (*intravenous* or *descending*) *pyelography*. When the dye is injected directly into the ureter, through a ureteric catheter guided through a cystoscope, the technique is called *retrograde* (*instrumental* or *ascending*) *pyelography*.

Excretory (Intravenous or Descending) Pyelography

Preparation

In addition to routine abdomen preparation:

(a) For 8 hours before pyelography, the patient is not given anything orally, all fluids are withheld, and diuretics are discontinued.

(b) Patient is asked to empty his bladder just before the injection of the dye (Fig. 36.3).

Administration of the Dye

20–40 cc of a warm iodine compound (urograffin 60% or 76% Conray 420 or Conray 280) which is selectively excreted by the kidneys, is slowly injected intravenously. Care is taken not to push any dye outside the vein because it is an irritant and may cause sloughing.

Exposures

Serial skiagram (excretory pyelograms) are taken at 5, 15 and 30 minutes, after the injection of the dye. Maximum concentration is reached in 15 to 20 minutes, and by 30 minutes the dye fills the urinary bladder.

Reading

Intravenous pyelography is an anatomical as well as a physiological test because it permits not only visualization of the urinary tract but also helps in assessment of the functional status of the kidney. Normally:

(a) Minor calices are cup-shaped due to the renal papillae projecting into them.

(b) Renal pelvis is funnel-shaped.

(c) Course of the ureter is clearly seen along the tips of the lumbar transverse processes, the sacroiliac joint, and the ischial spine, up to the bladder.

(d) Bladder appears oval or triangular in shape.

Retrograde (Instrumental or Ascending) Pyelography

Preparation

Preparation of the patient is similar to that for descending pyelography.

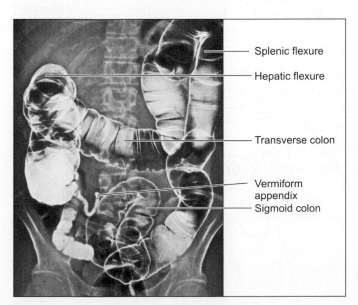

Fig. 36.2: Barium enema.

Splenic flexure

Hepatic flexure

Transverse colon

Vermiform appendix

Sigmoid colon

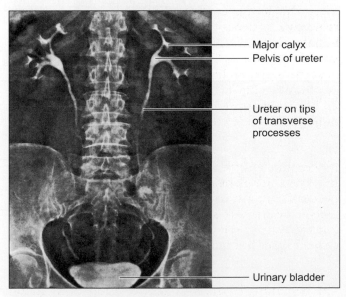

Fig. 36.3: Intravenous pyelogram.

Major calyx

Pelvis of ureter

Ureter on tips of transverse processes

Urinary bladder

Injection of Dye

The technique is quite difficult and can be done only by urologists. A cystoscope is passed into the urinary bladder through the urethra. Then the ureteric catheter is guided into the ureteric opening and passed up to the renal pelvis. Through the catheter, 5 to 10 ml of a sterile solution of 6–8% sodium iodide (or Conray 280) are injected. As the renal pelvis is filled to its capacity, the patient begins to complain of pain, when further injection must be stopped. General anaesthesia is, therefore, contraindicated because of the risk of overdistension of the pelvis. If the renal pelvis admits more than 10 ml of the dye, hydronephrosis is suspected.

An ascending pyelogram can be distinguished from a descending pyelogram because:

(a) Only one pelvis is outlined.

(b) The catheter through which the dye is injected can be seen.

BILIARY APPARATUS

Investigation of Choice

The investigation of choice for gall bladder is *ultrasonography*. It can be undertaken on a fasting patient. Gall bladder is seen as a cystic oval shadow with a narrow neck in the right upper quadrant along with visualisation of the common bile duct and portal vein. Besides, liver parenchyma, pancreas and both kidneys can be easily visualised. Also it helps in the visualisation of abdominal vessels and the spleen. However, endoscopic retrograde cholangio-pancreaticography (ERCP) can be carried out to outline the intrahepatic radicals, common bile duct, pancreatic duct and gall bladder through the oral route via an endoscope through which a catheter is inserted and the contrast is injected into the common bile duct.

Oral cholecystography is an outdated method for visualising the gall bladder by taking radiopaque dye which is exclusively excreted by the liver and concentrated by the gall bladder. The contrast is taken overnight and X-rays are taken 14–16 hours after the intake of the dye and gall bladder, cystic duct and bile duct can be seen. It is, however, dependent on the proper absorption from intestines.

Ultrasound done at the level of 1st lumbar vertebra reveals various structures (Fig. 36.4).

Liver, gall bladder, some blood vessels can also be seen by ultrasonography (Fig. 36.5).

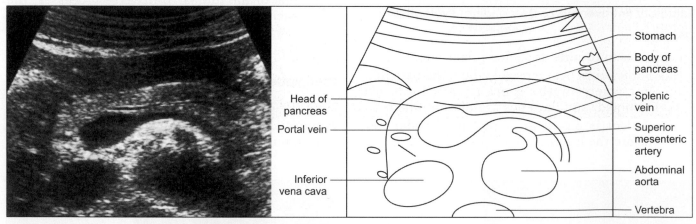

Fig. 36.4: Ultrasound image of pancreas with line drawing.

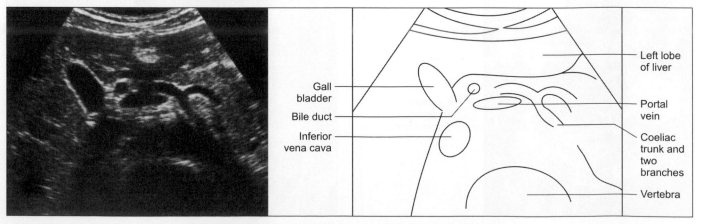

Fig. 36.5: Ultrasound image of coeliac trunk with line drawing.

HYSTEROSALPINGOGRAPHY

This is a radiological method by which the uterus and uterine tubes are visualized and their patency confirmed. The radiograph thus obtained is called a *hysterosalpingogram.*

The investigation is done preferably within the first 5 to 10 days of the menstrual cycle. A tight-fitting cannula is introduced into the internal os of the cervix. The cannula is connected to a syringe through which 5 to 10 ml of an iodized oil (lipiodol) are injected, and the skiagram taken.

The shape and size of the uterus and of the uterine tubes are studied. Spilling of the dye into the peritoneal cavity is noted (Fig. 36.6).

Hysterosalpingography is usually done to determine the patency of the uterine tubes in cases of sterility. However, it is also of value in the diagnosis of anomalies of the female genital tract. The female pelvic organs can also be seen by ultrasound.

FOETOGRAM

Plain X-ray of the abdomen in a full-term pregnant lady showing the foetus with vertex presentation. The shaft of bones of upper and lower limbs and body of vertebrae can easily be identified and appreciated (Fig. 36.7).

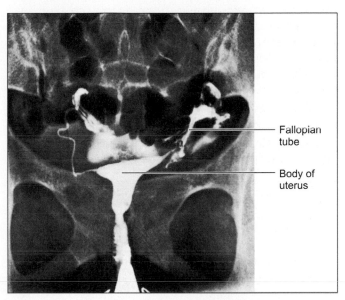

Fallopian tube

Body of uterus

Fig. 36.6: Hysterosalpingogram.

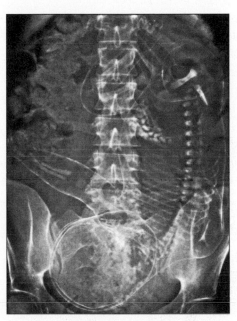

Fig. 36.7: Foetogram.

Appendix 2

NERVES OF ABDOMEN

LOWER INTERCOSTAL NERVES

Course

The ventral rami of T7–T11 pass forwards in the intercostal spaces below respective intercostal vessels. At the back of chest they lie between the pleura and posterior intercostal membrane but in most of their course they lie between internal intercostal and intercostalis intimi. As they reach the anterior ends of their respective spaces, the 7th and 8th nerves curve upwards and medially across the deep surface of costal margin, passing between digitations of transverses abdominis then piercing the posterior layer of internal oblique, to enter the rectus sheath, and continue to run upwards and medially parallel to the costal margin. After supplying rectus abdominis, they pierce the anterior wall of the rectus sheath to reach the skin. 7th nerve supplies skin of the epigastrium and 8th below it. At the anterior ends of 9th, 10th and 11th intercostal spaces, the 9th, 10th and 11th intercostal nerves pass between digitations of transversus abdominis to lie between it and the internal oblique and run in this plane. 9th nerve runs horizontally, but 10th and 11th run downwards and medially.

When they reach the lateral margin of rectus abdominis, they pierce the posterior layer of rectus sheath, enter it, pierce the muscle and its anterior sheath to supply the skin. The 10th nerve supplies the band of skin which includes the umbilicus.

The ventral ramus of T12 is larger than the others. It accompanies the subcostal artery along the lower border of 12th rib and passes behind the lateral arcuate ligament. It lies behind the kidney, anterior to quadratus lumborum, pierces the aponeurosis of transversus abdominis and runs in the interval between transversus and internal oblique.

Branches

Muscular

The intercostal and subcostal nerves and their collateral branches supply intercostal muscles and muscles of anterolateral abdominal wall. T12 supplies pyramidalis also, if present.

Cutaneous

The terminal parts of T7–T12 nerves are called as the anterior cutaneous branches. These supply the skin close to the anterior median line. T10 supplying the skin around umbilicus; T7, the skin of epigastrium and T8, T9 the intervening skin between epigastrium and the umbilicus. T11, T12 and iliohypogastric (L1) supply the skin between umbilicus and pubic symphysis. The lateral cutaneous branches of the T7–T11 intercostal nerves divide into anterior and posterior branches to supply the skin of lateral side of abdomen and back.

The lateral cutaneous branch of T12 supplies the skin of anterior part of the gluteal region.

UPPER LUMBAR NERVES

1. Iliohypogastric.
2. Ilioinguinal.
3. Genitofemoral.
4. Lateral cutaneous nerve of thigh.

All these nerves are described in Chapter 27.

LUMBAR PLEXUS

Formed by ventral rami of L1, L2, L3 and part of L4. These rami divide into dorsal and ventral divisions. From the ventral divisions of these rami arise ilioinguinal (L1), genitofemoral (L1, L2), obturator (L2, L3, L4), accessory obturator (L3, L4) nerves.

The dorsal divisions of these rami give rise to lateral cutaneous nerve of thigh (L2, L3), femoral nerve (L2, L3, L4) (Appendix 1). Iliohypogastric contains fibres of both ventral and dorsal divisions (L1).

SACRAL PLEXUS

It is formed by ventral rami of part of L4, L5, S1, S2, S3. Few muscular branches are given off from the rami. Then these divide into ventral and dorsal divisions.

Branches arising from ventral divisions are:

- Nerve to quadratus femoris (L4, L5, S1): Supplies quadratus femoris, inferior gemellus and hip joint.
- Nerve to obturator internus (L5, S1, S2): Supplies obturator internus and superior gemellus.
- Pudendal nerve (S2, S3, S4) is described below.
- Perforating cutaneous nerve (S3, S4): Supplies small area of skin of gluteal region.
- Tibial part of sciatic nerve (L4, L5, S1, S2, S3): Supplies all muscles of the calf and of the sole.
- Posterior cutaneous nerve of thigh (S1, S2): Supplies skin of back of thigh.

Branches from dorsal divisions are:

- Superior gluteal nerve (L4, L5, S1): Supplies gluteus medius, gluteus minimus and tensor fascia latae.
- Inferior gluteal nerve (L5, S1, S2): Supplies only gluteus maximus.
- Common peroneal part of sciatic nerve (L4, L5, S1, S2): Supplies evertors and foot and dorsiflexors of ankle joint and extensor digitorum brevis.

PUDENDAL NERVE

Pudendal nerve supplies the skin, external genital organs and muscles of perineum. It is concerned with micturition, defaecation, erection, ejaculation and in females, with parturition. It is accompanied by internal pudendal vessels.

Root value: It arises from the sacral plexus in the pelvis. Its root value is ventral rami of S2, S3, S4 nerves.

Course: It starts in the pelvis, enters the gluteal region through greater sciatic notch, lies on the sacrospinous ligament, leaves the gluteal region through lesser sciatic notch. It just peeps into the gluteal region to enter the pudendal canal in the lateral wall of the ischiorectal fossa.

Branches

1. **Inferior rectal nerve:** Skin around anus, external anal sphincter and lining of anal canal below the pectinate line.
2. **Perineal nerve:** Medial and lateral scrotal/labial branches. Muscular branches to sphincter urethrae, deep transversus perinei,

ischiocavernosus, bulbospongiosus, external anal sphincter, levator ani, corpus spongiosum, penis and urethra, lower 2.5 cm of vagina.

3. **Dorsal nerve of penis/clitoris:** Passes through deep perineal space, then runs on the dorsum of penis/clitoris and ends in the glans; supplying skin of body of penis/clitoris and of the glans.

Clinical Anatomy

Pudendal nerve block is given in some vaginal operations.

ABDOMINAL PART OF SYMPATHETIC TRUNK

Sympathetic trunk runs along the medial border of psoas major muscle. It is continuous with the pelvic part by passing behind the common iliac vessels. There are 4 ganglia in the lumbar or abdominal part. Only upper two ganglia receive white ramus communicans from the ventral primary rami of first and second lumbar nerves.

Branches

1. Grey rami communicans to the lumbar spinal nerves. These pass along the spinal nerves to be distributed to the sweat glands, cutaneous blood vessels and arrector pili muscles (sudomotor, vasomotor and pilomotor).
2. Postganglionic fibres pass medially to the aortic plexus.
3. Postganglionic fibres pass in front of common iliac vessels to form hypogastric plexus, which is also supplemented by branches of aortic plexus.

Aortic Plexus

This plexus is formed by preganglionic sympathetic, postganglionic sympathetic, preganglionic parasympathetic and visceral afferent fibres around the abdominal aorta. The plexus is concentrated around the origin of ventral and lateral branches of abdominal aorta. These are known as coeliac plexus, superior mesenteric plexus, inferior mesenteric plexus, and renal plexus.

Pelvic Part of Sympathetic Trunk

It runs in front of sacrum, medial to ventral sacral foramina. Caudally the two trunks unite and fuse into a single ganglion impar in front of coccyx. There are 4 ganglia in this part of sympathetic trunk. Their branches are:

1. Grey rami communicans to the sacral and coccygeal nerves.
2. Branches to the pelvic plexuses.

Collateral or Prevertebral Ganglia and Plexuses

Coeliac Plexus

It is the largest of the three autonomic plexuses, e.g. coeliac, superior mesenteric and inferior mesenteric plexuses. It is a dense network of nerve fibres which unite the two coeliac ganglia. The ganglia receive the greater splanchnic nerves, lesser splanchnic nerves of both sides including some filaments of vagi and phrenic nerves.

Coeliac ganglia are two irregularly shaped ganglia. Each ganglion receives greater splanchnic nerve. The lower part of the ganglion receives lesser splanchnic nerve and is also called as aorticorenal ganglion. The aorticorenal ganglion gives off the renal plexus which accompanies the renal vessels.

Secondary plexuses arising from coeliac and aorticorenal plexus are distributed along the branches of the aorta, namely phrenic, splenic, left gastric, hepatic, intermesenteric, suprarenal, renal, gonadal, superior and inferior mesenteric plexuses, and abdominal aortic plexus.

Superior hypogastric plexus: This plexus lies between the two common iliac arteries and is formed by:

1. Aortic plexus.
2. Branches from third and fourth lumbar sympathetic ganglia.

It divides into right and left inferior hypogastric plexus (pelvic plexus); which runs on the medial side of internal iliac artery and is supplemented by pelvic splanchnic nerves (parasympathetic nerves). Thus inferior hypogastric plexus contains both sympathetic and parasympathetic nerves. These are for the supply of the pelvic viscera along the branches of the arteries. The plexuses supply gastrointestinal tract and genitourinary tract.

The autonomic nerve supply of various organs and their effects are described.

Gastrointestinal Tract

Oesophagus

It receives its nerve supply from vagus and sympathetic.

Cervical part of oesophagus receives branches from recurrent laryngeal nerve of vagus and middle cervical ganglion of sympathetic trunk.

Thoracic part gets branches from vagal trunks and oesophageal plexus as well as from sympathetic trunks and greater splanchnic nerves.

Abdominal part receives fibres from vagal trunk (i.e. anterior and posterior gastric nerves), thoracic part of sympathetic trunks, greater splanchnic nerves and plexus around left gastric artery. The nerves form a plexus called myenteric plexus between two layers of the muscularis externa and another one in the submucous layer.

Stomach

Sympathetic supply reaches from coeliac plexus along gastric and gastroepiploic arteries. A few branches also reach from thoracic and lumbar sympathetic trunks.

Parasympathetic supply is derived from vagus nerves. The left vagus forms anterior gastric, while right vagus comprises posterior gastric nerve. The anterior gastric nerve supplies cardiac orifice, anterior surface of body as well as fundus of stomach, pylorus and liver.

Posterior gastric nerve supplies posterior surface of body and fundus till pyloric antrum. It gives a number of coeliac branches, which form part of the coeliac plexus.

Vagus is secretomotor to stomach. Its stimulation causes secretion which is rich in pepsin. Sympathetic inhibits peristalsis and is motor to the pyloric sphincter. It also carries pain fibres from stomach. Spasm, ischaemia and distension causes pain.

Small intestine

The nerves of this part of the gut are derived from coeliac ganglia formed by posterior gastric nerve (parasympathetic) and the plexus around superior mesenteric artery. These nerves form myenteric plexus and submucous plexus. Parasympathetic fibres relay in the ganglion cells present in these plexuses. Sympathetic inhibits the peristaltic movements of intestine but stimulates the sphincters.

Large intestine

Large intestine except the lower half of anal canal is supplied by both components of autonomic nervous system. The derivatives of midgut, i.e. caecum, vermiform appendix, ascending colon and right two-thirds of transverse colon receive their sympathetic nerve supply from coeliac and superior mesenteric ganglia and parasympathetic from vagus nerve.

Left one-third of transverse colon, descending colon, sigmoid colon, rectum and upper half of anal canal (developed from hindgut and anorectal canal) receive their sympathetic nerve supply from lumbar part of sympathetic trunk and superior hypogastric plexus through the plexuses on the branches of inferior mesenteric artery. Its effect is chiefly vasomotor. Parasympathetic supply of colon is received from pelvic splanchnic nerves.

Pelvic splanchnic nerves give fibres to inferior hypogastric plexuses to supply rectum and upper half of anal canal. Some fibres of inferior hypogastric plexus pass up through superior hypogastric plexus and get distributed along the branches of inferior mesenteric artery to the left one-third of transverse colon, descending and sigmoid colon.

Rectum and Anal Canal

Sympathetic fibres pass along inferior mesenteric and superior rectal arteries also via superior and inferior hypogastric plexuses.

Parasympathetic supply is from pelvic splanchnic nerve, which joins inferior hypogastric plexus. This supply is motor to muscles of rectum and inhibitory to internal sphincter.

The external anal sphincter is supplied by inferior rectal branch of pudendal nerve. Afferent impulses of physiological distension of rectum and sigmoid colon are carried by parasympathetic, whereas pain impulses are conveyed both by sympathetic and parasympathetic nerves.

Pancreas

Branches of coeliac plexus pass along the arteries. Sympathetic is vasomotor. The nerve fibres make synaptic contact with acinar cells before innervating the islets. The parasympathetic ganglia lies in sparse connective tissue of the gland and the islet cells.

Liver

Nerves of the liver are derived from hepatic plexus which contain both sympathetic and para-sympathetic fibres. These accompany the blood vessels and bile ducts. Both types of nerve fibres also reach the liver through various peritoneal folds.

Gall Bladder

Parasympathetic and sympathetic nerves of gall bladder are derived from coeliac plexus, along the hepatic artery (hepatic plexus) and its branches. Fibres from the right phrenic nerve (C4) through the communication of coeliac and phrenic plexus also reach gall bladder in the hepatic plexus. The reason of pain in the right shoulder (from where impulses are carried by lateral supraclavicular nerve C4) in cholecystitis is the stimulation of phrenic nerve fibres (C4) due to the communication of phrenic plexus and hepatic plexus via coeliac plexus.

Genitourinary Tract

Kidneys

The kidneys are supplied by renal plexus formed from coeliac ganglion, coeliac plexus, lowest thoracic splanchnic nerve, and first lumbar splanchnic nerve. The plexus runs along the branches of renal artery to supply the vessels, renal glomeruli and tubules. These are chiefly vasomotor in function.

Ureter is supplied in its upper part from renal and aortic plexus, middle part from superior hypogastric plexus and lower part from hypogastric nerve and inferior hypogastric plexus.

Vesical Plexus

Sympathetic fibres arise from T11 and T12 segments L1 and L2 segments of spinal cord. Parasympathetic fibres arise from sacral S2, S3, S4 segments of spinal cord, which relay in the neurons present in and near the wall of urinary bladder. Parasympathetic is motor to the muscular coat and inhibitory to the sphincter; sympathetic is chiefly vasomotor. Emptying and filling of bladder is normally controlled by parasympathetic only.

Male Reproductive Organs

Testicular plexus accompanies the testicular artery to reach the testis. It is formed by renal and aortic plexus, and also from superior and inferior hypogastric plexuses. This plexus supplies the epididymis and ductus deferens.

Prostatic plexus is formed from inferior hypogastric plexus and branches are distributed to prostate, seminal vesicle, prostatic urethra, ejaculatory ducts, erectile tissue of penis, penile part of urethra and bulbourethral glands. Sympathetic nerves cause vasoconstriction, parasympathetic nerves cause vasodilatation.

Female Reproductive Organs

Ovary and uterine tube receive their nerve supply from plexus around the ovarian vessels. This plexus is derived from renal, aortic plexuses and also superior and inferior hypogastric plexuses. Sympathetic fibres derived from T10 and T11 segments of spinal cord are vasomotor in nature whereas parasympathetic fibres are probably vasodilator in function.

Uterus

It is supplied by uterovaginal plexus, formed from the inferior hypogastric plexus. The sympathetic fibres are derived from T12 and L1 segments of spinal cord. Parasympathetic fibres arise from S2, S3, S4 segments of spinal cord. Sympathetic causes uterine contraction and vasoconstriction, while para-sympathetic nerves produce vasodilatation and uterine inhibition. Vagina is supplied by nerves arising from inferior hypogastric plexus and uterovaginal plexus. These supply wall of vagina including vestibular glands and clitoris. Para-sympathetic fibres contain vasodilator effect on the erectile tissue.

CLINICAL ANATOMY

- In some diseases affecting the nerve trunks near their origins, the pain is referred to their peripheral terminations. In tuberculosis of thoracic vertebrae, the pain is referred to abdomen either as constricting pain when one nerve is involved or general diffuse pain when more nerves are involved.

- The muscle and skin of the anterolateral abdominal wall is supplied by thoracic 7–12 spinal nerves. These muscles protect the underlying viscera effectively. Any blow to the abdominal wall will do no harm to the viscera if the muscles are firmly contracted. If the muscles are caught unawares, blow can do a lot of damage to viscera. Mostly there is reflex contraction of muscles if there is any attack to the skin (Fig. A2.1).

- The lower intercostal nerves are connected to sympathetic ganglia via the rami communicans. From these ganglia arise greater splanchnic nerves which supply abdominal viscera. In injury to the viscera or peritonitis, the muscles of abdominal wall firmly contract, giving rise to "board-like rigidity" to prevent any further insult to the viscera.

- If the lateral cutaneous nerve of thigh gets compressed as it pierces the inguinal ligament, there is pain tingling, numbness and anaesthesia over the anterolateral aspect of thigh. This is called "meralgia paraesthetica" (Fig. A2.2).

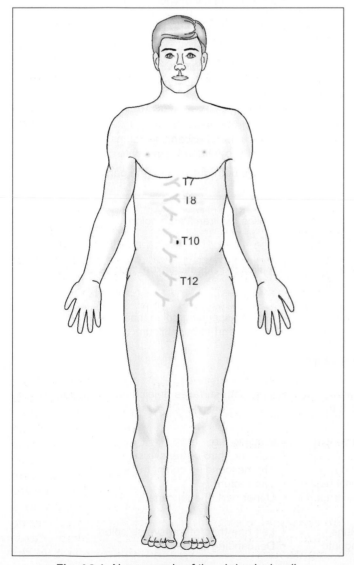

Fig. A2.1: Nerve supply of the abdominal wall.

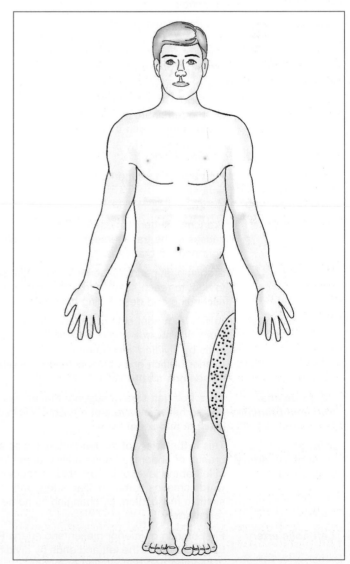

Fig. A2.2: Site of meralgia paraesthetica.

ARTERIES OF ABDOMEN AND PELVIS

VENTRAL BRANCHES OF ABDOMINAL AORTA

Artery	Origin, course, termination	Distribution
Coeliac trunk (Fig. 21.3)	It is the artery of foregut and the first ventral visceral branch of abdominal aorta arising at upper border of L1 vertebra. It has a course of 1.25 cm and ends by dividing into left gastric, common hepatic and splenic arteries	Coeliac trunk supplies the derivatives of foregut, namely oesophagus, stomach, proximal part of duodenum, spleen, greater part of pancreas, liver and gall bladder
Left gastric artery	Smallest branch of coeliac trunk. First it courses upward till the cardiac end of stomach, then it enters lesser omentum to run along lesser curvature of stomach. Ends by anastomosing with right gastric artery	Oesophageal branches to lower part of oesophagus. This part is also supplied by oesophageal branches of thoracic aorta. Gives gastric branches to both surfaces of stomach
Common hepatic artery	Branch of coeliac trunk. First descends till the upper border of duodenum, where it gives gastroduodenal artery, and continues as proper hepatic artery	Gastroduodenal supplies the stomach and 1st part of duodenum
Proper hepatic artery	It runs upwards in lesser omentum and ends at porta hepatis by dividing into right and left hepatic branches	Right gastric supplies stomach. Cystic artery for gall bladder from right hepatic artery. Two hepatic arteries to supply oxygen to the hepatic cells
Splenic artery	It is the largest branch of coeliac trunk. Runs sinuously along upper border of pancreas to reach hilum of spleen, where it ends by dividing 5–7 splenic branches	• Gives numerous pancreatic branches • 5–7 short gastric branches for fundus of stomach • Left gastroepiploic to supply stomach along greater curvature and greater omentum also
Superior mesenteric artery (Fig. 21.8)	It is the artery of midgut, arising from aorta at lower border of L1 vertebra. Courses downwards and to right to terminate in the right iliac fossa by anastomosing with a branch of ileocolic artery	• Distal part of duodenum below the opening of bile duct • Jejunum and ileum • Vermiform appendix • Caecum and ascending colon • Right two-thirds of transverse colon
Inferior pancreatico-duodenal artery	First branch of superior mesenteric artery from its right side	Supplies both duodenum and pancreas
Middle colic	Branch of superior mesenteric from its right side, it passes in the transverse mesocolon and divides into right and left branches	Supplies the transverse colon
Right colic	Branch of superior mesenteric from right side passes to right to reach ascending colon and divides into ascending and descending branches	Supplies the hepatic flexure and ascending colon
Ileocolic artery	Arises from right side of superior mesenteric artery. Runs downwards and to right till the caecum and ends by dividing into superior and inferior branches. Inferior branch ends by anastomosing with superior mesenteric artery	Supplies ascending colon, caecum, vermiform appendix and terminal ileum
12–15 Jejunal and ileal branches	Arise from left side of superior mesenteric artery course between layers of mesentery to reach the jejunum and ileum	Supply both surfaces of jejunum and ileum
Inferior mesenteric artery (Fig. 21.10)	This is the artery of the hindgut. It is also a ventral branch of abdominal aorta arising at the left, crosses to left at the level of L3 vertebra. It courses downwards crosses common iliac artery and continues in sigmoid mesocolon, by changing its name to superior rectal artery	It supplies the: • Left one-third of transverse colon • The descending colon, the sigmoid colon • The rectum • Upper part of anal canal
Left colic artery	First branch of inferior mesenteric artery. Runs upwards and to the left and ends by dividing into ascending and descending branches	• Left one-third of transverse colon • Descending colon

Artery	Origin, course, termination	Distribution
Sigmoid arteries	2–4 sigmoid arteries pass downwards and to left and anastomose with each other, lowest branch anastomoses with superior rectal artery	• Descending colon • Sigmoid colon
Superior rectal artery	Continuation of inferior mesenteric artery at the pelvic brim. Divides into right and left branches	Muscles and mucous membrane of rectum Rectum and upper part of anal canal

OTHER BRANCHES OF ABDOMINAL AORTA

Artery	Origin, course, termination	Distribution
Inferior phrenic arteries	Right and left inferior phrenic arteries give branches to the respective suprarenal glands and end in the thoracoabdominal diaphragm	Suprarenal glands and muscle of the diaphragm
Middle suprarenal arteries	Right and left arteries run upwards on the muscle of diaphragm to end in the suprarenal glands	Suprarenal glands
Renal arteries (Fig. 27.1)	These two large arteries arise at the level of L2 vertebra. Reach the hila of respective kidney to supply kidney	Suprarenals, ureters and kidneys
Gonadal	Arise at level of L2 vertebra. Each artery runs downwards and laterally	Runs as ovarian artery in female and as testicular artery in male
Ovarian arteries	Ovarian artery crosses the pelvic brim to enter the suspensory ligament of ovary. It then enters the hila of respective ovary	Supplies ovary and lateral part of oviduct
Testicular arteries	Each testicular artery joins the spermatic cord at the deep inguinal ring, courses through the inguinal canal. At the upper pole of testis, it divides into branches which supply testis and epididymis	Testis and epididymis
Lumbar arteries	Four pairs of lumbar arteries arise from the dorsal aspect of abdominal aorta. These pass laterally and dorsally to supply muscles of posterior abdominal wall. Gives branch to the vertebral canal also	Muscles of anterolateral and posterior abdominal wall. Spinal cord, muscles and skin of the back are also supplied
Median sacral artery	Single artery from back of aorta above its bifurcation. Ends in front of coccyx	Rectum and muscles of the pelvis
Common iliac artery	The two terminal branches of abdominal aorta. Each runs downwards and laterally and ends by dividing into larger external iliac and smaller internal iliac in front of sacroiliac joint at the level of L5 and S1 vertebrae	No branches are given off

EXTERNAL ILIAC ARTERY

Artery	Origin, course, termination	Distribution
External iliac artery	Larger terminal branch of common iliac artery Courses downwards and laterally till the midinguinal point from where it continues as the femoral artery	• Deep circumflex iliac for the muscles attached to the iliac crest • Inferior epigastric which enters the rectus sheath to supply the muscle and overlying skin

INTERNAL ILIAC ARTERY

Artery	Origin, course, termination	Distribution
Internal iliac artery (Fig. 34.1)	Smaller terminal branch of common iliac artery Begins in front of sacroiliac joint, crosses the pelvic brim and ends by dividing into anterior and posterior divisions	The artery supplies most of the pelvic organs, perineum and the gluteal region
Anterior division		
Superior vesical	Branch of internal iliac artery. Ends by giving branches to urinary bladder and ductus deferens	Superior surface of urinary bladder and the muscular wall of ductus deferens
Obturator artery	Branch of internal iliac artery. Runs on the lateral wall of pelvis, passes through obturator foramen to enter the thigh	Gives branches to obturator internus and iliacus muscles. In thigh it supplies the adductor muscles

Artery	Origin, course, termination	Distribution
Middle rectal artery	Branch of internal iliac artery. Ends by supplying muscle coats of rectum	Supplies muscle coats of rectum, prostate and seminal vesicles
Inferior vesical artery	Branch of internal iliac artery. Only in male ends by supplying trigone of urinary bladder	Supplies urinary bladder, prostate, seminal vesicle and lower part of ureter
Inferior gluteal artery	Largest and one of the terminal branches of internal iliac artery. It leaves the pelvis through greater sciatic notch to enter the gluteal region	Branches to muscles of gluteal region It is the axial artery of lower limb
Internal pudendal artery	Smaller terminal branch of internal iliac artery. Runs out of pelvis through greater sciatic notch and leaves the gluteal region by passing through lesser sciatic foramen to enter the pudendal canal. Then it runs in pudendal canal in the lateral wall of ischioanal fossa. Lastly it enters the deep perineal space where it ends by dividing into deep and dorsal arteries	In ischiorenal fossa, inferior rectal artery is given off which supplies mucous membrane, musculature of anal canal including skin overlying it. In perineum it gives perineal artery for muscles, scrotal or labial branches, deep and dorsal arteries of penis or clitoris
Vaginal artery	Branches of internal iliac artery only in female It ends by supplying the vagina	Supplies vagina, base of urinary bladder
Uterine artery	It is branch of internal iliac artery only in female. It runs downwards and medially till the lateral fornix of vagina and then upwards along vagina, cervix and uterus with a tortuous course and ends by anastomosing with the ovarian artery	Supplies vagina, uterus, medial two-thirds of oviduct The artery crosses in front of ureter
Posterior division		
Iliolumbar artery	Runs upwards in front of sacroiliac joint and ends by dividing into iliac branch and lumbar branch	Iliac branch supplies iliacus and lumbar branch supplies muscles of back and through its spinal branch, cauda equina is also supplied
Lateral sacral arteries	2 lateral sacral arteries which divide to enter 4 ventral sacral foramina to supply sacral canal and muscles of back of sacrum	Supply cauda equina and muscles of back of sacrum
Superior gluteal artery	Passes out through greater sciatic notch to reach gluteal region	It supplies muscles of gluteal region, especially gluteus medius and minimus

CLINICAL TERMS

Paramedian incision: These are given to open up the abdominal cavity. In paramedian incision the rectus abdominis muscle is pushed laterally so that the various nerves supplying the rectus muscle are not pulled or injured (Fig. 16.38).

Inguinal hernia: Hernia is the protrusion of the contents of a cavity through any of its walls. Hernia is common at any weak spot in any of the walls. Testis descends down along a peritoneal process called processes vaginalis. The connection is usually obliterated. In some cases the connection between peritoneal cavity and processus vaginalis remains open giving rise to congenital inguinal hernia.

Femoral hernia: The femoral canal is the medial compartment of the femoral sheath. It permits dilatation of femoral vein whenever required. This canal is wider in females than males because of the broad pelvis and smaller vessels. Sometimes a part of intestine or peritoneum may project in the femoral canal and be seen as a swelling below and lateral to pubic tubercle. The condition is called femoral hernia (Fig. 16.39).

Abdominal paracentesis: Collection of fluid in the peritoneal cavity is called "ascitis". In these cases the excess fluid may require removal. For the removal, abdominal paracentesis is done with a trocar and cannula. The site is usually midway between umbilicus and pubic symphysis.

Peritonitis: Inflammation of the peritoneum is called peritonitis. It is usually secondary to perforation of any viscera. The anterior abdominal muscles are in a state of contraction, and the condition is called "board-like rigidity".

Peritonitis is common in females, as the peritoneal cavity communicates with outside through fallopian tubes, uterus, vagina.

Internal hernia: Sometimes a loop of intestines enters a foramen, fossae, fold within the abdominal cavity itself, but cannot come out. It may become obstructed or strangulated (lack of blood supply). The condition is acute and needs immediate attention and treatment. Femoral and inguinal hernia are external hernia (Fig. 18.32).

Morisons pouch: The intraperitoneal space or pouch between the posterior surface of liver, right kidney and hepatic flexure is called *Morisons* or *hepatorenal pouch.* When a person is lying down, this pouch is the deepest. So pus or fluid tend to gravitate in this pouch (Fig. 18.27).

Abdominal policeman: The greater omentum is a four-layered peritoneum between greater curvature of stomach and transverse colon. It hangs down and covers all the abdominal viscera like an apron. It also moves. Any infected viscera or perforating viscera may be sealed by greater omentum. So it does try to limit the infection and hence is called *abdominal policeman* (Fig. 18.37).

Pouch of Douglas: The rectouterine pouch in females is the deepest or most dependent part of peritoneal cavity in sitting position. It lies at a depth of 5.5 cm from the skin of perineum (Fig. 18.17b).

Gastric ulcers: The gastric ulcers are common along the lesser curvatures as the fluids (hot/cold), alcoholic beverages pass along lesser curvature. The blood supply is also relatively less along the lesser curvature so the ulcers are common here. Gastric pain is felt in the epigastrium because the stomach is supplied from segments T6–T10 of the spinal cord, which also supply the upper part of the abdominal wall (Fig. 19.12).

Referred pain in early appendicitis: The visceral peritoneum over vermiform appendix is supplied by lesser splanchnic nerve which arises from thoracic 10 sympathetic ganglion. T10 spinal segment also receives the sensation of pain from umbilical area. Since somatic pain is better appreciated than visceral pain, pain of early appendicitis is referred to umbilical region. Later on there is pain in right fossa due to inflammation of local parietal peritoneum.

Intestinal obstruction: Intestinal obstruction is caused by tubercular ulcers not typhoid ulcers. In tubercular ulcers, the lymph vessels are affected, these pass circularly around the gut wall. During healing, these cause constriction of the gut wall and subsequent obstruction. Typhoid ulcers lie longitudinally along the antimesenteric border of the gut. These do not cause obstruction during healing.

Intussusception: Rarely a segment of intestine enters into the lumen of proximal segment of intestine, causing obstruction, and strangulation. It may be ileoileal or ileocolic.

Meckel's diverticulum: The apex of midgut loop is connected to secondary yolk sac by vitellointestinal duct. The proximal part of vitellointestinal duct may persist as Meckel's diverticulum. It is 2 inches long present at the antimesenteric border of ileum, 2 feet away from ileocaecal junction. Meckel's diverticulum may be connected to umbilicus by a fibrous band around which intestine may rotate and get obstructed (Fig. 20.10).

Internal haemorrhoids: The superior rectal artery divides into right and left branches. Only the right branch divides further into anterior and posterior branches. The veins follow the arteries. The venous radicles are in 3, 7, 11 O'clock positions. The internal piles are accordingly in 3, 7, 11 O'clock positions (Fig. 33.9).

Cholecystitis: Inflammation of the gall bladder is called cholecystitis. There is pain over right hypochondrium, radiating to the inferior angle of right scapula or to the right shoulder (Fig. 22.12).

Cholelithiasis: Stone formation in the gall bladder is called cholelithiasis (Fig. 22.10).

Splenomegaly: Enlargement of spleen is called splenomegaly. It occurs mostly in malaria and blood disorders (Fig. 23.28).

Splenectomy: Removal of spleen is called splenectomy. One must be careful of the tail of pancreas during splenectomy.

Diabetes mellitus: Deficiency of insulin causes diabetes mellitus.

Carcinoma of head of pancreas: Carcinoma of head of pancreas causes pressure over the underlying bile duct which leads to persistent obstructive jaundice.

Hepatitis: Inflammation of liver is referred to as hepatitis. It may be *infective* or *amoebic* hepatitis.

Cirrhosis: Due to malnutrition or alcohol abuse, the liver tissue undergoes fibrosis and shrinks. This is called cirrhosis of the liver.

Common diseases of kidney: The common diseases of kidney are nephritis, pyelonephritis, tuberculosis of kidney, renal stones and tumours. Common manifestations of a kidney disease are renal oedema and hypertension. Renal transplantation can be tried in selected cases. Lithotripsy is being used for removal of stones.

Ureteric colic: The ureteric colic is referred to T11-T12 segments. The pain radiates from loin to the groin (Fig. 24.22).

Hysterectomy: The procedure of removing uterus for various reasons is called hysterectomy. One has to carefully ligate the uterine artery, which crosses the ureter lying below the base of broad ligament. The integrity of ureter has to be maintained.

Tubectomy: This is a simple operative procedure done in females for family welfare. The peritoneal cavity has to be opened in females. The fallopian tube or uterine tube is ligated at two places and intervening segment is removed. The procedure is done on both sides (Figs 31.19 and 31.20).

Rupture of male urethra: The membranous part of urethra is likely to be ruptured. The urine fills superficial perineal space, scrotum, penis and lower part of anterior abdominal wall. It cannot go into the thighs because of firm attachment of membranous layer of superficial fascia to their boundaries (Fig. 28.26).

Tubal pregnancy: Sometimes the fertilized ovum instead of reaching the uterus adheres to the walls of the uterine tube and starts developing there. This is known as *tubal pregnancy*. The enlarging embryo mostly leads to rupture of the fallopian tube.

Prolapse of the uterus: Sometimes the uterus passes downwards into the vagina, invaginating it. It is called the prolapse of the uterus, and is caused by weakened supports of the uterus (Fig. 29.14).

Intrauterine contraceptive device: Insertion of a foreign body into the uterus can prevent implantation of the fertilized ovum. This is the basic principle underlying the use of various intrauterine contraceptive devices for preventing pregnancy (Fig. 31.24).

Enucleation of the prostatic adenoma: The prostate has a false capsule and a true capsule. The prostatic venous plexus lies between the true and false capsules.

In benign hypertrophy of prostate the adenoma only is enucleated, leaving both the capsules and the venous plexus and normal peripheral part of gland.

Vasectomy: It is a simple surgical procedure done for family welfare. A segment of vas deferens is exposed from a small incision on the upper part of scrotum. The two ends are tied and a small piece of vas deferens is removed. The procedure is done on both sides. Since hormones continue to be produced and circulated through blood, person remains potent. But, since the sperms cannot pass in the distal part of vas and into ejaculatory duct, the person becomes sterile after 3–4 months (Fig. 32.9).

Hydrocoele: The testis invaginates the processus vaginalis so that there is a visceral layer and a parietal layer of peritoneum. Collection of fluid in between the two layers is called *hydrocoele* (Fig. 17.13).

Cryptorchidism: If testis do not come down to the scrotum at birth or soon after, these are hidden anywhere along its path or these may have gone astray (Figs 17.11 and 17.12).

The testis may be undescended and be in lumbar region, iliac fossa, inguinal canal, superficial inguinal ring or at the upper end of scrotum. The testes may have gone astray (ectopic testis) to be in the region of inguinal canal and may be seen at superficial inguinal ring, root of penis, in perineum or in thigh.

Varicocoele: The dilatation and tortuosity of the pampiniform plexus in the spermatic cord is called *varicocoele*. It occurs more commonly on the left side. The factors are:

(a) Left testis hangs a little lower than right.
(b) Left testicular vein drains into left renal vein at right angle.
(c) Loaded pelvic colon may press upon the left testicular vein and prevent its proper drainage.

Varicocoele may lead to infertility (Fig. 17.5d).

Ischioanal abscess: Ischioanal abscess is common as it is situated on the two sides of the anal canal, deep to the skin of perineum. It is less painful compared to the perianal abscess. The perianal space is situated between ischial tuberosity and subcutaneous part of sphincter ani externus. The septa in this space are small and fat is tightly disposed, so infections are very painful.

Pudendal nerve block: This is an anaesthetic procedure used during vaginal deliveries or forceps delivery. The pudendal nerve is the nerve of perineum and after anaesthesia, the vaginal delivery becomes almost painless. The nerve is blocked by the anaesthetic drug as it lies on the ischial spine. The blockage can be done through vagina or from the perineum (Fig. 28.25).

CLINICOANATOMICAL PROBLEMS

1. A patient was to have laparotomy for intestinal obstruction. The surgeon asked the resident about the incision. The resident suggested a lateral rectus incision.

Clinicoanatomical problems:
• Why is lateral rectus incision not the incision of choice?

• Which is better incision and why?

Ans. Lateral rectus incision cuts the nerve supply to the rectus muscle entering from its lateral side. A paramedian incision is preferred, with rectus abdominis retracted laterally. This saves all the nerves supplying this important muscle.

2. During clinical rounds, students were asked the key landmark of abdomen. One of them said that L1 is the important landmark.

Clinicoanatomical problems:
- How does one locate L1 vertebra? What organs are located at this level?

Ans. L1 is important, as it is at the level of trans-pyloric plane. It is midway between jugular notch and the pubic symphysis. It passes through tips of 9th costal cartilages, fundus of gall bladder, neck of pancreas, hila of the kidneys, origin of superior mesenteric artery, and the splenic vein.

3. A man was referred for vasectomy. A few problems were posed to the medical student.

Clinicoanatomical problems:
- Is vasectomy done on one or both sides?
- How does one feel the vas deferens?
- How is vasectomy done?
- Does the patient need hospitalisation?

Ans. Vasectomy is done on both sides at the same sitting, one after the other. Vas deferens is palpated as a firm muscular tube in the spermatic cord. The vas is pulled out from the incision at the upper posterior part of scrotum and ligated at two places one cm apart. The intervening part is removed and sent for histopathological examination to confirm that the tissue removed is vas deferens only. It is an outpatient procedure and needs no hospitalisation.

4. A young male felt pain in the region of umbilicus. He also had nausea, temperature, and increased pulse rate with leucocytosis. Later on the pain was localised in right iliac fossa.

Clinicoanatomical problems:
- Discuss the referred pain of appendicitis.

Where is his appendix likely to be located? What is McBurney's point?

Ans. Initially the pain of acute appendicitis is referred to the skin in the region of umbilicus. Afferent nerve fibres from appendix are carried in lesser splanchnic nerve to T10 segment of spinal cord. The afferent impulses from the skin of umbilicus also reach T10 segment through 10th intercostal nerve. Since both the somatic and visceral impulses reach the same segment, and somatic impulses being appreciated better by brain, the pain is referred to the skin of the umbilicus. The most common position of appendix is retrocaecal, and since the patient's pain is in right iliac fossa, the position of the appendix is likely to be retrocaecal.

McBurney's point lies at the junction of lateral one-third and medial two-thirds of a line joining anterior superior iliac spine to the umbilicus.

5. During cholecystectomy by open surgery, the surgeon noticed severe bleeding. The bleeding was quickly stopped by treating the bleeding vessel by electrocautery.

Clinicoanatomical problems:
- How can one stop bleeding vessel without using clamps?
- What other surgical procedures are available to remove the gall bladder?

Ans. The bleeding of cystic artery can be stopped by compressing the hepatic artery between the thumb and index finger, as it lies in the anterior wall of the epiploic foramen. Cystic artery is a branch of the hepatic artery. The cystic artery was treated by electrocautery.

Gall bladder can also be removed by laparoscopic surgery.

MULTIPLE CHOICE QUESTIONS

A. Select the best response.

1. **The skin around the umbilicus is innervated by which of the following segments?**
   (a) T8   (b) T9
   (c) T10   (d) T11

2. **Which of the following does not contribute to the formation of the posterior wall of the inguinal canal?**
   (a) Fascia transversalis
   (b) Conjoint tendon
   (c) Reflected part of inguinal ligament
   (d) Lacunar ligament

3. **Testis is supplied by sympathetic nerves arising from which of the following segments?**
   (a) T10   (b) T11
   (c) T12   (d) L1

4. **Lymphatics from glans penis drain into:**
   (a) External iliac   (b) Internal iliac
   (c) Superficial inguinal
   (d) Deep inguinal

5. **Which of the following is not a retroperitoneal organ?**
   (a) Pancreas   **(b) Spleen**
   (c) Ascending colon   (d) Kidney

6. **Ligamentum teres is a remnant of:**
   (a) Lesser omentum
   (b) Ductus venosus
   (c) Left umbilical vein
   (d) Left umbilical artery

7. **Blood vessel related to paraduodenal fossa is:**
   (a) Portal vein
   (b) Gonadal vein
   (c) Superior mesenteric vein
   (d) Inferior mesenteric vein

8. **Posterior relation of foramen of Winslow is:**
   (a) Liver   (b) Duodenum
   (c) Inferior vena cava (d) Pancreas

9. **The following structures form part of the stomach bed except:**
   (a) Left suprarenal gland
   (b) Coeliac trunk
   (c) Splenic artery
   (d) Pancreas

10. **Which of the following is not present in the bed of stomach?**
    (a) Splenic artery
    (b) Transverse mesocolon
    (c) Fourth part of duodenum
    (d) Transverse colon

11. **A posteriorly perforating peptic ulcer will most likely produce peritonitis in the following:**
    (a) Greater sac
    (b) Lesser sac
    (c) Bare area of liver
    (d) Morisson's pouch

12. **Which of the following arteries supplies the fundus of stomach?**
    (a) Right gastric artery
    (b) Splenic artery
    (c) Short gastric arteries
    (d) Gastroduodenal artery

13. **Which of the following is not a characteristic feature of large intestine?**
    (a) Villi
    (b) Sacculations
    (c) Taenia coli
    (d) Appendices epiploicae

14. **Which of the following is true about Meckel's diverticulum?**
    (a) Length is about 9 inches
    (b) 2 inches proximal to ileocaecal valve
    (c) 2 feet proximal to ileocaecal valve
    (d) Attached to mesenteric border of the ileum

15. **Peyer's patches are present in:**
    (a) Duodenum
    (b) Jejunum
    (c) Ileum
    (d) Transverse colon

16. **Appendices epiploicae are seen in:**
    (a) Stomach
    (b) Ileum
    (c) Duodenum
    (d) Colon

17. **False regarding appendix is:**
    (a) Is covered by peritoneum
    (b) Commonest site is retrocaecal
    (c) Supplied by appendicular artery
    (d) Superior to caecum

18. **Most common position of vermiform appendix is:**
    (a) Pelvic
    (b) Retrocaecal
    (c) Preileal
    (d) Postileal

19. **First inch of 1st part of duodenum is not supplied by:**
    (a) Superior pancreaticoduodenal artery
    (b) Right gastroepiploic artery
    (c) Right gastric artery
    (d) Hepatic artery

20. **Meckel's diverticulum is a remnant of:**
    (a) Müllerian duct
    (b) Wolffian duct
    (c) Mesonephric duct
    (d) Vitellointestinal duct

21. **Inferior mesenteric vein opens into:**
    (a) Portal vein
    (b) Inferior vena cava
    (c) Splenic vein
    (d) Superior mesenteric vein

22. **Which of the following is not a direct branch of coeliac trunk?**
    (a) Left gastric   (b) Common hepatic
    (c) Splenic   **(d) Inferior pancreatico-
                               duodenal**

23. **Cystic artery is a branch of:**
    (a) **Right hepatic**
    (b) Left hepatic
    (c) Coeliac trunk
    (d) Common hepatic

24. **Ovarian artery is a branch of:**
    (a) **Abdominal aorta**
    (b) Common iliac artery
    (c) Internal iliac
    (d) External iliac

25. **Blood supply of liver is:**
    (a) 80% arterial, 20% venous
    (b) 70% arterial, 30% venous
    (c) **80% venous, 20% arterial**
    (d) 60% arterial, 40% venous

26. **Accessory pancreatic duct is also called as:**
    (a) Wirsung duct
    (b) **Santorini duct**
    (c) Hensen's duct
    (d) Hoffmann's duct

27. **All of the following are related to the anterior surface of left kidney except:**
    (a) Spleen
    (b) Pancreas
    (c) **Duodenum**
    (d) Left colic flexure

28. **Which of the following muscles is not forming posterior relation of kidney:**
    (a) **Latissimus dorsi**
    (b) Transversus abdominis
    (c) Psoas major
    (d) Quadratus lumborum

29. **Structure not lying anterior to left ureter is:**
    (a) Gonadal artery
    (b) Left colic artery
    (c) Pelvic colon
    (d) **Internal iliac artery**

30. **Right suprarenal vein drains into:**
    (a) **Inferior vena cava**
    (b) Right renal vein
    (c) Left renal vein
    (d) Lumbar vein

31. **Suprarenal gland does not receive blood supply from:**
    (a) Inferior phrenic artery
    (b) Renal artery
    (c) Abdominal aorta
    (d) **Superior mesenteric artery**

32. **Which of the following does not pass through the diaphragm?**
    (a) Oesophagus
    (b) Aorta
    (c) **Cisterna chyli**
    (d) Inferior vena cava

33. **Which of the following structures does not pass through oesophageal hiatus?**
    (a) Gastric nerve
    (b) Oesophagus
    (c) Left gastric artery
    (d) **Thoracic duct**

34. **Left gonadal vein drains into:**
    (a) Internal iliac vein
    (b) Inferior vena cava
    (c) **Left renal vein**
    (d) Vena azygos

35. **All the following are the characteristic features of female bony pelvis except:**
    (a) Pelvic inlet is round or oval
    (b) **Subpubic angle is 50 to 60 degrees**
    (c) Obturator foramen is small and triangular
    (d) Sciatic notches are wider

36. **Which of the following is true regarding the innervation of urinary bladder?**
    (a) **Parasympathetic fibres are motor to detrusor muscle**
    (b) Sympathetic nerves are motor to sphincter urethrae
    (c) Pudendal nerve innervates sphincter vesicae
    (d) Awareness of distension of bladder is mediated through lateral spinothalamic tract

37. **Which of the following is the shortest part of male urethra?**
    (a) **Membranous**
    (b) Prostatic
    (c) Bulbar
    (d) Penile

38. **Normal position of uterus is:**
    (a) **Anteverted and anteflexed**
    (b) Retroverted and retroflexed
    (c) Anteverted and retroflexed
    (d) Retroverted and anteflexed

39. **Cervix is supplied by which of the following nerves?**
    (a) Pudendal
    (b) **Pelvic splanchnic nerve**
    (c) Sacral 1
    (d) Lumbar 5, sacral 1

40. **Which of the following is not a content of broad ligament?**
    (a) Uterine tube
    (b) Ovarian ligament
    (c) Round ligament
    (d) Cervix

41. **Uterine artery is a branch of which artery?**
    (a) External iliac
    (b) Internal iliac
    (c) Abdominal aorta
    (d) Common iliac

42. **Which of the following is formed by mesonephric duct?**
    (a) Uterus
    (b) Penis
    (c) Ureter
    (d) Uterine tube

B. **Match the following on the left side with their appropriate answers on the right side.**

1. **Plane**   **Vertebral level**
   (a) Subcostal plane   (i) L1
   (b) Transtubercular plane   (ii) L3
   (c) Transpyloric plane   (iii) L4
   (d) Highest point of iliac crest (iv) L5

2. **Arterial branches and their origin**
   (a) Splenic artery   (i) Aorta
   (b) Testicular artery   (ii) Superior mesenteric artery
   (c) Ileocolic artery   (iii) Coeliac trunk
   (d) Inferior rectal artery   (iv) Internal pudendal artery

3. **Lymphatic drainage**
   (a) Greater curvature of stomach   (i) Pancreaticosplenic nodes
   (b) Testis   (ii) Internal iliac nodes
   (c) Prostate gland   (iii) Superior mesenteric nodes
   (d) Head of pancreas   (iv) Para-aortic nodes

4. **Venous drainage**
   (a) Left gastric vein   (i) Splenic vein
   (b) Inferior mesenteric vein (ii) Left renal vein

(c) Left testicular vein   (iii) Inferior vena cava
(d) Right testicular vein (iv) Portal vein

C. **For each of the statements or questions below, one or more answers given is/are correct.**
   A. If only 1, 2, 3 are correct
   B. If only 1, 3 are correct
   C. If only 2, 4 are correct
   D. If 1, 2, 3, 4 are correct
   E. If only 4 is correct
   F. If all are correct

1. **Contents of spermatic cord is/are**
   1. Ductus deferens
   2. Testicular artery
   3. Pampiniform plexus of veins
   4. Ilioinguinal nerve

2. **Epiploic foramen is bounded**
   1. Superiorly by the left lobe of the liver
   2. Posteriorly by the inferior vena cava
   3. Inferiorly by pylorus of stomach
   4. Anteriorly by lesser omentum containing hepatic artery, portal vein and bile duct

3. **Parasympathetic nerves innervating stomach**
   1. Increase the mobility of the stomach
   2. Are inhibitory to pyloric sphincter
   3. Increase the secretion of pepsin and HCl
   4. Are the chief pathway for pain sensation

4. **The following statements are true regarding appendix**
   1. Appendicular orifice is situated on the posterolateral aspect of caecum.
   2. Sympathetic innervation is derived from T10 spinal segment.
   3. Pelvic position is the most common position of appendix.
   4. Referred pain caused by appendicitis is first felt in the region of umbilicus.

5. **Lymphatics of the uterus drain into the following lymph nodes.**
   1. External iliac
   2. Internal iliac
   3. Superficial inguinal
   4. Deep inguinal.

Answers

B. 1. (a)–(ii), (b)–(iv), (c)–(i), (d)–(iii)
   2. (a)–(iii), (b)–(i), (c)–(ii), (d)–iv
   3. (a)–(i),   (b)–iv,   (c)–(ii), (d)–(iii)
   4. (a)–(iv), (b)–(i), (c)–(ii), (d)–(iii)

C. 1. D
   2. C
   3. A
   4. C
   5. A

MNEMONICS

1. **Meckel's diverticulum details (Note: "di-" means "two", so diverticulum is the thing with all the twos.)**

   2 inches long

   2 feet from end of ileum

   2 times more common in men

   2% occurrence in population

   2 types of tissues may be present

2. **Inferior vena cava tributaries "I like To Rise So High"**

   Iliac veins

   Lumbar veins

   Testicular veins

   Renal veins

   Suprarenal veins

   Hepatic veins

3. **Spleen: dimensions, weight, surface anatomy "1, 3, 5, 7, 8, 11"**

   Spleen dimensions are 1 inch × 3 inches × 5 inches.

   Weight is 7 ounces.

   It underlies ribs 9 through 11.

4. **Spermatic cord contents "3 arteries, 3 nerves, 3 other things"**

   3 arteries: testicular artery, artery to ductus deferens, cremasteric artery

   3 nerves: genital branch of the genitofemoral, ilioinguinal, autonomies

   3 other things: ductus deferens, pampiniform plexus, remains of processus vaginalis

5. **Ureter to uterine artery relations "Water under the bridge"**

   The ureters (which carry water), are posterior to the uterine artery.

   Clinically important, since a common surgical error is to ligate and cut ureter with uterine artery when removing uterus.

6. **Female pelvic organs "3 organs, each gets 2 blood supplies"**

   Vagina: uterine, vaginal

   Rectum: middle rectal, inferior rectal (inferior rectal is the branch of pudendal)

   Bladder in male: superior vesical, inferior vesical

   Bladder in female: superior vesical, vaginal

7. **Rule of 25 cm**

   Oesophagus, ureter, duodenum

8. **Structures at porta hepatis**

   From posterior to anterior side—VAD

   V – Portal vein

   A – Hepatic artery

   D – Hepatic duct

9. **Structures at hilum of kidney:**

   From anterior to posterior aspect—VAU

   V – Renal vein

   A – Renal artery

   U – Pelvis of ureter

10. **Diaphragm apertures: spinal levels "I 8 10 Eggs at 12"**

    Inferior vena cava (8)

    Oesophagus (10)

    Aorta (12)

FURTHER READING

- Brodel M. The intrinsic blood vessels of the kidney and their significance in nephrotomy. John Hopkins Hosp *Bull* 1911; 12:10–13.
- Buccione R, Schroeder AC, Eppig JJ. Interactions between somatic cells and germ cells throughout mammalian oogenesis *Biol Reprod* 1990; 43:543–7.
- Burkhill GJC, Healy JC. Anatomy of the retroperitoneum. *Imaging* 2000; 12:10–20.
- Buschard K, Kjaeldgaard A. Investigations and analysis of the positions, fixation, length and embryology of the vermiform appendix, *Acta Chir Scand* 1973; 139:293–8.
- Chanecellor MB, Yoshimura N. *Physiology and pharmacology of the bladder and urethra.* In: Walsh PC et al (eds) Campbell's Urology study Guide, 2nd edn. Philadelphia; Saunders; Chapter 23 2002.
- D, Panjabi MM. Normal motion of the lumbar spine related to age and gender. *Eur Spine J* 1995; 4:18–23.
- Delancey JO. Anatomy. In: Stanton SL, Monga A (eds) *Clinical Urogynaecology*, 2nd edition. London: Churchill Livingstone 2000.
- Didio L J, Anderson MC. The 'Sphinctres' of the Digestive System. Baltimore: Williams and Wilkins 1968.
- Dunaif A, Thomas A. Current concepts in the polycystic ovarian syndrome. *Annu Rev Med* 2001; 52:401–19.
- Ellis H (eds) Applied Radiological Anatomy. Cambridge, UK: Cambridge University Press.
- Jackson JE. Vascular anatomy of the gastrointestinal tract. In: Butler P, Mitchell AWM 1999.
- Kerr JB. Ultrastructure of the seminiferous epithelium and intertubular tissue of the human testis. *J electron Microsc Tech* 1991; 19:215– 40.

- Klutke CG, Siegel CL. Functional female pelvic anatomy. *Urol Clin North Am* 1995; 22 (3): 487–98.
- Kruyt RH, Delemarre JB, Doornbos J, Vogel HJ. Normal anorectum, dynamic MR imaging anatomy. *Radiology* 1991; 179 (1):159–63.
- Lunnis PJ, Phillips RK. Anatomy and function of anal longitudinal muscle. *Br J Surg* 1992; 79 : 882–4.
- Lytle WJ. Inguinal anatomy. *J Anatomy* 1979; 128:581–94.
- Meyers M. Dynamic Radiology of the Abdomen. Normal and pathologic Anatomy. New York: Springer 1994.
- Mitchell AWM, Dick R. Liver, gall bladder, pancreas and spleen. In: Butler P, Mitchell AWM, Ellis H (eds) Applied Radiological Anatomy. Cambridge: Cambridge University Press; 1999; 239–58.
- Mundy AR, Fitzpatrick J, Neal D, George N (eds). Male sexual function. In: The Scientific Basis of Urology, Chapter 12. Isis Medical Media: 1999; 243–53.
- Mundy AR, Fitzpatrick J, Neal D, George N (eds). The prostate and benign prostatic hyperplasia. In : The Scientific Basis of Urology, Chapter 13. Oxford; *Isis Medical Media*: 1999; 257–76.
- Novick AC. Anatomic approaches in nephron-sparing surgery for renal cell carcinoma. *Atlas Urol Clin North Am* 1998; 6:39.
- Paquet KJ. Causes and pathomechanics of oesophageal varices development. *Med Sci Monit* 6: 2000; 915–28.55.Dvorak J, Vajda EG, Grob
- Pearcy M, Protek I, Shepherd J. a. Three-dimensional X-ray analysis of normal movement in lumbar spine. Spine 1984; 9:582–7.
- Reilly FD. Innervation and vascular pharmaco-dynamics of the mammalian spleen. *Experientia* 1985; 41:187–92.
- Rizk NN. A new description of the anterior abdominal wall in man and mammals *J Anat* 1980; 131:373–85.
- Shah PM, Scarton HA, Tsapogas MJ. Geometric anatomy of the aortocommon iliac bifurcation. *J Anat* 1978; 126: 451–8.
- Smith PH, Porte D Jr. Neuropharmacology of the pancreatic islets. *Annu Rev Pharmacol Toxicol* 1976; 16:269–85.
- Spornitz UM. The functional morphology of the human endometrium and decidua. *Adv Anat Embryol Cell Biol* 1992; 124:1–99.
- Suzuki M, Akasihi S, Rikiyama T, Naitoh T, Rahman MM, Mastsuno S. Laparoscopic cholecystectomy, Calot's triangle and variations in cystic arterial supply. *Surgical Endoscopy* 2000; 14:141–4.
- Taylar JR, Twomey LT. Sexual dimorphism in human vertebral shape. *J Anat* 1984; 138:281–6.
- Vinecnt JM, Morrison ID, Armstrong P, Reznek RH. The size of normal adrenal glands on computed tomography. *Clin Radiol* 1994; 49:453–55.
- Wendell Smith CP, Wilson PM. The vulva, vagina and urethra and the musculature of the pelvic floor. In: Philipp E, Setchell M, Ginsburg J (eds) *Scientific Foundations of Obstetrics and Gynecology*. Oxford: Butterworth–Heinemann; 1991; 84–100.
- Yamaguchi S, Kuroyanagi H, Milson JW, Sim R, Shimada H. Venous anatomy of the right colon, Precise structure of the major veins and gastrocolic trunk in 58 cadavers. *Dis Colon Rectum* 2002; 45:1337–40.

Index

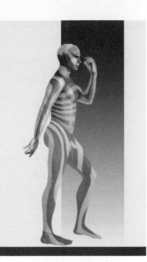